Y0-ADX-977

# MICHIGAN COMPILED LAWS SERVICE

## VOLUME 71

791 to 830

Prisons and Jails

*By the Editorial Staff of the Publisher*

2001 EDITION

LexisNexis

LEXIS, NEXIS, SHEPARD'S and Martindale-Hubbell are registered trademarks, LEXIS Publishing and MICHIE are trademarks and *lexis.com* is a service mark of Reed Elsevier Properties Inc., used under license. Matthew Bender is a registered trademark of Matthew Bender Properties Inc.

©2001 Matthew Bender & Company, Inc., one of the LEXIS Publishing™ companies. All rights reserved

No copyright is claimed in the text of statutes, regulations and excerpts from opinions quoted within this work. Permission to copy material exceeding fair use, 17 U.S.C. § 107, may be licensed for a fee of $1 per page per copy from the Copyright Clearance Center, 222 Rosewood Drive, Danvers, MA 01923, telephone (978) 750-8400

Editorial Offices
701 East Water Street, Charlottesville, VA 22902 (800) 446-3410
www.lexis.com

ISBN 0-327-16001-2

4418210

# THIS VOLUME CONTAINS

**Statutes:**

The 2001 Edition of the Michigan Compiled Laws Service contains the full text of the general laws of a permanent nature enacted by, and in force through, Pub. Act No. 200 of the 2000 Regular Legislative Session.

For the latest enactments and annotations, consult the pocket supplement to this volume, as well as the MCLS Advance Legislative Service and MCLS Quarterly Updates. You can also call LEXIS-NEXIS™ at 1-800-833-9844.

**Case notes and other annotation and reference materials:**

The case notes and other annotation and reference materials construing and applying the statutes in this volume have been updated through the following:

461 Mich 756

239 Mich App 733

609 NW2d 930

146 L Ed 2d 753

208 F3d 228

89 F Supp 2d 228

Mich Atty Gen Op 7055 (2000)

1998 Det C L Rev 293

79 Mich B J 1236

7 Mich J Gender & L 107

21 Mich J Int'l L 527

5 Mich J Race & L 711

98 Mich L Rev 2154

16 Thomas M Cooley L Rev 479

77 U Det Mercy L Rev 591

33 U Mich J L Ref 173

46 Wayne L Rev 391

---

**SHEPARD'S®** Citations Service. For further research of authorities referenced here, use SHEPARD'S to be sure your case or statute is still good law and to find additional authorities that support your position. SHEPARD'S is available exclusively from LEXIS Publishing™.

# MICHIGAN COMPILED LAWS SERVICE

**PUBLICATION EDITOR**
John A. Frey, J.D.

**Senior Legal Analyst**
Larry W. Schimmels, J.D.

**Legal Analysts**
Karen Lussen Blair, J.D.
Daniel A. Klein, J.D.

**Coordinating Editors**
Laureen M. Fiannaca
Cathie Schaefer

**Customer Relations Consultant**
Daniel Arban

# MICHIGAN COMPILED LAWS SERVICE
## TABLE OF CHAPTERS

| | |
|---|---|
| Chapter 1 | CONSTITUTION OF MICHIGAN OF 1963 |
| Chapter 2 | STATE |
| Chapter 3 | FEDERAL AND INTERSTATE RELATIONS |
| Chapter 4 | LEGISLATURE |
| Chapter 5 | EMERGENCY APPROPRIATIONS |
| Chapter 6 | IMPEACHMENTS |
| Chapter 8 | STATUTES |
| Chapter 10 | GOVERNOR |
| Chapter 11 | SECRETARY OF STATE |
| Chapter 12 | STATE TREASURER |
| Chapter 13 | AUDITOR GENERAL |
| Chapter 14 | ATTORNEY GENERAL |
| Chapter 15 | PUBLIC OFFICERS AND EMPLOYEES |
| Chapter 16 | EXECUTIVE ORGANIZATION |
| Chapter 17 | STATE ADMINISTRATIVE BOARD |
| Chapter 18 | DEPARTMENT OF MANAGEMENT AND BUDGET |
| Chapter 19 | BOARD OF STATE AUDITORS |
| Chapter 21 | BUDGET AND STATE ACCOUNTS |
| Chapter 24 | PRINTING AND STATE DOCUMENTS |
| Chapter 26 | SUPREME COURT REPORTS |
| Chapter 28 | MICHIGAN STATE POLICE |
| Chapter 29 | FIRE PREVENTION |
| Chapter 30 | CIVILIAN DEFENSE |
| Chapter 31 | SUCCESSION TO OFFICE |
| Chapter 32 | MILITARY ESTABLISHMENT |
| Chapter 33 | NAVAL MILITIA |
| Chapter 35 | VETERANS AND MEMBERS OF ARMED FORCES |
| Chapter 36 | MICHIGAN VETERANS' FACILITY |
| Chapter 37 | CIVIL RIGHTS |
| Chapter 38 | CIVIL SERVICE AND RETIREMENT |

# TABLE OF CHAPTERS

| | |
|---|---|
| Chapter 41 | TOWNSHIPS |
| Chapter 42 | CHARTER TOWNSHIPS |
| Chapter 43 | FENCES AND FENCE VIEWERS |
| Chapter 45 | COUNTIES |
| Chapter 46 | COUNTY BOARDS OF COMMISSIONERS |
| Chapter 47 | COUNTY AUDITORS |
| Chapter 48 | COUNTY TREASURERS |
| Chapter 49 | PROSECUTING ATTORNEYS |
| Chapter 50 | COUNTY CLERKS |
| Chapter 51 | SHERIFFS |
| Chapter 52 | CORONERS |
| Chapter 53 | REGISTER OF DEEDS |
| Chapter 54 | SURVEYORS |
| Chapter 55 | NOTARIES PUBLIC |
| Chapters 61 - 75 | VILLAGES |
| Chapter 78 | VILLAGES |
| Chapter 79 | VILLAGES |
| Chapters 81 - 113 | FOURTH CLASS CITIES |
| Chapter 115 | FOURTH CLASS CITIES |
| Chapter 117 | HOME RULE CITIES |
| Chapter 119 | METROPOLITAN DISTRICTS |
| Chapter 120 | PORT DISTRICTS |
| Chapter 121 | CHARTER WATER AUTHORITY |
| Chapter 123 | LOCAL GOVERNMENTAL AFFAIRS |
| Chapter 124 | MUNICIPALITIES |
| Chapter 125 | PLANNING, HOUSING, AND ZONING |
| Chapter 128 | CEMETERIES |
| Chapter 129 | PUBLIC FUNDS |
| Chapters 131 - 139 | MUNICIPAL FINANCE ACT |
| Chapter 141 | MUNICIPAL FINANCING |
| Chapter 168 | MICHIGAN ELECTION LAW |
| Chapter 169 | CAMPAIGN FINANCING AND ADVERTISING |
| Chapter 200 | MISCELLANEOUS ELECTION ACTS |

# TABLE OF CHAPTERS

| | |
|---|---|
| Chapter 201 | VACANCIES IN OFFICE |
| Chapter 205 | TAXATION |
| Chapter 206 | INCOME TAX ACT OF 1967 |
| Chapter 207 | TAXATION |
| Chapter 208 | SINGLE BUSINESS TAX ACT |
| Chapter 209 | STATE ASSESSMENT AND EQUALIZATION |
| Chapter 211 | TAXATION OF REAL AND PERSONAL PROPERTY |
| Chapter 213 | CONDEMNATION |
| Chapters 220 - 244 | GENERAL HIGHWAY LAW |
| Chapter 247 | HIGHWAYS |
| Chapter 249 | HIGHWAYS |
| Chapter 250 | HIGHWAYS |
| Chapter 252 | HIGHWAYS |
| Chapter 253 | GRADE CROSSINGS |
| Chapter 254 | BRIDGES |
| Chapter 255 | FERRIES |
| Chapter 256 | MOTOR VEHICLES |
| Chapter 257 | MOTOR VEHICLES |
| Chapter 259 | AVIATION |
| Chapter 260 | TRANSPORTATION SYSTEMS |
| Chapter 279 | DRAINS |
| Chapter 280 | DRAIN CODE OF 1956 |
| Chapter 281 | LAKES AND RIVERS |
| Chapter 282 | SOIL CONSERVATION |
| Chapter 285 | AGRICULTURE |
| Chapter 286 | AGRICULTURAL INDUSTRY |
| Chapter 287 | ANIMAL INDUSTRY |
| Chapter 288 | DAIRY INDUSTRY |
| Chapter 289 | PURE FOODS AND STANDARDS |
| Chapter 290 | WEIGHTS, MEASURES, AND STANDARDS |
| Chapter 291 | STATE FAIRS |
| Chapter 295 | STATE WEATHER SERVICE |
| Chapter 299 | NATURAL RESOURCES |

## TABLE OF CHAPTERS

| Chapter 300 | FISH AND GAME |
|---|---|
| Chapter 307 | FISHING |
| Chapter 308 | COMMERCIAL FISHING |
| Chapter 316 | HUNTING AND FISHING LICENSES |
| Chapter 317 | GAME BREEDING AND PROTECTION |
| Chapter 318 | STATE PARKS |
| Chapter 319 | OIL, GAS, AND MINERALS |
| Chapter 320 | FORESTS |
| Chapter 321 | GEOLOGICAL AND OTHER SURVEYS |
| Chapter 322 | STATE LANDS |
| Chapter 323 | WATER RESOURCES |
| Chapter 324 | NATURAL RESOURCES AND ENVIRONMENTAL PROTECTION ACT |
| Chapter 325 | HEALTH |
| Chapter 326 | VITAL STATISTICS |
| Chapter 327 | LOCAL HEALTH BOARDS |
| Chapter 328 | DEAD HUMAN BODIES |
| Chapter 329 | COMMUNICABLE DISEASES |
| Chapter 330 | MENTAL HEALTH CODE |
| Chapter 331 | HOSPITALS |
| Chapter 332 | TUBERCULOSIS SANATORIA |
| Chapter 333 | HEALTH |
| Chapter 335 | DRUGS |
| Chapter 336 | AIR POLLUTION |
| Chapter 338 | PROFESSIONS AND OCCUPATIONS |
| Chapter 339 | OCCUPATIONAL CODE |
| Chapter 340 | EDUCATION |
| Chapter 380 | SCHOOL CODE OF 1976 |
| Chapter 388 | SCHOOLS AND SCHOOL AID |
| Chapter 389 | COMMUNITY COLLEGES |
| Chapter 390 | UNIVERSITIES AND COLLEGES |
| Chapter 393 | DEAF AND BLIND |
| Chapter 395 | VOCATIONAL TRAINING |
| Chapter 397 | LIBRARIES |

# TABLE OF CHAPTERS

| Chapter 399 | HISTORICAL RECORDS AND SITES |
| Chapter 400 | SOCIAL SERVICES |
| Chapters 401 - 403 | THE POOR LAW |
| Chapter 404 | WELFARE AND CHARITY |
| Chapter 408 | LABOR |
| Chapter 409 | YOUTH EMPLOYMENT |
| Chapter 418 | WORKER'S DISABILITY COMPENSATION |
| Chapter 419 | MISCELLANEOUS LABOR LAWS |
| Chapter 421 | EMPLOYMENT SECURITY |
| Chapter 423 | LABOR DISPUTES AND EMPLOYMENT RELATIONS |
| Chapter 425 | MINES |
| Chapter 426 | FOREST PRODUCTS |
| Chapter 427 | HOTELS |
| Chapter 429 | BRANDS, LABELS, AND TRADEMARKS |
| Chapter 430 | NAMES, TITLES, INSIGNIA, AND EMBLEMS |
| Chapter 431 | RACING, BOXING, AND EXHIBITIONS |
| Chapter 432 | GAMING |
| Chapter 433 | ANIMALS RUNNING AT LARGE |
| Chapter 434 | LOST AND UNCLAIMED PROPERTY |
| Chapter 435 | SUNDAYS AND HOLIDAYS |
| Chapter 436 | ALCOHOLIC BEVERAGES |
| Chapter 438 | MONEY AND INTEREST |
| Chapter 439 | NEGOTIABLE INSTRUMENTS LAW |
| Chapter 440 | UNIFORM COMMERCIAL CODE |
| Chapter 441 | FIDUCIARY SECURITY TRANSFERS |
| Chapter 442 | SALES |
| Chapter 443 | UNIFORM WAREHOUSE RECEIPTS ACT |
| Chapter 444 | WAREHOUSES |
| Chapter 445 | TRADE AND COMMERCE |
| Chapter 446 | AUCTIONEERS, PAWNBROKERS, AND VENDORS |
| Chapter 447 | FOREIGN TRADE |
| Chapter 449 | PARTNERSHIPS |
| Chapter 450 | CORPORATIONS |

# TABLE OF CHAPTERS

| Chapter 451 | SECURITIES, REAL ESTATE, AND DEBT MANAGEMENT |
| Chapter 453 | AGRICULTURAL ASSOCIATIONS |
| Chapter 454 | TRADE AND LABOR ASSOCIATIONS |
| Chapter 455 | SUMMER RESORT AND PARK ASSOCIATIONS |
| Chapter 456 | CEMETERY ASSOCIATIONS |
| Chapter 457 | FRATERNAL ASSOCIATIONS |
| Chapter 458 | ECCLESIASTICAL CORPORATIONS |
| Chapter 460 | PUBLIC UTILITIES |
| Chapter 462 | RAILROADS |
| Chapter 468 | RAILROAD RATES, FINANCING, AND REGULATION |
| Chapter 469 | RAILROAD PROPERTY, EQUIPMENT, AND SERVICES |
| Chapter 470 | RAILROAD EMPLOYEES |
| Chapter 471 | UNION DEPOT COMPANIES |
| Chapter 472 | STREET RAILWAYS |
| Chapter 473 | CONSOLIDATED PUBLIC UTILITY COMPANIES |
| Chapter 474 | STATE TRANSPORTATION |
| Chapters 475 - 479 | MOTOR CARRIER ACT |
| Chapter 480 | MOTOR CARRIER SAFETY |
| Chapter 482 | BILLS OF LADING |
| Chapter 483 | OIL, GAS, AND BRINE LINES |
| Chapter 484 | TELEPHONE, TELEGRAPH, AND RADIO |
| Chapter 485 | CANAL, HARBOR, AND RIVER IMPROVEMENT COMPANIES |
| Chapter 486 | WATER AND POWER COMPANIES |
| Chapter 487 | FINANCIAL INSTITUTIONS |
| Chapter 488 | ELECTRONIC FUNDS TRANSFERS |
| Chapter 489 | SAVINGS AND LOAN ASSOCIATIONS |
| Chapter 490 | CREDIT UNIONS |
| Chapter 491 | COOPERATIVE SAVINGS ASSOCIATIONS |
| Chapter 492 | INSTALLMENT SALES OF MOTOR VEHICLES |
| Chapter 493 | REGULATORY LOANS |
| Chapter 494 | INVESTMENT COMPANIES AND TONTINES |
| Chapter 500 | INSURANCE CODE OF 1956 |
| Chapter 550 | GENERAL INSURANCE LAWS |

# TABLE OF CHAPTERS

| | |
|---|---|
| Chapter 551 | MARRIAGE |
| Chapter 552 | DIVORCE |
| Chapter 554 | REAL AND PERSONAL PROPERTY |
| Chapter 555 | USES AND TRUSTS |
| Chapter 556 | POWERS OF APPOINTMENT |
| Chapter 557 | PROPERTY OF HUSBAND AND WIFE |
| Chapter 558 | ESTATES IN DOWER |
| Chapter 559 | CONDOMINIUMS |
| Chapter 560 | SUBDIVISION CONTROL ACT OF 1967 |
| Chapter 561 | LOSS OR DESTRUCTION OF PUBLIC RECORDS |
| Chapter 564 | FAIR HOUSING ACT OF 1968 |
| Chapter 565 | CONVEYANCES OF REAL PROPERTY |
| Chapter 566 | FRAUDULENT CONVEYANCES AND CONTRACTS |
| Chapter 567 | ESCHEATS |
| Chapter 570 | LIENS |
| Chapter 600 | REVISED JUDICATURE ACT OF 1961 |
| Chapter 691 | JUDICIARY |
| Chapter 692 | JUDICIARY |
| Chapter 700 | ESTATES AND PROTECTED INDIVIDUALS CODE |
| Chapters 701 - 713 | PROBATE CODE |
| Chapter 720 | PROBATE |
| Chapter 722 | CHILDREN |
| Chapter 725 | MUNICIPAL COURTS OF RECORD |
| Chapter 726 | RECORDER'S COURT OF DETROIT |
| Chapter 727 | SUPERIOR COURT OF GRAND RAPIDS |
| Chapter 728 | COMMON PLEAS COURT |
| Chapter 729 | POLICE COURTS |
| Chapter 730 | JUSTICE COURTS AND MUNICIPAL COURTS |
| Chapter 750 | MICHIGAN PENAL CODE |
| Chapter 752 | CRIMES AND OFFENSES |
| Chapters 760 - 777 | CODE OF CRIMINAL PROCEDURE |
| Chapter 780 | CRIMINAL PROCEDURE |
| Chapter 791 | DEPARTMENT OF CORRECTIONS |

## TABLE OF CHAPTERS

| | |
|---|---|
| Chapter 798 | CORRECTIONS |
| Chapter 800 | PRISONS |
| Chapter 801 | JAILS AND WORKHOUSES |
| Chapter 802 | HOUSES OF CORRECTION |
| Chapter 803 | YOUTH TRAINING AND REHABILITATION |
| Chapter 804 | GIRLS' TRAINING SCHOOLS |
| Chapter 830 | STATE BUILDING PROGRAMS |

# CHAPTER 791
# DEPARTMENT OF CORRECTIONS

**Act 4 of 1947 (2nd Ex Sess) [Repealed]**

§§791.1–791.123 [Repealed]

## DEPARTMENT OF CORRECTIONS

**Act 232 of 1953**

### CHAPTER I
### DEPARTMENT OF CORRECTIONS

| | |
|---|---|
| § 791.201 | Establishment; administration by Michigan corrections commission; membership of commission, political affiliation, oath, holding other position, term, vacancies, removal, compensation and expenses; director; executive office, place of meetings. |
| § 791.202 | Commission, organization; meetings; quorum; administrative authority and duty; Open Meetings Act, compliance. |
| § 791.203 | Director of corrections; appointment, qualifications, term, removal, compensation and expenses, chief administrative officer of commission, powers and duties. |
| § 791.204 | Jurisdiction of department. |
| § 791.205 | Assistant directors; appointment, powers and duties. |
| § 791.205a | Employment or appointment by department of person convicted or charged with felony. |
| § 791.206 | Rules generally. |
| § 791.207 | Commission, annual report to governor and legislature; printing and distribution. |
| § 791.207a | Records of department; accessibility by governing bodies of senate and house fiscal agency. |
| § 791.208 | Criminal statistics; reports, duty of local and state officers, courts and judges. |
| § 791.209 | Crime prevention and research in criminology. |
| § 791.210 | Bond, officers and employees. |
| § 791.211 | Interstate compacts, commission's authority. |
| § 791.211a | Interstate corrections compact; contracts; suitability of institutions for confinement; out-of-state transfer of prisoners; conditions; report. |
| § 791.212 | Seal; use; copies of records and papers as evidence; filing; body corporate; authority; leases, easements; Freedom of Information Act, compliance. |
| § 791.213 | Acceptance of grant, devise, bequest, etc., by commission; enforcement of property rights, duty of attorney general. |
| § 791.214 | Budget, submission to department of administration. |
| § 791.215 | Correctional facility defined. |
| § 791.216 | Comprehensive plan for establishment of correctional facilities, development; approval by legislature; determination of need for facility; notice of proposed establishment of facility; local advisory board, creation; duties; officers; public hearing as to potential site; time; attendance; procedures for addressing; exclusion; public notice; minutes; final site selection; finding of compliance with act; |

# Department of Corrections

§ 791.217     transmittal of finding and notice; option to lease or purchase property; time for exercising.
§ 791.217     Action against department for failure to abide by site selection process; limitations period.
§ 791.218     Continuing relations between department and city, township or village in which facility located; advisory committee or board, duties.
§ 791.219     Applicability.
§§791.220–791.220c     [Repealed]
§ 791.220d     [Repealed]
§ 791.220e     Correctional facilities; establishment, operation, or maintenance in local government; limitations; applicability; "local unit of government" defined; use of real property adjoining former Detroit house of corrections.
§ 791.220f     Construction of correctional facilities; requirements; definition.
§ 791.220g     Youth correctional facility.
§ 791.220h     Order of restitution; deductions and payments.

## CHAPTER II

## BUREAU OF PROBATION

§ 791.221     Establishment of bureau; supervision by assistant director.
§ 791.222     Probation officers for courts; appointment, supervision and removal; grounds; misdemeanor, probation recovery camps.
§ 791.223     Assistant director; powers and duties; reports of probation officers.
§ 791.223a     Probation personnel, circuit and recorders court, state employees, supervision and direction; county probation personnel, transfer to state classified civil service; election; date; new employees, status; remaining employee of county, funds to county, use; plan, civil service commission, provisions; applicability of act; county responsibilities.
§ 791.224     [Repealed]
§ 791.225     Expenses of administering probation service covering more than one county; service grants, uniform rules.
§ 791.225a     Supervision fees; amount; collection; records; payment; waiver; determination; allocation of money collected for other obligations; administrative costs; enhanced services; unpaid amounts; time payable; exception; waiver of fee for person transferred to another state; supervision fee for offender transferred to Michigan.
§ 791.226     [Repealed]
§ 791.227     [Repealed]
§ 791.228     Juvenile probation, duty to furnish information; furnishing assistance; access to information and records.
§ 791.229     Privileged or confidential communications; access to records, reports, and case histories; confidential relationship inviolate.
§ 791.230     [Repealed]
§ 791.230a     Exemptions from disclosure under freedom of information act.

## CHAPTER III

## BUREAU OF PARDONS AND PAROLES; PAROLE BOARD

§ 791.231     Bureau of field services; establishment; supervision by deputy director, appointment, tenure, powers, duties; parole officers; secretarial; assistants; quarters.
§ 791.231a     Parole board; establishment; members; terms, reappointment, re-

# Department of Corrections

|  |  |
|---|---|
|  | moval, vacancies, qualifications; compensation; chairperson; designation, powers and duties; appointment and training function. |
| § 791.232 | [Repealed] |
| § 791.233 | Grant of parole; conditions; paroles-in-custody; rules. |
| § 791.233a | [Repealed] |
| § 791.233b[1] | Major controlled substance offense, definition. |
| § 791.233b | Eligibility for parole; minimum term required to be served; ineligibility for special parole. |
| § 791.233c | "Prisoner subject to disciplinary time" defined. |
| § 791.233d | Samples for chemical testing. |
| § 791.233e | Parole guidelines; purpose; mandatory and discretionary factors; nondiscrimination; promulgation of rules; departure from guidelines; review of guidelines; proposed revisions. |
| § 791.234 | Prisoners subject to jurisdiction of parole board; indeterminate and other sentences; termination of sentence; interview; release on parole; discretion of parole board; appeal to circuit court; cooperation with law enforcement by prisoner violating § 333.7401; definitions. |
| § 791.234a | Placement in special alternative incarceration unit; eligibility requirements; minimum sentence required for certain violations; participation prohibited by sentencing judge; eligibility determination by department; notice; prisoner consent to placement; minimum and maximum placement period; parole; suspension or revocation of parole; annual report to legislature. |
| § 791.235 | Release of prisoner on parole; procedure. |
| § 791.236 | Order of parole; signature of chairperson; notice; amendment; rescission; conditions; supervision; restitution; payment of parole supervision fee; condition requiring payment of assessment; compliance with §§28.721 to 28.732; violation of §§333.7401 to 333.7545; condition requiring housing in community corrections center or community residential home; condition requiring payment by parolee; review to ensure payment of restitution; report of violation; registration of parolee; condition to protect named person; "violent felony" defined. |
| § 791.236a | Collection of supervision fee by parole board; limit; payment; determination of amount; enforcement; parole oversight fee; fee for offender transferred to state under interstate compact; administrative costs; fee for offender transferred to Michigan; only one fee to apply at a time; waiver of fees; unpaid amounts; allocation of moneys collected. |
| § 791.237 | Paroled or discharged prisoner; furnishing clothing, transportation, and money; repayment of money; cost of implementing section. |
| § 791.238 | Custody of paroled prisoner; warrant for return; incarceration pending hearing; treatment as escaped prisoner; time during parole violation not counted as time served; forfeiture of good time; committing crime while on parole; construction of parole. |
| § 791.239 | Prisoner on parole, arrest without warrant on reasonable suspicion of parole violation. |
| § 791.239a | Parole violation; preliminary or fact-finding hearing; procedure. |
| § 791.240 | [Repealed] |
| § 791.240a | Parole violation; right to hearing; hearing, notice, time, location; rights; postponement; sufficiency of evidence; reinstatement to parole, or finding of violation and revocation of parole; noncompliance with restitution order; notice; hearing; representation by counsel; rights; finding, recommendation, disposition of charges; written statement, findings of fact, reasons. |
| § 791.241 | Decision of parole board; order. |

# Department of Corrections

§ 791.242    Certificate of discharge; minimum period of parole respecting certain crimes.

§ 791.243    Pardons, reprieves and commutations; form and contents of application.

§ 791.244    Parole board interview of prisoner serving sentence for first degree murder or sentence of imprisonment for life without parole; board duties upon own initiation of receipt of application for reprieve, commutation, or pardon; files as public record.

§ 791.245    Oath to witness, member of parole board may administer.

§ 791.246    Parole board, decisions and recommendations by majority vote of board or panel.

## CHAPTER IIIA
## [HEARINGS DIVISION]

§ 791.251    Hearings division; creation; appointment and duties of hearing administrator; duties of hearings division; supervision and qualifications of hearing officer.

§ 791.252    Hearing; procedures.

§ 791.253    Official record of hearings, inclusions; exclusions, inclusion on appeal.

§ 791.254    Rehearing; motion of department or request of party; circumstances; time for filing request; procedure; amendment or vacation of decision; rules.

§ 791.255    Judicial review, petition by prisoner.

§ 791.256    Prisoners confined in another state; right to hearings.

## CHAPTER IV
## BUREAU OF PENAL INSTITUTIONS

§ 791.261    Establishment of bureau; supervision by assistant director.

§ 791.262    Definitions; administration of facilities by bureau; supervision and inspection of jails and lockups; variance; limit on supervision, inspection and promulgation of rules and standards; provision of advice and services; enforcement of orders; sheriff's residence; commission member, visitation and inspection of jail or lockup; recordkeeping; violations.

§ 791.262a    Lockup advisory board, creation; membership; term; expenses; chairperson; quorum; policy; annual meeting.

§ 791.262b    Housing of two inmates in cell; conditions; classification system; considerations; submission for approval by department; housing of inmate with no prior convictions; visual supervision; authorization of sentencing judge; indemnification of state for damages resulting from housing two inmates in cell; limitations on housing.

§ 791.262c    Housing of two inmates in cell; designation as housing for two or more inmates; conditions; classification system; submission and approval of classification system; single occupancy of high security and segregation cells; visual supervision.

§ 791.263    Wardens; appointment; personnel; "correctional facility" explained.

§ 791.263a    Compensation of correctional or youth correctional facility employees injured by inmate assault or injured during riot; exception; definitions.

§ 791.263b    Housing of two inmates in a cell; conditions; classification system for housing inmates; considerations; submission and approval of classification system by judge; housing of inmate with no prior convictions; visual supervision; authorization of sentencing judge;

## Department of Corrections

| | |
|---|---|
| | indemnification of state for damages resulting from housing of two inmates in cell; limitations on housing; applications of subsections. |
| § 791.264 | Classification of prisoners; committee, duties, records; information with regard to prisoners, filing with parole board. |
| § 791.265 | Transfer or retransfer of prisoners; confinement in secure correctional facility; "offender" defined; transfer of offenders to country of citizenship; notification to judge and prosecutor; objections; "secure correctional facility" defined. |
| § 791.265a | Extending limits of confinement; rules; escape from custody; eligibility for extensions of limits of confinement; placement in community residential home; definitions. |
| § 791.265b | Disabled prisoner, power of director to transfer, duration of transfer; powers and duties of department; terms defined. |
| § 791.265c | Work camp; construction, maintenance, operation, purpose; assignment of prisoners; displacement of employed persons or workers on strike or locked out; agreement of bargaining unit; citizens advisory committee; report; escape; reimbursement of department; collecting and dispersing wages; amount of wages; prevailing wages; rules; restrictions; conditions. |
| § 791.265d | Occurrences requiring entry in law enforcement information network; occurrences requiring certain information to be made available on line; time limitation; scope of entry; "state correctional facility" defined. |
| § 791.265e | Transfer of prisoner to community placement facility, notice to sheriffs, police posts and local police department; notice contents. |
| § 791.265f | Type of housing for prisoners convicted of assaultive crimes; prohibition of opening facilities or entering contracts for dwellings originally intended to house one family. |
| § 791.265g | Definitions. |
| § 791.265h | Placement of prisoner not meeting community status criteria; criteria requirements; location of community corrections center for prisoner placement; operation of center serving more than one county; conditions; limit on number of prisoners to be placed in center; prisoner curfew; random checking of prisoners allowed off premises. |
| § 791.265i | Citizens' council in municipality where community corrections center located; members, appointment, residency requirements; chairperson; meetings; meeting with center supervisor; report by supervisor on prisoner numbers, activities, etc.; designee to act on supervisor's behalf; notice by council of placement believed in violation of criteria; review of record, reclassification of prisoner; annual report by council; duties of council. |
| § 791.266 | Commitment for classification; place. |
| § 791.267 | Temporary confinement; study of prisoner; suitability of prisoner to type of rehabilitation required; report; execution of confinement order; test for HIV or antibody to HIV; applicability of subsection (2); housing prisoner in administrative segregation, inpatient health care unit, or unit separate from general prisoner population; reporting positive test result; exposure of employee to blood or body fluid of prisoner; testing employee; employee equipment; HIV positive prisoner not to work in health facility; seroprevalence study; disclosure of test results; counseling; AIDS education program; report; definitions. |
| § 791.267a | Nonemergency medical, dental, or optometric services; intentional injury; copayment or payment by prisoner; on-site medical treatment; report on feasibility and cost. |
| § 791.267b | Exposure of employee to blood or body fluid of prisoner; request to test prisoner for HIV or HBV infection; form and contents of |

§ 791.268 request; determination; prisoner consent not required; counseling; determination not requiring HIV or HBV infection testing; notice of HIV or HBV test results; confidentiality; forms; violation of subsection (8) as misdemeanor; report; definitions.
§ 791.268 Payment of filing fees or costs by prisoner; court order to make monthly payments; removal of amount from prisoner institutional account.
§ 791.269 [Repealed]
§ 791.269a Subjecting visitor to pat down search; condition; waiver; definitions.

## CHAPTER V
## BUREAU OF PRISON INDUSTRIES

§ 791.270 Monitoring of telephone communications; conditions; disclosure of obtained information; evidence in criminal prosecution; definitions.
§ 791.271 Control and supervision of industrial plants by assistant director; bureau personnel, appointment.

## CHAPTER VI
## MISCELLANEOUS

§ 791.281 Transfer of powers and duties to new department of corrections; abolition of and successor to former department; pending hearings or proceedings not to abate; transfer of records and files; continuation of former orders, rules and regulations.
§ 791.282 Transfers of appropriations.
§ 791.283 Repeal of other provisions.

## MICHIGAN DEPARTMENT OF CORRECTIONS–MICHIGAN CORRECTIONS COMMISSION

### Executive Reorganization Order 1991-12

§ 791.302 Department of Corrections; transfer to new Department of Corrections.

## MICHIGAN DEPARTMENT OF CORRECTIONS BUREAU OF FIELD SERVICES DEPUTY DIRECTOR IN CHARGE OF FIELD SERVICES–EXECUTIVE REORGANIZATION

### Executive Reorganization Order 1992-3

§ 791.303 Transfer of services from Bureau of Field Services to director of Department of Corrections.

## COMMUNITY CORRECTIONS ACT

### Act 511 of 1988

§ 791.401 Title.
§ 791.402 Definitions.
§ 791.403 Office of community alternatives; powers and duties; board; executive director; staff; state community corrections board; policy making duties; members; fair demographic representation; term of office; chairperson; filling vacancies; compensation; reimbursement of expenses.

## Department of Corrections

§ 791.404  Duties of state board.
§ 791.405  Duties of office of community alternatives.
§ 791.406  County application for funding; regional advisory board; joint county and city funding applications; city application for funding, city advisory board.
§ 791.407  Board memberships; appointment of members; fair representation of women and minorities; publication of advance notice of appointments; request for interested persons.
§ 791.408  Funding application; comprehensive corrections plan; contents; development; approval of proposed comprehensive corrections plan; preparation by advisory board; intended participants; nonviolent offenders.
§ 791.409  Community corrections program; retention of jurisdiction by sentencing court.
§ 791.410  Application by nonprofit service agency other than board; notification of application; subsequent appointment of advisory board; contracts with nonprofit service agency; provision of services; limitations on direct funding.
§ 791.411  Authorization for payment of appropriated funds; limitations on funding for administration; funding and current spending.
§ 791.412  Annual and biannual reports, office of community alternatives; contents; submission.
§ 791.413  Transfer of appropriations and resources; time.
§ 791.414  Promulgation of rules.

### CORRECTIONAL OFFICERS' TRAINING ACT OF 1982

**Act 415 of 1982**

§ 791.501  Short title.
§ 791.502  Definitions.
§ 791.503  Correctional officer's training council, creation, appointment of members.
§ 791.504  Term of office; appointment of successors; filling vacancy, reappointment.
§ 791.505  Chairperson; meetings, special meetings; procedures, requirements; open meetings, notice; compensation of members, expenses.
§ 791.506  Members of council; disqualification from other public office or employment.
§ 791.507  Executive secretary, appointment, duties, compensation.
§ 791.508  Administrative support services, appropriation by council.
§ 791.509  Certification of correction officers; requirement of employment.
§ 791.510  Certification, automatic; recertification, requirements, training, minimum standards; approval by state civil service commission.
§ 791.511  Employment after effective date of act, requirements, standards; approval by state civil service commission.
§ 791.512  Certification and recertification, employment after certain date; requirements; correctional officers and immediate supervisors, Detroit house of correction; automatic certification and recertification dependent on date of employment; requirements; employee of state facility converted to state correctional facility; automatic certification and recertification, conversion date; approval by state civil service commission.
§ 791.513  Minimum standards and requirements, development by council; recruitment, training, certification, recertification, decertification;

|  |  |
|---|---|
|  | approval by civil service commission; approval by commission of corrections; approval by state civil service commission. |
| § 791.514 | Local correctional officers; minimum standards and requirements. |
| § 791.515 | Training academy; establishment, funding. |
| § 791.516 | Annual report. |
| § 791.517 | Promulgation of rules. |

OFFICE OF COMMUNITY ALTERNATIVES – MICHIGAN DEPARTMENT OF CORRECTIONS – EXECUTIVE REORGANIZATION

**Executive Reorganization Order 1995-14**

|  |  |
|---|---|
| § 791.601 | Transfer of powers and duties of office of community alternatives to department of corrections by type II transfer. |

Act 4, 1947 (2nd Ex Sess), p 18, imd eff November 12, 1947.

## [Repealed]

AN ACT to revise, consolidate and codify the laws relating to probationers and probation officers as herein defined, to pardons, reprieves, commutations and paroles, to the administration of penal institutions, correctional farms and probation recovery camps, to prison labor and prison industries, and the supervision and inspection of local jails and houses of correction; to create a state department of corrections, and to prescribe its powers and duties; to provide for the transfer to and vesting in said department of powers and duties vested by law in certain other state boards, commissions and officers, and to abolish the department of corrections created by Act No. 255 of the Public Acts of 1937 and its certain boards, commissions and offices the powers and duties of which are hereby transferred; to create a state advisory council of corrections and to prescribe the duties thereof; to prescribe penalties for the violation of the provisions of this act; and to repeal all acts and parts of acts inconsistent with the provisions of this act.

**§§791.1–791.123.** **[Repealed]** [MSA §§28.2141–28.2263]

**History:**
Pub Acts 1947 (2nd Ex Sess), No. 4, imd eff November 12, 1947; **repealed** by Pub Acts 1953, No. 232, § 83, eff October 2, 1953.

**Editor's notes:**
Pub Acts 1953, No. 232, § 83, see § 791.283.

## DEPARTMENT OF CORRECTIONS

Act 232, 1953, p 407, eff October 2, 1953.

AN ACT to revise, consolidate, and codify the laws relating to probationers and probation officers, to pardons, reprieves, com-

**Department of Corrections** § 791.201

mutations, and paroles, to the administration of correctional institutions, correctional farms, and probation recovery camps, to prisoner labor and correctional industries, and to the supervision and inspection of local jails and houses of correction; to provide for the siting of correctional facilities; to create a state department of corrections, and to prescribe its powers and duties; to provide for the transfer to and vesting in said department of powers and duties vested by law in certain other state boards, commissions, and officers, and to abolish certain boards, commissions, and offices the powers and duties of which are transferred by this act; to allow for the operation of certain facilities by private entities; to prescribe the powers and duties of certain other state departments and agencies; to provide for the creation of a local lockup advisory board; to prescribe penalties for the violation of the provisions of this act; to make certain appropriations; to repeal certain parts of this act on specific dates; and to repeal all acts and parts of acts inconsistent with the provisions of this act. (Amended by Pub Acts 1988, No. 510, eff March 30, 1989, by § 2 eff January 1, 1989; 1992, No. 22, imd eff March 19, 1992; 1993, No. 184, imd eff September 30, 1993 (see 1993 note below); 1996, No. 164, eff April 17, 1996 (see 1996 note below).).

*The People of the State of Michigan enact:*

**Popular Name:**
Department of Corrections Act.

**Editor's notes:**
**Pub Acts 1993, No. 184, § 2,** imd eff September 30, 1993, provides:
"Section 2. This amendatory act shall not take effect unless all of the following bills of the 87th Legislature are enacted into law:
"(a) House Bill No. 4875 [which became Act No. 185 of 1993].
"(b) House Bill No. 4876 [which became Act No. 169 of 1993]."
**Pub Acts 1996, No. 164, § 2,** eff April 17, 1996, provides:
"Section 2. This amendatory act shall not take effect unless all of the following bills of the 88th Legislature are enacted into law:
"(a) Senate Bill No. 696 [Act No. 243 of 1996].
"(b) House Bill No. 4723 [Act No. 263 of 1996]."

**Effect of amendment notes:**
**The 1996 amendment** inserted "; to allow for the operation of certain facilities by private entities;".

CHAPTER I

DEPARTMENT OF CORRECTIONS

**§ 791.201. Establishment; administration by Michigan corrections commission; membership of commission, political affiliation, oath, holding other position, term, vacancies, removal, compensation and expenses; director; executive office, place of meetings.** [MSA § 28.2271]

Sec. 1. There is hereby created a state department of corrections, hereinafter called the department, which shall possess the powers and perform the duties granted and conferred. The department shall consist of and be administered by a commission of 6 members appointed by the governor, by and with the advice and consent of the senate, to be known as the Michigan corrections commission, hereinafter called the commission, not more than 3 of whom shall be members of the same political party, each of whom shall qualify by taking the constitutional oath of office, and filing the same in the office of the secretary of state, and of such other officers and assistants as may be appointed or employed in the department, including a director as its executive head. A person holding a position either state or federal, or a person drawing a salary from a municipal unit of the state, shall not be eligible for appointment to the commission, without having first resigned from that position. The term of office of each member of the commission shall be 6 years. The governor shall fill a vacancy occurring in the membership of the commission for the unexpired term only, and for cause established on hearing may remove a member. Each member of the commission shall hold office until his successor shall be appointed and shall qualify. The per diem compensation of the commission and the schedule for reimbursement of expenses shall be established annually by the legislature. The department and commission shall have its executive office at Lansing. The department of management and budget shall provide suitable office accommodations. Meetings of the commission may be held at other suitable places as the commission may designate.

**History:**
Pub Acts 1953, No. 232, § 1, eff October 2, 1953; amended by Pub Acts 1975, No. 59, imd eff May 20.

**Former acts:**
This act, with certain alterations and omissions, is a substantial reenactment of Act 4 of 1947 (2nd Ex Sess), which was repealed hereby.

**Cross references:**
Legislative corrections ombudsman, Act No. 46 of 1974, §§4.351 et seq.
Transfer of the department of corrections created under this section to the department of corrections created by section 275 of the Executive Organization Act [ § 16.375], § 16.377.

**Michigan Digest references:**
Officers and Public Employees §§1 et seq.
Pardons and Paroles §§1 et seq., 4 et seq.
Prisons and Jails § 1.
Zoning § 18.

**LEXIS-NEXIS™ Michigan analytical references:**
Michigan Law and Practice, Convicts and Prisons § 2.

**L Ed annotations:**
Termination of public employment: right to hearing under due process clause of Fifth or Fourteenth Amendment–Supreme Court cases, 48 L Ed 2d 996.

**ALR notes:**
Validity, construction, and application of statutes making public proceedings open to the public, 38 ALR3d 1070.

**Michigan Civ Jur references:**
Buildings § 4.
Minors § 72.

**Research references:**
60 Am Jur 2d, Penal and Correctional Institutions §§3–5.

CASE NOTES

**1. Partial repeal.**
The provisions of this section creating the corrections commission were arguably repealed by implication by § 278 of Pub Acts 1965, No. 380 (§ 16.478), creating a commission composed of 5 members, not more than 3 of whom shall be members of the same political party, for terms of 5 years, the latter provision being so at variance with the earlier that both could not be given effect. Op Atty Gen, November 5, 1965, No. 4485.

**2. Validity and construction of former act.**
Words "all laws now in force," as used in former § 802.55, referred to laws in force at time offense was committed by person confined in house of correction, and not to laws in force at time former section was enacted. People v Reese (1961) 363 Mich 329, 109 NW2d 868.

Respondent was appointed while the senate was not in session, on December 20, 1910, to fill a vacancy in the board of control of the state prison at Jackson, by a governor whose term expired December 31, 1910. Said appointment was confirmed by the senate January 10, 1911, a new governor having meanwhile succeeded to office. Held, under former § 800.2, respondent held office only until the convening of the senate and not until the expiration of the term for which he was appointed. People ex rel. Attorney Gen. v Haggerty (1911) 167 Mich 682, 133 NW 828; Phillips v Kuhn (1911) 167 Mich 687, 133 NW 830.

Former Prison Code, as originally adopted, did not embrace an object not expressed in its title, in that it contained a provision for the punishment of convicts committing crimes in prison and prescribed penalties and punishment for such crimes. People v Huntley (1897) 112 Mich 569, 71 NW 178.

A valid contract made by the board of inspectors of the state house of correction for the keeping of female prisoners in the Detroit House of Correction, was not abrogated by former Prison Code, which, while superseding all prior acts relating to the management of the penal institutions of the state, expressly saved all existing rights and penalties. Rich v Chamberlain (1895) 107 Mich 381, 65 NW 235.

Public Acts 1875, No. 213; 1877, No. 176; 1885, No. 148, were superseded by former Prison Code. Rich v Chamberlain (1895) 107 Mich 381, 65 NW 235.

The failure to reenact and publish at length the laws relating to the penal institutions of the state when former Prison Code, revising and consolidating those laws, was passed, did not render said act obnoxious to the constitutional provision forbidding revision by reference to title only and requiring the revised sections "to be set out at length." Ellis ex rel. Fuller v Parsell (1894) 100 Mich 170, 58 NW 839.

Former Prison Code covered the entire management and control of three institutions, and superseded prior laws. Ellis ex rel. Fuller v Parsell (1894) 100 Mich 170, 58 NW 839.

Former Prison Code, vesting the government of the house of correction at Ionia in a board of control to consist of three members, not more than two of whom shall be of the same political party, was constitutional. Ellis ex rel. Fuller v Parsell (1894) 99 Mich 381, 58 NW 335.

Provision of former act for a nonpartisan board was passed for a salutary purpose, and violated no provision of the constitution. Ellis ex rel. Fuller v Parsell (1894) 99 Mich 381, 58 NW 335.

Provision of former § 802.55 that laws applicable to persons confined in state prison were applicable to persons in house of correction for any offense punishable by confinement in state prison would be held to have manifested intent that female defendant sentenced to house of correction for felonies of forgery, and uttering and publishing, be subject to § 750.193 upon her escape from house of correction, notwithstanding failure of statute to expressly include house of correction in definition of prison. People v Ransom (1974) 54 Mich App 738, 221 NW2d 466.

Where female defendant, after conviction under §§750.248 and 750.249, was sentenced to Detroit House of Correction (Dehoco) as required by former § 802.51, and after her escape from Dehoco was charged with and convicted of escaping from prison contrary to § 750.193, court of appeals, reading together provisions of §§750.193, 750.194 and former section, would hold that it found an intentional distinction between categories of prisoners, which emerged as function of crime for which they had been convicted, that all persons convicted of crimes punishable in state prisons, and only those persons, came under § 750.193 if they escaped or attempted to escape from Dehoco, that everyone else lawfully committed to Dehoco was controlled by § 750.194, and that, in this respect, men and women were treated under the law alike. People v Ransom (1974) 54 Mich App 738, 221 NW2d 466.

### 3. Constitutionality.

Statute conferring on department of corrections exclusive jurisdiction over penal institutions and authorizing department to determine all matters relating to their unified development, and to coordinate such institutions within its jurisdiction so that each shall form integral part of general penal system, coupled with title to statute repealing all statutory provisions inconsistent therewith, would be held to have manifested legislative intent to vest in corrections department complete jurisdiction over state's penal institutions and full power to develop in unified manner general system of state's correctional institutions, subject only to constitutional powers of executive and judiciary and not subject in any way to other legislative acts, such as zoning enabling act or local zoning ordinances enacted pursuant thereto. Dearden v Detroit (1978) 403 Mich 257, 269 NW2d 139, reh den (1978) 403 Mich 957.

In view of substantial authority and control exercised by state penal authorities over management and policies of Detroit House of Correction and clear statutory scheme for spreading costs of operating the facility among city, county and state users, legislature did not unconstitutionally delegate legislative power to city of Detroit by enactment of statutes concerning Detroit House of Correction, notwithstanding that such statutes give Detroit common council and its appointees power to exercise various responsibilities in day-to-day management of the facility. People v Andrea (1973) 48 Mich App 310, 210 NW2d 474.

### 4. Appointment.

The commission of corrections is composed of five members to be appointed by the governor by and with the advice and consent of the senate for a term of four years as required by 1965 PA 380, § 278. Op Atty Gen, October 3, 1983, No. 6187.

A person seeking appointment to the office of member of the commission of corrections must meet the eligibility requirements contained in 1953 PA 232, § 1. Op Atty Gen, October 3, 1983, No. 6187.

Governor is empowered, under § 16.378, to appoint members of commission of corrections. Op Atty Gen, November 5, 1965, No. 4485.

### 5. Compensation and expenses.

Expenses incurred by former board of control of prisons in attending convention of corrections and charities constituted claim against state which board of auditors in exercise of discretion might allow or not. Op Atty Gen, 1898, p 54.

### 6. Departmental powers.

Statute conferring on department of corrections exclusive jurisdiction over penal institutions and authorizing it to develop general system of state correctional institutions under its exclusive jurisdiction, coupled with silence of zoning enabling act on matter, would be held to have manifested legislative intent to grant department immunity from local zoning ordinances in establishing correctional institutions, thereby precluding city zoning ordinance from operating to prohibit department's use of leased property as convict rehabilitation center in city neighborhood. Dearden v Detroit (1978) 403 Mich 257, 269 NW2d 139, reh den (1978) 403 Mich 957.

The powers which the legislature has extended to the department of corrections are related solely to the administration of penal institutions, probation, pardons, paroles and commutations and other aspects of the department's corrections functions; the department is not charged with the enforcement of the general criminal laws of the state. In re Faketty (1982) 121 Mich App 266, 328 NW2d 551.

### 7. Tort liability.

In civil rights action by prisoners chal-

**Department of Corrections** § 791.202

lenging their transfer to maximum security institution, where defendant prison officials acted in good faith and in accordance with existing prescribed procedures of state department of corrections in making the transfer, it would be inappropriate to require defendants to answer for damages. Stone v Egeler (1973, WD Mich) 377 F Supp 115, mod on other grounds (1974, CA6 Mich) 506 F2d 287.

## § 791.202. Commission, organization; meetings; quorum; administrative authority and duty; Open Meetings Act, compliance. [MSA § 28.2272]

Sec. 2. (1) The commission shall elect annually a chairperson and other officers as it considers expedient. A meeting shall be held not less than once each month or at other times as considered necessary. A majority of the total membership of the commission shall constitute a quorum for the transaction of business. The commission shall constitute the responsible authority for the administration of the correctional facilities, correctional industries, parole, and probation of the state, subject to the limitations set forth in this act. The commission shall determine all matters relating to the unified development of the correctional facilities, correctional industries, parole, and probation of the state and shall coordinate and adjust the agencies and correctional facilities within its jurisdiction so that each shall form an integral part of a general system.

(2) The business which the commission may perform shall be conducted at a public meeting held in compliance with Act No. 267 of the Public Acts of 1976, being sections 15.261 to 15.275 of the Michigan Compiled Laws. Public notice of the time, date, and place of the meeting shall be given in the manner required by Act No. 267 of the Public Acts of 1976.

**History:**
 Pub Acts 1953, No. 232, § 2, eff October 2, 1953; amended by Pub Acts 1978, No. 413, imd eff September 28, 1978; 1987, No. 79, imd eff June 29, 1987.

**Michigan Digest references:**
 Officers and Public Employees §§1 et seq.
 Pardons and Paroles §§1 et seq., 4 et seq.
 Prisons and Jails § 1.
 Zoning § 18.

**LEXIS-NEXIS™ Michigan analytical references:**
 Michigan Law and Practice, Convicts and Prisons § 2.

**L Ed annotations:**
 Termination of public employment: right to hearing under due process clause of Fifth or Fourteenth Amendment–Supreme Court cases, 48 L Ed 2d 996.

**ALR notes:**
 Validity, construction, and application of statutes making public proceedings open to the public, 38 ALR3d 1070.

**Michigan Civ Jur references:**
 Buildings § 4.
 Minors § 72.

**Research references:**
 60 Am Jur 2d, Penal and Correctional Institutions §§3–5.

## CASE NOTES

The Michigan Parole Board is exempt from the requirements of the Open Meeting Act. Glover v Parole Bd. (1999) 460 Mich 511, 596 NW2d 598.

The Michigan Parole Board is exempt from the requirements of the Open Meeting Act. Glover v Parole Bd. (1999) 460 Mich 511, 596 NW2d 598.

A quorum of the former board, including member to whom the notice required by former § 800.23 had not been given, might take action on the appointment of a warden. Op Atty Gen, 1911, p 125.

## § 791.203. Director of corrections; appointment, qualifications, term, removal, compensation and expenses, chief administrative officer of commission, powers and duties. [MSA § 28.2273]

Sec. 3. The commission shall appoint a director of corrections who shall be qualified by training and experience in penology. He shall hold office at the pleasure of the commission except that he may be removed for cause and only after a public hearing before the commission. He shall receive such salary as shall be appropriated by the legislature, together with actual and necessary traveling and other expenses. The director shall be the chief administrative officer of the commission and shall be responsible to the commission for the exercise of the powers and duties prescribed and conferred by this act, and for such other powers and duties as may be assigned by the commission, subject at all times to its control. Subject to the provisions of this act, and to the rules and regulations adopted by the commission, the director shall have full power and authority to supervise and control the affairs of the department, and the several bureaus thereof, and he shall carry out the orders of the commission.

**History:**
Pub Acts 1953, No. 232, § 3, eff October 2, 1953.

**Michigan Digest references:**
Officers and Public Employees §§1 et seq.
Pardons and Paroles §§1 et seq., 4 et seq.
Prisons and Jails § 1.

**LEXIS-NEXIS™ Michigan analytical references:**
Michigan Law and Practice, Convicts and Prisons § 2.

**L Ed annotations:**
Termination of public employment: right to hearing under due process clause of Fifth or Fourteenth Amendment–Supreme Court cases, 48 L Ed 2d 996.

**ALR notes:**
Validity, construction, and application of statutes making public proceedings open to the public, 38 ALR3d 1070.

**Michigan Civ Jur references:**
Buildings § 4.
Minors § 72.

**Research references:**
60 Am Jur 2d, Penal and Correctional Institutions §§3–5.

**Department of Corrections** § 791.204

## § 791.204. Jurisdiction of department. [MSA § 28.2274]

Sec. 4. Subject to constitutional powers vested in the executive and judicial departments of the state, the department shall have exclusive jurisdiction over the following: (a) Probation officers of this state, and the administration of all orders of probation, (b) pardons, reprieves, commutations and paroles, and (c) penal institutions, correctional farms, probation recovery camps, prison labor and industry, wayward minor programs and youthful trainee institutions and programs for the care and supervision of youthful trainees.

**History:**
Pub Acts 1953, No. 232, § 4, eff October 2, 1953; amended by Pub Acts 1966, No. 210, imd eff July 11, 1966.

**Cross references:**
Probation and probation officers generally, §§771.1 et seq. and 791.221 et seq.
Penal and correctional institutions, §§791.262 et seq.
Probation recovery camps, §§798.1 et seq., 791.222 and 791.262.
Interstate compacts relating to probation and parole, §§798.101 et seq. and 791.211.
Correctional and prison industries, §§800.321 et seq.

**Michigan Digest references:**
Constitutional Law §§66, 89.
Officers and Public Employees §§1 et seq.
Pardons and Paroles §§1 et seq., 2, 4 et seq., 5, 6.
Prisons and Jails §§1, 1.05, 1.25, 1.35, 1.45, 1.50, 4.
State of Michigan § 25.
Statutes § 26.
Zoning § 18.

**LEXIS-NEXIS™ Michigan analytical references:**
Michigan Law and Practice, Convicts and Prisons § 2.

**L Ed annotations:**
Termination of public employment: right to hearing under due process clause of Fifth or Fourteenth Amendment–Supreme Court cases, 48 L Ed 2d 996.

**ALR notes:**
Validity, construction, and application of statutes making public proceedings open to the public, 38 ALR3d 1070.

**Michigan Civ Jur references:**
Buildings § 4.
Minors § 72.

**Research references:**
60 Am Jur 2d, Penal and Correctional Institutions §§3–5.

### CASE NOTES

**1. Powers.**
Legislature created department of corrections for purpose of concentrating with that department primary, but not exclusive, responsibility for well-being as well as disciplinary rehabilitation of state-sentenced prisoners, whenever such prisoners are held in any penal institution over which department of corrections has jurisdiction and power, whether exercised or not, to promulgate rules and standards relating thereto. Green v State Corrections Dep't (1971) 386 Mich 459, 192 NW2d 491.

The department has exclusive jurisdiction over paroles, commutations, and penal institutions, subject to the powers of the judicial and executive departments; a sentencing judge is not empowered to make the full payment of restitution a prerequisite to obtaining parole or early release, however, any restitution ordered shall be a condition of parole and the parole board may revoke parole if the defendant fails to comply. People v Greenberg (1989) 176 Mich App 296, 439 NW2d 336, app den (1989) 433 Mich 900.

The department of corrections has exclusive jurisdiction over pardons, reprieves, commutations and paroles. Collins v Director, Dep't of Corrections (1986) 153 Mich App 477, 395 NW2d 77, app den (1987) 428 Mich 867, 400 NW2d 605, cert den (1987) 483 US 1026, 97 L Ed 2d 774, 107 S Ct 3276, habeas corpus dismissed (1994, CA6 Mich) 1994 US App LEXIS 3878.

The statute by which a sentencing judge or his successor in office may, upon written objection, veto the release on parole of a prisoner who has completed at least ten years of a sentence for a conviction other than first-degree murder or a major controlled substances offense does not violate the constitutional provision for the separation of powers; the statute does not vest a judge with the power to pardon a prisoner or commute his sentence, which is vested by the constitution upon the governor, nor does it infringe upon the exclusive jurisdiction of the department of corrections over pardons, reprieves, commutations and paroles. Collins v Director, Dep't of Corrections (1986) 153 Mich App 477, 395 NW2d 77, app den (1987) 428 Mich 867, 400 NW2d 605, cert den (1987) 483 US 1026, 97 L Ed 2d 774, 107 S Ct 3276, habeas corpus dismissed (1994, CA6 Mich) 1994 US App LEXIS 3878.

A section of the Department of Corrections act concerning the department's jurisdiction grants exclusive jurisdiction to the department over, among other areas, penal institutions; the section is not an express limitation on the supervisory powers of the department but simply provides that no other agency of the state government can regulate the area. Davis v Detroit (1986) 149 Mich App 249, 386 NW2d 169, app den (1986) 426 Mich 856 and (disapproved on other grounds by Wade v Department of Corrections (1992) 439 Mich 158, 483 NW2d 26).

The department of corrections has jurisdiction over, and authority to control, the activities in penal institutions of this state and has the primary responsibility over the well-being of incarcerated state prisoners whenever such prisoners are held in any penal institution over which the department has jurisdiction. Cross v Department of Corrections (1981) 103 Mich App 409, 303 NW2d 218.

Statutory power conferred on corrections commission to have jurisdiction over and authority to supervise and inspect penal institutions, and to appoint director who in turn makes rules and regulations for management and control of such institutions, includes Detroit House of Correction within such powers. Green v State (1971) 30 Mich App 648, 186 NW2d 792, affd (1971) 386 Mich 459, 192 NW2d 491.

## § 791.205. Assistant directors; appointment, powers and duties. [MSA § 28.2275]

Sec. 5. The director, subject to the approval of the commission, shall appoint an assistant director in charge of probation, an assistant director in charge of pardons and paroles, an assistant director in charge of penal institutions, an assistant director in charge of prison industries, and an assistant director in charge of a youth division. The assistant directors shall exercise and perform the respective powers and duties prescribed and conferred by this act, and such other powers and duties as may be assigned by the director, subject at all times to his control.

**History:**
Pub Acts 1953, No. 232, § 5, eff October 2, 1953.

**Michigan Digest references:**
Officers and Public Employees §§1 et seq.

**Department of Corrections** § 791.206

Pardons and Paroles §§1 et seq., 4 et seq.
Prisons and Jails § 1.

**L Ed annotations:**
Termination of public employment: right to hearing under due process clause of Fifth or Fourteenth Amendment–Supreme Court cases, 48 L Ed 2d 996.

**ALR notes:**
Validity, construction, and application of statutes making public proceedings open to the public, 38 ALR3d 1070.

**Michigan Civ Jur references:**
Buildings § 4.
Minors § 72.

**Research references:**
60 Am Jur 2d, Penal and Correctional Institutions §§3–5.

## § 791.205a. Employment or appointment by department of person convicted or charged with felony. [MSA § 28.2275a]

Sec. 5a. (1) Beginning on the effective date of this section, an individual who has been convicted of a felony, or who is subject to any pending felony charges, shall not be employed by or appointed to a position in the department.

(2) If records available to the department show that an applicant for employment or appointment has been convicted of a felony or is subject to pending felony charges, the department shall inform the applicant of that fact and of his or her resulting ineligibility for employment or appointment. At the request of the applicant, the department shall permit the applicant to review the relevant portion of the records. If the applicant disputes the accuracy of the records, the department shall allow the applicant a reasonable period of time to contact the responsible agency or agencies in order to correct the alleged inaccuracies, and shall allow the applicant to reapply for employment or appointment if the records, as corrected, would remove the ineligibility imposed by this section.

(3) This section does not apply to a person employed by or appointed to a position in the department before the effective date of this section.

**History:**
Pub Acts 1953, No. 232, § 5a, as added by Pub Acts 1996, No. 140, imd eff March 25, 1996.

## § 791.206. Rules generally. [MSA § 28.2276]

Sec. 6. (1) The director may promulgate rules pursuant to the administrative procedures act of 1969, Act No. 306 of the Public Acts of 1969, being sections 24.201 to 24.328 of the Michigan Compiled Laws, which may provide for all of the following:

(a) The control, management, and operation of the general affairs of the department.

(b) Supervision and control of probationers an d probation officers throughout this state.

(c) The manner in which applications for pardon, reprieve, medical commutation, or commutation shall be made to the governor; the procedures for handling applications and recommendations by the parole board; the manner in which paroles shall be considered, the criteria to be used to reach release decisions, the procedures for medical and special paroles, and the duties of the parole board in those matters; interviews on paroles and for the notice of intent to conduct an interview; the entering of appropriate orders granting or denying paroles; the supervision and control of paroled prisoners; and the revocation of parole.

(d) The management and control of state penal institutions, correctional farms, probation recovery camps, and programs for the care and supervision of youthful trainees separate and apart from persons convicted of crimes within the jurisdiction of the department. Except as provided for in section 62(3), this subdivision shall not apply to detention facilities operated by local units of government used to detain persons less than 72 hours. The rules may permit the use of portions of penal institutions in which persons convicted of crimes are detained. The rules shall provide that decisions as to the removal of a youth from the youthful trainee facility or the release of a youth from the supervision of the department shall be made by the department and shall assign responsibility for those decisions to a committee.

(e) The management and control of prison labor and industry.

(2) The director may promulgate rules providing for a parole board structure consisting of 3-member panels.

(3) The director may promulgate further rules with respect to the affairs of the department as the director considers necessary or expedient for the proper administration of this act. The director may modify, amend, supplement, or rescind a rule.

(4) The director and the corrections commission shall not promulgate a rule or adopt a guideline that does either of the following:

(a) Prohibits a probation officer or parole officer from carrying a firearm while on duty.

(b) Allows a prisoner to have his or her name changed. If the Michigan supreme court rules that subsection 4(b) is violative of constitutional provisions under the first and fourteenth amendments to the United States constitution and article I, sections 2 and 4 of the Michigan constitution of 1963, the remaining provisions of the code shall remain in effect.

(5) If the Michigan supreme court rules that sections 45 and 46 of the administrative procedures act of 1969, Act No. 306 of the Public Acts of 1969, being sections 24.245 and 24.246 of the Michigan Compiled Laws, are unconstitutional, and a statute requiring legislative review of administrative rules is not enacted within 90 days after the Michigan supreme court ruling, the department shall not promulgate rules under this section.

**History:**
Pub Acts 1953, No. 232, § 6, eff October 2, 1953; amended by Pub Acts 1966, No. 210, imd eff July 11, 1966; 1982, No. 314, imd eff October 15,

1982; 1984, No. 102, imd eff May 7, 1984; 1986, No. 271, imd eff December 19, 1986 (see 1986 note below).

Amended by Pub Acts 1996, No. 104, imd eff March 5, 1996, by § 2 eff April 1, 1996 (see 1996 note below).

**Editor's notes:**
**Pub Acts 1986, No. 271, § 2,** imd eff December 19, 1986, provides:

"Section 2. Upon the expiration of 2 years after the effective date of this amendatory act, section 6 of Act No. 232 of the Public Acts of 1953, being section 791.206 of the Michigan Compiled Laws [this section], is repealed." However, the repeal provision was (**Repealed** by Pub Acts 1988, No. 364, § 1), which provides:

"Section 1. Enacting section 2 of Act No. 271 of the Public Acts of 1986 is repealed".

**Pub Acts 1996, No. 104, § 3,** imd eff March 5, 1996, by § 2 eff April 1, 1996, provides:

"Section 3. This amendatory act shall not take effect unless Senate Bill No. 346 of the 88th Legislature [Pub Acts 1996, No. 106] is enacted into law."

**Effect of amendment notes:**
**The 1996 amendment** made changes throughout the section.

**Statutory references:**
Section 62 is § 791.262.

**Michigan Administrative Code:**
Michigan Administrative Code R 791.1101–791.9930.

**Michigan Digest references:**
Mandamus § 115.
Prisons and Jails §§1.05, 1.35, 1.50, 4.

## CASE NOTES

**1. Construction, operation and effect.**

Statutory language governing parole board decision-making process does not require that majority vote be reached at a collegial meeting of the board members; thus, parole board's practice of circulating parole file from one board member to another, allowing for independent determination to be made by each member until majority decision was reached, did not constitute violation of board's statutory power. In re Parole of Franciosi (1998) 231 Mich App 607, 586 NW2d 542.

1986 PA 271, construed to provide that neither the Director of the Department of Corrections nor the Corrections Commission is authorized to adopt rules, guidelines or policy directives prohibiting probation or parole officers from carrying weapons while on duty, is constitutional under Const 1963, art 4, § 25. Op Atty Gen, April 27, 1987, No. 6435.

**2. Rules and regulations.**

Martin v Department of Corrections, 424 Mich 553 (1986), which held that the Department of Corrections is subject to the rule-making requirements of the Administrative Procedures Act when promulgating policy directives that penalize inmates for major misconduct violations, applies retroactively only with respect to cases pending on March 28, 1986, at the administrative, trial court, or appellate court levels where the issue of compliance with the act was properly raised and preserved. Jahner v Department of Corrections (1992) 197 Mich App 111, 495 NW2d 168.

In light of legislative repeal as obsolete and inoperative of §§800.1 et seq., dealing with duties of wards, clerk, and physician in correction facilities, thereby creating void correctable only by promulgation of proper rules, and in light of use of words "shall" in provision of this section that corrections commission shall promulgate rules and regulations for operation of correction facilities, such statute would be held to contain clear and legal mandate for commission to promulgate such rules so as to warrant issuance of writ of mandamus in event commission would fail to initiate within 90 days formal rule-making procedures under Administrative Procedures Act. Lundberg v Corrections Com. (1975) 57 Mich App 327, 225 NW2d 752.

Regulations for administration and discipline of prisons, promulgated and enforced by duly authorized officials, are not subject to judicial review unless defendant clearly demonstrates they interfere with fundamental constitutional right. People v Robinson (1972) 41 Mich App 259, 199 NW2d 878.

While courts generally refuse to interfere with prison regulations and policy, prisoner's showing of constitutional deprivation of due process of law warrants court's intervention. Wojnicz v Michigan Dep't of Corrections (1971) 32 Mich App 121, 188 NW2d 251.

Inmate confined to penal institution upon conviction of crime cannot enjoy same rights of personal freedom as other members of society. Op Atty Gen, March 16, 1977, No. 5179.

In absence of showing that prison warden's discretionary power has been arbitrarily exercised, no objection can be raised to curtailment of visiting privileges of prison inmate. Op Atty Gen, March 16, 1977, No. 5179.

Rules adopted by Department of Corrections must be promulgated pursuant to Michigan's Administrative Procedures Act. Spruytte v Walters (1985, CA6 Mich) 753 F2d 498 (criticized on other grounds by Walker v Mintzes (1985, CA6 Mich) 771 F2d 920) and cert den (1986) 474 US 1054, 88 L Ed 2d 767, 106 S Ct 788.

**3. Moneys and funds.**

In view of substantial authority and control exercised by state penal authorities over management and policies of Detroit House of Correction under former statute, and clear statutory scheme for spreading costs of operating the facility among city, county and state users, legislature did not unconstitutionally delegate legislative power to city of Detroit by enactment of statutes concerning Detroit House of Correction, notwithstanding that such statutes gave Detroit common council and its appointees power to exercise various responsibilities in day-to-day management of the facility. People v Andrea (1973) 48 Mich App 310, 210 NW2d 474.

Michigan Department of Corrections could not constitutionally appropriate funds from prison inmate's account without affording him procedural due process of notice and hearing. Wojnicz v Michigan Dep't of Corrections (1971) 32 Mich App 121, 188 NW2d 251.

A provision in an act appropriating funds to the Department of Corrections which provides for the creation of a loan program for city lockups is in violation of Const 1963, art IV, § 24, where there is no appropriation in the act for such program and nothing in the title to suggest that the act purports to create such a loan program. Op Atty Gen, April 26, 1979, No. 5485.

Action of Michigan prison officials, in seizing sum of money from prisoner's person and placing it in inmate general benefit fund was properly regulated function of prison administration, and as such did not constitute violation of prisoner's civil rights. Kimble v Department of Corrections (1969, CA6 Mich) 411 F2d 990.

**4. Due process requirements.**

Due process procedural requirements still apply where prisoner is subjected to disciplinary confinement or segregation. Dickerson v Warden, Marquette Prison (1980) 99 Mich App 630, 298 NW2d 841.

**5. Carrying concealed weapons.**

Probation or parole officers employed by the Department of Corrections may carry concealed weapons only if they either (1) possess permits from a county concealed weapon licensing board to do so, or (2) if they have written authorization from the Director of the Department of Corrections to carry weapons while on duty and/or when traveling to or from work. Op Atty Gen, April 27, 1987, No. 6435.

## § 791.207. Commission, annual report to governor and legislature; printing and distribution. [MSA § 28.2277]

Sec. 7. On or before the 15th day of January of each year, the commission shall make to the governor and legislature a report of the department for the preceding fiscal year. Such report, if so ordered by the board of state auditors, shall be printed and distrib-

**Department of Corrections** § 791.208

uted in such manner and to such persons, organizations, institutions and officials as said board may direct.

**History:**
Pub Acts 1953, No. 232, § 7, eff October 2, 1953.

## § 791.207a. Records of department; accessibility by governing bodies of senate and house fiscal agency. [MSA § 28.2277a]

Sec. 7a. (1) Except as provided in subsection (2), the governing bodies of the senate and house fiscal agencies shall have access to all records of the department of corrections relating to individuals under the supervision of the department of corrections including, but not limited to, records contained in basic information reports and in the corrections management information system, the parole board information system, and any successor databases.

(2) Records shall not be accessible under subsection (1) if the department of corrections determines that any of the following applies:

(a) Access is restricted or prohibited by law.

(b) Access could jeopardize an ongoing investigation.

(c) Access could jeopardize the safety of a prisoner, employee, or other person.

(d) Access could jeopardize the safety, custody, or security of an institution or other facility.

(3) The records that are to be accessed, and the manner of access to those records, shall be determined under a written agreement entered into jointly between the governing board of the senate fiscal agency, the governing committee of the house fiscal agency, and the department of corrections. The agreement shall ensure the confidentiality of accessed records.

**History:**
Pub Acts 1953, No. 232, § 7a, as added by Pub Acts 1998, No. 315, imd eff July 30, 1998, by enacting § 1 eff December 15, 1998 (see 1998 note below).

**Editor's notes:**
Pub Acts 1998, No. 315, enacting § 2, imd eff July 30, 1998, by enacting § 1 eff December 15, 1998, provides:
"Enacting section 2. This amendatory act does not take effect unless all of the following bills of the 89th Legislature are enacted into law:
"(a) Senate Bill No. 826 [Pub Acts 1998, No. 316].
"(b) House Bill No. 4065 [Pub Acts 1998, No. 319].
"(c) House Bill No. 4444 [Pub Acts 1998, No. 311].
"(d) House Bill No. 4445 [Pub Acts 1998, No. 312].
"(e) House Bill No. 4446 [Pub Acts 1998, No. 313].
"(f) House Bill No. 4515 [Pub Acts 1998, No. 320].
"(g) House Bill No. 5419 [Pub Acts 1998, No. 317].
"(h) House Bill No. 5876 [Pub Acts 1998, No. 318]."

## § 791.208. Criminal statistics; reports, duty of local and state officers, courts and judges. [MSA § 28.2278]

Sec. 8. Within the department there shall be established a general division of criminal statistics under the supervision and control of the director. He shall have the power and it shall be his duty to obtain from all chiefs of police, sheriffs, state police, prosecuting attorneys, courts, judges, parole and probation officers and all others concerned in the control, apprehension, trial, probation, parole and commitments of adult criminals and delinquents in this state, periodical reports as to the number and kinds of offenses known to law enforcement officers; the numbers, age, sex, race, nativity and offenses of criminals and delinquents arrested, tried and otherwise disposed of; the sentences imposed and whether executed or suspended; the numbers placed on parole and probation and the reasons therefor and such other information as he may deem necessary. It shall be the duty of all such chiefs of police, sheriffs, state police, prosecuting attorneys, courts, judges, parole and probation officers and others concerned to make such reports at such times and in such manner, and to furnish such facilities for investigation as the director may reasonably require.

**History:**
Pub Acts 1953, No. 232, § 8, eff October 2, 1953.

**Cross references:**
Registration bureau in department of public safety, §§28.241 et seq.
Uniform crime reporting system, §§28.251 et seq.
Fingerprinting of inmates of penal and correctional institutions, § 28.261.

### CASE NOTES

Prison officials, in regular course of their duties and in absence of knowledge, may give names and addresses of relatives and friends on "wanted circulars" published for purpose of apprehending fugitives from justice without being subjected to liability for libel, as constituting privileged communications. Op Atty Gen, February 17, 1947, No. 0–5218.

Department of corrections has authority to require individualized reports from various law enforcement officers in such form and at such times as it may direct. (Construing similar provision of former act.) Op Atty Gen, February 1, 1944, No. 0–1793.

## § 791.209. Crime prevention and research in criminology. [MSA § 28.2279]

Sec. 9. The commission shall study the problem of crime prevention and foster research in criminology. It shall lend its aid in local crime prevention activities.

**History:**
Pub Acts 1953, No. 232, § 9, eff October 2, 1953.

**Cross references:**
Proceedings to prevent crime, §§772.1 et seq.

## § 791.210. Bond, officers and employees. [MSA § 28.2280]

Sec. 10. The commission may require a bond from any officer or employee appointed by or subject to the control of the commission, conditioned upon the faithful performance of his duties and the accounting for all money and property within his control.

**Department of Corrections** § 791.211a

**History:**
Pub Acts 1953, No. 232, § 10, eff October 2, 1953.

**Michigan Digest references:**
Officers and Public Employees §§85 et seq.

### CASE NOTES

The record kept by clerk under former §§800.13 and 800.14 was a public record and might be used in evidence. People v Kemp (1889) 76 Mich 410, 43 NW 439.

**§ 791.211. Interstate compacts, commission's authority.** [MSA § 28.2281]

Sec. 11. The commission shall exercise the powers and duties created by Act No. 89 of the Public Acts of 1935, being sections 798.101 to 798.103, inclusive, of the Compiled Laws of 1948, and by any interstate compact made and entered into pursuant to said act, in regard to the control and supervision of parolees and probationers, and in regard to cooperative effort and mutual assistance in the prevention of crime and in the enforcement of the penal laws and policies of the contracting states, and the commission may promulgate such rules and regulations as may be deemed necessary to more effectively carry out the terms of the aforesaid act and compacts made pursuant thereto.

**History:**
Pub Acts 1953, No. 232, § 11, eff October 2, 1953.

**§ 791.211a. Interstate corrections compact; contracts; suitability of institutions for confinement; out-of-state transfer of prisoners; conditions; report.** [MSA § 28.2281(1)]

Sec. 11a. (1) The director of corrections may enter into contracts on behalf of this state as the director considers appropriate to implement the participation of this state in the interstate corrections compact pursuant to article III of the interstate corrections compact. The contracts may authorize confinement of prisoners in, or transfer of prisoners from, correctional facilities under the jurisdiction of the department of corrections. A contract shall not authorize the confinement of a prisoner who is in the custody of the department in an institution of a state other than a state that is a party to the interstate corrections compact. When transferring prisoners to institutions of other states under this section, the director shall endeavor to ensure that the transfers do not disproportionately affect groups of prisoners according to race, religion, color, creed, or national origin.

(2) The director of corrections shall first determine, on the basis of an inspection made by his or her direction, that an institution of another state is a suitable place for confinement of prisoners committed to his or her custody before entering into a contract permitting that confinement, and shall, at least annually, redetermine the suitability of that confinement. In determining the suit-

ability of an institution of another state, the director shall determine that the institution maintains standards of care and discipline not incompatible with those of this state and that all inmates confined in that institution are treated equitably, regardless of race, religion, color, creed, or national origin.

(3) In considering transfers of prisoners out-of-state pursuant to the interstate corrections compact due to bed space needs the department shall do all of the following:
 (a) Consider first prisoners who volunteer to transfer as long as they meet the eligibility criteria for such transfer.
 (b) Provide law library materials including Michigan Compiled Laws, Michigan state and federal cases, and U.S. sixth circuit court cases.
 (c) Not transfer a prisoner who has a significant medical or mental health need.
 (d) Use objective criteria in determining which prisoners to transfer.

(4) Unless a prisoner consents in writing, a prisoner transferred under the interstate corrections compact due to bed space needs shall not be confined in another state for more than 1 year.

(5) A prisoner who is transferred to an institution of another state under this section shall receive all of the following while in the receiving state:
 (a) Mail services and access to the court.
 (b) Visiting and telephone privileges.
 (c) Occupational and vocational programs such as GED-ABE and appropriate vocational programs for his or her level of custody.
 (d) Programs such as substance abuse programs, sex offender programs, and life skills development.
 (e) Routine and emergency health care, dental care, and mental health services.

(6) One year after April 13, 1994 and annually after that date, the department shall report all of the following to the senate and house committees responsible for legislation concerning corrections and to the appropriations subcommittees on corrections:
 (a) The number of prisoners transferred to or from correctional facilities in this state pursuant to the interstate corrections compact.
 (b) The cost to the state of the transfers described in subdivision (a).
 (c) The reasons for the transfers described in subdivision (a).

**History:**
Pub Acts 1953, No. 232, § 11a, as added by Pub Acts 1994, No. 93, imd eff April 13, 1994 (see 1994 note below).
Amended by Pub Acts 1998, No. 204, imd eff June 30, 1998.

**Editor's notes:**
**Pub Acts 1994, No. 93, § 2,** imd eff April 13, 1994, provides:
"Section 2. This amendatory act shall not take effect unless Senate Bill

No. 794 of the 87th Legislature [which became Pub Acts 1994, No. 92] is enacted into law."

**Effect of amendment notes:**
The **1998 amendment** added material to subsection (1); deleted former subsection (3); added new subsections (3)-(5); redesignated former subsection (4) as (6); and made additions and deletions in subsection (6).

## § 791.212. Seal; use; copies of records and papers as evidence; filing; body corporate; authority; leases, easements; Freedom of Information Act, compliance. [MSA § 28.2282]

Sec. 12. (1) The commission shall devise a seal, and the rules of the commission shall be published over the seal of the commission. All orders of the commission shall be issued over the seal of the commission. A copy of the records and papers in the office of the department, certified by an authorized agent of the commission and authenticated by the seal of the commission, shall be evidence in all cases with the same effect as the originals. A description of the seal, with an impression of the seal, shall be filed in the office of the secretary of state. The commission shall be a body corporate, and may lease lands under its jurisdiction, grant easements over, through, under, or across those lands for a lawful purpose, and do any other act necessary to carry out this act.

(2) A writing prepared, owned, used, in the possession of, or retained by the commission in the performance of an official function shall be made available to the public in compliance with Act No. 442 of the Public Acts of 1976, being sections 15.231 to 15.246 of the Michigan Compiled Laws.

**History:**
Pub Acts 1953, No. 232, § 12, eff October 2, 1953; amended by Pub Acts 1974, No. 357, imd eff December 21, 1974; 1978, No. 413, imd eff September 28, 1978.

**Michigan Digest references:**
Evidence §§691 et seq.

**Research references:**
60 Am Jur 2d, Penal and Correctional Institutions §§3–5.

### CASE NOTES

Under former similar provision, it was ruled that commissioner of corrections could not sell, lease or grant easement over property of state except as provided in such section, but he was authorized to lease any lands under jurisdiction of department if necessary in carrying out provisions of this act. Op Atty Gen, December 12, 1947, No. 657.

Commissioner, however, could not sell property of state. Op Atty Gen, December 12, 1947, No. 658.

## § 791.213. Acceptance of grant, devise, bequest, etc., by commission; enforcement of property rights, duty of attorney general. [MSA § 28.2283]

Sec. 13. The commission may receive on behalf of the state of Michigan any grant, devise, bequest, donation, gift or assignment of money, bonds or chooses in action, or of any property, real or personal, and accept the same, so that the right and title to the same shall pass to the state of Michigan; and all such bonds, notes or chooses in action, or the proceeds thereof when collected, and all other property or thing of value so received by the commission shall be used for the purposes set forth in the grant, devise, bequest, donation, gift or assignment: Provided, That such purposes shall be within the powers conferred on said commission. Whenever it shall be necessary to protect or assert the right or title of the commission to any property so received or derived as aforesaid, or to collect or reduce into possession any bond, note, bill or chose in action, the attorney general is directed to take the necessary and proper proceedings and to bring suit in the name of the commission on behalf of the state of Michigan in any court of competent jurisdiction, state or federal, and to prosecute all such suits.

**History:**
Pub Acts 1953, No. 232, § 13, eff October 2, 1953.

**Research references:**
60 Am Jur 2d, Penal and Correctional Institutions §§3–5.

## § 791.214. Budget, submission to department of administration. [MSA § 28.2284]

Sec. 14. The commission shall prepare for submission to the department of administration the estimated needs and costs to operate the department, and the several penal institutions under the jurisdiction of the department, in accordance with the requirements of the laws of this state.

**History:**
Pub Acts 1953, No. 232, § 14, eff October 2, 1953.

**Research references:**
60 Am Jur 2d, Penal and Correctional Institutions §§3–5.

## § 791.215. Correctional facility defined. [MSA § 28.2285]

Sec. 15. As used in this act, "correctional facility" means a facility or institution which is maintained and operated by the department.

**History:**
Pub Acts 1953, No. 232, § 15, as added by Pub Acts 1980, No. 303, imd eff November 26, 1980.

**Research references:**
60 Am Jur 2d, Penal and Correctional Institutions §§3–5.

**§ 791.216. Comprehensive plan for establishment of correctional facilities, development; approval by legislature; determination of need for facility; notice of proposed establishment of facility; local advisory board, creation; duties; officers; public hearing as to potential site; time; attendance; procedures for addressing; exclusion; public notice; minutes; final site selection; finding of compliance with act; transmittal of finding and notice; option to lease or purchase property; time for exercising.** [MSA § 28.2286]

Sec. 16. (1) The department shall develop a comprehensive plan for determining the need for establishing various types of correctional facilities, for selecting the location of a correctional facility, and for determining the size of the correctional facility. The comprehensive plan shall not be implemented until the legislature, by concurrent resolution adopted by a majority of those elected and serving in each house by a record roll call vote, approves the comprehensive plan.

(2) The department shall determine the need for a correctional facility based upon the comprehensive plan developed pursuant to subsection (1).

(3) The department shall publish a notice that it proposes to establish a correctional facility in a particular city, village, or township. The notice shall appear in a newspaper of general circulation in the area. In addition, the department shall notify the following officials:

(a) The state senator and the state representative representing the district in which the correctional facility is to be located.

(b) The president of each state supported college or university whose campus is located within 1 mile of the proposed correctional facility.

(c) The chief elected official of the city, village, or township in which the correctional facility is to be located.

(d) Each member of the governing body of the city, village, or township in which the correctional facility is to be located.

(e) Each member of the county board of commissioners in which the correctional facility is to be located.

(f) The president of the local school board of the local school district in which the correctional facility is to be located.

(g) The president of the intermediate school board of the intermediate school district in which the correctional facility is to be located.

(4) With the notice, the department shall request the chairperson of the county board of commissioners of the county in which the correctional facility is to be located and the person notified pursuant to subsection (3)(c) to create a local advisory board to assist in the identification of potential sites for the correctional facility, to act as a liaison between the department and the local community, and to ensure that the comprehensive plan is being followed by the department. The officials requested to create a local advisory board pursuant to this subsection shall serve as co-chairpersons of that local advisory board.

(5) After the requirements of subsections (1), (2), (3), and (4) are completed and the department has selected a potential site, the department shall hold a public hearing in the city, village, or township in which the potential site is located. The department shall participate in the hearing and shall make a reasonable effort to respond in writing to concerns and questions raised on the record at the hearing. The hearing shall not be held until the local advisory board created by subsection (4) has organized, or sooner than 30 days after the notice is sent pursuant to subsection (3), whichever occurs first.

(6) Hearings the department shall conduct under subsection (5) shall be open to the public and shall be held in a place available to the general public. Any person shall be permitted to attend a hearing except as otherwise provided in this section. A person shall not be required as a condition to attendance at a hearing to register or otherwise provide his or her name or other information or otherwise to fulfill a condition precedent to attendance. A person shall be permitted to address the hearing under written procedures established by the department. A person shall not be excluded from a hearing except for a breach of the peace actually committed at the meeting.

(7) The following provisions shall apply with respect to public notice of hearings required under this section:

(a) A public notice shall always contain the name of the department, its telephone number, and its address.

(b) A public notice shall always be posted at the department's principal office and other locations considered appropriate by the department.

(c) The required public notice for a hearing shall be posted in the office of the county clerk of the county in which the facility is to be located and shall be published in a newspaper of general circulation in the county in which the facility is to be located.

(d) A public notice stating the date, time, and place of the hearing shall be posted at least 10 days before the hearing.

(8) Minutes of each hearing required under this section shall be kept showing the date, time, place, members of the local advisory board present, members of the local advisory board absent, and a summary of the discussions at the hearing. The minutes shall be public records open to public inspection and shall be available at the address designated on posted public notices pursuant to subsection (7). Copies of the minutes shall be available from the department to the public at the reasonable estimated cost for printing and copying.

(9) On the basis of the information developed by the department during the course of the site selection process, and after community concerns have been responded to by the department pursuant to subsection (5), the commission shall make a final site determination for the correctional facility. The commission shall make a finding that the site determination was made in compliance with this section. This finding and notice of final site selection shall be transmitted in writing by the commission to the local advisory

**Department of Corrections** § 791.217

board, the officials described in subsection (3), and the chairpersons of the senate and house appropriations committees.

(10) An option to lease, purchase, or use property may be obtained but shall not be exercised by the state for a correctional facility until the commission has made a final site determination and has transmitted a notice of final site selection as required in subsection (9).

**History:**
Pub Acts 1953, No. 232, § 16, as added by Pub Acts 1980, No. 303, imd eff November 26, 1980.

**LEXIS-NEXIS™ Michigan analytical references:**
Michigan Law and Practice, Convicts and Prisons § 2.

**ALR notes:**
Validity, construction, and application of statutes making public proceedings open to the public, 38 ALR3d 1070.

**Research references:**
60 Am Jur 2d, Penal and Correctional Institutions § 7.

### CASE NOTES

Model policies developed and promoted by a local lockup advisory board within the Michigan Department of Corrections are not subject to the rule-making or the guideline-making requirements of the Administrative Procedures Act of 1969. Op Atty Gen, August 29, 1997, No. 6950.

## § 791.217. Action against department for failure to abide by site selection process; limitations period. [MSA § 28.2287]

Sec. 17. (1) A person who resides in the city, village, or township in which the department has determined a need for a correctional facility may bring an action in a court of proper jurisdiction against the department if the department is not abiding by the site selection process provided in section 16.

(2) An action brought under this section shall not be maintained if it is filed more than 45 days after the commission sends notification of the final site selected to the officials as required in section 16(9).

**History:**
Pub Acts 1953, No. 232, § 17, as added by Pub Acts 1980, No. 303, imd eff November 26, 1980.

**Statutory references:**
Section 16, above referred to, is § 791.216.

**ALR notes:**
Validity, construction, and application of statutes making public proceedings open to the public, 38 ALR3d 1070.

**Research references:**
60 Am Jur 2d, Penal and Correctional Institutions § 7.

## § 791.218. Continuing relations between department and city, township or village in which facility located; advisory committee or board, duties. [MSA § 28.2288]

Sec. 18. After a correctional facility is established, the department shall maintain relations with the city, village, or township in which the facility is located. The department shall request the officials notified under section 16(3)(b) to (g) to appoint an advisory committee or continue the advisory board established pursuant to section 16(4) to meet with the department and correctional facility representatives to assist in the identification of community concerns, to assist in the identification of problems, and to recommend methods for resolving those concerns and problems.

**History:**
Pub Acts 1953, No. 232, § 18, as added by Pub Acts 1980, No. 303, imd eff November 26, 1980.

**Statutory references:**
Section 16, above referred to, is § 791.216.

**ALR notes:**
Validity, construction, and application of statutes making public proceedings open to the public, 38 ALR3d 1070.

**Research references:**
60 Am Jur 2d, Penal and Correctional Institutions § 7.

## § 791.219. Applicability. [MSA § 28.2289]

Sec. 19. This section and sections 15 to 18 shall apply to correctional facilities established or proposed after the effective date of the concurrent resolution approving the comprehensive plan and to correctional facilities which are proposed before the effective date of the concurrent resolution approving the comprehensive plan but for which sites have not been selected by the commission as of that date.

**History:**
Pub Acts 1953, No. 232, § 19, as added by Pub Acts 1980, No. 303, imd eff November 26, 1980.

**Statutory references:**
Sections 15 to 18, above referred to, are §§791.215, 791.216, 791.217 and 791.218.

**ALR notes:**
Validity, construction, and application of statutes making public proceedings open to the public, 38 ALR3d 1070.

**Research references:**
60 Am Jur 2d, Penal and Correctional Institutions § 7.

### CASE NOTES

The Department of Corrections need not promulgate rules establishing placement procedures in regional prisons until, at least, the Legislature passes a concurrent resolution approving the comprehensive plan for correctional facilities. Jansson v Department of Corrections (1985) 146 Mich App 172, 379 NW2d 410.

**Department of Corrections** § 791.220e

§§791.220–791.220c. [Repealed] [MSA §§28.2290–28.2290(3)]

**History:**
Pub Acts 1953, No. 232, §§20–20c, as added by Pub Acts 1980, No. 485, imd eff January 20, 1981; **repealed** by Pub Acts 1995, No. 28, imd eff May 10, 1995.

**Editor's notes:**
Former §§791.220–791.220c pertained to definitions, corrections regions, selection and recommendation of sites for regional prisons, procedures to maximize the placement of prisoners in regions where they reside, and the promulgation of rules for such placement.

§ 791.220d. [Repealed] [MSA § 28.2290(4)]

**History:**
Pub Acts 1953, No. 232, § 20d, as added by Pub Acts 1980, No. 485, imd eff January 20, 1981; **repealed** by Pub Acts 1987, No. 176, imd eff November 19, 1987.

**Editor's notes:**
Former § 791.220d pertained to demolition of the Michigan reformatory in Ionia.

**§ 791.220e. Correctional facilities; establishment, operation, or maintenance in local government; limitations; applicability; "local unit of government" defined; use of real property adjoining former Detroit house of corrections.** [MSA § 28.2290(5)]

Sec. 20e. (1) Notwithstanding any other provision of this act, after June 14, 1985, a correctional facility, including a prison or other penal institution, correctional farm, reformatory, or probation recovery camp, owned, operated, leased, supervised, or contracted for by the state, shall not be established, operated, or maintained in any local unit of government in which the following correctional facilities are located:
    (a) Scott correctional facility.
    (b) Western Wayne correctional facility.
(2) Subsection (1) does not apply to the following correctional facilities that are in accordance with the following:

| | MAXIMUM PRISONERS | SECURITY LEVEL |
|---|---|---|
| Scott correctional facility | 860 | Multi-security level prison |
| Western Wayne correctional facility | 775 | Medium security prison |

(3) Scott correctional facility shall be used for housing female prisoners only.
(4) As used in this section, "local unit of government" means a city, village, or township.
(5) Except with regard to the limitations on state prison facilities and total state prisoners provided for in this section, this section

**§ 791.220e**                  **Department of Corrections**

shall not be construed as limiting the use of the approximately 900 acres of real property owned by the city of Detroit which adjoins the former Detroit house of corrections.

**History:**
Pub Acts 1953, No. 232, § 20e, as added by Pub Acts 1985, No. 62, imd eff June 14, 1985; amended by Pub Acts 1991, No. 96, imd eff August 1, 1991 (see 1991 note below); 1995, No. 20, imd eff April 12, 1995.

**Editor's notes:**
Pub Acts 1991, No. 96, § 2, imd eff August 1, 1991, provides:
"Section 2. This amendatory act shall not take effect unless Senate Bill No. 348 of the 86th Legislature [which became Act No. 97 of 1991] is enacted into law."

**Effect of amendment notes:**
The **1995 amendment** in subsection (2) under the column headed "Security Level", inserted "Multi-security level" in place of "Regional", and for the maximum number of prisoners in Western Wayne correctional facility replaced "500" with "775"; and in subsection (5) substituted "former" for "existing" preceding "Detroit house of corrections".

## § 791.220f. Construction of correctional facilities; requirements; definition. [MSA § 28.2290(6)]

Sec. 20f. (1) A correctional facility constructed after the effective date of this section shall be constructed in compliance with at least 1 of the following requirements:

(a) A distance of not less than 300 feet exists between each adjacent residential dwelling and any part of the correctional facility or grounds that is within the security perimeter.

(b) A buffer zone is constructed between the correctional facility and all adjacent residential dwellings. The buffer zone shall be designed to block sight and to block or reduce sound, and may consist of an earth berm or trees or other plants, or materials that would have a substantially similar effect. A fence does not meet the requirements of this subdivision.

(2) As used in this section, "correctional facility" means any facility that houses prisoners under the jurisdiction of the department, but does not include a halfway house, community corrections center, or community residential home.

**History:**
Pub Acts 1953, No. 232, § 20f, as added by Pub Acts 1989, No. 107, imd eff June 23, 1989.

## § 791.220g. Youth correctional facility. [MSA § 28.2290(7)]

Sec. 20g. (1) The department may establish a youth correctional facility which shall house only prisoners committed to the jurisdiction of the department who are 19 years of age or less and who were within the jurisdiction of 1 of the following courts:

(a) The circuit court or the recorder's court of the city of Detroit under section 606 of the revised judicature act of 1961, 1961 PA 236, MCL 600.606, or section 10a(1)(c) of 1919 PA 369, MCL 725.10a.

**Department of Corrections** § 791.220g

(b) The court having general criminal jurisdiction pursuant to a waiver of jurisdiction by the juvenile division of the probate court or the family division of circuit court under section 4 of chapter XIIA of 1939 PA 288, MCL 712A.4.

(c) The juvenile division of the probate court or the family division of circuit court in a case designated under section 2d of chapter XIIA of 1939 PA 288, MCL 712A.2d.

(2) The department may establish and operate the youth correctional facility or may contract on behalf of the state with a private vendor for the construction or operation, or both, of the youth correctional facility. If the department contracts with a private vendor to construct, rehabilitate, develop, renovate, or operate any existing or anticipated facility pursuant to this section, the department shall require a written certification from the private vendor regarding all of the following:

(a) If practicable to efficiently and effectively complete the project, the private vendor shall follow a competitive bid process for the construction, rehabilitation, development, or renovation of the facility, and this process shall be open to all Michigan residents and firms. The private vendor shall not discriminate against any contractor on the basis of its affiliation or nonaffiliation with any collective bargaining organization.

(b) The private vendor shall make a good faith effort to employ, if qualified, Michigan residents at the facility.

(c) The private vendor shall make a good faith effort to employ or contract with Michigan residents and firms to construct, rehabilitate, develop, or renovate the facility.

(3) If the department contracts with a private vendor for the operation of the youth correctional facility, the department shall require by contract that the personnel employed by the private vendor in the operation of the facility be certified as correctional officers to the same extent as would be required if those personnel were employed in a correctional facility operated by the department. The department also shall require by contract that the private vendor meet requirements specified by the department regarding security, protection of the public, inspections by the department, programming, liability and insurance, conditions of confinement, educational services required under subsection (8), and any other issues the department considers necessary for the operation of the youth correctional facility. The department shall also require that the contract include provisions to protect the public's interest if the private vendor defaults on the contract. Before finalizing a contract with a private vendor for the construction or operation of the youth correctional facility, the department shall submit the proposed contract to the standing committees of the senate and the house of representatives having jurisdiction of corrections issues, the corrections subcommittees of the standing committees on appropriations of the senate and the house of representatives, and, with regard to proposed construction contracts, the joint committee on capital outlay. A contract between the department and a private vendor for

§ 791.220g  Department of Corrections

the construction or operation of the youth correctional facility shall be contingent upon appropriation of the required funding. If the department contracts with a private vendor under this section, the selection of that private vendor shall be by open, competitive bid.

(4) The department shall not site a youth correctional facility under this section in a city, village, or township unless the local legislative body of that city, village, or township adopts a resolution approving the location.

(5) A private vendor operating a youth correctional facility under a contract under this section shall not do any of the following, unless directed to do so by the department policy:

(a) Calculate inmate release and parole eligibility dates.

(b) Award good time or disciplinary credits, or impose disciplinary time.

(c) Approve inmates for extensions of limits of confinement.

(6) The youth correctional facility shall be open to visits during all business hours, and during nonbusiness hours unless an emergency prevents it, by any elected state senator or state representative.

(7) Once each year, the department shall report on the operation of the facility. Copies of the report shall be submitted to the chairpersons of the house and senate committees responsible for legislation on corrections or judicial issues, and to the clerk of the house of representatives and the secretary of the senate.

(8) Regardless of whether the department itself operates the youth correctional facility or contracts with a private vendor to operate the youth correctional facility, all of the following educational services shall be provided for juvenile prisoners housed at the facility who have not earned a high school diploma or received a general education certificate (GED):

(a) The department or private vendor shall require that a prisoner whose academic achievement level is not sufficient to allow the prisoner to participate effectively in a program leading to the attainment of a GED certificate participate in classes that will prepare him or her to participate effectively in the GED program, and shall provide those classes in the facility.

(b) The department or private vendor shall require that a prisoner who successfully completes classes described in subdivision (a), or whose academic achievement level is otherwise sufficient, participate in classes leading to the attainment of a GED certificate, and shall provide those classes.

(9) Neither the department nor the private vendor shall seek to have the youth correctional facility authorized as a public school academy under the revised school code, 1976 PA 451, MCL 380.1 to 380.1852.

(10) A private vendor that operates the youth correctional facility under a contract with the department shall provide written notice of its intention to discontinue its operation of the facility. This subsection does not authorize or limit liability for a breach or default of contract. If the reason for the discontinuance is that the private

**Department of Corrections** § 791.220h

vendor intends not to renew the contract, the notice shall be delivered to the director of the department at least 1 year before the contract expiration date. If the discontinuance is for any other reason, the notice shall be delivered to the director of the department at least 6 months before the date on which the private vendor will discontinue its operation of the facility. This subsection does not authorize or limit liability for a breach or default of contract.

**History:**
Pub Acts 1953, No. 232, § 20g, as added by Pub Acts 1996, No. 164, eff April 17, 1996 (see 1996 note below); amended by Pub Acts 1998, No. 512, imd eff January 8, 1999.

**Editor's notes:**
**Pub Acts 1996, No. 164, § 2,** eff April 17, 1996, provides:
"Section 2. This amendatory act shall not take effect unless all of the following bills of the 88th Legislature are enacted into law:
"(a) Senate Bill No. 696 [Act No. 243 of 1996].
"(b) House Bill No. 4723 [Act No. 263 of 1996]."

**Effect of amendment notes:**
**The 1998 amendment** modified the former last sentence of subsection (1) and redesignated part of it as subsections (1)(a) and (1)(b), added subsection (1)(c), and made changes to statutory references throughout subsection (1) and in subsection (9).

**LEXIS-NEXIS™ Michigan analytical references:**
Michigan Law and Practice, Convicts and Prisons § 2.

## § 791.220h. Order of restitution; deductions and payments.
[MSA § 28.2290(8)]

Sec. 20h. (1) If a prisoner is ordered to pay restitution to the victim of a crime and the department receives a copy of the restitution order from the court, the department shall deduct 50% of the funds received by the prisoner in a month over $50.00 for payment of restitution. The department shall promptly forward the restitution amount to the crime victim as provided in the order of restitution when the amount exceeds $100.00, or the entire amount if the prisoner is paroled, transferred to community programs, or is discharged on the maximum sentence. The department shall notify the prisoner in writing of all deductions and payments made under this section. The requirements of this subsection remain in effect until all of the restitution has been paid.

(2) Any funds owed by the Michigan department of corrections or to be paid on behalf of one or more of its employees to satisfy a judgment or settlement to a person for a claim that arose while the person was incarcerated, shall be paid to satisfy any order(s) of restitution imposed on the claimant that the department has a record of. The payment shall be made as described in subsection (1). The obligation to pay the funds, described in this section, shall not be compromised. As used in this section, "fund" or "funds" means that portion of a settlement or judgment that remains to be paid to a claimant after statutory and contractual court costs, attorney fees, and expenses of litigation, subject to the court's approval, have been deducted.

**§ 791.220h**    **Department of Corrections**

(3) The department shall not enter into any agreement with a prisoner that modifies the requirements of subsection (1). Any agreement in violation of this subsection is void.

**History:**
Pub Acts 1953, No. 232, § 20h, as added by Pub Acts 1996, No. 559, by § 2 eff June 1, 1997 (see 1996 note below).

**Editor's notes:**
**Pub Acts 1996, No. 559,** § 3, by § 2 eff June 1, 1997, provides:
"Section 3. This amendatory act shall not take effect unless Senate Bill No. 929 of the 88th Legislature [Pub Acts 1996, No. 560] is enacted into law."

**ALR notes:**
Measure and elements of restitution to which victim is entitled under state criminal statute, 15 ALR5th 391.

**Research references:**
21 Am Jur 2d, Crim L § 525.
60 Am Jur 2d, Penal Inst § 106.

## CHAPTER II
## BUREAU OF PROBATION

### § 791.221. Establishment of bureau; supervision by assistant director. [MSA § 28.2291]

Sec. 21. There is hereby established within the department a bureau of probation. This bureau shall be under the direction and supervision of the assistant director in charge of probation.

**History:**
Pub Acts 1953, No. 232, § 21, eff October 2, 1953.

**Michigan Digest references:**
Pardons and Paroles §§1 et seq., 4 et seq.

**Research references:**
21 Am Jur 2d, Criminal Law §§567, 570, 579.

### § 791.222. Probation officers for courts; appointment, supervision and removal; grounds; misdemeanor, probation recovery camps. [MSA § 28.2292]

Sec. 22. (1) The commission shall appoint, supervise, and remove probation officers for the circuit court and recorder's court of this state, in the manner provided by the laws of this state.

(2) The commission may remove a probation employee for incompetency, misconduct, or failure to carry out the orders of the department, or for neglect of duty.

(3) A probation employee who receives compensation from public funds under this act, and receives any compensation, gift, or gratuity from a person under probation or from a person, partnership, association, or corporation for doing or refraining from doing an official act connected with his or her work as a probation employee, or connected with a proceeding pending or about to be

instituted in the circuit court or recorder's court is guilty of a misdemeanor.

(4) The commission shall be vested with the powers and duties prescribed by the law with respect to probation recovery camps.

**History:**
Pub Acts 1953, No. 232, § 22, eff October 2, 1953; amended by Pub Acts 1979, No. 89, imd eff August 1, 1979, by § 4 eff April 1, 1980 (see 1979 notes below).

**Editor's notes:**
**Pub Acts 1979, No. 89,** § **3,** imd eff August 1, 1979, by § 4 eff April 1, 1980, provides:
"Section 3. This amendatory act shall not take effect unless the funds for its implementation are appropriated by the legislature and House Bill No. 4402 of the 1979 regular session of the legislature [which became Act No. 81 of 1979] is enacted into law."
Pub Acts 1979, No. 89, § 4 originally read "This amendatory act shall take effect December 31, 1979", but Pub Acts 1979, No. 210, § 2, imd eff January 10, 1980, amended it to read "This amendatory act shall take effect April 1, 1980."

**Cross references:**
Probation officers generally, §§771.7 et seq.
Probation recovery camps, § 798.1 et seq.

**Michigan Digest references:**
Pardons and Paroles §§1 et seq., 4 et seq.

**Research references:**
21 Am Jur 2d, Criminal Law §§567, 570, 579.

## § 791.223. Assistant director; powers and duties; reports of probation officers. [MSA § 28.2293]

Sec. 23. The assistant director in charge of probation shall be the administrative head of the bureau of probation subject to the authority and supervision of the director of the department of corrections, and the commission. The assistant director shall exercise general supervision over the administration of probation in the circuit court and recorder's court of the state. The assistant director, with the approval of the director, shall appoint personnel other than probation officers necessary for the conduct of the bureau. The assistant director shall endeavor to secure the effective application of the probation system in all courts of the state and the enforcement of probation laws. The assistant director shall supervise the work of probation personnel and shall have access to all probation offices and records. The assistant director shall prescribe the form of records to be kept and reports to be made by probation personnel and shall promulgate general rules which shall regulate the procedure for the administration of probation, including investigation, supervision, case work, record keeping, and accounting. The assistant director shall collect and maintain a complete file of presentence investigations made by probation officers throughout the state. The assistant director shall collect, compile, and publish statistical and other information relating to probation work in all courts and other information of value in probation service. All

§ 791.223   Department of Corrections

probation officers shall submit the required reports to the department of corrections on forms to be prescribed and furnished by the department of corrections.

**History:**
Pub Acts 1953, No. 232, § 23, eff October 2, 1953; amended by Pub Acts 1979, No. 89, imd eff August 1, 1979, by § 4 eff April 1, 1980 (see 1979 notes below).

**Editor's notes:**
Pub Acts 1979, No. 89, § 3, imd eff August 1, 1979, by § 4 eff April 1, 1980, provides:

"Section 3. This amendatory act shall not take effect unless the funds for its implementation are appropriated by the legislature and House Bill No. 4402 of the 1979 regular session of the legislature [which became Act No. 81 of 1979] is enacted into law."

Pub Acts 1979, No. 89, § 4 originally read "This amendatory act shall take effect December 31, 1979", but Pub Acts 1979, No. 210, § 2, imd eff January 10, 1980, amended it to read "This amendatory act shall take effect April 1, 1980."

**Cross references:**
§§771.7 et seq.

**Michigan Digest references:**
Pardons and Paroles §§1 et seq., 4 et seq.

**Research references:**
21 Am Jur 2d, Criminal Law §§567, 570, 579.

## § 791.223a. Probation personnel, circuit and recorders court, state employees, supervision and direction; county probation personnel, transfer to state classified civil service; election; date; new employees, status; remaining employee of county, funds to county, use; plan, civil service commission, provisions; applicability of act; county responsibilities. [MSA § 28.2293(1)]

Sec. 23a. (1) Effective April 1, 1980, all probation personnel in the circuit court of this state and recorder's court of the city of Detroit shall be considered state employees for purposes of supervision and direction. County probation personnel may transfer their employment from a county probation department to state classified civil service pursuant to procedures established by the civil service commission. County probation personnel who wish to remain county employees may elect to do so pursuant to this section. Not later than 6 years after the effective date of this section, all probation employees shall be members of the state classified civil service.

(2) Effective April 1, 1980, all new employees hired as probation personnel shall be members of the state classified civil service.

(3) If a county probation employee remains an employee of the county, the county shall receive an amount from the state equal to the base state civil service salary or county salary, whichever is the lesser. Funds provided by the state pursuant to this section shall be used exclusively for the purpose of compensating county probation employees. The county shall provide for all salary in excess of the state base salary, travel, fringe benefits, and retirement for person-

**Department of Corrections** § 791.223a

nel choosing to remain as county employees.

(4) The civil service commission, in consultation with the department of corrections and affected counties, shall develop a plan effective April 1, 1980, which shall include provisions relating to the transfer of seniority rights, longevity, and accumulated annual and sick leave of county probation office personnel electing to join the state classified civil service. The plan shall specify procedures for the supervision, direction, and disciplinary removal of county probation personnel. If applicable, Act No. 88 of the Public Acts of 1961, as amended, being sections 38.1101 to 38.1105 of the Michigan Compiled Laws, shall apply.

(5) All rents, contractual services, supplies, materials, and equipment which are a county responsibility on the effective date of this section, shall continue to be a county responsibility.

**History:**
Pub Acts 1953, No. 232, § 23a, as added by Pub Acts 1979, No. 89, imd eff August 1, 1979, by § 4 eff April 1, 1980 (see 1979 note below); amended by Pub Acts 1979, No. 210, imd eff January 10, 1980 (see 1979 note below).

**Editor's notes:**
**Pub Acts 1979, No. 89, § 3,** imd eff August 1, 1979, by § 4 eff April 1, 1980, provides:

"Section 3. This amendatory act shall not take effect unless the funds for its implementation are appropriated by the legislature and House Bill No. 4402 of the 1979 regular session of the legislature [which became Act No. 81 of 1979] is enacted into law."

**Pub Acts 1979, No. 210,** §§3, 4, imd eff January 10, 1980, provide:

"Section 3. The provisions of Act Nos. 81 and 89 of the Public Acts of 1979 shall not take effect in a county with a population of 1.5 million or more prior to a majority vote of the elected members of the county's board of commissioners to place the question of the creation of a charter commission under the terms of enacted Senate Bill No. 652 [which became Act No. 7 of 1980] before the county electorate. Subsequent to the above action by the board of commissioners, funds appropriated for probation services for a county with a population of 1.5 million or more shall become immediately effective, and shall be retroactive to the extent of the funds provided.

"Section 4. Implementation of Act Nos. 81 and 89 of the Public Acts of 1979 shall not be effective in counties which refuse to provide probation support costs as required in those acts."

Pub Acts 1979, No. 89, § 4 originally read "This amendatory act shall take effect December 31, 1979", but Pub Acts 1979, No. 210, § 2, imd eff January 10, 1980, amended it to read "This amendatory act shall take effect April 1, 1980."

Although this section was added and amended at the 1979 session of the legislature, only the last amendment is hereinabove set out, as under the rule of Detroit U. Ry. v Barnes Paper Co. (1912) 172 Mich 586, 138 NW 211, the last amendment was controlling.

**Michigan Digest references:**
Pardons and Paroles §§1 et seq., 4 et seq.

**Research references:**
21 Am Jur 2d, Criminal Law §§567, 570, 579.

§ 791.223a      Department of Corrections

CASE NOTES

Counties remain responsible for rent, contractual services, supplies, materials, and equipment costs supporting probation officers and personnel in the county, including any increases in such costs arising from an increase in probation services staffing. Op Atty Gen, June 29, 1987, No. 6448.

Where both retirement systems have elected to come under the provisions of the Reciprocal Retirement Act, a member of a county retirement system who became a state employee and a member of the State Employees' Retirement System, upon attainment of age 60, may apply for a county retirement benefit combining county and state service, but the amount of benefits from the county retirement system shall be computed solely on service performed for the county. Op Atty Gen, January 13, 1981, No. 5838.

The federal Employees' Retirement Income Security Act of 1974 does not apply to retirement plans established and maintained by the state or any public division thereof for their respective employees. Op Atty Gen, January 13, 1981, No. 5838.

## § 791.224. [Repealed] [MSA § 28.2294]

**History:**
Pub Acts 1953, No. 232, eff October 2, 1953; **repealed** by Pub Acts 1979, No. 89, imd eff August 1, 1979, by § 4 eff April 1, 1980 (see 1979 notes below).

**Editor's notes:**
Former § 791.224 dealt with probation districts and the duties of probation officers.

**Pub Acts 1979, No. 89, § 3,** imd eff August 1, 1979, by § 4 eff April 1, 1980, provides:

"Section 3. This amendatory act shall not take effect unless the funds for its implementation are appropriated by the legislature and House Bill No. 4402 of the 1979 regular session of the legislature [which became Act No. 81 of 1979] is enacted into law."

Pub Acts 1979, No. 89, § 4 originally read "This amendatory act shall take effect December 31, 1979", but Pub Acts 1979, No. 210, § 2, imd eff January 10, 1980, amended it to read "This amendatory act shall take effect April 1, 1980."

## § 791.225. Expenses of administering probation service covering more than one county; service grants, uniform rules. [MSA § 28.2295]

Sec. 25. Where the courts of more than 1 county are served by the same probation officer or officers, the compensation of such officer or officers and the expenses of administering probation service within such counties shall be met jointly by the boards of supervisors therein: Provided, That when it shall appear to the commission that any county is unable to adequately maintain its probation program according to the standards set by the state bureau of probation, then service grants to such an extent and under such conditions as the commission may determine, may be made available to said county: Provided, That uniform rules to be followed in making available such service grants first shall be promulgated by the commission.

**History:**
Pub Acts 1953, No. 232, § 25, eff October 2, 1953.

**Department of Corrections** § 791.225a

**Michigan Digest references:**
Constitutional Law § 48.
Counties § 39.
Pardons and Paroles §§1 et seq., 4 et seq.

**Research references:**
21 Am Jur 2d, Criminal Law §§567, 570, 579.

## CASE NOTES

Assuming that county seeking service grants from department of corrections to hire additional probation personnel could show or had shown requisite inability to properly maintain an adequate probation program, provision of this section for service grants did not impose a clear duty upon department to provide sums necessary to hire more probation personnel. County of Wayne v Corrections Com. of State Dep't of Corrections (1973) 45 Mich App 720, 207 NW2d 205.

It was not function of court of appeals to order promulgation of uniform rules by corrections commission with regard to granting of service grants as an ancillary action in proceedings by county for mandamus to compel commission to provide service grants for hiring additional probation personnel. County of Wayne v Corrections Com. of State Dep't of Corrections (1973) 45 Mich App 720, 207 NW2d 205.

Provision of this section for service grants by corrections commission to county for purpose of maintaining county's probation program does not require, or even infer, that service grants must be made from general funds of department of corrections. County of Wayne v Corrections Com. of State Dep't of Corrections (1973) 45 Mich App 720, 207 NW2d 205.

Under provision of this section for service grants by corrections commission to county for purpose of maintaining county's probation program, size of service grant is question left to determination of commission. County of Wayne v Corrections Com. of State Dep't of Corrections (1973) 45 Mich App 720, 207 NW2d 205.

Under provision of this section for service grants by corrections commission to county for purpose of maintaining county's probation program, service grants are dependent upon a finding by commission that county is unable to adequately maintain its probation program according to standards set by state bureau of probation; hence burden is on county seeking service grants to show that it is unable to maintain such program rather than merely unwilling to maintain such program, and it is doubtful whether mere fact that county faces admittedly sizable financial deficit constitutes necessary showing that it is unable to properly maintain probation program. County of Wayne v Corrections Com. of State Dep't of Corrections (1973) 45 Mich App 720, 207 NW2d 205.

Under provision of this section that when it shall appear to corrections commission that any county is unable to adequately maintain its probation program according to standards set by state bureau of probation, then "service grants to such an extent and under such conditions as the commission may determine, may be made available to said county," quoted language is clearly permissive and language of statute cannot be read to be a mandate by legislature to require commission to make such grants. County of Wayne v Corrections Com. of State Dep't of Corrections (1973) 45 Mich App 720, 207 NW2d 205.

**§ 791.225a. Supervision fees; amount; collection; records; payment; waiver; determination; allocation of money collected for other obligations; administrative costs; enhanced services; unpaid amounts; time payable; exception; waiver of fee for person transferred to another state; supervision fee for offender transferred to Michigan.** [MSA § 28.2295(1)]

Sec. 25a. (1) The department shall collect supervision fees ordered under section 13(2) of chapter II or section 1 or 3c of chapter XI of the code of criminal procedure, Act No. 175 of the Public Acts of

**§ 791.225a**  **Department of Corrections**

1927, being sections 762.13, 771.1, and 771.3c of the Michigan Compiled Laws. The department shall maintain records of supervision fees ordered by the court, including records of payment by persons subject to supervision fees and any amounts of supervision fees past due and owing.

(2) A supervision fee is payable when the order of delayed sentence or order of probation is entered, unless the court allows a person who is subject to a supervision fee to pay the fee in monthly installments.

(3) The department shall waive any applicable supervision fee for a person who is transferred to another state under the interstate compact entered into pursuant to Act No. 89 of the Public Acts of 1935, being sections 798.101 to 798.103 of the Michigan Compiled Laws, for the months during which he or she is in another state. The department shall collect a supervision fee of not more than $30.00 per month for each month of supervision in this state for an offender transferred to this state under that interstate compact. In determining the amount of the fee, the department shall consider the offender's projected income and financial resources. The department shall use the following table of projected monthly income in determining the amount of the fee:

| Projected Monthly Income | Amount of Fee |
| --- | --- |
| $     0-249.99 | $ 0.00 |
| $250.00-499.99 | $10.00 |
| $500.00-749.99 | $20.00 |
| $750.00 or more | $30.00 |

The department may collect a higher amount than indicated by the table, up to the maximum of $30.00 for each month of supervision in this state, if the department determines that the offender has sufficient assets or other financial resources to warrant the higher amount. If the department collects a higher amount, the amount and the reasons for collecting that amount shall be stated in the department records.

(4) If a person who is subject to a supervision fee is also subject to any combination of fines, costs, restitution orders, assessments, or payments arising out of the same criminal proceeding, the allocation of money collected for those obligations shall be as otherwise provided in the code of criminal procedure, Act No. 175 of the Public Acts of 1927, being sections 760.1 to 776.21 of the Michigan Compiled Laws.

(5) Twenty percent of the money collected by the department under this section shall be allocated for administrative costs incurred by the department in collecting supervision fees and for enhanced services, as described in this subsection. Enhanced services include, but are not limited to, the purchase of services for offenders such as counseling, employment training, employment placement, or education; public transportation expenses related to training, counseling, or employment; enhancement of staff performance through specialized training and equipment purchase; and purchase of items for offender employment. The department shall develop priorities for expending the money for enhanced services in

**Department of Corrections** § 791.226

consultation with circuit judges in this state. At the end of each fiscal year, the unexpended balance of the money allocated for administrative costs and enhanced services shall be available for carry forward to be used for the purposes described in this subsection in subsequent fiscal years. Money received by the department pursuant to this subsection in the fiscal year ending September 30, 1994 is appropriated for the purposes described in this subsection.

(6) If a person has not paid the full amount of a supervision fee upon being discharged from probation, or upon termination of the period of delayed sentence for a person subject to delayed sentence, the department shall review and compare the actual income of the person during the period of probation or delayed sentence with the income amount projected when the supervision fee was ordered. If the department determines that the person's actual income did not equal or exceed the projected income, the department shall waive any unpaid amount in excess of the total amount that the person would have been ordered to pay if the person's income had been accurately projected, unless the court order states that a higher amount was ordered due to available assets or other financial resources. Any unpaid amounts not waived by the department shall be reported to the department of treasury. The department of treasury shall attempt to collect the unpaid balances pursuant to section 30a of Act No. 122 of the Public Acts of 1941, being section 205.30a of the Michigan Compiled Laws. Money collected under this subsection shall not be allocated for the purposes described in subsection (5).

**History:**
Pub Acts 1953, No. 232, § 25a, as added by Pub Acts 1993, No. 184, imd eff September 30, 1993 (see 1993 note below).

**Editor's notes:**
**Pub Acts 1993, No. 184, § 2,** imd eff September 30, 1993, provides:
"Section 2. This amendatory act shall not take effect unless all of the following bills of the 87th Legislature are enacted into law:
"(a) House Bill No. 4875 [which became Act No. 185 of 1993].
"(b) House Bill No. 4876 [which became Act No. 169 of 1993]."

**Michigan Digest references:**
Pardons and Paroles §§1 et seq., 4 et seq.

**Research references:**
21 Am Jur 2d, Criminal Law §§567, 570, 579.

### § 791.226. [Repealed] [MSA § 28.2296]

**History:**
Pub Acts 1953, No. 232, § 26, eff October 2, 1953; **repealed** by Pub Acts 1972, No. 179, imd eff June 16, 1972.

**Editor's notes:**
Former § 791.226 which limited application of the chapter to exclude certain counties over 500,000 population, was held constitutionally invalid as local legislation, but such invalidity was held not to affect the balance of the act. Judges for Third Judicial Circuit v County of Wayne (1969) 383 Mich 10, 172 NW2d 436, set aside on other grounds (1971) 386 Mich 1, 190 NW2d 228, cert den (1972) 405 US 923, 30 L Ed 2d 794, 92 S Ct 961.

## § 791.227. [Repealed] [MSA § 28.2297]

**History:**
Pub Acts 1953, No. 232, § 27, eff October 2, 1953; **repealed** by Pub Acts 1979, No. 89, imd eff August 1, 1979, by § 4 eff April 1, 1980 (see 1979 note below).

**Editor's notes:**
Former § 791.227 stated that nothing in the act shall apply to juvenile probation.
**Pub Acts 1979, No. 89,** § 3, imd eff August 1, 1979, by § 4 eff April 1, 1980, provides:
"Section 3. This amendatory act shall not take effect unless the funds for its implementation are appropriated by the legislature and House Bill No. 4402 of the 1979 regular session of the legislature [which became Act No. 81 of 1979] is enacted into law."
Pub Acts 1979, No. 89, § 4 originally read "This amendatory act shall take effect December 31, 1979", but Pub Acts 1979, No. 210, § 2, imd eff January 10, 1980, amended it to read "This amendatory act shall take effect April 1, 1980."

## § 791.228. Juvenile probation, duty to furnish information; furnishing assistance; access to information and records. [MSA § 28.2298]

Sec. 28. (1) The department of social services and the probate court of this state shall furnish to the department information, on request, concerning any individual having a previous record as a juvenile probationer who comes within the jurisdiction of the department.

(2) A department, board, commission, official, or employee of this state or a political subdivision of this state, shall give and furnish to the assistant director or to his or her agent, any assistance requested by the assistant director or his or her agent in the performance of their duties. Free access shall be given to any books, records, files, and documents in the custody of the department, board, commission, official, or employee, relating to matters within the scope of the powers and duties of the assistant director, except those expressly prohibited by law or court rule.

**History:**
Pub Acts 1953, No. 232, § 28, eff October 2, 1953; amended by Pub Acts 1979, No. 89, imd eff August 1, 1979, by § 4 eff April 1, 1980 (see 1979 note below).

**Editor's notes:**
**Pub Acts 1979, No. 89,** § 3, imd eff August 1, 1979, by § 4 eff April 1, 1980, provides:
"Section 3. This amendatory act shall not take effect unless the funds for its implementation are appropriated by the legislature and House Bill No. 4402 of the 1979 regular session of the legislature [which became Act No. 81 of 1979] is enacted into law."
Pub Acts 1979, No. 89, § 4 originally read "This amendatory act shall take effect December 31, 1979", but Pub Acts 1979, No. 210, § 2, imd eff January 10, 1980, amended it to read "This amendatory act shall take effect April 1, 1980."

**Michigan Digest references:**
Pardons and Paroles §§1 et seq., 4 et seq.

**Research references:**
21 Am Jur 2d, Criminal Law §§567, 570, 579.

## § 791.229. Privileged or confidential communications; access to records, reports, and case histories; confidential relationship inviolate. [MSA § 28.2299]

Sec. 29. All records and reports of investigations made by a probation officer, and all case histories of probationers shall be privileged or confidential communications not open to public inspection. Judges and probation officers shall have access to the records, reports, and case histories. The probation officer, the assistant director of probation, or the assistant director's representative shall permit the attorney general, the auditor general, and law enforcement agencies to have access to the records, reports, and case histories and shall permit designated representatives of a private vendor that operates a youth correctional facility under section 20g to have access to the records, reports, and case histories pertaining to prisoners assigned to the youth correctional facility. The relation of confidence between the probation officer and probationer or defendant under investigation shall remain inviolate.

**History:**
Pub Acts 1953, No. 232, § 29, eff October 2, 1953; amended by Pub Acts 1979, No. 89, imd eff August 1, 1979, by § 4 eff April 1, 1980 (see 1979 note below).
Amended by Pub Acts 1998, No. 512, imd eff January 8, 1999.

**Editor's notes:**
**Pub Acts 1979, No. 89, § 3,** imd eff August 1, 1979, by § 4 eff April 1, 1980, provides:
"Section 3. This amendatory act shall not take effect unless the funds for its implementation are appropriated by the legislature and House Bill No. 4402 of the 1979 regular session of the legislature [which became Act No. 81 of 1979] is enacted into law."
Pub Acts 1979, No. 89, § 4 originally read "This amendatory act shall take effect December 31, 1979", but Pub Acts 1979, No. 210, § 2, imd eff January 10, 1980, amended it to read "This amendatory act shall take effect April 1, 1980."

**Effect of amendment notes:**
**The 1998 amendment** added material and made a grammatical change.

**Statutory references:**
Section 20g, above referred to, is § 791.220g.

**Michigan Digest references:**
Pardons and Paroles §§1 et seq., 4 et seq.
Records § 7.
Witnesses § 174.10.

**Research references:**
21 Am Jur 2d, Criminal Law §§567, 570, 579.

§ 791.229                                                  **Department of Corrections**

## CASE NOTES

**1. Construction and effect.**

The statute which preserves the confidentiality of all records and reports of investigations by a probation officer and all case histories of probationers provides an absolute privilege against the disclosure of this information. However, there are some constitutional rights, i.e., the right of confrontation in criminal cases, which may supersede the privilege. Peters v Bay Fresh Start, Inc. (1987) 161 Mich App 491, 411 NW2d 463, app den (1987) 429 Mich 867.

When this section preserving confidentiality of presentence reports conflicts with constitutionally protected rights of confrontation and impeachment through prior inconsistent statements, it must give way to constitutional rights. People v Rohn (1980) 98 Mich App 593, 296 NW2d 315.

Provision of this section that histories of probationers and all records and reports of investigation made by probation officer in criminal cases referred for such investigation shall be privileged, and that relation of confidence between probation officer and probationer or defendant "under investigation" shall remain inviolate, would be held to extend privilege only to records, reports, and case histories prepared by probation officer, and not to other communications between officer and probationer. People v Burton (1977) 74 Mich App 215, 253 NW2d 710.

**2. Impeachment.**

Prosecution may not impeach accomplice, called as its own witness, in absence of surprise. People v Rohn (1980) 98 Mich App 593, 296 NW2d 315.

**3. Presentence report.**

The statute preserving the confidentiality of presentence reports, where it conflicts with the rights of confrontation and impeachment through use of prior inconsistent statements, must give way to those rights. People v Hooper (1987) 157 Mich App 669, 403 NW2d 605, app den (1987) 428 Mich 900.

Where presentence reports containing prior inconsistent statements of witnesses are necessary for effective cross-examination, trial court commits reversible error in denying defendant's access to such reports. People v Rohn (1980) 98 Mich App 593, 296 NW2d 315.

**4. Probation officers' reports.**

In determining whether, in a civil action for defamation, a probation report prepared in connection with an unrelated criminal matter is privileged and immune from discovery, a court should begin its analysis with a presumption in favor of preserving the privilege; the burden of establishing a waiver rests on the party seeking discovery, and fairness requires that the privilege end where it can be shown that the claim and the probable defenses to it are enmeshed in important evidence that will be unavailable if the privilege prevails; the burden on the defendant is proportional to the importance of the privilege: the court should carefully weigh the interests involved, balancing the importance of the privilege against the defending party's need for the information to construct its most effective defense; if allowed, discovery should be narrowly limited to those portions of the privileged material that bear directly on the issues at hand. Howe v Detroit Free Press, Inc. (1992) 440 Mich 203, 487 NW2d 374.

Probation officers' reports are absolutely privileged and cannot be the subject of discovery. Havens v Roberts (1984) 139 Mich App 64, 360 NW2d 183.

## § 791.230. [Repealed] [MSA § 28.2300]

**History:**

Pub Acts 1953, No. 232, § 30, as added by Pub Acts 1988, No. 59, imd eff March 21, 1988; **repealed** by Pub Acts 1994, No. 131, imd eff May 19, 1994.

**Editor's notes:**

Former § 791.230 pertained to exemption from disclosure, under the freedom of information act, of certain records requested by prisoners. For similar provisions see § 791.230a.

**Department of Corrections** **§ 791.231**

### § 791.230a. Exemptions from disclosure under freedom of information act. [MSA § 28.2300a]

Sec. 30a. The home addresses, telephone numbers, and personnel records of employees of the department, employees of the center for forensic psychiatry, and employees of a psychiatric hospital that houses prisoners are exempt from disclosure under the freedom of information act, Act No. 442 of the Public Acts of 1976, being sections 15.231 to 15.246 of the Michigan Compiled Laws.

**History:**
Pub Acts 1953, No. 232, § 30a, as added by Pub Acts 1994, No. 433, imd eff January 6, 1995.

## CHAPTER III

## BUREAU OF PARDONS AND PAROLES; PAROLE BOARD

### § 791.231. Bureau of field services; establishment; supervision by deputy director, appointment, tenure, powers, duties; parole officers; secretarial; assistants; quarters. [MSA § 28.2301]

Sec. 31. There is established within the department a bureau of field services, under the direction and supervision of a deputy director in charge of field services, who shall be appointed by the director and who shall be within the state civil service. The deputy director shall direct and supervise the work of the bureau of field services and shall formulate methods of investigation and supervision and develop various processes in the technique of supervision by the parole staff. The deputy director is responsible for all investigations of persons eligible for release from state penal institutions, and for the general supervision of persons released from penal institutions. The deputy director in charge of the bureau of field services is responsible for the collection and preservation of records and statistics with respect to paroled prisoners as may be required by the director and the chairperson of the parole board. The deputy director shall employ parole officers and assistants as may be necessary, subject to the approval of the director. The deputy director shall select secretarial and other assistants as may be necessary and may obtain permanent quarters for the staff as may be necessary.

**History:**
Pub Acts 1953, No. 232, § 31, eff October 2, 1953; amended by Pub Acts 1982, No. 314, imd eff October 15, 1982.

**Michigan Digest references:**
Pardons and Paroles §§4 et seq.

**Research references:**
59 Am Jur 2d, Pardon and Parole § 19.

**Legal periodicals:**
Guerin, People v. Moore: The role of discretion in indeterminate sentencing, Det CL Rev 3:1275 (1989).

## § 791.231

**CASE NOTES**

The subject of parole of prisoners has no common-law background and the statute regulating it is exclusive. People v Bendoni (1933) 263 Mich 295, 248 NW 627.

### § 791.231a. Parole board; establishment; members; terms, reappointment, removal, vacancies, qualifications; compensation; chairperson; designation, powers and duties; appointment and training function. [MSA § 28.2301(1)]

Sec. 31a. (1) Beginning October 1, 1992, there is established in the department, a parole board consisting of 10 members who shall be appointed by the director and who shall not be within the state civil service.

(2) Members of the parole board shall be appointed to terms of 4 years each, except that of the members first appointed, 4 shall serve for terms of 4 years each, 3 shall serve for terms of 3 years each, and 3 shall serve for terms of 2 year each. A member may be reappointed. The director may remove a member of the parole board for incompetency, dereliction of duty, malfeasance, misfeasance, or nonfeasance in office. If a vacancy occurs on the parole board, the director shall make an appointment for the unexpired term in the same manner as an original appointment. At least 4 members of the parole board shall be persons who, at the time of their appointment, have never been employed by or appointed to a position in the department of corrections.

(3) Each member of the parole board shall receive an annual salary as established by the legislature and shall be entitled to necessary traveling expenses incurred in the performance of official duties subject to the standardized travel regulations of the state.

(4) The chairperson of the parole board shall be designated by the director. The chairperson of the parole board is responsible for the administration and operation of the parole board. The chairperson may conduct interviews and participate in the parole decision making process. The chairperson shall select secretaries and other assistants as the chairperson considers to be necessary.

(5) The parole board created in this section shall exist for purposes of appointment and training on October 1, 1992, and as of November 15, 1992, shall exercise and perform the powers and duties prescribed and conferred by this act.

**History:**
Pub Acts 1953, No. 232, § 31a, as added by Pub Acts 1992, No. 181, imd eff September 22, 1992.

**Research references:**
59 Am Jur 2d, Pardon and Parole § 19.

**Department of Corrections** **§ 791.233**

CASE NOTES

1-15. [Reserved for use in future supplementation.]

16. Former § 791.232.
State board of parole is not person within meaning of Civil Rights Act on both claims for damages and injunctive relief. Bricker v Michigan Parole Bd. (1975, ED Mich) 405 F Supp 1340.
Parole board members are entitled to more than qualified immunity in deciding to grant, deny, or revoke parole, they act in quasi-judicial capacity, as arm of sentencing judge, and decision to impose certain conditions of parole fell within such quasi-judicial functions so that board members were immune from suit under civil rights statute. Bricker v Michigan Parole Bd. (1975, ED Mich) 405 F Supp 1340.
Absent allegation that more rigorous supervision as alleged by parolee resulted from use of unjustifiable standard, parolee could not prevail in his civil rights action against board members. Bricker v Michigan Parole Bd. (1975, ED Mich) 405 F Supp 1340.
Michigan Parole Board is not a "person" within meaning of statute establishing civil action for deprivation of any rights, privileges or immunities secured by Constitution and laws of United States by any person under color of any statute, rather, it is a governmental agency or unit, and as such, without the pale of Civil Rights Act. Glancy v Parole Board of Michigan Dep't of Corrections (1968, WD Mich) 287 F Supp 34.
The legislature may designate a group, called a board, within the department of corrections, vest it with statutory and commission delegated duties to perform, and exact that the appointed members of the board be within the state civil service, and such exactment does not render the act, nor the section thereof so providing, unconstitutional. Op Atty Gen, August 17, 1953, No. 1692.

**§ 791.232. [Repealed]** [MSA § 28.2302]

**History:**
Pub Acts 1953, No. 232, § 32, eff October 2, 1953; amended by Pub Acts 1976, No. 234, imd eff August 4, 1976; 1982, No. 314, imd eff October 15, 1982; **repealed** by Pub Acts 1992, No. 181, imd eff September 22, 1992.

**Editor's notes:**
Former § 791.232 provided for the establishment of a parole board. For current provision, see § 791.231a.

**§ 791.233. Grant of parole; conditions; paroles-in-custody; rules.** [MSA § 28.2303]

Sec. 33. (1) The grant of a parole is subject to all of the following:

(a) A prisoner shall not be given liberty on parole until the board has reasonable assurance, after consideration of all of the facts and circumstances, including the prisoner's mental and social attitude, that the prisoner will not become a menace to society or to the public safety.

(b) Except as provided in section 34a, a parole shall not be granted to a prisoner other than a prisoner subject to disciplinary time until the prisoner has served the minimum term imposed by the court less allowances for good time or special good time to which the prisoner may be entitled by statute, except that a prisoner other than a prisoner subject to disciplinary time is eligible for parole before the expiration of his or her minimum term of imprisonment whenever the sentencing judge, or the judge's successor in office, gives written approval of the parole of the prisoner before the expiration of the minimum term of imprisonment.

(c) Except as provided in section 34a, and notwithstanding the provisions of subdivision (b), a parole shall not be granted to a prisoner other than a prisoner subject to disciplinary time sentenced for the commission of a crime described in section 33b(a) to (cc) until the prisoner has served the minimum term imposed by the court less an allowance for disciplinary credits as provided in section 33(5) of 1893 PA 118, MCL 800.33. A prisoner described in this subdivision is not eligible for special parole.

(d) Except as provided in section 34a, a parole shall not be granted to a prisoner subject to disciplinary time until the prisoner has served the minimum term imposed by the court.

(e) A prisoner shall not be released on parole until the parole board has satisfactory evidence that arrangements have been made for such honorable and useful employment as the prisoner is capable of performing, for the prisoner's education, or for the prisoner's care if the prisoner is mentally or physically ill or incapacitated.

(f) A prisoner whose minimum term of imprisonment is 2 years or more shall not be released on parole unless he or she has either earned a high school diploma or earned its equivalent in the form of a general education development (GED) certificate. The director of the department may waive the restriction imposed by this subdivision as to any prisoner who is over the age of 65 or who was gainfully employed immediately before committing the crime for which he or she was incarcerated. The department of corrections may also waive the restriction imposed by this subdivision as to any prisoner who has a learning disability, who does not have the necessary proficiency in English, or who for some other reason that is not the fault of the prisoner is unable to successfully complete the requirements for a high school diploma or a general education development certificate. If the prisoner does not have the necessary proficiency in English, the department of corrections shall provide English language training for that prisoner necessary for the prisoner to begin working toward the completion of the requirements for a general education development certificate. This subdivision applies to prisoners sentenced for crimes committed after December 15, 1998. In providing an educational program leading to a high school degree or general education development certificate, the department shall give priority to prisoners sentenced for crimes committed on or before December 15, 1998.

(2) Paroles-in-custody to answer warrants filed by local or out-of-state agencies, or immigration officials, are permissible if an accredited agent of the agency filing the warrant calls for the prisoner to be paroled in custody.

(3) Pursuant to the administrative procedures act of 1969, 1969 PA 306, MCL 24.201 to 24.328, the parole board may promulgate rules not inconsistent with this act with respect to conditions to be imposed upon prisoners paroled under this act.

**History:**
Pub Acts 1953, No. 232, § 33, eff October 2, 1953; amended by Pub Acts

**Department of Corrections** § **791.233**

1978, No. 81, imd eff March 29, 1978 (see 1978 note below); amended pursuant to initiative petition, Proposal B ratified at general election of November 7, 1978; 1982, No. 458, imd eff December 30, 1982 (see 1982 note below); 1994, No. 217, eff June 27, 1994 (see 1994 note below).

Amended by Pub Acts 1998, No. 320, imd eff July 30, 1998, by enacting § 1 eff December 15, 1998 (see 1998 note below).

**Editor's notes:**
**Pub Acts 1978, No. 81, § 2,** imd eff March 29, 1978, provides:
"Section 2. This amendatory act shall not take effect unless House Bill No. 4190 of the 1977 regular session of the legislature [which became Act No. 147 of 1978] is enacted into law. If House Bill No. 4190 of the 1977 regular session of the legislature [which became Act No. 147 of 1978] is enacted into law, this amendatory act shall take effect on the same date as that act takes effect."

**Pub Acts 1982, No. 458, § 2,** imd eff December 30, 1982, provides:
"Section 2. This amendatory act shall not take effect unless House Bill No. 6166 of the 81st Legislature [which became Act No. 442 of 1982] is enacted into law."

**Pub Acts 1994, No. 217, §§2, 3,** eff June 27, 1994, provide:
"Section 2. This amendatory act shall take effect on the date that sentencing guidelines are enacted into law after the sentencing commission submits its report to the secretary of the senate and the clerk of the house of representatives pursuant to sections 31 to 34 of chapter IX of the code of criminal procedure, Act No. 175 of the Public Acts of 1927, as added by the amendatory act resulting from House Bill No. 4782 of the 87th Legislature [Pub Acts 1994, No. 445]. (**Repealed** by Pub Acts 1998, No. 316, imd eff July 30, 1998, by enacting § 2 eff December 15, 1998.).

"Section 3. This amendatory act shall not take effect unless all of the following bills of the 87th Legislature are enacted into law:
"(a) Senate Bill No. 41 [Pub Acts 1994, No. 218].
"(b) House Bill No. 4782 [Pub Acts 1994, No. 445].
"(c) House Bill No. 5439 [Pub Acts 1994, No. 322]."

**Pub Acts 1998, No. 320, enacting § 2,** imd eff July 30, 1998, by enacting § 1 eff December 15, 1998, provides:
"Enacting section 2. This amendatory act does not take effect unless all of the following bills of the 89th Legislature are enacted into law:
"(a) Senate Bill No. 826 [Pub Acts 1998, No. 316].
"(b) House Bill No. 4065 [Pub Acts 1998, No. 319].
"(c) House Bill No. 4444 [Pub Acts 1998, No. 311].
"(d) House Bill No. 4445 [Pub Acts 1998, No. 312].
"(e) House Bill No. 4446 [Pub Acts 1998, No. 313].
"(f) House Bill No. 5398 [Pub Acts 1998, No. 315].
"(g) House Bill No. 5419 [Pub Acts 1998, No. 317].
"(h) House Bill No. 5876 [Pub Acts 1998, No. 318]."

**Effect of amendment notes:**
**The 1994 amendment** made revisions throughout this section.

**The 1998 amendment** deleted ", plus any disciplinary time accumulated pursuant to section 34 of Act No. 118 of the Public Acts of 1893, being section 800.34 of the Michigan Compiled Laws." following "court" in paragraph (d) of subsection (1); added paragraph (f) of subsection (1); and changed the style of statutory references throughout the section.

**Statutory references:**
Sections 33b and 34a are §§791.233b and 791.234a.

**Michigan Digest references:**
Pardons and Paroles §§4 et seq., 6.

**Research references:**
59 Am Jur 2d, Pardon and Parole §§81–84.

**Legal periodicals:**
Ward, A New Phenomenon—Prosecution Appeals of Decisions to Parole, 72 Mich B J 10:1058 (1993).

CASE NOTES

**1. In general.**

The court rule which governs procedures to be followed in accepting a plea of guilty does not require the trial court to advise a defendant relative to any consequences of the statute prescribing eligibility for parole until the minimum term of a sentence for certain crimes is served. People v Albert (1982) 120 Mich App 396, 327 NW2d 489.

Parole may be granted to a prisoner at the expiration of his net minimum sentence (the calendar minimum sentence less accumulated good time) and special parole may be granted at any time prior to the net minimum sentence if the sentencing court gives written approval. Lamb v Bureau of Pardons & Paroles (1981) 106 Mich App 175, 307 NW2d 754.

Conditions of parole may restrict prisoner's activities substantially beyond ordinary restrictions imposed by law on average citizen such as restriction to particular community, job, or home at direction of his parole officer. Bricker v Michigan Parole Bd. (1975, ED Mich) 405 F Supp 1340.

State is not constitutionally required to provide for parole, and, if state does so provide, it may stipulate its terms and conditions as well as status of parolee imposing reasonable conditions restricting state prisoners. Bricker v Michigan Parole Bd. (1975, ED Mich) 405 F Supp 1340.

Where reports from law enforcement sources indicated that ownership of company for which parolee wished to work was linked to organized crime, restriction against such employment was reasonably related to purpose of prisoner's parole. Bricker v Michigan Parole Bd. (1975, ED Mich) 405 F Supp 1340.

Difficulties of supervising self-employed broker for waste removal services were reasonable grounds for imposing conditions that parolee not be self-employed. Bricker v Michigan Parole Bd. (1975, ED Mich) 405 F Supp 1340.

Where a sentence for a fixed term of years is imposed upon an habitual offender, the offender must serve the full number of years imposed by the court. Op Atty Gen, October 16, 1979, No. 5583.

A prisoner who has served his or her maximum sentence less good time is entitled to be discharged even though the term served is less than the minimum sentence imposed. Op Atty Gen, October 16, 1979, No. 5583.

**2. Validity.**

Application of statute prohibiting possession of a firearm by a convicted felon to a person who is a convicted felon as a result of a conviction of a felony committed before the date that statute took effect does not violate the ex post facto clauses of the United States and Michigan Constitutions. People v Tice (1996) 220 Mich App 47, 558 NW2d 245.

A prisoner may be granted parole before having obtained employment where the parole is conditioned upon the prisoner not being released until satisfactory evidence of useful employment is provided to the Parole Board. Wayne County Prosecutor v Parole Bd. (1995) 210 Mich App 148, 532 NW2d 899.

Provisions of former §§802.104, 802.105, concerning parole considerations applicable to inmates in Detroit House of Correction who were more than 15 years of age and were common prostitutes did not govern parole procedures for women inmates generally and did not support contention that, for purposes of parole consideration, women state inmates of Detroit House of Correction were statutorily treated differently than male state prisoners in other state penal institutions under this act. People v Andrea (1973) 48 Mich App 310, 210 NW2d 474.

Since equal treatment of male and female convicts in state prisons with respect to good-time credits was mandated by former § 802.55, former statutes establishing Detroit House of Correction and requiring all female state prisoners to be incarcerated there did not unconstitutionally discriminate against such prisoners on ground that, under former § 802.20, they were not permitted to earn as much good-time credit per month for good behavior as men in other state penal institutions, under § 800.33. People v Andrea (1973) 48 Mich App 310, 210 NW2d 474.

Inasmuch as the descriptive ballot lan-

**Department of Corrections** § 791.233

guage used with respect to the adoption of 1978 initiated law provides a fair description of the impact of the proposal, it was validly adopted and is applicable to all of the offenses enumerated. Op Atty Gen, October 16, 1979, No. 5583.

**3. Construction.**
Title to Michigan bill which includes certain parole statutes provides that it is, in part, an act to revise, consolidate, and codify the laws relating to paroles. The statutes in question concern parole eligibility and, accordingly, fall within the objective of the act as expressed in its title. That they may also be viewed as imposing a form of punishment, a subject arguably not directly related to parole, is immaterial. Hawkins v Department of Corrections (1996) 219 Mich App 523, 557 NW2d 138.

Proposal B, which mandates that parole shall not be granted to persons committing certain offenses until the minimum sentence imposed by the court has been served, applies only to offenses committed after its effective date, December 12, 1978. People v Lewis (1988) 168 Mich App 255, 423 NW2d 637, app den (1988) 431 Mich 884, habeas corpus den, motion den (1994, CA6 Mich) 1994 US App LEXIS 37120.

The provision in the parole act requiring the serving of a mandatory minimum sentence before being eligible for parole applies only to indeterminate sentences; it binds the parole board, precluding release of a prisoner before the expiration of the minimum term fixed by the sentencing judge for crimes enumerated in the statute such as second-degree murder and has no application to a fixed or life sentence. People v Hutchinson (1986) 155 Mich App 84, 399 NW2d 448, app den (1987) 428 Mich 866.

The express purpose of 1978 Initiative Proposal B was to amend this section to eliminate the allowance for good time, special good time and special parole set forth in a subsection of that statute; the "special parole" eliminated by Proposal B is not the 10 calendar year minimum sentence provision set forth in the "lifer law," § 791.234, which minimum sentence provision was not repealed by implication with the passage of Proposal B. People v Waterman (1984) 137 Mich App 429, 358 NW2d 602.

The Michigan statute providing for early parole creates only an expectation or hope of an early parole, not a right to parole; the statute provides that parole should not be granted to a prisoner until the prisoner has served the minimum term imposed by the court, less allowance for good time or special good time; the statute provides for an early parole prior to the expiration of the minimum sentence if the sentencing judge approves the early release. Hurst v Department of Corrections Parole Bd. (1982) 119 Mich App 25, 325 NW2d 615.

The people of the state of Michigan, in enacting, by their powers of initiative, the sections of the Michigan Penal Code which provide that a person convicted of certain enumerated criminal offenses and sentenced to a minimum term of years exceeding ten years must serve the entire minimum sentence, undiminished by allowances for good time, special good time, or special parole, intended the law to apply to situations in which a person is sentenced to life in prison, and, because the Penal Code provides that no minimum term of years may be set where the maximum sentence is life, the minimum sentence in such a situation, for the purpose of applying the provision of the code allowing the diminishing of a sentence by parole, is life, precluding parole consideration for a person so sentenced; thus, where the record reveals on appeal that a trial court may have intended to sentence a criminal defendant to a parolable life term, the sentence should be vacated and the case remanded for resentencing. People v Anderson (1981) 112 Mich App 640, 317 NW2d 205 (criticized on other grounds by People v Waterman (1984) 137 Mich App 429, 358 NW2d 602) and related proceeding (1993) 199 Mich App 681, 503 NW2d 465, app den (1993) 444 Mich 852, 508 NW2d 498.

1978 initiated law precludes parole consideration for a prisoner with a life sentence. Op Atty Gen, October 16, 1979, No. 5583.

An attempt to commit a crime which is not included in the list of offenses enumerated in 1978 initiated law does not fall within its scope. Op Atty Gen, October 16, 1979, No. 5583.

**4. "Parole" defined.**
A "parole" is a conditional release, the condition being that if the party shows he can refrain from committing crime he will receive an absolute discharge from the balance of his sentence. In re Eddinger (1926) 236 Mich 668, 211 NW 54.

**5. Authority to sign written approval of parole.**
A judge, acting in pursuance of an appointment by the presiding circuit judge, in the place of a judge in the service of the armed forces and absent from his judicial circuit by reason thereof, was invested with authority to give written approval of the parole of any subjects under the jurisdiction of the board of pardons and paroles, and the parole board is authorized to act upon such written approval. (Construing similar provision of former act.) Op Atty Gen, June 18, 1943, No. 0-889.

**6. Good time.**
1978 initiated law denying good time from minimum sentence for certain crimes applies to only persons who have committed the enumerated offense on or after December 10, 1978 at 12:01 a.m. Op Atty Gen, October 16, 1979, No. 5583.

Good time and special good time could be credited on minimum terms which had been reduced by sentencing judge. (Construing similar provision of former act.) Op Atty Gen, September 17, 1942, No. 24544.

Parole board had power to grant regular good time and special good time upon recommendation of warden without approval of sentencing judge. (Construing similar provision of former act.) Op Atty Gen, September 17, 1942, No. 24544.

**7. Restitution as condition of parole.**
The department has exclusive jurisdiction over paroles, commutations, and penal institutions, subject to the powers of the judicial and executive departments; a sentencing judge is not empowered to make the full payment of restitution a prerequisite to obtaining parole or early release, however, any restitution ordered shall be a condition of parole and the parole board may revoke parole if the defendant fails to comply. People v Greenberg (1989) 176 Mich App 296, 439 NW2d 336, app den (1989) 433 Mich 900.

## § 791.233a. [Repealed] [MSA § 28.2303(1)]

**History:**
Pub Acts 1953, No. 232, § 33a, eff October 2, 1953; **repealed** by Pub Acts 1982, No. 314, imd eff October 15, 1982.

**Editor's notes:**
Former § 791.233a provided that in determining a prisoner's fitness for release on parole, the parole board may consider instances of the prisoner's voluntary assistance to medical and other scientific research, and his blood donations.

## § 791.233b[1]. Major controlled substance offense, definition. [MSA § 28.2303(2)]

Sec. 33b[1]. As used in section 34, "major controlled substance offense" means any of the following:

(a) A violation of section 7401(2)(a)(i) or (ii) of the public health code, Act No. 368 of the Public Acts of 1978, being section 333.7401 of the Michigan Compiled Laws.

(b) A violation of section 7403(2)(a)(i) or (ii) of Act No. 368 of the Public Acts of 1978, being section 333.7403 of the Michigan Compiled Laws.

(c) Conspiracy to commit an offense listed in subdivision (a) or (b).

**History:**
Pub Acts 1953, No. 232, § 33b[1], as added by Pub Acts 1978, No. 81, imd eff March 29, 1978 (see 1978 note below); amended by Pub Acts 1988, No. 143, imd eff June 3, 1988, by § 2 eff June 1, 1988.

**Editor's notes:**
**Pub Acts 1978, No. 81, § 2,** imd eff March 29, 1978, provides:

**Department of Corrections** § 791.233b

> "Section 2. This amendatory act shall not take effect unless House Bill No. 4190 of the 1977 regular session of the legislature [Act No. 147 of 1978] is enacted into law. If House Bill No. 4190 of the 1977 regular session of the legislature [Act No. 147 of 1978] is enacted into law, this amendatory act shall take effect on the same date as that act takes effect."

**Research references:**
59 Am Jur 2d, Pardon and Parole §§81–84.

## § 791.233b. Eligibility for parole; minimum term required to be served; ineligibility for special parole. [MSA § 28.2303(3)]

Sec. 33b. A person convicted and sentenced for the commission of any of the following crimes other than a prisoner subject to disciplinary time is not eligible for parole until the person has served the minimum term imposed by the court less an allowance for disciplinary credits as provided in section 33(5) of Act No. 118 of the Public Acts of 1893, being section 800.33 of the Michigan Compiled Laws, and is not eligible for special parole:

(a) Section 13 of the Michigan penal code, Act No. 328 of the Public Acts of 1931, as amended, being section 750.13 of the Michigan Compiled Laws.

(b) Section 14 of Act No. 328 of the Public Acts of 1931, as amended, being section 750.14 of the Michigan Compiled Laws.

(c) Section 72, 73, or 75 of Act No. 328 of the Public Acts of 1931, as amended, being section 750.72, 750.73, or 750.75 of the Michigan Compiled Laws.

(d) Section 80, 82, 83, 84, 86, 87, 88, 89, or 90 of Act No. 328 of the Public Acts of 1931, as amended, being section 750.80, 750.82, 750.83, 750.84, 750.86, 750.87, 750.88, 750.89, or 750.90 of the Michigan Compiled Laws, or under former section 85 of Act No. 328 of the Public Acts of 1931.

(e) Section 91 or 92 of Act No. 328 of the Public Acts of 1931, as amended, being section 750.91 or 750.92 of the Michigan Compiled Laws.

(f) Section 110, 112, or 116 of Act No. 328 of the Public Acts of 1931, as amended, being section 750.110, 750.112, or 750.116 of the Michigan Compiled Laws.

(g) Section 135, 136b(2), or 136b(3) of Act No. 328 of the Public Acts of 1931, as amended, being section 750.135 or 750.136b of the Michigan Compiled Laws, or under former section 136a of Act No. 328 of the Public Acts of 1931.

(h) Section 158 of Act No. 328 of the Public Acts of 1931, as amended, being section 750.158 of the Michigan Compiled Laws.

(i) Section 160 of Act No. 328 of the Public Acts of 1931, as amended, being section 750.160 of the Michigan Compiled Laws.

(j) Section 171 of Act No. 328 of the Public Acts of 1931, as amended, being section 750.171 of the Michigan Compiled Laws.

(k) Section 196 of Act No. 328 of the Public Acts of 1931, as amended, being section 750.196 of the Michigan Compiled Laws, or under former section 194 of Act No. 328 of the Public Acts of

§ 791.233b                                   Department of Corrections

1931.

(l) Section 204, 205, 206, 207, 208, 209, or 213 of Act No. 328 of the Public Acts of 1931, as amended, being section 750.204, 750.205, 750.206, 750.207, 750.208, 750.209, or 750.213 of the Michigan Compiled Laws.

(m) Section 224, 226, or 227 of Act No. 328 of the Public Acts of 1931, as amended, being section 750.224, 750.226, or 750.227 of the Michigan Compiled Laws.

(n) Section 316, 317, 319, 321, 322, 323, 327, 328, or 329 of Act No. 328 of the Public Acts of 1931, as amended, being section 750.316, 750.317, 750.319, 750.321, 750.322, 750.323, 750.327, 750.328, or 750.329 of the Michigan Compiled Laws.

(o) Former section 333 of Act No. 328 of the Public Acts of 1931.

(p) Section 338, 338a, or 338b of Act No. 328 of the Public Acts of 1931, as amended, being section 750.338, 750.338a, or 750.338b of the Michigan Compiled Laws, or under former section 341 of Act No. 328 of the Public Acts of 1931.

(q) Section 349, 349a, or 350 of Act No. 328 of the Public Acts of 1931, as amended, being section 750.349, 750.349a, or 750.350 of the Michigan Compiled Laws.

(r) Section 357 of Act No. 328 of the Public Acts of 1931, as amended, being section 750.357 of the Michigan Compiled Laws.

(s) Section 386 or 392 of Act No. 328 of the Public Acts of 1931, as amended, being section 750.386 or 750.392 of the Michigan Compiled Laws.

(t) Section 397 or 397a of Act No. 328 of the Public Acts of 1931, as amended, being section 750.397 or 750.397a of the Michigan Compiled Laws.

(u) Section 436 of Act No. 328 of the Public Acts of 1931, as amended, being section 750.436 of the Michigan Compiled Laws.

(v) Section 511 or 517 of Act No. 328 of the Public Acts of 1931, as amended, being section 750.511 or 750.517 of the Michigan Compiled Laws.

(w) Section 520b, 520c, 520d, or 520g of Act No. 328 of the Public Acts of 1931, as amended, being section 750.520b, 750.520c, 750.520d, or 750.520g of the Michigan Compiled Laws.

(x) Section 529, 529a, 530, or 531 of Act No. 328 of the Public Acts of 1931, as amended, being section 750.529, 750.529a, 750.530, or 750.531 of the Michigan Compiled Laws.

(y) Section 544 of Act No. 328 of the Public Acts of 1931, as amended, being section 750.544 of the Michigan Compiled Laws, or under former section 545a of Act No. 328 of the Public Acts of 1931.

(z) Former section 2 of Act No. 38 of the Public Acts of the Extra Session of 1950.

(aa) Former section 6 of Act No. 117 of the Public Acts of 1952.

(bb) Section 1, 2, or 3 of Act No. 302 of the Public Acts of 1968, as amended, being section 752.541, 752.542, or 752.543 of the Michigan Compiled Laws.

(cc) Section 7401(2)(a), 7401(2)(b), 7402(2)(a), or 7402(2)(b) of

# Department of Corrections § 791.233b

the public health code, Act No. 368 of the Public Acts of 1978, being section 333.7401 or 333.7402 of the Michigan Compiled Laws.

**History:**
Pub Acts 1953, No. 232, § 33b, as added pursuant to initiative petition, Proposal B, ratified at general election of November 7, 1978; amended by Pub Acts 1982, No. 458, imd eff December 30, 1982 (see 1982 note below); 1989, No. 252, eff March 29, 1990; 1994, No. 199, imd eff June 21, 1994, by § 2 eff October 1, 1994 (see 1994 note below); 1994, No. 217, eff June 27, 1994 (see 1994 note below).

**Editor's notes:**
Another section 33b was added by Act No. 81 of 1978 and was assigned § 791.233b[1]. The above section 33b was added by initiative petition, Proposal B, ratified at the general election of November 7, 1978 and was designated as § 791.232.

**Pub Acts 1982, No. 458, § 2,** imd eff December 30, 1982, provides:
"Section 2. This amendatory act shall not take effect unless House Bill No. 6166 of the 81st Legislature [which became Act No. 442 of 1982] is enacted into law."

**Pub Acts 1994, No. 199, § 3,** imd eff June 21, 1994, by § 2 eff October 1, 1994, provides:
"Section 3. This amendatory act shall not take effect unless Senate Bill No. 773 of the 87th Legislature (which became Pub Acts 1994, No. 191) is enacted into law."

**Pub Acts 1994, No. 217, §§2, 3,** eff June 27, 1994, provide:
"Section 2. This amendatory act shall take effect on the date that sentencing guidelines are enacted into law after the sentencing commission submits its report to the secretary of the senate and the clerk of the house of representatives pursuant to sections 31 to 34 of chapter IX of the code of criminal procedure, Act No. 175 of the Public Acts of 1927, as added by the amendatory act resulting from House Bill No. 4782 of the 87th Legislature [which became Pub Acts 1994, No. 445]. (**Repealed** by Pub Acts 1998, No. 316, imd eff July 30, 1998, by enacting § 2 eff December 15, 1998.).

"Section 3. This amendatory act shall not take effect unless all of the following bills of the 87th Legislature are enacted into law:
"(a) Senate Bill No. 41 [Pub Acts 1994, No. 218].
"(b) House Bill No. 4782 [Pub Acts 1994, No. 445].
"(c) House Bill No. 5439 [Pub Acts 1994, No. 322]."

**Effect of amendment notes:**
**The first 1994 amendment (Pub Act 199)** made revisions throughout this section but did not add or delete any subsections or paragraphs.

**The second 1994 amendment (Pub Act 217)** likewise made revisions throughout this section but did not add or delete any subsections or paragraphs.

**Michigan Digest references:**
Assault and Battery § 1.
Constitutional Law § 67.
Criminal Sexual Conduct § 43.
Homicide § 148.
Pardons and Paroles §§4—6.
Prisons and Jails § 2.40.
Statutes § 189.

**LEXIS-NEXIS™ Michigan analytical references:**
Michigan Law and Practice, Criminal Law §§715, 717.
Michigan Law and Practice, Statutes § 34.

**Research references:**
59 Am Jur 2d, Pardon and Parole §§81–84.

**Legal periodicals:**
Dagher-Margosian, Life Means Life: Parole Rarely Granted on Nonmandatory Life Terms, 73 Mich BJ 11:1184 (1994).

Guerin, People v. Moore: The role of discretion in indeterminate sentencing, Det CL Rev 3:1275 (1989).

## CASE NOTES

**1. Construction and effect**

The provision in the parole act requiring the serving of a mandatory minimum sentence before being eligible for parole applies only to indeterminate sentences; it binds the parole board, precluding release of a prisoner before the expiration of the minimum term fixed by the sentencing judge for crimes enumerated in the statute such as second-degree murder and has no application to a fixed or life sentence. People v Johnson (1984) 421 Mich 494, 364 NW2d 654.

A person convicted of a Proposal B offense and receiving good-time credits against the maximum sentence before December 30, 1982, is thereafter entitled to continue receiving good-time credits against the maximum sentence and to receive disciplinary credits against the minimum sentence. Lowe v Department of Corrections (1994) 206 Mich App 128, 521 NW2d 336.

Neither unintentional reference to ballot proposal as "referendum" nor Board of Canvassers' solicitation of Attorney General's legal opinion would operate to invalidate proposal as "mixed petition" for both initiative and referendum or as violative of separation of powers as alleged on challenge to constitutionality of resulting statute which eliminated good time allowances in determining eligibility for parole for certain crimes. LaFountain v Attorney Gen. (1993) 200 Mich App 262, 503 NW2d 739.

A person convicted and sentenced for a crime listed in "Proposal B" is not eligible for parole until the person has served his or her minimum sentence, less any disciplinary credits. People v Robinson (1988) 172 Mich App 650, 432 NW2d 390 (criticized on other grounds by People v Legree (1989) 177 Mich App 134, 441 NW2d 433) and app den (1989) 433 Mich 908.

Third-offense habitual offenders may be sentenced to imprisonment for life or for a lesser term; a sentence of 80 to 120 years imprisonment for a third offense habitual offender convicted of a crime listed in Proposal B is neither a sentence of life imprisonment nor for a lesser term where the minimum sentence of 80 years far exceeds the defendant's life expectancy. People v Robinson (1988) 172 Mich App 650, 432 NW2d 390 (criticized on other grounds by People v Legree (1989) 177 Mich App 134, 441 NW2d 433) and app den (1989) 433 Mich 908.

Michigan's "lifer law" allows any prison inmate under a sentence of life or for a term of years, other than those who have been convicted of first-degree murder or of a major controlled substance offense, to be considered for parole after serving 10 calendar years of his or her sentence; the electorate's approval of Proposal B in 1978 and the 1982 amendment of that statute modified the "lifer law" to the effect that inmates serving indeterminate sentences for any of the crimes enumerated in the statute are no longer eligible for parole until the minimum term is served less any time earned in disciplinary credits; Proposal B does not apply to life sentences. People v Hurst (1986) 155 Mich App 573, 400 NW2d 685, appeal after remand (1988) 169 Mich App 160, 425 NW2d 752, app den (1989, Mich) 1989 Mich LEXIS 365.

1978 Initiative Proposal B, which eliminated allowances for good time, special good time and special parole for certain specified crimes, did not affect the statute providing that a defendant receiving a nonmandatory life sentence is eligible for parole consideration after serving ten years of his sentence. People v Clark (1985) 141 Mich App 1, 366 NW2d 62.

A defendant receiving a nonmandatory life sentence is eligible for parole consideration after serving 10 calendar years of his sentence; Proposal B, which eliminated the allowances for good time, special good time, and special parole to reduce the ten-year minimum on nonmandatory life sentences, did not repeal the "lifer law," the statute which, in effect, sets the minimum term on all life sentences other than those for first-degree murder and major controlled substance offenses at 10 calendar years. People v Martin (1984) 139 Mich App 738, 363 NW2d 24.

Statute prohibiting "good time" reduction from minimum sentence applies only to criminal offenses that were committed after effective date of statute. People v Kildow (1980) 99 Mich App 446, 298 NW2d 123.

**2. Duties of trial court**

A trial court is not required to inform a defendant charged with a crime requiring service of a minimum term before there can be eligibility for parole that the minimum term cannot be diminished by parole or by allowances for good time, special good time, or special parole prior to accepting the defendant's guilty plea. People v Armstrong (1982) 118 Mich App 733, 325 NW2d 555.

A trial court errs in failing to inform a defendant as to the consequences of pleading guilty to a crime which requires service of the minimum term imposed before there can be eligibility for parole only if there is a sentence bargain with the judge, as distinguished from a bargain for a prosecutor's recommendation, or if the record establishes that the defendant was misled as to the effect of his plea to such a crime. People v Hadley (1982) 114 Mich App 117, 318 NW2d 625.

A trial court is required to inform a defendant who pleads guilty of the maximum and minimum sentence he could receive, but is not required to inform the defendant of all sentencing consequences of the plea, including the fact that, in the case of certain enumerated crimes, the mandatory minimum sentence may not be diminished by allowances for good time, special good time or special parole. People v Gooch (1982) 114 Mich App 309, 319 NW2d 343.

A trial court is not required to inform a defendant charged with a crime requiring service of a minimum term before parole that the minimum term cannot be diminished by allowances for good time, special good time, or special parole prior to accepting the defendant's guilty plea. People v Richards (1981) 106 Mich App 16, 307 NW2d 692.

**3. Conviction of delivery of LSD**

Conviction of the delivery of LSD in violation of Public Health Code is a crime subject to the provisions of 1978 PA Initiated Measure amending 1953 PA 232. Op Atty Gen, April 16, 1981, No. 5875.

**4. Nonparolable offense**

Where defendant entered guilty plea to second degree murder pursuant to plea bargain for reduced sentence in exchange for his testimony against codefendants, resulting life sentence was required to be vacated and proceedings remanded for resentencing on record disclosing that court intended to sentence defendant to parolable life term, but that department of corrections could not carry out such intent because of Attorney General's binding opinion that life sentence was nonparolable regarding second-degree murder. People v Penn (1981) 102 Mich App 731, 302 NW2d 298.

## § 791.233c. "Prisoner subject to disciplinary time" defined.
[MSA § 28.2303(4)]

Sec. 33c. As used in this act, "prisoner subject to disciplinary time" means that term as defined in section 34 of Act No. 118 of the Public Acts of 1893, being section 800.34 of the Michigan Compiled Laws.

**History:**
Pub Acts 1953, No. 232, § 33c, as added Pub Acts 1994, No. 217, eff June 27, 1994 (see 1994 note below).

**Editor's notes:**
**Pub Acts 1994, No. 217, §§2, 3,** eff June 27, 1994, provide:

"Section 2. This amendatory act shall take effect on the date that sentencing guidelines are enacted into law after the sentencing commission submits its report to the secretary of the senate and the clerk of the house of representatives pursuant to sections 31 to 34 of chapter IX of the code of criminal procedure, Act No. 175 of the Public Acts of 1927, as added by the amendatory act resulting from House Bill No. 4782 of the 87th Legislature [which became Pub Acts 1994, No. 445]. (**Repealed** by Pub Acts 1998, No. 316, imd eff July 30, 1998, by enacting § 2 eff December 15, 1998.).

"Section 3. This amendatory act shall not take effect unless all of the following bills of the 87th Legislature are enacted into law:

"(a) Senate Bill No. 41 [Pub Acts 1994, No. 218].

**§ 791.233c**

"(b) House Bill No. 4782 [Pub Acts 1994, No. 445].
"(c) House Bill No. 5439 [Pub Acts 1994, No. 322]."

**§ 791.233d. Samples for chemical testing.** [MSA § 28.2303(5)]

Sec. 33d. (1) A prisoner serving a sentence for a violation of section 91, 316, or 317 of the Michigan penal code, Act No. 328 of the Public Acts of 1931, being section 750.91, 750.316, and 750.317 of the Michigan Compiled Laws, or a violation or attempted violation of section 349, 520b, 520c, 520d, 520e, or 520g of Act No. 328 of the Public Acts of 1931, being sections 750.349, 750.520b, 750.520c, 750.520d, 750.520e, and 750.520g of the Michigan Compiled Laws, shall not be released on parole, placed in a community placement facility of any kind, including a community corrections center or a community residential home, or discharged upon completion of his or her maximum sentence until he or she has provided samples for chemical testing for DNA identification profiling or a determination of the sample's genetic markers and has provided samples for a determination of his or her secretor status. However, if at the time the prisoner is to be released, placed, or discharged the department of state police already has a sample from the prisoner that meets the requirements of the rules promulgated under the DNA identification profiling system act, Act No. 250 of the Public Acts of 1990, being sections 28.171 to 28.176 of the Michigan Compiled Laws, the prisoner is not required to provide another sample.

(2) The samples required to be collected under this section shall be collected by the department and transmitted by the department to the department of state police in the manner prescribed by rules promulgated under the DNA identification profiling system act, Act No. 250 of the Public Acts of 1990.

(3) The department may collect a sample under this section regardless of whether the prisoner consents to the collection. The department is not required to give the prisoner an opportunity for a hearing or obtain a court order before collecting the sample.

(4) As used in this section, "sample" means a portion of a prisoner's blood, saliva, or tissue collected from the prisoner.

**History:**
Pub Acts 1953, No. 232, § 33d, as added by Pub Acts 1990, No. 251, eff March 28, 1991 (see 1990 note below); amended by Pub Acts 1994, No. 164, imd eff June 17, 1994, by § 3 eff September 1, 1994 (see 1994 note below); 1996, No. 509, imd eff January 9, 1997, by § 2 eff January 1, 1997 (see 1996 note below).

**Editor's notes:**
**Pub Acts 1990, No. 251, § 2,** eff March 28, 1991, provides:
"Section 2. This amendatory act shall not take effect unless the sponsor of this bill provides an enacted source of revenue to fully fund the program and the legislature appropriates sufficient money to fund the program it creates."
The sponsor of the bill did not provide an enacted source of revenue to fully fund this program. However, this condition, or "enacting section", was repealed by Pub Acts 1994, No. 165.
§ 791.233d is reported in the bound volume as being repealed, when only

**Department of Corrections** § 791.233e

its enacting section was repealed, as explained above. The correct provisions are now set forth herein.

**Pub Acts 1994, No. 164, § 3,** imd eff June 17, 1994, by § 2 eff September 1, 1994, provides:

"Section 3. This amendatory act shall not take effect unless all of the following bills of the 87th Legislature are enacted into law:

"(a) Senate Bill No. 1003 [which became Pub Acts 1994, No. 166].

"(b) House Bill No. 5414 [which became Pub Acts 1994, No. 163].

"(c) House Bill No. 5415 [which became Pub Acts 1994, No. 164]."

**Pub Acts 1996, No. 509, § 3,** imd eff January 9, 1997, by § 2 eff January 1, 1997, provides:

"Section 3. This amendatory act shall not take effect unless all of the following bills of the 88th Legislature are enacted into law:

"(a) House Bill No. 5912 [Pub Acts 1996, No. 508].

"(b) House Bill No. 5914 [Pub Acts 1996, No. 510]."

**Effect of amendment notes:**

The **1996 amendment** redesignated and revised existing text as subsections (1) and (2); and added subsections (3) and (4).

**§ 791.233e. Parole guidelines; purpose; mandatory and discretionary factors; nondiscrimination; promulgation of rules; departure from guidelines; review of guidelines; proposed revisions.** [MSA § 28.2303(6)]

Sec. 33e. (1) The department shall develop parole guidelines that are consistent with section 33(1)(a) and that shall govern the exercise of the parole board's discretion pursuant to sections 34 and 35 as to the release of prisoners on parole under this act. The purpose of the parole guidelines shall be to assist the parole board in making release decisions that enhance the public safety.

(2) In developing the parole guidelines, the department shall consider factors including, but not limited to, the following:

(a) The offense for which the prisoner is incarcerated at the time of parole consideration.

(b) The prisoner's institutional program performance.

(c) The prisoner's institutional conduct.

(d) The prisoner's prior criminal record. As used in this subdivision, "prior criminal record" means the recorded criminal history of a prisoner, including all misdemeanor and felony convictions, probation violations, juvenile adjudications for acts that would have been crimes if committed by an adult, parole failures, and delayed sentences.

(e) Other relevant factors as determined by the department, if not otherwise prohibited by law.

(3) In developing the parole guidelines, the department may consider both of the following factors:

(a) The prisoner's statistical risk screening.

(b) The prisoner's age.

(4) The department shall ensure that the parole guidelines do not create disparities in release decisions based on race, color, national origin, gender, religion, or disability.

(5) The department shall promulgate rules pursuant to the administrative procedures act of 1969, Act No. 306 of the Public Acts of 1969, being sections 24.201 to 24.328 of the Michigan Compiled

## § 791.233e — Department of Corrections

Laws, which shall prescribe the parole guidelines. The department shall submit the proposed rules to the joint committee on administrative rules not later than April 1, 1994. Until the rules take effect, the director shall require that the parole guidelines be considered by the parole board in making release decisions. After the rules take effect, the director shall require that the parole board follow the parole guidelines.

(6) The parole board may depart from the parole guideline by denying parole to a prisoner who has a high probability of parole as determined under the parole guidelines or by granting parole to a prisoner who has a low probability of parole as determined under the parole guidelines. A departure under this subsection shall be for substantial and compelling reasons stated in writing. The parole board shall not use a prisoner's gender, race, ethnicity, alienage, national origin, or religion to depart from the recommended parole guideline.

(7) Not less than once every 2 years, the department shall review the correlation between the implementation of the parole guidelines and the recidivism rate of paroled prisoners, and shall submit to the joint committee on administrative rules any proposed revisions to the administrative rules that the department considers appropriate after conducting the review.

### History:
Pub Acts 1953, No. 232, § 33e, as added by Pub Acts 1992, No. 181, imd eff September 22, 1992.

### Statutory references:
Sections 33, 34 and 35, above referred to, are §§791.233, 791.234 and 791.235.

### Michigan Digest references:
Pardons and Paroles § 5.

### LEXIS-NEXIS™ Michigan analytical references:
Michigan Law and Practice, Criminal Law § 717.

### Research references:
59 Am Jur 2d, Pardon and Parole § 79.

### Legal periodicals:
Van Ochten, Prison Disciplinary Hearings: Enforcing the Rules, 77 Mich B J 178 (1998).

### CASE NOTES

While the parole guidelines provide greater restrictions on the Parole Board's exercise of discretion concerning a prisoner of either low or high probability, the guidelines allow for a broader exercise of discretion in the case of a prisoner with an average probability of parole; the Parole Board's denial of parole to a prisoner with an average probability was not an abuse of discretion, and the circuit court erred in so holding, where there was no evidence that the board made its decision on a purely subjective basis or that the decision otherwise represented the product of the board's improper prejudice, and where the denial of parole was based on the prisoner's history of assaultive behavior and parole failure. Killebrew v Department of Corrections (1999) 237 Mich App 650, 604 NW2d 696, app den, motion gr (2000) 461 Mich 996.

**§ 791.234. Prisoners subject to jurisdiction of parole board; indeterminate and other sentences; termination of sentence; interview; release on parole; discretion of parole board; appeal to circuit court; cooperation with law enforcement by prisoner violating § 333.7401; definitions.** [MSA § 28.2304]

Sec. 34. (1) Except as provided in section 34a, a prisoner sentenced to an indeterminate sentence and confined in a state correctional facility with a minimum in terms of years other than a prisoner subject to disciplinary time is subject to the jurisdiction of the parole board when the prisoner has served a period of time equal to the minimum sentence imposed by the court for the crime of which he or she was convicted, less good time and disciplinary credits, if applicable.

(2) Except as provided in section 34a, a prisoner subject to disciplinary time sentenced to an indeterminate sentence and confined in a state correctional facility with a minimum in terms of years is subject to the jurisdiction of the parole board when the prisoner has served a period of time equal to the minimum sentence imposed by the court for the crime of which he or she was convicted.

(3) If a prisoner other than a prisoner subject to disciplinary time is sentenced for consecutive terms, whether received at the same time or at any time during the life of the original sentence, the parole board has jurisdiction over the prisoner for purposes of parole when the prisoner has served the total time of the added minimum terms, less the good time and disciplinary credits allowed by statute. The maximum terms of the sentences shall be added to compute the new maximum term under this subsection, and discharge shall be issued only after the total of the maximum sentences has been served less good time and disciplinary credits, unless the prisoner is paroled and discharged upon satisfactory completion of the parole.

(4) If a prisoner subject to disciplinary time is sentenced for consecutive terms, whether received at the same time or at any time during the life of the original sentence, the parole board has jurisdiction over the prisoner for purposes of parole when the prisoner has served the total time of the added minimum terms. The maximum terms of the sentences shall be added to compute the new maximum term under this subsection, and discharge shall be issued only after the total of the maximum sentences has been served, unless the prisoner is paroled and discharged upon satisfactory completion of the parole.

(5) If a prisoner other than a prisoner subject to disciplinary time has 1 or more consecutive terms remaining to serve in addition to the term he or she is serving, the parole board may terminate the sentence the prisoner is presently serving at any time after the minimum term of the sentence has been served.

(6) A prisoner under sentence for life, other than a prisoner sentenced for life for murder in the first degree, or sentenced for life for a violation of chapter XXXIII of the Michigan penal code, 1931 PA 328, MCL 750.200 to 750.212a, who has served 10 calendar years of the sentence in the case of a prisoner sentenced for any other

§ 791.234          Department of Corrections

crime committed before October 1, 1992, or, except as provided in subsection (10), who has served 20 calendar years of the sentence in the case of a prisoner sentenced to imprisonment for life for violating or conspiring to violate section 7401(2)(a)(i) of the public health code, 1978 PA 368, MCL 333.7401, who has another conviction for a serious crime, or, except as provided in subsection (10), who has served 17-1/2 calendar years of the sentence in the case of a prisoner sentenced to imprisonment for life for violating or conspiring to violate section 7401(2)(a)(i) of the public health code, 1978 PA 368, MCL 333.7401, who does not have another conviction for a serious crime, or who has served 15 calendar years of the sentence in the case of a prisoner sentenced for any other crime committed on or after October 1, 1992, is subject to the jurisdiction of the parole board and may be released on parole by the parole board, subject to the following conditions:

(a) At the conclusion of 10 calendar years of the prisoner's sentence and thereafter as determined by the parole board until the prisoner is paroled, discharged, or deceased, and in accordance with the procedures described in subsection (7), 1 member of the parole board shall interview the prisoner. The interview schedule prescribed in this subdivision applies to all prisoners to whom this subsection is applicable, regardless of the date on which they were sentenced.

(b) In addition to the interview schedule prescribed in subdivision (a), the parole board shall review the prisoner's file at the conclusion of 15 calendar years of the prisoner's sentence and every 5 years thereafter until the prisoner is paroled, discharged, or deceased. A prisoner whose file is to be reviewed under this subdivision shall be notified of the upcoming file review at least 30 days before the file review takes place and shall be allowed to submit written statements or documentary evidence for the parole board's consideration in conducting the file review.

(c) A decision to grant or deny parole to a prisoner so sentenced shall not be made until after a public hearing held in the manner prescribed for pardons and commutations in sections 44 and 45. Notice of the public hearing shall be given to the sentencing judge, or the judge's successor in office, and parole shall not be granted if the sentencing judge, or the judge's successor in office, files written objections to the granting of the parole within 30 days of receipt of the notice of hearing. The written objections shall be made part of the prisoner's file.

(d) A parole granted under this subsection shall be for a period of not less than 4 years and subject to the usual rules pertaining to paroles granted by the parole board. A parole ordered under this subsection is not valid until the transcript of the record is filed with the attorney general whose certification of receipt of the transcript shall be returnable to the office of the parole board within 5 days. Except for medical records protected under section 2157 of the revised judicature act of 1961, 1961 PA 236, MCL 600.2157, the file of a prisoner granted a parole under this subsection is a public record.

**Department of Corrections** § **791.234**

(e) A parole shall not be granted under this subsection in the case of a prisoner who is otherwise prohibited by law from parole consideration. In such cases the interview procedures in section 44 shall be followed.

(7) An interview conducted under subsection (6)(a) is subject to both of the following requirements:

(a) The prisoner shall be given written notice, not less than 30 days before the interview date, stating that the interview will be conducted.

(b) The prisoner may be represented at the interview by an individual of his or her choice. The representative shall not be another prisoner. A prisoner is not entitled to appointed counsel at public expense. The prisoner or representative may present relevant evidence in favor of holding a public hearing as described in subsection (6)(b).

(8) In determining whether a prisoner convicted of violating or conspiring to violate section 7401(2)(a)(i) of the public health code, 1978 PA 368, MCL 333.7401, and sentenced to imprisonment for life before October 1, 1998 is to be released on parole, the parole board shall consider all of the following:

(a) Whether the violation was part of a continuing series of violations of section 7401 or 7403 of the public health code, 1978 PA 368, MCL 333.7401 and 333.7403, by that individual.

(b) Whether the violation was committed by the individual in concert with 5 or more other individuals.

(c) Any of the following:

(i) Whether the individual was a principal administrator, organizer, or leader of an entity that the individual knew or had reason to know was organized, in whole or in part, to commit violations of section 7401 or 7403 of the public health code, 1978 PA 368, MCL 333.7401 and 333.7403, and whether the violation for which the individual was convicted was committed to further the interests of that entity.

(ii) Whether the individual was a principal administrator, organizer, or leader of an entity that the individual knew or had reason to know committed violations of section 7401 or 7403 of the public health code, 1978 PA 368, MCL 333.7401 and 333.7403, and whether the violation for which the individual was convicted was committed to further the interests of that entity.

(iii) Whether the violation was committed in a drug-free school zone.

(iv) Whether the violation involved the delivery of a controlled substance to an individual less than 17 years of age or possession with intent to deliver a controlled substance to an individual less than 17 years of age.

(9) Except as provided in section 34a, a prisoner's release on parole is discretionary with the parole board. The action of the parole board in granting a parole is appealable by the prosecutor of

§ 791.234                      **Department of Corrections**

the county from which the prisoner was committed or the victim of the crime for which the prisoner was convicted. The appeal shall be to the circuit court in the county from which the prisoner was committed, by leave of the court.

(10) If the sentencing judge, or his or her successor in office, determines on the record that a prisoner described in subsection (6) sentenced to imprisonment for life for violating or conspiring to violate section 7401(2)(a)(i) of the public health code, 1978 PA 368, MCL 333.7401, has cooperated with law enforcement, the prisoner is subject to the jurisdiction of the parole board and may be released on parole as provided in subsection (6), 2-1/2 years earlier than the time otherwise indicated in subsection (6). The prisoner is considered to have cooperated with law enforcement if the court determines on the record that the prisoner had no relevant or useful information to provide. The court shall not make a determination that the prisoner failed or refused to cooperate with law enforcement on grounds that the defendant exercised his or her constitutional right to trial by jury. If the court determines at sentencing that the defendant cooperated with law enforcement, the court shall include its determination in the judgment of sentence.

(11) As used in this section:

(a) "Serious crime" means violating or conspiring to violate article 7 of the public health code, 1978 PA 368, MCL 333.7101 to 333.7545, that is punishable by imprisonment for more than 4 years, or an offense against a person in violation of section 83, 84, 86, 87, 88, 89, 316, 317, 321, 349, 349a, 350, 397, 520b, 520c, 520d, 520g, 529, 529a, or 530 of the Michigan penal code, 1931 PA 328, MCL 750.83, 750.84, 750.86, 750.87, 750.88, 750.89, 750.316, 750.317, 750.321, 750.349, 750.349a, 750.350, 750.397, 750.520b, 750.520c, 750.520d, 750.520g, 750.529, 750.529a, and 750.530.

(b) "State correctional facility" means a facility that houses prisoners committed to the jurisdiction of the department, and includes a youth correctional facility operated under section 20g by the department or a private vendor.

**History:**

Pub Acts 1953, No. 232, § 34, eff October 2, 1953; amended by Pub Acts 1955, No. 107, imd eff June 3, 1955; 1957, No. 192, eff September 27, 1957; 1958, No. 210, eff September 13, 1958; 1978, No. 81, imd eff March 29, 1978 (see 1978 note below); 1982, No. 314, imd eff October 15, 1982; 1992, No. 22, imd eff March 19, 1992 (see 1992 note below); 1992, No. 181, imd eff September 22, 1992; 1994, No. 217, imd eff June 27, 1994 (see 1994 note below); 1994, No. 345, imd eff December 15, 1994, by § 2 eff January 1, 1995.

Amended by Pub Acts 1998, No. 209, imd eff July 1, 1998, by enacting § 1 eff October 1, 1998 (see 1998 note below); 1998, No. 314, imd eff July 30, 1998, by enacting § 1 eff October 1, 1998; 1998, No. 315, imd eff July 30, 1998, by enacting § 1 eff December 15, 1998 (see 1998 note below); 1998, No. 512, imd eff January 8, 1999; 1999, No. 191, eff March 10, 2000 (see Mich. Const. note below).

**Editor's notes:**

**Pub Acts 1978, No. 81, § 2,** imd eff March 29, 1978, provides:

"Section 2. "This amendatory act shall not take effect unless House Bill

**Department of Corrections** § 791.234

No. 4190 of the 1977 regular session of the legislature [Act No. 147 of 1978] is enacted into law. If House Bill No. 4190 of the 1977 regular session of the legislature [Act No. 147 of 1978] is enacted into law, this amendatory act shall take effect on the same date as that act takes effect."

**Pub Acts 1992, No. 22, § 2,** imd eff March 19, 1992, provides:
"Section 2. "This amendatory act shall not take effect unless all of the following bills of the 86th Legislature are enacted into law:
"(a) Senate Bill No. 145 [Act No. 21 of 1992].
"(b) Senate Bill No. 335 [Act No. 23 of 1992]."

**Pub Acts 1994, No. 217, §§2, 3,** imd eff June 27, 1994, provide:
"Section 2. This amendatory act shall take effect on the date that sentencing guidelines are enacted into law after the sentencing commission submits its report to the secretary of the senate and the clerk of the house of representatives pursuant to sections 31 to 34 of chapter IX of the code of criminal procedure, Act No. 175 of the Public Acts of 1927, as added by the amendatory act resulting from House Bill No. 4782 of the 87th Legislature. [House Bill No. 4782 became Pub Acts 1994, No. 445. Sections 31 to 34 of chapter IX of the code of criminal procedure are §§769.31–769.34.] (**Repealed** by Pub Acts 1998, No. 316, imd eff July 30, 1998, by enacting § 2 eff December 15, 1998.).
"Section 3. This amendatory act shall not take effect unless all of the following bills of the 87th Legislature are enacted into law:
"(a) Senate Bill No. 41 [Pub Acts 1994, No. 218].
"(b) House Bill No. 4782 [Pub Acts 1994, No. 445].
"(c) House Bill No. 5439 [Pub Acts 1994, No. 322]."

**Pub Acts 1998, No. 209, enacting § 2,** imd eff July 1, 1998, by enacting § 1 eff October 1, 1998, provides:
"Enacting section 2. This amendatory act does not take effect unless all of the following bills of the 89th Legislature are enacted into law:
"(a) Senate Bill No. 97 [Pub Acts 1998, No. 208].
"(b) House Bill No. 4289 [Pub Acts 1998, No. 206]."

**Pub Acts 1998, No. 315, enacting § 2,** imd eff July 30, 1998, by enacting § 1 eff December 15, 1998, provides:
"Enacting section 2. This amendatory act does not take effect unless all of the following bills of the 89th Legislature are enacted into law:
"(a) Senate Bill No. 826 [Pub Acts 1998, No. 316].
"(b) House Bill No. 4065 [Pub Acts 1998, No. 319].
"(c) House Bill No. 4444 [Pub Acts 1998, No. 311].
"(d) House Bill No. 4445 [Pub Acts 1998, No. 312].
"(e) House Bill No. 4446 [Pub Acts 1998, No. 313].
"(f) House Bill No. 4515 [Pub Acts 1998, No. 320].
"(g) House Bill No. 5419 [Pub Acts 1998, No. 317].
"(h) House Bill No. 5876 [Pub Acts 1998, No. 318]."

**Michigan Constitution of 1963, Art. IV, § 27,** provides:
"No act shall take effect until the expiration of 90 days from the end of the session at which it was passed, but the legislature may give immediate effect to acts by a two-thirds vote of the members elected to and serving in each house."

**Effect of amendment notes:**
**The first 1994 amendment (Pub Act 217)** added subsection (2), pertaining to prisoners subject to disciplinary time, and subsection (4), pertaining to prisoners subject to disciplinary time and sentenced for consecutive terms, and renumbered the remaining subsections accordingly; in subsections (1), (3) (formerly (2)), and (5) (formerly (3)), added "other than a prisoner subject to disciplinary time"; in subsection (6) (formerly (4)) paragraph (b), substituted "44(2)(f) to (h)" for "44(d) to (f)"; and made grammatical changes.

**The second 1994 amendment (Pub Act 345)** in subsection (7), added "in the county from which the prisoner was committed," and added subsection (8).

**The first 1998 amendment (Pub Act 209)** made stylistic changes to the statutory citations in subsection (2), paragraph (c) of subsection (6), and subsection (8); and added "or sentenced for life for a violation of chapter XXXIII of the Michigan penal code, 1931 PA 328, MCL 750.200 to 750.212," in the introductory paragraph of subsection (6).

**The second 1998 amendment (Pub Act 314)** substantially revised the initial paragraph of subsection (6); deleted "such time as" preceding "the prisoner" and substituted "regardless of the date on which they were sentenced" for "whether sentenced before, on, or after the effective date of the 1992 amendatory act that amended this subdivision" in paragraph (a) of subsection (6); deleted "44(2)(f) to (h) 44" preceding "and 45" in paragraph (b) of subsection (6); added subsections (7), (10) and (11); and redesignated former subsections (7) and (8) as subsections (8) and (9).

**The third 1998 amendment (Pub Act 315)** deleted ", plus any disciplinary time accumulated pursuant to section 34 of 1893 PA 118, MCL 800.34." following "convicted" in subsection (2); deleted ", plus any disciplinary time." following "minimum terms" in subsection (4); substantially revised the introductory paragraph of subsection (6); substantially revised paragraph (a) of subsection (6); deleted "44(2)(f) to (h) 44" preceding "and 45" in paragraph (b) of subsection (6); added subsection (7); deleted former subsection (8), as such subsection was numbered prior to the amendments made by 1998 PA 314; redesignated former subsection (7), as such subsection was numbered prior to the amendments made by 1998 PA 314, as subsection (8); added subsections (9) and (10), as such subsections would have been numbered prior to the amendments made by 1998 PA 314; and made minor grammatical changes.

**The fourth 1998 amendment (Pub Act 512)** made changes to cross-references in subsection (6), redesignated part of subsection (10) as (10)(a), and added subsection (10(b).

**The 1999 amendment** in subsection (6), deleted "or for a term of years," after "life" and substituted "(10)" for "(9)" after "subsection"; in subsection (6)(a), deleted "every 5 years" before "thereafter" and added "as determined by the parole board" after "thereafter", substituted "subsection (7)" for "section 35(4) to (6)"; and added a new subsection (6)(b); redesignated former subsection (6)(b) through (d) as (c) through (e); in new subsection (6)(c), substituted "decision to grant of deny parole to" for "parole shall not be granted", and inserted "shall not be made" after "sentenced"; added a new subsection (7) and redesignated former subsections (7) through (10) as (8) through (11); in redesignated subsection (9), deleted "or dying" after "granting", and deleted "the prisoner" before "the prosecutor".

**Statutory references:**
Sections 20g, 34a, 35, 44 and 45, above referred to, are §§791.220g, 791.234a, 791.235, 791.244 and 791.245.

**Cross references:**
Hearings for pardons and commutations, § 791.244.

**Michigan Digest references:**
Assault and Battery § 1.
Contracts Substances §§1, 20.
Criminal Sexual Conduct § 43.
Former Jeopardy § 3.
Habeas Corpus §§37.50, 38.
Homicide § 149.
Pardons and Paroles §§4, 5, 9.
Prisons and Jails § 9.

**LEXIS-NEXIS™ Michigan analytical references:**
Michigan Law and Practice, Criminal Law § 621.

**Research references:**
59 Am Jur 2d, Pardon and Parole §§81–84.
18A Am Jur Pl & Pr Forms, Rev, Pardon and Parole, Form 35.

# Department of Corrections § 791.234

**Legal periodicals:**

Special parole: challenges to the imposition of special punishment for drug law violators, 3 Crim JJ 55.

Ward, A New Phenomenon—Prosecution Appeals of Decisions to Parole, 72 Mich B J 10:1058(1993).

Girard et al., Prosecution Appeals of Decisions to Parole—A Different Perspective, 73 Mich B J 2:188 (1994).

Rubenstein, Comment, Let the Punishment Fit the Crime: Does Michigan's Drug Lifer Law Violate the Prohibition Against "Cruel and/or Unusual Punishment?", 10 Thomas M. Cooley L Rev 1:211 (1993).

Friedman, Hurdling the 6.500 Barrier: A Guide to Michigan Post-Conviction Remedies, 14 Thomas M. Cooley L Rev 1:65 (1997).

Mones, Battered Child Syndrome: Understanding Parricide, 30 Trial 2:24 (1994).

Guerin, People v. Moore: The role of discretion in indeterminate sentencing, Det CL Rev 3:1275 (1989).

## CASE NOTES

**1. In general.**

Prisoner sentenced in 1940 for crime committed while on parole from 1931 sentence was prisoner sentenced for consecutive terms within meaning of 1953 statute providing for computing new maximum terms of such person by adding maximums of his previous terms. In re Petition of Callahan (1957) 348 Mich 77, 81 NW2d 669.

Fact the prisoner, upon whose case parole board had failed to act, was eligible for parole by such board, did not permit trial judge to reduce nunc pro tunc valid sentence, after part thereof had been served, since such amendment of sentence would have violated jurisdiction of parole board. People v Fox (1945) 312 Mich 577, 20 NW2d 732, 168 ALR 703.

The statute unequivocally forbids the granting of parole to any prisoner who fails to overcome any of the statutory hurdles for eligibility; until all the statutory conditions are met, the Parole Board lacks the discretion to parole a prisoner and the Parole Board's decision to take no action on an inmate's application for parole on the grounds that the inmate failed to overcome the interview, hearing, and objection hurdles is not reviewable by the court. Johnson v Parole Bd. (In re Johnson) (1999) 235 Mich App 21, 596 NW2d 202.

The statute unequivocally forbids the granting of parole to any prisoner who fails to overcome any of the statutory hurdles for eligibility; until all the statutory conditions are met, the Parole Board lacks the discretion to parole a prisoner and the Parole Board's decision to take no action on an inmate's application for parole on the grounds that the inmate failed to overcome the interview, hearing, and objection hurdles is not reviewable by the court. Johnson v Parole Bd. (In re Johnson) (1999) 235 Mich App 21, 596 NW2d 202.

Parole may not be granted by the parole board in certain circumstances if the sentencing judge or his successor objects. People v McKendrick (1983) 123 Mich App 631, 333 NW2d 45, revd on other grounds (1983) 418 Mich 189, 341 NW2d 436.

In class action by inmates who committed crimes on or before September 22, 1992, and were in custody of Michigan Department of Corrections, Michigan Parole Board's 1992 amendments to parole laws restricting frequency of parole review hearings, from an initial four years and every two years thereafter to an initial ten years and five years thereafter, were ex post facto laws violating U.S. Constitution as applied to all inmates who committed their crimes and were convicted between 1977 and 1982 receiving parolable life sentences or long, indeterminate sentences, and all inmates who committed their crimes and were convicted after 1982 receiving mandatory life sentences, parolable life sentences or long, indeterminate sentences because the nexus between parole hearings and parole eligibility under the Michigan parole system created a "sufficient risk" of increased punishment of inmates who would otherwise be eligible for parole after an earlier hearing and the parole board failed to make a meaningful exercise of its retained discretion to conduct a hearing by not inquiring into an inmate's likelihood of receiving a favorable parole recommendation at his or her next review. Shabazz v Gabry (1995, ED Mich) 900 F Supp 118, app dismd (1995, CA6 Mich) 1995 US App LEXIS 38885.

Jurisdiction of parole board with respect to consecutive sentences discussed. Op Atty Gen, November 28, 1955, No. 1924.

**2. Constitutionality.**

The statutory penalty of mandatory life in prison without possibility of parole for possession of 650 grams or more of any mixture containing cocaine is so grossly disproportionate as to be cruel or unusual. People v Bullock (1992) 440 Mich 15, 485 NW2d 866, reh den (1992) 440 Mich 1203, 486 NW2d 744.

A statutory amendment increasing the interval between parole interviews for prisoners serving parolable life sentences did not violate the ex post facto clauses of the federal and state constitutions because the legislative change was merely procedural and did not affect prisoners' substantive rights. In re Parole of Glover (1997) 226 Mich App 655, 575 NW2d 772, appeal granted (1998) 458 Mich 866.

The statute by which a sentencing judge or his successor in office may, upon written objection, veto the release on parole of a prisoner who has completed at least ten years of a sentence for a conviction other than first-degree murder or a major controlled substances offense does not violate the constitutional provision for the separation of powers; the statute does not vest a judge with the power to pardon a prisoner or commute his sentence, which is vested by the constitution upon the governor, nor does it infringe upon the exclusive jurisdiction of the department of corrections over pardons, reprieves, commutations and paroles. Collins v Director, Dep't of Corrections (1986) 153 Mich App 477, 395 NW2d 77, app den (1987) 428 Mich 867, 400 NW2d 605, cert den (1987) 483 US 1026, 97 L Ed 2d 774, 107 S Ct 3276, habeas corpus dismissed (1994, CA6 Mich) 1994 US App LEXIS 3878.

In class action by inmates who committed crimes on or before September 22, 1992, and were in custody of Michigan Department of Corrections, Michigan Parole Board's 1992 amendments to parole laws restricting frequency of parole review hearings, from an initial four years and every two years thereafter to an initial ten years and five years thereafter, were ex post facto laws violating U.S. Constitution as applied to all inmates who committed their crimes and were convicted between 1977 and 1982 receiving parolable life sentences or long, indeterminate sentences, and all inmates who committed their crimes and were convicted after 1982 receiving mandatory life sentences, parolable life sentences or long, indeterminate sentences because the nexus between parole hearings and parole eligibility under the Michigan parole system created a "sufficient risk" of increased punishment of inmates who would otherwise be eligible for parole after an earlier hearing and the parole board failed to make a meaningful exercise of its retained discretion to conduct a hearing by not inquiring into an inmate's likelihood of receiving a favorable parole recommendation at his or her next review. Shabazz v Gabry (1995, ED Mich) 900 F Supp 118, app dismd (1995, CA6 Mich) 1995 US App LEXIS 38885.

Statute extending initial parole eligibility from 10 to 15 years for parolable non-drug life sentences imposed as of 1992 violated no procedural or substantive rights of inmate whose eligibility for parole after first 10 years remained unchanged under 1978 life sentence, thus affording inmate no ground for claiming violation of ex post facto clause absent retrospective application or disadvantage to him from change in frequency of hearings as result of parole board rules enacted on basis of statute, which in any event were not "laws" within meaning of ex post facto clause. Canales v Gabry (1994, ED Mich) 844 F Supp 1167.

**3. Construction, operation and effect.**

The Parole Board is required to provide substantial and compelling reasons in writing for departing from the parole guidelines' recommendation; brief conclusory statements do not constitute substantial and compelling reasons for denying parole; when the Parole Board denies parole, it must state the reasons in writing and in sufficient detail to facilitate appellate review for an abuse of discretion. In Re Parole of Scholtz (1998) 231 Mich App 104, 585 NW2d 352.

Where the prosecution does not object at the time of sentencing to the trial court allowing defendant to participate in the Special Alternative Incarceration (SAI) program, the prosecution waives its objection to placement; the applicable

**Department of Corrections** § 791.234

statute specifically provides that the trial court should make this decision at the time of sentencing and include it in the judgment of sentence, and, as a matter of policy, the prosecution cannot raise postsentencing objections to matters that could have been raised at the time of sentencing. People v Krim (1996) 220 Mich App 314, 559 NW2d 366.

In construing statute providing that a prisoner's release is discretionary with parole board once comes under jurisdiction of board upon serving minimum term of sentence minus allowances for good time and special good time, together with statute providing that habitual offenders shall not be eligible for parole prior to expiration of minimum term fixed by sentencing judge without permission of sentencing judge or his successor, release on parole of a prisoner sentenced under habitual offender statute would be held to be proscribed prior to expiration of calendar year minimum sentence imposed by sentencing judge in absence of written consent of such judge or his successor. People ex rel. Oakland County Prosecuting Attorney v State, Bureau of Pardons & Paroles (1977) 78 Mich App 111, 259 NW2d 385.

Contention that sentence of "natural life" upon conviction of armed robbery was impermissible as forever prohibiting review of defendants' files by parole board was specious, since word "natural" added to word "life" was mere surplusage. People v Rowls (1970) 28 Mich App 190, 184 NW2d 332.

In class action by inmates who committed crimes on or before September 22, 1992, and were in custody of Michigan Department of Corrections, Michigan Parole Board's 1992 amendments to parole laws restricting frequency of parole review hearings, from an initial four years and every two years thereafter to an initial ten years and five years thereafter, were ex post facto laws violating U.S. Constitution as applied to all inmates who committed their crimes and were convicted between 1977 and 1982 receiving parolable life sentences or long, indeterminate sentences, and all inmates who committed their crimes and were convicted after 1982 receiving mandatory life sentences, parolable life sentences or long, indeterminate sentences because the nexus between parole hearings and parole eligibility under the Michigan parole system created a "sufficient risk" of increased punishment of inmates who would otherwise be eligible for parole after an earlier hearing and the parole board failed to make a meaningful exercise of its retained discretion to conduct a hearing by not inquiring into an inmate's likelihood of receiving a favorable parole recommendation at his or her next review. Shabazz v Gabry (1995, ED Mich) 900 F Supp 118, app dismd (1995, CA6 Mich) 1995 US App LEXIS 38885.

Under similar provision of former act, parole board had no jurisdiction over prisoners in county jails. Op Atty Gen, December 11, 1946, No. 0–5286.

**4. Parole eligibility; life imprisonment.**

A person sentenced to life imprisonment for conspiracy to commit first-degree murder is eligible for parole consideration. People v Jahner (1989) 433 Mich 490, 446 NW2d 151.

The mandatory sentence of not less than twenty years nor more than thirty years of imprisonment without parole for possession of more than 225 grams but less than 650 grams of cocaine is not cruel or unusual punishment under the state constitution. People v DiVietri (1994) 206 Mich App 61, 520 NW2d 643.

Person convicted of conspiracy to commit first-degree murder is not eligible for parole. People v Jones (1988) 167 Mich App 424, 423 NW2d 590.

Person convicted of conspiracy to commit first-degree murder is eligible for release on parole upon serving ten calendar years of his mandatory sentence of life in prison. People v Fernandez (1987) 164 Mich App 485, 417 NW2d 540 (criticized by People v Jones (1988) 167 Mich App 424, 423 NW2d 590).

Michigan's "lifer law" allows any prison inmate under a sentence of life or for a term of years, other than those who have been convicted of first-degree murder or of a major controlled substance offense, to be considered for parole after serving 10 calendar years of his or her sentence; the electorate's approval of Proposal B in 1978 and the 1982 amendment of that statute modified the "lifer law" to the effect that inmates serving indeterminate sentences for any of the crimes enumerated in the statute are no longer eligible for parole until the minimum term is served less any time earned in disciplinary credits; Proposal B does not apply to life sentences. People v Hurst (1986) 155 Mich App 573, 400 NW2d 685, appeal after remand (1988)

§ 791.234            Department of Corrections

169 Mich App 160, 425 NW2d 752, app den (1989, Mich) 1989 Mich LEXIS 365.

A person sentenced to life imprisonment for any crime other than first-degree murder or a major controlled substance offense is eligible for parole consideration after serving 10 calendar years of the life sentence; 1978 Initiative Proposal B did not repeal the statute providing for such parole consideration. People v Dziuba (1984) 139 Mich App 789, 363 NW2d 33, app den (1985, Mich) 366 NW2d 7.

In the department of corrections act, the legislature has provided that the parole board may not grant a parole to a person convicted prior to June 3, 1988, of the crime of conspiracy to possess cocaine and sentenced to life imprisonment. Op Atty Gen, October 14, 1991, No. 6702.

**5. Date of minimum expiration.**

Where more than five years had elapsed since petitioner had been sentenced in state courts for sentences bearing three-year minimums, imposed while petitioner was serving five-year federal sentence, petitioner was properly within jurisdiction of state parole board, under provision of this section that date of minimum expiration determines when parole board receives jurisdiction. Petition of Carey (1964) 372 Mich 378, 126 NW2d 727.

A defendant sentenced as a habitual offender, receiving good-time credit, comes under the jurisdiction of the parole board following expiration of his net minimum sentence, at which time the parole board may grant parole subject to the approval of the sentencing judge; the action of the parole board in releasing prisoners is not reviewable if in compliance with law and failure to obtain the prior approval of the sentencing judge in such a case is not in compliance with law. Lamb v Bureau of Pardons & Paroles (1981) 106 Mich App 175, 307 NW2d 754.

A prisoner sentenced to an indeterminate sentence for a crime listed in 1978 PA Initiated Law (Proposal B) may not be considered for parole until the prisoner has served the minimum term imposed by the sentencing judge. Op Atty Gen, February 25, 1986, No. 6346.

**6. Discretion of parole board.**

The time of a prisoner's release on parole is discretionary with the parole board, although a prisoner sentenced to an indeterminate sentence becomes subject to the jurisdiction of the parole board when he has served the minimum sentence imposed, less any good time allowance. Phillips v Warden, State Prison (1986) 153 Mich App 557, 396 NW2d 482, app den (1987) 428 Mich 859.

Parole consideration determinations are left to the parole board's discretion and are not subject to the enhanced procedural safeguards applicable to prison disciplinary hearings. Shields v Department of Corrections (1983) 128 Mich App 380, 340 NW2d 95.

The power to grant or deny parole is vested in the parole board. People v McKendrick (1983) 123 Mich App 631, 333 NW2d 45, revd on other grounds (1983) 418 Mich 189, 341 NW2d 436.

Parole board is vested with broad discretionary power in determining whether or not prisoner is entitled to parole. (Construing similar provision of former act.) Ex parte McBride (1946, DC Mich) 68 F Supp 139.

**7. Parole hearings.**

The Parole Board is not exempt from the public meeting and notice requirements of the Open Meetings Act and the Parole Board violated the Open Meetings Act when it made a parole decision in a closed meeting without providing the public with notice of its action. In re Parole of Glover (1997) 226 Mich App 655, 575 NW2d 772, app gr (1998) 458 Mich 866.

A public hearing by the parole board concerning parole for a prisoner is not required by statute until after an initial decision by the board to proceed toward a grant of parole. Middleton v Parole Bd. (1995) 208 Mich App 563, 528 NW2d 791.

Michigan parole board's authorized discretionary amendment of its rules to extend time between parole hearings in accord with parole statute did not violate procedural or substantive due process rights of inmate where his hope of parole from life sentence created no protectable expectation or liberty interest, rules were not penal "laws" subject to ex post facto clause, and law under which inmate was convicted and sentenced for life remained unchanged as to ten year period before his initial eligibility for parole. Canales v Gabry (1994, ED Mich) 844 F Supp 1167.

Under this section notice of public hearing must be given to the sentencing judge, if alive, and if written objections are filed by said judge, parole may not be granted, and failure of sentencing judge, if alive, to file written objections leaves matter of parole to discretion of parole board. (Construing similar provision of former act.) Op Atty Gen, 1941–1942, p 637, No. 24084.

**8. Review of action of parole board.**

The trial court possesses the discretionary right to determine minimum sentences and, within the statutes, the parole board possesses the same discretion in determining the length of parole. Lane v Michigan Dep't of Corrections, Parole Board (1970) 383 Mich 50, 173 NW2d 209.

A parole board's decision on whether to consider a prisoner for parole is expressly exempted from judicial review as long as the decision is made pursuant to law, and it matters not whether the decision falls within the formal definition of a "contested case." Shields v Department of Corrections (1983) 128 Mich App 380, 340 NW2d 95.

Federal court would not superimpose its own judgment on exercise of parole board's discretion. Bricker v Michigan Parole Bd. (1975, ED Mich) 405 F Supp 1340.

Federal court would not examine factual basis for parole board's determination that parole violation occurred. Bricker v Michigan Parole Bd. (1975, ED Mich) 405 F Supp 1340.

Federal courts are loathe to interfere in administration of state prisons, absent violation of federal constitutional right, for parole system is part of state correctional system in that parole is form of custody whereby prisoner leaves his place of incarceration while remaining in legal custody and control of board of parole until termination of his sentence. Bricker v Michigan Parole Bd. (1975, ED Mich) 405 F Supp 1340.

Plaintiff's attack on reincarceration in state prison could not be cast as civil rights claim in order to avoid requirement of exhaustion of state remedies. Bricker v Michigan Parole Bd. (1975, ED Mich) 405 F Supp 1340.

Petitioner alleging denial of parole in violation of his constitutional rights is not entitled to bring habeas corpus in federal district court unless he has exhausted his remedies in state courts, and he has not exhausted those remedies where his petition for habeas corpus in state supreme court has been denied and he has not sought review in United States Supreme Court. Ex parte McBride (1946, DC Mich) 68 F Supp 139.

Federal district court should not interfere, in habeas corpus proceedings, with management of state prison and treatment accorded prisoner, unless petitioner alleges facts which clearly indicate his right to discharge, and not merely legal conclusion that he has been denied due process of law. Ex parte McBride (1946, DC Mich) 68 F Supp 139.

It is not province of federal district court in habeas corpus proceedings to inquire into discretionary action of parole board. Ex parte McBride (1946, DC Mich) 68 F Supp 139.

A court has no power to review action of parole board in granting or denying parole to person serving life term or indeterminate sentence where there has been compliance with statutory requirements. Op Atty Gen, October 12, 1944, No. 0–2781.

**§ 791.234a. Placement in special alternative incarceration unit; eligibility requirements; minimum sentence required for certain violations; participation prohibited by sentencing judge; eligibility determination by department; notice; prisoner consent to placement; minimum and maximum placement period; parole; suspension or revocation of parole; annual report to legislature.** [MSA § 28.2304(1)]

Sec. 34a. (1) A prisoner sentenced to an indeterminate term of imprisonment under the jurisdiction of the department, regardless of when he or she was sentenced, shall be considered by the department for placement in a special alternative incarceration unit established under section 3 of the special alternative incarceration act, 1988 PA 287, MCL 798.13, if the prisoner meets the eligibility requirements of subsections (2) and (3). For a prisoner committed to the jurisdiction of the department on or after March 19, 1992, the department shall determine before the prisoner leaves the reception center whether the prisoner is eligible for placement in a special alternative incarceration unit, although actual placement may take place at a later date. A determination of eligibility does not guarantee placement in a unit.

(2) To be eligible for placement in a special alternative incarceration unit, the prisoner shall meet all of the following requirements:

(a) The prisoner's minimum sentence does not exceed either of the following limits, as applicable:

(i) 24 months or less for a violation of section 110 of the Michigan penal code, 1931 PA 328, MCL 750.110, if the violation involved any occupied dwelling house.

(ii) 36 months or less for any other crime.

(b) The prisoner has never previously been placed in a special alternative incarceration unit as either a prisoner or a probationer, unless he or she was removed from a special alternative incarceration unit for medical reasons as specified in subsection (6).

(c) The prisoner is physically able to participate in the program.

(d) The prisoner does not appear to have any mental disability that would prevent participation in the program.

(e) The prisoner is serving his or her first prison sentence.

(f) At the time of sentencing, the judge did not prohibit participation in the program in the judgment of sentence.

(g) The prisoner is otherwise suitable for the program, as determined by the department.

(h) The prisoner is not serving a sentence for any of the following crimes:

(i) A violation of section 11, 49, 80, 83, 89, 91, 157b, 158, 207, 260, 316, 317, 327, 328, 335a, 338, 338a, 338b, 349, 349a, 350, 422, 436, 511, 516, 517, 520b, 529, 529a, 531, or 544 of the Michigan penal code, 1931 PA 328, MCL 750.11, 750.49, 750.80, 750.83, 750.89, 750.91, 750.157b, 750.158, 750.207, 750.260, 750.316, 750.317, 750.327, 750.328, 750.335a, 750.338, 750.338a, 750.338b, 750.349, 750.349a, 750.350, 750.422, 750.436, 750.511, 750.516, 750.517, 750.520b, 750.529, 750.529a, 750.531, and 750.544.

(ii) A violation of section 145c, 520c, 520d, or 520g of the Michigan penal code, 1931 PA 328, MCL 750.145c, 750.520c, 750.520d, and 750.520g.

(iii) A violation of section 72, 73, or 75 of the Michigan penal code, 1931 PA 328, MCL 750.72, 750.73, and 750.75.

(iv) A violation of section 86, 112, 136b, 193, 195, 213, 319, 321, 329, or 397 of the Michigan penal code, 1931 PA 328, MCL 750.86, 750.112, 750.136b, 750.193, 750.195, 750.213, 750.319, 750.321, 750.329, and 750.397.

(v) A violation of section 2 of 1968 PA 302, MCL 752.542.

(vi) An attempt to commit a crime described in subparagraphs (i) to (v).

**Department of Corrections** § **791.234a**

(vii) A violation occurring on or after January 1, 1992, of section 625(4) or (5) of the Michigan vehicle code, 1949 PA 300, MCL 257.625.

(viii) A crime for which the prisoner was punished pursuant to section 10, 11, or 12 of chapter IX of the code of criminal procedure, 1927 PA 175, MCL 769.10, 769.11, and 769.12.

(3) A prisoner who is serving a sentence for a violation of section 7401 or 7403 of the public health code, 1978 PA 368, MCL 333.7401 and 333.7403, and who has previously been convicted for a violation of section 7401 or 7403(2)(a), (b), or (e) of the public health code, 1978 PA 368, MCL 333.7401 and 333.7403, is not eligible for placement in a special alternative incarceration unit until after he or she has served the equivalent of the mandatory minimum sentence prescribed by statute for that violation.

(4) If the sentencing judge prohibited a prisoner's participation in the special alternative incarceration program in the judgment of sentence, that prisoner shall not be placed in a special alternative incarceration unit. If the sentencing judge permitted the prisoner's participation in the special alternative incarceration program in the judgment of sentence, that prisoner may be placed in a special alternative incarceration unit if the department determines that the prisoner also meets the requirements of subsections (2) and (3). If the sentencing judge neither prohibited nor permitted a prisoner's participation in the special alternative incarceration program in the judgment of sentence, and the department determines that the prisoner meets the eligibility requirements of subsections (2) and (3), the department shall notify the judge or the judge's successor, the prosecuting attorney for the county in which the prisoner was sentenced, and any victim of the crime for which the prisoner was committed if the victim has submitted to the department a written request for any notification pursuant to section 19(1) of the crime victim's rights act, 1985 PA 87, MCL 780.769, of the proposed placement of the prisoner in the special alternative incarceration unit not later than 30 days before placement is intended to occur. The department shall not place the prisoner in a special alternative incarceration unit unless the sentencing judge, or the judge's successor, notifies the department, in writing, that he or she does not object to the proposed placement. In making the decision on whether or not to object, the judge, or judge's successor, shall review any impact statement submitted pursuant to section 14 of the crime victim's rights act, 1985 PA 87, MCL 780.764, by the victim or victims of the crime of which the prisoner was convicted.

(5) Notwithstanding subsection (4), a prisoner shall not be placed in a special alternative incarceration unit unless the prisoner consents to that placement and agrees that the department may suspend or restrict privileges generally afforded other prisoners including, but not limited to, the areas of visitation, property, mail, publications, commissary, library, and telephone access. However, the department may not suspend or restrict the prisoner's access to the prisoner grievance system.

(6) A prisoner may be placed in a special alternative incarceration program for a period of not less than 90 days or more than 120 days. If, during that period, the prisoner misses more than 5 days of program participation due to medical excuse for illness or injury occurring after he or she was placed in the program, the period of placement shall be increased by the number of days missed, beginning with the sixth day of medical excuse, up to a maximum of 20 days. However, the total number of days a prisoner may be placed in this program, including days missed due to medical excuse, shall not exceed 120 days. A medical excuse shall be verified by a physician's statement. A prisoner who is medically unable to participate in the program for more than 25 days shall be returned to a state correctional facility but may be reassigned to the program if the prisoner meets the eligibility requirements of subsections (2) and (3).

(7) Upon certification of completion of the special alternative incarceration program, the prisoner shall be placed on parole. A prisoner paroled under this section shall have conditions of parole as determined appropriate by the parole board and shall be placed on parole for not less than 18 months, or the balance of the prisoner's minimum sentence, whichever is greater, with at least the first 120 days under intensive supervision.

(8) The parole board may suspend or revoke parole for any prisoner paroled under this section subject to sections 39a and 40a. For a prisoner other than a prisoner subject to disciplinary time, if parole is revoked before the expiration of the prisoner's minimum sentence, less disciplinary credits, the parole board shall forfeit, pursuant to section 33(13) of 1893 PA 118, MCL 800.33, all disciplinary credits that were accumulated during special alternative incarceration, and the prisoner shall be considered for parole pursuant to section 35.

(9) On March 19, 1993, and annually after that time, the department shall report to the legislature the impact of the operation of this section, including a report concerning recidivism.

**History:**
Pub Acts 1953, No. 232, § 34a, as added by Pub Acts 1992, No. 22, imd eff March 19, 1992; amended by Pub Acts 1994, No. 199, imd eff June 21, 1994, by § 2 eff October 1, 1994 (see 1994 note below); 1994, No. 217, eff June 27, 1994 (see 1994 note below); 1994, No. 427, imd eff January 6, 1995.

Amended by Pub Acts 1998, No. 84, imd eff May 13, 1998; 1998, No. 315, imd eff July 30, 1998, by enacting § 1 eff December 15, 1998 (see 1998 note below).

**Editor's notes:**
**Pub Acts 1992, No. 22,** § **2,** imd eff March 19, 1992, provides:

"Section 2. This amendatory act shall not take effect unless all of the following bills of the 86th Legislature are enacted into law:

"(a) Senate Bill No. 145 [which became Act No. 21 of 1992].

"(b) Senate Bill No. 335 [which became Act No. 23 of 1992]."

**Pub Acts 1994, No. 199,** § **3,** imd eff June 21, 1994, by § 2 eff October 1, 1994, provides:

"Section 3. This amendatory act shall not take effect unless Senate Bill

**Department of Corrections** § 791.234a

No. 773 of the 87th Legislature (which became Pub Acts 1994, No. 191) is enacted into law."

**Pub Acts 1994, No. 217, §§2 and 3,** eff June 27, 1994, provide:

"Section 2. This amendatory act shall take effect on the date that sentencing guidelines are enacted into law after the sentencing commission submits its report to the secretary of the senate and the clerk of the house of representatives pursuant to sections 31 to 34 of chapter IX of the code of criminal procedure, Act No. 175 of the Public Acts of 1927, as added by the amendatory act resulting from House Bill No. 4782 of the 87th Legislature [Pub Acts 1994, No. 445]. (**Repealed** by Pub Acts 1998, No. 316, imd eff July 30, 1998, by enacting § 2 eff December 15, 1998.).

"Section 3. This amendatory act shall not take effect unless all of the following bills of the 87th Legislature are enacted into law:

"(a) Senate Bill No. 41 [Pub Acts 1994, No. 218].
"(b) House Bill No. 4782 [Pub Acts 1994, No. 445].
"(c) House Bill No. 5439 [Pub Acts 1994, No. 322]."

**Pub Acts 1998, No. 315, enacting** § **2,** imd eff July 30, 1998, by enacting § 1 eff December 15, 1998, provides:

"Enacting section 2. This amendatory act does not take effect unless all of the following bills of the 89th Legislature are enacted into law:

"(a) Senate Bill No. 826 [Pub Acts 1998, No. 316].
"(b) House Bill No. 4065 [Pub Acts 1998, No. 319].
"(c) House Bill No. 4444 [Pub Acts 1998, No. 311].
"(d) House Bill No. 4445 [Pub Acts 1998, No. 312].
"(e) House Bill No. 4446 [Pub Acts 1998, No. 313].
"(f) House Bill No. 4515 [Pub Acts 1998, No. 320].
"(g) House Bill No. 5419 [Pub Acts 1998, No. 317].
"(h) House Bill No. 5876 [Pub Acts 1998, No. 318]."

**Effect of amendment notes:**

**The first 1994 amendment (Pub Act 199)** in subsection (1) paragraph (h) subparagraph (i), inserted "529a," and "750.529a"; in subsection (9) substituted "By March 19, 1993" for "One year after the effective date of the 1992 amendatory act that added this section"; in subsection (10) substituted "March 19, 1995" for "upon the expiration of 3 years after the date of its enactment"; and made grammatical changes.

**The second 1994 amendment (Pub Act 217)** in subsection (1), substituted "March 19, 1992" for "the effective date of the amendatory act that added this section"; in subsection (2), paragraph (h), subparagraph (i), inserted "529a" and "750.529a"; in subsection (3) deleted ", being sections 333.7401 and 333.7403 of the Michigan Compiled Laws,"; in subsection (8) substituted "For a prisoner other than a prisoner subject to disciplinary time, if" for "If", deleted "all disciplinary credits granted" following "shall forfeit" and inserted "all disciplinary credits" preceding "that were accumulated"; in subsection (9) substituted "On March 19, 1993," for "One year after the effective date of the 1992 amendatory act that added this section" and in subsection (10) substituted "March 19, 1995" for "upon the expiration of 3 years after the date of its enactment".

**The third 1994 amendment (Pub Act 427)** in subsection (2), paragraph (i), substituted "A violation of section" for "Section"; and in subsection (10) substituted "The provisions of this section regarding prisoners subject to disciplinary time take effect beginning on the effective date of Act No. 217 of the Public Acts of 1994, as prescribed in enacting section 2 of that amendatory act." for "This section is repealed March 19, 1995."

**The first 1998 amendment (Pub Act 84)** in subsection (1), substituted "January 6, 1995" for "the effective date of the amendatory act that added this section"; in subsection (2)(d), substituted "disability" for "handicap"; and changed the form of statutory references throughout the section.

**The second 1998 amendment (Pub Act 315)** deleted "either before, on, or after January 6, 1995" following preceding "to an indeterminate" and inserted ", regardless of when he or she was sentenced" in subsection (1); deleted ", as that term is defined in that section." following "house" in

## § 791.234a

subparagraph (i) of paragraph (a) of subsection (2); and deleted former subsection (10).

**Statutory references:**
Sections 35, 39a and 40a are §§791.235, 791.239a and 791.240a.

**Michigan Digest references:**
Pardons and Paroles §§2, 5.

**Legal periodicals:**
Ward, A New Phenomenon—Prosecution Appeals of Decisions to Parole, 72 Mich B J 10:1058 (1993).

### CASE NOTES

Greater penalty mandated on conviction of statutory felony murder than for predicate crime of armed robbery manifested legislative intent not to impose punishments for both predicate and underlying crimes, thus rendering earlier sentence for armed robbery violating Double Jeopardy Clauses of State and Federal Constitutions on subsequent conviction of defendant for felony murder of victim who died four years from effects of gunshot wounds inflicted in armed robbery. People v Harding (1993) 443 Mich 693, 506 NW2d 482.

### § 791.235. Release of prisoner on parole; procedure. [MSA § 28.2305]

Sec. 35. (1) The release of a prisoner on parole shall be granted solely upon the initiative of the parole board. The parole board may grant a parole without interviewing the prisoner. However, beginning on the date on which the administrative rules prescribing parole guidelines pursuant to section 33e(5) take effect, the parole board may grant a parole without interviewing the prisoner only if, after evaluating the prisoner according to the parole guidelines, the parole board determines that the prisoner has a high probability of being paroled and the parole board therefore intends to parole the prisoner. Except as provided in subsection (2), a prisoner shall not be denied parole without an interview before 1 member of the parole board. The interview shall be conducted at least 1 month before the expiration of the prisoner's minimum sentence less applicable good time and disciplinary credits for a prisoner eligible for good time and disciplinary credits, or at least 1 month before the expiration of the prisoner's minimum sentence for a prisoner subject to disciplinary time. The parole board shall consider any statement made to the parole board by a crime victim under the crime victim's rights act, 1985 PA 87, MCL 780.751 to 780.834, or under any other provision of law. The parole board shall not consider any of the following factors in making a parole determination:

(a) A juvenile record that a court has ordered the department to expunge.

(b) Information that is determined by the parole board to be inaccurate or irrelevant after a challenge and presentation of relevant evidence by a prisoner who has received a notice of intent to conduct an interview as provided in subsection (4). This subdivision applies only to presentence investigation reports prepared before April 1, 1983.

**Department of Corrections** § 791.235

(2) Beginning on the date on which the administrative rules prescribing the parole guidelines take effect pursuant to section 33e(5), if, after evaluating a prisoner according to the parole guidelines, the parole board determines that the prisoner has a low probability of being paroled and the parole board therefore does not intend to parole the prisoner, the parole board shall not be required to interview the prisoner before denying parole to the prisoner.

(3) The parole board may consider but shall not base a determination to deny parole solely on either of the following:

(a) A prisoner's marital history.

(b) Prior arrests not resulting in conviction or adjudication of delinquency.

(4) If an interview is to be conducted, the prisoner shall be sent a notice of intent to conduct an interview at least 1 month before the date of the interview. The notice shall state the specific issues and concerns that shall be discussed at the interview and that may be a basis for a denial of parole. A denial of parole shall not be based on reasons other than those stated in the notice of intent to conduct an interview except for good cause stated to the prisoner at or before the interview and in the written explanation required by subsection (12). This subsection does not apply until April 1, 1983.

(5) Except for good cause, the parole board member conducting the interview shall not have cast a vote for or against the prisoner's release before conducting the current interview. Before the interview, the parole board member who is to conduct the interview shall review pertinent information relative to the notice of intent to conduct an interview.

(6) A prisoner may waive the right to an interview by 1 member of the parole board. The waiver of the right to be interviewed shall be given not more than 30 days after the notice of intent to conduct an interview is issued and shall be made in writing. During the interview held pursuant to a notice of intent to conduct an interview, the prisoner may be represented by an individual of his or her choice. The representative shall not be another prisoner or an attorney. A prisoner is not entitled to appointed counsel at public expense. The prisoner or representative may present relevant evidence in support of release. This subsection does not apply until April 1, 1983.

(7) At least 90 days before the expiration of the prisoner's minimum sentence less applicable good time and disciplinary credits for a prisoner eligible for good time or disciplinary credits, or at least 90 days before the expiration of the prisoner's minimum sentence for a prisoner subject to disciplinary time, or the expiration of a 12-month continuance for any prisoner, a parole eligibility report shall be prepared by appropriate institutional staff. The parole eligibility report shall be considered pertinent information for purposes of subsection (5). The report shall include all of the following:

(a) A statement of all major misconduct charges of which the prisoner was found guilty and the punishment served for the misconduct.

(b) The prisoner's work and educational record while confined.

(c) The results of any physical, mental, or psychiatric examinations of the prisoner that may have been performed.

(d) Whether the prisoner fully cooperated with the state by providing complete financial information as required under section 3a of the state correctional facility reimbursement act, 1935 PA 253, MCL 800.403a.

(e) For a prisoner subject to disciplinary time, a statement of all disciplinary time submitted for the parole board's consideration pursuant to section 34 of 1893 PA 118, MCL 800.34.

(8) The preparer of the report shall not include a recommendation as to release on parole.

(9) Psychological evaluations performed at the request of the parole board to assist it in reaching a decision on the release of a prisoner may be performed by the same person who provided the prisoner with therapeutic treatment, unless a different person is requested by the prisoner or parole board.

(10) The parole board may grant a medical parole for a prisoner determined to be physically or mentally incapacitated. A decision to grant a medical parole shall be initiated upon the recommendation of the bureau of health care services and shall be reached only after a review of the medical, institutional, and criminal records of the prisoner.

(11) The department shall submit a petition to the appropriate court under section 434 of the mental health code, 1974 PA 258, MCL 330.1434, for any prisoner being paroled or being released after serving his or her maximum sentence whom the department considers to be a person requiring treatment. The parole board shall require mental health treatment as a special condition of parole for any parolee whom the department has determined to be a person requiring treatment whether or not the petition filed for that prisoner is granted by the court. As used in this subsection, "person requiring treatment" means that term as defined in section 401 of the mental health code, 1974 PA 258, MCL 330.1401.

(12) When the parole board makes a final determination not to release a prisoner, the prisoner shall be provided with a written explanation of the reason for denial and, if appropriate, specific recommendations for corrective action the prisoner may take to facilitate release.

(13) This section does not apply to the placement on parole of a person in conjunction with special alternative incarceration under section 34a(7).

**History:**

Pub Acts 1953, No. 232, § 35, eff October 2, 1953; amended by Pub Acts 1982, No. 314, imd eff October 15, 1982; 1984, No. 414, eff March 29, 1985 (see 1984 note below); 1992, No. 22, imd eff March 19, 1992 (see 1992 note below); 1992, No. 181, imd eff September 22, 1992; 1994, No. 217, eff June 27, 1994 (see 1994 note below).

Amended by Pub Acts 1998, No. 315, imd eff July 30, 1998, by enacting § 1 eff December 15, 1998 (see 1998 note below).

**Editor's notes:**
**Pub Acts 1984, No. 414, § 2,** eff March 29, 1985, provides:
"Section 2. This amendatory act shall not take effect unless Senate Bill No. 684 of the 82nd Legislature [which became Act No. 282 of 1984] is enacted into law."
**Pub Acts 1992, No. 22, § 2,** imd eff March 19, 1992, provides:
"Section 2. This amendatory act shall not take effect unless all of the following bills of the 86th Legislature are enacted into law:
"(a) Senate Bill No. 145 [which became Act No. 21 of 1992].
"(b) Senate Bill No. 335 [which became Act No. 23 of 1992]."
**Pub Acts 1994, No. 217, §§2, 3,** eff June 27, 1994, provide:
"Section 2. This amendatory act shall take effect on the date that sentencing guidelines are enacted into law after the sentencing commission submits its report to the secretary of the senate and the clerk of the house of representatives pursuant to sections 31 to 34 of chapter IX of the code of criminal procedure, Act No. 175 of the Public Acts of 1927, as added by the amendatory act resulting from House Bill No. 4782 of the 87th Legislature [which became Pub Acts 1994, No. 445]. (**Repealed** by Pub Acts 1998, No. 316, imd eff July 30, 1998, by enacting § 2 eff December 15, 1998.).
"Section 3. This amendatory act shall not take effect unless all of the following bills of the 87th Legislature are enacted into law:
"(a) Senate Bill No. 41 [Pub Acts 1994, No. 218].
"(b) House Bill No. 4782 [Pub Acts 1994, No. 445].
"(c) House Bill No. 5439 [Pub Acts 1994, No. 322]."
**Pub Acts 1998, No. 315, enacting § 2,** imd eff July 30, 1998, by enacting § 1 eff December 15, 1998, provides:
"Enacting section 2. This amendatory act does not take effect unless all of the following bills of the 89th Legislature are enacted into law:
"(a) Senate Bill No. 826 [Pub Acts 1998, No. 316].
"(b) House Bill No. 4065 [Pub Acts 1998, No. 319].
"(c) House Bill No. 4444 [Pub Acts 1998, No. 311].
"(d) House Bill No. 4445 [Pub Acts 1998, No. 312].
"(e) House Bill No. 4446 [Pub Acts 1998, No. 313].
"(f) House Bill No. 4515 [Pub Acts 1998, No. 320].
"(g) House Bill No. 5419 [Pub Acts 1998, No. 317].
"(h) House Bill No. 5876 [Pub Acts 1998, No. 318]."

**Effect of amendment notes:**
**The 1994 amendment** in subsection (1), inserted "for a prisoner eligible for good time and disciplinary credits, or at least 1 month before the expiration of the prisoner's minimum sentence plus disciplinary time for a prisoner subject to disciplinary time" and in subsection (7), inserted "less applicable good time and disciplinary credits for a prisoner eligible for good time or disciplinary credits, or at least 90 days before the expiration of the prisoner's minimum sentence plus disciplinary time for a prisoner subject to disciplinary time" and "for any prisoner", respectively.
**The 1998 amendment** in the initial paragraph of subsection (1), deleted "plus disciplinary time" following "sentence" in the fifth sentence, and changed the style of statutory references; in subsection (7), deleted "plus disciplinary time" in the first sentence of the initial paragraph, changed the style of statutory references in paragraph (d), and added paragraph (e); and, in subsection (11) substituted "appropriate" for "probate", deleted "probate" preceding "court" in the second sentence, and changed the style of statutory references.

**Statutory references:**
Sections 33e and 34a, above referred to, are §§791.233e and 791.234a.

**Cross references:**
Information assembled by classification committees of penal institutions to be filed with parole board, § 791.264.

**Michigan Digest references:**
Pardons and Paroles §§2, 4, 5.

**LEXIS-NEXIS™ Michigan analytical references:**
Michigan Law and Practice, Criminal Law § 717.
Michigan Law and Practice, Criminal Law § 717.

**Research references:**
59 Am Jur 2d, Pardon and Parole §§81–84.
18A Am Jur Pl & Pr Forms, Rev, Pardon and Parole, Form 35.

### CASE NOTES

The statute barring an attorney from acting as a prisoner's representative at a parole interview does not violate federal or state guaranties of equal protection of the law; however, the statute does not prevent a lawyer from attending and participating in a parole interview in the same manner that a nonlawyer could. Franciosi v Michigan Parole Bd. (2000) 461 Mich 347, 604 NW2d 675.

Inmates serving parolable life terms and denied parole are statutorily entitled to a sufficiently detailed written explanation for the board's decision and, where appropriate, specific recommendations for corrective action the prisoner may take to facilitate release; an inmate does not have a federal or state due process right to a detailed written explanation denying the inmate's request for parole. Glover v Parole Bd. (1999) 460 Mich 511, 596 NW2d 598.

Statutory requirement that parole hearing be had before parole board required at least a quorum and hearings before one or two board members failed to fulfill statutory requirement. Young v Parole Bd. (1982) 413 Mich 536, 321 NW2d 374.

Statute prohibiting presence of attorneys at parole interviews does not violate Equal Protection Clauses of the federal and Michigan constitutions, as prohibition is rationally related to state's legitimate interest in assessing an inmate's readiness for parole through interview process that "fosters openness, sincerity and candor"; presence of attorneys would formalize process and impede parole board's ability to fairly assess inmate's readiness based on "the inmate's own words, unguided by the promptings of counsel". In re Parole of Franciosi (1998) 231 Mich App 607, 586 NW2d 542.

The parole board may grant a parole without conducting an interview of the convict but may not deny a parole without the prisoner's being interviewed by at least one member of the board; an interview is not required upon a prisoner's initial eligibility for parole but, once the board passes-over an inmate, rehearings must be held every twelve months. Phillips v Warden, State Prison (1986) 153 Mich App 557, 396 NW2d 482, app den (1987) 428 Mich 859.

Federal habeas corpus petitioner's contention that state parole board's consideration of prior invalid conviction resulted in delayed discretionary parole review on subsequent conviction asserted, at most, violation of state procedural rule which did not rise to federal constitutional proportions, since state prisoners have no federal constitutional right to parole. Gavin v Wells (1990, CA6 Mich) 914 F2d 97.

### § 791.236. Order of parole; signature of chairperson; notice; amendment; rescission; conditions; supervision; restitution; payment of parole supervision fee; condition requiring payment of assessment; compliance with §§28.721 to 28.732; violation of §§333.7401 to 333.7545; condition requiring housing in community corrections center or community residential home; condition requiring payment by parolee; review to ensure payment of restitution; report of violation; registration of parolee; condition to protect named person; "violent felony" defined. [MSA § 28.2306]

Sec. 36.

**Department of Corrections** § 791.236

(1) All paroles shall be ordered by the parole board and shall be signed by the chairperson. Written notice of the order shall be given to the sheriff or other police officer of the municipality or county in which the prisoner was convicted, and to the sheriff or other local police officer of the municipality or county to which the paroled prisoner is sent.

(2) A parole order may be amended or rescinded at the discretion of the parole board for cause. If a paroled prisoner who is required to register pursuant to the sex offenders registration act, 1994 PA 295, MCL 28.721 to 28.732, willfully violates that act, the parole board shall rescind the parole. If a prisoner convicted of violating or conspiring to violate section 7401(2)(a)(i) or (ii) or 7403(2)(a)(i) or (ii) o f the public health code, 1978 PA 368, MCL 333.7401 and 333.7403, is released on parole and violates or conspires to violate article 7 of the public health code, 1978 PA 368, MCL 333.7401 to 333.7545, and that violation or conspiracy to violate is punishable by imprisonment for 4 or more years, or commits a violent felony during his or her release on parole, parole shall be revoked.

(3) A parole shall not be rescinded unless an interview is conducted by 1 member of the parole board. The purpose of the interview is to consider and act upon information received by the board after the original parole release decision. A rescission interview shall be conducted within 45 days after receiving the new information. At least 10 days before the interview, the parolee shall receive a copy or summary of the new evidence that is the basis for the interview. An amendment to a parole order shall be in writing and is not effective until notice of the amendment is given to the parolee.

(4) When a parole order is issued, the order shall contain the conditions of the parole and shall specifically provide proper means of supervision of the paroled prisoner in accordance with the rules of the bureau of field services.

(5) The parole order shall contain a condition to pay restitution to the victim of the prisoner's crime or the victim's estate if the prisoner was ordered to make restitution pursuant to the crime victim's rights act, 1985 PA 87, MCL 780.751 to 780.834, or the code of criminal procedure, 1927 PA 175, MCL 760.1 to 776.22.

(6) The parole order shall contain a condition requiring the parolee to pay a parole supervision fee as prescribed in section 36a.

(7) The parole order shall contain a condition requiring the parolee to pay any assessment the prisoner was ordered to pay pursuant to section 5 of 1989 PA 196, MCL 780.905.

(8) If the parolee is required to be registered under the sex offenders registration act, 1994 PA 295, MCL 28.721 to 28.732, the parole order shall contain a condition requiring the parolee to comply with that act.

(9) If a prisoner convicted of violating or conspiring to violate section 7401(2)(a)(i) or (ii) or 7403(2)(a)(i) or (ii) of the public health code, 1978 PA 368, MCL 333.7401 and 333.7403, is released on

## § 791.236                  Department of Corrections

parole, the parole order shall contain a notice that if the parolee violates or conspires to violate article 7 of the public health code, 1978 PA 368, MCL 333.7401 to 333.7545, and that violation or conspiracy to violate is punishable by imprisonment for 4 or more years, or commits a violent felony during his or her release on parole, parole shall be revoked.

(10) A parole order issued for a prisoner subject to disciplinary time may contain a condition requiring the parolee to be housed in a community corrections center or a community residential home for not less than the first 30 days but not more than the first 180 days of his or her term of parole. As used in this subsection, "community corrections center" and "community residential home" mean those terms as defined in section 65a.

(11) The parole order shall contain a condition requiring the parolee to pay the following amounts owed by the prisoner, if applicable:

    (a) The balance of filing fees and costs ordered to be paid under section 2963 of the revised judicature act of 1961, 1961 PA 236, MCL 600.2963.

    (b) The balance of any filing fee ordered to be paid by a federal court under section 1915 of title 28 of the United States Code, 28 U.S.C. 1915 and any unpaid order of costs assessed against the prisoner.

(12) In each case in which payment of restitution is ordered as a condition of parole, a parole officer assigned to a case shall review the case not less than twice yearly to ensure that restitution is being paid as ordered. The final review shall be conducted not less than 60 days before the expiration of the parole period. If the parole officer determines that restitution is not being paid as ordered, the parole officer shall file a written report of the violation with the parole board on a form prescribed by the parole board. The report shall include a statement of the amount of arrearage and any reasons for the arrearage known by the parole officer. The parole board shall immediately provide a copy of the report to the court, the prosecuting attorney, and the victim.

(13) If a parolee is required to register pursuant to the sex offenders registration act, 1994 PA 295, MCL 28.721 to 28.732, the parole officer shall register the parolee as provided in that act.

(14) If the parole order contains a condition intended to protect 1 or more named persons, the department shall enter those provisions of the parole order into the corrections management information system, accessible by the law enforcement information network. If the parole board revokes a parole order described in this subsection, the department within 3 business days shall remove from the corrections management information system the provisions of that parole order.

(15) As used in this section, "violent felony" means an offense against a person in violation of section 82, 83, 84, 86, 87, 88, 89, 316, 317, 321, 349, 349a, 350, 397, 520b, 520c, 520d, 520e, 520g, 529, 529a, or 530 of the Michigan penal code, 1931 PA 328, MCL 750.82,

**Department of Corrections** § **791.236**

750.83, 750.84, 750.86, 750.87, 750.88, 750.89, 750.316, 750.317, 750.321, 750.349, 750.349a, 750.350, 750.397, 750.520b, 750.520c, 750.520d, 750.520e, 750.520g, 750.529, 750.529a, and 750.530.

**History:**
Pub Acts 1953, No. 232, § 36, eff October 2, 1953; amended by Pub Acts 1982, No. 314, imd eff October 15, 1982; 1985, No. 85, imd eff July 5, 1985 (see 1985 note below); 1989, No. 185, imd eff August 24, 1989, by § 2 eff October 1, 1989; 1993, No. 346, imd eff January 10, 1994, by § 2 eff May 1, 1994 (see 1993 note below); 1994, No. 217, eff June 27, 1994 (see 1994 note below); 1994, No. 287, by § 2 eff October 1, 1995 (see 1994 note below).

Amended by Pub Acts 1996, No. 554, by § 3 eff June 1, 1997 (see 1996 note below); 1998, No. 314, imd eff July 30, 1998, by enacting § 1 eff October 1, 1998; 1998, No. 315, imd eff July 30, 1998, by enacting § 1 eff December 15, 1998 (see 1998 note below); 1999, No. 271, by enacting § 1 eff July 1, 2000.

**Editor's notes:**
**Pub Acts 1985, No. 85, § 2,** imd eff July 5, 1985, provides:
"Section 2. This amendatory act shall not take effect unless all of the following bills of the 83rd Legislature are enacted into law:
"(a) House Bill No. 4009 [which became Act No. 87 of 1985].
"(b) House Bill No. 4370 [which became Act No. 89 of 1985]."
**Pub Acts 1993, No. 346, § 3,** imd eff January 10, 1994, by § 2 eff May 1, 1994, provides:
"Section 3. This amendatory act shall not take effect unless all of the following bills of the 87th Legislature are enacted into law:
"(a) Senate Bill No. 137 [which became Act No. 341 of 1993].
"(b) Senate Bill No. 138 [which became Act No. 342 of 1993].
"(c) Senate Bill No. 139 [which became Act No. 343 of 1993].
"(d) Senate Bill No. 469 [which became Act No. 344 of 1993].
"(e) Senate Bill No. 470 [which became Act No. 345 of 1993].
"(f) Senate Bill No. 473 [which became Act No. 347 of 1993]."
**Pub Acts 1994, No. 217, §§2, 3,** eff June 27, 1994, provide:
"Section 2. This amendatory act shall take effect on the date that sentencing guidelines are enacted into law after the sentencing commission submits its report to the secretary of the senate and the clerk of the house of representatives pursuant to sections 31 to 34 of chapter IX of the code of criminal procedure, Act No. 175 of the Public Acts of 1927, as added by the amendatory act resulting from House Bill No. 4782 of the 87th Legislature [Pub Acts 1994, No. 445]. (**Repealed** by Pub Acts 1998, No. 316, imd eff July 30, 1998, by enacting § 2 eff December 15, 1998.).
"Section 3. This amendatory act shall not take effect unless all of the following bills of the 87th Legislature are enacted into law:
"(a) Senate Bill No. 41 [Pub Acts 1994, No. 218].
"(b) House Bill No. 4782 [Pub Acts 1994, No. 445].
"(c) House Bill No. 5439 [Pub Acts 1994, No. 322]."
**Pub Acts 1994, No. 287, § 3,** by § 2 eff October 1, 1995, provides:
"Section 3. This amendatory act shall not take effect unless all of the following bills of the 87th Legislature are enacted into law:
"(a) Senate Bill No. 193 [Pub Acts 1994, No. 286].
"(b) Senate Bill No. 397 [Pub Acts 1994, No. 295].
"(c) Senate Bill No. 400 [Pub Acts 1994, No. 294].
"(d) House Bill No. 4601 [Pub Acts 1994, No. 355]."
**Pub Acts 1996, No. 554, § 2,** by § 3 eff June 1, 1997, provides:
"Section 2. This amendatory act shall not take effect unless all of the following bills of the 88th Legislature are enacted into law:
"(a) Senate Bill No. 1215 [Pub Acts 1996, No. 555].
"(b) House Bill No. 4990 [Pub Acts 1996, No. 556]."
**Pub Acts 1998, No. 315, enacting** § **2,** imd eff July 30, 1998, by enacting § 1 eff December 15, 1998, provides:

§ 791.236                                                    Department of Corrections

"Enacting section 2. This amendatory act does not take effect unless all of the following bills of the 89th Legislature are enacted into law:
"(a) Senate Bill No. 826 [Pub Acts 1998, No. 316].
"(b) House Bill No. 4065 [Pub Acts 1998, No. 319].
"(c) House Bill No. 4444 [Pub Acts 1998, No. 311].
"(d) House Bill No. 4445 [Pub Acts 1998, No. 312].
"(e) House Bill No. 4446 [Pub Acts 1998, No. 313].
"(f) House Bill No. 4515 [Pub Acts 1998, No. 320].
"(g) House Bill No. 5419 [Pub Acts 1998, No. 317].
"(h) House Bill No. 5876 [Pub Acts 1998, No. 318]."

**Effect of amendment notes:**
**The first 1994 amendment (Pub Act 217)** inserted a new subsection (7) and redesignated former subsection (7) as (8).

**The second 1994 amendment (Pub Act 287)** in subsection (2), inserted "If a paroled prisoner who is required to register pursuant to the sex offenders registration act willfully violates that act, the parole board shall rescind the parole.", redesignated former subsection (7) as (9), and inserted new subsections (7), (8) and (10).

**The 1996 amendment** in subsection (8), replaced "its report" with "recommended sentencing guidelines"; added new subsection (9); and updated the statutory citations contained throughout the section.

**The first 1998 amendment (Pub Act 314)** added the third sentence of subsection (2); redesignated the former second paragraph of subsection (2) as subsection (3); added subsections (9) and (14); redesignated former subsections (3)–(7) as subsections (4)–(8); redesignated former subsections (8)–(11) as subsections (10)–(13); changed the style of statutory references throughout; and made grammatical changes throughout.

**The second 1998 amendment (Pub Act 315)** added the third sentence of subsection (2); redesignated the former second paragraph of subsection (2) as subsection (3); added subsections (9) and (14); deleted the former third sentence of subsections (10); redesignated former subsections (3)–(7) as subsections (4)–(8); redesignated former subsections (8)–(11) as subsections (10)–(13); changed the style of statutory references throughout; and made grammatical changes throughout.

**The 1999 amendment** added new subsection (14) and redesignated former subsection (14) as subsection (15).

**Statutory references:**
Sections 36a and 65a are §§791.236a and 791.265a.

**Michigan Digest references:**
Pardons and Paroles §§5, 9.

**Research references:**
59 Am Jur 2d, Pardon and Parole §§81–84.
18A Am Jur Pl & Pr Forms, Rev, Pardon and Parole, Form 35.

**Legal periodicals:**
Post, The constitutionality of parole departments disclosing the HIV status of parolees, 1992 Wis L Rev 1993.

### CASE NOTES

The setting of conditions of parole is left to the discretion of the parole board. Triplett v Deputy Warden, Jackson Prison (1985) 142 Mich App 774, 371 NW2d 862.

**Department of Corrections** § 791.236a

§ 791.236a. Collection of supervision fee by parole board; limit; payment; determination of amount; enforcement; parole oversight fee; fee for offender transferred to state under interstate compact; administrative costs; fee for offender transferred to Michigan; only one fee to apply at a time; waiver of fees; unpaid amounts; allocation of moneys collected. [MSA § 28.2306(1)]

Sec. 36a. (1) The parole board shall include in each order of parole that the department of corrections shall collect a parole supervision fee of not more than $30.00 multiplied by the number of months of parole ordered, but not more than 60 months. The fee is payable when the parole order is entered, but the fee may be paid in monthly installments if the parole board approves installment payments for that parolee. In determining the amount of the fee, the parole board shall consider the parolee's projected income and financial resources. The parole board shall use the following table of projected monthly income in determining the amount of the fee to be ordered:

| Projected Monthly Income | Amount of Fee |
| --- | --- |
| $0-249.99 | $ 0.00 |
| $250.00-499.99 | $10.00 |
| $500.00-749.99 | $20.00 |
| $750.00 or more | $30.00 |

The parole board may order a higher amount than indicated by the table, up to the maximum of $30.00 multiplied by the number of months of parole ordered but not more than 60 months, if the parole board determines that the parolee has sufficient assets or other financial resources to warrant the higher amount. If the parole board orders a higher amount, the amount and the reasons for ordering that amount shall be stated in the parole order.

| | |
| --- | --- |
| $500.00-749.99 | $10.00 |
| $750.00-999.99 | $20.00 |
| $1,000.00 or more | $30.00 |

(2) A parole oversight fee ordered before October 1, 1993, pursuant to this section as it existed before this section was amended by Act No. 184 of the Public Acts of 1993 remains enforceable according to the terms of that parole order notwithstanding the amendments to this section made by Act No. 184 of the Public Acts of 1993.

(3) If a person who is subject to a supervision fee imposed on or after May 1, 1994 is also subject to any combination of fines, costs, restitution, assessments, or payments arising out of the same criminal proceeding, the allocation of money collected for those obligations shall be as provided in section 22 of chapter XV of the code of criminal procedure, Act No. 175 of the Public Acts of 1927, being section 775.22 of the Michigan Compiled Laws.

(4) A person shall not be subject to more than 1 parole supervision fee at the same time. If a parole supervision fee is ordered for a parolee for any month or months during which that parolee already is subject to a parole supervision fee, the department shall waive the fee having the shorter remaining duration.

**§ 791.236a**                         **Department of Corrections**

(5) The department shall waive the parole supervision fee for a parolee who is transferred to another state under the interstate compact entered into pursuant to Act No. 89 of the Public Acts of 1935, being sections 798.101 to 798.103 of the Michigan Compiled Laws, for the months during which he or she is in another state. The department shall collect a parole supervision fee of not more than $30.00 per month for each month of parole supervision in this state for an offender transferred to this state under that interstate compact. In determining the amount of the fee, the department shall consider the parolee's projected income and financial resources. The department shall use the following table of projected monthly income in determining the amount of the fee:

| Projected Monthly Income | Amount of Fee |
|---|---|
| $ 0-249.99 | $ 0.00 |
| $250.00-499.99 | $10.00 |
| $500.00-749.99 | $20.00 |
| $750.00 or more | $30.00 |

The department may collect a higher amount than indicated by the table, up to the maximum of $30.00 for each month of parole supervision in this state, if the department determines that the parolee has sufficient assets or other financial resources to warrant the higher amount. If the department collects a higher amount, the amount and the reasons for collecting that amount shall be stated in the department records.

(6) Twenty percent of the money collected by the department under this section shall be allocated for administrative costs incurred by the department in collecting parole supervision fees and for enhanced services, as described in this subsection. Enhanced services include, but are not limited to, the purchase of services for parolees such as counseling, employment training, employment placement, or education; public transportation expenses related to training, counseling, or employment; enhancement of staff performance through specialized training and equipment purchase; and purchase of items for parolee employment. At the end of each fiscal year, the unexpended balance of the money allocated for administrative costs and enhanced services shall be available for carryforward to be used for the purposes described in this subsection in subsequent fiscal years. Money received by the department pursuant to this subsection in the fiscal year ending September 30, 1994 is appropriated for the purposes described in this subsection.

(7) If a parolee has not paid the full amount of the parole supervision fee upon being discharged from parole, the department shall review and compare the actual income of the person during the period of parole with the income amount projected when the parole supervision fee was ordered. If the department determines that the parolee's actual income did not equal or exceed the projected income, the department shall waive any unpaid amount in excess of the total amount that the parolee would have been ordered to pay if the parolee's income had been accurately projected, unless the parole order states that a higher amount was ordered due to available assets or other financial resources. Any unpaid amounts not waived

**Department of Corrections** § 791.237

by the department shall be reported to the department of treasury. The department of treasury shall attempt to collect the unpaid balances pursuant to section 30a of Act No. 122 of the Public Acts of 1941, being section 205.30a of the Michigan Compiled Laws. Money collected under this subsection shall not be allocated for the purposes described in subsection (6).

**History:**
Pub Acts 1953, No. 232, § 36a, as added by Pub Acts 1989, No. 185, imd eff August 23, 1989, by § 2 eff October 1, 1989; amended by Pub Acts 1993, No. 184, imd eff September 30, 1993 (see 1993 note below); 1993, No. 346, imd eff January 10, 1994, by § 2 eff May 1, 1994 (see 1993 note below).

**Editor's notes:**
Pub Acts 1992, No. 181, § 2, provided for the repeal of this section on October 1, 1993. However, Pub Acts 1993, No. 185, § 3, repealed section 2 of 1992 Pub Act No. 181, effectively rendering the repeal void.
**Pub Acts 1993, No. 184, § 2,** imd eff September 30, 1993, provides:
"Section 2. This amendatory act shall not take effect unless all of the following bills of the 87th Legislature are enacted into law:
"(a) House Bill No. 4875 [which became Act No. 185 of 1993].
"(b) House Bill No. 4876 [which became Act No. 169 of 1993]."
**Pub Acts 1993, No. 346, § 3,** imd eff January 10, 1994, by § 2 eff May 1, 1994, provides:
"Section 3. This amendatory act shall not take effect unless all of the following bills of the 87th Legislature are enacted into law:
"(a) Senate Bill No. 137 [which became Act No. 341 of 1993].
"(b) Senate Bill No. 138 [which became Act No. 342 of 1993].
"(c) Senate Bill No. 139 [which became Act No. 343 of 1993].
"(d) Senate Bill No. 469 [which became Act No. 344 of 1993].
"(e) Senate Bill No. 470 [which became Act No. 345 of 1993].
"(f) Senate Bill No. 473 [which became Act No. 347 of 1993]."

**Research references:**
21 Am Jur 2d, Criminal Law §§570, 575.

## § 791.237. Paroled or discharged prisoner; furnishing clothing, transportation, and money; repayment of money; cost of implementing section. [MSA § 28.2307]

Sec. 37. (1) When a prisoner is released upon parole, the department shall provide the prisoner with clothing and a nontransferable ticket to the place in which the paroled prisoner is to reside. At the discretion of the deputy director in charge of the bureau of field services, the paroled prisoner may be advanced the expense of the transportation to the place of residence and a sum of money necessary for reasonable maintenance and subsistence for a 2-week period, as determined by the deputy director. A sum of money given under this section shall be repaid to the state by the paroled prisoner within 180 days after the money is received by the paroled prisoner.

(2) If a prisoner who is discharged without being paroled has less than $75.00 in his or her immediate possession, has no visible means of support, and has conserved personal funds in a reasonable manner, the department shall furnish to that prisoner the following:
(a) Clothing that is appropriate for the season.

(b) A sum of $75.00 including that amount already in the prisoner's possession.

(c) Transportation to a place in this state where the prisoner will reside or work or to the place where the prisoner was convicted or sentenced.

(3) When providing for transportation, the department shall:

(a) Use the most economical available public transportation.

(b) Arrange for and purchase the prisoner's transportation ticket.

(c) Assume responsibility for delivering that prisoner to the site of departure and confirming the prisoner's departure from the site.

(4) The cost of implementing this section shall be paid out of the general fund of the state.

**History:**
Pub Acts 1953, No. 232, § 37, eff October 2, 1953; amended by Pub Acts 1980, No. 22, imd eff March 7, 1980; 1982, No. 314, imd eff October 15, 1982; 1994, No. 217, eff June 27, 1994 (see 1994 note below).

**Editor's notes:**
**Pub Acts 1994, No. 217, §§2, 3,** eff June 27, 1994, provide:

"Section 2. This amendatory act shall take effect on the date that sentencing guidelines are enacted into law after the sentencing commission submits its report to the secretary of the senate and the clerk of the house of representatives pursuant to sections 31 to 34 of chapter IX of the code of criminal procedure, Act No. 175 of the Public Acts of 1927, as added by the amendatory act resulting from House Bill No. 4782 of the 87th Legislature [which became Pub Acts 1994, No. 445]. (**Repealed** by Pub Acts 1998, No. 316, imd eff July 30, 1998, by enacting § 2 eff December 15, 1998.).

"Section 3. This amendatory act shall not take effect unless all of the following bills of the 87th Legislature are enacted into law:

"(a) Senate Bill No. 41 [Pub Acts 1994, No. 218].

"(b) House Bill No. 4782 [Pub Acts 1994, No. 445].

"(c) House Bill No. 5439 [Pub Acts 1994, No. 322]."

**Effect of amendment notes:**
**The 1994 amendment** in subsection (2), opening paragraph, substituted "without being paroled" for "on his or her maximum sentence less good time", and in subsection (2), paragraph (a), substituted "that" for "which".

**Research references:**
59 Am Jur 2d, Pardon and Parole §§81–84.
18A Am Jur Pl & Pr Forms, Rev, Pardon and Parole, Form 35.

### CASE NOTES

Under the provisions of a former act, it was mandatory upon the wardens of the various penal institutions of the state, upon the discharge of a prisoner therefrom, to furnish prisoner with a suit of clothing not to exceed in value $10, at least $5 in money, and a railroad ticket from the place where the prison was located to the place from which the prisoner was sentenced. Op Atty Gen, 1921–1922, p 225.

Warden of Michigan state prison had no authority to award a prisoner, previously under his charge but transferred to Ionia state asylum, the gratuity payable under former § 800.62 when such prisoner was discharged at end of sentence. Op Atty Gen, 1912, p 134.

**§ 791.238. Custody of paroled prisoner; warrant for return; incarceration pending hearing; treatment as escaped prisoner; time during parole violation not counted as time served; forfeiture of good time; committing crime while on parole; construction of parole.** [MSA § 28.2308]

Sec. 38. (1) Each prisoner on parole shall remain in the legal custody and under the control of the department. The deputy director of the bureau of field services, upon a showing of probable violation of parole, may issue a warrant for the return of any paroled prisoner. Pending a hearing upon any charge of parole violation, the prisoner shall remain incarcerated.

(2) A prisoner violating the provisions of his or her parole and for whose return a warrant has been issued by the deputy director of the bureau of field services is treated as an escaped prisoner and is liable, when arrested, to serve out the unexpired portion of his or her maximum imprisonment. The time from the date of the declared violation to the date of the prisoner's availability for return to an institution shall not be counted as time served. The warrant of the deputy director of the bureau of field services is a sufficient warrant authorizing all officers named in the warrant to detain the paroled prisoner in any jail of the state until his or her return to the state penal institution.

(3) If a paroled prisoner fails to return to prison when required by the deputy director of the bureau of field services or if the paroled prisoner escapes while on parole, the paroled prisoner shall be treated in all respects as if he or she had escaped from prison and is subject to be retaken as provided by the laws of this state.

(4) The parole board, in its discretion, may cause the forfeiture of all good time to the date of the declared violation.

(5) A prisoner committing a crime while at large on parole and being convicted and sentenced for the crime shall be treated as to the last incurred term as provided under section 34.

(6) A parole shall be construed as a permit to the prisoner to leave the prison, and not as a release. While at large, the paroled prisoner shall be considered to be serving out the sentence imposed by the court and, if he or she is eligible for good time, shall be entitled to good time the same as if confined in a state correctional facility.

**History:**
Pub Acts 1953, No. 232, § 38, eff October 2, 1953; amended by Pub Acts 1968, No. 192, eff November 15, 1968; 1982, No. 314, imd eff October 15, 1982; 1994, No. 217, eff June 27, 1994 (see 1994 note below).

**Editor's notes:**
**Pub Acts 1994, No. 217, §§2, 3,** eff June 27, 1994, provide:
"Section 2. This amendatory act shall take effect on the date that sentencing guidelines are enacted into law after the sentencing commission submits its report to the secretary of the senate and the clerk of the house of representatives pursuant to sections 31 to 34 of chapter IX of the code of criminal procedure, Act No. 175 of the Public Acts of 1927, as added by the amendatory act resulting from House Bill No. 4782 of the 87th Legislature [which became Pub Acts 1994, No. 445]. (**Repealed** by Pub Acts 1998, No. 316, imd eff July 30, 1998, by enacting § 2 eff December 15, 1998.).

## § 791.238            Department of Corrections

"Section 3. This amendatory act shall not take effect unless all of the following bills of the 87th Legislature are enacted into law:
"(a) Senate Bill No. 41 [Pub Acts 1994, No. 218].
"(b) House Bill No. 4782 [Pub Acts 1994, No. 445].
"(c) House Bill No. 5439 [Pub Acts 1994, No. 322]."

**Effect of amendment notes:**
**The 1994 amendment** in subsection (1), substituted "department" for "commission", in subsections (2) and (3), substituted "is" for "shall be" in four instances, and in subsection (6), inserted ", if he or she is eligible for good time," and substituted "a state correctional facility" for "prison".

**Statutory references:**
Section 34, above referred to, is § 791.234.

**Michigan Digest references:**
Habeas Corpus § 37.50.
Pardons and Paroles §§4, 7 et seq., 9.
Statutes §§80, 80.60, 99.

**Legal periodicals:**
Ward, The Young Decision Should Save County Tax Dollars, 75 Mich B J 11:1186 (1996).

### CASE NOTES

**1. In general.**

Object of parole is to keep prisoner in legal custody while allowing him to live beyond prison enclosure to give him chance to show that he can shun crime. Ex parte Dawsett (1945) 311 Mich 588, 19 NW2d 110, cert den (1946) 329 US 786, 91 L Ed 674, 67 S Ct 299.

Parole of prisoner is permission to live outside prison during good behavior, and on condition that misconduct will warrant his return to prison to serve remainder of term. Ex parte Dawsett (1945) 311 Mich 588, 19 NW2d 110, cert den (1946) 329 US 786, 91 L Ed 674, 67 S Ct 299.

Where petitioner after serving part of sentence was paroled, violated his parole, was treated as escaped prisoner, returned to prison for maximum term of his sentence, and time earned for good behavior was forfeited, date upon which petitioner could be released held date upon which maximum term was served less any time earned for good behavior after his return to prison. In re Holton (1943) 304 Mich 534, 8 NW2d 628.

Warrant for arrest of parole violator which was signed by the commissioner of pardons and paroles and which recited that it was done "at the direction" of the governor was permissible under the former act. Robinson v Gries (1936) 277 Mich 15, 268 NW 794.

This section authorizes parole board, in its discretion, to forfeit for violation of parole all or any part of the good time earned by the convict to the date of his delinquency. Op Atty Gen, August 1, 1955, No. 2141.

**2. Validity.**

Applying credit for time spent on parole while failing to give credit for time spent on probation when imposing sentence following probation revocation hearing would be held to be justified by compelling state interest in conformity with equal protection of laws, since credit for time spent on probation could discourage courts in necessary exercise of discretion in sentencing defendants in manner relevant to their respective characteristics and to crime involved, and such credit would work against state interest in avoiding expense attendant to incarceration and in seeking effective rehabilitation and continued usefulness of its citizens outside of prison walls. People v Lacy (1974) 54 Mich App 471, 221 NW2d 199.

Failure to grant defendant credit for time spent on probation against prison sentence imposed after revocation of such probation would be held to have constituted reprosecution in violation of double jeopardy prohibition. People v Lacy (1974) 54 Mich App 471, 221 NW2d 199.

**3. Construction.**

This section, relating to "dead time," must be read in pari materia with interstate parole compact to effect constitu-

# Department of Corrections § 791.238

tionally approved and well established legislative intent against consecutive sentences, which abides absent some clearly expressed contrary provision. Browning v Michigan Dep't of Corrections (1971) 385 Mich 179, 188 NW2d 552.

Presumption arose that, when legislature revised this section in 1968, legislature was aware of adoption and content of interstate parole compact to which Michigan is signatory and which had been in existence for some time. Browning v Michigan Dep't of Corrections (1971) 385 Mich 179, 188 NW2d 552.

A paroled prisoner remains in the custody of the Department of Corrections until all the conditions and obligations of the parole have been faithfully performed; unless and until parole is successfully completed, the prisoner is deemed to be serving the sentence imposed by the trial court. Harper v Department of Corrections, 215 Mich App 648, 546 NW2d 718.

The constitutional requirement that a warrant be supported by oath or affirmation is not applicable to warrants for the revocation of parole. Triplett v Deputy Warden, Jackson Prison (1985) 142 Mich App 774, 371 NW2d 862.

**4. Parole jurisdiction.**

Jurisdiction of commissioner of pardons and paroles did not terminate upon deportation of prisoner pursuant to commutation of sentence on condition of deportation and that prisoner never return to United States, and where such prisoner illegally reentered United States after being deported commissioner had jurisdiction to act upon violation. In re Petition for Cammarata (1954) 341 Mich 528, 67 NW2d 677, cert den (1955) 349 US 953, 99 L Ed 1278, 75 S Ct 881.

Where deportee reentered United States in violation of parole, and parole authorities believed their failure to act would result in redeportation as desired by them, and parole authorities issued parole violation warrant upon receipt of letter from immigration and naturalization service that deportation within reasonable time was improbable, parole authorities would not be held to have waived jurisdiction over such deportee notwithstanding delay of about four years before attempting to incarcerate deportee. In re Petition for Cammarata (1954) 341 Mich 528, 67 NW2d 677, cert den (1955) 349 US 953, 99 L Ed 1278, 75 S Ct 881.

Statute places paroled prisoners under control of state corrections commission and its bureau of pardons and paroles, and courts may not interfere with performance of administrative functions thus vested. Ex parte Casella (1946) 313 Mich 393, 21 NW2d 175.

Under authority expressly granted by Michigan Constitution, legislature properly made granting and revocation of paroles purely administrative functions within exclusive jurisdiction of parole board. Ex parte Casella (1946) 313 Mich 393, 21 NW2d 175.

The executive department is authorized to revoke paroles. Ex parte Frencavage (1926) 234 Mich 384, 208 NW 462.

Parole board does not lose jurisdiction over parolee by deferring execution of warrant for parole violation until termination of other impending criminal proceedings against parolee. Ward v Parole Board, Dep't of Corrections (1971) 35 Mich App 456, 192 NW2d 537.

Where department of corrections had only constructive knowledge of parolee's whereabouts since they knew that there was likelihood of his being in certain city and could have inquired as to his whereabouts and there was no showing of any affirmative action from which decision not to execute warrant may be reasonably inferred, waiver of jurisdiction over parolee was not shown. Saunders v Michigan Dep't of Corrections (1976, ED Mich) 406 F Supp 1364.

Actual knowledge of parolee's whereabouts by department of corrections would permit inference of waiver of jurisdiction over parolee if not acted upon, but constructive knowledge would permit inference of waiver if it were shown that department of corrections made decision not to act, but mere inaction in such situation would not permit inference of waiver. Saunders v Michigan Dep't of Corrections (1976, ED Mich) 406 F Supp 1364.

**5. Status and control of paroled convict.**

Even though parolee is not in actual custody of corrections commission, he is in its legal custody and control. Jurczyszyn v Pascoe (1946) 316 Mich 529, 25 NW2d 609, cert den (1948) 335 US 834, 93 L Ed 387, 69 S Ct 23.

A prisoner while at large by virtue of his parole is deemed to be serving the sentence imposed upon him and remains in the legal custody and under the control of the warden of the prison from which he is paroled. People v Bendoni (1933) 263 Mich 295, 248 NW 627; Ex parte Dawsett (1945) 311 Mich 588, 19 NW2d 110, cert den (1946) 329 US 786, 91 L Ed 674, 67 S Ct 299.

A paroled prisoner is still regarded as under the control of the prison authorities. People v Cook (1907) 147 Mich 127, 110 NW 514.

It is not function of attorney general to promulgate rules of behavior for paroled prisoners, such authority having been vested exclusively in the parole board. Op Atty Gen, August 1, 1955, No. 2141.

The state is not liable for the maintenance and care of indigent paroled prisoners. Op Atty Gen, 1921–1922, p 224.

### 6. Violation of parole.

When paroled prisoner has been returned to custody for parole violation, question whether his conduct was in violation of parole order is for determination of parole board. Ex parte Casella (1946) 313 Mich 393, 21 NW2d 175.

For a prisoner, paroled to a person in another state under a condition that he remain out of this state for the period of his maximum sentence, to return to and be found in this state, constitutes no crime. People v Bendoni (1933) 263 Mich 295, 248 NW 627.

A contention that a paroled prisoner, who had violated his parole, cannot be required to serve the balance of his sentence because no proceedings to return him to prison were taken before the parole period expired, is without merit. In re Eddinger (1926) 236 Mich 668, 211 NW 54.

When a prisoner applies for parole he applies under the provisions of the law, and agrees to its terms, and fully understands that for any misconduct provided in the statute he may be taken back to serve out his sentence. This power of recall was formerly lodged in the warden, subject to review by the board of pardons. People v Cook (1907) 147 Mich 127, 110 NW 514.

While crime resulting in commitment of parolee as criminal sexual psychopath did not of itself constitute parole violation under former act, connected noncriminal offense prohibited by terms and conditions of parole may, after hearing, be determined such a violation. Op Atty Gen, February 18, 1948, No. 710.

There is no practical way of compelling one who has violated terms of parole to return from Canada except through extradition. Op Atty Gen, 1916, p 95.

### 7. Reimprisonment of parolee.

Where warrant for parole violation was issued in 1927 and parole officers had it within their power to take parolee into custody in 1934 and 1937 and since such time parolee's maximum sentence had expired, reimprisonment of parolee was without warrant in law. Colin v Bannon (1953) 337 Mich 491, 60 NW2d 431.

Parole officers, in exercising right to imprison parole violator, may not withhold such action indefinitely and exercise it at some remote time, since exercise of such power at whim or caprice of parole officers would deprive parolee of due process of law. Colin v Bannon (1953) 337 Mich 491, 60 NW2d 431.

Where 18-year delay in parolee's arrest for parole violation was occasioned by his failure to report and to keep the authorities advised as to his whereabouts, as required by the terms of his parole, the long period of inaction followed by his eventual arrest and imprisonment did not constitute denial of due process. Ginivalli v Frisbie (1953) 336 Mich 101, 57 NW2d 457.

### 8. Serving of interrupted sentence.

Where record contained nothing to controvert allegation in answer and return that from issuance of parole violation warrant to arrest of plaintiff parole violator more than six years later upon charges of criminal offenses, the corrections department and its officers had no knowledge or information concerning whereabouts of plaintiff, the parole board which passed plaintiff's case for consideration in three years, requiring plaintiff meanwhile to continue to serve his maximum prison term, after plaintiff pleaded guilty to counts of parole violation, would be held to have properly refused to count as served on sentence the time which elapsed from date of plaintiff's delinquency to date of his arrest. In re Carpenter (1957) 348 Mich 408, 83 NW2d 326, cert den (1957) 355 US 850, 2 L Ed 2d 59, 78 S Ct 77.

Statutory provision that convict violating parole and for whose return a warrant has been issued shall be treated as an escaped prisoner owing service to the state and shall be liable to serve out unexpired portion of maximum imprisonment, and that the time from the date of his declared delinquency to the date of his arrest shall not be counted as time

**Department of Corrections** § **791.238**

served and the provision of the Constitution authorizing its enactment are not in conflict with the United States Constitution. Ginivalli v Frisbie (1953) 336 Mich 101, 57 NW2d 457.

Under statutory provision that a parole violator shall be liable to serve out the unexpired portion of maximum imprisonment and that the time from the date of his declared delinquency to the date of his arrest shall not be counted as time served, a parolee arrested after the expiration date of his maximum term was liable to serve out the unexpired portion of his maximum imprisonment, the period from his parole violation to the time of his arrest therefor being eliminated from the computation. Ginivalli v Frisbie (1953) 336 Mich 101, 57 NW2d 457.

Person who has violated parole may be required to serve remainder of his sentence after the expiration date of his maximum term as originally imposed by the court. Ginivalli v Frisbie (1953) 336 Mich 101, 57 NW2d 457.

Interrupted sentence of parole violator commences to run upon issuance of parole violation warrant if parolee is then in custody. Op Atty Gen, February 18, 1948, No. 710.

**9. Serving sentence for crime committed on parole.**

Deletion, consonant with supreme court's prior construction, of language that parole violator shall serve second sentence only after first sentence is served or annulled, from last two revisions of this section, reflects and confirms legislative intent that parole violator should serve his sentences concurrently. Browning v Michigan Dep't of Corrections (1971) 385 Mich 179, 188 NW2d 552.

Presumption obtained that, when legislature revised this section in 1968, legislature realized that Michigan, unlike most states, had qualifiably renounced consecutive sentencing in favor of concurrent sentencing on grounds that to allow consecutive sentences would render second sentence uncertain and indefinite and subject to undefined and uncertain contingencies. Browning v Michigan Dep't of Corrections (1971) 385 Mich 179, 188 NW2d 552.

Provision of former statute that sentence for felony committed while on parole shall commence at the expiration of service of the prior sentence was not violative of the constitutional limit on powers of offices on ground that it provided for invasion of judicial province by agency of the administrative branch of government. In re Petition of Callahan (1957) 348 Mich 77, 81 NW2d 669.

Under former statute providing that a sentence for felony committed while on parole shall commence at expiration of service of the prior sentence, sentence imposed in 1940 for crime committed while prisoner was on parole from 1931 sentence was automatically suspended until 1931 sentence had been served. In re Petition of Callahan (1957) 348 Mich 77, 81 NW2d 669.

Under statute providing that a sentence for felony committed while on parole shall commence at the expiration of service of the prior sentence, prisoner was not entitled to release under sentence imposed in 1940 while prisoner was on parole from 1931 sentence on theory that 1940 sentence began running as of the date of its imposition. In re Petition of Callahan (1957) 348 Mich 77, 81 NW2d 669.

Under former statute providing that a sentence for a felony committed while on parole shall commence at the expiration of service of the prior sentence, order of parole board suspending commencement of prisoner's 1940 sentence until his 1931 sentence had been served was unnecessary since suspension was automatic. In re Petition of Callahan (1957) 348 Mich 77, 81 NW2d 669.

Provision of former statute that paroled prisoner convicted of crime while on parole should continue to serve out first sentence prior to beginning to serve second sentence was mandatory and operated automatically on prisoners contemplated by it. Canfield v Commissioner of Pardons & Paroles (1937) 280 Mich 305, 273 NW 578.

Where Michigan prisoner was on parole under 1929 sentence at time he committed crimes for which he was sentenced in 1941 and 1942, parole board's order that he began serving latter sentences after his 1929 sentence was cancelled and annulled by board was proper, notwithstanding provision in 1941 and 1942 sentences for definite term "from and including this date," and did not constitute violation of his constitutional rights. Brown v Jacques (1950, DC Mich) 90 F Supp 165.

Action of Michigan parole board in ordering Michigan parole violator to commence serving 1941 and 1942 sentences for crimes committed at time he was on parole on day following termination of his prior sentence, did not constitute violation of his constitutional rights, notwithstanding that 1941 and 1942 sentences provided for definite term "from and including this date." Brown v Jacques (1950, DC Mich) 90 F Supp 165.

Discussion of order of service of consecutive sentences. Op Atty Gen, November 28, 1955, No. 1924.

All sentences for crimes committed while on parole shall be concurrent with each other but consecutive to the sentence upon which such convict was paroled, the test being that the crime was committed while on parole rather than when the sentence was imposed. (Modifying Opinion No. 1010, dated August 8, 1949.) Op Atty Gen, November 19, 1954, No. 1010a.

Juvenile committed by probate court to corrections commission, who was convicted of crime while on parole therefrom, was subject to service of maximum term of juvenile commitment before service of criminal sentence. Op Atty Gen, January 27, 1948, No. 513.

Construction placed on former provision by Michigan Supreme Court, to effect that second sentence did not commence as of date of its imposition, but began from time defendant's first sentence has been served, was binding on federal court. Lundy v Michigan State Prison Board (1950, CA6 Mich) 181 F2d 772.

**10. Credit for time on parole.**

Phrase "date of availability," within this section, means actual or constructive availability for return to Michigan penal system, and arrest of a parolee, irrespective of location of arrest, coupled with good faith effort to retake parolee, constitutes constructive availability. Browning v Michigan Dep't of Corrections (1971) 385 Mich 179, 188 NW2d 552.

For all practical purposes, arrest of in-state parole violator terminates his "dead time" which is period, created by this section, during which running of parole violator's sentence is suspended. Browning v Michigan Dep't of Corrections (1971) 385 Mich 179, 188 NW2d 552.

When language of this section relating to "dead time" was revised in 1968 to expressly provide that time from declared violation to date of his availability for return to penal institution under control of corrections commission shall not be counted as part or portion of time to be served, no change in basic meaning of "dead time" was intended or accomplished. Browning v Michigan Dep't of Corrections (1971) 385 Mich 179, 188 NW2d 552.

Where consecutive terms of prisoner convicted in 1940 for crime committed while on parole from 1931 sentence had not expired on October 2, 1953, the effective date of statute providing for computing new maximum term by adding the maximums of his previous terms, act of parole board discharging prisoner from 1931 sentence prior to effective date did not affect rights of prisoner to benefits under the act. In re Petition of Callahan (1957) 348 Mich 77, 81 NW2d 669.

Period of so-called "dead time" of parole violator ends when warrant for parole violation is issued and parole board has it within its power to place parolee in confinement. Colin v Bannon (1953) 337 Mich 491, 60 NW2d 431.

Time from issuance of warrant for return of prisoner for parole violation until he called at office of parole bureau was "dead time," i.e., could not be counted as any part of time to be served, even though that interval had been spent in army of allied nation during war, such military service not being capable of changing plain terms of statute. Ex parte Davis (1945) 312 Mich 154, 20 NW2d 141.

When warrant for parole violation was issued against parolee in custody awaiting trial and sentence for crime other than that for which he was originally sentenced, period of so-called "dead time," for which parolee could not be given credit against original sentence, ended, since at that time parole board had it within its power to place parolee in actual confinement in state prison. In re Holton (1943) 304 Mich 534, 8 NW2d 628.

Time during which parolee was in custody awaiting trial and sentence for crime other than that for which he was originally sentenced was so-called "dead time" and could not be credited to remainder of parolee's sentence. In re Holton (1943) 304 Mich 534, 8 NW2d 628.

**11. Habeas corpus by parolee.**

Where prisoner serving consecutive sentences was entitled to be released when total maximum terms, less statutory good time and special good time

**Department of Corrections** § 791.239

allowances, had been served, but record failed to disclose all pertinent facts relative to special good time allowances, writ of habeas corpus would be held in abeyance pending prompt determination of special good time allowances and computation of total maximum term remaining unserved. In re Petition of Callahan (1957) 348 Mich 77, 81 NW2d 669.

Habeas corpus proceeding by paroled prisoner who had been returned to custody for parole violation should have been dismissed on filing of answer to petition for writ and introduction in evidence of warrant, showing that prisoner was lawfully in custody, granting and revocation of paroles being purely administrative function over which parole board has exclusive jurisdiction. Ex parte Casella (1946) 313 Mich 393, 21 NW2d 175.

Where prisoner who had been released on parole was returned to custody for parole violation, his discharge in habeas corpus proceedings was erroneous when based on failure of assistant director of bureau of pardons and paroles to show that warrant for prisoner's arrest was issued upon showing of probable violation of parole, and where there was no contention that warrant was not in form required by statute, granting and revocation of paroles being administrative function within exclusive jurisdiction of parole board. Ex parte Casella (1946) 313 Mich 393, 21 NW2d 175.

**12. Michigan parolee extradited to another state.**

Warrant of rendition, granted by Michigan governor, whereby parolee under Michigan robbery sentence was taken to Ohio to answer robbery indictment in that state, did not waive Michigan's jurisdiction over parolee so as to preclude Michigan parole board from holding him guilty of parole violation upon his return to Michigan, and requiring him to serve remainder of his sentence. Jurczyszyn v Pascoe (1946) 316 Mich 529, 25 NW2d 609, cert den (1948) 335 US 834, 93 L Ed 387, 69 S Ct 23.

Governor's parole of felon, serving life sentence, to Missouri authorities to stand trial for murder and robbery, who was to be returned to Michigan if acquitted, constituted surrender of jurisdiction of parolee upon his conviction in Missouri, and executive clemency authorizing Missouri parole would not restore Michigan jurisdiction. Op Atty Gen, June 30, 1948, No. 800.

## § 791.239. Prisoner on parole, arrest without warrant on reasonable suspicion of parole violation. [MSA § 28.2309]

Sec. 39. A probation officer, a parole officer, a peace officer of this state, or an employee of the department other than a probation or parole officer who is authorized by the director to arrest parole violators may arrest without a warrant and detain in any jail of this state a paroled prisoner, if the probation officer, parole officer, peace officer, or authorized departmental employee has reasonable grounds to believe that the prisoner has violated parole or a warrant has been issued for his or her return under section 38.

**History:**
Pub Acts 1953, No. 232, § 39, eff October 2, 1953; amended by Pub Acts 1968, No. 192, eff November 15, 1968; 1982, No. 314, imd eff October 15, 1982; 1988, No. 293, imd eff August 4, 1988.

**Statutory references:**
Section 38, above referred to, is § 791.238.

**Michigan Digest references:**
Pardons and Paroles §§6, 7.
Search and Seizure § 2.

**LEXIS-NEXIS™ Michigan analytical references:**
Michigan Law and Practice, Searches and Seizures §§2, 7.

**Legal periodicals:**
Ward, The Young Decision Should Save County Tax Dollars, 75 Mich B J 11:1186 (1996).

### CASE NOTES

Arrest of paroled prisoner by parole officer without warrant is authorized when arresting officer has reasonable grounds to believe that paroled prisoner has violated his parole. (Construing former act.) Ex parte Casella (1946) 313 Mich 393, 21 NW2d 175.

Evidence seized in warrantless search of parolee's home was admissible under Fourth Amendment where arrest of parolee was based on reasonable suspicion supported by articulable facts that parolee had engaged in criminal conduct or had violated his parole, a lower standard than probable cause, but higher than mere suspicion. United States v Carnes (1997, ED Mich) 987 F Supp 551.

In parole/probation context, warrant requirement under Fourth Amendment must give way to warrantless searches based on reasonable regulations because of the special needs of the parole/probation system; considerations of rehabilitation, supervision, and community safety and deterrence require quick response to parole violations and a close officer-parolee relationship. United States v Carnes (1997, ED Mich) 987 F Supp 551.

Parolees have limited protection of their privacy interests under Fourth Amendment with a lower standard than probable cause, but one that is higher than mere suspicion; complete search of parolee's home pursuant to arrest under regulations allowing administrative warrantless searches of parolees is not violation of Fourth Amendment where arrest of parolee is based on reasonable suspicion supported by articulable facts that parolee has engaged in criminal conduct or has violated his parole. United States v Carnes (1997, ED Mich) 987 F Supp 551.

In parole/probation context, warrant requirement under Fourth Amendment must give way to warrantless searches based on reasonable regulations because of the special needs of the parole/probation system; considerations of rehabilitation, supervision, and community safety and deterrence require quick response to parole violations and a close officer-parolee relationship. United States v Carnes (1997, ED Mich) 987 F Supp 551.

Evidence seized in warrantless search of parolee's home was admissible under Fourth Amendment where arrest of parolee was based on reasonable suspicion supported by articulable facts that parolee had engaged in criminal conduct or had violated his parole, a lower standard than probable cause, but higher than mere suspicion. United States v Carnes (1997, ED Mich) 987 F Supp 551.

A district court probation officer has no authority to use a warrantless detainer causing an individual arrested on an unrelated charge to be held in custody for an alleged violation of a district court probation order. Op Atty Gen, April 27, 1988, No. 6515.

## § 791.239a. Parole violation; preliminary or fact-finding hearing; procedure. [MSA § 28.2309(1)]

Sec. 39a. (1) Within 10 days after an arrest for an alleged violation of parole, the parolee shall be entitled to a preliminary hearing to determine whether there is probable cause to believe that the conditions of parole have been violated or a fact-finding hearing held pursuant to section 40a.

(2) Prior to the preliminary hearing, the accused parolee shall be given written notice of the charges, time, place, and purpose of the preliminary hearing.

(3) At the preliminary hearing, the accused parolee is entitled to the following rights:

(a) Disclosure of the evidence against him or her.

(b) The right to testify and present relevant witnesses and documentary evidence.

(c) The right to confront and cross-examine adverse witnesses unless the person conducting the preliminary hearing finds on the record that a witness may be subjected to risk of harm if his or her identity is revealed.

(4) A preliminary hearing may be postponed beyond the 10-day time limit on the written request of the parolee, but shall not be postponed by the department.

(5) If a preliminary hearing is not held pursuant to subsection (1), an accused parolee shall be given written notice of the charges against him or her, the time, place and purpose of the fact-finding hearing and a written summary of the evidence to be presented against him or her.

(6) If a preliminary hearing is not held pursuant to subsection (1), an accused parolee may not be found guilty of a violation based on evidence that was not summarized in the notice provided pursuant to subsection (5) except for good cause stated on the record and included in the written findings of fact provided to the parolee.

**History:**
Pub Acts 1953, No. 232, § 39a, as added by Pub Acts 1982, No. 314, imd eff October 15, 1982.

**Legal periodicals:**
Ward, The Young Decision Should Save County Tax Dollars, 75 Mich B J 11:1186 (1996).

### CASE NOTES

A parolee was not denied due process of law by the failure to hold a preliminary hearing on a charge of violation of parole where there was no statutory requirement for a preliminary hearing and the final parole-revocation hearing was not substantially delayed after his arrest and he was not detained in a location distant from the site of the parole-revocation hearing. Triplett v Deputy Warden, Jackson Prison (1985) 142 Mich App 774, 371 NW2d 862.

## § 791.240. [Repealed] [MSA § 28.2310]

**History:**
Pub Acts 1953, No. 232, eff October 2, 1953; **repealed** by Pub Acts 1968, No. 192, eff November 15, 1968.

**Editor's notes:**
For current provisions, see § 791.240a.

## § 791.240a. Parole violation; right to hearing; hearing, notice, time, location; rights; postponement; sufficiency of evidence; reinstatement to parole, or finding of violation and revocation of parole; noncompliance with restitution order; notice; hearing; representation by counsel; rights; finding, recommendation, disposition of charges; written statement, findings of fact, reasons. [MSA § 28.2310(1)]

Sec. 40a. (1) Within 45 days after a paroled prisoner has been returned or is available for return to a state correctional facility under accusation of a parole violation other than conviction for a felony or misdemeanor punishable by imprisonment under the laws of this state, the United States, or any other state or territory of the United States, the prisoner is entitled to a fact-finding hearing on the charges before 1 member of the parole board or an attorney hearings officer designated by the chairperson of the parole board. The fact-finding hearing shall be conducted only after the accused parolee has had a reasonable amount of time to prepare a defense. The fact-finding hearing may be held at a state correctional facility or at or near the location of the alleged violation.

(2) An accused parolee shall be given written notice of the charges against him or her and the time, place, and purpose of the fact-finding hearing. At the fact-finding hearing, the accused parolee may be represented by an appointed or retained attorney and is entitled to the following rights:

(a) Full disclosure of the evidence against him or her.

(b) To testify and present relevant witnesses and documentary evidence.

(c) To confront and cross-examine adverse witnesses unless the person conducting the fact-finding hearing finds on the record that a witness is subject to risk of harm if his or her identity is revealed.

(d) To present other relevant evidence in mitigation of the charges.

(3) A fact-finding hearing may be postponed for cause beyond the 45-day time limit on the written request of the parolee, the parolee's attorney, or, if a postponement of the preliminary hearing has been granted beyond the 10-day time limit, by the parole board.

(4) If the evidence presented is insufficient to support the allegation that a parole violation occurred, the parolee shall be reinstated to parole status.

(5) If the parole board member or hearings officer conducting the fact-finding hearing determines from a preponderance of the evidence that a parole violation has occurred, the member or hearings officer shall present the relevant facts to the parole board and make a recommendation as to the disposition of the charges.

(6) If a preponderance of the evidence supports the allegation that a parole violation occurred, the parole board may revoke parole, and the parolee shall be provided with a written statement of the findings of fact and the reasons for the determination within 60 days after the paroled prisoner has been returned or is available for return to a state correctional facility.

(7) A parolee who is ordered to make restitution under the crime victim's rights act, Act No. 87 of the Public Acts of 1985, being sections 780.751 to 780.834 of the Michigan Compiled Laws, or the code of criminal procedure, Act No. 175 of the Public Acts of 1927, being sections 760.1 to 776.21 of the Michigan Compiled Laws, or to pay an assessment ordered under section 5 of Act No. 196 of the Public Acts of 1989, being section 780.905 of the Michigan Compiled Laws, as a condition of parole may have his or her parole revoked by

**Department of Corrections** § 791.240a

the parole board if the parolee fails to comply with the order and if the parolee has not made a good faith effort to comply with the order. In determining whether to revoke parole, the parole board shall consider the parolee's employment status, earning ability, and financial resources, the willfulness of the parolee's failure to comply with the order, and any other special circumstances that may have a bearing on the parolee's ability to comply with the order.

**History:**
Pub Acts 1953, No. 232, § 40a, as added by Pub Acts 1968, No. 192, eff November 15, 1968; amended by Pub Acts 1982, No. 314, imd eff October 15, 1982; 1985, No. 85, imd eff July 5, 1985 (see 1985 note below); 1993, No. 346, imd eff January 10, 1994, by § 2 eff May 1, 1994 (see 1993 note below).

**Editor's notes:**
**Pub Acts 1985, No. 85, § 2,** imd eff July 5, 1985, provides:
"Section 2. This amendatory act shall not take effect unless all of the following bills of the 83rd Legislature are enacted into law:
"(a) House Bill No. 4009 [which became Act No. 87 of 1985].
"(b) House Bill No. 4370 [which became Act No. 89 of 1985]."
**Pub Acts 1993, No. 346, § 3,** imd eff January 10, 1994, by § 2 eff May 1, 1994, provides:
"Section 3. This amendatory act shall not take effect unless all of the following bills of the 87th Legislature are enacted into law:
"(a) Senate Bill No. 137 [which became Act No. 341 of 1993].
"(b) Senate Bill No. 138 [which became Act No. 342 of 1993].
"(c) Senate Bill No. 139 [which became Act No. 343 of 1993].
"(d) Senate Bill No. 469 [which became Act No. 344 of 1993].
"(e) Senate Bill No. 470 [which became Act No. 345 of 1993].
"(f) Senate Bill No. 473 [which became Act No. 347 of 1993]."

**Cross references:**
Rights of accused in criminal prosecutions, Constitution of 1963, Art. I, § 20.

**Michigan Digest references:**
Mandamus § 95.
Pardons and Paroles §§5, 7 et seq., 9.

**L Ed annotations:**
Validity, under equal protection clause of Fourteenth Amendment, of state statutes relating to parole or pardon of convicted criminal, 35 L Ed 2d 775.
Comment Note–Procedural requirements, under Federal Constitution, applicable to revocation of probation or parole, 36 L Ed 2d 1077.

**ALR notes:**
Right to notice and hearing before revocation of suspension of sentence, parole, conditional pardon, or probation, 29 ALR2d 1074.

**Research references:**
59 Am Jur 2d, Pardon and Parole §§95–97.
18A Am Jur Pl & Pr Forms, Rev, Pardon and Parole, Form 35.

**Legal periodicals:**
Ward, The Young Decision Should Save County Tax Dollars, 75 Mich B J 11:1186 (1996).

## CASE NOTES

**1. Constitutionality.**

Parole revocation statute, although not violative of due process on its face where it merely provided that hearing was not matter of right upon conviction-based revocation, was unconstitutional as applied by parole board in failing to accord petitioner notice and full hearing on issue of mitigation regarding misdemeanor-based revocation. Witzke v Withrow (1988, WD Mich) 702 F Supp 1338.

**2. Construction and effect.**

Intent of legislature that paroles can be extended without hearings was held to have been established by the explicit, unambiguous wording of pertinent provisions of the parole statutes, the silence and absence of legislative objection during the extended period the parole board has construed the statute as giving the right to extend paroles without hearings, and recent legislative change limiting a parolee's rights when charged with violating parole. Lane v Michigan Dep't of Corrections, Parole Board (1970) 383 Mich 50, 173 NW2d 209.

That defendant was not tried and convicted for possession of drugs and weapons would not foreclose valid revocation of parole for violating conditions prohibiting such possession where no charges were brought against defendant with respect to weapons, and drugs possession charges were dismissed prior to trial, thereby obviating any issue of collateral estoppel, and where conduct prohibited by parole conditions was broader than that prohibited by criminal law and not dependent on conviction thereunder as prerequisite to parole revocation. Smith v Michigan Parole Board (1977) 78 Mich App 753, 261 NW2d 193.

Provision of former § 791.240 for revocation of parole without formal hearing upon conviction of felony or misdemeanor under laws of state would be held not to include violation of municipal ordinances. Lobaido v Department of Corrections, Parole Board (1971) 37 Mich App 171, 194 NW2d 444.

The 30-day period in which a parole violator was entitled to hearing under this section would be held to commence from time defendant was incarcerated pursuant to parole violation warrant, and not from time of original arrest for possession of uncased shotgun, from which arrest parole violation warrant resulted. Feazel v Department of Corrections (1971) 31 Mich App 425, 188 NW2d 59.

For purposes of provision of this section entitling a parole violator to hearing within 30 days of his return to state penal institution, violator would be deemed to have been "returned to state penal institution" upon issuance of parole violation warrant and arrest and his incarceration in any penal institution in state. Feazel v Department of Corrections (1971) 31 Mich App 425, 188 NW2d 59.

This section, although not expressly providing therefor, would be held to provide within concept "hearing" for introduction of evidence and production of witnesses. Feazel v Department of Corrections (1971) 31 Mich App 425, 188 NW2d 59.

Former § 791.240 was intended to provide alleged violator with same safeguards as trial itself provided. People v Bess (1968) 11 Mich App 109, 157 NW2d 455.

Parole revocation statute, although not violative of due process on its face where it merely provided that hearing was not matter of right on conviction-based revocation, was unconstitutional as applied by parole board in failing to accord petitioner notice and full hearing on issue of mitigation regarding misdemeanor-based revocation. Witzke v Withrow (1988, WD Mich) 702 F Supp 1338.

**3. Parole violation.**

Conviction of paroled prisoner for a felony while on parole and constitutional rights available to prisoner before he is so convicted permit enactment by legislature of a conclusive statutory presumption that parole has been violated. Shadbolt v Michigan Dep't of Corrections (1971) 386 Mich 232, 191 NW2d 344.

In habeas corpus proceedings involving legality of incarceration as parole violator, record establishing that petitioner while under release to Missouri authorities had in fact not violated Michigan parole conditions, necessitated his discharge from custody as on parole under order of February 19, 1961. In re Vaughan (1963) 371 Mich 386, 124 NW2d 251.

Parolee, by not reporting to person to

**Department of Corrections** § 791.240a

whom he is paroled, violates terms of his parole. Colin v Bannon (1953) 337 Mich 491, 60 NW2d 431.

Judicial review of a revocation of parole may be pursued under the provisions of the Administrative Procedures Act or upon a complaint for habeas corpus. Triplett v Deputy Warden, Jackson Prison (1985) 142 Mich App 774, 371 NW2d 862.

Criminal conviction was not prerequisite to revocation of parole for violation of parole condition prohibiting conduct broader than that covered by criminal law. Smith v Michigan Parole Board (1977) 78 Mich App 753, 261 NW2d 193.

Testimony that person on parole left restaurant with companion whom he then knew possessed a revolver was sufficient to establish violation of parole condition prohibiting such person from being in company of any person possessing a firearm. In re Litton (1971) 30 Mich App 281, 185 NW2d 910.

If allegedly delinquent parolee is in custody, parole board, having issued warrant charging him with parole violation, must seek to execute it with reasonable diligence and to hold revocation hearing within reasonable time. Evans v Department of Corrections (1969) 18 Mich App 426, 171 NW2d 499.

While crime resulting in commitment of parolee as criminal sexual psychopath did not of itself constitute parole violation under former act, connected noncriminal offense prohibited by terms and conditions of parole may, after hearing, be determined such a violation. Op Atty Gen, February 18, 1948, No. 710.

**4. Right to counsel.**

Equal protection clause of Fourteenth Amendment requires that an indigent parolee who contests parole revocation be afforded the same right to counsel that a parolee with means enjoys. Hawkins v Michigan Parole Board (1973) 390 Mich 569, 213 NW2d 193.

If parolee who is subject to having his parole revoked for any reason other than conviction of a felony or misdemeanor punishable by imprisonment alleges indigency and requests appointment of counsel, circuit court in county in which parolee is confined shall determine if parolee is indigent and, upon a finding of indigency, shall appoint counsel. Hawkins v Michigan Parole Board (1973) 390 Mich 569, 213 NW2d 193.

The statutory right to counsel at parole revocation hearings cannot be limited to those who can afford to hire an attorney, but must be extended also to indigents. Hawkins v Michigan Parole Board (1973) 390 Mich 569, 213 NW2d 193.

Before parole revocation hearing takes place, parolee must be advised of his right to counsel, if his parole is being revoked for any reason other than conviction of a felony or misdemeanor punishable by imprisonment. Hawkins v Michigan Parole Board (1973) 390 Mich 569, 213 NW2d 193.

Paroled prisoner had no right to hearing on charge of violating his parole where violation consisted of a felony conviction; hence prisoner's claim of right to counsel predicated on his right to a hearing was without merit. Shadbolt v Michigan Dep't of Corrections (1971) 386 Mich 232, 191 NW2d 344.

Prior to parole revocation hearing, a parolee must be advised of his right to counsel where his parole is being revoked for any reason other than conviction of felony or misdemeanor punishable by imprisonment. Callison v Michigan Dep't of Corrections (1974) 56 Mich App 260, 223 NW2d 738.

Parole board's advice to alleged parole violator that he was entitled to public hearing with counsel, hearing with witnesses without counsel, or hearing before board, was insufficient to apprise defendant of his right to counsel at revocation hearing if indigent. Callison v Michigan Dep't of Corrections (1974) 56 Mich App 260, 223 NW2d 738.

An indigent parolee who contests parole revocation is constitutionally entitled to appointed counsel. Callison v Michigan Dep't of Corrections (1974) 56 Mich App 260, 223 NW2d 738.

Petitioner whose revocation of parole was grounded on offense punishable by fine only, coupled with classification of parole reports, and who contended that his acts did not justify revocation and was deprived of opportunity to examine for accuracy certain material upon which revocation was based, was deprived of proper revocation hearing by failure of parole hearing board to properly advise him of his right to counsel if indigent. Callison v Michigan Dep't of Corrections (1974) 56 Mich App 260, 223 NW2d 738.

Where parolee, who was charged with parole violation by allegedly moving from one place to another without permission of his parole officer and violating special condition of parole that he refrain from association with minor females, was not represented by attorney at parole revocation hearing, allegedly because he was indigent, and no hearing to determine whether parolee was indigent had been held prior to revocation hearing, court of appeals would order that indigency hearing be held and that counsel be appointed if parolee was found to be indigent; and mandamus compelling release of parolee from custody pending de novo revocation hearing would be granted. Hawkins v Michigan Parole Board (1973) 45 Mich App 529, 206 NW2d 764, affd (1973) 390 Mich 569, 213 NW2d 193.

In view of provisions of former § 791.240, permitting representation by attorney when parolee has sufficient funds to hire one at parole revocation hearing, equal protection of laws would be held to require furnishing such counsel for indigent parolee at such hearing where it involves a factual dispute. Warren v Michigan Parole Bd. (1970) 23 Mich App 754, 179 NW2d 664.

Indigent criminal not entitled to counsel at public expense in proceeding to revoke his parole after sentencing. Saunders v Michigan Parole Board (1968) 15 Mich App 183, 166 NW2d 278.

### 5. Counsel costs and fees.

Costs of counsel appointed for indigent parolee in proceedings to revoke his parole shall be paid from general operating budget of department of corrections until such time as legislature shall otherwise provide. Hawkins v Michigan Parole Board (1973) 390 Mich 569, 213 NW2d 193.

### 6. Habeas corpus.

Administrative procedure prescribed by statute and requiring fair and impartial hearing before parole board for paroled prisoner returned to custody for parole violation adequately protects rights of parolee, and in habeas corpus proceeding to obtain his release it may not be assumed that arbitrary action will be taken or that requirements of statute will not be observed. (Construing similar provision of former act.) Ex parte Casella (1946) 313 Mich 393, 21 NW2d 175.

Habeas corpus petition by person returned to prison for parole violation was properly dismissed where prisoner failed to sustain his burden of showing that conditions of parole had been met. Ex parte Dawsett (1945) 311 Mich 588, 19 NW2d 110, cert den (1946) 329 US 786, 91 L Ed 674, 67 S Ct 299.

A prisoner whose paroles were revoked by the executive department was not entitled to discharge on habeas corpus on the ground that the paroles were not revoked by the warden of the prison, as was provided for by former provision. Ex parte Frencavage (1926) 234 Mich 384, 208 NW 462.

Where defendant was in federal custody at time parole board issued warrant charging him with parole violation but defendant was not arrested by parole officers until he was released from federal prison and placed on parole by federal authorities several years later, after his Michigan sentence would have expired had he been given credit for time spent in federal custody, parole board was held to have abused its discretion by not attempting to execute its warrant with reasonable diligence and by not giving defendant a timely hearing, and cause was remanded for issuance of writ of habeas corpus and termination of defendant's parole. Evans v Department of Corrections (1969) 18 Mich App 426, 171 NW2d 499.

Habeas corpus was not proper remedy for parole violator who was not given hearing within 30 days as required by this section. In re Lane (1965) 2 Mich App 140, 138 NW2d 541.

### 7. Mandamus.

Absence of manifest injustice precluded grant of defendant's mandamus complaint seeking release from confinement under parole revocation order entered at hearing in which defendant appeared pro se and produced no witnesses where parole board apprised defendant of his right to hearing some seven days prior thereto upon his confinement under parole violation warrant, and parole agent's affidavit recited that defendant four days before hearing stated that he would prefer to act on his own behalf at hearing if he did not secure retained counsel. Smith v Michigan Parole Board (1977) 78 Mich App 753, 261 NW2d 193.

Where appellate court was without jurisdiction to hear appeal as of right from order of state parole board resulting in defendant's parole, such court would dismiss appeal without prejudice to defendant to proceed properly by writ of mandamus pursuant to applicable general court rule. People v White (1975) 58 Mich App 229, 227 NW2d 296.

Failure of parole board to hold hearing within 30 days as required by this sec-

## Department of Corrections § 791.240a

tion, may be remedied by petition for writ of mandamus. In re Lane (1965) 2 Mich App 140, 138 NW2d 541.

**8. Notice of rights.**
Provisions of former § 791.240 entitling a parole violator to fair and impartial hearing required that accused be properly apprised of rules governing such hearing in advance thereof, either by submitting to accused a copy of rules adopted by parole board for such hearings, or through publication of such rules in usual manner for publishing rules in administrative bodies. In re Lane (1965) 2 Mich App 140, 138 NW2d 541.

Parole revocation statute, although not violative of due process on its face where it merely provided that hearing was not matter of right on conviction-based revocation, was unconstitutional as applied by parole board in failing to accord petitioner notice and full hearing on issue of mitigation regarding misdemeanor-based revocation. Witzke v Withrow (1988, WD Mich) 702 F Supp 1338.

Former act provided for hearing to determine if parole violation in fact occurred, and required board to give reasonable notice to alleged violator, as to time and place of such hearing, and of right to representation by counsel as provided herein. Op Atty Gen, September 4, 1962, No. 4102.

**9. Hearing.**
There is valid basis for denying a prisoner accused of violating his parole a hearing in the case of conviction for a felony, since such a conviction cannot occur before prisoner has been accorded his full constitutional rights including right to counsel and right to speedy and public trial. Shadbolt v Michigan Dep't of Corrections (1971) 386 Mich 232, 191 NW2d 344.

Where alleged violations of parole were not "a felony or misdemeanor under the laws of this state," within meaning of former § 791.240, failure of parole board to conduct parole violation hearing provided for by statute within 30 days constituted waiver of any claim based upon such violations and alleged violator was entitled to be discharged from prison but under jurisdiction of parole board under its prior order granting parole. Stewart v Parole Board (1969) 382 Mich 474, 170 NW2d 16.

Alleged parole violator is entitled to hearing provided by statute regardless of whether or not he admits his guilt. Stewart v Parole Board (1969) 382 Mich 474, 170 NW2d 16.

Upon determining that alleged parole violator was entitled to release from custody until proper parole revocation hearing could be held in which alleged violator would be entitled to appointed counsel if indigent, preliminary hearing to determine whether reasonable grounds existed for parole revocation would be held not to be required as prerequisite to subsequent revocation under particular factual circumstances on record revealing reason to believe that alleged violator's acts constituted parole violation, thereby warranting commencement of formal hearing wherein all relevant factors would be considered in determining whether parole should, in fact, be revoked. Callison v Michigan Dep't of Corrections (1974) 56 Mich App 260, 223 NW2d 738.

Parolee would be entitled to full evidentiary hearing in proceedings to revoke parole grounded on his conviction for careless driving in violation of municipal ordinance, which conviction was not felony or misdemeanor under laws of state, within meaning of provision of former § 791.240, obviating necessity for such hearing. Lobaido v Department of Corrections, Parole Board (1971) 37 Mich App 171, 194 NW2d 444.

If there is no reason for deferring service of parole violation warrant, parolee is entitled to have service made and his hearing conducted within reasonable time after issuance of warrant. Ward v Parole Board, Dep't of Corrections (1971) 35 Mich App 456, 192 NW2d 537.

Where parolee is confined on separate criminal charge and demands hearing on alleged parole violation, parolee has burden to make himself available for hearing before parole board, either by furnishing bail or obtaining his liberty by other possible means, and state is not required to seek judicial process or judicial consent to assure parolee's physical presence in state penal institution from which he was paroled in order to conduct hearing. Ward v Parole Board, Dep't of Corrections (1971) 35 Mich App 456, 192 NW2d 537.

Although a parole revocation hearing is not a trial with full constitutional implications, the allegedly delinquent parolee has a right to have the parole board exercise reasonable diligence in seeking to hold a revocation hearing, and if he is at large and if the parole board has knowledge of his whereabouts, either actual or constructive, it must seek to execute its warrant within a reasonable time. Evans v Department of Corrections (1969) 18 Mich App 426, 171 NW2d 499.

Denial of bond to armed-robbery accused without hearing because robbery also constituted parole violation, would be held not to have deprived accused of due process of law under former § 791.240. People v Bess (1968) 11 Mich App 109, 157 NW2d 455.

Under former § 791.240, alleged parole violator had right to fair and impartial hearing on parole violation only if alleged violation was not commission of, and conviction for, a felony or misdemeanor under laws of Michigan. Stewart v Buchkoe (1968, WD Mich) 283 F Supp 1021.

**10. – Defect in hearing.**

Record, in habeas corpus proceedings to test legality of incarceration as parole violator, established that petitioner had not been afforded opportunity to meet witnesses against him as required by former act, and that proceedings before Michigan parole board and its findings were nullity, and would accordingly be set aside. In re Vaughan (1963) 371 Mich 386, 124 NW2d 251.

Petitioner who was not sufficiently advised of right to counsel in parole violation proceeding would be entitled to new revocation hearing conducted in conformity with due process requirements, including prior hearing on indigency if alleged, and appointment of counsel upon determination of indigency. Callison v Michigan Dep't of Corrections (1974) 56 Mich App 260, 223 NW2d 738.

Where petitioner was denied opportunity to cross-examine accusers and to bring forth affirmative rebuttal on his own behalf at parole revocation hearing held in interim between repeal of statute expressly providing for fair hearing standards and effective date of hearing regulations adopted by director of department of corrections, petitioner would be entitled to rehearing, in accord with procedures outlined by director of department of corrections, in light of statute in effect at time of original hearing and providing for "hearing," which hearing would necessarily require introduction of witness and introduction concerning evidence of alleged parole violation even though such statute did not specifically provide therefor. Crawford v Michigan Parole Board (1971) 35 Mich App 185, 192 NW2d 358.

Parole board's finding of parole violation was not statutorily or constitutionally infirm by reason of admission of hearsay testimony and lack of confrontation, where parole officer testified from personal knowledge and his testimony sustained finding of board. Ward v Parole Board, Dep't of Corrections (1971) 35 Mich App 456, 192 NW2d 537.

**11. – Time of hearing.**

Mere notice of parole violation charges does not suffice for the purpose of placing a parolee "under accusation" and, therefore, does not trigger the statutory requirement that a prisoner is entitled to a hearing within 45 days after the paroled prisoner "has been returned or is available for return to a state correctional facility under accusation of a parole violation;" parole revocation hearing was timely because it was held within 45 days after a parole board issued a parole violation warrant for the parolee's arrest. Persichino v Parole Bd. (1998) 229 Mich App 450, 582 NW2d 523.

A parolee detained on local criminal charges and accused of a parole violation is entitled to a hearing on his parole violation within 45 days of his release on the local criminal charges where a parole violation warrant has been issued but not executed. Hinton v Parole Bd. (1986) 148 Mich App 235, 383 NW2d 626.

Paroled prisoners who are under accusation of violation of parole are entitled to parole revocation hearings within 45 days of their return to state prison or of their availability for return to prison; such hearings may take place at the prison or locally and are to be preceded by preliminary probable cause hearings or written notice of the charges and the evidence to be presented against the parolee at the fact-finding parole revocation hearing; only if a violation of parole is established by a preponderance of the evidence can parole be revoked and, even if a violation of parole is established, the parole board may decline to revoke parole. People v Wright (1983) 128 Mich App 374, 340 NW2d 93.

Failure to hold parole revocation hearing within 30 days of defendant's arrest on charges on which parole revocation was based did not deprive parole board of jurisdiction to proceed on parole violation warrant or invalidate revocation where defendant was free on bond fol-

**Department of Corrections** § 791.242

lowing arrest and until confinement under parole violation warrant, and parole violation hearing was held within 30 days of such confinement as required by statute, thereby foreclosing any prejudice to defendant. Smith v Michigan Parole Board (1977) 78 Mich App 753, 261 NW2d 193.

Where no proper revocation hearing was held within 30 days of petitioner's confinement for alleged parole violation, as required by this section, petitioner would be entitled to writ of mandamus compelling his release from custody until proper revocation hearing could be held. Callison v Michigan Dep't of Corrections (1974) 56 Mich App 260, 223 NW2d 738.

Conviction of parolee for violation of municipal ordinance against careless driving was not conviction of felony or misdemeanor under laws of state, within meaning of provision of former § 791.240, authorizing revocation of parole without formal hearing and, accordingly, failure of parole board to conduct statutorily-required full hearing within 30 days of such municipal ordinance conviction constituted waiver of any claim for parole revocation grounded on such conviction. Lobaido v Department of Corrections, Parole Board (1971) 37 Mich App 171, 194 NW2d 444.

Although warrant for parole violation was issued on March 6 and requested parole violation hearing was not held until November 1, statutory 30-day period within which hearing was required to be held did not expire where parolee was confined on another separate criminal charge on March 13 and thus was "unavailable" to parole board until parolee's October 4th acquittal on separate charge. Ward v Parole Board, Dep't of Corrections (1971) 35 Mich App 456, 192 NW2d 537.

Failure to hold hearing within thirty days as required by former act did not bar further proceedings, since such act was not statute of limitations. In re Lane (1965) 2 Mich App 140, 138 NW2d 541.

**12. – Evidence.**

Alleged parole violator would not be deprived of his right, under this section, to present evidence and produce witnesses at parole violation hearing by mere fact that he was accused of parole violation prior to issuance of specific regulations governing hearings before parole board. Feazel v Department of Corrections (1971) 31 Mich App 425, 188 NW2d 59.

Where testimony at hearing before parole board was sufficient to prove violation of conditions of parole, it was unnecessary to take further testimony with respect to a second alleged violation; hence petitioner's claim that hearsay was received concerning second alleged violation did not "militate" against board's finding concerning the proved violation. In re Litton (1971) 30 Mich App 281, 185 NW2d 910.

**§ 791.241. Decision of parole board; order.** [MSA § 28.2311]

Sec. 41. When the parole board has determined the matter it shall enter an order rescinding such parole, or reinstating the original order of parole or enter such other order as it may see fit.

**History:**
Pub Acts 1953, No. 232, § 41, eff October 2, 1953.

**§ 791.242. Certificate of discharge; minimum period of parole respecting certain crimes.** [MSA § 28.2312]

Sec. 42. When any paroled prisoner has faithfully performed all of the conditions and obligations of his parole for the period of time fixed in such order, and has obeyed all of the rules and regulations adopted by the parole board, he shall be deemed to have served his full sentence, and the parole board shall enter a final order of discharge and issue to the paroled prisoner a certificate of discharge.

No parole shall be granted for a period less than 2 years in all cases of murder, actual forcible rape, robbery armed, kidnapping,

§ 791.242                  **Department of Corrections**

extortion, or breaking and entering an occupied dwelling in the night time except where the maximum time remaining to be served on the sentence is less than 2 years.

**History:**
Pub Acts 1953, No. 232, § 42, eff October 2, 1953; amended by Pub Acts 1961, No. 92, eff September 8, 1961.

**Michigan Digest references:**
Pardons and Paroles § 4.

**Research references:**
59 Am Jur 2d, Pardon and Parole §§86–88.

**Legal periodicals:**
Ward, A New Phenomenon—Prosecution Appeals of Decisions to Parole, 72 Mich B J 10:1058 (1993).

Ward, The Young Decision Should Save County Tax Dollars, 75 Mich B J 11:1186 (1996).

### CASE NOTES

Discharge from balance of prison sentence, like pardon, is gift from executive, and like any other gift becomes effective only when delivered and accepted, and after delivery cannot be recalled. (Construing similar provision of former act.) Ex parte Dawsett (1945) 311 Mich 588, 19 NW2d 110, cert den (1946) 329 US 786, 91 L Ed 674, 67 S Ct 299.

Absolute discharge at end of parole is more than release from parole, but is remission of remaining portion of sentence. (Construing similar provision of former act.) Ex parte Dawsett (1945) 311 Mich 588, 19 NW2d 110, cert den (1946) 329 US 786, 91 L Ed 674, 67 S Ct 299.

Where delivery of an absolute discharge of a paroled prisoner was made only to his first friend, the governor had power to revoke the discharge for violation of the parole and cause the prisoner to be apprehended and returned to prison to serve the balance of his sentence. In re Eddinger (1926) 236 Mich 668, 211 NW 54.

A parole is not the same as a pardon, commutation, or reprieve and is subject to certain statutory restrictions; although a parole, and a discharge from parole, is granted through the executive branch, a parole may not be granted unless the terms of § 791.242; MCL § 791.242 have been met. People v Young (1996) 220 Mich App 420, 559 NW2d 670.

A paroled prisoner remains in the custody of the Department of Corrections until all the conditions and obligations of the parole have been faithfully performed; unless and until parole is successfully completed, the prisoner is deemed to be serving the sentence imposed by the trial court. Harper v Department of Corrections, 215 Mich App 648, 546 NW2d 718.

### § 791.243. Pardons, reprieves and commutations; form and contents of application. [MSA § 28.2313]

Sec. 43. All applications for pardons, reprieves and commutations shall be filed with the parole board upon forms provided therefor by the parole board, and shall contain such information, records and documents as the parole board may by rule require.

**History:**
Pub Acts 1953, No. 232, § 43, eff October 2, 1953.

**Michigan Digest references:**
Pardons and Paroles §§1 et seq., 10.

§ 791.244. Parole board interview of prisoner serving sentence for first degree murder or sentence of imprisonment for life without parole; board duties upon own initiation of receipt of application for reprieve, commutation, or pardon; files as public record. [MSA § 28.2314]

Sec. 44. (1) Subject to the constitutional authority of the governor to grant reprieves, commutations, and pardons, 1 member of the parole board shall interview a prisoner serving a sentence for murder in the first degree or a sentence of imprisonment for life without parole at the conclusion of 10 calendar years and thereafter as determined appropriate by the parole board, until such time as the prisoner is granted a reprieve, commutation, or pardon by the governor, or is deceased. The interview schedule prescribed in this subsection applies to all prisoners to whom this section is applicable, regardless of when they were sentenced.

(2) Upon its own initiation of, or upon receipt of any application for, a reprieve, commutation, or pardon, the parole board shall do all of the following, as applicable:

(a) Not more than 60 days after receipt of an application, conduct a review to determine whether the application for a reprieve, commutation, or pardon has merit.

(b) Deliver either the written documentation of the initiation or the original application with the parole board's determination regarding merit, to the governor and retain a copy of each in its file, pending an investigation and hearing.

(c) Within 10 days after initiation, or after determining that an application has merit, forward to the sentencing judge and to the prosecuting attorney of the county having original jurisdiction of the case, or their successors in office, a written notice of the filing of the application or initiation, together with copies of the application or initiation, any supporting affidavits, and a brief summary of the case. Within 30 days after receipt of notice of the filing of any application or initiation, the sentencing judge and the prosecuting attorney, or their successors in office, may file information at their disposal, together with any objections, in writing, which they may desire to interpose. If the sentencing judge and the prosecuting attorney, or their successors in office, do not respond within 30 days, the parole board shall proceed on the application or initiation.

(d) If an application or initiation for commutation is based on physical or mental incapacity, direct the bureau of health care services to evaluate the condition of the prisoner and report on that condition. If the bureau of health care services determines that the prisoner is physically or mentally incapacitated, the bureau shall appoint a specialist in the appropriate field of medicine, who is not employed by the department, to evaluate the condition of the prisoner and to report on that condition. These reports are protected by the doctor-patient privilege of confidentiality, except that these reports shall be provided to the governor for his or her review.

(e) Within 270 days after initiation by the parole board or receipt of an application that the parole board has determined to have merit pursuant to subdivision (a), make a full investigation and determination on whether or not to proceed to a public hearing.

(f) Conduct a public hearing not later than 90 days after making a decision to proceed with consideration of a recommendation for the granting of a reprieve, commutation, or pardon. The public hearing shall be held before a formal recommendation is transmitted to the governor. One member of the parole board who will be involved in the formal recommendation may conduct the hearing, and the public shall be represented by the attorney general or a member of the attorney general's staff.

(g) At least 30 days before conducting the public hearing, provide written notice of the public hearing by mail to the attorney general, the sentencing trial judge, and the prosecuting attorney, or their successors in office, and each victim who requests notice pursuant to the crime victim's rights act, 1985 PA 87, MCL 780.751 to 780.834.

(h) Conduct the public hearing pursuant to the rules promulgated by the department. Except as otherwise provided in this subdivision, any person having information in connection with the pardon, commutation, or reprieve shall be sworn as a witness. A person who is a victim shall be given an opportunity to address and be questioned by the parole board at the hearing or to submit written testimony for the hearing. In hearing testimony, the parole board shall give liberal construction to any technical rules of evidence.

(i) Transmit its formal recommendation to the governor.

(j) Make all data in its files available to the governor if the parole board recommends the granting of a reprieve, commutation, or pardon.

(3) Except for medical records protected by the doctor-patient privilege of confidentiality, the files of the parole board in cases under this section shall be matters of public record.

**History:**

Pub Acts 1953, No. 232, § 44, eff October 2, 1953; amended by Pub Acts 1982, No. 314, imd eff October 15, 1982; 1992, No. 181, imd eff September 22, 1992.

Amended by Pub Acts 1999, No. 191, eff March 10, 2000 (see Mich. Const. note below).

**Editor's notes:**

**Michigan Constitution of 1963, Art. IV, § 27,** provides:

"No act shall take effect until the expiration of 90 days from the end of the session at which it was passed, but the legislature may give immediate effect to acts by a two-thirds vote of the members elected to and serving in each house."

**Effect of amendment notes:**

**The 1999 amendment** in subsection (1), deleted "but not later than every 5 years" after "board", and substituted "regardless of when they are sentenced." for "whether sentenced before, on, or after the effective date of the 1992 amendatory act that amended this subsection"; and updated the statutory reference.

**Michigan Digest references:**
Pardons and Paroles §§1 et seq., 5, 10.

**ALR notes:**
Validity, construction, and application of statutes making public proceedings open to the public, 38 ALR3d 1070.

**Research references:**
59 Am Jur 2d, Pardon and Parole §§34, 64, 65, 82.

**Legal periodicals:**
Koenig, Advocating Consistent Sentencing of Prisoners: Deconstructing the Michigan Myth that Retroactive Application of Lesser Penalties for Crimes Violates the Governor's Power of Commutation, 16 T.M. Cooley L Rev 61 (1999).

### CASE NOTES

The parole board in not required to conduct a hearing on every application for commutation of sentence it receives; the statute governing the procedure for processing applications for reprieves, commutations, or pardons requires a public hearing only if the parole board is inclined to recommend clemency. Berry v Department of Corrections (1982) 117 Mich App 494, 324 NW2d 65.

In class action by inmates who committed crimes on or before September 22, 1992, and were in custody of Michigan Department of Corrections, Michigan Parole Board's 1992 amendments to parole laws restricting frequency of parole review hearings, from an initial four years and every two years thereafter to an initial ten years and five years thereafter, were ex post facto laws violating U.S. Constitution as applied to all inmates who committed their crimes and were convicted between 1977 and 1982 receiving parolable life sentences or long, indeterminate sentences, and all inmates who committed their crimes and were convicted after 1982 receiving mandatory life sentences, parolable life sentences or long, indeterminate sentences because the nexus between parole hearings and parole eligibility under the Michigan parole system created a "sufficient risk" of increased punishment of inmates who would otherwise be eligible for parole after an earlier hearing and the parole board failed to make a meaningful exercise of its retained discretion to conduct a hearing by not inquiring into an inmate's likelihood of receiving a favorable parole recommendation at his or her next review. Shabazz v Gabry (1995, ED Mich) 900 F Supp 118, app dismd (1995, CA6 Mich) 1995 US App LEXIS 38885.

## § 791.245. Oath to witness, member of parole board may administer. [MSA § 28.2315]

Sec. 45. In the conduct of any hearing or investigation as herein provided any member of the parole board may administer the oath to any witness.

**History:**
Pub Acts 1953, No. 232, § 45, eff October 2, 1953.

## § 791.246. Parole board, decisions and recommendations by majority vote of board or panel. [MSA § 28.2316]

Sec. 46. All decisions and recommendations of the parole board required by this act shall be by a majority vote of the parole board or a parole board panel created pursuant to section 6(2).

## § 791.246            Department of Corrections

**History:**
    Pub Acts 1953, No. 232, § 46, as added by Pub Acts 1982, No. 314, imd eff October 15, 1982.

**Statutory references:**
    Section 6, above referred to, is § 791.206.

**Research references:**
    59 Am Jur 2d, Pardon and Parole § 19.

## CHAPTER IIIA
## [HEARINGS DIVISION]

Added by Pub Acts 1979, No. 140, imd eff November 7, 1979.

### § 791.251. Hearings division; creation; appointment and duties of hearing administrator; duties of hearings division; supervision and qualifications of hearing officer. [MSA § 28.2320(51)]

Sec. 51. (1) There is created within the department a hearings division. The division is under the direction and supervision of the hearings administrator who is appointed by the director of the department.

(2) Except as provided in subsection (4), the hearings division is responsible for each prisoner hearing the department conducts that may result in the loss by a prisoner of a right, including but not limited to any 1 or more of the following matters:

    (a) An infraction of a prison rule that may result in punitive segregation, loss of disciplinary credits, or the loss of good time.

    (b) A security classification that may result in the placement of a prisoner in administrative segregation.

    (c) A special designation that permanently excludes, by department policy or rule, a person under the jurisdiction of the department from community placement.

    (d) Visitor restrictions.

    (e) High or very high assaultive risk classifications.

(3) The hearings division is responsible for each prisoner hearing that may result in the accumulation of disciplinary time.

(4) The hearings division is not responsible for a prisoner hearing that is conducted as a result of a minor misconduct charge that would not cause a loss of good time or disciplinary credits, or result in placement in punitive segregation.

(5) Each hearings officer of the department is under the direction and supervision of the hearings division. Each hearings officer hired by the department after October 1, 1979, shall be an attorney.

**History:**
    Pub Acts 1953, No. 232, § 51, as added by Pub Acts 1979, No. 140, imd eff November 7, 1979 (see 1979 note below); amended by Pub Acts 1983, No. 155, imd eff July 24, 1983, by § 2 eff October 1, 1983; 1994, No. 217, eff June 27, 1994 (see 1994 note below).
    Amended by Pub Acts 1998, No. 204, imd eff June 30, 1998.

**Editor's notes:**
    **Pub Acts 1979, No. 140, §§2, 3,** imd eff November 7, 1979, provide:

**Department of Corrections** § 791.251

"Section 2. The procedures provided for in sections 52, 53, 54, and 55 [which became §§791.252–791.255] shall take effect on February 1, 1980.

"Section 3. This amendatory act shall not take effect unless House Bill No. 4105 of the 1979 regular session of the legislature [which became Act No. 139 of 1979] is enacted into law."

**Pub Acts 1994, No. 217, §§2, 3,** eff June 27, 1994, provide:

"Section 2. This amendatory act shall take effect on the date that sentencing guidelines are enacted into law after the sentencing commission submits its report to the secretary of the senate and the clerk of the house of representatives pursuant to sections 31 to 34 of chapter IX of the code of criminal procedure, Act No. 175 of the Public Acts of 1927, as added by the amendatory act resulting from House Bill No. 4782 of the 87th Legislature [Pub Acts 1994, No. 445]. (**Repealed** by Pub Acts 1998, No. 316, imd eff July 30, 1998, by enacting § 2 eff December 15, 1998.).

"Section 3. This amendatory act shall not take effect unless all of the following bills of the 87th Legislature are enacted into law:

"(a) Senate Bill No. 41 [Pub Acts 1994, No. 218].
"(b) House Bill No. 4782 [Pub Acts 1994, No. 445].
"(c) House Bill No. 5439 [Pub Acts 1994, No. 322]."

**Effect of amendment notes:**
**The 1994 amendment** redesignated former subsections (3) and (4) as (4) and (5), added a new subsection (3), substituted "is" for "shall be" and "that" for "which" throughout, and made other grammatical changes.

**The 1998 amendment** in subsection (2), added "Except as provided in subsection (4)".

**Michigan Digest references:**
Administrative Law § 4.10.
Civil Rights §§25, 36.
Convicts § 1.
Libel and Slander § 40.
Officers and Public Employees § 69.
Prisons and Jails §§1.05, 2.110, 2.115, 2.15, 2.120, 2.125, 2.55, 4.20, 6, 6.10, 6.40.

**Research references:**
60 Am Jur 2d, Penal and Correctional Institutions §§42, 44, 45, 65.

### CASE NOTES

Where an inmate had a full hearing under the statute on a major sexual assault charge, the inmate was not entitled to another hearing before the corrections department could apply the special designation of homosexual predator to the inmate where the designation was based on the finding after the first hearing that the inmate was guilty of sexual assault; the legislature did not intend that separate hearings would be needed in cases where a single instance of alleged misconduct might result in the loss of more than one right. Gee v Department of Corrections (1999) 235 Mich App 291, 597 NW2d 223.

Where an inmate had a full hearing under the statute on a major sexual assault charge, the inmate was not entitled to another hearing before the corrections department could apply the special designation of homosexual predator to the inmate where the designation was based on the finding after the first hearing that the inmate was guilty of sexual assault; the legislature did not intend that separate hearings would be needed in cases where a single instance of alleged misconduct might result in the loss of more than one right. Gee v Department of Corrections (1999) 235 Mich App 291, 597 NW2d 223.

The judicial review of a final decision or order of a hearing officer of the Department of Corrections provided for under § 791.255 applies to those decisions regarding hearings covered by § 791.251; namely, matters that may result in the loss by a prisoner of a right, e.g., loss of good time or disciplinary credits or placement in punitive segregation. Martin v Stine, 214 Mich App 403,

**§ 791.251**                               **Department of Corrections**

542 NW2d 884.

A prison disciplinary hearing is a judicial proceeding, and its participants are entitled to an absolute privilege from liability for defamation for relevant, material, or pertinent statements made therein. Couch v Schultz (1992) 193 Mich App 292, 483 NW2d 684, app den (1992) 441 Mich 855, 489 NW2d 764.

Absolute immunity from an action brought under 42 USCS 1983 accorded officers of the hearings division of the department of corrections does not extend to a hearing officer of that department who is not a member of the hearings division. Spruytte v Owens (1991) 190 Mich App 127, 475 NW2d 382.

An inmate's right to possess a particular piece of property while incarcerated is not a right subject to the hearing requirements applicable to the hearings division of the department of corrections; due process is satisfied where prison officials give a written response to an inmate's request to possess a particular piece of property as long as the reply, if a denial, states the reasons for the denial and the reasons are based on the criteria of the administrative rule pertaining to an inmate's possession of property. Spruytte v Department of Corrections (1990) 184 Mich App 423, 459 NW2d 52.

A prisoner in Michigan is entitled to a hearing before being deprived of a right or significant privilege. De Walt v Warden, Marquette Prison (1982) 112 Mich App 313, 315 NW2d 584.

Department of Corrections hearing officer, as attorney empowered by statute to conduct formal adversary proceedings in prison misconduct cases, was analogous to federal administrative law judge and absolutely immune from monetary damage liability arising out of challenged acts in conduct of prison misconduct hearings. Branham v Spurgis (1989, WD Mich) 720 F Supp 605, app dismd without op (1989, CA6 Mich) 889 F2d 1086.

Under the Michigan statutory scheme, a prison hearing officer is a specially appointed judicial officer who acts independently of other prison officials in role similar to that of administrative law judge, thereby entitling him to absolute judicial immunity on civil rights claim of prison inmate grounded on acts taken in the officer's official capacity in prison disciplinary proceedings (42 USCS 1983). Shelly v Johnson (1988, CA6 Mich) 849 F2d 228.

In action for due process violation under 42 USCS § 1983, arising from officials' removal of funds deposited in inmate's prison account, district court's grant of summary judgment for property sergeant and acting assistant deputy warden was proper because inmate failed to plead and prove that state remedies available to redress wrong were inadequate or that resort to state remedies would be futile. Copeland v Machulis (1995, CA6 Mich) 57 F3d 476.

## § 791.252. Hearing; procedures. [MSA § 28.2320(52)]

Sec. 52. The following procedures shall apply to each prisoner hearing conducted pursuant to section 51(2):

    (a) The parties shall be given an opportunity for an evidentiary hearing without undue delay.

    (b) The parties shall be given reasonable notice of the hearing.

    (c) If a party fails to appear at a hearing after proper service of notice, the hearings officer, if an adjournment is not granted, may proceed with the hearing and make a decision in the absence of the party.

    (d) Each party shall be given an opportunity to present evidence and oral and written arguments on issues of fact.

    (e) A prisoner may not cross-examine a witness, but may submit rebuttal evidence. A prisoner may also submit written questions to the hearings officer to be asked of a witness or witnesses. The hearings officer may present these questions to and receive answers from the witness or witnesses. The questions presented and the evidence received in response to these questions shall become a part of the record. A hearings officer may refuse to present the prisoner's questions to the witness or witnesses. If the hearings officer does not present the questions to the witness or witnesses, the reason for the decision not to present the questions shall be entered into the record.

(f) The hearings officer may administer an oath or affirmation to a witness in a matter before the officer, certify to official acts, and take depositions.

(g) The hearings officer may admit and give probative effect to evidence of a type commonly relied upon by reasonably prudent persons in the conduct of their affairs. Irrelevant, immaterial, or unduly repetitious evidence may be excluded. The reason for the exclusion of the evidence shall be entered into the record. An objection to an offer of evidence may be made and shall be noted in the record. The hearings officer, for the purpose of expediting a hearing and if the interest [sic] of the parties are not substantially prejudiced by the action, may provide for the submission of all or part of the evidence in written form.

(h) Evidence, including records and documents in possession of the department of which the hearings officer wishes to avail himself or herself, shall be offered and made a part of the record. A hearings officer may deny access to the evidence to a party if the hearings officer determines that access may be dangerous to a witness or disruptive of normal prison operations. The reason for the denial shall be entered into the record.

(i) The hearings conducted under this chapter shall be conducted in an impartial manner. On the filing in good faith by a party of a timely and sufficient affidavit of personal bias or disqualification of a hearings officer, the department shall determine the matter as a part of the record of the hearing, and the determination shall be subject to judicial review at the conclusion of the hearing. If a hearings officer is disqualified or it is impracticable for the hearings officer to continue the hearing, another hearings officer may be assigned to continue the hearing unless it is shown that substantial prejudice to a party will result from the continuation.

(j) Except as otherwise authorized by subdivision (e), a hearings officer, after the notice of the hearing is given, shall not communicate, directly or indirectly, in connection with an issue of fact, with a person or party, except on notice and opportunity for all parties to participate. A hearings officer may communicate with other members of the department and may have the aid and advice of department employees other than employees which have been or are engaged in investigating or prosecuting functions in connection with the hearing or a factually related matter which may be the subject of a hearing.

(k) A final decision or order of a hearings officer in a hearing shall be made, within a reasonable period, in writing or stated in the record and shall include findings of fact, and shall state any sanction to be imposed against a prisoner as a direct result of a hearing conducted under this chapter. The final decision shall be made on the basis of a preponderance of the evidence presented. Findings of fact shall be based exclusively on the evidence and on matters officially noticed. Findings of fact, if set forth in statutory language, shall be accompanied by a concise and explicit statement of the underlying facts supporting them. A decision or order shall not be made except upon consideration of the record as a whole or a portion of the record as may be cited by a party to the proceeding and as supported by and pursuant to competent, material, and substantial evidence. A copy of the decision or order shall be delivered or mailed immediately to the prisoner. The final disposition shall be posted for the information of the reporting officer.

**History:**
Pub Acts 1953, No. 232, § 52, as added by Pub Acts 1979, No. 140, imd eff November 7, 1979 (see 1979 note below).

**Editor's notes:**
**Pub Acts 1979, No. 140, §§2, 3,** imd eff November 7, 1979, provide:
"Section 2. The procedures provided for in sections 52, 53, 54, and 55 [which became §§791.252–791.255] shall take effect on February 1, 1980.
"Section 3. This amendatory act shall not take effect unless House Bill No. 4105 of the 1979 regular session of the legislature [which became Act No. 139 of 1979] is enacted into law."

**Statutory references:**
Section 51, above referred to, is § 791.251.

**Michigan Digest references:**
Prisons and Jails §§2.110, 2.15, 2.55, 6, 6.10.

**Research references:**
60 Am Jur 2d, Penal and Correctional Institutions §§42, 44, 45, 65.

**Legal periodicals:**
Van Ochten, Prison Disciplinary Hearings: Enforcing the Rules, 77 Mich B J 178 (1998).

## CASE NOTES

**1. Construction and effect.**
A prisoner may not personally question a witness at prison disciplinary hearings, but may submit written questions to the hearing officer to be asked of the witness. Tauber v Department of Corrections (1988) 172 Mich App 332, 431 NW2d 506, certificate for ques declined (1989) 432 Mich 906, 444 NW2d 522 and (criticized on other grounds by Jahner v Department of Corrections (1992) 197 Mich App 111, 495 NW2d 168).

Prisoners classified as "drug traffickers" and thereby excluded from consideration for eligibility in community placement programs under an administrative rule adopted by the Department of Corrections have a right to an administrative hearing to challenge that classification. Edmond v Department of Corrections (1985) 143 Mich App 527, 373 NW2d 168.

A state prisoner is entitled to due process notice and some kind of hearing in connection with disciplinary determinations involving serious misconduct; the Legislature has fashioned misconduct hearing procedures designed to comply with the due process mandate. Van Grimmett v Warden, Marquette Prison (1984) 136 Mich App 237, 355 NW2d 637, revd on other grounds, motion den (1985) 422 Mich 935, 369 NW2d 461.

A party who fails to challenge the impartiality of a Department of Corrections hearing officer at the time of a hearing before such hearing officer waives any alleged error on the issue of impartiality of the hearing officer. Van

## Department of Corrections § 791.252

Grimmett v Warden, Marquette Prison (1984) 136 Mich App 237, 355 NW2d 637, revd on other grounds, motion den (1985) 422 Mich 935, 369 NW2d 461.

A prisoner whose classification is changed as a result of a determination of misconduct is not denied due process of law by the failure of the prison authorities to hold a separate hearing on the reclassification issue. Custer v Marquette Prison Warden (1983) 128 Mich App 524, 340 NW2d 314.

A decision of a hearing officer at a department of corrections prisoner misconduct hearing must be based on a preponderance of the evidence and the officer's findings of fact must be accompanied by a concise and explicit statement of the underlying facts supporting the findings. Custer v Marquette Prison Warden (1983) 128 Mich App 524, 340 NW2d 314.

A prisoner in Michigan is entitled to notice and a hearing before being deprived of a right or significant privilege; such a hearing must include: (1) advance written notice of the charges at least 24 hours prior to the disciplinary hearing; (2) a written statement by the factfinder explaining the reason for any disciplinary action, such statement to be supplied to the prisoner; and (3) the opportunity to call witnesses and present documentary evidence, if this would not be unduly hazardous to institutional safety or correctional goals. Tocco v Marquette Prison Warden (1983) 123 Mich App 395, 333 NW2d 295.

The transfer of state prisoners from one state institution to another state institution in which conditions are less favorable to the prisoners does not infringe upon a liberty interest of the prisoners within the meaning of the due process clause of the Fourteenth Amendment, absent a state law or practice conditioning such transfers on proof of serious misconduct or the occurrence of other events. De Walt v Warden, Marquette Prison (1982) 112 Mich App 313, 315 NW2d 584.

While convicted prisoner does not forfeit all his constitutional protection when entering prison, prison disciplinary proceedings are not part of criminal prosecution and thus do not call into play all those rights due accused in criminal prosecution. Dickerson v Warden, Marquette Prison (1980) 99 Mich App 630, 298 NW2d 841.

Before prisoner could be denied "good time credits" following due process requirements must be met: advance written notice of charges of at least 24 hours prior to disciplinary hearing; written statement by factfinders explaining reason for disciplinary action must be supplied to prisoner; and opportunity to call witnesses and present documentary evidence, if this would not be unduly hazardous to institutional safety or correctional goals, must be afforded to prisoner. Dickerson v Warden, Marquette Prison (1980) 99 Mich App 630, 298 NW2d 841.

Where plaintiff-prisoners were given alleged "sham" hearing and remained in solitary confinement for some eight months before given full hearing, plaintiffs' pleadings in circuit court, alleging deprivation of federal constitutional rights under color of state law was sufficient. Dickerson v Warden, Marquette Prison (1980) 99 Mich App 630, 298 NW2d 841.

Department of Corrections hearing officer, as attorney empowered by statute to conduct formal adversary proceedings in prison misconduct cases, was analogous to federal administrative law judge and absolutely immune from monetary damage liability arising out of challenged acts in conduct of prison misconduct hearings. Branham v Spurgis (1989, WD Mich) 720 F Supp 605, app dismd without op (1989, CA6 Mich) 889 F2d 1086.

**2. Segregated confinement.**

Classification of segregated confinement as administrative confinement did not take such confinement outside scope either constitutional due process requirements or statutory mandate relative to necessary notice and hearings that must be afforded to prisoner before imposition of segregated confinement. Dickerson v Warden, Marquette Prison (1980) 99 Mich App 630, 298 NW2d 841.

Classification of segregated confinement of prison inmate as "administrative confinement" rather than "disciplinary confinement" did not release prison officials from duty to conduct evidentiary hearing with proper notice to prisoner where such segregated confinement was not of short duration. Dickerson v Warden, Marquette Prison (1980) 99 Mich App 630, 298 NW2d 841.

## § 791.253. Official record of hearings, inclusions; exclusions, inclusion on appeal. [MSA § 28.2320(53)]

Sec. 53. (1) The department shall prepare an official record of a hearing which shall include:

(a) Questions and offers of proof, objections, and rulings on the objections.

(b) Matters officially noticed, except a matter so obvious that a record would not serve a useful purpose.

(c) A decision or order by the hearings officer.

(2) The official record shall not include evidence, access to which a hearings officer has determined would be disruptive of normal prison operations. However, on an appeal from a final decision made to a court of this state, that evidence shall be included in the official record.

**History:**
Pub Acts 1953, No. 232, § 53, as added by Pub Acts 1979, No. 140, imd eff November 7, 1979 (see 1979 note below).

**Editor's notes:**
**Pub Acts 1979, No. 140, §§2, 3,** imd eff November 7, 1979, provide:
"Section 2. The procedures provided for in sections 52, 53, 54, and 55 [which became §§791.252–791.255] shall take effect on February 1, 1980.
"Section 3. This amendatory act shall not take effect unless House Bill No. 4105 of the 1979 regular session of the legislature [which became Act No. 139 of 1979] is enacted into law."

**Research references:**
60 Am Jur 2d, Penal and Correctional Institutions §§42, 44, 45, 65.

### CASE NOTES

Department of Corrections hearing officer, as attorney empowered by statute to conduct formal adversary proceedings in prison misconduct cases, was analogous to federal administrative law judge and absolutely immune from monetary damage liability arising out of challenged acts in conduct of prison misconduct hearings. Branham v Spurgis (1989, WD Mich) 720 F Supp 605, app dismd without op (1989, CA6 Mich) 889 F2d 1086.

## § 791.254. Rehearing; motion of department or request of party; circumstances; time for filing request; procedure; amendment or vacation of decision; rules. [MSA § 28.2320(54)]

Sec. 54. (1) The department shall provide for a rehearing of a matter that was subject to a hearing, pursuant to this section. A rehearing may be ordered by the hearings administrator after a review of the record of the hearing. A rehearing may be held upon the request of a party or upon the department's own motion.

(2) A rehearing shall be ordered if any of the following occurs:

(a) The record of testimony made at the hearing is inadequate for purposes of judicial review.

(b) The hearing was not conducted pursuant to applicable statutes or policies and rules of the department and the departure from the statute, rule, or policy resulted in material prejudice to either party.

**Department of Corrections** § 791.254

(c) The prisoner's due process rights were violated.

(d) The decision of the hearings officer is not supported by competent, material, and substantial evidence on the record as a whole.

(e) It is determined, based on fact, that the hearings officer conducting the hearing was personally biased in favor of 1 of the parties.

(3) A request for a rehearing shall be filed within 30 days after the final decision or order is issued after the initial hearing. A rehearing shall be conducted in the same manner as an original hearing. The evidence received at the rehearing shall be included in the record for department reconsideration and for judicial review. A decision or order may be amended or vacated after the rehearing.

(4) Pursuant to the administrative procedures act of 1969, Act No. 306 of the Public Acts of 1969, being sections 24.201 to 24.315 of the Michigan Compiled Laws, the department shall promulgate the rules necessary to implement this chapter.

**History:**
Pub Acts 1953, No. 232, § 54, as added by Pub Acts 1979, No. 140, imd eff November 7, 1979 (see 1979 note below); amended by Pub Acts 1983, No. 155, imd eff July 24, 1983, by § 2 eff October 1, 1983.

**Editor's notes:**
**Pub Acts 1979, No. 140, §§2, 3,** imd eff November 7, 1979, provide:
"Section 2. The procedures provided for in sections 52, 53, 54, and 55 [which became §§791.252–791.255] shall take effect on February 1, 1980.
"Section 3. This amendatory act shall not take effect unless House Bill No. 4105 of the 1979 regular session of the legislature [which became Act No. 139 of 1979] is enacted into law."

**Michigan Administrative Code:**
Michigan Administrative Code R 791.1101–791.9930.

**Research references:**
60 Am Jur 2d, Penal and Correctional Institutions §§42, 44, 45, 65.

### CASE NOTES

**1. Grounds for rehearing.**
Hearing officer's alleged wrongful refusal to permit inmate to present certain documents in state prison misconduct hearing gave rise to no federal due process claim, where the deprivation was not pursuant to established state procedure, and postdeprivation remedies provided by state statute were adequate to ensure compliance with inmate's due process rights. Branham v Spurgis (1989, WD Mich) 720 F Supp 605, app dismd without op (1989, CA6 Mich) 889 F2d 1086.

**2. due process violations.**
Hearing officer's alleged wrongful refusal to permit inmate to present certain documents in state prison misconduct hearing gave rise to no federal due process claim, where the deprivation was not pursuant to established state procedure, and postdeprivation remedies provided by state statute were adequate to ensure compliance with inmate's due process rights. Branham v Spurgis (1989, WD Mich) 720 F Supp 605, app dismd without op (1989, CA6 Mich) 889 F2d 1086.

**3. Hearing officers.**
Department of Corrections hearing officer, as attorney empowered by statute to conduct formal adversary proceedings in prison misconduct cases, was analogous to federal administrative law judge and absolutely immune from monetary damage liability arising out of challenged acts in conduct of prison misconduct hearings. Branham v Spurgis

**§ 791.254**                                **Department of Corrections**

(1989, WD Mich) 720 F Supp 605, app dismd without op (1989, CA6 Mich) 889 F2d 1086.

### § 791.255. Judicial review, petition by prisoner. [MSA § 28.2320(55)]

Sec. 55. (1) A prisoner aggrieved by a final decision or order of a hearings officer shall file a motion or application for rehearing in order to exhaust his or her administrative remedies before seeking judicial review of the final decision or order.

(2) Within 60 days after the date of delivery or mailing of notice of the decision on the motion or application for the rehearing, if the motion or application is denied or within 60 days after the decision of the department or hearing officer on the rehearing, a prisoner aggrieved by a final decision or order may file an application for direct review in the circuit court in the county where the petitioner resides or in the circuit court for Ingham county.

(3) Within 60 days after the application is filed and the department is served, the department shall transmit to the court a certified copy of the entire record of the proceedings. In the case of alleged irregularity in procedure which is not shown on the record, proof may be submitted to the court.

(4) The review shall be confined to the record and any supplemental proofs submitted pursuant to subsection (3). The scope of review shall be limited to whether the department's action is authorized by law or rule and whether the decision or order is supported by competent, material and substantial evidence on the whole record.

(5) The court may affirm, reverse or modify the decision or order or remand the case for further proceedings.

**History:**
    Pub Acts 1953, No. 232, § 55, as added by Pub Acts 1979, No. 140, imd eff November 7, 1979 (see 1979 note below); amended by Pub Acts 1983, No. 155, imd eff July 24, 1983, by § 2 eff October 1, 1983.

**Editor's notes:**
    **Pub Acts 1979, No. 140, §§2, 3,** imd eff November 7, 1979, provide:
    "Section 2. The procedures provided for in sections 52, 53, 54, and 55 [which became §§791.252–791.255] shall take effect on February 1, 1980.
    "Section 3. This amendatory act shall not take effect unless House Bill No. 4105 of the 1979 regular session of the legislature [which became Act No. 139 of 1979] is enacted into law."

**Michigan Digest references:**
    Prisons and Jails §§1.05, 2.105, 2.110, 2.140, 2.15, 2.55.

**LEXIS-NEXIS™ Michigan analytical references:**
    Michigan Law and Practice, Convicts and Prisons § 4.

**Research references:**
    60 Am Jur 2d, Penal and Correctional Institutions §§42, 44, 45, 65.

## CASE NOTES

Prisoner's petition for judicial review was untimely where, although given to prison authorities for mailing to the court clerk within the applicable 60-day period for filing, it was not received by the clerk within the 60-day deadline. Walker-Bey v Department of Corrections (1997) 222 Mich App 605, 564 NW2d 171.

The judicial review of a final decision or order of a hearing officer of the Department of Corrections provided for under § 791.255 applies to those decisions regarding hearings covered by § 791.251; namely, matters that may result in the loss by a prisoner of a right, e.g., loss of good time or disciplinary credits or placement in punitive segregation. Martin v Stine, 214 Mich App 403, 542 NW2d 884.

A prisoner aggrieved by a final decision or order of a hearings officer must file a motion or application for rehearing and receive a response to his or her motion prior to seeking judicial review in circuit court. Seaton-El v Department of Corrections (1990) 184 Mich App 454, 458 NW2d 910, app den (1991) 437 Mich 976.

The court of appeals may decline to declare void a decision of the Michigan Department of Corrections on the mere possibility that a necessary rule may not have been implemented by the department under the hearings division act where the petitioner has failed to present facts establishing that a procedure was followed by the department that necessarily had to be implemented by rule. Acrey v Department of Corrections (1986) 152 Mich App 554, 394 NW2d 415.

Prison disciplinary hearings are contested cases for the purposes of the Administrative Procedures Act and, while the APA provisions governing procedure in contested cases do not apply to such hearings, the judicial review provisions of the APA do apply. Tocco v Marquette Prison Warden (1983) 123 Mich App 395, 333 NW2d 295.

Federal courts do not have jurisdiction to relitigate de novo the determinations made in state prison disciplinary hearings, so long as some evidence in the record supports the fact finder's resolution of factual issues, including questions of credibility of conflicting testimony of different witnesses. Mullins v Smith (1998, ED Mich) 14 F Supp 2d 1009.

Department of Corrections hearing officer, as attorney empowered by statute to conduct formal adversary proceedings in prison misconduct cases, was analogous to federal administrative law judge and absolutely immune from monetary damage liability arising out of challenged acts in conduct of prison misconduct hearings. Branham v Spurgis (1989, WD Mich) 720 F Supp 605, app dismd without op (1989, CA6 Mich) 889 F2d 1086.

## § 791.256. Prisoners confined in another state; right to hearings. [MSA § 28.2320(56)]

Sec. 56. (1) A prisoner sentenced under the laws of this state who is imprisoned in another state pursuant to the interstate corrections compact is entitled to hearings pursuant to subsection (6) of article IV of the interstate corrections compact.

(2) A prisoner is not entitled to a hearing prior to his or her transfer to an institution of another state pursuant to the interstate corrections compact.

(3) This section shall not impair or abrogate the rights of crime victims, including but not limited to those rights provided under the crime victim's rights act, 1985 PA 87, MCL 780.751 to 780.834.

**History:**
Pub Acts 1953, No. 232, § 56, as added by Pub Acts 1994, No. 93, imd eff April 13, 1994 (see 1994 note below).
Amended by Pub Acts 1998, No. 204, imd eff June 30, 1998.

**§ 791.256**                                        **Department of Corrections**

**Editor's notes:**
**Pub Acts 1994, No. 93, § 2,** imd eff April 13, 1994, provides:
"Section 2. This amendatory act shall not take effect unless Senate Bill No. 794 of the 87th Legislature [which became Pub Acts 1994, No. 92] is enacted into law."

**Effect of amendment notes:**
**The 1998 amendment** substantially rewrote the section.

**Statutory references:**
Subsection (6) of article IV of the interstate corrections compact is § 3.983.

## CHAPTER IV
## BUREAU OF PENAL INSTITUTIONS

### § 791.261. Establishment of bureau; supervision by assistant director. [MSA § 28.2321]

Sec. 61. There is hereby established within the department, a bureau of prisons. This bureau shall be under the direction and supervision of the assistant director in charge of the bureau of penal institutions.

**History:**
Pub Acts 1953, No. 232, § 61, eff October 2, 1953.

**Research references:**
60 Am Jur 2d, Penal and Correctional Institutions §§4–6, 8–10.

### § 791.262. Definitions; administration of facilities by bureau; supervision and inspection of jails and lockups; variance; limit on supervision, inspection and promulgation of rules and standards; provision of advice and services; enforcement of orders; sheriff's residence; commission member, visitation and inspection of jail or lockup; recordkeeping; violations. [MSA § 28.2322]

Sec. 62. (1) As used in this section:

(a) "Holding cell" means a cell or room in a facility of a local unit of government that is used for the detention of 1 or more persons awaiting processing, booking, court appearances, transportation to a jail or lockup, or discharge for not to exceed 12 hours.

(b) "Holding center" means a facility that is operated by a local unit of government for the detention of persons awaiting processing, booking, court appearances, transportation to a jail or lockup, or discharge; for not to exceed 24 hours.

(c) "Jail" means a facility that is operated by a local unit of government for the detention of persons charged with, or convicted of, criminal offenses or ordinance violations; persons found guilty of civil or criminal contempt; or a facility which houses prisoners pursuant to an agreement authorized under Act No. 164 of the Public Acts of 1861, being sections 802.1 to 802.21 of the Michigan Compiled Laws, for not more than 1 year.

(d) "Local unit of government" means any county, city, village, township, charter township, community college, college, or university.

(e) "Lockup" means a facility that is operated by a local unit of government for the detention of persons awaiting processing, booking, court appearances, or transportation to a jail, for not to exceed 72 hours.

(f) "State correctional facility" means a facility or institution maintained and operated by the department.

(2) State correctional facilities shall be administered by the bureau of prisons.

(3) The department shall supervise and inspect jails and lockups that are under the jurisdiction of the county sheriff to obtain facts concerning the proper management of the jails and lockups and their usefulness. The department shall promulgate rules and standards promoting the proper, efficient, and humane administration of jails and lockups that are under the jurisdiction of the county sheriff pursuant to the administrative procedures act of 1969, Act No. 306 of the Public Acts of 1969, being sections 24.201 to 24.315 of the Michigan Compiled Laws.

(4) The department may grant a variance to the rules and standards promulgated under subsection (3).

(5) Except as provided in subsection (3), the department shall not supervise and inspect, or promulgate rules and standards for the administration of, holding cells, holding centers, or lockups. However, the department shall provide advice and services concerning the efficient and humane administration of holding cells, holding centers, and lockups at the request of a local unit of government.

(6) The commission may enforce any reasonable order with respect to jails and lockups subject to supervision and inspection pursuant to subsection (3) through mandamus or injunction in the circuit court of the county where the jail is located through proceedings instituted by the attorney general on behalf of the commission.

(7) The county board of commissioners may determine whether the sheriff's residence is to be part of the county jail.

(8) The sheriff or the administrator of a jail or lockup, subject to supervision and inspection under subsection (3), shall admit to the jail or lockup any member of the commission or an authorized designee of the commission, for the purpose of visitation and inspection.

(9) The sheriff or the administrator of a jail or lockup subject to supervision and inspection under subsection (3) shall keep records of a type and in a manner reasonably prescribed by the commission. The commission shall provide the forms required for keeping the records.

(10) Any person who violates subsections (8) or (9) shall be guilty of a misdemeanor.

**History:**
Pub Acts 1953, No. 232, § 62, eff October 2, 1953; amended by Pub Acts 1964, No. 111, eff August 28, 1964; 1984, No. 102, imd eff May 7, 1984;

§ 791.262    Department of Corrections

amended by Pub Acts 1987, No. 251, imd eff December 28, 1987, by § 2 eff January 1, 1988 (see 1987 note below).

**Editor's notes:**
 Pub Acts 1987, No. 251, § 3, imd eff December 28, 1987, by § 2 eff January 1, 1988, provides:
 "Section 3. This amendatory act shall not take effect unless Senate Bill No. 498 of the 84th Legislature [which became Act No. 252 of 1987] is enacted into law."

**Cross references:**
 County jails and lockups, § 45.16–45.18.
 Administration and control of probation recovery camps, § 798.1.
 Local jails, workhouses and houses of correction, §§801.1 et seq and §§801.201 et seq.

**Michigan Digest references:**
 Constitutional Law § 89.
 Nuisances § 28.
 Prisons and Jails §§1 et seq., 1.05, 1.20, 1.25, 1.35, 1.45, 1.50, 2.110, 2.135, 4.
 State of Michigan § 25.
 Statutes § 160.

**Research references:**
 60 Am Jur 2d, Penal and Correctional Institutions §§4–6, 8–10.

**Legal periodicals:**
 Women in crime, 3 Crim JJ 175.
 Legal issues surrounding private operation of prisons, 22 Crim L Bull 309 (1986).

### CASE NOTES

**1. Validity.**

The 1984 amendment of a section of the Department of Corrections act to take away the Department of Corrections' supervisory and rule-making power over local detention facilities changed existing substantive law and should be limited to prospective application. Davis v Detroit (1986) 149 Mich App 249, 386 NW2d 169, app den (1986) 426 Mich 856 and (disapproved on other grounds by Wade v Department of Corrections (1992) 439 Mich 158, 483 NW2d 26).

Acts establishing Detroit House of Correction are not unconstitutional as being special and local legislation, since Detroit House of Correction is a state, not local, prison. People v Andrea (1973) 48 Mich App 310, 210 NW2d 474.

In view of substantial authority and control exercised by state penal authorities over management and policies of Detroit House of Correction and clear statutory scheme for spreading costs of operating the facility among city, county and state users, legislature did not unconstitutionally delegate legislative power to city of Detroit by enactment of statutes concerning Detroit House of Correction, notwithstanding that such statutes give Detroit common council and its appointees power to exercise various responsibilities in day-to-day management of the facility. People v Andrea (1973) 48 Mich App 310, 210 NW2d 474.

Provisions of former §§802.51 et seq. requiring female state prisoners to be committed to Detroit House of Correction did not violate provision of article IV, § 24, of the Constitution of 1963 that no law should embrace more than one object which should be expressed in its title, since such Act had but one object; namely, to supplement former Act, which was described fully by its title. People v Andrea (1973) 48 Mich App 310, 210 NW2d 474.

**2. Powers.**

No matter where department of corrections may choose lawfully or need lawfully to incarcerate or permit incarceration of state-sentenced prisoner, its duty to him remains constant and may not be subjected to delegation, whether or not others are concurrently account-

**Department of Corrections** § 791.262

able for breach of same or corresponding legal duty. Green v State Corrections Dep't (1971) 386 Mich 459, 192 NW2d 491.

The 1984 amendment of a section of the Department of Corrections act to take away the Department of Corrections' supervisory and rule-making power over local detention facilities changed existing substantive law and should be limited to prospective application. Hickey v Zezulka (1989) 177 Mich App 606, 443 NW2d 180, app gr, in part, motion gr (1990) 435 Mich 861, 457 NW2d 345, later proceeding (1991) 438 Mich 1202 and amd on other grounds, motion den (1992) 440 Mich 1203.

Statutory power conferred on corrections commission to have jurisdiction over and authority to supervise and inspect penal institutions, and to appoint director who in turn makes rules and regulations for management and control of such institutions, includes Detroit house of correction within such powers. Green v State (1971) 30 Mich App 648, 186 NW2d 792, affd (1971) 386 Mich 459, 192 NW2d 491.

**3. Jails and houses of correction.**

Regulations of state corrections department, as proper exercise of police power, could constitutionally be applied to county jail buildings constructed prior to adoption of regulations. Wayne County Jail Inmates v Lucas (1974) 391 Mich 359, 216 NW2d 910, later proceeding (1989) 432 Mich 882, 453 NW2d 656, on remand on other grounds (1989) 178 Mich App 634, 444 NW2d 549.

Provision of this section authorizing department of corrections to prescribe housing regulations for prisoners did not authorize department to ignore local housing ordinances or statutes which were properly applicable to county jail in addition to department regulations. Wayne County Jail Inmates v Lucas (1974) 391 Mich 359, 216 NW2d 910, later proceeding (1989) 432 Mich 882, 453 NW2d 656, on remand on other grounds(1989) 178 Mich App 634, 444 NW2d 549.

The provisions of former § 802.2, that the Detroit House of Correction is subject to periodical inspection in the discretion of the state authorities, includes inspection by representatives of the state dairy and food commissioner. People v Jacob (1915) 184 Mich 77, 150 NW 363.

While the legislature has required the city of Detroit to pay the expenses of the Detroit House of Correction to the extent that they shall be found to exceed its earnings, the management and appropriations of said institution are not within the control of the common council, but are confided to officers provided for by the law, except as the assent and concurrence of the council are necessary to extraordinary appropriations. Detroit v Board of Water Comm'rs (1896) 108 Mich 494, 66 NW 377.

The Detroit House of Correction is not entitled to be supplied with water free of charge by the Detroit water commissioners. Detroit v Board of Water Comm'rs (1896) 108 Mich 494, 66 NW 377.

The board of water commissioners of Detroit is not obliged to furnish water gratuitously to the Detroit House of Correction as to a city public institution. It is not such. Detroit v Board of Water Comm'rs (1896) 108 Mich 494, 66 NW 377.

There is no conflict between a city's authority to maintain a jail and detain suspects under the home rule act and the Department of Corrections' supervisory power, contained in a section of the Department of Corrections act, to insure that such facilities are maintained in a safe and humane condition. Davis v Detroit (1986) 149 Mich App 249, 386 NW2d 169, app den (1986) 426 Mich 856 and (disapproved on other grounds by Wade v Department of Corrections (1992) 439 Mich 158, 483 NW2d 26).

The city of Detroit may close the Detroit house of correction when it has no agreement to take custody of any committed persons. Recorder's Court of Detroit v Detroit (1984) 134 Mich App 239, 351 NW2d 289.

Personnel of the department of corrections who have experience in handling the affairs of prisoners are in a far better position to ascertain whether an act constitutes a threat to the institutional order of a prison than are the courts, and the judiciary should not interfere with the personnel's exercise of discretion unless that discretion has been clearly abused. Meadows v Marquette Prison Warden (1982) 117 Mich App 794, 324 NW2d 507.

The power granted to the department of corrections to make orders concerning the administration of local jails is insufficient to constitute control of a local jail for purposes of an action against the department based on nuisance. Mitchell v Michigan Dep't of Corrections (1982)

113 Mich App 739, 318 NW2d 507.

The Legislature has not authorized a city to confine persons convicted for violation of its ordinances in a jail owned and operated by a private company. Op Atty Gen, October 21, 1987, No. 6474.

Under prior provision, department of corrections was authorized to require that a county, in building a county jail, include space in the building for the sheriff's living quarters. Op Atty Gen, November 16, 1955, No. 2288.

**4. Sentence to Detroit house of correction.**

A person convicted under the former occupational license tax statute and sentenced for a minimum term of 65 days is properly sentenced to the Detroit House of Correction. In re Kreiner (1909) 156 Mich 296, 120 NW 785.

No court outside of Wayne county can sentence persons convicted of state prison offenses to the Detroit House of Correction until the state prison inspectors have contracted for their confinement and maintenance therein as authorized by statute. It is discretionary with such inspectors whether they shall make such contract. Dorsey v People (1877) 37 Mich 382; Humphrey v People (1878) 39 Mich 207.

Conviction outside of Wayne county in proceedings under the prohibitory liquor-law did not authorize imprisonment in the Detroit House of Correction. In re Sorenson (1874) 29 Mich 475.

Except under former § 802.9, no court outside of Wayne county can sentence to imprisonment in said house of correction for offenses not punishable by imprisonment in the state prison. In re Sorenson (1874) 29 Mich 475.

A person convicted under the former statutes as a common prostitute in any other county than Wayne could not be punished by imprisonment in the Detroit House of Correction. In re Weinrich (1870) 20 Mich 14.

**5. Records.**

Department of corrections has authority to prescribe contents and type of records to be kept by sheriffs and superintendents of each local house of correction. (Construing similar provision of former act.) Op Atty Gen, February 1, 1944, No. 0–1793.

**§ 791.262a. Lockup advisory board, creation; membership; term; expenses; chairperson; quorum; policy; annual meeting.** [MSA § 28.2322(1)]

Sec. 62a. (1) A local lockup advisory board is created within the bureau of prisons. The board shall consist of 7 members appointed for a period of 4 years. The director of each of the following shall appoint 1 member:

(a) The department of state police.
(b) The Michigan association of chiefs of police.
(c) The Michigan municipal league.
(d) The Michigan townships association.
(e) The Michigan judges' association.
(f) The Michigan district judges' association.
(g) The Michigan sheriffs' association.

(2) The members appointed under subsection (1) shall serve without compensation but shall be entitled to actual and necessary expenses incurred in the performance of official duties.

(3) The first meeting of the advisory board shall be convened within 60 days after the effective date of this section, at which time the members appointed under subsection (1) shall elect a chairperson. A quorum shall consist of 4 members.

(4) The local lockup advisory board shall develop and promote a model policy for use in the administration of local lockups, holding cells, and holding centers. The model policy shall be developed within 6 months after the date of the first meeting. The advisory board shall convene annually to review the model policy.

**Department of Corrections** § 791.262b

**History:**
Pub Acts 1953, No. 232, § 62a, as added by Pub Acts 1984, No. 102, imd eff May 7, 1984.

**§ 791.262b. Housing of two inmates in cell; conditions; classification system; considerations; submission for approval by department; housing of inmate with no prior convictions; visual supervision; authorization of sentencing judge; indemnification of state for damages resulting from housing two inmates in cell; limitations on housing.** [MSA § 28.2322(2)]

Sec. 62b. (1) The rules and standards promulgated under section 62(3) shall not prohibit the housing of 2 inmates in a county jail cell which is designed and constructed for single occupancy and which meets both of the following conditions:

(a) The basic cell is at least 65 square feet in area.

(b) The cell provides unrestricted access to a day area which is available for use by the inmates other than those inmates being disciplined. The day area shall be available at least 14 hours per day and shall contain an average of at least 20 additional square feet of space per inmate.

(2) For purposes of housing inmates as provided for under this section, the sheriff of the county shall develop and implement a classification system classifying the county jail population according to all of the following:

(a) Behavior characteristics.

(b) Similar physical characteristics.

(c) Age.

(d) Type of crime committed and criminal history.

(e) Gender.

(3) The classification system under subsection (2) shall be submitted to and approved by the department. Any classification system in effect on December 31, 1987, shall continue in effect until changed as provided in this subsection.

(4) A person who has no prior criminal convictions may only be housed with another inmate who does not have a prior felony conviction.

(5) Cells in which 2 inmates are housed shall have doors which allow visual supervision, and inmates shall be under visual supervision at least every hour.

(6) An inmate who is subject to section 33b(a) to (cc) of Act No. 232 of the Public Acts of 1953, being section 791.233b of the Michigan Compiled Laws, shall not be housed in a cell with another inmate as provided for under this section, unless the sentencing judge authorizes the inmate for such housing.

(7) If the state incurs any expense or is liable for damages on any judgment for an action brought as the result of a county housing 2 inmates in a cell as provided for under this section, the county in which the action arose shall fully indemnify the state for the expense or damages.

(8) No more than 75% of the total inmate population may be

§ 791.262b                                    Department of Corrections

housed 2 to a cell and pretrial inmates must be housed in separate cell blocks or housing units from sentenced inmates. In any jail facility with 5 or more floors, pretrial inmates shall be housed on separate floors from sentenced inmates.

**History:**
Pub Acts 1953, No. 232, § 62b, eff October 2, 1953; amended by Pub Acts 1987, No. 252, imd eff December 28, 1987 (see 1987 note below); 1988, No. 492, imd eff December 29, 1988.

**Editor's notes:**
Pub Acts 1987, No. 251, § 3, imd eff December 28, 1987, by § 2 eff January 1, 1988, provides:
"Section 3. This amendatory act shall not take effect unless Senate Bill No. 498 of the 84th Legislature [which became Act No. 252 of 1987] is enacted into law."

**Statutory references:**
Section 62 is 791.262.

### CASE NOTES

The [former] Prison Overcrowding Emergency Powers Act is constitutional and does not contravene the governor's exclusive power of commutation with respect to sentences imposed after January 26, 1981, and with respect to sentences imposed before that date only insofar as the governor's actions which trigger the reductions in sentence are discretionary rather than mandatory. Oakland County Prosecuting Attorney v Michigan Dep't of Corrections (1981) 411 Mich 183, 305 NW2d 515.

The Department of Corrections is without authority by variance or otherwise to permit a county jail to house three or more inmates in a cell. Op Atty Gen, April 28, 1987, No. 6436.

The legislature has set a limit of two inmates to be housed in a county jail cell. Op Atty Gen, April 28, 1987, No. 6436.

The governor, upon appropriate certification of the commission of corrections, shall formally rescind the previous declaration of prison overcrowding state of emergency before declaring a new prison overcrowding state of emergency. Op Atty Gen, April 5, 1984, No. 6215.

The governor may, upon appropriate certification by the commission of corrections, declare a prison overcrowding state of emergency in the event the population of the prison system exceeds the rated design capacity for thirty consecutive days. A formal rescission of a previous emergency declaration, which has served its purpose, is not requisite to a new declaration of emergency. Op Atty Gen, August 30, 1983, No. 6182.

**§ 791.262c. Housing of two inmates in cell; designation as housing for two or more inmates; conditions; classification system; submission and approval of classification system; single occupancy of high security and segregation cells; visual supervision.** [MSA § 28.2322(3)]

Sec. 62c. (1) The rules and standards promulgated under section 62(3) shall not prohibit the housing of 2 or more inmates in a county jail cell which is designed and constructed for housing 2 or more inmates, and which meets all of the following conditions:

(a) The basic cell has at least 52 square feet in area per inmate. This subdivision shall only apply to cells constructed after January 1, 1988.

(b) The cell provides access to a day area which is available for use by other than those being disciplined. The day area shall

**Department of Corrections** § 791.263

contain at least 20 additional square feet of space per inmate. This subdivision shall only apply to cells constructed after January 1, 1988.

(c) The cell complies with other rules and standards for multiple occupancy housing in jails, as promulgated under section 62(3).

(2) For purposes of housing inmates as provided for under this section, the sheriff of the county shall develop and implement a classification system classifying the county jail population according to all of the following:

(a) Behavior characteristics.

(b) Similar physical characteristics.

(c) Age.

(d) Type of crime committed and criminal history.

(e) Gender.

(3) The classification system under subsection (2) shall be submitted to and approved by the department.

(4) High security and segregation cells shall not be constructed to house multiple inmates.

(5) Cells in which 2 or more inmates are housed shall have doors which allow visual supervision, and inmates shall be under visual supervision at least every hour.

**History:**
Pub Acts 1953, No. 232, § 62c, as added by Pub Acts 1987, No. 251, imd eff December 28, 1987, by § 2 eff January 1, 1988 (see 1987 note below); amended by Pub Acts 1988, No. 293, imd eff August 4, 1988.

**Editor's notes:**
**Pub Acts 1987, No. 251,** § 3, imd eff December 28, 1987, by § 2 eff January 1, 1988, provides:

"Section 3. This amendatory act shall not take effect unless Senate Bill No. 498 of the 84th Legislature [which became Act No. 252 of 1987] is enacted into law."

**Statutory references:**
Section 62, above referred to, is § 791.262.

## § 791.263. Wardens; appointment; personnel; "correctional facility" explained. [MSA § 28.2323]

Sec. 63. (1) The wardens of the correctional facilities of this state shall be appointed by the director of corrections and shall be within the state civil service. The assistant director in charge of the bureau of correctional facilities shall, subject to the approval of the director, appoint personnel within the bureau as may be necessary. Members of the staff and employees of each correctional facility shall be appointed by the warden subject to the approval of the director.

(2) As used in this section, "correctional facility" does not include a youth correctional facility authorized under section 20g if that facility is operated by a private vendor.

**History:**
Pub Acts 1953, No. 232, § 63, eff October 2, 1953.
Amended by Pub Acts 1998, No. 512, imd eff January 8, 1999.

## § 791.263

**Effect of amendment notes:**
The **1998 amendment** redesignated the existing section as subsection (1), substituted "correctional facility" and "correctional facilities" for "penal institution" and "penal institutions" in subsection (1), added subsection (2), and made grammatical changes.

**Statutory references:**
Section 20g, above referred to, is § 791.220g.

**Michigan Digest references:**
Prisons and Jails §§2.110, 2.135, 5.

**LEXIS-NEXIS™ Michigan analytical references:**
Michigan Law and Practice, Convicts and Prisons § 2.

**Research references:**
60 Am Jur 2d, Penal and Correctional Institutions §§4–6, 8–10.

### CASE NOTES

**1. Powers and duties of warden generally.**

A former provision, empowering the warden of a prison to sue and be sued, was repealed by former § 800.12. McDowell v Fuller (1912) 169 Mich 332, 135 NW 265.

The state can only be sued with legislative consent, which may be withdrawn at any time without impairing contractual rights. McDowell v Fuller (1912) 169 Mich 332, 135 NW 265.

Under former § 800.9, warden of state prison had general superintendence of matters of internal discipline. Parshay v Buchkoe (1971) 30 Mich App 556, 186 NW2d 859.

**2. Deputy warden.**

Under former law, deputy warden of a prison might, in the absence of the warden, issue a warrant for retaking and returning a paroled convict to the prison for a breach of his parole. Ex parte Fox (1907) 147 Mich 189, 110 NW 517.

**3. Removal of personnel.**

Former act did not require a notice of an order removing the warden of the state house of correction to be served upon him before quo warranto proceedings were instituted against him, and the fact that he was represented by counsel when the order was made was required to be treated as sufficient notice of said order. Ellis ex rel. Fuller v Parsell (1894) 99 Mich 381, 58 NW 335.

Under former act, the board of control of the state house of correction and reformatory at Ionia had power to remove the warden for lack of capacity and diligence without regard to the question of moral turpitude. Fuller v Ellis (1893) 98 Mich 96, 57 NW 33.

The provision of former § 800.5, relative to removal for cause, was not in conflict with the constitutional provision vesting in governor powers of removal, nor with the provision prohibiting exercise of the powers of one department by members of another. Fuller v Ellis (1893) 98 Mich 96, 57 NW 33; Ellis ex rel. Fuller v Parsell (1894) 99 Mich 381, 58 NW 335.

**4. Compensation and emoluments.**

Under former law, salary of warden of state prison could be increased by the state prison board upon approval of the governor. Op Atty Gen, 1928–1930, p 515.

Under former law, prison guards and employees were not entitled to payment for overtime service. Op Atty Gen, 1923–1924, p 75.

Employees occupying dwelling houses furnished them as part payment for their services were not tenants of the board of control of the Michigan state prison, and the board of control was entitled to the possession of said premises upon the termination of their employment. Op Atty Gen, 1919, p 102.

Under former law, deputy warden acting as warden could not claim the salary of warden, unless he had been so appointed by the board of control. Op Atty Gen, 1919, p 107.

**5. Discipline and control.**

Former § 800.40 was not intended to provide for the punishment of crimes committed in prison but merely for the good government of the prison, and to aid the officers thereof to maintain discipline. People v Huntley (1897) 112 Mich 569, 71 NW 178.

# Department of Corrections § 791.263a

State has duty to assure safety of prison inmate. People v Harmon (1974) 53 Mich App 482, 220 NW2d 212, affd (1975) 394 Mich 625, 232 NW2d 187.

Persons in charge of prisons and jails are obliged to take reasonable precautions in order to provide a place of confinement where a prisoner is safe from gang rapes and beatings by fellow inmates, safe from guard ignorance of pleas for help and safe from intentional placement into situations where an assault of one type or another is likely to result. People v Harmon (1974) 53 Mich App 482, 220 NW2d 212, affd (1975) 394 Mich 625, 232 NW2d 187.

**6. Disciplinary hearings.**

A prisoner in Michigan must be afforded minimal due process in connection with prison disciplinary hearings in which the prisoner may be deprived of a right or significant privilege. Casper v Marquette Prison Warden (1983) 126 Mich App 271, 337 NW2d 56.

Minimum due process in prison disciplinary hearings requires a disciplinary committee to establish in good faith to its own satisfaction the credibility and reliability of a confidential informant, and there must be some information on the record to convince an appellate tribunal that the disciplinary committee undertook such an inquiry in good faith. Casper v Marquette Prison Warden (1983) 126 Mich App 271, 337 NW2d 56.

Prisoners in Michigan are not constitutionally entitled to full rights of confrontation and cross-examination at prison disciplinary hearings; the scope of confrontation and cross-examination is left to the sound discretion of prison officials. Casper v Marquette Prison Warden (1983) 126 Mich App 271, 337 NW2d 56.

**§ 791.263a. Compensation of correctional or youth correctional facility employees injured by inmate assault or injured during riot; exception; definitions.** [MSA § 28.2323(1)]

Sec. 63a. (1) A person employed by the department of corrections in a correctional facility who is injured as a result of an assault by a prisoner housed in the correctional facility or injured during a riot shall receive his or her full wages by the department of corrections until worker's compensation benefits begin and then shall receive in addition to worker's compensation benefits a supplement from the department which together with the worker's compensation benefits shall equal but not exceed the weekly net wage of the employee at the time of the injury. This supplement shall only apply while the person is on the department's payroll and is receiving worker's compensation benefits. Fringe benefits normally received by an employee shall be in effect during the time the employee receives the supplement provided by this section from the department.

(2) Subsection (1) also applies to a person who is employed by the department of corrections who, while performing his or her duties in a youth correctional facility, is injured as a result of an assault by a prisoner housed in the youth correctional facility or is injured during a riot in the youth correctional facility. However, subsection (1) does not apply to any person employed by, or retained under contract by, a private vendor that operates a youth correctional facility.

(3) For purposes of this section:

(a) "Correctional facility" means a facility that houses prisoners committed to the jurisdiction of the department, including a community corrections center.

(b) "Youth correctional facility" means a facility authorized under section 20g.

## § 791.263a — Department of Corrections

**History:**
Pub Acts 1953, No. 232, § 63a, as added by Pub Acts 1975, No. 293, imd eff December 10, 1975.
Amended by Pub Acts 1998, No. 512, imd eff January 8, 1999.

**Effect of amendment notes:**
**The 1998 amendment** made various substitutions and deletions in subsection (1), added new subsection (2), redesignated former subsection (2) as (3), and substantially rewrote that subsection.

**Statutory references:**
Section 20g, above referred to, is § 791.220g.

**Michigan Digest references:**
Prisons and Jails §§2.35, 3, 5, 5.70, 7.

**Michigan Civ Jur references:**
Workers' Compensation § 108.45.

**Legal periodicals:**
Legal aspects of prison riots, 16 Harv Civil Rights L Rev 735 (1982).

### CASE NOTES

**1. Construction and effect.**
A person employed by a state penal institution who is injured and becomes unable to work as a result of an assault by an inmate shall be eligible to receive a supplemental benefit in addition to workers' compensation benefits as long as he remains on the payroll of the Department of Corrections and continues to receive workers' compensation benefits. Michigan State Employees Asso. v Michigan Dep't of Corrections (1988) 172 Mich App 155, 431 NW2d 411.

Prison-inmate relationship is not an employer-employee arrangement within contemplation of Labor Standards Act. Green v State (1971) 30 Mich App 648, 186 NW2d 792, affd (1971) 386 Mich 459, 192 NW2d 491.

**2. Nature of institution.**
The Detroit House of Correction is a prison for the confinement of persons convicted of offenses. No one can be received into it except in pursuance of some express statute. In re Kaminsky (1888) 70 Mich 653, 38 NW 659.

Detroit House of Correction is not a city prison but exists as creation of state legislature and is subject to same standard of supervision and inspection by corrections commission as is applicable to other state prison facilities, even though it is managed by a city appointed superintendent and every prisoner therein may not be a state prisoner. Green v State (1971) 30 Mich App 648, 186 NW2d 792, affd (1971) 386 Mich 459, 192 NW2d 491.

**3. License to carry concealed weapon.**
The superintendent, deputy superintendent and guards of the Detroit house of correction may not carry a concealed weapon without first having obtained a license as required by 1931 PA 328, § 227. Op Atty Gen, May 4, 1984, No. 6223.

**4. Liability for injuries.**
Detroit House of Correction, in which plaintiff was incarcerated as state-sentenced prisoner when he sustained personal injury as result of alleged negligence, was a public building within meaning of § 691.1406 and plaintiff was a member of public community for whose benefit the building was operated and maintained. Green v State Corrections Dep't (1971) 386 Mich 459, 192 NW2d 491.

State, through department of corrections, may be held to respond in damages for tortuous injury sustained by state-sentenced convict while he is incarcerated in Detroit House of Correction. Green v State Corrections Dep't (1971) 386 Mich 459, 192 NW2d 491.

Plaintiff who was sentenced for state statutory offense and committed to state corrections commission which in turn delivered him to Detroit House of Correction would be held to be state prisoner at time he was injured in machine shop of House of Correction and thereby entitled to name state as proper party defendant in subsequent action for damages resulting from such injury. Green v State

**Department of Corrections** § 791.263b

(1971) 30 Mich App 648, 186 NW2d 792, affd (1971) 386 Mich 459, 192 NW2d 491.

Permanently attached fixtures in public buildings are part of buildings, and accordingly, defective planing machine securely anchored to floor in shop of public prison building thereby became part of such building for purposes of determining liability of state, under § 691.1406, for injuries caused by defects in public buildings. Green v State (1971) 30 Mich App 648, 186 NW2d 792, affd (1971) 386 Mich 459, 192 NW2d 491.

Plaintiff's failure to file 60-day notice of claim, required by § 691.1406, for injury sustained as he worked on defective machine while incarcerated as state prisoner would be held not to have barred plaintiff's subsequent cause of action against state in light of facts that at time of injury prison authority was already aware of defect in machine, that plaintiff was incapacitated from bringing action during his incarceration, and that inequity would result by permitting state to imprison plaintiff, instruct him to work at knowingly defective machine, and then escape liability for ensuing injury. Green v State (1971) 30 Mich App 648, 186 NW2d 792, affd (1971) 386 Mich 459, 192 NW2d 491.

Detroit House of Correction would be held to be "public building" for purpose of determining liability of state, under §§691.1401–691.1415, for injuries caused by defects in public building. Green v State (1971) 30 Mich App 648, 186 NW2d 792, affd (1971) 386 Mich 459, 192 NW2d 491.

State prison corrections officer who was taken captive by male prisoner and raped during course of negotiations for her release could not maintain federal civil rights action against prison authorities whose alleged negligence in matter did not amount to deliberate indifference shocking to conscience, and whose conduct afforded no basis for establishing requisite violation of due process in view of fact that acts in question were committed by prisoner not acting under color of state law, custom or usage. Nobles v Brown (1992, CA6 Mich) 985 F2d 235.

**§ 791.263b. Housing of two inmates in a cell; conditions; classification system for housing inmates; considerations; submission and approval of classification system by judge; housing of inmate with no prior convictions; visual supervision; authorization of sentencing judge; indemnification of state for damages resulting from housing of two inmates in cell; limitations on housing; applications of subsections.** [MSA § 28.2323(2)]

Sec. 63b. (1) The rules and standards promulgated under section 62(3) shall not prohibit the housing of 2 inmates in any cell in a county jail as prescribed under this section which meets both of the following conditions:

(a) The basic cell is at least 65 square feet in area.

(b) The cell provides unrestricted access to a day area which is available for use by the inmates other than those inmates being disciplined. The day area shall be available at least 14 hours per day and shall contain an average of at least 20 additional square feet of space per inmate.

(2) For purposes of housing inmates as provided for under this section, the sheriff of the county shall develop and implement a classification system classifying the county jail population according to all of the following:

(a) Behavior characteristics.

(b) Similar physical characteristics.

(c) Age.

(d) Type of crime committed and criminal history.

(e) Gender.

(3) The classification system under subsection (2) shall be submitted to and approved by the chief judge of the circuit court for the county.

(4) A person who has no other prior convictions shall not be housed with another inmate as provided for under this section.

(5) Cells in which 2 inmates are housed shall have doors which allow visual supervision, and inmates shall be under visual supervision at least every hour.

(6) An inmate who is subject to section 33b(a) to (cc) of Act No. 232 of the Public Acts of 1953, being section 791.233b of the Michigan Compiled Laws, shall not be housed in a cell with another inmate as provided for under this section, unless the sentencing judge authorizes the inmate for such housing.

(7) If the state incurs any expense or is liable for damages on any judgment for an action brought as the result of a county housing 2 inmates in a cell as provided for under this section, the county in which the action arose shall fully indemnify the state for the expense or damages.

(8) No more than 75% of the total inmate population may be housed 2 to a cell and pretrial inmates must be housed in separate cell blocks or housing units from sentenced inmates. In any jail facility with 5 or more floors, pretrial inmates must be housed on separate floors from sentenced inmates.

(9) Subsections (1) to (6) shall not apply after April 30, 1990.

**History:**
Pub Acts 1953, No. 232, § 63b, as added by Pub Acts 1984, No. 145, imd eff June 25, 1984.

**Statutory references:**
Section 62 is § 791.262.

## § 791.264. Classification of prisoners; committee, duties, records; information with regard to prisoners, filing with parole board. [MSA § 28.2324]

Sec. 64. The assistant director in charge of the bureau of penal institutions shall have authority and it shall be his duty to classify the prisoners in the several penal institutions. He shall, subject to the approval of the director, promulgate regulations under which there shall be organized in each penal institution, a classification committee from the staff of such penal institution, which committee shall perform such services and in such manner as the assistant director in charge of the bureau of penal institutions shall require. It shall be the duty of each such classification committee to obtain and file complete information with regard to each prisoner sentenced under an indeterminate sentence at the time such prisoner is received in any penal institution. It shall be the duty of the clerk of the court and of all probation officers and other officials to send such information as may be in their possession or under their control to each such classification committee when and in such manner as they may be directed. When all such existing available records have been assembled, each such classification committee shall determine whether any further investigation is necessary, and, if so, it shall make such investigation. All such information shall be filed with the parole board so as to be readily available when the parole of the prisoner is to be considered.

**History:**
Pub Acts 1953, No. 232, § 64, eff October 2, 1953.

**Michigan Digest references:**
Prisons and Jails § 4.

**Research references:**
60 Am Jur 2d, Penal and Correctional Institutions §§8–10.

**Legal periodicals:**
A new classification system for criminal offenders, VI: Differences among the types on the adjective checklist, 11 Crim Justice & Behavior 349 (1984).

### CASE NOTES

The legislature, by explicitly defining eligibility requirements for prisoners convicted of violent or assaultive crimes and prisoners convicted of first-degree murder for community placement, did not intend to preclude the Department of Corrections from defining eligibility for community placement for additional categories such as offenders classified as drug traffickers. Luttrell v Department of Corrections (1984) 421 Mich 93, 365 NW2d 74, on remand (1985) 143 Mich App 527, 373 NW2d 168.

**§ 791.265. Transfer or retransfer of prisoners; confinement in secure correctional facility; "offender" defined; transfer of offenders to country of citizenship; notification to judge and prosecutor; objections; "secure correctional facility" defined.** [MSA § 28.2325]

Sec. 65. (1) Under rules promulgated by the director of the department, the assistant director in charge of the bureau of correctional facilities, except as otherwise provided in this section, may cause the transfer or re-transfer of a prisoner from a correctional facility to which committed to any other correctional facility, or temporarily to a state institution for medical or surgical treatment. In effecting a transfer, the assistant director of the bureau of correctional facilities may utilize the services of an executive or employee within the department and of a law enforcement officer of the state.

(2) A prisoner who is subject to disciplinary time and is committed to the jurisdiction of the department shall be confined in a secure correctional facility for the duration of his or her minimum sentence, except for periods when the prisoner is away from the secure correctional facility while being supervised by an employee of the department or by an employee of a private vendor that operates a youth correctional facility under section 20g for 1 of the following purposes:

(a) Visiting a critically ill relative.

(b) Attending the funeral of a relative.

(c) Obtaining medical services not otherwise available at the secure correctional facility.

(d) Participating in a work detail.

(3) As used in this section, "offender" means a citizen of the United States or a foreign country who has been convicted of a crime and been given a sentence in a country other than the country of which he or she is a citizen. If a treaty is in effect between the United States and a foreign country, which provides for the transfer of offenders from the jurisdiction of 1 of the countries to the jurisdiction of the country of which the offender is a citizen, and if the offender requests the transfer, the governor of this state or a person designated by the governor may give the approval of this state to a transfer of an offender, if the conditions of the treaty are satisfied.

(4) Not less than 45 days before approval of a transfer pursuant to subsection (3) from this state to another country, the governor, or the governor's designee, shall notify the sentencing judge and the prosecuting attorney of the county having original jurisdiction, or their successors in office, of the request for transfer. The notification shall indicate any name changes of the offender subsequent to sentencing. Within 20 days after receiving such notification, the judge or prosecutor may send to the governor, or the governor's designee, information about the criminal action against the offender or objections to the transfer. Objections to the transfer shall not preclude approval of the transfer.

(5) As used in this section, "secure correctional facility" means a facility that houses prisoners under the jurisdiction of the department according to the following requirements:

(a) The facility is enclosed by a locked fence or wall that is designed to prevent prisoners from leaving the enclosed premises and that is patrolled by correctional officers.

(b) Prisoners in the facility are restricted to the area inside the fence or wall.

(c) Prisoners are under guard by correctional officers 7 days per week, 24 hours per day.

**History:**
Pub Acts 1953, No. 232, § 65, eff October 2, 1953; amended by Pub Acts 1980, No. 150, imd eff June 10, 1980; 1982, No. 179, imd eff June 14, 1982; 1994, No. 217, eff June 27, 1994 (see 1994 note below).

Amended by Pub Acts 1998, No. 512, imd eff January 8, 1999.

**Editor's notes:**
**Pub Acts 1994, No. 217, §§2, 3,** eff June 27, 1994, provide:

"Section 2. This amendatory act shall take effect on the date that sentencing guidelines are enacted into law after the sentencing commission submits its report to the secretary of the senate and the clerk of the house of representatives pursuant to sections 31 to 34 of chapter IX of the code of criminal procedure, Act No. 175 of the Public Acts of 1927, as added by the amendatory act resulting from House Bill No. 4782 of the 87th Legislature [Pub Acts 1994, No. 445]. (**Repealed** by Pub Acts 1998, No. 316, imd eff July 30, 1998, by enacting § 2 eff December 15, 1998.).

"Section 3. This amendatory act shall not take effect unless all of the following bills of the 87th Legislature are enacted into law:

"(a) Senate Bill No. 41 [Pub Acts 1994, No. 218].

"(b) House Bill No. 4782 [Pub Acts 1994, No. 445].

"(c) House Bill No. 5439 [Pub Acts 1994, No. 322]."

**Effect of amendment notes:**
The **1994 amendment** redesignated former subsections (2) and (3) as (3) and (4); inserted new subsections (2) and (5); and made grammatical changes.
The **1998 amendment** added and deleted material in subsection (2).

**Statutory references:**
Section 20g, above referred to, is § 791.220g.

**Michigan Digest references:**
Prisons and Jails § 6.

**LEXIS-NEXIS™ Michigan analytical references:**
Michigan Law and Practice, Convicts and Prisons § 4.

**Research references:**
60 Am Jur 2d, Penal and Correctional Institutions §§53, 54, 56.

### CASE NOTES

The serious misconduct of a prisoner is not a prerequisite to his interfacility transfer; the department of corrections has discretion to transfer prisoners to protect other inmates and advance the smooth operation of the institution. De Walt v Warden, Marquette Prison (1982) 112 Mich App 313, 315 NW2d 584.

To provide equal protection of laws to prisoners involuntarily committed to mental institution, probate court hearing must be accorded before transfer, hearing to be conducted in same manner as civil commitment of a nonprisoner. Op Atty Gen, July 19, 1977, No. 5144.

Under former law, if there was no emergency, parental consent was required to be obtained for an operation upon unemancipated minor, and surgeon performed such operation at his own peril in absence of parental consent, but in case of emergency, rule was not required to be adhered to, and ordinary diligence was required in attempting to locate parent or person in loco parentis for consent, if practicable or possible before the operation. Op Atty Gen, May 14, 1956, No. 2435.

Department of corrections has authority to temporarily transfer prisoner from penal institution to which he was committed to some other state institution for neurological examination. (Construing similar provision of former act.) Op Atty Gen, August 23, 1944, No. 0–2614.

## § 791.265a. Extending limits of confinement; rules; escape from custody; eligibility for extensions of limits of confinement; placement in community residential home; definitions.
[MSA § 28.2325(1)]

Sec. 65a. (1) Under prescribed conditions, the director may extend the limits of confinement of a prisoner when there is reasonable assurance, after consideration of all facts and circumstances, that the prisoner will not become a menace to society or to the public safety, by authorizing the prisoner to do any of the following:

(a) Visit a specifically designated place or places. An extension of limits may be granted only to a prisoner housed in a state correctional facility to permit a visit to a critically ill relative, attendance at the funeral of a relative, or contacting prospective employers. The maximum amount of time a prisoner is eligible for an extension of the limits of confinement under this subdivision shall not exceed a cumulative total period of 30 days.

(b) Obtain medical services not otherwise available to a prisoner housed in a state correctional facility.

**§ 791.265a**                      **Department of Corrections**

(c) Work at paid employment, participate in a training or educational program, or participate in a community residential drug treatment program while continuing as a prisoner housed on a voluntary basis at a community corrections center or in a community residential home.

(2) The director shall promulgate rules to implement this section.

(3) The willful failure of a prisoner to remain within the extended limits of his or her confinement or to return within the time prescribed to an institution or facility designated by the director shall be considered an escape from custody as provided in section 193 of the Michigan penal code, 1931 PA 328, MCL 750.193.

(4) Subject to subsection (8), a prisoner, other than a prisoner subject to disciplinary time, who is convicted of a crime of violence or any assaultive crime is not eligible for the extensions of the limits of confinement provided in subsection (1) until the minimum sentence imposed for the crime has less than 180 days remaining.

(5) Subject to subsection (8), a prisoner subject to disciplinary time is not eligible for the extensions of the limits of confinement provided in subsection (1) until he or she has served the minimum sentence imposed for the crime.

(6) However, notwithstanding subsections (4) or (5), if the reason for the extension is to visit a critically ill relative, attend the funeral of a relative, or obtain medical services not otherwise available, the director may allow the extension under escort as provided in subsection (1).

(7) A prisoner serving a sentence for murder in the first degree is not eligible for the extensions of confinement under this section until a parole release date is established by the parole board and in no case before serving 15 calendar years with a good institutional adjustment.

(8) A prisoner who is convicted of a crime of violence or any assaultive crime, and whose minimum sentence imposed for the crime is 10 years or more, shall not be placed in a community residential home during any portion of his or her sentence.

(9) As used in this section:

(a) "Community corrections center" means a facility either contracted for or operated by the department in which a security staff is on duty 7 days per week, 24 hours per day.

(b) "Community residential home" means a location where electronic monitoring of prisoner presence is provided by the department 7 days per week, 24 hours per day, except that the department may waive the requirement that electronic monitoring be provided as to any prisoner who is within 3 months of his or her parole date.

(c) "State correctional facility" means a facility owned or leased by the department. State correctional facility does not include a community corrections center or community residential home.

**History:**
    Pub Acts 1953, No. 232, § 65a, as added by Pub Acts 1974, No. 68, imd eff April 1, 1974; amended by Pub Acts 1987, No. 271, imd eff December 29,

# Department of Corrections § 791.265a

1987; 1988, No. 272, imd eff July 15, 1988, by § 2 eff December 1, 1988; 1994, No. 217, eff June 27, 1994 (see 1994 note below).

Amended by Pub Acts 1997, No. 13, imd eff June 5, 1997; 1998, No. 315, imd eff July 30, 1998, by enacting § 1 eff December 15, 1998 (see 1998 note below).

**Editor's notes:**
**Pub Acts 1994, No. 217, §§2, 3,** eff June 27, 1994, provide:

"Section 2. This amendatory act shall take effect on the date that sentencing guidelines are enacted into law after the sentencing commission submits its report to the secretary of the senate and the clerk of the house of representatives pursuant to sections 31 to 34 of chapter IX of the code of criminal procedure, Act No. 175 of the Public Acts of 1927, as added by the amendatory act resulting from House Bill No. 4782 of the 87th Legislature [Pub Acts 1994, No. 445]. (**Repealed** by Pub Acts 1998, No. 316, imd eff July 30, 1998, by enacting § 2 eff December 15, 1998.).

"Section 3. This amendatory act shall not take effect unless all of the following bills of the 87th Legislature are enacted into law:

"(a) Senate Bill No. 41 [Pub Acts 1994, No. 218].

"(b) House Bill No. 4782 [Pub Acts 1994, No. 445].

"(c) House Bill No. 5439 [Pub Acts 1994, No. 322]."

**Pub Acts 1998, No. 315, enacting § 2,** imd eff July 30, 1998, by enacting § 1 eff December 15, 1998, provides:

"Enacting section 2. This amendatory act does not take effect unless all of the following bills of the 89th Legislature are enacted into law:

"(a) Senate Bill No. 826 [Pub Acts 1998, No. 316].

"(b) House Bill No. 4065 [Pub Acts 1998, No. 319].

"(c) House Bill No. 4444 [Pub Acts 1998, No. 311].

"(d) House Bill No. 4445 [Pub Acts 1998, No. 312].

"(e) House Bill No. 4446 [Pub Acts 1998, No. 313].

"(f) House Bill No. 4515 [Pub Acts 1998, No. 320].

"(g) House Bill No. 5419 [Pub Acts 1998, No. 317].

"(h) House Bill No. 5876 [Pub Acts 1998, No. 318]."

**Effect of amendment notes:**
**The 1994 amendment** made changes throughout the section.

**The 1997 amendment** in subsection (3), revised the statutory reference appearing at the end of the subsection; in subsection (4), twice added, "Subject to subsection (6), a"; added subsections (6) and (7); and in subsection (8), paragraph (b), replaced "facility" with "location" before "where electronic monitoring".

**The 1998 amendment** substituted "(8)" for "(6)" in subsection (4); redesignated the former second and third sentences of subsection (4) as subsections (5) and (6); substituted "(8)" for "(6)" and deleted "plus any disciplinary time" following "crime" in the redesignated subsection (5); inserted "notwithstanding subsections (4) or (5)," in the redesignated subsection (6); deleted former subsection (7); and redesignated former subsections (5), (6), and (8) as subsections (7), (8) and (9).

**Michigan Digest references:**
Convicts § 1.
Statutes § 55.

**ALR notes:**
Propriety of conditioning probation on defendant's not entering specified geographical area, 28 ALR4th 725.

## CASE NOTES

The legislature intended to allow the Department of Corrections to promulgate rules to address prison escape situations and also intended that the state prosecute individuals who fail to remain within the extended limits of their confinement under the prison escape statute. People v Roupe (1986) 150 Mich App 469, 389 NW2d 449, app den (1986) 426 Mich 863.

This section, providing that willful failure of a prisoner to return to prison facility following authorized furlough constitutes escape, would be held to be sufficiently germane, auxiliary or incidental to scope of mandatory legislation dealing with temporary furlough or work release programs under department of corrections act referring in its title to administration of penal institutions and powers and duties of department, thereby complying with "title-object" clause of constitution. People v Wade (1977) 77 Mich App 554, 258 NW2d 750.

State prison inmate who was removed from prison work-pass program had no protected liberty interest or other constitutional rights under § 1983 of Civil Rights Act, where inmate was removed pursuant to authorized discretionary generalized policy determination that prisoners under life sentences were ineligible for program, inmate was afforded opportunity for pre-termination hearing to contest his inclusion in this category and in addition was categorically ineligible to participate in program because of enabling statute itself excluding prisoners convicted of crimes of violence or any assaultive crime. Codd v Brown (1991, CA6 Mich) 949 F2d 879.

## § 791.265b. Disabled prisoner, power of director to transfer, duration of transfer; powers and duties of department; terms defined. [MSA § 28.2325(2)]

Sec. 65b. (1) As used in this section:

(a) "Medical institution" means that term as defined in section 106(2) of Act No. 280 of the Public Acts of 1939, as amended, being section 400.106 of the Michigan Compiled Laws.

(b) "Mentally or physically disabled prisoner" means a prisoner whose physical or mental health has deteriorated to a point which renders the prisoner a minimal threat to society.

(c) "Office of health care" means the office of health care in the department of corrections.

(2) The director may transfer a mentally or physically disabled prisoner to a medical institution for treatment and care. The transfer shall be effective for the duration of the prisoner's sentence, the duration of the existing medical condition causing the prisoner to be mentally or physically disabled, or for any other length of time considered necessary by the director, but shall not exceed the term of the sentence.

(3) The office of health care, upon the request of the director, shall determine whether a prisoner is mentally or physically disabled. The department of corrections shall continue its financial responsibility for the maintenance and care of any inmate transferred to a medical institution under this act. The department shall develop regulations for reimbursement to the institutions to which the parties are transferred.

**History:**
Pub Acts 1953, No. 232, § 65b, as added by Pub Acts 1980, No. 491, imd eff January 21, 1981.

**Michigan Digest references:**
Prisons and Jails §§4.30, 6.10, 6.50.

**Research references:**
60 Am Jur 2d, Penal and Correctional Institutions §§52, 56.

**Department of Corrections** § 791.265c

CASE NOTES

Summary judgment precluded where genuine issue of material fact existed as to whether inmate's transfer to psychiatric facility without determination that inmate was mentally or physically disabled constituted loss of protected liberty interest. Witzke v Johnson (1987, WD Mich) 656 F Supp 294.

**§ 791.265c. Work camp; construction, maintenance, operation, purpose; assignment of prisoners; displacement of employed persons or workers on strike or locked out; agreement of bargaining unit; citizens advisory committee; report; escape; reimbursement of department; collecting and dispersing wages; amount of wages; prevailing wages; rules; restrictions; conditions.** [MSA § 28.2325(3)]

Sec. 65c. (1) As used in this section, "work camp" means a correctional facility that houses prisoners who are made available for work as provided in subsection (3).

(2) The department may construct, maintain, and operate work camps for the purpose of housing prisoners who are under its jurisdiction.

(3) Prisoners assigned to work camps may be provided an opportunity to do any of the following, as long as the department has reasonable cause to believe the prisoner will honor the trust placed in him or her by such an assignment:

(a) Perform meaningful work at paid employment in the community.

(b) Provide labor on public works projects.

(c) Perform meaningful work on projects that serve the public interest or a charitable purpose and are operated by organizations that are exempt from taxation under section 501(c)(3) of the internal revenue code. Work performed by prisoners pursuant to this subdivision shall not result in a competitive disadvantage to a for profit enterprise.

(4) Prisoners made available for work under subsection (3)(c) shall not be assigned to work on projects in a manner that results in the displacement of employed persons in the community or the replacement of workers on strike or locked out of work. If a collective bargaining agreement is in effect at a place of employment that is the site of a proposed work project under subsection (3)(c), that bargaining unit must agree to the assignment of prisoners at the place of employment before the assignment is made.

(5) The warden at a correctional facility that makes prisoners available for work under subsection (3)(c) shall appoint a 7-member citizens advisory committee for the purpose of obtaining public input on proposals for assigning prisoners to work on those projects. The committee shall include broad representation from the community in which the proposed work project is to be located, including representatives of business, community service, and religious organizations and the president of the local AFL-CIO central labor council, or his or her designee. Before prisoners are assigned to a

**§ 791.265c**  **Department of Corrections**

proposed work project, the proposed assignment shall be reviewed by the citizens advisory committee.

(6) The department annually shall submit to the house and senate appropriations subcommittees on corrections a report on work projects in which prisoners are made available for work under subsection (3)(c), including, but not limited to, the number of work projects, the number of prisoners placed on each work project, the type of work performed, and any problems raised by an advisory committee with respect to the work project.

(7) The willful failure of a prisoner to report to or return from an assignment to paid employment in the community or on a public work project within the time prescribed, or to remain within the prescribed limits of such an assignment, shall be considered an escape from lawful custody as provided in section 193(3) of the Michigan penal code, Act No. 328 of the Public Acts of 1931, as amended, being section 750.193 of the Michigan Compiled Laws.

(8) Prisoners employed at paid employment in the community shall reimburse the department for food, clothing, and daily travel expenses to and from work for days worked.

(9) The wages of prisoners employed at paid employment in the community shall be collected by the work camp responsible for the prisoner's care.

(10) A work camp collecting wages of a prisoner pursuant to subsection (9) shall disperse wages collected in the following priority order:

(a) Reimbursement to the department pursuant to subsection (8).

(b) Support of the prisoner's dependents who are receiving public assistance up to the maximum of the public assistance benefit but not exceeding 50% of the prisoner's net earnings.

(c) For prisoners without dependents receiving public assistance, 50% of the prisoner's net earnings shall be placed, at the prisoner's option, in either the prisoner's personal noninstitutional savings account or in escrow by the department for use by the prisoner upon release.

(d) The balance, if any, to the prisoner's institutional account.

(11) An employer who employs a prisoner pursuant to this section for work to which Act No. 166 of the Public Acts of 1965, as amended, being sections 408.551 to 408.558 of the Michigan Compiled Laws, applies shall pay the prisoner the prevailing wage as provided in that act.

(12) An employer who employs a prisoner pursuant to this section for work that is not under Act No. 166 of the Public Acts of 1965, as amended, shall pay the prisoner not less than the wage the employer pays to other employees with similar skills and experience.

(13) The department shall promulgate rules pursuant to the Administrative procedures act of 1969, Act No. 306 of the Public Acts of 1969, as amended, being sections 24.201 to 24.328 of the Michigan Compiled Laws, to establish criteria by which the department shall determine eligibility for participation in the programs of paid

**Department of Corrections** § 791.265d

employment in the community established by this section.

**History:**
Pub Acts 1953, No. 232, § 65c, as added by Pub Acts 1981, No. 119, imd eff July 19, 1981; amended by Pub Acts 1993, No. 34, imd eff May 3, 1993.

**Research references:**
60 Am Jur 2d, Penal and Correctional Institutions §§34, 37–39.

### CASE NOTES

The Michigan Supreme Court has approved of an exclusion-by-category policy for use in defining eligibility for community placement residence programs; such a policy may be based upon statutory mandate or legislative intent or policy. Jansson v Department of Corrections (1985) 147 Mich App 774, 383 NW2d 152.

**§ 791.265d. Occurrences requiring entry in law enforcement information network; occurrences requiring certain information to be made available on line; time limitation; scope of entry; "state correctional facility" defined.** [MSA § 28.2325(4)]

Sec. 65d. (1) If 1 or more of the following occur, the department shall make an entry in the law enforcement information network:

(a) A prisoner escapes from a state correctional facility.

(b) A parole violation warrant is issued.

(2) If 1 or more of the following occur, the department shall make available on line to the law enforcement information network, by way of the corrections management information system, the following information:

(a) A prisoner is transferred into a community residential program.

(b) A prisoner is transferred into a minimum custody correctional facility of any kind, including a correctional camp or work camp.

(c) A person's parole status changes.

(3) An entry under subsection (1), or information under subsection (2), shall be entered or made available not later than 24 hours after the event occurs, and shall include the prisoner's name and former name, if any, physical descriptors, the remaining term of his or her sentence, and any other information determined relevant by the department.

(4) As used in this section, "state correctional facility" means a facility or institution which houses a prisoner population under the jurisdiction of the department.

**History:**
Pub Acts 1953, No. 232, § 65d, as added by Pub Acts 1988, No. 401, eff March 30, 1989, by § 2 eff upon expiration of 270 days after date of enactment.
Amended by Pub Acts 1996, No. 104, imd eff March 5, 1996, by § 2 eff April 1, 1996 (see 1996 note below).

**Editor's notes:**
**Pub Acts 1996, No. 104,** § 3, imd eff March 5, 1996, by § 2 eff April 1, 1996, provides:

**§ 791.265d**  **Department of Corrections**

"Section 3. This amendatory act shall not take effect unless Senate Bill No. 346 of the 88th Legislature [Pub Acts 1996, No. 106] is enacted into law."

**Effect of amendment notes:**
The **1996 amendment** made changes throughout the section.

## § 791.265e. Transfer of prisoner to community placement facility, notice to sheriffs, police posts and local police department; notice contents. [MSA § 28.2325(5)]

Sec. 65e. When a prisoner is transferred into a community placement facility of any kind, including a community corrections center, halfway house, or resident home, the department shall send notice of the transfer from the corrections management information system via the law enforcement information network to the sheriff and the Michigan state police post having jurisdiction over the county where the prisoner was originally sentenced, and to the local police department, the county sheriff and the Michigan state police post having jurisdiction over the community placement facility in which the prisoner is placed. The notice required under this section shall include the prisoner's name, the name of the community placement facility, crimes for which the prisoner is serving a sentence, and any other information determined relevant by the department.

**History:**
Pub Acts 1953, No. 232, § 65e, as added by Pub Acts 1988, No. 392, eff March 30, 1989, by § 2 eff upon expiration of 270 days after date of enactment.

## § 791.265f. Type of housing for prisoners convicted of assaultive crimes; prohibition of opening facilities or entering contracts for dwellings originally intended to house one family. [MSA § 28.2325(6)]

Sec. 65f. (1) Beginning September 30, 1990, a prisoner who is serving a sentence for conviction of an assaultive crime shall not be placed in a privately owned, noncommercial residential dwelling used for housing prisoners.

(2) Beginning on the effective date of this section, for the purpose of housing prisoners, the department shall not open a facility in, or enter into a new contract for, a dwelling originally constructed and intended to be used to house 1 family.

**History:**
Pub Acts 1953, No. 232, § 65f, as added by Pub Acts 1990, No. 160, imd eff July 2, 1990.

**LEXIS-NEXIS™ Michigan analytical references:**
Michigan Law and Practice, Convicts and Prisons § 4.

## § 791.265g. Definitions. [MSA § 28.2325(7)]

Sec. 65g. As used in this section and sections 65h and 65i:
(a) "Community corrections center" means that term as defined in section 65a.

(b) "Community residential home" means that term as defined in section 65a.

(c) "Community status criteria" means the criteria for determining which prisoners are eligible to be placed in community corrections facilities as prescribed in section 65(g)(1).

(d) "Council" means a citizens' council formed under section 65i(1).

(e) "Prisoner" means a person who is under the jurisdiction of the department and has not been released on parole or discharged.

(f) "State correctional facility" means that term as defined in section 65a.

**History:**
Pub Acts 1953, No. 232, § 65g, as added by Pub Acts 1990, No. 353, imd eff December 26, 1990.

**Statutory references:**
Sections 65, 65a, 65h and 65i, above referred to, are §§791.265, 791.265a, 791.265h and 791.265i.

**Michigan Digest references:**
Prisons and Jails § 8.

## § 791.265h. Placement of prisoner not meeting community status criteria; criteria requirements; location of community corrections center for prisoner placement; operation of center serving more than one county; conditions; limit on number of prisoners to be placed in center; prisoner curfew; random checking of prisoners allowed off premises. [MSA § 28.2325(8)]

Sec. 65h. (1) A prisoner who does not meet the community status criteria shall not be placed in a community corrections center or community residential home. The community status criteria include all of the following requirements:

(a) The prisoner has been given a level I security classification by the department's bureau of correctional facilities, on a scale of 6 levels in which level I is the least restrictive level.

(b) The prisoner is not serving a sentence for conviction of a crime of escape under section 193 of the Michigan penal code, Act No. 328 of the Public Acts of 1931, being section 750.193 of the Michigan Compiled Laws.

(c) The prisoner is not serving a sentence for conviction of a criminal sexual conduct offense listed in section 2a(1) of chapter IX of the code of criminal procedure, Act No. 175 of the Public Acts of 1927, being section 769.2a of the Michigan Compiled Laws.

(d) The prisoner is not classified as a very high assault risk according to the department's risk screening criteria.

(e) The prisoner does not have any pending felony charges against him or her, and is not subject to a detainer request from another jurisdiction by which the prisoner, upon his or her release, would be returned to that other jurisdiction to begin serving another felony sentence.

(f) The prisoner has not been given a special designation by the department which would prevent his or her placement.

(g) If the prisoner is serving a sentence for conviction of a crime of violence or an assaultive crime, as defined by rules of the department, the prisoner has less than 180 days remaining on his or her minimum sentence, and otherwise meets the community placement requirements of section 65a.

(h) If the prisoner is not subject to the 180-day rule described in subdivision (g), the prisoner is being placed no earlier in that prisoner's sentence than is allowed by the administrative rules of the department.

(2) Except as provided in subsections (3) and (4), a prisoner who is placed in a community corrections center shall be placed in a center that is located in 1 of the following:

(a) The county of the prisoner's most recent residence as listed on the prisoner's presentence report.

(b) A county in which the prisoner's spouse, parent, grandparent, brother, sister, or child resides.

(3) Subsection (2) does not prohibit the department from operating a community corrections center that serves more than 1 county. Any prisoner placed in such a center shall meet the conditions of subsection (2)(a) or (b) of the counties the center serves.

(4) Notwithstanding subsection (2), not more than 10% of the prisoner population of any community corrections center, at any 1 time, may consist of prisoners who would not be placed in that community corrections center according to the provisions of subsection (2).

(5) The department shall establish a curfew for every prisoner placed in a community corrections center.

(6) Random checks shall be conducted for all prisoners who are allowed off the premises of the community corrections center for purposes of employment, seeking employment, attending school, receiving treatment, or for any other approved reason. The random checks shall be for the purpose of verifying that each prisoner allowed off the premises is participating as scheduled in the function for which he or she is allowed off the premises.

**History:**
Pub Acts 1953, No. 232, § 65h, as added by Pub Acts 1990, No. 353, imd eff December 26, 1990.

**Statutory references:**
Section 65a is § 791.265a.

**LEXIS-NEXIS™ Michigan analytical references:**
Michigan Law and Practice, Convicts and Prisons § 4.

**§ 791.265i. Citizens' council in municipality where community corrections center located; members, appointment, residency requirements; chairperson; meetings; meeting with center supervisor; report by supervisor on prisoner numbers, activities, etc.; designee to act on supervisor's behalf; notice by council of placement believed in violation of criteria; review of record, reclassification of prisoner; annual report by council; duties of council.** [MSA § 28.2325(9)]

Sec. 65i. (1) The legislative body of a city, village, or township in which a community corrections center is located may form a 5-member citizens' council by sending written notice of its intention to form a citizens' council to the board of commissioners of the county in which the city, village, or township is located.

(2) Within 30 days after receiving the notice, the county board of commissioners or, in a county that has a county executive, the county executive subject to the concurrence of the county board of commissioners, shall appoint 5 members to the council. Three of the members shall be residents of the city, village, or township in which the community corrections center is located. The remaining 2 members need not be residents of that city, village, or township, but shall be residents of the county. Each member shall serve at the pleasure of the county board of commissioners or county executive that appointed that member.

(3) A citizens' council shall select a chairperson from among its members and other officers necessary for conducting the council's business. A citizens' council shall meet at a place and time determined by the chairperson.

(4) The supervisor of a community corrections center, at the request of the chairperson of the citizens' council in whose jurisdiction that community corrections center is located, shall meet with the council and, if requested by the chairperson, shall provide to the council any of the following information for that community corrections center for the reporting period agreed to by the chairperson and the center supervisor:

(a) The number of prisoners placed in the community corrections center and the number of prisoners returned from the community corrections center to a state correctional facility.

(b) The institutional number, record of convictions, and term of sentence of each prisoner placed in the center, and a summary of the disciplinary problems or major misconduct citations, if any, for each of those prisoners while in the center; and written documentation verifying that the prisoners in the community corrections center were in compliance with the community status criteria on the date of their placement into the community corrections center. The written information provided under this subsection, and all copies of that information, may be distributed to the committee only for the duration of the meeting, and after the meeting shall be retained by the supervisor of the community corrections center or his or her designee.

(c) The number of prisoners in the center who, while in the

**§ 791.265i**                      **Department of Corrections**

center, tested positive for the presence of alcohol or controlled substances, resulting in a major misconduct violation.

(d) The number of prisoners who were apprehended and charged with the commission of a new criminal offense while in the center, or after they had escaped from the center and before they had been recaptured.

(e) The number of incidents resulting in a major misconduct violation in which a prisoner placed in the center was absent from the center without authorization, or failed to report to employment, school, treatment, or other destination as to which the prisoner's absence from the center was authorized.

(f) The number of prisoners in the center who are in treatment programs, and a summary of the services offered by those programs.

(g) The number of prisoners in the center who are employed, and the number who are in education programs.

(h) The number of personnel employed at the center and their job classifications, and the number and job classification of any personnel positions at the center that are not filled at the time of the report.

(5) A center supervisor shall not be required to meet with a citizens' council more often than once each month. If the center supervisor is unavailable at the time of a meeting called pursuant to subsection (4), the regional supervisor may appoint a designee to act on the center supervisor's behalf. If a community corrections center does not have a center supervisor, the duties of the center supervisor under this section shall be performed by a regional supervisor, field agent, or other person designated by the department as being generally responsible for overseeing the daily operation of that community corrections center.

(6) If a citizens' council believes that the placement of a prisoner into a community corrections center within its jurisdiction was made in violation of the community status criteria, the council shall give written or verbal notice to the center supervisor. If the center supervisor believes that the council was incorrect in its determination, the center supervisor or his or her designee shall meet with the council or chairperson of the council within 2 business days after receiving the notice, and shall review the prisoner's record and the community placement criteria and shall determine whether or not the placement violates the community placement criteria. If it is determined by the center supervisor that the placement does violate the community placement criteria, the department shall reclassify the prisoner to be returned to a state correctional facility.

(7) Each citizens' council may report annually to the county board of commissioners for that county or, in a county that has a county executive, to the county executive, and the state representatives and state senators for that district. The report shall describe the effect on the city, village, or township and the surrounding communities of the community corrections centers in the council's jurisdiction, and shall include a summary of information provided to the council under subsection (4).

(8) A citizens' council also shall do all of the following:
(a) Act as a liaison between the residents of the area affected by the community corrections center or centers in its jurisdiction and the department as to issues concerning the center or centers.
(b) Review policies and procedures governing the operation of the center or centers in its jurisdiction, including placement and supervision standards.

**History:**
Pub Acts 1953, No. 232, § 65i, as added by Pub Acts 1990, No. 353, imd eff December 26, 1990.

**LEXIS-NEXIS™ Michigan analytical references:**
Michigan Law and Practice, Convicts and Prisons § 4.

## § 791.266. Commitment for classification; place. [MSA § 28.2326]

Sec. 66. For the purpose of classification, all convicted prisoners shall be committed by courts of criminal jurisdiction of the state, to the commission, at a place to be designated by the commission.

**History:**
Pub Acts 1953, No. 232, § 66, eff October 2, 1953.

**Michigan Digest references:**
Criminal Law and Procedure § 739.
Prisons and Jails § 4.

**Research references:**
60 Am Jur 2d, Penal and Correctional Institutions § 8.

### CASE NOTES

The legislature seems to have the right to prescribe where persons convicted of crime shall be confined. Detroit v Wayne County Auditors (1880) 43 Mich 169, 5 NW 77 (superseded on other grounds by statute as stated in Recorder's Court of Detroit v Detroit (1984) 134 Mich App 239, 351 NW2d 289).

Where commitment form used by justice of the peace of Genesee county to commit a woman as a common prostitute to the Detroit House of Correction, held that the woman's imprisonment in that institution was unlawful, not being authorized under former statutes with respect to persons convicted in counties other than Wayne. In re Weinrich (1870) 20 Mich 14.

Writ of superintending control to prevent placement of certain persons detained for trial or sentence in Detroit House of Correction would not issue where there was statutorily authorized agreement between city and county for such placement, and terms of such agreement were not breached by defendant county officials. Detroit v Sullivan (1973) 47 Mich App 106, 209 NW2d 255.

State prisoner in Detroit House of Correction would be held to be member of public community even though, while incarcerated, he was prevented by law from exercising rights and privileges he enjoyed as free member of society. Green v State (1971) 30 Mich App 648, 186 NW2d 792, affd (1971) 386 Mich 459, 192 NW2d 491.

Contempt of court was not a crime which came within meaning of former section. Op Atty Gen, November 30, 1948, No. 853.

**§ 791.267. Temporary confinement; study of prisoner; suitability of prisoner to type of rehabilitation required; report; execution of confinement order; test for HIV or antibody to HIV; applicability of subsection (2); housing prisoner in administrative segregation, inpatient health care unit, or unit separate from general prisoner population; reporting positive test result; exposure of employee to blood or body fluid of prisoner; testing employee; employee equipment; HIV positive prisoner not to work in health facility; seroprevalence study; disclosure of test results; counseling; AIDS education program; report; definitions.** [MSA § 28.2327]

Sec. 67. (1) Quarters for temporary confinement apart from those of regular inmates shall be provided for convicted prisoners upon commitment at each of the state correctional facilities, which the director shall designate as a reception center. Within 60 days after the arrival of a convicted prisoner at such a state correctional facility, the classification committee shall make and complete a comprehensive study of the prisoner, including physical and psychiatric examinations, to ensure that the prisoner is confined in the state correctional facility suited to the type of rehabilitation required in his or her case. The warden of the state correctional facility shall deliver a report of the study of the classification committee to the deputy director of the correctional facilities administration, who shall, within 5 days after receipt of the report, execute an order to confine the prisoner in the state correctional facility determined as suitable by the deputy director.

(2) Immediately upon arrival at a reception center designated pursuant to subsection (1), each incoming prisoner shall undergo a test for HIV or an antibody to HIV. This subsection does not apply if an incoming prisoner has been tested for HIV or an antibody to HIV under section 5129 of the public health code, Act No. 368 of the Public Acts of 1978, being section 333.5129 of the Michigan Compiled Laws, within the 3 months immediately preceding the date of the prisoner's arrival at the reception center, as indicated by the record transferred to the department by the court under that section.

(3) If a prisoner receives a positive test result and is subsequently subject to discipline by the department for sexual misconduct that could transmit HIV, illegal intravenous use of controlled substances, or assaultive or predatory behavior that could transmit HIV, the department shall house that prisoner in administrative segregation, an inpatient health care unit, or a unit separate from the general prisoner population, as determined by the department.

(4) The department shall report each positive test result to the department of community health, in compliance with section 5114 of Act No. 368 of the Public Acts of 1978, being section 333.5114 of the Michigan Compiled Laws.

(5) If an employee of the department sustains a percutaneous, mucous membrane, or open wound exposure to the blood or body

**Department of Corrections** § 791.267

fluid of a prisoner, the employee may, and the department shall, proceed under section 67b.

(6) Upon the request of an employee of the department, the department shall provide or arrange for a test for HIV or an antibody to HIV for that employee, free of charge.

(7) Upon the request of an employee of the department, the department shall provide to that employee the equipment necessary to implement universal precautions to prevent transmission of HIV infection.

(8) A prisoner who receives a positive HIV test result under subsection (5) shall not work in a health facility operated by the department.

(9) The department shall conduct a seroprevalence study of the prisoners in all state correctional facilities to determine the percentage of prisoners who are HIV infected.

(10) The results of a test for HIV or an antibody to HIV conducted under this section shall be disclosed by the department pursuant to section 67b.

(11) The deputy director of the correctional facilities administration shall take steps to ensure that all prisoners who receive HIV testing receive counseling regarding AIDS including, at a minimum, treatment, transmission, and protective measures.

(12) The department, in conjunction with the department of community health, shall develop and implement a comprehensive AIDS education program designed specifically for correctional environments. The program shall be conducted by the bureau within the department responsible for health care, for staff and for prisoners at each state correctional facility.

(13) By March 30, 1991, the department shall submit a report regarding the testing component, managerial aspects, and effectiveness of subsections (2) to (12) to the senate and house committees with jurisdiction over matters pertaining to corrections, and to the senate and house committees with jurisdiction over matters pertaining to public health.

(14) As used in this section:

(a) "AIDS" means acquired immunodeficiency syndrome.

(b) "HIV" means human immunodeficiency virus.

(c) "Positive test result" means a double positive enzyme-linked immunosorbent assay test, combined with a positive western blot assay test, or a positive test under an HIV test that is considered reliable by the federal centers for disease control and is approved by the department of community health.

**History:**
Pub Acts 1953, No. 232, § 67, eff October 2, 1953; amended by Pub Acts 1960, No. 103, imd eff April 26, 1960; 1988, No. 510, eff March 30, 1989, by § 2 eff January 1, 1989.
Amended by Pub Acts 1996, No. 565, imd eff January 16, 1997.

**Effect of amendment notes:**
The **1996 amendment** made changes throughout the section.

**Statutory references:**
Section 67b is § 791.267b.

**§ 791.267**

**Cross references:**
Classification of prisoners, §§791.264, 791.266.

**Michigan Digest references:**
Prisons and Jails § 4.

**Research references:**
60 Am Jur 2d Penal and Correctional Institutions §§8–10, 53, 54.

### CASE NOTES

MCL 333.5127, which allows minors to consent to the provision of medical or surgical care, treatment or services by a hospital, clinic or physician if the minor is or professes to be infected with a venereal disease or HIV, applies to minors in the custody of the Michigan Department of Corrections. Op Atty Gen, November 29, 1994, No. 6823.

### § 791.267a. Nonemergency medical, dental, or optometric services; intentional injury; copayment or payment by prisoner; on-site medical treatment; report on feasibility and cost. [MSA § 28.2327(1)]

Sec. 67a. (1) A prisoner who receives nonemergency medical, dental, or optometric services at his or her request is responsible for a copayment fee to the department for those services, as determined by the department. If the prisoner is a minor, the prisoner's parent or guardian is also responsible for services.

(2) A prisoner who intentionally injures himself or herself, and receives emergency medical care for that injury is responsible for the entire cost of the medical care, rather than the copayment described in subsection (1).

(3) The department shall determine whether those prisoners who injure themselves intentionally shall be housed in a facility designed to allow on-site medical treatment of those injuries. Not later than 6 months after the effective date of this section, the director of the department shall report to the legislature on the feasibility and cost of implementing this subsection.

**History:**
Pub Acts 1953, No. 232, § 67a, as added by Pub Acts 1996, No. 234, eff 90 days from end of 1996 legislative session (see Mich. Const. note below).

**Editor's notes:**
**Michigan Constitution of 1963, Art. IV, § 27,** provides:
"No act shall take effect until the expiration of 90 days from the end of the session at which it was passed, but the legislature may give immediate effect to acts by a two-thirds vote of the members elected to and serving in each house."

**LEXIS-NEXIS™ Michigan analytical references:**
Michigan Law and Practice, Convicts and Prisons § 4.

**Department of Corrections** § 791.267b

**§ 791.267b. Exposure of employee to blood or body fluid of prisoner; request to test prisoner for HIV or HBV infection; form and contents of request; determination; prisoner consent not required; counseling; determination not requiring HIV or HBV infection testing; notice of HIV or HBV test results; confidentiality; forms; violation of subsection (8) as misdemeanor; report; definitions.** [MSA § 28.2327(2)]

Sec. 67b. (1) If an employee of the department sustains a percutaneous, mucous membrane, or open wound exposure to the blood or body fluids of a prisoner, the employee may request that the prisoner be tested for HIV infection or HBV infection, or both, pursuant to this section.

(2) An employee shall make a request described in subsection (1) to the department in writing on a form provided by the department within 72 hours after the exposure occurs. The request form shall be dated and shall contain at a minimum the name and address of the employee making the request and a description of his or her exposure to the blood or other body fluids of the prisoner. The request form shall contain a space for the information required under subsection (6) and a statement that the requester is subject to the confidentiality requirements of subsection (8) and section 5131 of the public health code, Act No. 368 of the Public Acts of 1978, being section 333.5131 of the Michigan Compiled Laws. The request form shall not contain information that would identify the prisoner.

(3) Upon receipt of a request under this section, The department shall make a determination as to whether or not there is reasonable cause to believe that the exposure described in the request occurred and if it was a percutaneous, mucous membrane, or open wound exposure pursuant to R 325.70001 to R 325.70018 of the Michigan administrative code. If the department determines that there is reasonable cause to believe that the exposure described in the request occurred and was a percutaneous, mucous membrane, or open wound exposure, the department shall test the prisoner for HIV infection or HBV infection, or both, as indicated in the request, subject to subsection (4).

(4) In order to protect the health, safety, and welfare of department employees, the department may test a prisoner under subsection (3) whether or not the prisoner consents to the test. The department is not required to give the prisoner an opportunity for a hearing or to obtain an order from a court of competent jurisdiction before administering the test.

(5) The department is not required to provide HIV counseling pursuant to section 5133(1) of Act No. 368 of the Public Acts of 1978, being section 333.5133 of the Michigan Compiled Laws, to an employee who requests that a prisoner be tested for HIV under this section, unless the department tests the employee for HIV.

(6) The department shall comply with this subsection if the department receives a request under this section and determines either that there is not reasonable cause to believe the requester's description of his or her exposure or that the exposure was not a

percutaneous, mucous membrane, or open wound exposure and as a result of the determination the department is not required to test the prisoner for HIV infection or HBV infection, or both. The department shall state in writing on the request form the reason it determined there was not reasonable cause to believe the requester's description of his or her exposure or for the department's determination that the exposure was not a percutaneous, mucous membrane, or open wound exposure, as applicable. The department shall transmit a copy of the completed request form to the requesting individual within 2 days after the date the department makes the determination described in this subsection.

(7) The department shall notify the requesting employee of the HIV or HBV test results, or both, whether positive or negative, within 2 days after the test results are obtained by the department. The notification shall be transmitted directly to the requesting employee or, upon request of the requesting employee, to his or her primary care physician or other health professional designated by the employee. The notice required under this subsection shall include an explanation of the confidentiality requirements of subsection (8).

(8) The notice required under subsection (7) shall not contain information that would identify the prisoner who tested positive or negative for HIV or HBV. The information contained in the notice is confidential and is subject to this section, the rules promulgated under section 5111(2) of Act No. 368 of the Public Acts of 1978, being section 333.5111 of the Michigan Compiled Laws, and section 5131 of Act No. 368 of the Public Acts of 1978, being section 333.5131 of the Michigan Compiled Laws. A person who receives confidential information under this section shall disclose the information to others only to the extent consistent with the authorized purpose for which the information was obtained.

(9) The department shall develop and distribute the forms required under this section.

(10) In addition to the penalties prescribed in the rules promulgated under section 5111(2) of Act No. 368 of the Public Acts of 1978 and in section 5131 of Act No. 368 of the Public Acts of 1978, a person who discloses information in violation of subsection (8) is guilty of a misdemeanor.

(11) The department shall report to the department of community health each test result obtained under this section that indicates that an individual is HIV infected, in compliance with section 5114 of Act No. 368 of the Public Acts of 1978, being section 333.5114 of the Michigan Compiled Laws.

(12) As used in this section:

(a) "Employee" means an individual who is employed by or under contract to the department of corrections.

(b) "HBV" means hepatitis B virus.

(c) "HBV infected" or "HBV infection" means the status of an individual who is tested as HBsAg-positive.

(d) "HIV" means human immunodeficiency virus.

(e) "HIV infected" means that term as defined in section 5101 of Act No. 368 of the Public Acts of 1978, being section 333.5101 of the Michigan Compiled Laws.

**History:**
Pub Acts 1953, No. 232, § 67b, as added by Pub Acts 1996, No. 565, imd eff January 16, 1997.

**LEXIS-NEXIS™ Michigan analytical references:**
Michigan Law and Practice, Convicts and Prisons § 4.

**§ 791.268. Payment of filing fees or costs by prisoner; court order to make monthly payments; removal of amount from prisoner institutional account.** [MSA § 28.2328]

Sec. 68. If a prisoner is ordered by a court to make monthly payments for the purpose of paying the balance of filing fees or costs under section 2963 of the revised judicature act of 1961, Act No. 236 of the Public Acts of 1961, being section 600.2963 of the Michigan Compiled Laws, the department shall remove those amounts from the institutional account of the prisoner subject to the order and, when an amount equal to the balance of the filing fees or costs due is removed, remit that amount as directed in the order.

**History:**
Pub Acts 1953, No. 232, § 68, as added by Pub Acts 1996, No. 556, eff January 16, 1997 (see 1996 note below).

**Editor's notes:**
Former § 791.268 was added by Pub Acts 1968, No. 306 and repealed by Pub Acts 1974, No. 258, by § 1102(1) eff August 6, 1975. It dealt with, inter alia, psychiatric examination of prisoners. For current provisions, see §§330.2000 et seq.
**Pub Acts 1996, No. 556, § 2,** eff January 16, 1997, provides:
"Section 2. This amendatory act shall not take effect unless all of the following bills of the 88th Legislature are enacted into law:
"(a) Senate Bill No. 1214 [Pub Acts 1996, No. 554].
"(b) Senate Bill No. 1215 [Pub Acts 1996, No. 555]."

**§ 791.269. [Repealed]** [MSA § 28.2329]

**History:**
Pub Acts 1953, No. 232, § 69, as added by Pub Acts 1988, No. 469, imd eff December 27, 1988; **repealed** by Pub Acts 1995, No. 18, imd eff April 12, 1995.

**Editor's notes:**
Former § 791.269 pertained to cell occupancy requirements for new housing or facilities.

**CASE NOTES**

It is improper for a sentencing court to lengthen a defendant's sentence as a buffer against possible sentence time reductions resulting from invocation of the Prison Overcrowding Emergency Powers Act. People v King (1987) 158 Mich App 672, 405 NW2d 116.

A trial court may not increase a defendant's sentence based on speculation and conjecture that the 90-day time-cut provisions of the Prison Overcrowding Emergency Powers Act will continue to be implemented in the future or be utilized with the same frequency and regu-

**§ 791.269**            **Department of Corrections**

larity as in the past. People v Lundy (1985) 145 Mich App 847, 378 NW2d 622.

### § 791.269a. Subjecting visitor to pat down search; condition; waiver; definitions. [MSA § 28.2329(1)]

Sec. 69a. (1) A visitor to a state correctional facility shall not be subjected to a pat down search unless every person performing or assisting in performing the pat down search is of the same sex as the person being searched. If the necessary personnel are not readily available, a visitor at his or her option may sign a waiver provided by the department of corrections, waiving the provisions of this subsection.

(2) As used in this section:

(a) "Pat down search" means a search of a person in which the person conducting the search touches the body or clothing, or both, of the person being searched to detect the presence of concealed objects.

(b) "State correctional facility" includes a youth correctional facility operated under section 20g by the department or a private vendor.

**History:**
Pub Acts 1953, No. 232, § 69a, as added by Pub Acts 1990, No. 42, imd eff March 20, 1990.
Amended by Pub Acts 1998, No. 512, imd eff January 8, 1999.

**Effect of amendment notes:**
**The 1998 amendment** redesignated part of subsection (2) as (2)(a), added subsection (2)(b), and made grammatical changes.

**Statutory references:**
Section 20g, above referred to, is § 791.220g.

**LEXIS-NEXIS™ Michigan analytical references:**
Michigan Law and Practice, Convicts and Prisons § 4.

## CHAPTER V

## BUREAU OF PRISON INDUSTRIES

### § 791.270. Monitoring of telephone communications; conditions; disclosure of obtained information; evidence in criminal prosecution; definitions. [MSA § 28.2330]

Sec. 70. (1) A correctional facility may monitor telephone communications over telephones available for use by prisoners in the correctional facility if all of the following conditions are met:

(a) The director promulgates rules under which the monitoring is to be conducted, and the monitoring is conducted in accordance with those rules. The rules shall include provisions for minimizing the intrusiveness of the monitoring and shall prescribe a procedure by which a prisoner may make telephone calls to his or her attorney, and any federal, state, or local public official if requested by that public official, that are not monitored.

(b) The monitoring is routinely conducted for the purpose of preserving the security and orderly management of the correctional facility, interdicting drugs and other contraband, and protecting the public, and is performed by employees of the department or, in the case of a youth correctional facility operated by a private vendor under section 20g, is conducted by employees of the private vendor.

(c) Notices are prominently posted on or near each telephone subject to monitoring informing users of the telephone that communications over the telephone may be monitored.

(d) In addition to the posting of notices under subdivision (c), the prisoners in the correctional facility are given reasonable notice of the rules promulgated under subdivision (a).

(e) Each party to the conversation is notified by voice that the conversation is being monitored.

(2) A correctional facility shall disclose information obtained pursuant to this section regarding a crime or attempted crime to any law enforcement agency having jurisdiction over that crime or attempted crime.

(3) Evidence obtained pursuant to this section regarding a crime or attempted crime may be considered as evidence in a criminal prosecution for that crime or attempted crime.

(4) As used in this section:

(a) "Correctional facility" includes a youth correctional facility operated under section 20g by the department or a private vendor.

(b) "Monitor" means to listen to or record, or both.

**History:**
Pub Acts 1953, No. 232, § 70, as added by Pub Acts 1993, No. 255, imd eff November 29, 1993 (see 1993 note below).
Amended by Pub Acts 1998, No. 512, imd eff January 8, 1999.

**Editor's notes:**
**Pub Acts 1993, No. 255, § 2,** imd eff November 29, 1993, provides:
"Section 2. This amendatory act shall not take effect unless House Bill No. 4223 of the 87th Legislature [Act No. 227 of 1993] is enacted into law."

**Effect of amendment notes:**
**The 1998 amendment** added and deleted material in subsection (1)(b), redesignated part of subsection (4) as (4)(b), and added subsection (4)(a).

**Statutory references:**
Section 20g, above referred to, is § 791.220g.

**Michigan Administrative Code:**
Michigan Administrative Code R 791.1101–791.9930.

**LEXIS-NEXIS™ Michigan analytical references:**
Michigan Law and Practice, Convicts and Prisons § 4.

## § 791.271. Control and supervision of industrial plants by assistant director; bureau personnel, appointment. [MSA § 28.2331]

Sec. 71. The assistant director of the bureau of prison industries is hereby vested with the control, management, coordination and supervision of the industrial plants connected with the several penal

§ 791.271                        Department of Corrections

institutions, and subject to the approval of the director shall appoint all bureau personnel as may be necessary.

**History:**
Pub Acts 1953, No. 232, § 71, eff October 2, 1953.

**Michigan Digest references:**
Prisons and Jails §§1, 3.

## CHAPTER VI

## MISCELLANEOUS

**§ 791.281. Transfer of powers and duties to new department of corrections; abolition of and successor to former department; pending hearings or proceedings not to abate; transfer of records and files; continuation of former orders, rules and regulations.** [MSA § 28.2341]

Sec. 81. The powers and duties vested by law in the state department of corrections created under the provisions of Act No. 4 of the Public Acts of the Second Extra Session of 1947, as amended, being sections 791.1 to 791.123, inclusive, of the Compiled Laws of 1948, are hereby transferred to and vested in the state department of corrections herein created. Immediately on the taking effect of this act the state department of corrections created under said Act No. 4 of the Public Acts of the Second Extra Session of 1947, as amended, shall be abolished, and the state department of corrections herein created shall be the successor to all the powers, duties and responsibilities thereof, and whenever reference is made in any law of the state to the department of corrections reference shall be deemed to be intended to be made to the state department of corrections herein created. Any hearing or other proceeding pending before the state department of corrections created under Act No. 4 of the Public Acts of the Second Extra Session of 1947, as amended, shall not be abated but shall be deemed to be transferred to the department created under the provisions of this act, and shall be conducted and determined thereby in accordance with the provisions of the law governing such hearing or proceeding. All records, files and other papers belonging to the state department of corrections created under Act No. 4 of the Public Acts of the Second Extra Session of 1947, as amended, shall be turned over to the state department of corrections created under this act and shall be continued as a part of the records and files thereof. All orders and rules and regulations shall continue in effect at the pleasure of the department created under the provisions of this act, acting within its lawful authority. All of the powers and duties vested in the state department of corrections created under Act No. 4 of the Public Acts of the Second Extra Session of 1947, as amended, shall be transferred to and vested in the department of corrections created under this act.

**History:**
Pub Acts 1953, No. 232, § 81, eff October 2, 1953.

**Former acts:**
See Pub Acts 1921, No. 163, § 5, and Pub Acts 1937, No. 257, which were repealed by Pub Acts 1939, No. 280; Pub Acts 1921, No. 403, § 1, which was repealed by Pub Acts 1937, No. 255; Pub Acts 1947 (2nd Ex Sess), No. 4.

Chapter V, § 1, of Act 255 of 1937, which was repealed by Pub Acts 1947 (2nd Ex Sess), No. 4, abolished state prison commission and offices of director of prison industry and commissioner of pardons and paroles and transferred their powers and duties to department of corrections created by Act 255 of 1937.

### CASE NOTES

Department of corrections could convey land by authority of former Michigan Statues Annotated section 28.1661. (Construing former act.) Op Atty Gen, July 13, 1942, No. 24166.

## § 791.282. Transfers of appropriations. [MSA § 28.2342]

Sec. 82. The provisions of any other law to the contrary notwithstanding, for the fiscal year ending June 30, 1954, the commission may, with the approval of the state administrative board, make such transfers of appropriations as are necessary to carry out the intent of this act.

**History:**
Pub Acts 1953, No. 232, § 82, eff October 2, 1953.

## § 791.283. Repeal of other provisions. [MSA § 28.2343]

Sec. 83. Act No. 4 of the Public Acts of the Second Extra Session of 1947, as amended, being sections 791.1 to 791.123, inclusive, of the Compiled Laws of 1948, is hereby repealed.

**History:**
Pub Acts 1953, No. 232, § 83, eff October 2, 1953.

## MICHIGAN DEPARTMENT OF CORRECTIONS–MICHIGAN CORRECTIONS COMMISSION

Executive Reorganization Order 1991-12, p 1282, eff April 23, 1991

### § 791.302. Department of Corrections; transfer to new Department. [MSA § 28.2355(101)]

Whereas, Article V, Section 1, of the Constitution of the State of Michigan of 1963 vests the executive power in the Governor; and

Whereas, Article V, Section 2, of the Constitution of the State of Michigan of 1963 empowers the Governor to make changes in the organization of the Executive Branch or in the assignment of functions among its units which he considers necessary for efficient administration; and

Whereas, Article V, Section 8, of the Constitution of the State of Michigan of 1963 provides that each principal department shall be under the supervision of the Governor, unless otherwise provided by the Constitution; and

Whereas, the Department of Corrections was created by Act No. 232 of the Public Acts of 1953, as amended, being Section 791.201 et seq. of the Michigan Compiled Laws; and

Whereas, the Michigan Corrections Commission was created by, and given certain functions, duties, and responsibilities in Act No. 232 of the Public Acts of 1953, as amended, being Section 791.201 et seq. of the Michigan Compiled Laws; and

Whereas, the functions, duties, and responsibilities assigned to the Michigan Corrections Commission can be more effectively carried out by the Director of Corrections and the Governor; and

Whereas, it is necessary in the interests of efficient administration and effectiveness of government to effect changes in the organization of the Executive Branch of government.

Now, Therefore, I, John Engler, Governor of the State of Michigan, pursuant to the powers vested in me by Article V, Section 1, Article V, Section 2, and Article V, Section 8 of the Constitution of the State of Michigan of 1963 and the laws of the State of Michigan, do hereby order the following:

1. The Department of Corrections, created under Section 1 of Act No. 232 of the Public Acts of 1953, as amended, being Section 791.201 of the Michigan Compiled Laws, is transferred by a Type I transfer, as defined by Section 3 of Act No. 380 of the Public Acts of 1965, being Section 16.103 of the Michigan Compiled Laws, to a new Michigan Department of Corrections.

2. All the statutory authority, powers, duties, functions, and responsibilities of the Michigan Corrections Commission are hereby transferred to the Director of the new Michigan Department of Corrections, as head of the Michigan Department of Corrections, by a Type III transfer, as defined by Section 3 of Act

**Department of Corrections** § 791.302

No. 380 of the Public Acts of 1965, being Section 16.103 of the Michigan Compiled Laws, except the power to appoint the Director of Corrections contained in Section 3 of Act No. 232 of the Public Acts of 1953, being Section 791.203 of the Michigan Compiled Laws.

3. Pursuant to Article V, Section 1, Article V, Section 2, and Article V, Section 8 of the Constitution of the State of Michigan of 1963, the power to appoint the Director of the new Michigan Department of Corrections is hereby vested in the Governor.

4. The Director of the new Michigan Department of Corrections shall provide executive direction and supervision for the implementation of the transfer. The assigned functions, except the power to appoint the Director, shall be administered under the direction and supervision of the Director, and all prescribed functions of rule making, licensing, and registration, including the prescription of rules, regulations, standards, and adjudications, shall be transferred to the Director of the new Michigan Department of Corrections.

5. All records, personnel, property, and unexpended balances of appropriations, allocations, and other funds used, held, employed, available, or to be made available to the Michigan Corrections Commission for the activities transferred to the new Michigan Department of Corrections by this Order are hereby transferred to the new Michigan Department of Corrections.

6. The Director of the new Michigan Department of Corrections shall immediately develop a memorandum of record identifying any pending settlements, issues of compliance with applicable federal and State laws and regulations, or other obligations to be resolved by the Michigan Corrections Commission.

7. All rules, orders, contracts, and agreements relating to the assigned functions lawfully adopted prior to the effective date of this Order shall continue to be effective until revised, amended, or repealed.

8. Any suit, action, or other proceeding lawfully commenced by, against, or before any entity affected by this Order shall not abate by reason of the taking effect of this Order. Any suit, action, or other proceeding may be maintained by, against, or before the appropriate successor of any entity affected by this Order.

In fulfillment of the requirement of Article V, Section 2, of the Constitution of the State of Michigan of 1963, the provisions of this Executive Order shall become effective 60 days after the filing of this Executive Order.

**History:**
Executive Reorganization Order 1991-12 was promulgated February 21, 1991, as Executive Order 1991-12, eff April 23, 1991.

## CASE NOTES

The [former] Prison Overcrowding Emergency Powers Act is constitutional and does not contravene the governor's exclusive power of commutation with respect to sentences imposed after January 26, 1981, and with respect to sentences imposed before that date only insofar as the governor's actions which trigger the reductions in sentence are discretionary rather than mandatory. Oakland County Prosecuting Attorney v Michigan Dep't of Corrections (1981) 411 Mich 183, 305 NW2d 515.

The governor, upon appropriate certification of the commission of corrections, shall formally rescind the previous declaration of prison overcrowding state of emergency before declaring a new prison overcrowding state of emergency. Op Atty Gen, April 5, 1984, No. 6215.

The governor may, upon appropriate certification by the commission of corrections, declare a prison overcrowding state of emergency in the event the population of the prison system exceeds the rated design capacity for thirty consecutive days. A formal rescission of a previous emergency declaration, which has served its purpose, is not requisite to a new declaration of emergency. Op Atty Gen, August 30, 1983, No. 6182.

**Department of Corrections** § 791.303

## MICHIGAN DEPARTMENT OF CORRECTIONS BUREAU OF FIELD SERVICES DEPUTY DIRECTOR IN CHARGE OF FIELD SERVICES–EXECUTIVE REORGANIZATION

Executive Reorganization Order 1992-3, eff June 1, 1992

**§ 791.303. Transfer of services from Bureau of Field Services to director of Department of Corrections.** [MSA § 28.2355(201)]

Whereas, Article V, Section 2, of the Constitution of the State of Michigan of 1963 empowers the Governor to make changes in the organization of the Executive Branch or in the assignment of functions among its units which he considers necessary for efficient administration; and

Whereas, the Bureau of Field Services and the position of deputy director in charge of field services was created by Section 31 of Act No. 232 of the Public Acts of 1953, as amended by Act No. 314 of the Public Acts of 1982, being Section 791.231 of the Michigan Compiled Laws, in the Michigan Department of Corrections; and

Whereas, the functions, duties and responsibilities assigned to the Bureau of Field Services, and the deputy director in charge of field services, can be more effectively organized and carried out under the supervision and direction of the head of the Michigan Department of Corrections; and

Whereas, it is necessary in the interest of efficient administration and effectiveness of government to effect changes in the organization of the Executive Branch of government.

Now, Therefore, I, John Engler, Governor of the State of Michigan, pursuant to the powers vested in me by the Constitution of the State of Michigan of 1963 and the laws of the State of Michigan, do hereby order the following:

(1) All the statutory authority, powers, duties, functions and responsibilities, including the functions of budgeting, procurement and management-related functions, created under Section 31 of Act No. 232 of the Public Acts of 1953, as amended by Act No. 314 of the Public Acts of 1982, being Section 791.231 of the Michigan Compiled Laws, are hereby transferred from the Bureau of Field Services and the deputy director in charge of field services to the Director of the Michigan Department of Corrections by a Type III transfer, as defined by Section 3 of Act No. 380 of the Public Acts of 1965, as amended, being Section 16.103 of the Michigan Compiled Laws. The Bureau of Field Services and the position of deputy director in charge of field services are hereby abolished.

(2) The Director of the Michigan Department of Corrections shall provide executive direction and supervision for the implementation of the transfer. The transferred functions shall be administered under the direction and supervision of the Director of the Michigan Department of Corrections who may administer

the transferred functions himself or may administer the transferred functions in other ways to promote efficient administration. All prescribed functions of rule making, licensing and registration, including the prescription of rules, regulations, standards and adjudications, shall be transferred to the Director of the Michigan Department of Corrections.

(3) All records, personnel, property and unexpended balances of appropriations, allocations and other funds used, held, employed, available or to be made available to the Bureau of Field Services or the deputy director in charge of field services, for the activities transferred to the Director of the Michigan Department of Corrections by this Order, are hereby transferred to the Michigan Department of Corrections.

(4) The Director of the Michigan Department of Corrections shall make internal organizational changes as may be administratively necessary to complete the realignment of responsibilities prescribed by this Order.

(5) The Director of the Michigan Department of Corrections shall immediately initiate coordination to facilitate the transfer and develop a memorandum of record identifying any pending settlements, issues of compliance with applicable federal and State laws and regulations, or other obligations to be resolved by the Bureau of Field Services or the deputy director in charge of field services.

(6) All rules, orders, contracts and agreements relating to the assigned functions lawfully adopted prior to the effective date of this Order shall continue to be effective until revised, amended or repealed.

(7) Any suit, action or other proceeding lawfully commenced by, against or before any entity affected by this Order shall not abate by reason of the taking effect of this Order. Any suit, action or other proceeding may be maintained by, against or before the appropriate successor of any entity affected by this Order.

In fulfillment of the requirement of Article V, Section 2, of the Constitution of the State of Michigan of 1963, the provisions of this Order shall become effective 60 days from the filing of this Order.

**History:**
Executive Reorganization Order 1992-3 was promulgated April 1, 1992, as Executive Order 1992-4, eff June 1, 1992.

# COMMUNITY CORRECTIONS ACT

Act 511, 1988, p 2098, imd eff December 29, 1988.

AN ACT to provide for the funding of community-based corrections programs through local governmental subdivisions or certain nonprofit agencies; to prescribe the powers and duties of certain state officers and agencies; to provide for community corrections advisory boards and prescribe their powers and duties; to create an office of community alternatives and a state community corrections board within the department of corrections and prescribe their powers and duties; and to provide for the promulgation of rules.

*The People of the State of Michigan enact:*

### § 791.401. Title. [MSA § 28.2354(1)]

Sec. 1. This act shall be known and may be cited as the "community corrections act".

**History:**
 Pub Acts 1988, No. 511, § 1, imd eff December 29, 1988.

### § 791.402. Definitions. [MSA § 28.2354(2)]

Sec. 2. As used in this act:

(a) "City advisory board" means a community corrections advisory board created by a city pursuant to sections 6 and 7.

(b) "City-county advisory board" means a community corrections advisory board created by a county and the largest city by population within that county pursuant to sections 6 and 7.

(c) "Community corrections program" means a program that is operated by or contracted for by a city, county, or group of counties, or is operated by a nonprofit service agency, and is an alternative to incarceration in a state correctional facility or jail.

(d) "County advisory board" means a community corrections advisory board created by a county pursuant to sections 6 and 7.

(e) "Department" means the department of corrections.

(f) "Nonprofit service agency" means a nonprofit organization that provides treatment, guidance, training, or other rehabilitative services to individuals, families, or groups in such areas as health, education, vocational training, special education, social services, psychological counseling, alcohol and drug treatment, community service work, victim restitution, and employment.

(g) "Office" means the office of community alternatives created in section 3.

(h) "Plan" means a comprehensive corrections plan submitted by a county, city, or regional advisory board pursuant to section 8.

(i) "Regional advisory board" means a community corrections advisory board created by a group of 2 or more counties pursuant to sections 6 and 7.

(j) "State board" means the state community corrections board created in section 3.

**History:**
 Pub Acts 1988, No. 511, § 2, imd eff December 29, 1988.

**Statutory references:**
 Sections 3 and 6–8, above referred to, are §§791.403, 791.406, 791.407 and 791.408.

§ 791.403. Office of community alternatives; powers and duties; board; executive director; staff; state community corrections board; policy making duties; members; fair demographic representation; term of office; chairperson; filling vacancies; compensation; reimbursement of expenses. [MSA § 28.2354(3)]

Sec. 3. (1) An office of community alternatives is created within the department. The office shall exercise its powers and duties including budgeting and management as an autonomous entity, independent of the director of the department. The office shall consist of the board and an executive director, and such staff as the executive director may appoint to carry out the duties of the office. The executive director shall be appointed by the board, and shall carry out the duties of the office subject to the policies established by the board.

(2) A state community corrections board is created in the office. The board shall act as the policy making body for the office, as provided in this act.

(3) Not later than 90 days after the effective date of this act, the governor shall appoint, and the senate shall confirm, the 13 members of the state board as follows:

(a) One member shall be a county sheriff.

(b) One member shall be a chief of a city police department.

(c) One member shall be a judge of the circuit court or recorder's court.

(d) One member shall be a judge of the district court.

(e) One member shall be a county commissioner.

(f) One member shall be a member of city government.

(g) One member shall represent an existing community alternatives program.

(h) One member shall be the director of the department of corrections or his or her designee.

(i) One member shall be a county prosecutor.

(j) One member shall be a criminal defense attorney.

(k) Three members shall be representatives of the general public.

(4) The governor shall ensure fair geographic representation of the state board membership and that minority persons and women are fairly represented.

(5) Members of the state board shall serve for terms of 4 years each, except that of the members first appointed, 5 shall serve for terms of 4 years each, 4 shall serve for terms of 3 years each, and 4 shall serve for terms of 2 years each.

(6) A vacancy on the state board shall be filled in the same manner as the original appointment.

(7) Members of the state board shall serve without compensation, but shall be reimbursed by the department for actual and necessary expenses incurred in attending meetings.

(8) The governor shall annually appoint a chairperson from among the members of the board.

**Department of Corrections** § 791.405

**History:**
Pub Acts 1988, No. 511, § 3, imd eff December 29, 1988.

### § 791.404. Duties of state board. [MSA § 28.2354(4)]

Sec. 4. The state board shall do all of the following:

(a) Develop and establish goals, offender eligibility criteria, and program guidelines for community corrections programs.

(b) Adopt minimum program standards, policies, and rules for community corrections programs.

(c) Adopt an application process and procedures for funding community corrections programs, including the format for comprehensive corrections plans.

(d) Adopt criteria for community corrections program evaluations.

(e) Hire an executive director, who shall serve at the pleasure of the board.

**History:**
Pub Acts 1988, No. 511, § 4, imd eff December 29, 1988.

### § 791.405. Duties of office of community alternatives. [MSA § 28.2354(5)]

Sec. 5. The office shall do all of the following:

(a) Provide technical assistance and training to cities, counties, regions, or nonprofit service agencies in developing, implementing, evaluating, and operating community corrections programs.

(b) Enter into agreements with city, county, city-county, or regional advisory boards or nonprofit service agencies for the operation of community corrections programs by those boards or agencies, and monitor compliance with those agreements.

(c) Act as an information clearinghouse regarding community corrections programs for cities, counties, regions, or nonprofit service agencies that receive funding under this act.

(d) Review and approve local plans and proposals pursuant to sections 8 and 10.

(e) In instances of substantial noncompliance, halt funding to cities, counties, regions, or agencies, except that before halting funding, the office shall do both of the following:

(i) Notify the city, county, region, or agency of the allegations and allow 30 days for a response.

(ii) If an agreement is reached concerning a remedy, allow 30 days following that agreement for the remedy to be implemented.

**History:**
Pub Acts 1988, No. 511, § 5, imd eff December 29, 1988.

**Statutory references:**
Sections 8 and 10, above referred to, are §§791.408 and 791.410.

## § 791.406. County application for funding; regional advisory board; joint county and city funding applications; city application for funding, city advisory board. [MSA § 28.2354(6)]

Sec. 6. (1) A county may elect to apply for funding and other assistance under this act by a vote of the county board of commissioners approving the decision to apply, and by appointing a county advisory board. Two or more counties, by vote of the county board of commissioners of each county, may agree to create a regional advisory board instead of a county advisory board. A regional advisory board shall perform the same functions as a county advisory board for each county that participates in establishing the regional board.

(2) A county and the largest city by population within that county may elect to jointly apply for funding and other assistance under this act. An application for funding requires a vote of the board of commissioners approving the decision to apply and a majority resolution of the city council, and the appointment of a city-county advisory board.

(3) A city may elect to apply for funding and other assistance under this act by a majority resolution of the city council, and by appointing a city advisory board.

**History:**
Pub Acts 1988, No. 511, § 6, imd eff December 29, 1988.

## § 791.407. Board memberships; appointment of members; fair representation of women and minorities; publication of advance notice of appointments; request for interested persons. [MSA § 28.2354(7)]

Sec. 7. (1) A county advisory board, regional advisory board, city-county advisory board, or city advisory board shall consist of the following:

(a) One member shall be a county sheriff, or his or her designee.

(b) One member shall be a chief of a city police department, or his or her designee.

(c) One member shall be a judge of the circuit court or his or her designee.

(d) One member shall be a judge of the district court or his or her designee.

(e) One member shall be a judge of the probate court or his or her designee.

(f) One member shall be a county commissioner or city councilperson. In the case of a regional advisory board or a city-county advisory board, 1 county commissioner or councilperson from each participating city and county shall serve as a member.

(g) One member shall be selected from 1 of the following service areas: mental health, public health, substance abuse, employment and training, or community alternative programs.

(h) One member shall be a county prosecuting attorney or his or her designee.

(i) One member shall be a criminal defense attorney.

(j) One member shall be from the business community.

(k) One member shall be from the communications media.

(l) One member shall be either a circuit court probation agent or a district court probation officer.

(m) One member shall be a representative of the general public.

(2) In the case of a county or regional advisory board, the members shall be appointed by the county board or boards of commissioners. In the case of a city advisory board, the members shall be appointed by the city council. In the case of the city-county advisory board, the members shall be appointed by the county board of commissioners and the city council. In appointing the members of an advisory board, the county and city shall ensure that minority persons and women are fairly represented.

(3) Before an appointment is made under this section, the appointing authority shall publish advance notice of the appointments and shall request that the names of persons interested in being considered for appointment be submitted to the appointing authority.

**History:**
Pub Acts 1988, No. 511, § 7, imd eff December 29, 1988.

## § 791.408. Funding application; comprehensive corrections plan; contents; development; approval of proposed comprehensive corrections plan; preparation by advisory board; intended participants; nonviolent offenders. [MSA § 28.2354(8)]

Sec. 8. (1) A county, city, city-county, or regional advisory board, on behalf of the city, county, or counties it represents, may apply for funding and other assistance under this act by submitting to the office a comprehensive corrections plan that meets the requirements of this section, and the criteria, standards, rules, and policies developed by the state board pursuant to section 4.

(2) The plan shall be developed by the county, city, city-county, or regional advisory board and shall include all of the following for the county, city, or counties represented by the advisory board:

(a) A system for the development, implementation, and operation of community corrections programs and an explanation of how the state prison commitment rate for the city, county, or counties will be reduced, and how the public safety will be maintained, as a result of implementation of the comprehensive corrections plan. The plan shall include, where appropriate, provisions that detail how the city, county, or counties plan to substantially reduce, within 1 year, the use of prison sentences for felons for which the state felony sentencing guidelines upper limit for the recommended minimum sentence is 12 months or less as validated by the department of corrections. Continued funding in the second and subsequent years shall be contingent upon substantial compliance with this subdivision.

(b) A data analysis of the local criminal justice system including a basic description of jail utilization detailing such areas as sentenced versus unsentenced inmates, sentenced felons versus sentenced misdemeanants, and any use of a jail classification system. The analysis also shall include a basic description of offenders sentenced to probation and to prison and a review of the rate of commitment to the state corrections systems from the city, county, or counties for the preceding 3 years. The analysis also shall compare actual sentences with the sentences recommended by the state felony sentencing guidelines.

(c) An analysis of the local community corrections programs used at the time the plan is submitted and during the preceding 3 years, including types of offenders served and funding levels.

(d) A system for evaluating the effectiveness of the community corrections program, which shall utilize the criteria developed pursuant to section 4(d).

(e) The identity of any designated subgrant recipient.

(f) In the case of a regional or city-county plan, provisions for the appointment of 1 fiscal agent to coordinate the financial activities pertaining to the grant award.

(3) The county board or boards of commissioners of the county or counties represented by a county, city-county, or regional advisory board, or the city council of the city represented by a city or city-county advisory board, shall approve the proposed comprehensive corrections plan prepared by their advisory board before the plan is submitted to the office pursuant to subsection (1).

(4) This section is intended to encourage the participation in community corrections programs of offenders who would likely be sentenced to imprisonment in a state correctional facility or jail, would not increase the risk to public safety, have not demonstrated a pattern of violent behavior, and do not have a criminal record that indicates a pattern of violent offenses.

**History:**
Pub Acts 1988, No. 511, § 8, imd eff December 29, 1988.

**Statutory references:**
Section 4, above referred to, is § 791.404.

## § 791.409. Community corrections program; retention of jurisdiction by sentencing court. [MSA § 28.2354(9)]

Sec. 9. A sentencing court that places a person in a community corrections program shall retain jurisdiction over the person as a probationer under chapter XI of the code of criminal procedure, Act No. 175 of the Public Acts of 1927, being sections 771.1 to 771.14a of the Michigan Compiled Laws.

**History:**
Pub Acts 1988, No. 511, § 9, imd eff December 29, 1988.

**§ 791.410. Application by nonprofit service agency other than board; notification of application; subsequent appointment of advisory board; contracts with nonprofit service agency; provision of services; limitations on direct funding.** [MSA § 28.2354(10)]

Sec. 10. (1) In any jurisdiction that has not elected to apply for funding under this act and has not appointed an advisory board or participated in the creation of an advisory board, a nonprofit service agency that operates in that jurisdiction may apply for and receive direct state funding in that jurisdiction.

(2) The office promptly shall notify the county board of commissioners of a county described in subsection (1) of the fact that the nonprofit service agency has submitted an application for funding. The county shall have 30 days after receiving notice to apply for funding under this act, and to take steps to appoint a county advisory board or participate in the creation of a regional advisory board, in which case the application of the nonprofit service agency shall be denied.

(3) An advisory board may contract with a nonprofit service agency for the provision of services as described in the comprehensive corrections plan.

(4) A nonprofit service agency that receives direct funding under subsection (1) shall not receive the direct funding for a period of more than 24 consecutive months.

**History:**
Pub Acts 1988, No. 511, § 10, imd eff December 29, 1988.

**§ 791.411. Authorization for payment of appropriated funds; limitations on funding for administration; funding and current spending.** [MSA § 28.2354(11)]

Sec. 11. (1) The office shall authorize payments from funds appropriated to the office for community corrections programs to cities, counties, regions, or agencies for the community corrections programs described in the plan submitted pursuant to section 8 or the proposal submitted pursuant to section 10 if the plan or proposal is approved by the office.

(2) Of the total funding recommended for the implementation of the comprehensive corrections plan, not more than 30% may be used by the city, county, or counties for administration.

(3) The funds provided to a city, county, or counties under this section shall not supplant current spending by the city, county, or counties for community corrections programs.

**History:**
Pub Acts 1988, No. 511, § 11, imd eff December 29, 1988.

**Statutory references:**
Sections 8 and 10, above referred to, are §§791.408 and 791.410.

## § 791.412. Annual and biannual reports, office of community alternatives; contents; submission. [MSA § 28.2354(12)]

Sec. 12. (1) The office shall submit an annual report not later than November 1 of each year, detailing the individual requests received by the state board for funding under this act, and the programs and plans approved for funding.

(2) The office shall submit a biannual report not later than March 1 and September 1 of each year, detailing the effectiveness of the programs and plans funded under this act, including an explanation of how the rate of commitment of prisoners to the state prison system has been affected by the programs and plans funded under this act and listing any instances of noncompliance as required under section 5(b).

(3) All of the reports required in this section shall be submitted to the department of management and budget, the department of corrections, the members of the senate standing committee on criminal justice, urban affairs and economic development, the members of the house standing committee on corrections, the members of the senate and house appropriations subcommittees on corrections, and the senate and house fiscal agencies.

**History:**
Pub Acts 1988, No. 511, § 12, imd eff December 29, 1988.

**Statutory references:**
Section 5, above referred to, is § 791.405.

## § 791.413. Transfer of appropriations and resources; time. [MSA § 28.2354(13)]

Sec. 13. Not later than 180 days after the effective date of this act, any records, property, personnel, and unexpended balances of appropriations and other resources necessary to the operation of the office shall be transferred to the office by the department of corrections.

**History:**
Pub Acts 1988, No. 511, § 13, imd eff December 29, 1988.

## § 791.414. Promulgation of rules. [MSA § 28.2354(14)]

Sec. 14. The office, with the approval of the state board, shall promulgate rules pursuant to the administrative procedures act of 1969, Act No. 306 of the Public Acts of 1969, being sections 24.201 to 24.328 of the Michigan Compiled Laws, necessary to implement this act.

**History:**
Pub Acts 1988, No. 511, § 14, imd eff December 29, 1988.

## CORRECTIONAL OFFICERS' TRAINING ACT OF 1982

Act 415, 1982, p 1616, eff March 30, 1983.

AN ACT to improve the training and education of state and local correctional officers; to provide for the certification of state correctional officers and the development of standards and requirements for state and local correctional officers; to provide for the creation of a correctional officers' training council and a central training academy; and to prescribe the powers and duties of certain state agencies.

*The People of the State of Michigan enact:*

### § 791.501. Short title. [MSA § 28.2355(1)]

Sec. 1. This act shall be known and may be cited as the "correctional officers' training act of 1982".

**History:**
Pub Acts 1982, No. 415, § 1, eff March 30, 1983.

**CASE NOTES**

The Correctional Officers Training Act of 1982 has imposed no new or increased activities or services upon local units of government necessitating state funding under Const 1963, art 9, § 29. Op Atty Gen, November 4, 1988, No. 6546.

### § 791.502. Definitions. [MSA § 28.2355(2)]

Sec. 2. As used in this act:

(a) "Central training academy" means the central training academy established pursuant to section 15.

(b) "Correctional facility" means either of the following:

(i) A facility or institution which houses an inmate population under the jurisdiction of the department of corrections.

(ii) A municipal or county jail, work camp, lockup, holding center, halfway house, community corrections center, or any other facility maintained by a municipality or county which houses adult prisoners.

(c) "Council" means the correctional officers' training council created under section 3.

(d) "Department" means the state department of corrections.

(e) "Executive secretary" means the executive secretary of the council.

(f) "Local correctional officer" means any person employed by a unit of local government in a correctional facility as a correctional officer, or that person's immediate supervisor.

(g) "State correctional officer" means any person employed by the department in a correctional facility as a correctional officer or a corrections medical aide, or that person's immediate supervisor.

### § 791.502                                  Department of Corrections

**History:**
Pub Acts 1982, No. 415, § 2, eff March 30, 1983.

**Statutory references:**
Sections 3 and 15, above referred to, are §§791.503 and 791.515.

### § 791.503. Correctional officer's training council, creation, appointment of members. [MSA § 28.2355(3)]

Sec. 3. The correctional officer's training council is created within the department and shall establish standards regarding training and education as prescribed in this act. The council shall consist of 10 members appointed by the governor. The members shall be appointed as follows:

    (a) One member shall represent state corrections officers.
    (b) One member shall represent local corrections officers.
    (c) One member shall represent local agencies which maintain jails, corrections, or temporary holding facilities.
    (d) One member shall represent the Michigan commission of corrections.
    (e) One member shall represent the office of criminal justice.
    (f) One member shall represent the state personnel director.
    (g) Two members shall represent the public at large.
    (h) Two members shall represent the academic community at least 1 of whom shall represent Michigan community colleges.

**History:**
Pub Acts 1982, No. 415, § 3, eff March 30, 1983.

### § 791.504. Term of office; appointment of successors; filling vacancy, reappointment. [MSA § 28.2355(4)]

Sec. 4. (1) All members of the council shall hold office for a term of 3 years, except that of the members first appointed 3 shall have a term of 1 year, 4 shall have a term of 2 years, and 3 shall have a term of 3 years. Successors shall be appointed in the same manner as the original appointment.

(2) A person appointed as a member to fill a vacancy created other than by expiration of a term shall be appointed in the same manner as the original appointment for the remainder of the unexpired term of the member whom the person is to succeed.

(3) Any member may be reappointed for additional terms.

**History:**
Pub Acts 1982, No. 415, § 4, eff March 30, 1983.

### § 791.505. Chairperson; meetings, special meetings; procedures, requirements; open meetings, notice; compensation of members, expenses. [MSA § 28.2355(5)]

Sec. 5. (1) The council shall designate from among its members a chairperson and a vice-chairperson who shall serve for 1-year terms and who may be reelected.

(2) The council shall meet at least 4 times in each year at

Lansing. The council shall hold special meetings when called by the chairperson or, in the absence of the chairperson, by the vice-chairperson, or when called by the chairperson upon the written request of 5 members of the council. The council shall establish its own procedures and requirements with respect to quorum, place, and conduct of its meeting and other matters.

(3) The business which the council may perform shall be conducted at a public meeting of the council held in compliance with the open meetings act, Act No. 267 of the Public Acts of 1976, as amended, being sections 15.261 to 15.275 of the Michigan Compiled Laws. Public notice of the time, date, and place of the meeting shall be given in the manner required by Act No. 267 of the Public Acts of 1976, as amended.

(4) The members of the council shall serve without compensation but shall be entitled to their actual expenses in attending meetings and in the performance of their duties under this act.

**History:**
Pub Acts 1982, No. 415, § 5, eff March 30, 1983.

### § 791.506. Members of council; disqualification from other public office or employment. [MSA § 28.2355(6)]

Sec. 6. A member of the council shall not be disqualified from holding any public office or employment by reason of his or her appointment or membership on the council, nor shall he or she forfeit any such office or employment, by reason of his or her appointment under this act, notwithstanding the provisions of any local or special act or any local law, ordinance, or charter.

**History:**
Pub Acts 1982, No. 415, § 6, eff March 30, 1983.

### § 791.507. Executive secretary, appointment, duties, compensation. [MSA § 28.2355(7)]

Sec. 7. There shall be an executive secretary of the council who shall be appointed by the council upon recommendations from the director of the department. The executive secretary shall be an employee of the department and shall perform such functions and duties as may be assigned by the council. The executive secretary shall receive compensation and reimbursement for expenses within the amounts appropriated under section 8.

**History:**
Pub Acts 1982, No. 415, § 7, eff March 30, 1983.

**Statutory references:**
Section 8, above referred to, is § 791.508.

### § 791.508. Administrative support services, appropriation by council. [MSA § 28.2355(8)]

Sec. 8. Administrative support services for the council and executive secretary shall be provided by the department as provided by separate appropriation for the council.

**History:**
Pub Acts 1982, No. 415, § 8, eff March 30, 1983.

## § 791.509. Certification of correction officers; requirement of employment. [MSA § 28.2355(9)]

Sec. 9. Beginning 6 months after the effective date of this act, a person shall not be a state correctional officer unless he or she is certified or recertified by the Michigan commission of corrections as provided in section 10, 11, or 12. The Michigan commission of corrections shall certify those persons and recertify on an annual basis those persons who satisfy the criteria set forth in sections 10 to 12.

**History:**
Pub Acts 1982, No. 415, § 9, eff March 30, 1983.

**Statutory references:**
Sections 10–12, above referred to, are §§791.510, 791.511 and 791.512.

## § 791.510. Certification, automatic; recertification, requirements, training, minimum standards; approval by state civil service commission. [MSA § 28.2355(10)]

Sec. 10. (1) Beginning September 30, 1983, a person who is employed as a state correctional officer on March 30, 1983, shall automatically be certified and annually recertified by the commission of corrections until December 31, 1985. Beginning January 1, 1986, a person who is employed as a state correctional officer on March 30, 1983, shall not be recertified unless he or she has done both of the following:

(a) Completed successfully 320 hours of training with credit for training provided by the department allowed but limited to 160 hours of credit for training received prior to July 1, 1982.

(b) Fulfilled other minimum standards and requirements for recertification developed pursuant to section 13 by the council and approved by the commission of corrections.

(2) All minimum standards and requirements for recertification of persons under this section shall be subject to approval by the state civil service commission.

**History:**
Pub Acts 1982, No. 415, § 10, eff March 30, 1983; amended by Pub Acts 1989, No. 4, imd eff April 14, 1989, by § 2 eff upon expiration of 60 days after date of enactment.

**Statutory references:**
Section 13, above referred to, is § 791.513.

## § 791.511. Employment after effective date of act, requirements, standards; approval by state civil service commission. [MSA § 28.2355(11)]

Sec. 11. (1) A person who is not employed as a state correctional officer on March 30, 1983, but who becomes employed as a state correctional officer before January 1, 1985, shall not be certified or recertified by the commission of corrections unless he or she has done both of the following:

(a) Obtained a high school diploma or attained a passing score on the general education development test indicating a high school graduation level.

(b) Fulfilled other minimum standards and requirements developed pursuant to section 13 by the council and approved by the commission of corrections for certification and subsequently for recertification.

(2) All minimum standards and requirements for certification and subsequently for recertification of persons under this section shall be subject to approval by the state civil service commission.

**History:**
Pub Acts 1982, No. 415, § 11, eff March 30, 1983; amended by Pub Acts 1989, No. 4, imd eff April 14, 1989, by § 2 eff upon expiration of 60 days after date of enactment.

**Statutory references:**
Section 13, above referred to, is § 791.513.

**§ 791.512. Certification and recertification, employment after certain date; requirements; correctional officers and immediate supervisors, Detroit house of correction; automatic certification and recertification dependent on date of employment; requirements; employee of state facility converted to state correctional facility; automatic certification and recertification, conversion date; approval by state civil service commission.** [MSA § 28.2355(12)]

Sec. 12. (1) Except as provided for in subsections (2) and (3), a person who is not employed as a state correctional officer on March 30, 1983 and who is not employed as a state correctional officer until after December 31, 1984, shall not be certified or recertified by the Michigan commission of corrections unless he or she has done all of the following:

(a) Obtained a high school diploma or attained a passing score on the general education development test indicating a high school graduation level.

(b) Successfully completed all of the following:

(i) One of the following:

(A) A vocational certificate program as determined by the council, earned from an accredited postsecondary educational institution, which program shall require a minimum of 15 semester credit hours or 23 term credit hours.

(B) Equivalent course work to a vocational certificate program, as determined by the council, earned from an accredited postsecondary educational institution, which course work shall require a minimum of 15 semester credit hours or 23 term credit hours. The credit hours required under this subparagraph may be earned before or after the effective date of the amendatory act that added this subparagraph.

(C) A degree granted by an accredited postsecondary educational institution in a major discipline of study that is relevant to the position of state correctional officer, as determined by the council. A degree required under this subparagraph may be earned before or after the effective date of the amendatory act that added this subparagraph.

(ii) A minimum of 2 months of supervised, paid internship, as determined by the council, as an intern in a correctional facility.

(iii) A minimum of 320 hours of new employee training, as determined by the council, at the central training academy.

(c) Fulfilled other minimum standards and requirements developed pursuant to section 13 by the council and approved by the commission of corrections for certification and subsequently for recertification.

(2) A person who is employed as a correctional officer or an immediate supervisor of a correctional officer at the former Detroit house of correction on December 31, 1984 shall automatically be certified and annually recertified by the Michigan commission of corrections until December 31, 1985. Beginning January 1, 1986, a person who is employed as a correctional officer or an immediate supervisor of a correctional officer at the former Detroit house of correction on December 31, 1984 shall not be recertified unless he or she has done both of the following:

(a) Completed successfully a minimum of 160 hours of training provided by the department.

(b) Fulfilled other minimum standards and requirements for recertification developed pursuant to section 13 by the council and approved by the commission of corrections.

(3) A department of mental health direct care employee of a state facility officially designated for closure or phase-down due to deinstitutionalization, or a forensic security aide II or III employed by the department of mental health center for forensic psychiatry, or a work camp supervisor employed by the department of corrections shall automatically be certified and annually recertified by the commission of corrections for 3 years following the date he or she became employed as a state correctional officer provided he or she has done all of the following:

(a) Within 1 year of the date he or she became employed as a state correctional officer, obtained a high school diploma or attained a passing score on the general education development test indicating a high school graduation level.

(b) Within 1 year of the date he or she became employed as a state correctional officer, completed successfully 320 hours of new employee training with a credit up to 160 hours of previously acquired training, as approved by the council.

(c) Within 3 years of the date he or she became employed as a state correctional officer, completed 1 of the following:

(i) A vocational certificate program, as determined by the

**Department of Corrections** § 791.513

council, earned from an accredited postsecondary educational institution, which program shall require a minimum of 15 semester credit hours or 23 term credit hours.

(ii) Equivalent course work to a vocational certificate program, as determined by the council, earned from an accredited postsecondary educational institution which course work shall require a minimum of 15 semester credit hours or 23 term credit hours. The credit hours required under this subparagraph may be earned before or after the effective date of the amendatory act that added this subparagraph.

(iii) A degree granted by an accredited postsecondary educational institution in a major discipline of study that is relevant to the position of state correctional officer, as determined by the council. A degree required under this subparagraph may be earned before or after the effective date of the amendatory act that added this subparagraph.

(d) Fulfilled other minimum standards and requirements developed pursuant to section 13 by the council and approved by the commission of corrections for certification and subsequently for recertification.

(4) All minimum standards and requirements for certification and subsequently for recertification of persons under subsections (1), (2), and (3) shall be subject to approval by the state civil service commission.

**History:**
Pub Acts 1982, No. 415, § 12, eff March 30, 1983; amended by Pub Acts 1985, No. 44, imd eff June 14, 1985; 1989, No. 4, imd eff April 14, 1989, by § 2 eff upon expiration of 60 days after date of enactment.

**Statutory references:**
Section 13, above referred to, is § 791.513.

**§ 791.513. Minimum standards and requirements, development by council; recruitment, training, certification, recertification, decertification; approval by civil service commission; approval by commission of corrections; approval by state civil service commission.** [MSA § 28.2355(13)]

Sec. 13. (1) Not later than June 30, 1983, and as often as necessary after that, the council shall develop minimum standards and requirements for state correctional officers with respect to the following:

(a) Recruitment, selection, and certification of new state correctional officers based upon at least, but not limited to, work experience, educational achievement, and physical and mental fitness.

(b) New employee and continuing training programs.

(c) Recertification process.

(d) Course content of the vocational certificate program, required in section 12, the central training academy, and continuing training programs.

(e) Decertification process.

(2) Standards and requirements developed by the council under this section shall be effective only if they are approved by the commission of corrections.

(3) Standards and requirements approved by the commission of corrections under this section shall be subject to approval by the state civil service commission.

**History:**
Pub Acts 1982, No. 415, § 13, eff March 30, 1983; amended by Pub Acts 1989, No. 4, imd eff April 14, 1989, by § 2 eff upon expiration of 60 days after date of enactment.

**Statutory references:**
Section 12, above referred to, is § 791.512.

## § 791.514. Local correctional officers; minimum standards and requirements. [MSA § 28.2355(14)]

Sec. 14. Not later than 3 years after the effective date of this act, the council shall develop minimum standards and requirements for certification, recertification and decertification of local correctional officers.

**History:**
Pub Acts 1982, No. 415, § 14, eff March 30, 1983.

### CASE NOTES

The Correctional Officers Training Act of 1982 does not require local correctional officers to be certified by the Commission of Corrections. Op Atty Gen, November 4, 1988, No. 6546.

## § 791.515. Training academy; establishment, funding. [MSA § 28.2355(15)]

Sec. 15. The department shall establish a central training academy for use as an employee training center for state and local correctional officers. Funds necessary for the establishment and use of the training academy shall be provided by the department and supported by separate appropriation.

**History:**
Pub Acts 1982, No. 415, § 15, eff March 30, 1983.

## § 791.516. Annual report. [MSA § 28.2355(16)]

Sec. 16. The council shall make an annual report to the governor which includes pertinent data regarding the standards and requirements established and an evaluation on the effectiveness of correctional officer training programs.

**History:**
Pub Acts 1982, No. 415, § 16, eff March 30, 1983.

**Department of Corrections** § 791.517

### § 791.517. Promulgation of rules. [MSA § 28.2355(17)]

Sec. 17. The council shall promulgate rules necessary to implement this act pursuant to Act No. 306 of the Public Acts of 1969, as amended, being sections 24.201 to 24.315 of the Michigan Compiled Laws.

**History:**
Pub Acts 1982, No. 415, § 17, eff March 30, 1983.

## OFFICE OF COMMUNITY ALTERNATIVES – MICHIGAN DEPARTMENT OF CORRECTIONS – EXECUTIVE REORGANIZATION

Executive Reorganization Order 1995-14, p 2425, eff September 10, 1995

### § 791.601. Transfer of powers and duties of office of community alternatives to department of corrections by type II transfer. [MSA § 28.2360(1)]

WHEREAS, Article V, Section 2, of the Constitution of the State of Michigan of 1963, empowers the Governor to make changes in the organization of the Executive Branch or in the assignment of functions among its units which he considers necessary for efficient administration; and

WHEREAS, Act No. 511 of the Public Acts of 1988 ("Act No. 511"), the Community Corrections Act, created an Office of Community Alternatives as an autonomous entity within the Department of Corrections; and

WHEREAS, the purpose of Act No. 511 is to fund qualifying community corrections alternative programs that reduce state prison commitments by encouraging participation of offenders likely to be sentenced to imprisonment in a state correctional facility or jail, who would not increase the risk to public safety, have not demonstrated a pattern of violent behavior, and do not have a criminal record that indicates a pattern of violent offenses; and

WHEREAS, Act No. 511 expressly requires that continued funding shall be contingent upon substantial compliance with this objective; and

WHEREAS, Sec. 1006 of Enrolled House Bill 4418, the FY 1996 appropriations bill for the Department of Corrections, for the first time affords the Office of Community Alternatives (Corrections) express authority to approve use of its funds for the construction of facilities, which are to be minimum security facilities; it is essential that such decisions be integrated into and coordinated with comprehensive facilities planning for the Department of Corrections; and

WHEREAS, this goal can be achieved only by coordination of corrections and corrections alternative policies; and

WHEREAS, it is necessary in the interests of efficient administration and effectiveness of government to effect changes in the organization of the Executive Branch of government.

NOW, THEREFORE, I, John Engler, Governor of the State of Michigan, pursuant to the powers vested in me by the Constitution of the State of Michigan of 1963, and the laws of the State of Michigan, do hereby order the following:

1. All the statutory authority, powers, duties, functions and responsibilities, including the functions of budgeting, procurement and management-related functions, created under Act No. 511 of the Public Acts of 1988, are hereby transferred from the

**Department of Corrections** § 791.601

Office of Community Alternatives to the Department of Corrections by Type II transfer, as defined by Section 3 of Act No. 380 of the Public Acts of 1965, being Section 16.103 of the Michigan Compiled Laws.

2. The Director of the Department of Corrections may appoint the Executive Director of the Office of Community Alternatives or may administer the assigned functions in other ways to promote efficient administration.

3. The Director of the Department of Corrections shall provide executive direction and supervision for the implementation of the transfer. The assigned functions shall be administered under the direction and supervision of the Director, and all prescribed functions of rule-making, licensing and registration, including the prescription of rules, regulations, standards and adjudications, shall be transferred to the Director of the Department of Corrections.

4. All records, personnel, property and unexpended balances of appropriations, allocations and other fluids used, held, employed, available or to be made available to the Office of Community Alternatives for the activities transferred to the Department of Corrections by this Order are hereby transferred to the Department of Corrections.

5. The Director of the Department of Corrections shall make internal organizational changes as may be administratively necessary to complete the realignment of responsibilities prescribed by this Order.

6. The Executive Director of the Office of Community Alternatives and the Director of the Department of Corrections shall immediately initiate coordination to facilitate the transfer and develop a memorandum of record identifying any pending settlements, issues of compliance with applicable federal and state laws and regulations, or other obligations to be resolved by the Office of Community Alternatives.

7. All rules, orders, contracts and agreements relating to the assigned functions lawfully adopted prior to the effective date of this Order shall continue to be effective until revised, amended or repealed.

8. Any suit, action or other proceeding lawfully commenced by or against any entity affected by this Order shall not abate by reason of the taking effect of this Order. Any suit, action or other proceeding may be maintained by or against the appropriate successor of any entity affected by this Order.

In fulfillment of the requirement of Article V, Section 2, of the Constitution of the State of Michigan of 1963, the provisions of this Executive Order shall become effective 60 days after filing.

**History:**
Executive Reorganization Order No. 1995-14 was promulgated on July 11, 1995, as Executive Order No. 1995-16, eff. September 10, 1995.

**Legal periodicals:**
Braunlich, Day Report--An Alternative to Incarceration, 75 Mich B J 2:156 (1996).

# CHAPTER 798

# CORRECTIONS

## PROBATION RECOVERY CAMPS

### Act 195 of 1935

| | |
|---|---|
| § 798.1 | Probation recovery camps; establishment and maintenance by state prison commission. |
| § 798.2 | Rules and regulations; segregation of inmates; courses of instruction. |
| § 798.3 | Persons eligible. |
| § 798.4 | Transfers of inmates; written notice. |
| § 798.5 | Agreements with state departments for joint undertakings. |
| § 798.6 | Construction of act. |

## SPECIAL ALTERNATIVE INCARCERATION ACT

### Act 287 of 1988

| | |
|---|---|
| § 798.11 | Title of act. |
| § 798.12 | Definitions. |
| § 798.13 | Special alternative incarceration units; housing and training probationers; transportation; transfer; housing and training, prisoners. |
| § 798.14 | Program of work and exercise; term of incarceration; aftercare residential pilot program; facility construction. |
| § 798.15 | Certification, probationer's satisfactory completion of training; certification, prisoner's satisfactory completion of training. |
| § 798.16 | Probationer, failure; prisoner, failure; disciplinary procedures, program applicability. |
| § 798.17 | Effective date. |
| § 798.18 | Enactment of other bill. |

## INTERSTATE COMPACTS

### Act 89 of 1935

| | |
|---|---|
| § 798.101 | Probation and parole; interstate compact; permitting paroled prisoner to reside in other state; supervision by receiving state; retaking paroled person from receiving state; transporting retaken prisoner; regulations; ratification of compact; renunciation of compact; effect; notice. |
| § 798.102 | Declaration of necessity. |
| § 798.103 | Prevention of crime; interstate compacts. |

## DISCHARGE FROM PAROLE FOR HONORABLY DISCHARGED VETERANS [Repealed]

### Act 277 of 1945 [Repealed]

§§798.201, 798.202 [Repealed]

## Corrections

### LANDS FOR SHORT TERM PRISONERS; QUARRIES [Repealed]

#### Act 301 of 1931 [Repealed]

§§798.301–798.303 [Repealed]

### CAMPS FOR PRISON INMATES WITHIN CONSERVATION AREAS [Repealed]

#### Act 274 of 1949 [Repealed]

§ 798.351 [Repealed]
§§798.352, 798.353 [Repealed]

### JACKSON; SALE OF STATE LAND [Repealed]

#### Act 171 of 1939 [Repealed]

§§798.401–798.405 [Repealed]

### WATER SALES TO LOCAL INDUSTRY

#### Act 386 of 1974

| | |
|---|---|
| § 798.411 | Supplying water from southern Michigan prison; contract; contents. |
| § 798.412 | Approval by attorney general. |
| § 798.413 | Revenues, disposition; limitation of civil liability. |

### JACKSON; SALE OF PROPERTY [Repealed]

#### Act 192 of 1939 [Repealed]

§§798.421, 798.422 [Repealed]

---

## PROBATION RECOVERY CAMPS

Act 195, 1935, p 321, imd eff June 6, 1935.

AN ACT to provide for the establishment of probation recovery camps; to prescribe the powers and duties of the state prison commission with respect thereto; to designate persons eligible for entrance in said camps, and to declare the effect of this act.

*The People of the State of Michigan enact:*

### § 798.1. Probation recovery camps; establishment and maintenance by state prison commission. [MSA § 28.1681]

Sec. 1. The state prison commission is hereby authorized and it shall be the duty of said commission to provide and establish probation recovery camps, to be located in such regions of the state which are adapted to reforestation and the development and conservation of the natural resources of the state, other than agricultural. Said camps shall be under the complete and exclusive supervision of the state prison commission. Said commission shall have the power to acquire by purchase, gift, grant or devise, or condemnation under the provisions of act number one hundred forty-nine [149] of the public acts of nineteen hundred eleven [1911], as amended, being sections three thousand seven hundred sixty-three [3763] to three thousand seven hundred eighty-three [3783], inclusive, of the compiled laws of nineteen hundred twenty-nine [1929], suitable sites and acreage; to erect and maintain appropriate buildings thereon; and to otherwise equip and furnish the said camps. The said commission is hereby authorized to engage teachers, trainers and other employees and incur such other expenses as shall be necessary to the proper functioning of this act.

**History:**
Pub Acts 1935, No. 195, § 1, imd eff June 6, 1935.

**Cross references:**
Jurisdiction over probation recovery camps is vested in department of corrections, § 791.204.
Authority of director and commission with respect thereto, §§791.206, 791.222.
To be administered within bureau of penal institutions, § 791.262.

**Research references:**
59 Am Jur 2d, Pardon and Parole §§78, 83.

## § 798.2. Rules and regulations; segregation of inmates; courses of instruction. [MSA § 28.1682]

Sec. 2. The said commission shall adopt and enforce rules and regulations for the government and discipline of the camps: Provided, That parolees shall be segregated from probationers and confined in separate camps and that no camp shall confine both probationers and parolees. The commission shall provide educational and instructive courses of both a civil and semi-military character: Provided, That such courses shall not be other than vocational or physical and shall be best suited to equip and train the inmates as good citizens.

**History:**
Pub Acts 1935, No. 195, § 2, imd eff June 6, 1935.

**Research references:**
59 Am Jur 2d, Pardon and Parole §§78, 83.

## § 798.3. Persons eligible. [MSA § 28.1683]

Sec. 3. Any person convicted of a crime in this state who has been or shall be declared eligible to probation, under the laws of this state, by a court of competent jurisdiction, or who, in the opinion of the state prison commission, is qualified to parole from any penal institution, is eligible to confinement in the camps herein provided for.

**History:**
Pub Acts 1935, No. 195, § 3, imd eff June 6, 1935.

**Research references:**
59 Am Jur 2d, Pardon and Parole §§78, 83.

## § 798.4. Transfers of inmates; written notice. [MSA § 28.1684]

Sec. 4. The said commission shall have the discretionary power to transfer an inmate from one camp to another whenever it shall deem such change wise for the welfare of the inmate or the interests of the camps. Written notice of any such transfer shall be given to the committing authority within fifteen [15] days from the date thereof.

**History:**
Pub Acts 1935, No. 195, § 4, imd eff June 6, 1935.

**Research references:**
59 Am Jur 2d, Pardon and Parole §§78, 83.

## § 798.5. Agreements with state departments for joint undertakings. [MSA § 28.1685]

Sec. 5. The commission shall have the power and authority to enter into agreements with the department of conservation or any other department or agency of the state for joint undertakings for the conservation and development of the natural resources of the state and for the recovery and reclamation of any inmate of the camps, or for any other kindred purpose wherein the facilities of any such department or agencies may be useful and available and of mutual benefit and advantage. The various agencies of the state shall establish, as far as possible, reciprocal relations for the efficient functioning of this act.

**History:**
Pub Acts 1935, No. 195, § 5, imd eff June 6, 1935.

**Research references:**
59 Am Jur 2d, Pardon and Parole §§78, 83.

## § 798.6. Construction of act. [MSA § 28.1686]

Sec. 6. This act shall be construed as supplementary to the laws of this state with respect to pardons, paroles and probation.

**History:**
Pub Acts 1935, No. 195, § 6, imd eff June 6, 1935.

**Research references:**
59 Am Jur 2d, Pardon and Parole §§78, 83.

# SPECIAL ALTERNATIVE INCARCERATION ACT

Act 287, 1988, p 760, imd eff August 1, 1988.

AN ACT to establish special alternative incarceration units; and to

**Corrections** § 798.13

prescribe certain powers and duties of the department of corrections and county sheriffs.

*The People of the State of Michigan enact:*

## § 798.11. Title of act. [MSA § 28.2356(1)]

Sec. 1. This act shall be known and may be cited as the "special alternative incarceration act".

**History:**
Pub Acts 1988, No. 287, § 1, imd eff August 1, 1988.

**Michigan Digest references:**
Pardons and Paroles § 8.

### CASE NOTES

The prosecution may be deemed to have waived a post-sentencing challenge to a sentencing court's grant of permission for a defendant's placement in a special alternative incarceration unit or "boot camp" where the prosecution did not object to the court's grant of permission at the sentencing hearing. People v Krim (1996) 220 Mich App 314, 559 NW2d 366.

## § 798.12. Definitions. [MSA § 28.2356(2)]

Sec. 2. As used in this act:

(a) "Department" means the department of corrections.

(b) "Prisoner" means a person serving a term of incarceration under the jurisdiction of the department.

(c) "Probationer" means a person placed on probation pursuant to chapter XI of the code of criminal procedure, Act No. 175 of the Public Acts of 1927, being sections 771.1 to 771.14a of the Michigan Compiled Laws.

(d) "Unit" means a special alternative incarceration unit.

**History:**
Pub Acts 1988, No. 287, § 2, imd eff August 1, 1988; amended by Pub Acts 1992, No. 23, imd eff March 19, 1992 (see 1992 note below).

**Editor's notes:**
**Pub Acts 1992, No. 23, § 2,** imd eff March 19, 1992, provides:
"Section 2. This amendatory act shall not take effect unless all of the following bills of the 86th Legislature are enacted into law:
"(a) Senate Bill No. 145 [which became Act No. 21 of 1992].
"(b) Senate Bill No. 334 [which became Act No. 22 of 1992]". .

## § 798.13. Special alternative incarceration units; housing and training probationers; transportation; transfer; housing and training, prisoners. [MSA § 28.2356(3)]

Sec. 3. (1) The department shall establish special alternative incarceration units for the purpose of housing and training probationers eligible for special alternative incarceration pursuant to section 3b of chapter XI of the code of criminal procedure, Act No. 175 of the Public Acts of 1927, being section 771.3b of the Michigan Compiled

### § 798.13 — Corrections

Laws. A probationer who is placed in a unit by a court shall be transported by the county sheriff directly to a unit and shall not be processed through the department's reception center for prisoners. The department may transfer a probationer from 1 unit to another unit at the department's discretion, during the probationer's incarceration in a unit.

(2) The department shall establish special alternative incarceration units for the purpose of housing and training prisoners eligible for special alternative incarceration pursuant to section 34a of Act No. 232 of the Public Acts of 1953, being section 791.234a of the Michigan Compiled Laws.

**History:**
Pub Acts 1988, No. 287, § 3, imd eff August 1, 1988; amended by Pub Acts 1992, No. 23, imd eff March 19, 1992 (see 1992 note below).

**Editor's notes:**
Pub Acts 1992, No. 23, § 2, imd eff March 19, 1992, provides:
"Section 2. This amendatory act shall not take effect unless all of the following bills of the 86th Legislature are enacted into law:
"(a) Senate Bill No. 145 [which became Act No. 21 of 1992].
"(b) Senate Bill No. 334 [which became Act No. 22 of 1992]"..

### § 798.14. Program of work and exercise; term of incarceration; aftercare residential pilot program; facility construction. [MSA § 28.2356(4)]

Sec. 4. (1) The units shall provide a program of physically strenuous work and exercise, patterned after military basic training, and other programming as determined by the department. The term of any probationer's or prisoner's incarceration in a unit shall not exceed 120 days except that the probationer also shall be required to complete a period of not less than 120 days of probation under intensive supervision, and a prisoner also shall be required to complete a period of not less than 120 days of parole under intensive supervision. A probationer also may be required to complete a period of not more than 120 days in a residential program, if ordered by the sentencing court to do so under section 3b(9) of chapter XI of the code of criminal procedure, Act No. 175 of the Public Acts of 1927, being section 771.3b of the Michigan Compiled Laws, or if required by the department to do so under section 3b(10) of chapter XI of Act No. 175 of the Public Acts of 1927.

(2) The department shall develop and operate a special alternative incarceration aftercare residential pilot program. The program shall be a residential program in which probationers may be required to participate pursuant to section 3b(10) of chapter XI of Act No. 175 of the Public Acts of 1927 and in which prisoners may be required to participate. The construction of the facility used for the purposes of the program shall be governed by a written agreement between the department, the department of management and budget, and the city, village, or township in which the program is operated.

**History:**
Pub Acts 1988, No. 287, § 4, imd eff August 1, 1988; amended by Pub Acts

**Corrections** § 798.16

1989, No. 303, imd eff January 3, 1990; 1992, No. 23, imd eff March 19, 1992 (see 1992 note below).

**Editor's notes:**
**Pub Acts 1992, No. 23, § 2,** imd eff March 19, 1992, provides:
"Section 2. This amendatory act shall not take effect unless all of the following bills of the 86th Legislature are enacted into law:
"(a) Senate Bill No. 145 [which became Act No. 21 of 1992].
"(b) Senate Bill No. 334 [which became Act No. 22 of 1992]". . .

### CASE NOTES

A defendant who serves time in a special alternative incarceration unit of the Department of Corrections as part of a sentence of probation and subsequently is convicted and sentenced for violating probation is entitled to sentencing credit for the time served in the special alternative incarceration unit. People v Hite (1993) 200 Mich App 1, 503 NW2d 692.

**§ 798.15. Certification, probationer's satisfactory completion of training; certification, prisoner's satisfactory completion of training.** [MSA § 28.2356(5)]

Sec. 5. (1) At any time during a probationer's incarceration in a unit, but not less than 5 days before the probationer's expected date of release, the department shall certify to the sentencing court as to whether the probationer has satisfactorily completed the course of training at the unit.

(2) At least 10 days before the prisoner's expected date of release, the department shall certify to the parole board as to whether the prisoner has satisfactorily completed the course of training at the unit.

**History:**
Pub Acts 1988, No. 287, § 5, imd eff August 1, 1988; amended by Pub Acts 1992, No. 23, imd eff March 19, 1992 (see 1992 note below).

**Editor's notes:**
**Pub Acts 1992, No. 23, § 2,** imd eff March 19, 1992, provides:
"Section 2. This amendatory act shall not take effect unless all of the following bills of the 86th Legislature are enacted into law:
"(a) Senate Bill No. 145 [which became Act No. 21 of 1992].
"(b) Senate Bill No. 334 [which became Act No. 22 of 1992]". . .

**§ 798.16. Probationer, failure; prisoner, failure; disciplinary procedures, program applicability.** [MSA § 28.2356(6)]

Sec. 6. (1) A probationer who fails to work diligently and productively at the program of the unit, or who fails to obey the rules of behavior established for the unit, may be reported to the sentencing court for possible revocation of probation and may be housed in a county jail while awaiting a probation revocation determination.

(2) A prisoner who fails to work diligently and productively at the program of the unit, or who fails to obey the rules of behavior established for the unit, shall be returned to a state correctional facility and shall no longer be eligible for placement in the program. A prisoner removed from a unit for this purpose shall be credited for

**§ 798.16**      Corrections

the time served in the unit except that all disciplinary credits accumulated in the unit may be forfeited.

(3) Disciplinary procedures required by sections 51 to 55 of Act No. 232 of the Public Acts of 1953, being sections 791.251 to 791.255 of the Michigan Compiled Laws, are not applicable in determining whether the rules of behavior established for the unit have been violated, except where the removal from the unit and the forfeiture of disciplinary credits are at issue.

**History:**
Pub Acts 1988, No. 287, § 6, imd eff August 1, 1988; amended by Pub Acts 1992, No. 23, imd eff March 19, 1992 (see 1992 note below).

**Editor's notes:**
Pub Acts 1992, No. 23, § 2, imd eff March 19, 1992, provides:
"Section 2. This amendatory act shall not take effect unless all of the following bills of the 86th Legislature are enacted into law:
"(a) Senate Bill No. 145 [which became Act No. 21 of 1992].
"(b) Senate Bill No. 334 [which became Act No. 22 of 1992]"..

**CASE NOTES**

A defendant who serves time in a special alternative incarceration unit of the Department of Corrections as part of a sentence of probation and subsequently is convicted and sentenced for violating probation is entitled to sentencing credit for the time served in the special alternative incarceration unit. People v Hite (1993) 200 Mich App 1, 503 NW2d 692.

**§ 798.17. Effective date.** [MSA § 28.2356(7)]

Sec. 7. This act shall take effect July 1, 1988.

**History:**
Pub Acts 1988, No. 287, § 7, imd eff August 1, 1988.

**§ 798.18. Enactment of other bill.** [MSA § 28.2356(8)]

Sec. 8. This act shall not take effect unless Senate Bill No. 691 of the 84th Legislature is enacted into law.

**History:**
Pub Acts 1988, No. 287, § 8, imd eff August 1, 1988.

## INTERSTATE COMPACTS

Act 89, 1935, p 143, imd eff May 27, 1935.

AN ACT providing that the state of Michigan may enter into a compact or compacts with any of the United States for mutual helpfulness in relation to persons convicted of crime or offenses or who are or may be at large on probation or parole, and providing that the state may enter into a compact or compacts with any of the United States that will provide for cooperative effort and mutual assistance amongst them in the prevention of crime and in the enforcement of their respective penal laws and policies and to

**Corrections** § 798.101

establish such agencies, joint or otherwise, as said states may deem desirable for making effective such agreements and compacts.

*The People of the State of Michigan enact:*

**§ 798.101. Probation and parole; interstate compact; permitting paroled prisoner to reside in other state; supervision by receiving state; retaking paroled person from receiving state; transporting retaken prisoner; regulations; ratification of compact; renunciation of compact; effect; notice.** [MSA § 28.1361]

Sec. 1. The governor of this state is hereby authorized and directed to enter into a compact on behalf of the state of Michigan with any of the United States legally joining therein in the form substantially as follows:

A COMPACT

Entered into by and among the contracting states, signatories hereto, with the consent of Congress of the United States of America, granted by an act entitled "An act granting the consent of Congress to any two [2] or more states to enter into agreements or compacts for cooperative effort and mutual assistance in the prevention of crime and for other purposes."

The contracting states solemnly agree:

(1) That it shall be competent for the duly constituted judicial and administrative authorities of a state party to this compact, (herein called "sending state") to permit any person convicted of an offense within such state and placed on probation or released on parole to reside in any other state party to this compact, (herein called "receiving state") while on probation or parole, if

(a) Such person is in fact a resident of or has his family residing within the receiving state and can obtain employment there;

(b) Though not a resident of the receiving state and not having his family residing there, the receiving state consents to such person's being sent there.

Before granting such permission, opportunity shall be granted to the receiving state to investigate the home and prospective employment of such person.

A resident of the receiving state, within the meaning of this section, is one who has been an actual inhabitant of such state continuously for more than one year prior to his coming to the sending state and has not resided within the sending state for more than six continuous months immediately preceding the commission of the offense for which he has been convicted.

(2) That each receiving state will assume the duties of visitation of and supervision over probationers or parolees of

§ 798.101

any sending state and in the exercise of those duties will be governed by the same standards that prevail for its own probationers and parolees.

(3) That duly accredited officers of a sending state may at all times enter a receiving state and there apprehend and retake any person on probation or parole. For that purpose no formalities will be required other than establishing the authority of the officer and the identity of the person to be retaken. All legal requirements to obtain extradition or [of] fugitives from justice are hereby expressly waived. The decision of the sending state to retake a person on probation or parole shall be conclusive upon and not reviewable within the receiving state: Provided, however, That if at the time when a state seeks to retake a probationer or parolee there should be pending against him within the receiving state any criminal charge, or he should be suspected of having committed within such state a criminal offense, he shall not be retaken without the consent of the receiving state until discharged from prosecution or from imprisonment for such offense.

(4) That the duly accredited officers of the sending state will be permitted to transport prisoners being retaken through any and all states parties to this compact, without interference.

(5) That the governor of each state may designate an officer who, acting jointly with like officers of other contracting states, if and when appointed, shall promulgate such rules and regulations as may be deemed necessary to more effectively carry out the terms of this compact.

(6) That this compact shall become operative immediately upon its ratification by any state as between it and any other state or states so ratifying. When ratified, it shall have the full force and effect of law within such state; the form of ratification to be in accordance with the laws of the ratifying state.

(7) That this compact shall continue in force and remain binding upon each ratifying state until renounced by it. The duties and obligations hereunder of a renouncing state shall continue as to parolees or probationers residing therein at the time of withdrawal until retaken or finally discharged by the sending state. Renunciation of this compact shall be by the same authority which ratified it, by sending six [6] months' notice in writing of its intention to withdraw from the compact.

**History:**
Pub Acts 1935, No. 89, § 1, imd eff May 27, 1935.

**Cross references:**
Jurisdiction of probation and parole matters is vested in department of corrections, § 791.204.
Corrections commission authorized to exercise powers and duties created by this act, § 791.211.

**Michigan Digest references:**
Extradition § 1.
Pardons and Paroles §§4 et seq.
Statutes §§80, 99.

## CASE NOTES

Provisions of § 791.238, relating to "dead time," must be read in pari materia with interstate parole compact to effect constitutionally approved and well-established legislative intent against consecutive sentences, which abides absent some clearly expressed contrary provision. Browning v Michigan Dep't of Corrections (1971) 385 Mich 179, 188 NW2d 552.

Where inmate of Michigan state prison was paroled to sheriff of county in New York, under statute authorizing compacts with other states in relation to paroled persons, Michigan rules governing conduct while on parole remaining operative in New York, such surrender was not extradition to New York, even though prisoner was arraigned in latter state for larceny committed there prior to his Michigan imprisonment, and was given suspended New York sentence on condition that he should make restitution and meet requirements of Michigan parole board, and prisoner's status remained that of parolee whose supervision had been assumed by state of New York. Ex parte Dawsett (1945) 311 Mich 588, 19 NW2d 110, cert den (1946) 329 US 786, 91 L Ed 674, 67 S Ct 299.

There was no relinquishment of jurisdiction by Michigan over its paroled prisoner in delivering him to New York sheriff under statute authorizing compacts with other states in relation to paroled persons where Michigan rules governing prisoner's conduct on parole remained operative in New York, even though latter state assumed supervision of him and imposed suspended sentence upon him on his plea of guilty to larceny committed before his imprisonment in Michigan. Ex parte Dawsett (1945) 311 Mich 588, 19 NW2d 110, cert den (1946) 329 US 786, 91 L Ed 674, 67 S Ct 299.

## § 798.102. Declaration of necessity. [MSA § 28.1362]

Sec. 2. Whereas an emergency exists for the immediate taking effect of this act, the same shall become effective immediately upon its passage and, when the governor of this state shall sign and seal this compact or any compact with any other state, pursuant to the provisions of this act. Such compact or compacts as between the state of Michigan and such other state so signing shall have the force and effect of law immediately upon the enactment by such other state of a law giving it similar effect.

**History:**
Pub Acts 1935, No. 89, § 2, imd eff May 27, 1935.

## § 798.103. Prevention of crime; interstate compacts. [MSA § 28.1363]

Sec. 3. The governor of the state of Michigan is further authorized and empowered to enter into any other agreements or compacts with any of the United States not inconsistent with the laws of this state or of the United States, or the other agreeing states, for cooperative effort and mutual assistance in the prevention of crime and in the enforcement of the penal laws and policies of the contracting states and to establish agencies, joint or otherwise, as may be deemed desirable for making effective such agreements and compacts. The intent and purpose of this act is to grant to the governor of the state of Michigan administrative power and authority if and when conditions of crime make it necessary to bind the state in a cooperative

§ 798.103 Corrections

effort to reduce crime and to make the enforcement of the criminal laws of agreeing states more effective, all pursuant to the consent of the Congress of the United States heretofore granted.

**History:**
Pub Acts 1935, No. 89, § 3, imd eff May 27, 1935.

## DISCHARGE FROM PAROLE FOR HONORABLY DISCHARGED VETERANS [Repealed]

Act 277, 1945, p 451, imd eff May 25, 1945.
[Repealed]

AN ACT to authorize the granting of discharges from paroles to persons honorably discharged from the armed forces of the United States.

§§ 798.201, 798.202. **[Repealed]** [MSA §§ 28.1347(1), 28.1347(2)]

**History:**
Pub Acts 1945, No. 277, imd eff May 25, 1945; **repealed** by Pub Acts 1964, No. 256, eff August 28, 1964.

## LANDS FOR SHORT TERM PRISONERS; QUARRIES [Repealed]

Act 301, 1931, p 494, eff September 18, 1931.
[Repealed]

AN ACT to authorize the state administrative board to purchase lands for the purpose of providing employment and establishing barracks for the housing of short term prisoners, and to agriculturally develop said lands, also the developing of stone quarries on said lands for the purpose of securing crushed rock to be used for highway or other purposes, as may be designated by the said state administrative board and to provide for an appropriation for the purchase of the same.

§§ 798.301–798.303. **[Repealed]** [MSA §§ 28.1671–28.1673]

**History:**
Pub Acts 1931, No. 301, eff September 18, 1931; **repealed** by Pub Acts 1964, No. 256, eff August 28, 1964.

**Corrections** 798.405

## CAMPS FOR PRISON INMATES WITHIN CONSERVATION AREAS [Repealed]

Act 274, 1949, p 401, imd eff June 7, 1949.
[Repealed]

AN ACT to authorize the construction of camps for inmates of state prisons on state-owned lands within conservation areas, to authorize the use of inmate labor on conservation projects on state-owned lands, and to make an appropriation therefor.

### § 798.351. [Repealed] [MSA § 28.1715]

**History:**
Pub Acts 1949, No. 274, imd eff June 7, 1949; **repealed** by Pub Acts 1981, No. 119, imd eff July 19, 1981.

### §§798.352, 798.353. [Repealed] [MSA §§28.1716, 28.1717]

**History:**
Pub Acts 1949, No. 274, imd eff June 7, 1949; **repealed** by Pub Acts 1964, No. 256, eff August 28, 1964.

## JACKSON; SALE OF STATE LAND [Repealed]

Act 171, 1939, p 331, imd eff June 6, 1939.
[Repealed]

AN ACT to authorize the Michigan corrections commission to sell and dispose of certain lands acquired for the use of the old prison of southern Michigan at Jackson, Michigan, and to provide for the disposition of the proceeds of such sale.

### §§798.401–798.405. [Repealed] [MSA §§13.788(1)–13.788(5)]

**History:**
Pub Acts 1939, No. 171, imd eff June 6, 1939; **repealed** by Pub Acts 1964, No. 256, eff August 28, 1964.

## WATER SALES TO LOCAL INDUSTRY

Act 386, 1974, p 1348, imd eff December 23, 1974.

AN ACT to authorize the department of corrections to sell water to local industry; and to provide for the disposition of revenues derived therefrom.

*The People of the State of Michigan enact:*

## § 798.411. Supplying water from southern Michigan prison; contract; contents. [MSA § 28.1674(1)]

Sec. 1. (1) The director of the department of corrections may contract with the Jackson area industrial development corporation to supply water from southern Michigan prison to local industry.

(2) The contract shall provide:

(a) That the water shall be used solely for fire protection and fire extinguishing systems.

(b) That the water shall be sold at not less than its fair market value.

(c) That all water main and other installation and maintenance costs shall be paid by the corporation.

**History:**
Pub Acts 1974, No. 386, § 1, imd eff December 23, 1974.

## § 798.412. Approval by attorney general. [MSA § 28.1674(2)]

Sec. 2. The contract authorized by this act shall be approved by the attorney general.

**History:**
Pub Acts 1974, No. 386, § 2, imd eff December 23, 1974.

## § 798.413. Revenues, disposition; limitation of civil liability. [MSA § 28.1674(3)]

Sec. 3. The revenues received under this act shall be deposited in the state treasury and credited to the general fund. The state of Michigan and the Michigan department of corrections and all personnel shall not be held liable for any damages which might result from the failure or inability of the prison water system to supply the private corporation with water under any circumstances.

**History:**
Pub Acts 1974, No. 386, § 3, imd eff December 23, 1974.

# JACKSON; SALE OF PROPERTY [Repealed]

Act 192, 1939.
[Repealed]

## §§798.421, 798.422. [Repealed]

**History:**
Pub Acts 1939, No. 192, §§1, 2; **repealed** by Pub Acts 1964, No. 256, eff August 28, 1964.

# CHAPTER 800

# PRISONS

## PRISON CODE

### Act 118 of 1893

§§800.1–800.32 [Repealed]
§ 800.33  Record of major misconduct charges as part of parole eligibility report; reduction from sentence; good time, disciplinary credits, special disciplinary credits; forfeiture; disciplinary credit committee; rules; good time committee; powers of warden and parole board; prisoner subject to disciplinary time; reduction of credits by court order.
§ 800.34  Disciplinary time; receipt for each major misconduct; accumulation; consideration for concurrent or consecutive sentences; reduction; "prisoner subject to disciplinary time" defined.
§ 800.35  Rules.
§§800.36–800.40 [Repealed]
§ 800.41  Enforcement of discipline; attempted escapes; "correctional facility" defined.
§ 800.42  Prisoner in correctional facility having security classification of I, II, III, IV, V, or VI; personal property; disposal; definitions.
§ 800.43  Receipt or possession of certain material; prohibition; list; notice; appeal; limits on amount.
§ 800.44  Uniform; color.
§§800.45–800.47 [Repealed]
§ 800.48  Removal of person to prison; duty of sheriff.
§ 800.49  Fees and expenses for conveying convicts to prison, payment.
§ 800.50  Delivery of convict; certified copy of sentence, delivery to warden; certificate of delivery; use as evidence.
§§800.51–800.60 [Repealed]
§ 800.61  Escaped convicts, measures for recapture; reward; sentence.
§§800.62–800.66 [Repealed]

## PRISON OVERCROWDING EMERGENCY POWERS ACT [Repealed]

### Act 519 of 1980 [Repealed]

§ 800.71  [Repealed]
§ 800.72  [Repealed]
§ 800.73  [Repealed]
§ 800.74  [Repealed]
§ 800.75  [Repealed]
§ 800.76  [Repealed]
§ 800.77  [Repealed]
§ 800.78  [Repealed]
§ 800.79  [Repealed]

# Prisons

## MICHIGAN REFORMATORY [Repealed]

### Act 75 of 1901 [Repealed]

§ 800.91 [Repealed]

## EMPLOYMENT OF CONVICTS FOR PUBLIC PROJECTS

### Act 181 of 1911

| | |
|---|---|
| § 800.101 | Convicts; employment on public projects; control; compensation; disposition of moneys. |
| § 800.101a | Employment on state highways; requisition, order; control; compensation, disposition. |
| § 800.102 | Class of labor prohibited. |
| § 800.103 | [Repealed] |

## COMMITMENT RESTRICTIONS [Repealed]

### Act 2 of 1885 [Repealed]

§ 800.151 [Repealed]

## IONIA COUNTY PROSECUTOR [Repealed]

### Act 176 of 1877 [Repealed]

§ 800.167 [Repealed]

## BERTILLON SYSTEM [Repealed]

### Act 183 of 1891 [Repealed]

§§ 800.201–800.203 [Repealed]

## CENTRAL RECORDS BUREAU [Repealed]

### Act 27 of 1903 [Repealed]

§§ 800.231–800.234 [Repealed]

## LIQUOR, NARCOTICS AND WEAPONS

### Act 17 of 1909

| | |
|---|---|
| § 800.281 | Liquor, drugs and controlled substances; prohibited distribution. |
| § 800.281a | Definitions. |
| § 800.282 | Exceptions; physician's certificate; clergy, wine; hospital supply; owner or operator of privately owned community corrections center, resident home. |
| § 800.283 | Weapons or implements for escape; furnishing prohibited; possession or control of weapons or implements. |
| § 800.284 | Searching of visitors. |
| § 800.285 | Felony; penalty. |

**Prisons**

## ADMISSION OF CLERGYMEN

### Act 185 of 1859

§ 800.291 Admission of clergymen; time.
§ 800.292 Duty of keeper.

## PRISON LABOR AND INDUSTRIES [Repealed]

### Act 210 of 1935 [Repealed]

§§800.301–800.319 [Repealed]

## CORRECTIONAL INDUSTRIES ACT

### Act 15 of 1968

§ 800.321 Short title.
§ 800.322 "Correctional industries products" and "youth correctional facility" defined.
§ 800.323 Jurisdiction of commission.
§ 800.324 Commission of corrections; powers.
§ 800.325 Correctional industries revolving fund; crediting money collected from inmate labor; expenditures.
§ 800.326 Sale, exchange, or purchase of correctional industries products; availability of agricultural products to nonprofit charitable organizations or family independence agency; use of inmate labor.
§ 800.327 Employment of inmates; types of employment.
§ 800.327a Assignment of inmates to work in private manufacturing or service enterprise.
§ 800.328 Specifications and standards; inspection, acceptance or rejection.
§ 800.329 Purchase and sale of finished goods, material or equipment; purposes.
§ 800.330 Institutions maintained by political subdivisions; disposition of products; exceptions.
§ 800.331 Intent of act; correctional industries as total self-supporting system; methods of purchasing and accounting.
§ 800.332 Schedule of payments or allowances to inmates or dependents.
§ 800.333 Violations by officers; effect.
§ 800.334 Violation; misdemeanor.
§ 800.335 [Repealed]

### Executive Reorganization Order 1993-8

§ 800.341 Michigan state industries advisory board, creation.

## STATE CORRECTIONAL FACILITY REIMBURSEMENT ACT

### Act 253 of 1935

§ 800.401 Title of act.
§ 800.401a Definitions.

| | |
|---|---|
| § 800.401b | Information regarding assets of prisoners, form; form submitted to every prisoner; date; resubmission, purpose; completion of form; oath or affirmation; department to develop form, time. |
| § 800.402 | Report to attorney general by director, contents. |
| § 800.403 | Reports, investigation; cost of care of prisoner, reimbursement of state; reimbursement of state; limitation. |
| § 800.403a | Complete financial information, cooperation by prisoner; failure to cooperate, effect |
| § 800.404 | Exclusive jurisdiction of circuit court; complaint by attorney general, contents; order to show cause, issuance; service of complaint and order upon prisoner; methods; time; hearing; finding of assets subject to claim; order to reimburse state; amount of reimbursement; prisoner's obligation to provide support, consideration at hearing; order to reimburse state, failure to comply; order to show cause; contempt of court; cost of proceedings, liability of prisoner's assets; proceedings by state to recover cost of care of prisoner, commencement. |
| § 800.404a | Cost of care of prisoner, reimbursement to state; attorney general; remedies; enforcement procedure; restraining order; exception; appointment of receiver; enforcement of judgment, prohibition. |
| § 800.404b | Enforcement of provisions of act; assistance of prosecuting attorney; reimbursement for cost of care of prisoner in work camp; prohibition. |
| § 800.405 | Information and assistance to attorney general and prosecuting attorney by certain officials. |
| § 800.406 | Cost of investigation, payment; balance, credited to general fund; determination of amount due state; evidence. |
| § 800.407 | [Repealed] |

## REIMBURSEMENT OF COUNTY FOR PROSECUTION AND PRISON MAINTENANCE EXPENSES

### Act 16 of 1978

| | |
|---|---|
| § 800.451 | State correctional facility, definition. |
| § 800.452 | Reimbursement of county by state; expenses for fees of jurors, witnesses and attorneys; new felonies; submission of monthly costs to department of corrections; payment; determination of reasonableness conclusive; state agency's responsibility for duties; dates; reimbursement for fees; calculation; limit; exceptions. |
| § 800.453 | Reimbursement of county by state; additional jurisdictional duties in circuit court; submission of quarterly itemized costs to state court administrative officer; payment; determination of reasonableness conclusive. |
| § 800.454 | Reimbursement of county for costs of previously incarcerated state prisoner; conditions for reimbursement; daily limitation; inapplicability of provision; submission of monthly itemized costs to department of corrections; payment; determination of reasonableness conclusive. |
| § 800.455 | Cost of proceedings, transfer or treatment of mentally ill prisoner; reimbursement of county; itemized costs; determination of reasonableness; payment. |

## COUNTY ESCAPED PRISONER PROSECUTION PROGRAM; MICHIGAN DEPARTMENT OF MANAGEMENT AND BUDGET; MICHIGAN DEPARTMENT OF CORRECTIONS

**Executive Reorganization Order 1993-4**

§ 800.461   County escaped prisoner prosecution program, transfer from Department of Management and Budget.

## PRISON CODE

Act 118, 1893, p 170, imd eff May 26, 1893.

AN ACT to revise and consolidate the laws relative to state prisons, to state houses of correction, and branches of state prisons and reformatories, and the government and discipline thereof and to repeal all acts inconsistent therewith. (Amended by Pub Acts 1978, No. 80, imd eff March 29, 1978.).

**Popular Name:**
Prison Code

### §§800.1–800.32.   [Repealed]   [MSA §§28.1371–28.1402]

**History:**
Pub Acts 1893, No. 118, imd eff May 26, 1893; **repealed** by Pub Acts 1972, No. 179, imd eff June 16, 1972.

**Editor's notes:**
Former § 800.1 provided for the maintenance of various state prisons and a house of correction and reformatory. Former § 800.2 provided for prison boards of control, together with manner of appointment, terms of office. Former § 800.3 provided for payment of expenses of the boards of control. Former § 800.4 dealt with officers of prisons, and their oath. Former § 800.5 provided for the appointment of a warden of each prison, together with his term of office. Former § 800.6 provided for the appointment of deputy wardens and other personnel. Former § 800.7 dealt with the attendance of the warden at the prison, and the performance of his duties, in his absence, by his deputy. Former § 800.8 required the warden to keep a daily journal, specified its contents, and provided for its inspection. Former § 800.9 outlined the general duties of the warden. Former § 800.10 required the warden to make a monthly report to the board of receipts and expenditures of moneys. Former § 800.11 dealt with the custody, care and return of convicts' property. Former § 800.12 dealt with the manner of conducting fiscal transactions and litigation, and determination of certain controversies.

Former § 800.13 provided for the clerk's bond. Former § 800.14 outlined the duties of the clerk. Former § 800.15 outlined the duties of the physician. Former § 800.16 dealt with the physician's examination of sick convicts, and provided for certification of the convict's disability to labor. Former § 800.17 dealt with purchase of medicine and hospital stores with the advice of the physician. Former § 800.18 outlined the duties of the chaplain. Former § 800.19 required the warden and other officers to admit the board to the prison for purposes of inspection. Former § 800.20 dealt with the salaries of the prison officers, the warden's house, and provisions for lodging and boarding of employees. Former § 800.21 dealt with conflicts of interests, and prohibited convict labor for prison officials. Former § 800.22 exempted prison personnel from military and jury duties. For current provisions as to jury service, see § 600.1307. Former § 800.23 dealt with board meetings. Former § 800.24 dealt with classification of prisoners.

Former § 800.25 empowered the board to make regulations respecting food, clothing, etc., and required that all diets, clothing, and the like be of good quality and in sufficient quantity for the sustenance and comfort of the convicts. Former § 800.26 required reports by the warden to the board, and by the board to the governor. Former § 800.27 dealt with the wearing of a uniform by certain officers while on duty. Former § 800.28 dealt with the transfer of prisoners. Former § 800.29 empowered courts of criminal jurisdiction to sentence males within specified age categories to certain penal institutions. Former § 800.30 required the keeping of a register, containing specified data, respecting the prisoners. Former § 800.31 authorized the warden to employ convicts in specified occupations in and about the prison. For current provisions as to employment, see the Correctional Industries Act, §§800.321 et seq., and especially § 800.327. Former § 800.32 made aiding escape a felony.

Former §§800.24 and 800.28 were previously repealed by Pub Acts 1937, No. 255, imd eff July 22, 1937, ordered to take eff July 1, 1937 which, in turn, was repealed by Pub Acts 1947 (2nd Ex Sess), No. 4, imd eff November 12, 1947, former §§791.1 et seq., which, in turn, was repealed by Pub Acts 1953, No. 232, eff October 2, 1953.

For current provisions relative to the Department of Corrections and its various bureaus including the bureau of penal institutions and the bureau of prison industries, see §§791.201 et seq.

## § 800.33. Record of major misconduct charges as part of parole eligibility report; reduction from sentence; good time, disciplinary credits, special disciplinary credits; forfeiture; disciplinary credit committee; rules; good time committee; powers of warden and parole board; prisoner subject to disciplinary time; reduction of credits by court order. [MSA § 28.1403]

Sec. 33. (1) A record of all major misconduct charges for which a prisoner has been found guilty shall be maintained and given to the parole board as part of the parole eligibility report prepared for each prisoner pursuant to section 35 of 1953 PA 232, MCL 791.235.

(2) Except as otherwise provided in this section, a prisoner who is serving a sentence for a crime committed before April 1, 1987, and who has not been found guilty of a major misconduct or had a violation of the laws of this state recorded against him or her shall receive a reduction from his or her sentence as follows:

(a) During the first and second years of his or her sentence, 5 days for each month.

(b) During the third and fourth years, 6 days for each month.

(c) During the fifth and sixth years, 7 days for each month.

(d) During the seventh, eighth, and ninth years, 9 days for each month.

(e) During the tenth, eleventh, twelfth, thirteenth, and fourteenth years, 10 days for each month.

(f) During the fifteenth, sixteenth, seventeenth, eighteenth, and nineteenth years, 12 days for each month.

(g) From and including the twentieth year, up to and including the period fixed for the expiration of the sentence, 15 days for each month.

**Prisons** § 800.33

(3) Except as provided in section 34, all prisoners serving a sentence for a crime that was committed on or after April 1, 1987 are eligible to earn disciplinary and special disciplinary credits as provided in subsection (5). Disciplinary credits shall be earned, forfeited, and restored as provided in this section. Accumulated disciplinary credits shall be deducted from a prisoner's minimum and maximum sentence in order to determine his or her parole eligibility date and discharge date.

(4) This section shall not be construed to allow good time, disciplinary credits, or special disciplinary credits in cases of commuted sentences unless so stipulated in the executive order commuting the sentence.

(5) Except as provided in section 34, all prisoners serving a sentence on December 30, 1982, or incarcerated after December 30, 1982, for the conviction of a crime enumerated in section 33b(a) to (cc) of 1953 PA 232, MCL 791.233b, are eligible to earn a disciplinary credit of 5 days per month for each month served after December 30, 1982. Accumulated disciplinary credits shall be deducted from a prisoner's minimum and maximum sentence in order to determine his or her parole eligibility dates.

A prisoner shall not earn disciplinary credits under this subsection during any month in which the prisoner is found guilty of having committed a major misconduct. The amount of disciplinary credits not earned as a result of being found guilty of a major misconduct shall be limited to the disciplinary credits that would have been earned for the month in which the major misconduct occurred. Any disciplinary credits not earned as a result of the prisoner being found guilty of a major misconduct shall never be earned or restored. The warden may order that a prisoner found guilty of a major misconduct, including but not limited to charges of rioting, inciting to riot, escape, homicide, or assault and battery, forfeit all or a portion of the disciplinary credits accumulated prior to the month in which the misconduct occurred. An order forfeiting accumulated disciplinary credits shall be based upon a review of the prisoner's institutional record.

The disciplinary credit committee, which is comprised of the prisoner's resident unit manager, custody officers in the resident unit with direct supervisory responsibilities over the prisoner, and the appropriate work or school assignment supervisor, shall be a part of the reclassification process and shall review, at least annually, the status of each prisoner in the housing unit who has forfeited disciplinary credits. The committee may recommend to the warden whether any forfeited disciplinary credits should be restored to the prisoner.

In addition to disciplinary credits, a prisoner eligible for disciplinary credits under this subsection may be awarded 2 days per month special disciplinary credits for good institutional conduct on the recommendation of the disciplinary credit committee and the concurrence of the warden based on an annual review of the

§ 800.33                                                              Prisons

prisoner's institutional record. Special disciplinary credits shall not be awarded for any month in which a prisoner has been found guilty of a major misconduct.

The department of corrections shall promulgate rules pursuant to the administrative procedures act of 1969, 1969 PA 306, MCL 24.201 to 24.328, necessary to implement this subsection not more than 180 days after December 30, 1982.

(6) On and after April 1, 1987, a prisoner shall not earn good time under this section during any month in which the prisoner is found guilty of having committed a major misconduct. The amount of good time not earned as a result of being found guilty of a major misconduct shall be limited to the amount of good time that would have been earned during the month in which the major misconduct occurred. Any good time not earned as a result of the prisoner being found guilty of a major misconduct shall never be earned or restored.

(7) The department of corrections shall promulgate rules pursuant to the administrative procedures act of 1969, 1969 PA 306, MCL 24.201 to 24.328, prescribing how much of his or her accumulated good time or accumulated disciplinary credits the prisoner may forfeit if found guilty of 1 or more major misconducts.

(8) The warden may order that a prisoner found guilty of a major misconduct forfeit all or a portion of the good time accumulated prior to the month in which the misconduct occurred.

(9) The good time committee, which is comprised of the prisoner's resident unit manager, custody officer in the resident unit with direct supervisory responsibility over the prisoner, and the appropriate work or school assignment supervisor, shall be part of the reclassification process. The good time committee shall recommend to the war den the amount of special good time to be awarded and the restoration of any accumulated good time that has been forfeited.

(10) The warden, as a reward for good conduct, may restore to a prisoner the whole or any portion of the good time or disciplinary credits forfeited because of a finding of guilty for a major misconduct. However, forfeited good time or disciplinary credits shall not be restored without the recommendation of the disciplinary credit committee or good time committee and the prior written approval of the deputy director in charge of the bureau of correctional facilities or the deputy director in charge of the bureau of field services. Disciplinary credits or good time allowances that have not been earned because of institutional misconduct shall not be restored.

(11) A prisoner who has been sentenced concurrently for separate convictions shall have his or her good time or disciplinary credits computed on the basis of the longest of the concurrent sentences. If a prisoner is serving consecutive sentences for separate convictions, his or her good time or disciplinary credits shall be computed and accumulated on each sentence individually and all good time or disciplinary credits that have been earned on any of the sentences shall be subject to forfeiture pursuant to subsections (5) and (8).

(12) The warden of an institution may grant special good time

allowances to eligible prisoners who are convicted of a crime that is committed before April 1, 1987. Special good time credit shall not exceed 50% of the good time allowances under the schedule in subsection (2). Special good time shall be awarded for good conduct only and shall not be awarded for any month in which a prisoner has been found guilty of a major misconduct.

(13) The parole board shall be exclusively empowered to cause the forfeiture of good time or disciplinary credits earned by a prisoner at the time of a parole violation.

(14) A prisoner subject to disciplinary time is not eligible for good time, special good time, disciplinary credits, or special disciplinary credits.

(15) The court may order the reduction or forfeiture of 1 or more of the following credits pursuant to section 5513 of the revised judicature act of 1961, 1961 PA 236, MCL 600.5513:

(a) Good time.
(b) Disciplinary.
(c) Special disciplinary.

**History:**
Pub Acts 1893, No. 118, § 33, imd eff May 26, 1893; amended by Pub Acts 1917, No. 17, eff August 10, 1917; 1921, No. 256, imd eff May 18, 1921; 1929, No. 300, imd eff May 23, 1929; 1931, No. 86, imd eff May 11, 1931; 1933, No. 252, eff October 17, 1933; 1953, No. 105, eff October 2, 1953; 1978, No. 80, imd eff March 29, 1978; 1982, No. 442, imd eff December 30, 1982; 1986, No. 322, imd eff December 26, 1986, by § 3 eff April 1, 1987; 1994, No. 218, eff June 27, 1994 (see 1994 note below).

Amended by Pub Acts 1999, No. 148, imd eff November 1, 1999 (see 1999 note below).

**Prior codification:**
CL 1929, § 17576; CL 1915, § 1732; CL 1897, § 2112.

**Editor's notes:**
**Pub Acts 1994, No. 218, §§2, 3,** eff June 27, 1994, provide:

"Section 2. Sections 33 and 34 of Act No. 118 of the Public Acts of 1893, as amended or as added by this amendatory act, shall take effect on the date that sentencing guidelines are enacted into law after the sentencing commission submits its report to the secretary of the senate and the clerk of the house of representatives pursuant to sections 31 to 34 of chapter IX of the code of criminal procedure, Act No. 175 of the Public Acts of 1927, as added by the amendatory act resulting from House Bill No. 4782 of the 87th Legislature [Pub Acts 1994, No. 445]. (**Repealed** by Pub Acts 1998, No. 316, imd eff July 30, 1998, by enacting § 2 eff December 15, 1998.).

"Section 3. This amendatory act shall not take effect unless all of the following bills of the 87th Legislature are enacted into law:

"(a) Senate Bill No. 40 [Pub Acts 1994, No. 217].
"(b) House Bill No. 4782 [Pub Acts 1994, No. 445].
"(c) House Bill No. 5439 [Pub Acts 1994, No. 322]."

**Pub Acts 1999, No. 148, enacting § 1,** imd eff November 1, 1999, provides:

"Enacting section 1. This amendatory act does not take effect unless Senate Bill No. 419 of the 90th Legislature [Pub Act 1999, No. 147] is enacted into law."

**Effect of amendment notes:**
**The 1994 amendment** substituted "April 1, 1987" for "the effective date of this 1986 amendatory act" in several locations; in subsections (3) and (5) inserted "Except as provided in section 34"; in subsection (5), fourth

## § 800.33

paragraph, inserted "eligible for disciplinary credits under this subsection"; added subsection (14); and made grammatical changes.

**The 1999 amendment** in subsections (1), (5), and (7), changed the style of statutory references; and added subsection (15).

**Statutory references:**
Section 34 is § 800.34.

**Michigan Digest references:**
Administrative Law § 3.60.
Former Jeopardy §§4, 7.
Pardons and Paroles §§4, 10.
Prisons and Jails §§1.05, 2, 2.10, 2.35, 2.40, 2.50, 2.80, 2.110, 5.
Probate Courts § 5.

**LEXIS-NEXIS™ Michigan analytical references:**
Michigan Law and Practice, Convicts and Prisons §§2, 6.

**ALR notes:**
Computation of incarceration time under work-release or "hardship" sentences, 28 ALR4th 1265.

**Research references:**
60 Am Jur 2d, Penal and Correctional Institutions §§58, 59, 61–64.
22 Am Jur Trials 1, Prisoners' Rights Litigation.

### CASE NOTES

**1. Validity.**

The amendment of the statute authorizing a prison warden to order, without a hearing officer's recommendation, the automatic forfeiture of five days of disciplinary credits and the discretion to order a forfeiture of up to two years of accumulated disciplinary credits upon finding a prisoner guilty of a major misconduct charge following a hearing does not violate due process or provide the warden with unfettered discretion; due process does not require that the prisoner receive a written explanation of the reasons for the forfeiture. Tessin v Department of Corrections (1992) 197 Mich App 236, 495 NW2d 397.

Due process does not require that a prison warden provide a prisoner a written explanation of the reasons for ordering forfeiture of the prisoner's accumulated disciplinary credits following a hearing and a finding that the prisoner committed a major misconduct offense; however, the submission of a written explanation is necessary to enable a trial court to determine whether there was an abuse of the warden's discretion in the imposition of the penalty; the written statement must take into account the prisoner's institutional record and the nature of the major misconduct committed. Tessin v Department of Corrections (1992) 197 Mich App 236, 495 NW2d 397.

Due process does not require that a prison warden provide a prisoner a written explanation of the reasons for ordering forfeiture of the prisoner's accumulated disciplinary credits following a hearing and a finding that the prisoner committed a major misconduct offense; however, the submission of a written explanation is necessary to enable a trial court to determine whether there was an abuse of the warden's discretion in the imposition of the penalty; the written statement must take into account the prisoner's institutional record and the nature of the major misconduct committed. Tessin v Department of Corrections (1992) 197 Mich App 236, 495 NW2d 397.

Since equal treatment of male and female convicts in state prisons with respect to good-time credits was mandated by former § 802.55, former statutes establishing Detroit House of Correction and requiring all female state prisoners to be incarcerated there did not unconstitutionally discriminate against such prisoners on ground that, under former § 802.20, they were not permitted to earn as much good-time credit per month for good behavior as men in other state penal institutions under this section. People v Andrea (1973) 48 Mich App 310, 210 NW2d 474.

**2. Construction, operation and effect.**

Sentence of 75–150 years, along with

consideration of possible disciplinary credits, was affirmed on review of conviction for second-degree murder. People v Rushlow (1991) 437 Mich 149, 468 NW2d 487, motion den (1991) 437 Mich 1255, 472 NW2d 286.

The Department of Corrections' use of the "immediate usage" method for calculating regular good-time and special good-time credits for prisoners does not violate the statute that authorizes the credits; the immediate usage method permits prisoners to use immediately their good-time credit as earned to reduce both their minimum and maximum sentences; the next year of a sentence begins not upon the actual service of a calendar year in prison, but upon completion of a year reduced by good-time credits; the method allows a prisoner to become eligible for the higher accrual rates of good-time credits sooner than the corresponding calendar year and thus to become eligible for parole or discharge at an earlier date. Michigan ex rel. Oakland County Prosecutor v Department of Corrections (1993) 199 Mich App 681, 503 NW2d 465, app den (1993) 444 Mich 852, 508 NW2d 498.

The Legislature's failure to amend the statutory provision regarding good-time credits for prisoners so as to require the Department of Corrections to calculate the credits in a manner other than the "immediate usage" method employed by the department indicates consent or acquiescence with regard to the method. Michigan ex rel. Oakland County Prosecutor v Department of Corrections (1993) 199 Mich App 681, 503 NW2d 465, app den (1993) 444 Mich 852, 508 NW2d 498.

Michigan's "lifer law" allows any prison inmate under a sentence of life or for a term of years, other than those who have been convicted of first-degree murder or of a major controlled substance offense, to be considered for parole after serving 10 calendar years of his or her sentence; the electorate's approval of Proposal B in 1978 and the 1982 amendment of that statute modified the "lifer law" to the effect that inmates serving indeterminate sentences for any of the crimes enumerated in the statute are no longer eligible for parole until the minimum term is served less any time earned in disciplinary credits; Proposal B does not apply to life sentences. People v Hurst (1986) 155 Mich App 573, 400 NW2d 685, appeal after remand (1988) 169 Mich App 160, 425 NW2d 752, app den (1989, Mich) 1989 Mich LEXIS 365.

Prisoners currently under the jurisdiction of the Department of Corrections who were convicted of controlled substance offenses set forth in § 333.7403(2)(a)(i), (ii), or (iii); MCL § 333.7403(2)(a)(i), (ii), or (iii), and who were under the five-day sentence reduction limitation of the former provisions of MCL § 800.33(4), may be allowed sentence reduction pursuant to MCL § 800.33(2), commencing April 1, 1987, the effective date of 1986 PA 322. Op Atty Gen, April 22, 1988, No. 6514.

### 3. Statute as ex post facto.

A statute denying to convicts under sentence for a second offense the same reductions from their sentence for good behavior that are allowed to other convicts is not ex post facto as applied to the punishment of an offense subsequently committed, although the offender had been convicted of his first offense before the passage of the act. In re Miller (1896) 110 Mich 676, 68 NW 990.

A statute which impliedly provides for estimating the credits of convicts in the state prison upon a schedule less favorable than the one in force when they were sentenced, diminishes the right given them by the former statute to earn by good behavior a certain reduction of sentence, and is to that extent ex post facto, its effect being to increase, not to mitigate, punishment. In re Canfield (1894) 98 Mich 644, 57 NW 807.

### 4. Good behavior allowance.

Where petitioner after serving part of sentence was paroled, violated his parole, was treated as escaped prisoner, returned to prison for maximum term of his sentence, and time earned for good behavior was forfeited, date upon which petitioner could be released held date upon which maximum term was served less any time earned for good behavior after his return to prison. In re Holton (1943) 304 Mich 534, 8 NW2d 628.

The question of good behavior time of a prisoner under the statute applies only to those whose expiration of sentence is fixed and the statute is not applicable to a life sentence. Meyers v Jackson (1929) 245 Mich 692, 224 NW 356.

A defendant who is convicted as an habitual offender must serve the minimum prison sentence imposed by the trial court prior to being eligible for disciplinary credits. People v Lincoln (1987) 167 Mich App 429, 423 NW2d 216.

This section, as amended in 1953, confers no arbitrary power on parole board to withhold approval of release or discharge of convict who has earned sufficient good time thereunder to be eligible therefor, the sole power conferred upon board being to determine from convict's prison record whether he has earned such good time and whether it is correctly computed, and the parole board is given no power to reverse or vacate orders or findings of warden or commissioner of corrections with respect to good-time allowances. Op Atty Gen, March 30, 1955, No. 1938.

Discussion of good-time credit to be given for time already served after new trial and conviction of person who had escaped under previous sentence. Op Atty Gen, June 30, 1948, No. 786.

Good time may not be deducted from sentence for contempt and such sentence, although it may be served in prison, is not a "term in prison" within meaning of good-time provisions of prison code. Op Atty Gen, November 7, 1947, No. 208.

Commissioner of pardons and paroles has exclusive power to grant or withhold allowance of additional good time to prisoners by virtue of this section. Op Atty Gen, January 10, 1935.

### 5. – Entitlement.

A prisoner's writ of mandamus directing prison officials to recalculate his maximum prison sentence to include the application of good-time credits was properly rejected where the prisoner had been convicted of delivery of cocaine greater than 22 grams but less than 650 grams and conspiracy to deliver cocaine; the plain language of the statute precludes persons convicted of certain offenses–including delivery and conspiracy to deliver a controlled substance–from good-time credit reductions. Rhode v Department of Corrections (1997) 227 Mich App 174, 578 NW2d 320.

A person convicted of a Proposal B offense and receiving good-time credits against the maximum sentence before December 30, 1982, is thereafter entitled to continue receiving good-time credits against the maximum sentence and to receive disciplinary credits against the minimum sentence. Lowe v Department of Corrections (1994) 206 Mich App 128, 521 NW2d 336.

All prisoners, including those prisoners sentenced as habitual offenders, are entitled to good-time credit. Lamb v Bureau of Pardons & Paroles (1981) 106 Mich App 175, 307 NW2d 754.

Since confinement of military prisoner in United States disciplinary barracks is not confinement within prison within meaning of this section and violation of article of war does not constitute crime within meaning of section unless such violation is also a crime recognized by civil law of jurisdiction in which act is committed, war veteran whose only previous sentence was confinement in United States disciplinary barracks was entitled to receive good-time allowance on high rate scale. Op Atty Gen, December 1, 1948, No. 856.

Convict whose only prior Commitment has been under federal Juvenile Delinquency Act is entitled to maximum good-time allowance provided by this section. Op Atty Gen, May 10, 1946, No. 0–4634.

One sentenced for nonpayment of alimony is not entitled to deduction from sentence on account of good time. Op Atty Gen, 1928–1930, p 576.

This section applies only to state prisons, and a prisoner serving a one-year sentence in a county jail is not eligible to have his term shortened by "good time," though he may make application for parole at the end of the minimum term, or for pardon or commutation of sentence. Op Atty Gen, 1926–1928, p 172.

Good time allowed convicts is deductible from the minimum sentence only; there is no authority for deducting good time from the maximum sentence. Op Atty Gen, 1923–1924, p 13.

The good time earned is a substantial right. A convict may earn good time after being transferred to a state hospital. Op Atty Gen, 1923–1924, p 24.

### 6. Second or subsequent term.

Provision for "low-grade good time" allowance was applicable to prisoner who had served time in federal penitentiary in Kansas under sentence on conviction by court-martial for crime which would have been a felony if committed in Michigan. Losinger v Department of Corrections (1950) 329 Mich 47, 44 NW2d 864.

This section, providing that a prisoner "who has already served a second term in the said prison" shall be allowed specified good time, does not include a term of imprisonment in the house of correction and reformatory imposed without jurisdiction. In re Harney (1903) 134 Mich 527, 96 NW 795.

Time being served under sentence for a subsequent conviction for a separate offense while a person has been admitted to bail on an appeal from a prior conviction and sentence may not be construed as time being served on first sentence when appeal is abandoned. Op Atty Gen, August 5, 1949, No. 1009.

Under good-time law, any convict sentenced and committed to serve any time in penitentiary should be considered as serving or having served a term in prison. Op Atty Gen, November 7, 1947, No. 208.

Commitment to prison for contempt under provisions of § 552.201, may not be computed against good time convict may earn under provisions of this section. Op Atty Gen, November 7, 1947, No. 208.

One who has served previous term in federal prison, regardless of where located, may not earn good time at so-called high rate authorized by this section. Op Atty Gen, November 7, 1947, No. 208.

Convict whose only prior commitment has been under federal Juvenile Delinquency Act is entitled to maximum good-time allowance provided by this section. Op Atty Gen, May 10, 1946, No. 0–4634.

Convict who has served term in federal prison upon conviction in general court-martial proceeding must be governed by lower scale in respect of good-time allowance under this section. Op Atty Gen, February 1, 1944, No. 0–1756.

Prison inmate serving two or more consecutive sentences, when commencing his second sentence should receive the benefit of the time served upon his first sentence and earn his good time upon an accelerated scale. Op Atty Gen, October 23, 1939.

Under this section, as amended by Pub Acts 1933, No. 252, (1) a first termer is entitled to make regular good time allowance from beginning of his term, and may also receive additional good time not to exceed 50 percent of regular allowance, (2) a second termer whose first term was served in Michigan is entitled to make regular low-rate good time from beginning of his term to October 17, 1933, and thereafter regular high-rate good time on the accelerated scale, and may also receive additional good time not to exceed 50 percent of regular good-time allowance, (3) a second termer whose first term was served outside Michigan is entitled to regular low-rate good time from beginning of his term and may also receive additional good time not to exceed 50 percent of his regular good-time allowance, (4) a third, fourth, etc., termer's good-time allowance starts from October 17, 1933, and is based on the low rate, but he may also receive additional good time not to exceed 50 percent of his good-time allowance, and (5) one convicted as a "subsequent offender" is entitled to the same allowances as if he had not been so convicted. Op Atty Gen, 1933–1934, pp 302–305.

A second termer, sentenced prior to effective date of 1929 amendment of this section (May 23), whose first term was served in Michigan, is entitled to regular good-time allowance computed on the basis of a first termer, but extra good-time allowance should not exceed 50 percent of what his regular good-time allowance would be if computed on the basis of a second termer. Op Atty Gen, 1933–1934, p 394.

Under prior statute the serving of two prior sentences at Jackson prison would bar "good time" in subsequent term at Marquette. Op Atty Gen, 1915, p 77.

A convict was regarded as serving a first term where a prior "first" sentence had been discharged on order of the supreme court. Op Atty Gen, 1914, p 520.

### 7. Commuted sentence.

Commutation by the governor of a life sentence to one of 15 years fixes the date of expiration of the sentence and the prisoner is not entitled to a further reduction under a statute providing for reduction of sentence for good behavior. Meyers v Jackson (1929) 245 Mich 692, 224 NW 356.

Where a commutation order commutes a sentence to "twenty to thirty years with good time allowance," the inmate is entitled to deduction for good time commencing with date of imposition of sentence. Op Atty Gen, 1930–1932, p 181.

Under prior statute where executive order commuting a sentence was silent regarding allowance for good time, good time must be allowed. Op Atty Gen, 1926–1928, p 452.

### 8. Forfeiture of good time.

Due process does not require that a prison warden provide a prisoner a written explanation of the reasons for ordering forfeiture of the prisoner's accumulated disciplinary credits following a hearing and a finding that the prisoner committed a major misconduct offense;

however, the submission of a written explanation is necessary to enable a trial court to determine whether there was an abuse of the warden's discretion in the imposition of the penalty; the written statement must take into account the prisoner's institutional record and the nature of the major misconduct committed. Tessin v Department of Corrections (1992) 197 Mich App 236, 495 NW2d 397.

Michigan prison code provision relating to forfeiture of good time which contains language relating to "serious act of insubordination" is apparently designed to deter, by punishing, acts of misconduct which are so flagrant that they represent threat to security and order of prison institution, and if inmate's behavior does not constitute "threat to institutional order" or "open defiance of authority" then it cannot be said to fall within meaning of statute. Butler v Warden, Marquette Prison (1980) 100 Mich App 179, 298 NW2d 701.

Conduct in question must be both serious and amount to act of insubordination in order to come within purview of good time statute permitting warden to forfeit good time on sentence by special order in absence of properly promulgated rules delineating how much good time would be forfeited by a convict for one or more actions of prison rules. Williams v Warden, Michigan Reformatory (1979) 88 Mich App 782, 279 NW2d 313.

In absence of rules properly promulgated by director of corrections delineating how much good time on sentence shall be forfeited for one or morections of prison rules in any month, good time may be forfeited under authority of good time statute by special order of warden only for serious act of insubordination, attempt to escape, or escape. Williams v Warden, Michigan Reformatory (1979) 88 Mich App 782, 279 NW2d 313.

Federal Supreme Court holding entitling state prison inmates to due process notice and hearing concerning discipline by department of corrections following serious misconduct committed by inmates is applicable prospectively only as of June 24, 1974, and, accordingly, would not apply to 1966 act of state prison warden in administratively forfeiting inmate's accumulated time as result of his conviction for felony committed while in prison. Parshay v Department of Corrections (1975) 61 Mich App 677, 233 NW2d 139.

Board of control of Michigan reformatory has power to adopt rule providing that convict on parole shall forfeit his good time for violation thereof. Op Atty Gen, 1913, p 393.

Prisoner guilty of a single action of prison rules in any month did not lose all his good time, and where guilty of more than one action lost only such good time as the board of control at regular meeting deemed meet. Op Atty Gen, 1912, p 124.

**9. – Escape.**

Lapse of approximately six months after sentence of prisoner for escape did not preclude warden from forfeiting prisoner's good time earned under original sentence, under provision authorizing warden to take away earned good time for any serious act of insubordination, including escaping prison. In re Evans (1958) 352 Mich 185, 89 NW2d 535.

Statute specifically authorizing warden to remove portion or all of earned good time where inmate escapes or attempts to escape precluded defendant escapee from successfully contending that removal of his earned good time could not be effected in absence of regulation promulgated by prison officials under Administrative Procedures Act. Pfefferle v Michigan Corrections Com. (1976) 86 Mich App 366, 272 NW2d 563.

Prison authorities' revocation of defendant inmate's earned good time because of escape was violative of due process and could not stand on record disclosing that authorities afforded defendant no prior notice or time to prepare defense in initial revocation hearing, failed to afford defendant opportunity to present defense witnesses at subsequent hearing, and made no finding that calling of witnesses would be unduly hazardous to institutional safety or goals, and no findings regarding evidence and reasons relied on for revocation. Pfefferle v Michigan Corrections Com. (1976) 86 Mich App 366, 272 NW2d 563.

Combination of administrative forfeiture of good time and sentence on criminal conviction for same act of escape did not violate double jeopardy provision of Fifth Amendment, since forfeiture proceeding does not amount to criminal prosecution in court of justice, and there was no identity of offenses in that single act of escape constituted both statutory criminal offense and offense against prison rules evoking good time forfeiture procedure under this section. People v Bachman (1973) 50 Mich App 682, 213

NW2d 800.

Administrative procedure whereby defendant as returned escapee was placed in solitary confinement, given booklet issued by warden regarding returning escapees, was taken before prison board for questioning, with resultant loss of good time, following which defendant was sentenced for escape, would be held not to have amounted to such acts as would demonstrate cruel and unusual punishment in violation of defendant's constitutional rights. People v Robinson (1972) 41 Mich App 259, 199 NW2d 878.

**10. – Parole violation.**

Parole violator's assault of a parole officer would justify the commissioner in holding him guilty of a serious act of insubordination and invest him with the discretion to cancel the prisoner's good time to the time of such assault. Robinson v Gries (1936) 277 Mich 15, 268 NW 794.

Under a statute providing that the prison board may by general rules prescribe for forfeiture of good time by prisoners, a prisoner cannot be deprived of the right to earn a reduction of his term while out on parole where there is no express rule covering his case, and the rules apply in terms only to those within the prison. In re Mann (1900) 125 Mich 402, 84 NW 612.

This section permits the revoking of all of the good time of a prisoner returned to prison for violation of parole up to the time of the violation. Op Atty Gen, 1930–1932, p 466.

**11. – Discretion of warden.**

The amendment of the statute authorizing a prison warden to order, without a hearing officer's recommendation, the automatic forfeiture of five days of disciplinary credits and the discretion to order a forfeiture of up to two years of accumulated disciplinary credits upon finding a prisoner guilty of a major misconduct charge following a hearing does not violate due process or provide the warden with unfettered discretion; due process does not require that the prisoner receive a written explanation of the reasons for the forfeiture. Tessin v Department of Corrections (1992) 197 Mich App 236, 495 NW2d 397.

Defendant warden did not abuse discretion in finding that act of throwing urine or human waste constitutes "serious act of insubordination" as phrase is used in statute relating to forfeiture of good time. Butler v Warden, Marquette Prison (1980) 100 Mich App 179, 298 NW2d 701.

For purposes of determining what constitutes "serious act of insubordination" as phrase is used in statute relating to forfeiture of good time, prison warden is in far better position to ascertain whether act constitutes threat to institutional order of prison than are courts, and judiciary should not interfere with warden's exercise of discretion unless that discretion has been clearly abused. Butler v Warden, Marquette Prison (1980) 100 Mich App 179, 298 NW2d 701.

Warden's forfeiture of plaintiff inmate's good time earned on sentence because of finding that plaintiff committed assault on another inmate in prison was violative of due process as failing to comply with good time statute where conduct in question did not qualify as serious act of insubordination for which warden could forfeit good time by special order under statute, and where department of corrections had promulgated no rules for delineating how much good time should be forfeited by one or more actions of prison rules, thereby entitling plaintiff to grant of writ of mandamus for restoration of forfeited good time. Williams v Warden, Michigan Reformatory (1979) 88 Mich App 782, 279 NW2d 313.

A prison warden's statutory discretion to forfeit escaped prisoner's earned good time may not be exercised in arbitrary manner or one resulting in substantial injustice. Pfefferle v Michigan Corrections Com. (1976) 86 Mich App 366, 272 NW2d 563.

**12. Judicial intervention.**

Prison authorities have the right to adopt reasonable restrictions governing the conduct of inmates and visitors and the courts ought not to interfere with prison operations in the absence of constitutional deprivation. Bessinger v Department of Corrections (1985) 142 Mich App 793, 371 NW2d 868.

Prisoners enjoy certain constitutional protections and may be entitled to judicial intervention upon a showing of a clear abuse of discretion on the part of prison officials; such intervention must be based on clear and articulable grounds. Bessinger v Department of Corrections (1985) 142 Mich App 793, 371 NW2d 868.

## § 800.34. Disciplinary time; receipt for each major misconduct; accumulation; consideration for concurrent or consecutive sentences; reduction; "prisoner subject to disciplinary time" defined. [MSA § 28.1404]

Sec. 34. (1) A prisoner subject to disciplinary time shall receive disciplinary time for each major misconduct for which he or she is found guilty as prescribed by rule pursuant to section 35.

(2) Accumulated disciplinary time shall be submitted to the parole board for the parole board's consideration at the prisoner's parole review or interview. A prisoner's minimum sentence, plus disciplinary time, shall not exceed his or her maximum sentence.

(3) A prisoner who has been sentenced concurrently for separate convictions shall have his or her disciplinary time considered by the parole board on each sentence individually. If a prisoner is serving consecutive sentences for separate convictions, his or her disciplinary time shall be considered by the parole board on each sentence individually.

(4) A prisoner subject to disciplinary time may have any or all of his or her accumulated disciplinary time reduced by the department if he or she has demonstrated exemplary good conduct during the term of imprisonment. Disciplinary time deducted pursuant to this section may be restored if the prisoner is found guilty of a major misconduct.

(5) As used in this act, "prisoner subject to disciplinary time" includes both of the following:

(a) A prisoner sentenced to an indeterminate term of imprisonment for any of the following crimes committed on or after December 15, 1998:

(i) A violation of section 625(4) or (5) of the Michigan vehicle code, 1949 PA 300, MCL 257.625.

(ii) A violation of section 80176(4) or (5) of part 801 (marine safety) of the natural resources and environmental protection act, 1994 PA 451, MCL 324.80176.

(iii) A violation of section 72, 73, 80, 82, 83, 84, 86, 87, 88, 89, 90, 110a(2), 112, 136b(2), 145c, 204, 204a, 205, 205a, 206, 207, 208, 210, 211, 211a, 213, 316, 317, 319, 321, 322, 327, 328, 329, 349, 349a, 350, 357, 397, 411i, 479b, 520b, 520c, 520d, 520e, 520g, 529, 529a, 530, or 531 of the Michigan penal code, 1931 PA 328, MCL 750.72, 750.73, 750.80, 750.82, 750.83, 750.84, 750.86, 750.87, 750.88, 750.89, 750.90, 750.110a, 750.112, 750.136b, 750.145c, 750.204, 750.204a, 750.205, 750.205a, 750.206, 750.207, 750.208, 750.210, 750.211, 750.211a, 750.213, 750.316, 750.317, 750.319, 750.321, 750.322, 750.327, 750.328, 750.329, 750.349, 750.349a, 750.350, 750.357, 750.397, 750.411i, 750.479b, 750.520b, 750.520c, 750.520d, 750.520e, 750.520g, 750.529, 750.529a, 750.530, and 750.531.

(iv) A violation of section 1 of 1931 PA 214, MCL 752.191.

(v) A violation of section 1, 2, or 2a of 1968 PA 302, MCL 752.541, 752.542, and 752.542a.

(vi) Any offense not listed in subparagraphs (i) to (v) that is punishable by life imprisonment.

(vii) An attempt, conspiracy, or solicitation to commit an offense described in subparagraphs (i) to (vi).

(b) A prisoner sentenced to an indeterminate term of imprisonment for any crime not listed in subdivision (a), if that crime was committed on or after December 15, 2000.

**History:**
Pub Acts 1893, No. 118, § 34, as added by Pub Acts 1994, No. 218, eff June 27, 1994 (see 1994 note below).

Amended by Pub Acts 1996, No. 83, imd eff February 27, 1996 (see 1996 note below); 1998, No. 316, imd eff July 30, 1998, by enacting § 2 eff December 15, 1998 (see 1998 note below).

**Editor's notes:**
Former § 34 was repealed by Pub Acts, 1921, No. 237, imd eff May 26, 1921. It provided for a joint meeting of the prison boards to determine the kinds of productive labor to be pursued in each prison.

Prior § 34 was repealed by Pub Acts 1972, No. 179, imd eff June 16, 1972. This section dealt with employment of prisoners in making articles for state institutions. For current provisions as to employment, see the Correctional Industries Act, §§800.321 et seq. and particularly § 800.327.

**Pub Acts 1994, No. 218, §§2, 3,** eff June 27, 1994, provide:
"Section 2. Sections 33 and 34 of Act No. 118 of the Public Acts of 1893, as amended or as added by this amendatory act, shall take effect on the date that sentencing guidelines are enacted into law after the sentencing commission submits its report to the secretary of the senate and the clerk of the house of representatives pursuant to sections 31 to 34 of chapter IX of the code of criminal procedure, Act No. 175 of the Public Acts of 1927, as added by the amendatory act resulting from House Bill No. 4782 of the 87th Legislature [which became Pub Acts 1994, No. 445]. (**Repealed** by Pub Acts 1998, No. 316, imd eff July 30, 1998, by enacting § 2 eff December 15, 1998.).

"Section 3. This amendatory act shall not take effect unless all of the following bills of the 87th Legislature are enacted into law:

"(a) Senate Bill No. 40 [Pub Acts 1994, No. 217].

"(b) House Bill No. 4782 [Pub Acts 1994, No. 445].

"(c) House Bill No. 5439 [Pub Acts 1994, No. 322]."

**Pub Acts 1996, No. 83, § 2,** imd eff February 27, 1996, provides:
"Section 2. This amendatory act shall take effect on the date that sentencing guidelines are enacted into law after the sentencing commission submits its report to the secretary of the senate and the clerk of the house of representatives pursuant to sections 31 to 34 of chapter IX of the code of criminal procedure, Act No. 175 of the Public Acts of 1927, being sections 769.31 to 769.34 of the Michigan Compiled Laws."

**Pub Acts 1998, No. 316, enacting** § 3, imd eff July 30, 1998, by enacting § 2 eff December 15, 1998, provides:

"Enacting section 3. This amendatory act does not take effect unless all of the following bills of the 89th Legislature are enacted into law:

"(a) House Bill No. 4065 [Pub Acts 1998, No. 319].

"(b) House Bill No. 4444 [Pub Acts 1998, No. 311].

"(c) House Bill No. 4445 [Pub Acts 1998, No. 312].

"(d) House Bill No. 4446 [Pub Acts 1998, No. 313].

"(e) House Bill No. 4515 [Pub Acts 1998, No. 320].

"(f) House Bill No. 5398 [Pub Acts 1998, No. 315].

"(g) House Bill No. 5419 [Pub Acts 1998, No. 317]."

"(h) House Bill No. 5876 [Pub Acts 1998, No. 318]. .

**Effect of amendment notes:**
**The 1996 amendment** updated the statutory reference stated in subsection (5), paragraph (b).

The **1998 amendment** substituted "submitted to the parole board for the parole board's consideration at the prisoner's parole review or interview" for "added to a prisoner's minimum sentence in order to determine his or her parole eligibility date" in subsection (2); substituted "considered by the parole board" for "computed and accumulated" twice in subsection (3); redesignated part of the former first sentence of subsection (5) as paragraph (a) and redesignated former paragraphs (a)–(g) as subparagraphs (i)–(vii) and changed references to these subdivisions accordingly; added paragraph (b) of subsection (5); and changed the style of statutory references throughout subsection (5).

**Statutory references:**
Section 35, above referred to, is § 800.35.

**LEXIS-NEXIS™ Michigan analytical references:**
Michigan Law and Practice, Convicts and Prisons § 2.

**Research references:**
60 Am Jur 2d, Penal Inst §§124, 125, 222 et seq.
22 Am Jur Trials 1, Prisoners' Rights Litigation.

## § 800.35. Rules. [MSA § 28.1405]

Sec. 35. The department shall promulgate rules prescribing the amount of disciplinary time to be submitted to the parole board for the parole board's consideration for each type of major misconduct for which a prisoner subject to disciplinary time is found guilty. The rules shall be promulgated pursuant to the administrative procedures act of 1969, 1969 PA 306, MCL 24.201 to 24.328.

**History:**
Pub Acts 1893, No. 118, § 35, as added by Pub Acts 1994, No. 218, eff June 27, 1994 (see 1994 note below).
Amended by Pub Acts 1998, No. 316, imd eff July 30, 1998, by enacting § 2 eff December 15, 1998 (see 1998 note below).

**Editor's notes:**
Former § 35 was repealed by Pub Acts 1972, No. 179, imd eff June 16, 1972. That section dealt with transfer of convicts from one kind of work to another.

**Pub Acts 1994, No. 218, §§2, 3,** eff June 27, 1994, provide:
"Section 2. Sections 33 and 34 of Act No. 118 of the Public Acts of 1893, as amended or as added by this amendatory act, shall take effect on the date that sentencing guidelines are enacted into law after the sentencing commission submits its report to the secretary of the senate and the clerk of the house of representatives pursuant to sections 31 to 34 of chapter IX of the code of criminal procedure, Act No. 175 of the Public Acts of 1927, as added by the amendatory act resulting from House Bill No. 4782 of the 87th Legislature [which became Pub Acts 1994, No. 445]. (**Repealed** by Pub Acts 1998, No. 316, imd eff July 30, 1998, by enacting § 2 eff December 15, 1998.).
"Section 3. This amendatory act shall not take effect unless all of the following bills of the 87th Legislature are enacted into law:
"(a) Senate Bill No. 40 [Pub Acts 1994, No. 217].
"(b) House Bill No. 4782 [Pub Acts 1994, No. 445].
"(c) House Bill No. 5439 [Pub Acts 1994, No. 322]."
**Pub Acts 1998, No. 316, enacting** § **3,** imd eff July 30, 1998, by enacting § 2 eff December 15, 1998, provides:
"Enacting section 3. This amendatory act does not take effect unless all of the following bills of the 89th Legislature are enacted into law:
"(a) House Bill No. 4065 [Pub Acts 1998, No. 319].

# Prisons § 800.41

"(b) House Bill No. 4444 [Pub Acts 1998, No. 311].
"(c) House Bill No. 4445 [Pub Acts 1998, No. 312].
"(d) House Bill No. 4446 [Pub Acts 1998, No. 313].
"(e) House Bill No. 4515 [Pub Acts 1998, No. 320].
"(f) House Bill No. 5398 [Pub Acts 1998, No. 315].
"(g) House Bill No. 5419 [Pub Acts 1998, No. 317]."
"(h) House Bill No. 5876 [Pub Acts 1998, No. 318]. .

**Effect of amendment notes:**
The **1998 amendment** substituted "submitted to the parole board for the parole board's consideration" for " received by prisoners subject to disciplinary time" and "a prisoner subject to disciplinary time" for "he or she"; and changed the style of statutory references.

**LEXIS-NEXIS™ Michigan analytical references:**
Michigan Law and Practice, Convicts and Prisons § 2.

**Research references:**
60 Am Jur 2d, Penal Inst §§124, 125, 222 et seq.
22 Am Jur Trials 1, Prisoners' Rights Litigation.

**Legal periodicals:**
Van Ochten, Prison Disciplinary Hearings: Enforcing the Rules, 77 Mich B J 178 (1998).

## §§800.36–800.40. [Repealed] [MSA §§28.1406–28.1409(1)]

**History:**
Pub Acts 1893, No. 118, §§36–40, imd eff May 26, 1893; **repealed** by Pub Acts 1972, No. 179, imd eff June 16, 1972.

**Editor's notes:**
Former § 800.36 related to the transfer of prisoners from one kind of work to another. Former § 800.37 dealt with employment of convicts in solitary confinement. Former § 800.38 required the employment of certain convicts at hard labor. Former § 800.39 required that whenever there was a sufficient number of cells, prisoners should be kept singly therein. Former § 800.40 outlined duties of guards and employees, and made specified types of misconduct a misdemeanor, and empowered the warden or his deputy to punish the convicts, but prohibited certain types of punishment, such as whipping.

## § 800.41. Enforcement of discipline; attempted escapes; "correctional facility" defined. [MSA § 28.1410]

Sec. 41. (1) If a prisoner or prisoners assault or batter any officer or guard of a correctional facility, or assault or batter another prisoner or any other person, or damage, or attempt to damage any part of a correctional facility, or attempt to escape, or resist or disobey any reasonable command, the officers or guards of the correctional facility shall use all suitable means to defend themselves, to enforce the observance of discipline, to secure the persons of offenders, and to prevent any such attempt to escape.

(2) As used in this section, "correctional facility" means a facility that houses prisoners committed to the jurisdiction of the department of corrections, and includes a youth correctional facility operated by the department of corrections or a private vendor under section 20g of 1953 PA 232, MCL 791.232.

§ 800.41

**History:**
Pub Acts 1893, No. 118, § 41, imd eff May 26, 1893.
Amended by Pub Acts 1998, No. 513, imd eff January 8, 1999.

**Prior codification:**
CL 1929, § 17583; CL 1915, § 1739; CL 1897, § 2120.

**Effect of amendment notes:**
The **1998 amendment**redesignated the existing section as subsection (1), added and deleted material in subsection (1), and added subsection (2).

**Michigan Digest references:**
Prisons and Jails § 2.

**LEXIS-NEXIS™ Michigan analytical references:**
Michigan Law and Practice, Convicts and Prisons § 2.

**ALR notes:**
Prosecutions of inmates of state or local penal institutions for crime of riot, 39 ALR4th 1170.

**Research references:**
27 Am Jur 2d, Escape, Prison Breaking, and Rescue § 25.
60 Am Jur 2d Penal and Correctional Institutions §§41, 42.
54 Am Jur Trials 425, Asserting Claims of Unconstitutional Prison Conditions.

### CASE NOTES

Where defendant, who was committed to state prison in 1953 and later transferred to Detroit House of Correction, escaped from House of Correction in 1954, at which time house of correction was not specifically mentioned in § 750.193, former § 802.55 would be read together with § 750.193, and defendant could be prosecuted under § 750.193. People v Reese (1961) 363 Mich 329, 109 NW2d 868.

## § 800.42. Prisoner in correctional facility having security classification of I, II, III, IV, V, or VI; personal property; disposal; definitions. [MSA § 28.1411]

Sec. 42. (1) A prisoner in a correctional facility assigned to a housing unit having a security classification of IV, V, or VI shall not have in his or her living area any personal clothing, except that a prisoner in a correctional facility assigned to a housing unit having a security classification of IV may keep 1 set of personal clothing as determined by the department in his or her living area and may wear such clothing for court appearances or during visits. A prisoner in a correctional facility assigned to a housing unit having a security classification of V or VI shall be provided civilian clothing by the institution for jury trials or as ordered by the court for other court appearances.

(2) A prisoner in a correctional facility assigned to a housing unit having a security classification of I, II, or III may have personal clothing in his or her living area and may wear such clothing as approved by the department of corrections.

(3) Except as provided in subsection (4), the amount of personal property a prisoner may have in his or her living area, including personal clothing, shall not exceed the following limits:

**Prisons** § 800.42

(a) For a prisoner in a correctional facility assigned to a housing unit having a security classification of IV, V, or VI, not more than the amount that can be contained in 1 duffel bag or 1 footlocker or similarly sized container as approved by the department of corrections.

(b) For a prisoner in a correctional facility assigned to a housing unit having a security classification of I, II, or III, not more than the amount that can be contained in 1 duffel bag and 1 footlocker or similarly sized container as approved by the department of corrections.

(4) A prisoner may possess property in excess of the amounts set forth in subsection (3) if that property consists of legal materials that are not available in the institutional law library to which the prisoner has access. This subsection does not require that a prisoner be allowed physical access to a law library.

(5) This section does not allow a prisoner to possess personal property of a type otherwise prohibited by the department of corrections for any reason.

(6) Within 121 days after the effective date of the 1997 amendatory act that amended this section, any personal clothing in the possession of or in the living area of a prisoner that is not permitted under this section shall be disposed of by the prisoner using 1 of the following methods:

(a) Sent home with visitors.

(b) Mailed at the department's expense, to a person identified by the prisoner and approved of by the department.

(c) Donated to charity.

If the prisoner does not dispose of the personal clothing within the 121-day period as provided in this subsection, the department shall dispose of the clothing in a manner determined by the department.

(7) As used in this section and section 44:

(a) "Legal materials" means either of the following:

(i) Pleadings and other documents ordinarily filed with a court, letters, research notes, necessary exhibits, books, periodicals, and similar items that are needed for litigation which the prisoner is currently pursuing on his or her own behalf, or on behalf of another prisoner if that assistance has been approved by the institution head.

(ii) Pleadings, transcripts, court orders, and court opinions arising out of the offense for which the prisoner is currently incarcerated.

(b) "Personal clothing" means any clothing that is not a uniform or other standardized clothing issued by the department but does not include undergarments.

(c) "Security classification" means 1 of 6 levels of restrictiveness enforced in housing units at each correctional facility, as determined by the department of corrections, with security level I being the least restrictive and security level VI being the most restrictive.

**History:**
Pub Acts 1893, No. 118, § 42, as added by Pub Acts 1989, No. 168, imd eff August 21, 1989.
Amended by Pub Acts 1998, No. 376, imd eff October 21, 1998.

**Effect of amendment notes:**
The **1998 amendment** completely rewrote subsection (6), and made substantive changes throughout the section.

**Statutory references:**
Section 44, above referred to, is § 800.44.

**LEXIS-NEXIS™ Michigan analytical references:**
Michigan Law and Practice, Convicts and Prisons § 2.

**ALR notes:**
Prison conditions as amounting to cruel and unusual punishment, 51 ALR3d 111.
Validity and construction of prison regulation of inmates' possession of personal property, 66 ALR4th 800.

**Research references:**
60 Am Jur 2d, Penal Institution § 106.
22 Am Jur Trials 1, Prisoners' Rights Litigation.
19 Am Jur Pl & Pr Forms, Rev, Penal and Correctional Institutions, Form 47.

## § 800.43. Receipt or possession of certain material; prohibition; list; notice; appeal; limits on amount. [MSA § 28.1412]

Sec. 43. (1) The department may prohibit a prisoner from receiving or possessing any material that the department determines under this section is detrimental to the security, good order, or discipline of the institution, or that may facilitate or encourage criminal activity, or that may interfere with the rehabilitation of any prisoner. The department shall not prohibit a prisoner from receiving or possessing any material solely because the content of that material is religious, philosophical, political, social, or sexual, or because it is unpopular or repugnant. Material that may be prohibited under this section includes, but is not limited to, any of the following:

(a) Material that depicts or describes procedures for constructing or using weapons, ammunition, bombs, or incendiary devices.

(b) Material that depicts, encourages, or describes methods of escaping from correctional facilities or that contains blueprints, drawings, or similar descriptions of department institutions or facilities.

(c) Material that depicts or describes procedures for manufacturing alcoholic beverages or drugs.

(d) Material that is written in code.

(e) Material that depicts, describes, or encourages activities that may lead to the use of physical violence or group disruption.

(f) Material that encourages or provides instruction in criminal activity.

(g) Material that is sexually explicit and that by its nature or content poses a threat to the security, good order, or discipline of the institution, facilitates criminal activity, or interferes with the rehabilitation of any prisoner.

(2) The department of corrections shall not establish a list of material that may be prohibited under this section before the material is reviewed. This subsection does not prevent the department from prohibiting other prisoners from receiving or possessing identical copies of the material without review after the material has been initially reviewed.

(3) If a publication is prohibited by the department, the department shall promptly notify the prisoner in writing that the material is prohibited and the reasons it is prohibited. The notice shall state the specific content upon which the prohibition is based. The department shall allow the prisoner to review the material to determine whether he or she wishes to administratively appeal the department's decision to prohibit the material unless the review would threaten the security, good order, or discipline of the institution, encourage or provide instruction in criminal activity, or interfere with the rehabilitation of any prisoner.

(4) This section does not prohibit the department from setting limits on the amount of material an inmate may receive or retain in his or her quarters for fire, sanitation, or housekeeping reasons.

**History:**
Pub Acts 1893, No. 118, § 43, as added by Pub Acts 1996, No. 549, imd eff January 15, 1997.

**LEXIS-NEXIS™ Michigan analytical references:**
Michigan Law and Practice, Convicts and Prisons § 2.

**ALR notes:**
Nature and elements of offense of conveying contraband to state prisoner, 64 ALR4th 902.

Validity and construction of prison regulation of inmates' possession of personal property, 66 ALR4th 800.

Validity, construction, and application of state statute criminalizing possession of contraband by individual in penal or correctional institution, 45 ALR5th 767.

**Research references:**
60 Am Jur 2d, Penal Inst §§80, 106.

## § 800.44. Uniform; color. [MSA § 28.1413]

Sec. 44. A prisoner in a correctional facility assigned to a housing unit having a security classification of I to VI shall wear a uniform provided by the department at all times except when personal clothing may be worn as provided in section 42. The color of a prisoner's uniform shall be determined by the department.

**History:**
Pub Acts 1893, No. 118, § 44, as added by Pub Acts 1998, No. 376, imd eff October 21, 1998.

**Editor's notes:**
Former § 800.44 making it the duty of the warden to practice rigid economy, and to take duplicate receipts for expenditures, was repealed by Pub Acts 1972, No. 179, imd eff June 16, 1972.

§ 800.44

**Statutory references:**
Section 42, above referred to, is § 800.42.

**LEXIS-NEXIS™ Michigan analytical references:**
Michigan Law and Practice, Convicts and Prisons § 2.

**Research references:**
61 Am Jur 2d, Penal and Correctional Institutions §§26, 27, 106.
22 Am Jur Trials 1, Prisoners' Rights Litigation.

## §§800.45–800.47. [Repealed] [MSA §§28.1414–28.1416]

**History:**
Pub Acts 1893, No. 118, §§45–47, imd eff May 26, 1893; **repealed** by Pub Acts 1972, No. 179, imd eff June 16, 1972.

**Editor's notes:**
Former § 800.45 provided for a monthly audit of the books. Former § 800.46 provided for payment of bills by the auditor general, and limited the amount of sums drawn at one time. Former § 800.47 dealt with inventory and settlement of accounts upon removal or resignation of the warden.

## § 800.48. Removal of person to prison; duty of sheriff. [MSA § 28.1417]

Sec. 48. It shall be the duty of the sheriff of every county in which any criminal is sentenced to confinement in a prison, to cause the convict to be removed from the county jail without needless delay after sentence, and conveyed to the proper prison and delivered to the warden of that prison.

**History:**
Pub Acts 1893, No. 118, § 48, imd eff May 26, 1893; amended by Pub Acts 1986, No. 114, imd eff May 27, 1986.

**Prior codification:**
CL 1929, § 17590; CL 1915, § 1746; CL 1897, § 2127.

**Effect of amendment notes:**
**The 1986 amendment** substituted "without needless delay" for "within forty-eight [48] hours", and made grammatical revisions.

**Cross references:**
Warrant to sheriff, § 769.17.

**Michigan Digest references:**
Sheriffs and Constables § 5.

**LEXIS-NEXIS™ Michigan analytical references:**
Michigan Law and Practice, Convicts and Prisons § 2.

**Michigan Civ Jur references:**
Sheriffs and Constables §§12, 30.

**Research references:**
70 Am Jur 2d, Sheriffs, Police, and Constables §§2, 3.

## CASE NOTES

Under prior provision, the governor had power to order that a woman sentenced to imprisonment in the state prison for life be transferred to the house of correction, without shortening the term of imprisonment. Rich v Chamberlain (1895) 107 Mich 381, 65 NW 235.

### § 800.49. Fees and expenses for conveying convicts to prison, payment. [MSA § 28.1418]

Sec. 49. The fees and actual expenses of sheriffs in conveying convicts to either prison shall be made out in a bill containing the items thereof, and shall be presented to the warden when the prisoner is delivered at the prison. The warden shall certify on it that the prisoner has been received, and the bill, including the sheriff's actual expenses in returning to the county from whence the prisoner was sent, shall be audited by the auditor general and paid from the state treasury. Before drawing his warrant, the auditor general shall correct any errors in said bill as to form, items or amount, and the sheriff shall be paid for such services, his actual traveling expenses and the expenses of the convict, and the sum of three [3] dollars for each and every day so employed.

**History:**
Pub Acts 1893, No. 118, § 49, imd eff May 26, 1893.

**Prior codification:**
CL 1929, § 17591; CL 1915, § 1747; CL 1897, § 2128.

**Michigan Digest references:**
Sheriffs and Constables § 19.

**LEXIS-NEXIS™ Michigan analytical references:**
Michigan Law and Practice, Convicts and Prisons § 2.

**Michigan Civ Jur references:**
Sheriffs and Constables §§12, 30.

**Research references:**
70 Am Jur 2d, Sheriffs, Police, and Constables §§2, 3.

## CASE NOTES

Discussion of fees of a sheriff for conveying a prisoner to the place of confinement being state charges, Hursley v Stone (1892) 90 Mich 439, 51 NW 530.

The compensation of a sheriff for conveying a prisoner sentenced to the Detroit House of Correction under former § 802.51 was a state charge. Hursley v Stone (1892) 90 Mich 439, 51 NW 530.

Sheriffs are entitled only to actual expenses in transporting convicts to prison. Op Atty Gen, March 27, 1940.

Where a local act provides for paying the sheriff of a particular county a fixed salary in lieu of fees, any fees collected by the sheriff under the provisions of this section must be turned over to the county. Op Atty Gen, 1930–1932, p 91.

### § 800.50. Delivery of convict; certified copy of sentence, delivery to warden; certificate of delivery; use as evidence. [MSA § 28.1419]

Sec. 50. When any convict shall be delivered to the warden of

## § 800.50

either prison, the officer having such convict in his charge shall deliver to such warden the certified copy of the sentence, received by such officer from the clerk of the court, and shall take from such warden a certificate of the delivery of such convict; and such certified copy of the sentence of any convict shall be evidence of the facts therein contained.

**History:**
Pub Acts 1893, No. 118, § 50, imd eff May 26, 1893.

**Prior codification:**
CL 1929, § 17592; CL 1915, § 1748; CL 1897, § 2129.

**Cross references:**
Copy of sentence to be part of record sent to warden, § 769.18.

**LEXIS-NEXIS™ Michigan analytical references:**
Michigan Law and Practice, Convicts and Prisons § 2.

**Research references:**
70 Am Jur 2d, Sheriffs, Police, and Constables §§2, 3.

### CASE NOTES

In trial of defendant for escape from prison, it was not necessary to introduce certificate of his confinement as a business record to prove that he was properly confined at time of escape, a certified copy of his sentence being sufficient. People v Noble (1969) 18 Mich App 300, 170 NW2d 916 (criticized on other grounds by People v Benevides (1994) 204 Mich App 188, 514 NW2d 208).

## §§800.51–800.60. [Repealed] [MSA §§28.1420–28.1429]

**History:**
Pub Acts 1893, No. 118, §§51–60, imd eff May 26, 1893; **repealed** by Pub Acts 1972, No. 179, imd eff June 16, 1972.

**Editor's notes:**
Former § 800.51 dealt with trafficking in letters or in certain implements, and made unlawful traffic therein a misdemeanor. Former § 800.52 specified the persons authorized to visit the prison. Former § 800.53 empowered the board to establish visiting rules and procedures, including the payment of a fee by visitors. Former § 800.54 outlined the procedure for the use of convicts as witnesses. Former § 800.55 required the establishment of a school in each prison. Former § 800.56 dealt with the maintenance of a prison library. Former § 800.57 dealt with health measures to be taken in case of an epidemic. Former § 800.58 dealt with the removal of the prisoners in case of a fire. Former § 800.59 dealt with the replacement of buildings destroyed or damaged by fire. Former § 800.60 made it the duty of the auditor general to examine and audit the warden's accounts.

## § 800.61. Escaped convicts, measures for recapture; reward; sentence. [MSA § 28.1430]

Sec. 61. Whenever any convict shall escape from either prison, it shall be the duty of the warden to take all proper measures for the apprehension of such convict, and for that purpose he may offer a reward not exceeding fifty [50] dollars for the apprehension and delivery of such convict; but with the consent of his board such reward may be increased to a sum not exceeding five hundred [500] dollars. All suitable rewards and other sums of money, necessarily paid for advertising and apprehending any convict who may escape from prison, shall be audited by the auditor general, and paid out of the state treasury. If any prisoner shall be retaken, the time between the escape and his recommittal shall not be computed as part of the term of imprisonment, but he shall remain in the prison a sufficient length of time after the term of his sentence would have expired, if he had not escaped, to equal the period of time he may have been absent by reason of such escape.

**History:**
Pub Acts 1893, No. 118, § 61, imd eff May 26, 1893.

**Prior codification:**
CL 1929, § 17603; CL 1915, § 1759; CL 1897, § 2140.

**Michigan Digest references:**
Prisons and Jails § 5.
Rewards §§1 et seq.

**LEXIS-NEXIS™ Michigan analytical references:**
Michigan Law and Practice, Convicts and Prisons § 2.

**Michigan Civ Jur references:**
Rewards §§1 et seq.

**Research references:**
27 Am Jur 2d, Escape, Prison Breaking, and Rescue § 26.
57 Am Jur 2d, Rewards §§1, 4 et seq.

### CASE NOTES

Claims for rewards for apprehending convicts escaped from the state prison should be audited by the auditor general. Op Atty Gen, 1910, pp 143, 145.

## §§800.62–800.66. [Repealed] [MSA §§28.1431–28.1433]

**History:**
Pub Acts 1893, No. 118, §§62, 63, 66; imd eff May 26, 1893; **repealed** by Pub Acts 1972, No. 179, imd eff June 16, 1972.

**Editor's notes:**
Former § 800.62 dealt with the furnishing of clothing, transportation, etc., to a prisoner upon his discharge. Former § 800.63 dealt with the effect of the passage of the statute upon existing rights, contracts and the like. Former § 800.66 contained a repealer and a savings clause.

Secs. 64, 65. (Repealed.).

Secs. 64 and 65, dealing respectively with the penalties for crimes committed in prisons and with the jurisdiction of courts in respect thereto, were repealed by Pub Acts 1927, No. 175, eff September 5, 1927. For present provisions applicable to the subject see §§768.6, 768.7.

# PRISON OVERCROWDING EMERGENCY POWERS ACT
[Repealed]

Act 519, 1980, p 2225, imd eff January 26, 1981.
[Repealed]

AN ACT to authorize the governor to declare a prison overcrowding state of emergency under certain circumstances; to prescribe the powers and duties of the governor and the commission of corrections; and to provide remedies for a prison overcrowding state of emergency.

### § 800.71. [Repealed] [MSA § 28.1437(1)]

**History:**
Pub Acts 1980, No. 519, § 1, imd eff January 26, 1981; **repealed** by Pub Acts 1987, No. 101, eff January 1, 1988 (see 1987 note below).

**Editor's notes:**
Former § 800.71 contained the short title of the act.
**Pub Acts 1987, No. 101, § 2,** eff January 1, 1988, provides:
"Section 2. This act shall not take effect unless House Bill No. 4006 of the 84th Legislature [which became Act No. 100 of 1987] is enacted into law."

### § 800.72. [Repealed] [MSA § 28.1437(2)]

**History:**
Pub Acts 1980, No. 519, § 2, imd eff January 26, 1981; amended by Pub Acts 1983, No. 255, imd eff December 29, 1983; **repealed** by Pub Acts 1987, No. 100, eff January 1, 1988 (see 1987 note below).

**Editor's notes:**
Former § 800.72 contained definitions in the prison overcrowding emergency powers act.
**Pub Acts 1987, No. 100, § 3,** eff January 1, 1988, provides:
"Section 3. This amendatory act shall not take effect unless Senate Bill No. 14 of the 84th Legislature [which became Act No. 101 of 1987] is enacted into law."

### § 800.73. [Repealed] [MSA § 28.1437(3)]

**History:**
Pub Acts 1980, No. 519, § 3, imd eff January 26, 1981; amended by Pub Acts 1983, No. 255, imd eff December 29, 1983; **repealed** by Pub Acts 1987, No. 101, eff January 1, 1988 (see 1987 note below).

**Editor's notes:**
Former § 800.73 dealt with the commission's request that the governor declare a state of emergency.
**Pub Acts 1987, No. 101, § 2,** eff January 1, 1988, provides:
"Section 2. This act shall not take effect unless House Bill No. 4006 of the 84th Legislature [which became Act No. 100 of 1987] is enacted into law."

### § 800.74. [Repealed] [MSA § 28.1437(4)]

**History:**
Pub Acts 1980, No. 519, § 4, imd eff January 26, 1981; amended by Pub Acts 1983, No. 255, imd eff December 29, 1983; **repealed** by Pub Acts 1987, No. 100, eff January 1, 1988 (see 1987 note below).

**Editor's notes:**
Former § 800.74 dealt with the declaration of a state of emergency and the reduction of minimum sentences.
**Pub Acts 1987, No. 100, § 3,** eff January 1, 1988, provides:
"Section 3. This amendatory act shall not take effect unless Senate Bill No. 14 of the 84th Legislature [which became Act No. 101 of 1987] is enacted into law."

## § 800.75. [Repealed] [MSA § 28.1437(5)]

**History:**
Pub Acts 1980, No. 519, § 5, imd eff January 26, 1981; amended by Pub Acts 1983, No. 255, imd eff December 29, 1983; **repealed** by Pub Acts 1987, No. 101, eff January 1, 1988 (see 1987 note below).

**Editor's notes:**
Former § 800.75 dealt with the failure to reduce the prison population at the time of a state of emergency.
**Pub Acts 1987, No. 101, § 2,** eff January 1, 1988, provides:
"Section 2. This act shall not take effect unless House Bill No. 4006 of the 84th Legislature [which became Act No. 100 of 1987] is enacted into law."

## § 800.76. [Repealed] [MSA § 28.1437(6)]

**History:**
Pub Acts 1980, No. 519, § 6, imd eff January 26, 1981; amended by Pub Acts 1983, No. 255, imd eff December 29, 1983; **repealed** by Pub Acts 1987, No. 100, eff January 1, 1988 (see 1987 note below).

**Editor's notes:**
Former § 800.76 dealt with the rescission of a state of emergency.
**Pub Acts 1987, No. 100, § 3,** eff January 1, 1988, provides:
"Section 3. This amendatory act shall not take effect unless Senate Bill No. 14 of the 84th Legislature [which became Act No. 101 of 1987] is enacted into law."

## § 800.77. [Repealed] [MSA § 28.1437(7)]

**History:**
Pub Acts 1980, No. 519, § 7, imd eff January 26, 1981; **repealed** by Pub Acts 1987, No. 101, eff January 1, 1988 (see 1987 note below).

**Editor's notes:**
Former § 800.77 dealt with the declaration of the end of a state of emergency.
**Pub Acts 1987, No. 101, § 2,** eff January 1, 1988, provides:
"Section 2. This act shall not take effect unless House Bill No. 4006 of the 84th Legislature [which became Act No. 100 of 1987] is enacted into law."

## § 800.78. [Repealed] [MSA § 28.1437(8)]

**History:**
Pub Acts 1980, No. 519, § 8, imd eff January 26, 1981; amended by Pub Acts 1983, No. 255, imd eff December 29, 1983; 1984, No. 315, imd eff December 21, 1984; **repealed** by Pub Acts 1988, No. 469, imd eff December 27, 1988.

**Editor's notes:**
Former § 800.78 pertained to occupancy of new housing and facilities. For current provisions, see § 791.269.

## § 800.79. [Repealed] [MSA § 28.1437(9)]

**History:**
Pub Acts 1980, No. 519, § 9, imd eff January 26, 1981; amended by Pub Acts 1983, No. 255, imd eff December 29, 1983; **repealed** by Pub Acts 1987, No. 101, eff January 1, 1988 (see 1987 note below).

**Editor's notes:**
Former § 800.79 stated certain conditions upon the occurrence of which this former act would not take effect.

**Pub Acts 1987, No. 101, § 2,** eff January 1, 1988, provides:
"Section 2. This act shall not take effect unless House Bill No. 4006 of the 84th Legislature [which became Act No. 100 of 1987] is enacted into law."

## MICHIGAN REFORMATORY [Repealed]

Act 75, 1901, p 109, imd eff April 22, 1901.
[Repealed]

AN ACT providing for changing the name of the state house of correction and reformatory at Ionia.

### § 800.91. [Repealed] [MSA § 28.1441]

**History:**
Pub Acts 1901, No. 75, § 1, imd eff April 22, 1901; **repealed** by Pub Acts 1964, No. 256, eff August 28, 1964.

## EMPLOYMENT OF CONVICTS FOR PUBLIC PROJECTS

Act 181, 1911, p 305, eff August 1, 1911.

AN ACT to provide for employing the convicts in the custody of the department of corrections upon public projects other than construction within any county . (Amended by Pub Acts 1970, No. 54, imd eff July 10, 1970.).

*The People of the State of Michigan enact:*

### § 800.101. Convicts; employment on public projects; control; compensation; disposition of moneys. [MSA § 28.1511]

Sec. 1. Upon the written request of a majority of the board of commissioners, the department of corrections may detail such able bodied convicts as in its discretion shall seem proper, not exceeding the number specified in the written request, to work upon public projects of a county. The county shall pay to the general fund a certain fixed amount of money per day for each man so detailed, which amount shall be decided upon by the corrections commission. The amount to be paid shall be a fair and just compensation for such labor. The county shall pay expenses of transportation to and from the county and shall provide or pay for the lodging and food of the convicts while employed by it and shall furnish all tools and materials necessary in the performance of the work. The convicts employed upon the public projects shall be under the care and custody of officers as the department of corrections shall designate, and the expense of guarding if guards are necessary shall be borne by the county. Where 2 or more applications shall be on file they shall be filled pro rata. All moneys collected under the provisions of this section shall be turned over to the state treasurer and credited to the general fund.

**History:**
Pub Acts 1911, No. 181, § 1, eff August 1, 1911; amended by Pub Acts 1970, No. 54, imd eff July 10, 1970.

**Prior codification:**
CL 1929, § 17637; CL 1915, § 1814.

**Cross references:**
Use of county jail prisoners on highway labor, §§801.10 et seq.

**Michigan Digest references:**
Prisons and Jails § 3.

**LEXIS-NEXIS™ Michigan analytical references:**
Michigan Law and Practice, Convicts and Prisons § 5.

**Research references:**
60 Am Jur 2d, Penal and Correctional Institutions §§34–39.

## § 800.101a. Employment on state highways; requisition, order; control; compensation, disposition. [MSA § 28.1512]

Sec. 1a. Any convicts mentioned in section one [1] of this act may be employed by the state highway department in this state in construction work upon the public highways of this state. The state highway commissioner shall make requisition for convicts desired for employment and in such requisition shall state the number desired, the place of such work and the time when desired. Such requisition shall be made to the commissioner of pardons and paroles who shall thereupon determine which of such convicts may be used for such employment. At the direction of the governor, the commissioner of pardons and paroles shall issue an order authorizing the transfer of such convicts from their place of confinement to such place of highway employment or prison camp, a copy of which order shall be authority to the warden for the temporary transfer of such convicts. In their employment in highway construction such convicts shall be under the direction of the state highway commissioner or his designated agents and employees. The wardens shall furnish at each place of employment sufficient guards to prevent insubordination or escape. The compensation for such employment shall be determined by the state highway commissioner and the commissioner of pardons and paroles. Such officers shall determine the amount to be paid to each convict and the amount to be paid the prison from which such convict is obtained. All sums so paid or allowed to the prison therefor shall be paid or credited to the fund of such prison.

**History:**
Pub Acts 1911, No. 181, § 1a, as added by Pub Acts 1927, No. 316, eff September 5, 1927.

**§ 800.101a**  **Prisons**

**Prior codification:**
CL 1929, § 17638.

**Statutory references:**
Section 1, above referred to, is § 800.101.

**Michigan Digest references:**
Prisons and Jails § 3.

**LEXIS-NEXIS™ Michigan analytical references:**
Michigan Law and Practice, Convicts and Prisons § 5.

**Research references:**
60 Am Jur 2d, Penal and Correctional Institutions §§34–39.

### CASE NOTES

Although there is no express authority for so doing, it would appear that the state prison board, with approval of the state administrative board, would have incidental power to establish prison camps as an outlet for prison labor and as an incident to probation and parole of prisoners. Op Atty Gen, 1933–1934, p 475.

## § 800.102. Class of labor prohibited. [MSA § 28.1513]

Sec. 2. Said convicts when employed under the provisions of section one [1] of this act shall not be used for the purpose of building any bridge or structure of like character which requires the employment of skilled labor.

**History:**
Pub Acts 1911, No. 181, § 2, eff August 1, 1911.

**Prior codification:**
CL 1929, § 17639; CL 1915, § 1815.

**Statutory references:**
Section 1, above referred to, is § 800.101.

**Michigan Digest references:**
Prisons and Jails § 3.

**LEXIS-NEXIS™ Michigan analytical references:**
Michigan Law and Practice, Convicts and Prisons § 5.

**Research references:**
60 Am Jur 2d, Penal and Correctional Institutions §§34–39.

## § 800.103. [Repealed] [MSA § 28.1514]

**History:**
CL 1929, § 17640; CL 1915, § 1816; Pub Acts 1911, No. 181, § 3, eff August 1, 1911; **repealed** by Pub Acts 1986, No. 322, by § 3, eff April 1, 1987.

**Editor's notes:**
Former § 800.103 dealt with special good time allowances for convicts employed on public works. For current provisions, see § 800.33.

## COMMITMENT RESTRICTIONS [Repealed]

Act 2, 1885, p 2, eff February 10, 1885.
[Repealed]

AN ACT to prohibit justices of the peace, or any judge or justice of any police court, from sentencing or committing persons to the state house of correction and reformatory at Ionia, in certain cases.

### § 800.151. [Repealed] [MSA § 28.1551]

**History:**
Pub Acts 1885, No. 2, eff February 10, 1885; **repealed** by Pub Acts 1964, No. 256, eff August 28, 1964.

---

## IONIA COUNTY PROSECUTOR [Repealed]

Act 176, 1877, p 171, imd eff May 22, 1877.
[Repealed]

AN ACT to regulate and govern the state house of correction and reformatory at Ionia.

### § 800.167. [Repealed] [MSA § 28.1561]

**History:**
Pub Acts 1877, No. 176, imd eff May 22, 1877; **repealed** by Pub Acts 1964, No. 256, eff August 28, 1964.

**Editor's notes:**
Sections 1–66. (Superseded.).
These sections have been superseded by Pub Acts 1893, No. 118, being §§800.1 et seq. As to the repeal of this act, see Attorney General v. Parsell, 100 Mich 170.
Former § 800.167 established the duties of the Ionia County prosecuting attorney.

---

## BERTILLON SYSTEM [Repealed]

Act 183, 1891, p 240, imd eff July 2, 1891.
[Repealed]

AN ACT to provide for the registration and identification of criminals in the penal institutions of this state, by the Bertillon system.

### §§800.201–800.203. [Repealed] [MSA §§28.1591–28.1593]

**History:**
Pub Acts 1891, No. 183, imd eff July 2, 1891; **repealed** by Pub Acts 1972, No. 179, imd eff June 16, 1972.

**Editor's notes:**
For provisions as to the Bureau of Criminal Identification, see §§28.241 et seq. and as to the uniform crime reporting system, §§28.251 et seq.

## CENTRAL RECORDS BUREAU [Repealed]

Act 27, 1903, p 32, eff September 17, 1903.
[Repealed]

AN ACT to provide for a central bureau for the receiving and compiling records of the description, measurements and histories of the convicts in the penal institutions of this and other states; to make such descriptions, measurements and histories available to the several circuit courts of this state, and to provide for the expenses necessarily incurred in so doing.

### §§800.231–800.234. [Repealed] [MSA §§28.1601–28.1604]

**History:**
Pub Acts 1903, No. 27, eff September 17, 1903; **repealed** by Pub Acts 1972, No. 179, imd eff June 16, 1972.

**Editor's notes:**
For provisions as to the Bureau of Criminal Identification, see §§28.241 et seq., and as to the uniform crime reporting system, §§28.251 et seq.

## LIQUOR, NARCOTICS AND WEAPONS

Act 17, 1909, p 32, eff September 1, 1909.

AN ACT to prohibit or limit the access by prisoners and by employees of correctional facilities to certain weapons and to alcoholic liquor, drugs, medicines, poisons, and controlled substances in, on, or outside of correctional facilities; to prohibit or limit the bringing into or onto certain facilities and real property, and the disposition of , certain weapons and substances; to prohibit or limit the selling , giving, or furnishing of certain weapons and substances to prisoners; to prohibit the control or possession of certain weapons and substances by prisoners; and to prescribe penalties. (Amended by Pub Acts 1977, No. 164, imd eff November 10, 1977; 1982, No. 343, imd eff December 21, 1982.).

*The People of the State of Michigan enact:*

### § 800.281. Liquor, drugs and controlled substances; prohibited distribution. [MSA § 28.1621]

Sec. 1. (1) Except as provided in section 2, a person shall not sell, give, or furnish, either directly or indirectly, any alcoholic liquor, prescription drug, poison, or controlled substance to a prisoner who

# Prisons § 800.281

is in or on a correctional facility or dispose of that liquor, drug, poison, or controlled substance in any manner that allows a prisoner or employee of the correctional facility who is in or on a correctional facility access to it.

(2) Except as provided in section 2, a person who knows or has reason to know that another person is a prisoner shall not sell, give, or furnish, either directly or indirectly, any alcoholic liquor, prescription drug, poison, or controlled substance to that prisoner anywhere outside of a correctional facility.

(3) Except as provided in section 2, a person shall not bring any alcoholic liquor, prescription drug, poison, or controlled substance into or onto a correctional facility.

(4) Except as provided in section 2, a prisoner shall not possess any alcoholic liquor, prescription drug, poison, or controlled substance.

**History:**
Pub Acts 1909, No. 17, § 1, eff September 1, 1909; amended by Pub Acts 1982, No. 343, imd eff December 21, 1982.

**Prior codification:**
CL 1929, § 17653; CL 1915, § 1827.

**Statutory references:**
Section 2, above referred to, is § 800.282.

**Federal aspects:**
Prison Traffic in Contraband Articles. 18 USCS § 1791.

**Michigan Digest references:**
Intoxicating Liquors §§78, 88.
Prisons and Jails §§1.05, 2.30, 4.
Statutes § 33.

**LEXIS-NEXIS™ Michigan analytical references:**
Michigan Law and Practice, Convicts and Prisons § 4.
Michigan Law and Practice, Poisons and Narcotics § 3.

**ALR notes:**
Validity, construction, and application of state statute criminalizing possession of contraband by individual in penal or correctional institution, 45 ALR5th 767.
Fourth Amendment as protecting prison visitor against unreasonable searches and seizures, 69 ALR Fed 856.

## CASE NOTES

**1. Construction and effect.**
The crime of prisoner in possession of contraband is a strict liability crime; the statute does not prohibit only the "knowing" control of weapons and controlled substances by prisoners. People v Ramsdell (1998) 230 Mich App 386, 585 NW2d 1.

Specific intent is not an element of the crime of being a prisoner in possession of a controlled substance. People v Wyngaard (1997) 226 Mich App 681, 575 NW2d 48.

A person need not be legally incarcerated in order to be convicted of being a prisoner in possession of a controlled substance. People v Ovalle (1997) 222 Mich App 463, 564 NW2d 147.

The sentencing guidelines do not apply to the offense of prisoner in possession of a controlled substance. People v Berry (1993) 198 Mich App 723, 499 NW2d 458.

The proscription of possession of marijuana by prisoners and the raising of that possession to felony status is not violative of equal protection. People v

Krajenka (1990) 188 Mich App 661, 470 NW2d 403.

The distinction between prisoners and nonprisoners is not arbitrary and is rationally related to the recognized and legitimate governmental interest in enhancing prisoner discipline. People v Krajenka (1990) 188 Mich App 661, 470 NW2d 403.

The statute which prohibits possession of certain contraband by prisoners does not violate the title-object clause of the Michigan Constitution; the statute involves the single object of maintaining order and discipline in prisons. People v Krajenka (1990) 188 Mich App 661, 470 NW2d 403.

Conviction under the statute which proscribes the possession of liquor in prison does not require proof of specific intent. People v Norman (1989) 176 Mich App 271, 438 NW2d 895.

The statute which prohibits the bringing of contraband into a prison is aimed at those who actually bring the contraband into the prison from outside, not at convicts who ultimately gain possession of the contraband. People v Goulett (1981) 103 Mich App 381, 303 NW2d 21.

Where accused employed agents to pick up whiskey and marijuana outside of prison and smuggle it inside in garbage trucks, where others would unload contraband, repackage it and deliver it to accused, accused was directly responsible for "bringing" contraband into prison in violation of statute. People v Lewis (1980) 97 Mich App 650, 296 NW2d 62.

Statute prohibiting bringing of enumerated contraband into prison does not violate title-object clause of Michigan Constitution. People v Lewis (1980) 97 Mich App 650, 296 NW2d 62.

Statute is designed to keep enumerated contraband out of prison, not to punish particular group of people. People v Lewis (1980) 97 Mich App 650, 296 NW2d 62.

This section, prohibiting as felony bringing opium, morphine, or any other kind or character of narcotics into state prison would be held to include marijuana as narcotic within definition of § 335.151. People v Sartin (1971) 33 Mich App 195, 189 NW2d 755.

**2. Searches.**

A search of a visitor at a prison is reasonable where notices posted on the prison grounds warn that visitors are subject to search and will be prosecuted for bringing alcohol, controlled substances, or weapons into the prison and visitors can avoid a search by choosing not to proceed with their visits. People v Demps (1992) 196 Mich App 433, 493 NW2d 466.

## § 800.281a. Definitions. [MSA § 28.1621(1)]

Sec. 1a. As used in this act:

(a) "Alcoholic liquor" means any spirituous, vinous, malt, or fermented liquor, liquid, or compound whether or not medicated, containing ½ of 1% or more of alcohol by volume and which is or readily can be made suitable for beverage purposes.

(b) "Chief administrator" means the warden, superintendent, or other employee approved or designated by the department of corrections as the chief administrative officer of a correctional facility.

(c) "Controlled substance" means a drug, substance, or immediate precursor in schedules 1 to 5 of part 72 of 1978 PA 368, MCL 333.7201 to 333.7231.

(d) "Department" means the department of corrections.

(e) "Correctional facility" means any of the following:

(i) A state prison, reformatory, work camp, or community corrections center.

(ii) A youth correctional facility operated by the department or a private vendor under section 20g of 1953 PA 232, MCL 791.232.

(iii) A privately operated community corrections center or

resident home which houses prisoners committed to the jurisdiction of the department.

(iv) The land on which a facility described in subparagraph (i), (ii), or (iii) is located.

(f) "Prescription drug" means prescription drug as defined in section 17708 of 1978 PA 368, MCL 333.17708.

(g) "Prisoner" means a person committed to the jurisdiction of the department who has not been released on parole or discharged.

**History:**
Pub Acts 1909, No. 17, § 1a, as added by Pub Acts 1982, No. 343, imd eff December 21, 1982.
Amended by Pub Acts 1998, No. 514, imd eff January 8, 1999.

**Effect of amendment notes:**
The **1998 amendment** added "approved or" in subsection (b), added new subsection (d), redesignated former subsections (d)–(f) as (e)–(g), redesignated former subsections (d)(ii) and (d)(iii) as (e)(iii) and (e)(iv), added new subsection (e)(ii), made changes to the statutory references in subsections (c) and (f), and substituted "jurisdiction of the department" for "Michigan commission on corrections" in subsection (g).

## § 800.282. Exceptions; physician's certificate; clergy, wine; hospital supply; owner or operator of privately owned community corrections center, resident home. [MSA § 28.1622]

Sec. 2. (1) A person is not in violation of section 1 if all of the following occur:

(a) A licensed physician certifies in writing that the alcoholic liquor, prescription drug, or controlled substance is necessary for the health of the prisoner or employee.

(b) The certificate contains the following information:

(i) The quality of the alcoholic liquor, prescription drug, or controlled substance which is to be furnished to the prisoner or employee.

(ii) The name of the prisoner or employee.

(iii) The time when the alcoholic liquor, prescription drug, or controlled substance is to be furnished.

(iv) The reason why the alcoholic liquor, prescription drug, or controlled substance is needed.

(c) The certificate has been delivered to the chief administrator of the correctional facility to which the prisoner is assigned or at which the employee works.

(d) The chief administrator of the correctional facility or the designee of the chief administrator approves in advance the sale, giving, furnishing, bringing, or possession of the alcoholic liquor, prescription drug, or controlled substance.

(e) The sale, giving, furnishing, bringing, or possession of the alcoholic liquor, prescription drug, or controlled substance is in compliance with the certificate.

(2) Not more than 2 ounces of wine for the use of the clergy may be brought into or onto a correctional facility by a person of the

clergy of any religious denomination for clergy purposes.

(3) Section 1(3) shall not apply to the bringing of alcoholic liquor, prescription drugs, or controlled substances into or onto a correctional facility for the ordinary hospital supply of the correctional facility.

(4) Section 1(3) shall not apply to the bringing of any alcoholic liquor, prescription drug, poison, or controlled substance into or onto a privately operated community corrections center or resident home which houses prisoners for the use of the owner, operator, or nonprisoner resident of that center or home if the owner or operator, lives in the center or home, or for the use of a nonprisoner guest of the owner, operator, or nonprisoner resident.

**History:**
Pub Acts 1909, No. 17, § 2, eff September 1, 1909; amended by Pub Acts 1977, No. 164, imd eff November 10, 1977; 1982, No. 343, imd eff December 21, 1982.

**Prior codification:**
CL 1929, § 17654; CL 1915, § 1828.

**Statutory references:**
Section 1, above referred to, is § 800.281.

## § 800.283. Weapons or implements for escape; furnishing prohibited; possession or control of weapons or implements.
[MSA § 28.1623]

Sec. 3. (1) Unless authorized by the chief administrator of the correctional facility, a weapon or other implement which may be used to injure a prisoner or other person, or in assisting a prisoner to escape from imprisonment, shall not be sold, given, or furnished, either directly or indirectly, to a prisoner who is in or on the correctional facility, or be disposed of in a manner or in a place that it may be secured by a prisoner who is in or on the correctional facility.

(2) Unless authorized by the chief administrator of the correctional facility, a person, who knows or has reason to know that another person is a prisoner, shall not sell, give, or furnish, either directly or indirectly, to that prisoner anywhere outside of a correctional facility a weapon or other implement which may be used to injure a prisoner or other person or in assisting a prisoner to escape from imprisonment.

(3) Unless authorized by the chief administrator of the correctional facility, a weapon or other implement which may be used to injure a prisoner or other person, or in assisting a prisoner to escape from imprisonment, shall not be brought into or onto any correctional facility.

(4) Unless authorized by the chief administrator of the correctional facility, a prisoner shall not have in his or her possession or under his or her control a weapon or other implement which may be used to injure a prisoner or other person, or to assist a prisoner to escape from imprisonment.

**History:**
Pub Acts 1909, No. 17, § 3, eff September 1, 1909; amended by Pub Acts 1972, No. 105, imd eff March 29, 1972; 1982, No. 343, imd eff December 21, 1982.

**Prior codification:**
CL 1929, § 17655; CL 1915, § 1829.

**Cross references:**
Aiding escapes, §§750.183 et seq.

**Michigan Digest references:**
Prisons and Jails §§1.05, 2.10, 2.100.
Statutes § 34.

**LEXIS-NEXIS™ Michigan analytical references:**
Michigan Practice – Criminal Law §§3.97–3.101.

## CASE NOTES

**1. Validity.**
The statute making it a crime for an inmate to be in possession of a dangerous weapon does not violate the title-object clause of the Michigan Constitution. People v Rau (1989) 174 Mich App 339, 436 NW2d 409, app den (1989, Mich) 1989 Mich LEXIS 2008.

The statute which prohibits the unauthorized transportation of a weapon or other implement which may be used to injure a prisoner or other person, or in assisting a prisoner to escape from imprisonment, into or onto any correctional facility is not unconstitutionally vague; a hypodermic syringe may be found to be an object with weapon-like qualities that can be used to harm others or make an escape. People v Osuna (1988) 174 Mich App 530, 436 NW2d 405.

This section, prohibiting unauthorized possession by prison inmate of implement which may be used to injure or assist in prison escape was not subject to attack as unconstitutionally vague as against defendant inmate upon person of whom prison authorities during routine shakedown discovered draftsman compass which was bent and sharpened to render it unfit for normal use and give it weapon like quality which could be used to harm others. People v Herron (1976) 68 Mich App 381, 242 NW2d 584.

This section, proscribing unauthorized possession by a prison inmate of implement which may be used to injure another or to assist in prison escape would be held not to be unconstitutionally vague on its face even though it did not specify every type of implement proscribed. People v Herron (1976) 68 Mich App 381, 242 NW2d 584.

**2. Construction and effect.**
The statute which prohibits the unauthorized transportation of a weapon or other implement which may be used to injure a prisoner or other person, or in assisting a prisoner to escape from imprisonment, into or onto any correctional facility is not unconstitutionally vague; a hypodermic syringe may be found to be an object with weapon-like qualities that can be used to harm others or make an escape. People v Osuna (1988) 174 Mich App 530, 436 NW2d 405.

The element which transforms an unauthorized article into a weapon within a prison setting is its potential to cause injury, not the inmate's subjective intent. People v Osuna (1988) 174 Mich App 530, 436 NW2d 405.

The element which transforms an unauthorized article into a weapon within a prison setting is its potential to cause injury, not the subjective intent of the inmate in possession of the article; a "weapon" within prison walls need not be equated with a "weapon" as that term is defined in the Penal Code. Acrey v Department of Corrections (1986) 152 Mich App 554, 394 NW2d 415.

**3. Defenses.**
The defense of duress was properly excluded from consideration by the jury in a trial where the defendant was charged with being an inmate in possession of a dangerous weapon and failed to show a factual basis of immediate threat for his claim of duress; furthermore, duress has not been specifically recognized by the Legislature as a defense to a charge of being an inmate in possession of a dangerous weapon. People v Rau

(1989) 174 Mich App 339, 436 NW2d 409, app den (1989, Mich) 1989 Mich LEXIS 2008.

The defense of duress is not available to the crime of possession of a weapon by a prison inmate. People v Crooks (1986) 151 Mich App 389, 390 NW2d 250, app den (1986) 426 Mich 870.

**4. Burden of proof.**

The prosecution in proceeding on a charge of possession of a weapon by a prisoner is not required to establish that the prisoner's possession of the weapon was not authorized, absent some indication that, in fact, the prisoner was authorized to possess the weapon. People v Perry (1985) 145 Mich App 778, 377 NW2d 911.

**5. Instructions.**

A prisoner being tried for possession of a weapon who claims that he came into possession of the weapon as a result of disarming another prisoner in self-defense is entitled to a jury instruction that, if the jury believed that the defendant had acquired the weapon purely in self-defense and had intended to give the weapon to the prison authorities at the first opportunity, the defendant would not be guilty of the crime of possession of a weapon by a prisoner. People v Perry (1985) 145 Mich App 778, 377 NW2d 911.

**6. Searches.**

A search of a visitor at a prison is reasonable where notices posted on the prison grounds warn that visitors are subject to search and will be prosecuted for bringing alcohol, controlled substances, or weapons into the prison and visitors can avoid a search by choosing not to proceed with their visits. People v Demps (1992) 196 Mich App 433, 493 NW2d 466.

## § 800.284. Searching of visitors. [MSA § 28.1624]

Sec. 4. The chief administrator of a correctional facility may search, or have searched, any person coming to the correctional facility as a visitor, or in any other capacity, who is suspected of having any weapon or other implement which may be used to injure a prisoner or other person or in assisting a prisoner to escape from imprisonment, or any alcoholic liquor, prescription drug, poison, or controlled substance upon his or her person.

**History:**
Pub Acts 1909, No. 17, § 4, eff September 1, 1909; amended by Pub Acts 1982, No. 343, imd eff December 21, 1982.

**Prior codification:**
CL 1929, § 17656; CL 1915, § 1830.

**LEXIS-NEXIS™ Michigan analytical references:**
Michigan Law and Practice, Convicts and Prisons § 4.

### CASE NOTES

1972 amendment to this section proscribing possession of weapons by convicts would be held to be violative of constitutional title-object clause as exceeding scope of its title which related to weapons brought into prison or sold or furnished to convicts, under which preamendment statutory proscription was aimed at persons other than convicts, who sold, gave, furnished or brought weapons to convicts in prison. People v Stanton (1977) 400 Mich 192, 253 NW2d 650.

A search of a visitor at a prison is reasonable where notices posted on the prison grounds warn that visitors are subject to search and will be prosecuted for bringing alcohol, controlled substances, or weapons into the prison and visitors can avoid a search by choosing not to proceed with their visits. People v Demps (1992) 196 Mich App 433, 493 NW2d 466.

A search of a visitor at a prison is reasonable where notices posted on the prison grounds warn that visitors are subject to search and will be prosecuted for bringing alcohol, controlled substances, or weapons into the prison and visitors can avoid a search by choosing not to proceed with their visits. People v Demps (1992) 196 Mich App 433, 493 NW2d 466.

## § 800.285. Felony; penalty. [MSA § 28.1625]

Sec. 5. (1) Except as provided in subsection (2), a person violating this act is guilty of a felony, punishable by a fine of not more than $1,000.00, or imprisonment for not more than 5 years, or both.

(2) If the delivery of a controlled substance is a felony punishable by imprisonment for more than 5 years under part 74 of Act No. 368 of the Public Acts of 1978, being sections 333.7401 to 333.7415 of the Michigan Compiled Laws, a person who gives, sells, or furnishes a controlled substance in violation of section 1 of this act shall not be prosecuted under this section for that giving, selling, or furnishing. If the possession of a controlled substance is a felony punishable by imprisonment for more than 5 years under part 74 of Act No. 368 of the Public Acts of 1978, a person who possesses, or brings into a correctional facility, a controlled substance in violation of section 1 of this act shall not be prosecuted under this section for that possession.

**History:**
Pub Acts 1909, No. 17, § 5, eff September 1, 1909; amended by Pub Acts 1982, No. 343, imd eff December 21, 1982.

**Prior codification:**
CL 1929, § 17657; CL 1915, § 1831.

**Statutory references:**
Section 1 is § 800.281.

**Michigan Digest references:**
Criminal Law and Procedure § 47.

### CASE NOTES

Defendant who pleaded guilty to bringing narcotics into state prison could not successfully contend that he was sentenced under wrong statute, in that he was sentenced under this act rather than under § 335.153, because docket number of sentence proceedings referred to dropped charge of narcotics possession growing out of same incident, where sentence was within maximum set by this section and docket number was subject to correction as clerical error in manner provided by MCR 2.613. People v Sartin (1971) 33 Mich App 195, 189 NW2d 755.

# ADMISSION OF CLERGYMEN

Act 185, 1859, p 516, eff May 18, 1859.

AN ACT to provide for the admission of clergymen to visit prisoners confined in any jail or prison in this state.

*The People if the State of Michigan enact:*

### § 800.291. Admission of clergymen; time. [MSA § 28.1631]

Sec. 1. That it shall be the duty of the keeper, or other persons having the control of any prison, jail, almshouse, house of correction, hospital, or poor-house in the state of Michigan to fix and appoint some suitable and convenient time, in each week, during which clergymen of all religious denominations may visit the inmates of such prison, jail, almshouse, house of correction, hospital or poor-house; and when any inmate of any jail, prison, almshouse, house of correction, hospital or poor-house, is dangerously sick, and desires religious counsel, the clergyman of his choice shall be admitted to visit such inmate, and be permitted to administer to such inmate the rites of his church.

**History:**
Pub Acts 1859, No. 185, § 1, eff May 18, 1859.

**Prior codification:**
CL 1929, § 17658; CL 1915, § 1832; HOW § 9901; CL 1897, § 2153; CL 1871, § 8189.

**ALR notes:**
Provision of religious facilities for prisoners, 12 ALR3d 1276.

**Research references:**
60 Am Jur 2d, Penal and Correctional Institutions § 46.

### § 800.292. Duty of keeper. [MSA § 28.1632]

Sec. 2. It shall be the duty of such keeper, or other person in control, during the time fixed, in pursuance of the first [1st] section of this act, to give free access to any clergyman of any religious denomination and to furnish such clergyman all reasonable facilities for interviews with the inmates, named in the first [1st] section: Provided, however, That the keeper or other persons having the control of said prison or jail, almshouse, workhouse, house of correction, hospital or poor-house, shall first be satisfied that such clergymen are in good and regular standing in their profession, and are pastors of any church or religious congregation in this state.

**History:**
Pub Acts 1859, No. 185, § 2, eff May 18, 1859.

**Prior codification:**
CL 1929, § 17659; CL 1915, § 1833; HOW § 9902; CL 1897, § 2154; CL 1871, § 8190.

**Statutory references:**
Section 1, above referred to, is § 800.291.

**ALR notes:**
Provision of religious facilities for prisoners, 12 ALR3d 1276.

**Research references:**
60 Am Jur 2d, Penal and Correctional Institutions § 46.

**Prisons** 800.319

## PRISON LABOR AND INDUSTRIES [Repealed]

Act 210, 1935, p 335, eff September 21, 1935.
[Repealed]

AN ACT to provide for the employment of prison labor in the penal institutions of this state; to establish a state use system of prison industries; to define the powers and duties of the prison commission, the governor and other officers and employes in relation thereto, and to provide for the abolition of certain employe positions; to provide for the requisitioning and disbursement of prison products; to provide for the sale and/or purchase of certain prison equipment; to create a revolving fund and otherwise provide for the disposition of the proceeds of said industry; to provide for purchasing and accounting procedures; to prohibit the sale, exchange or other distribution of prison products made in or transported into this state, except as herein provided; to provide for the requisitioning and/or purchase and supply of prison products for use or consumption by certain institutions and departments; to provide penalties for violations of this act; and to repeal certain acts and parts of acts.

### §§800.301–800.319.  [Repealed]  [MSA §§28.1521–28.1539]

**History:**
Pub Acts 1935, No. 210, eff September 21, 1935; **repealed** by Pub Acts 1968, No. 15, imd eff April 5, 1968.

**Editor's notes:**
For current provisions, see §§800.321 et seq.

## CORRECTIONAL INDUSTRIES ACT

Act 15, 1968, p 25, imd eff April 5, 1968.

An act to provide for the employment of inmate labor in the correctional institutions of this state; to provide for the employment of inmate labor in certain private enterprises under certain conditions; to provide for certain powers and duties of the department of corrections, the governor, and other officers and agencies in relation to correctional institutions; to provide for the requisitioning and disbursement of correctional industries products; to provide for the disposition of the proceeds of correctional industries and farms; to provide for purchasing and accounting procedures; to regulate the sale or disposition of inmate labor and products; to provide for the requisitioning, purchases, and supply of correctional industries products; to provide penalties for violations of this act; and to repeal acts and parts of acts. (Amended by Pub Acts 1990, No. 24, imd eff March 7, 1990; 1996, No. 537, imd eff January 13, 1997.).

*The People of the State of Michigan enact:*

**Effect of amendment notes:**
  **The 1996 amendment** inserted "to provide for the employment of inmate labor in certain private enterprises under certain conditions;"; substituted "department" for "commission"; and made a grammatical change.

## § 800.321. Short title. [MSA § 28.1540(1)]

Sec. 1. This act shall be known and may be cited as the "correctional industries act".

**History:**
  Pub Acts 1968, No. 15, § 1, imd eff April 5, 1968.

**Michigan Digest references:**
  Labor, § 11.
  Prisons and Jails § 3.

**LEXIS-NEXIS™ Michigan analytical references:**
  Michigan Law and Practice, Convicts and Prisons § 5.

**Research references:**
  60 Am Jur 2d, Penal and Correctional Institutions §§34–40.

## § 800.322. "Correctional industries products" and "youth correctional facility" defined. [MSA § 28.1540(2)]

Sec. 2. As used in this act:

(a) "Correctional industries products" means all services provided, goods, wares, and merchandise manufactured or produced, wholly or in part, by inmates in any state correctional institution, but does not include products manufactured with inmate labor or services rendered with inmate labor in a private manufacturing or service enterprise established under section 7a.

(b) "Youth correctional facility" means a facility established under section 20g of Act No. 232 of the Public Acts of 1953, being section 791.220g of the Michigan Compiled Laws.

**History:**
  Pub Acts 1968, No. 15, § 2, imd eff April 5, 1968; amended by Pub Acts 1980, No. 245, imd eff July 28, 1980, by § 3 eff October 1, 1980.
  Amended by Pub Acts 1996, No. 537, imd eff January 13, 1997.

**Effect of amendment notes:**
  **The 1996 amendment** in subsection (a), added what is not included as "correctional industries products"; and added paragraph (b).

**Statutory references:**
  Section 7a, above referred to, is § 800.327a.

**Michigan Digest references:**
  Prisons and Jails § 3.

**LEXIS-NEXIS™ Michigan analytical references:**
  Michigan Law and Practice, Convicts and Prisons § 5.

**Research references:**
  60 Am Jur 2d, Penal and Correctional Institutions §§34–40.

## § 800.323. Jurisdiction of commission. [MSA § 28.1540(3)]

Sec. 3. The authority and duties contained in this act are vested in the commission of corrections.

**History:**
Pub Acts 1968, No. 15, § 3, imd eff April 5, 1968; amended by Pub Acts 1980, No. 245, imd eff July 28, 1980, by § 3 eff October 1, 1980.

**Michigan Digest references:**
Prisons and Jails § 3.

**LEXIS-NEXIS™ Michigan analytical references:**
Michigan Law and Practice, Convicts and Prisons § 5.

**Research references:**
60 Am Jur 2d, Penal and Correctional Institutions §§34–40.

## § 800.324. Commission of corrections; powers. [MSA § 28.1540(4)]

Sec. 4. The department of corrections may do any of the following:

(a) Construct, use, equip, and maintain buildings, machinery, boilers, and equipment that may be necessary to provide for the employment of inmate labor in the state correctional institutions for the manufacture of goods, wares, and merchandise and the operation of services.

(b) Purchase new material to be used in the manufacture of goods, wares, merchandise, and operation of services.

(c) Dispose of the manufactured products or provide services in the manner provided by law.

(d) Continue to use and maintain the buildings, machinery, boilers, and equipment in the manufacture of goods, wares, and merchandise in the manner in the operation on April 5, 1968 and use the facilities in the operation of service programs.

(e) Recruit and employ agents and assistants through the department of civil service as may be necessary to carry out the purposes of this act and recommend to the department of civil service classes and selection procedures that recognize the unique needs of correctional industries in this state.

(f) Establish an advisory council for correctional industries in this state, which shall include representatives of organized labor, private industry, state government, and the general public.

(g) Enter into any agreements necessary for assigning inmates to employment in private manufacturing or service enterprises under section 7a.

**History:**
Pub Acts 1968, No. 15, § 4, imd eff April 5, 1968; amended by Pub Acts 1980, No. 245, imd eff July 28, 1980, by § 3 eff October 1, 1980.
Amended by Pub Acts 1996, No. 537, imd eff January 13, 1997.

**Effect of amendment notes:**
**The 1996 amendment** added paragraph (g); and made grammatical changes.

**Statutory references:**
Section 7a, above referred to, is § 800.327a.

**Cross references:**
Corrections commission, § 791.201 et seq.
Bureau of prison industries, § 791.271.

**Michigan Digest references:**
Prisons and Jails § 3.

**LEXIS-NEXIS™ Michigan analytical references:**
Michigan Law and Practice, Convicts and Prisons § 5.

**Research references:**
60 Am Jur 2d, Penal and Correctional Institutions §§34–40.

### CASE NOTES

In determining whether a prison inmate was employed by prison or by institution other than prison conducting program within prison walls, economic reality test would be applicable to consider as indicia which party had right to hire and fire inmate, to set work hours and pay wages, and supervise inmate's work performance. Manville v Bd. of Governors of Wayne State University (1978) 85 Mich App 628, 272 NW2d 162 (criticized on other grounds by People v Thomas (1982) 118 Mich App 667, 325 NW2d 536).

Relationship between state prison inmates and department of corrections, as created and governed by Correctional Industries Act, would be held to be custodial, rehabilitative relationship using employment as means to reach such ends, and not an employment relationship as would render inmates public employees subject to jurisdiction of employment relations commission. Prisoners' Labor Union v State (Dep't of Corrections) (1975) 61 Mich App 328, 232 NW2d 699.

Inmates of state prison, assigned, under former law, by prison officials to work in prison stamping plant upon parts and assemblies of shell casings which were to be furnished by manufacturer to ordinance division of war department, were not employees of manufacturer within meaning of Fair Labor Standards Act. Huntley v Gunn Furniture Co. (1948, DC Mich) 79 F Supp 110, 15 CCH LC ¶ 64646.

Under former law, labor of inmates of state prison belonged to state and such inmates could be lawfully employed only by state. Huntley v Gunn Furniture Co. (1948, DC Mich) 79 F Supp 110, 15 CCH LC ¶ 64646.

### § 800.325. Correctional industries revolving fund; crediting money collected from inmate labor; expenditures. [MSA § 28.1540(5)]

Sec. 5. Except as provided in section 7a, all money collected from the sale or disposition of goods, wares, and merchandise manufactured by inmate labor, or received for services provided by labor in the correctional institutions pursuant to this act, shall be turned over to the state treasurer and credited to the correctional industries revolving fund, and shall be paid out only for the cost of doing business incurred in carrying out the purpose of this act. An expenditure for a structure from the revolving fund that would otherwise require the approval of the joint capital outlay subcommittee of the legislature shall be submitted for approval to that subcommittee before the commencement of any construction.

**History:**
Pub Acts 1968, No. 15, § 5, imd eff April 5, 1968; amended by Pub Acts 1980, No. 245, imd eff July 28, 1980, by § 3 eff October 1, 1980.
Amended by Pub Acts 1996, No. 537, imd eff January 13, 1997.

**Effect of amendment notes:**
The **1996 amendment** added "Except as provided in section 7a, all"; and made a grammatical change.

**Statutory references:**
Section 7a, above referred to, is § 800.327a.

**Michigan Digest references:**
Prisons and Jails § 3.

**LEXIS-NEXIS™ Michigan analytical references:**
Michigan Law and Practice, Convicts and Prisons § 5.

**Research references:**
60 Am Jur 2d, Penal and Correctional Institutions §§34–40.

## § 800.326. Sale, exchange, or purchase of correctional industries products; availability of agricultural products to nonprofit charitable organizations or family independence agency; use of inmate labor. [MSA § 28.1540(6)]

Sec. 6. (1) Correctional industries products may be sold, exchanged, or purchased by institutions of this or any other state or political subdivision of this or any other state, the federal government or agencies of the federal government, a foreign government or agencies of a foreign government, a private vendor that operates the youth correctional facility, or any organization that is a tax exempt organization under section 501(c)(3) of the internal revenue code.

(2) An agricultural product that is produced on a correctional farm may be utilized within the correctional institutions or within a youth correctional facility notwithstanding its operation by a private vendor or sold to an institution, governmental agency, or organization described in subsection (1) or sold for utilization in the food production facilities of the department of corrections notwithstanding the operation of those facilities by a private vendor. An agricultural product that is not utilized or sold as provided in this subsection shall be made available without charge to nonprofit charitable organizations or to the family independence agency for use in food banks, bulk food distributions, or similar charitable food distribution programs. This subsection does not apply to an agricultural product that is not in a form suitable for use in the manner prescribed in this section, such as bulk grain, live cattle, and hogs, which may be sold on the open market.

(3) Except as provided in subsections (4) and (5), the labor of inmates shall not be sold, hired, leased, loaned, contracted for, or otherwise used for private or corporate profit or for any purpose other than the construction, maintenance, or operation of public works, ways, or property as directed by the governor. This act does not prohibit the sale at retail of articles made by inmates for the personal benefit of themselves or their dependents or the payment to inmates for personal services rendered in the correctional institutions, subject to regulations approved by the department of corrections, or the use of inmate labor upon agricultural land that has been rented or leased by the department of corrections upon a sharecropping or other basis.

(4) If more than 80% of a particular product sold in the United States is manufactured outside the United States and none of that product is manufactured in this state, or if a particular service is not performed in this state, as determined by the department of corrections in conjunction with the advisory council for correctional industries, inmate labor may be used in the manufacture of that product or the rendering of that service in a private manufacturing or service enterprise established under section 7a. A determination by the department of corrections under this subsection shall be made at the time the individual or business entity applies to the department for approval to produce that product or render that service pursuant to section 7a.

(5) Inmate labor may be used in the youth correctional facility notwithstanding the operation of that facility by a private vendor.

**History:**
Pub Acts 1968, No. 15, § 6, imd eff April 5, 1968; amended by Pub Acts 1980, No. 245, imd eff July 28, 1980, by § 3 eff October 1, 1980; 1990, No. 24, imd eff March 7, 1990.
Amended by Pub Acts 1996, No. 537, imd eff January 13, 1997.

**Effect of amendment notes:**
**The 1996 amendment** revised subsections (1)–(3); and added subsections (4) and (5).

**Statutory references:**
Section 7a, above referred to, is § 800.327a.

**Michigan Digest references:**
Prisons and Jails § 3.

**LEXIS-NEXIS™ Michigan analytical references:**
Michigan Law and Practice, Convicts and Prisons § 5.

**Research references:**
60 Am Jur 2d, Penal and Correctional Institutions §§34–40.

## CASE NOTES

**1. Prohibited sales and contracts.**
It was unlawful, under former statute, to sell prison products produced in the penal institutions of Michigan to the agencies of other states, except as permitted thereby. Op Atty Gen, December 26, 1956, No. 2846.

Under former statute, prison products could not be sold to foreign purchasers either public or private. Op Atty Gen, April 27, 1949, No. 958; Op Atty Gen, May 27, 1949, No. 958a.

Sharecropping contracts for use of prison labor were unlawful as not within scope of permissive use of prison labor under former statute. Op Atty Gen, February 17, 1948, No. 659.

Under former statute, prison labor could not be employed for personal and private purposes by individual, corporation or association, nor was it permissible for prison industries to purchase raw materials and equipment for resale to employees, private individuals or corporations. Op Atty Gen, July 9, 1947, No. 481.

Under former statute, prison-made goods could not be sold to church organizations, parochial schools, fraternal orders, hospitals, or other private charitable or nonprofit organizations. Op Atty Gen, March 29, 1946, No. 0–4517.

Under former statute, prison products could not be sold to Michigan municipal league as jobber for resale to Michigan municipalities. Op Atty Gen, December 30, 1946, No. 0–5314.

Formerly, Michigan national guard was legally qualified to be supplied and furnished with war materials manufactured by Michigan state industries, but manufacture of war materials for United States army and navy could not be undertaken. Op Atty Gen, June 21, 1940.

Under former statute, candy manufactured by prison industries could not be sold to inmate stores for resale to inmates. Op Atty Gen, October 19, 1939.

Livestock raised on prison farm was considered agricultural product under former statute and could not be sold on open market. Op Atty Gen, January 7, 1936.

Formerly, state prison industries could not sell highway signs manufactured in prison factory to county road commission. Op Atty Gen, January 8, 1936.

Under former statute state prison commission was prohibited from contracting to supply municipal subdivisions of state, such as counties, townships, villages and cities, with prison-made goods. Op Atty Gen, December 5, 1935.

Sale of farm products raised within this state by convicts or prisoners, would be in violation of former statute. Op Atty Gen, December 5, 1935.

**2. Wages and working conditions.**

Claim by prison inmates against drug companies operating prison research clinics, based on Michigan Prison Industries Act, involved factual allegations similar to those raising federal questions and was therefore before federal district court under its pendent jurisdiction. Sims v Parke Davis & Co. (1971, ED Mich) 334 F Supp 774, 15 FR Serv 2d 709, affd (1971, CA6 Mich) 453 F2d 1259, cert den (1972) 405 US 978, 31 L Ed 2d 254, 92 S Ct 1196.

Even if employment of prison inmates at prison research clinics operated by drug companies violated Prison Industries Act, such employment did not constitute violation of due process or equal protection rights of prisoners. Sims v Parke Davis & Co. (1971, ED Mich) 334 F Supp 774, 15 FR Serv 2d 709, affd (1971, CA6 Mich) 453 F2d 1259, cert den (1972) 405 US 978, 31 L Ed 2d 254, 92 S Ct 1196.

Failure to pay prison inmates, who worked in prison research clinics operated by drug companies, for their labor at its reasonable value was not denial of any fundamental constitutional right which followed prisoners into their cells. Sims v Parke Davis & Co. (1971, ED Mich) 334 F Supp 774, 15 FR Serv 2d 709, affd (1971, CA6 Mich) 453 F2d 1259, cert den (1972) 405 US 978, 31 L Ed 2d 254, 92 S Ct 1196.

Labor of inmates lawfully incarcerated in penitentiaries belongs to state, rather than inmates. Sims v Parke Davis & Co. (1971, ED Mich) 334 F Supp 774, 15 FR Serv 2d 709, affd (1971, CA6 Mich) 453 F2d 1259, cert den (1972) 405 US 978, 31 L Ed 2d 254, 92 S Ct 1196.

Provision of former § 800.305, that labor of prisoners might not be sold, hired, leased, loaned, contracted for or otherwise used for private or corporate profit or for any other purpose than construction, maintenance or operation of public works, ways or property, was never intended to protect inmates incarcerated in prisons from being compelled to perform services for private corporate profit, but rather was intended to protect work force outside prison walls; hence inmates could not maintain action for damages based on violation of act. Sims v Parke Davis & Co. (1971, ED Mich) 334 F Supp 774, 15 FR Serv 2d 709, affd (1971, CA6 Mich) 453 F2d 1259, cert den (1972) 405 US 978, 31 L Ed 2d 254, 92 S Ct 1196.

Since prison inmates had no right to their own labor, or to its fruits, at time they were ordered to work in prison research clinics operated by drug companies, utilization of inmates' labor did not deprive them of any property to which they were entitled or enable them to recover reasonable value of their services under any theory of action recognized by Michigan law. Sims v Parke Davis & Co. (1971, ED Mich) 334 F Supp 774, 15 FR Serv 2d 709, affd (1971, CA6 Mich) 453 F2d 1259, cert den (1972) 405 US 978, 31 L Ed 2d 254, 92 S Ct 1196.

Violation, if any, of former Prison Industries Act in furnishing inmates to drug companies for use in prison research clinics did not create cause of action for monetary damages in favor of inmates. Sims v Parke Davis & Co. (1971, ED Mich) 334 F Supp 774, 15 FR Serv 2d 709, affd (1971, CA6 Mich) 453 F2d 1259, cert den (1972) 405 US 978, 31 L Ed 2d 254, 92 S Ct 1196.

Where prison inmates, who worked in prison research clinics operated by drug companies, failed to show that prison officials purposely discriminated against them, and in fact such employment conferred tangible benefits on inmates, who received higher wages, more freedom and labored under better working conditions than did inmates in different prison industries, inmates suffered no denial of federally protected rights even if their labor was used contrary to Michigan law or prison officials acted under color of state law. Sims v Parke Davis & Co. (1971, ED Mich) 334 F Supp 774, 15 FR Serv 2d 709, affd (1971, CA6 Mich) 453 F2d 1259, cert den (1972) 405 US 978, 31 L Ed 2d 254, 92 S Ct 1196.

**3. Personal services.**
Under former statute, the department of corrections was not authorized to permit or allow inmates of state prisons to work for privately supported nonprofit institutions. Op Atty Gen, June 15, 1943, No. 0–870.

**4. Cost of production.**
Cost of production as provided for in former statute did not include items of food, clothing and maintenance of prisoners. Op Atty Gen, July 9, 1947, No. 481.

**§ 800.327. Employment of inmates; types of employment. [MSA § 28.1540(7)]**

Sec. 7. The department of corrections shall provide as fully as practicable for the employment of inmates in tasks consistent with the penal and rehabilitative purposes of their imprisonment and with the public economy. The types of employment shall be as follows:

(a) Routine maintenance and operation of correctional institutions.

(b) Educational and rehabilitation activities, whether formal or through productive or socialized activities, determined on the basis of individual needs and educability.

(c) Productive or maintenance labor on or in connection with the institution farms, or other land rented or leased by the department of corrections, factories, shops, or other available facilities for the production and distribution of correctional industries products and services.

(d) Labor assignments on state public works, ways, or properties when and as requisitioned by the governor or on county, township, or district roads when requested by the county board of commissioners pursuant to section 1 of Act No. 181 of the Public Acts of 1911, being section 800.101 of the Michigan Compiled Laws.

(e) Labor assignments in private manufacturing or service enterprises established under section 7a.

**History:**
Pub Acts 1968, No. 15, § 7, imd eff April 5, 1968; amended by Pub Acts 1980, No. 245, imd eff July 28, 1980, by § 3 eff October 1, 1980.
Amended by Pub Acts 1996, No. 537, imd eff January 13, 1997.

**Effect of amendment notes:**
**The 1996 amendment** added paragraph (e); and made grammatical changes.

**Statutory references:**
Section 7a is § 800.327a.

**Michigan Digest references:**
Prisons and Jails § 3.

**LEXIS-NEXIS™ Michigan analytical references:**
Michigan Law and Practice, Convicts and Prisons § 5.

**Research references:**
60 Am Jur 2d, Penal and Correctional Institutions §§34–40.

### CASE NOTES

Plaintiff prison inmate who was employed as clerk in state university education program conducted in prison for benefit of prison rehabilitation program, although arguably entitled to coverage under minimum wage law, would be held to be subject to more recently enacted and more specific Correctional Industries Act providing for payments to inmates on basis of need, motivation, or reward unrelated to any profits to state as result of work in question, thereby precluding plaintiff from maintaining cause of action upon which relief could be granted under minimum wage law. Manville v Bd. of Governors of Wayne State University (1978) 85 Mich App 628, 272 NW2d 162.

Prison inmates who work in the state prison system are not "employees" within the provisions of the Michigan Occupational Safety and Health Act. Op Atty Gen, December 23, 1987, No. 6485.

Sharecropping contracts for use of prison labor were unlawful as not within scope of permissive use of prison labor under former statute. Op Atty Gen, February 17, 1948, No. 659.

### § 800.327a. Assignment of inmates to work in private manufacturing or service enterprise. [MSA § 28.1540(7a)]

Sec. 7a. (1) Inmates may be assigned to work in a private manufacturing or service enterprise that meets all of the following requirements:

(a) The enterprise is suitably designed for the utilization of inmate labor. Prisoners shall not be granted access to any employee, customer or client information including, but not limited to, personal addresses, telephone numbers, E-mail addresses, credit card information or other financial information, health records, or any information contained in personnel, client or customer files.

(b) The enterprise either is located within 10 miles of a correctional facility or is located within a correctional facility pursuant to a lease agreement executed between the department of corrections and the enterprise. If the enterprise is located within a correctional facility, the enterprise shall pay to the local taxing authority an amount in lieu of ad valorem property taxes equivalent to the amount of ad valorem property taxes that would have been required if the enterprise had been located outside the correctional facility.

(c) The enterprise manufactures products or renders services that are permitted to be manufactured or rendered using inmate labor, as determined under section 6(4).

(d) The ratio of the number of employees of the enterprise to the number of inmates assigned to work in the enterprise shall not be less than 1 employee to 3 inmates.

(2) Only those inmates who reside in a correctional institution having a security designation of level I, who are not serving a sentence of life imprisonment, and who volunteer for the assignment are eligible to be assigned to work in a private manufacturing or service enterprise. As used in this subsection, "security designation" means 1 of 6 levels of restrictiveness enforced at each correc-

§ 800.327a                                                                                    **Prisons**

tional institution, as determined by the department, with security level I being the least restrictive and security level VI being the most restrictive.

(3) The contract between the department and the private manufacturing or service enterprise shall ensure that a wage that is the higher of the prevailing wage or the minimum wage established pursuant to the minimum wage law of 1964, Act No. 154 of the Public Acts of 1964, being sections 408.381 to 408.398 of the Michigan Compiled Laws, shall be paid by the department to the inmate for work performed by the inmate in the private manufacturing or service enterprise. The wages of an inmate under this section shall be distributed in the following order:

(a) The department shall withhold and pay the inmate's applicable state and local income taxes and federal income, social security, and medicare taxes.

(b) Of the balance remaining:

(i) If the inmate has been ordered by the court to pay restitution to the victim of his or her crime, 20% shall be paid for that restitution on the inmate's behalf, in accordance with the court order, until the amount of restitution is satisfied. If restitution is satisfied or if the inmate was not made subject to restitution, 10% shall be added to the escrow account under subparagraph (iv) and 10% shall be deposited with the state treasurer and credited to the crime victims rights fund created in section 4 of Act No. 196 of the Public Acts of 1989, being section 780.904 of the Michigan Compiled Laws, in addition to the amount in subparagraph (v).

(ii) If the inmate has a spouse or children, 20% shall be paid to the inmate's spouse or children for the purpose of family support. If the inmate's spouse or children receive aid to families with dependent children or general assistance under the social welfare act, Act No. 280 of the Public Acts of 1939, being sections 400.1 to 400.119b of the Michigan Compiled Laws, while the inmate is incarcerated, the 20% designated in this subdivision shall be deposited with the state treasurer and credited to the general fund as repayment of that aid or assistance, until that amount of aid or assistance is repaid.

(iii) Ten percent shall be paid to the inmate for his or her personal use while incarcerated.

(iv) Ten percent shall be held by the department in an escrow account for the inmate, and shall be returned to the inmate upon his or her release.

(v) The balance remaining after the deductions specified in subparagraphs (i) to (iv) shall be deposited with the state treasurer and credited to the general fund, as partial reimbursement to the state for the cost of that inmate's imprisonment and care.

(vi) The inmate shall not be eligible for unemployment compensation or retirement benefits upon his or her release from a work assignment or from imprisonment.

(4) The contract between the department and the private manufacturing or service enterprise shall provide that the department shall pay the applicable employer's share of federal social security and medicare taxes and state worker's disability compensation payments or contributions.

(5) The contract between the department and the private manufacturing or service enterprise shall provide that the enterprise shall reimburse the department for the amounts paid by the department for the purposes described in subsections (3) and (4). The contract also shall require the enterprise to pay to the department an annual administrative fee equal to 1% of the total amounts paid annually to the department by the enterprise for the purposes described in subsections (3) and (4).

(6) The contract provisions created in this section shall not be construed as making the prisoner an employee of the state of Michigan.

**History:**
Pub Acts 1968, No. 15, § 7a, as added by Pub Acts 1996, No. 537, imd eff January 13, 1997.

**Statutory references:**
Section 6 is § 800.326.

**LEXIS-NEXIS™ Michigan analytical references:**
Michigan Law and Practice, Convicts and Prisons § 5.

## § 800.328. Specifications and standards; inspection, acceptance or rejection. [MSA § 28.1540(8)]

Sec. 8. The director of the department of management and budget shall prescribe specifications, standards, quality tests, methods, and conditions of packaging and conditions and times of delivery for correctional industries products purchased by this state, and may inspect, accept, or reject correctional industries products to the same extent as if they were purchased from other sources.

**History:**
Pub Acts 1968, No. 15, § 8, imd eff April 5, 1968; amended by Pub Acts 1980, No. 245, imd eff July 28, 1980, by § 3 eff October 1, 1980.

**Michigan Digest references:**
Prisons and Jails § 3.

**LEXIS-NEXIS™ Michigan analytical references:**
Michigan Law and Practice, Convicts and Prisons § 5.

**Research references:**
60 Am Jur 2d, Penal and Correctional Institutions §§34–40.

## § 800.329. Purchase and sale of finished goods, material or equipment; purposes. [MSA § 28.1540(9)]

Sec. 9. Correctional industries, with the approval of the department of management and budget, may purchase finished goods, materials, or equipment of the same type as ordinarily produced by correctional industries. The industries may then sell the items to those entities for whom production by correctional industries is permitted by this act. The purpose of this section is to provide for the completing of orders when production is not sufficient or for other reasons of economy and good business practice which may make the purchases beneficial to the state.

**History:**
Pub Acts 1968, No. 15, § 9, imd eff April 5, 1968; amended by Pub Acts 1980, No. 245, imd eff July 28, 1980, by § 3 eff October 1, 1980.

**Michigan Digest references:**
Prisons and Jails § 3.

**LEXIS-NEXIS™ Michigan analytical references:**
Michigan Law and Practice, Convicts and Prisons § 5.

**Research references:**
60 Am Jur 2d, Penal and Correctional Institutions §§34–40.

## § 800.330. Institutions maintained by political subdivisions; disposition of products; exceptions. [MSA § 28.1540(10)]

Sec. 10. A correctional institution now maintained by a political subdivision of this state may sell or otherwise dispose of its correctional institution products to the institutions or departments of the county or political subdivision in which the institution is located. The provisions of sections 8 and 9 shall not apply to a correctional institution of a political subdivision.

**History:**
Pub Acts 1968, No. 15, § 10, imd eff April 5, 1968; amended by Pub Acts 1985, No. 55, imd eff June 14, 1985 (see 1985 note below).

**Editor's notes:**
**Pub Acts 1985, No. 55, § 3,** imd eff June 14, 1985, provides:
"Section 3. This amendatory act shall not take effect unless all of the following bills of the 83rd Legislature are enacted into law:
"(a) House Bill No. 4392 [which became Act No. 61 of 1985].
"(b) House Bill No. 4393 [which became Act No. 44 of 1985].
"(c) House Bill No. 4395 [which became Act No. 46 of 1985].
"(d) House Bill No. 4394 [which became Act No. 45 of 1985].
"(e) House Bill No. 4396 [which became Act No. 47 of 1985].
"(f) House Bill No. 4403 [which became Act No. 54 of 1985].
"(g) House Bill No. 4398 [which became Act No. 49 of 1985].
"(h) House Bill No. 4401 [which became Act No. 52 of 1985].
"(i) House Bill No. 4399 [which became Act No. 50 of 1985].
"(j) House Bill No. 4417 [which became Act No. 56 of 1985].
"(k) House Bill No. 4400 [which became Act No. 51 of 1985].
"(l) House Bill No. 4423 [which became Act No. 60 of 1985].
"(m) House Bill No. 4402 [which became Act No. 53 of 1985].
"(n) House Bill No. 4397 [which became Act No. 48 of 1985].
"(o) House Bill No. 4418 [which became Act No. 57 of 1985].
"(p) House Bill No. 4421 [which became Act No. 58 of 1985].
"(q) House Bill No. 4422 [which became Act No. 59 of 1985]."

**Statutory references:**
Sections 8 and 9, above referred to, are §§800.328 and 800.329.

**Michigan Digest references:**
Prisons and Jails § 3.

**LEXIS-NEXIS™ Michigan analytical references:**
Michigan Law and Practice, Convicts and Prisons § 5.

**Research references:**
60 Am Jur 2d, Penal and Correctional Institutions §§34–40.

## § 800.331. Intent of act; correctional industries as total self-supporting system; methods of purchasing and accounting. [MSA § 28.1540(11)]

Sec. 11. (1) It is the intent of this act to do all of the following:

(a) Provide adequate, regular, diversified, and suitable employment for inmates of the state for the purpose of enhancing job skills consistent with proper penal purposes.

(b) Utilize the labor of inmates for self-maintenance and for reimbursing the state for expenses incurred by reason of their crimes and imprisonment, and for employment in private manufacturing or service enterprises established under section 7a.

(c) Provide a means for inmates to earn wages for support of their families, reimbursement to the state for part of the cost of their imprisonment, restitution to crime victims, and other purposes consistent with their imprisonment.

(d) Effect the requisitioning and disbursement of correctional industries products and services directly through established state authorities without possibility of private profits and without any intermediating financial considerations, appropriations, or expenditures.

(e) Permit the management of correctional industries to operate in a manner as similar as possible to similar private industrial operations.

(2) Within 5 years after October 1, 1980, correctional industries shall be changed from a system that requires intermediating financial assistance to a total self-supporting system.

(3) The governor shall require the director of the department of management and budget to establish suitable methods of purchasing and accounting, which shall provide as may be necessary or advisable for all of the following:

(A) The purchasing and supply of supplies and materials necessary for the institutional manufacture or production of correctional industries products.

(B) Crediting correctional industries accounts and debiting accounts of consuming institutions or departments for products requisitioned and disbursed, at prices fixed to recapture all direct and indirect costs. In addition, the methods of purchasing, accounting, and pricing may provide for the setting of a margin in excess of direct and indirect costs, which may be expended for purposes consistent with this act.

(C) The purchase of all commodities or requirements other than correctional industries products as provided in this act, by competitive bidding or other methods established by law or approved practice. All agencies, offices, and departments of this state shall order goods from correctional industries if the goods are produced by correctional industries of this state, are comparable in price and quality to the goods normally purchased by governmental agencies, and can be supplied in a reasonable time period as determined by the department of management and budget.

(D) An equitable basis to be proposed by the department of corrections and approved by the department of management and budget for determining costs between the correctional institutions and correctional industries that requires the institutions to absorb that portion of the supervisory costs that directly relate to custody and security responsibilities.

**History:**
Pub Acts 1968, No. 15, § 11, imd eff April 5, 1968; amended by Pub Acts 1980, No. 245, imd eff July 28, 1980, by § 3 eff October 1, 1980.
Amended by Pub Acts 1996, No. 537, imd eff January 13, 1997.

**Effect of amendment notes:**
The **1996 amendment** in subsection (1), paragraph (a), added "for the purpose of enhancing job skills" after "state"; in subsection (1), paragraph (b), added "and for employment in private manufacturing or service enterprises established under section 7a"; added a new subsection (1), paragraph (c); in subsection (2), added "October 1, 1980"; in subsection (3), paragraph (A), deleted "pursuant to sections 2, 6, and 7" after "products"; and made grammatical changes.

**Statutory references:**
Section 7a, above referred to, is § 800.327a.

**Michigan Digest references:**
Prisons and Jails § 3.

**LEXIS-NEXIS™ Michigan analytical references:**
Michigan Law and Practice, Convicts and Prisons § 5.

**Research references:**
60 Am Jur 2d, Penal and Correctional Institutions §§34–40.

### CASE NOTES

Correctional institutions may not make profit from manufacture of products by correctional industries. Op Atty Gen, February 23, 1976, No. 4948.

## § 800.332. Schedule of payments or allowances to inmates or dependents. [MSA § 28.1540(12)]

Sec. 12. The department of corrections may adopt a schedule of payments or allowances to inmates or to their dependents from the funds as may be provided for the payment. This section does not apply to the payment of wages to inmates assigned to work in private manufacturing or service enterprises under section 7a.

**History:**
Pub Acts 1968, No. 15, § 12, imd eff April 5, 1968; amended by Pub Acts 1980, No. 245, imd eff July 28, 1980, by § 3 eff October 1, 1980.
Amended by Pub Acts 1996, No. 537, imd eff January 13, 1997.

**Effect of amendment notes:**
The **1996 amendment** substituted "department" for "commission"; and added the second sentence.

**Statutory references:**
Section 7a, above referred to, is § 800.327a.

**Michigan Digest references:**
Prisons and Jails §§3, 3.40.

**LEXIS-NEXIS™ Michigan analytical references:**
Michigan Law and Practice, Convicts and Prisons § 5.

**Research references:**
60 Am Jur 2d, Penal and Correctional Institutions §§34–40.

### CASE NOTES

State has right to fruits of an inmate's labor performed for state and need not pay minimum wage for it. Manville v Bd. of Governors of Wayne State University (1978) 85 Mich App 628, 272 NW2d 162 (criticized on other grounds by People v Thomas (1982) 118 Mich App 667, 325 NW2d 536).

Services performed by plaintiff inmate's labor performed for state education program operating entirely within prison walls for benefit of prison rehabilitation program would be held to have come within scope of Correctional Industries Act providing for employment of inmate labor in correctional institutions and payment therefor on basis of need or motivation or reward for industry or behavior unrelated to any profits to state. Manville v Bd. of Governors of Wayne State University (1978) 85 Mich App 628, 272 NW2d 162 (criticized on other grounds by People v Thomas (1982) 118 Mich App 667, 325 NW2d 536).

In action in which plaintiff prison inmate sought relief under minimum wage law for services rendered as clerk in education program conducted by defendant state university for benefit of prison rehabilitation, plaintiff's employment by defendant rather than by prison under economic reality test was properly asserted in pleadings alleging that he was employee of defendant, hired and supervised, fired and paid by agent acting on behalf of defendant, that no prison official participated in job selection or set work hours, and that his pay did not go through prison payroll system but came directly from defendant. Manville v Bd. of Governors of Wayne State University (1978) 85 Mich App 628, 272 NW2d 162 (criticized on other grounds by People v Thomas (1982) 118 Mich App 667, 325 NW2d 536).

## § 800.333. Violations by officers; effect. [MSA § 28.1540(13)]

Sec. 13. Wilful violations of any of the provisions of this act by an officer of the state or of any political subdivision thereof, or by any officer of any institution of either, shall be sufficient cause for removal from office, and subject such officer to prosecution as provided in section 14.

**History:**
Pub Acts 1968, No. 15, § 13, imd eff April 5, 1968.

**Statutory references:**
Section 14, above referred to, is § 800.334.

**Michigan Digest references:**
Prisons and Jails § 3.

**LEXIS-NEXIS™ Michigan analytical references:**
Michigan Law and Practice, Convicts and Prisons § 5.

**Research references:**
60 Am Jur 2d, Penal and Correctional Institutions §§34–40.

## § 800.334. Violation; misdemeanor. [MSA § 28.1540(14)]

Sec. 14. Any person, firm or corporation who wilfully violates any of the provisions of this act is guilty of a misdemeanor.

**History:**
Pub Acts 1968, No. 15, § 14, imd eff April 5, 1968.

**Cross references:**
Punishment for misdemeanor, § 750.504.

**Michigan Digest references:**
Prisons and Jails § 3.

**LEXIS-NEXIS™ Michigan analytical references:**
Michigan Law and Practice, Convicts and Prisons § 5.

**Research references:**
60 Am Jur 2d, Penal and Correctional Institutions §§ 34–40.

## § 800.335. [Repealed] [MSA § 28.1540(15)]

**History:**
Pub Acts 1968, No. 15, § 15, imd eff April 5, 1968; **repealed** by Pub Acts 1980, No. 245, imd eff July 28, 1980, by § 3 eff October 1, 1980.

Executive Reorganization Order 1993-8, eff October 9, 1993

## § 800.341. Michigan state industries advisory board, creation. [MSA § 28.1540(20)]

Whereas, Article V, Section 2, of the Constitution of the State of Michigan of 1963 empowers the Governor to make changes in the organization of the Executive Branch or in the assignment of functions among its units which he considers necessary for efficient administration; and

Whereas, the Michigan State Industries Advisory Council was created by Act No. 245 of the Public Acts of 1980, as amended, being Section 800.324(f) of the Michigan Compiled Laws, in the Corrections Commission, now the Department of Corrections; and

Whereas, the functions, duties and responsibilities assigned to the Michigan State Industries Advisory Council can be more effectively carried out by the new Michigan State Industries Advisory Board; and

Whereas, it is necessary in the interests of efficient administration and effectiveness of government to effect changes in the organization of the Executive Branch of government.

Now, Therefore, I, John Engler, Governor of the State of Michigan, pursuant to the powers vested in me by the Constitution of the State of Michigan of 1963 and the laws of the State of Michigan, do hereby order the following:

1. There is hereby established a new Michigan State Industries Advisory Board (the "Board") within the Department of Corrections on the following terms and conditions:

    (a) The Board shall consist of the following eleven members:
    i. Two representatives of labor unions;
    ii. One representative of a financial institution;
    iii. Two representatives of small business;
    iv. Two representatives of manufacturers;
    v. One public member;
    vi. The Director of the Department of Corrections or his/her designee;
    vii. The Business Ombudsman; and
    viii. One representative from the Department of Management and Budget.

    (b) Each member of the Board shall be appointed by the Governor and shall serve for a term of three years, except that of the members first appointed, three shall be appointed for a term of one year, four shall be appointed for a term of two years and four shall be appointed for a term of three years. The Governor shall appoint one member of the Board as Chairperson and that member shall serve as Chairperson at the pleasure of the Governor.

    (c) The Board shall make recommendations to the Governor and the Director of the Department of Corrections on ways to better integrate Michigan State Industries into the business community and foster its growth while ensuring that competition with the private sector is minimized.

(d) The duties of the Board shall be consistent with the above recommendations, including, but not limited to:

i. Meet with Michigan State Industries management and the Director of the Department of Corrections to review operations;

ii. Assist in making capital expenditure recommendations;

iii. Review the annual report and operating statements;

iv. Assist in developing Michigan State Industries' five-year plan;

v. Assist in product development; and

vi. Assist in developing marketing plans to advise the Director of the Department of Corrections on matters related to Michigan State Industries.

2. All the statutory authority, powers, duties, functions, and responsibilities of the Michigan State Industries Advisory Council are hereby transferred to the new Michigan State Industries Advisory Board created by Section 1 of this Order by a Type III transfer, as defined by Section 3 of Act No. 380 of the Public Acts of 1965, being Section 16.103 of the Michigan Compiled Laws, and the Michigan State Industries Advisory Council is hereby abolished. The transfer shall take place under the following conditions:

(a) The Director of the Department of Corrections shall provide executive direction and supervision for the implementation of the transfer.

(b) All records, personnel, property and unexpended balances of appropriations, allocations and other funds used, held, employed, available or to be made available to the Michigan State Industries Advisory Council for the activities transferred to the Michigan State Industries Advisory Board by this Order are hereby transferred to the new Michigan State Industries Advisory Board.

(c) All rules, orders, contracts and agreements relating to the assigned functions lawfully adopted prior to the effective date of this order shall continue to be effective until revised, amended, or repealed.

(d) Any suit, action or other proceeding lawfully commenced by, against or before any entity affected by this Order shall not abate by reason of the taking effect of this Order. Any suit, action or other proceeding may be maintained by, against or before the appropriate successor of any entity affected by this Order.

The provisions of the Order shall become effective immediately upon filing.

**History:**

Executive Reorganization Order No. 1993–8 was promulgated as Executive Order No. 1993–15, eff October 9, 1993.

# STATE CORRECTIONAL FACILITY REIMBURSEMENT ACT

Act 253, 1935, p 434, imd eff June 8, 1935.

AN ACT to provide procedures for securing reimbursement to the state of the expenses incurred by the state for the cost of care of certain prisoners in state correctional facilities; to provide procedures for securing the reimbursement of expenses to be incurred by the state in regard to the future cost of care of such prisoners; and to prescribe certain powers and duties of certain state and local public officers and officials. (Amended by Pub Acts 1984, No. 282, imd eff December 20, 1984.).

*The People of the State of Michigan enact:*

## § 800.401. Title of act. [MSA § 28.1701]

Sec. 1. This act shall be known and may be cited as "the state correctional facility reimbursement act."

**History:**
Pub Acts 1935, No. 253, § 1, imd eff June 8, 1935; amended by Pub Acts 1984, No. 282, imd eff December 20, 1984.

**Michigan Digest references:**
Infants § 54.
Limitations of Actions § 52.
Prisons and Jails §§1.05, 1.20, 4, 4.50, 5.

**LEXIS-NEXIS™ Michigan analytical references:**
Michigan Law and Practice, Convicts and Prisons § 4.
Michigan Law and Practice, Education § 136.

**Research references:**
60 Am Jur 2d, Penal and Correctional Institutions § 11.

**Legal periodicals:**
Sable, Casenote, The Fruits of Crime, Victims, & New York's Son of Sam Law: Simon and Schuster, Inc. v. Members of the New York State Crime Victims Board, 1992 Detroit C L Rev 4:1185.
Fryer, Note, Bearing the Burden of Strict Scrutiny In the Wake of Simon & Shuster, Inc. v. Members of the New York State Crime Victims Board: A Constitutional Analysis of Michigan's "Son of Sam" Law, 70 U Det Mercy L R 1:191 (1992).

### CASE NOTES

Because the obligations of a prisoner to compensate the citizenry for the cost of incarceration imposed by the State Correctional Facility Reimbursement Act does not create a debtor-creditor relationship, the limits on garnishment of earnings imposed by the federal Consumer Credit Protection Act are not applicable. State Treasurer v Gardner (1998) 459 Mich 1, 583 NW2d 687.

The Prison Reimbursement Act was intended to apply to all inmates of the state penal system and was not limited to the inmates of the three penal institutions named in the act and in existence at the time of its passage; nor is the act violative of the constitutional guarantee of equal protection. State Treasurer v

## § 800.401                                                Prisons

Wilson (1985) 423 Mich 138, 377 NW2d 703, on remand (1986) 150 Mich App 78, 388 NW2d 312.

The State Correctional Facility Reimbursement Act creates an obligation on the part of a prisoner to pay the cost of care during incarceration and a right on the part of the state to reimbursement for such cost; any common-law right that the prisoner may have to prefer creditors does not apply to actions under the act and the prisoner may not impede the state's right to reimbursement by claiming that he would prefer to use his assets to pay the obligation of his choice. State Treasurer v Sheko (1996) 218 Mich App 185, 553 NW2d 654, app den (1997) 455 Mich 856.

### § 800.401a. Definitions. [MSA § 28.1701(1)]

Sec. 1a. As used in this act:

(a) "Assets" means property, tangible or intangible, real or personal, belonging to or due a prisoner or former prisoner including income or payments to such prisoner from social security, worker's compensation, veteran's compensation, pension benefits, previously earned salary or wages, bonuses, annuities, retirement benefits, or from any other source whatsoever, but does not include any of the following:

(i) The homestead of the prisoner up to $50,000.00 in value.

(ii) Money saved by the prisoner from wages and bonuses paid the prisoner while he or she was confined to a state correctional facility.

(b) "Cost of care" means the cost to the department for providing transportation, room, board, clothing, security, medical, and other normal living expenses of prisoners, and the cost to the department for providing college-level classes or programs to prisoners, as determined by the department.

(c) "Department" means the department of corrections of this state.

(d) "Director" means the director of the department.

(e) "Prisoner" means any person who is under the jurisdiction of the department and is either confined in any state correctional facility or is under the continuing jurisdiction of the department.

(f) "State correctional facility" means a facility or institution which houses a prisoner population under the jurisdiction of the department. State correctional facility includes a correctional camp, community correction center, state prison, and a state reformatory.

**History:**

Pub Acts 1935, No. 253, § 1a, as added by Pub Acts 1984, No. 282, imd eff December 20, 1984.

Amended by Pub Acts 1996, No. 286, imd eff June 17, 1996.

**Effect of amendment notes:**

**The 1996 amendment** in paragraph (a), deleted former subparagraphs (ii) and (iii); and revised paragraph (b).

**Michigan Digest references:**

Poor Persons § 11.

Prisons and Jails §§ 1.05, 4, 4.50, 5.

**LEXIS-NEXIS™ Michigan analytical references:**
Michigan Law and Practice, Convicts and Prisons § 4.
Michigan Law and Practice, Education § 136.

**Research references:**
60 Am Jur 2d, Penal and Correctional Institutions § 11.

### CASE NOTES

State Correctional Facility Reimbursement Act, which specifically includes pension benefits as assets that may be subject to a prisoner's statutory obligation to reimburse the state for his incarceration costs, has priority over the Public School Employees Retirement Act's nonassignment provision, which protects a public employee's pension from legal process; therefore, the nonassignment provision does not insulate a public school employee's pension from the reimbursement provision. State Treasurer v Schuster (1998) 456 Mich 408, 572 NW2d 628.

A retirement allowance received pursuant to the Public School Employees Retirement Act by a state prison inmate is not subject to the State Correctional Facility Reimbursement Act as a source for the reimbursement of the state for the cost of the inmate's incarceration. State Treasurer v Schuster, 215 Mich App 347, 547 NW2d 332.

## § 800.401b. Information regarding assets of prisoners, form; form submitted to every prisoner; date; resubmission, purpose; completion of form; oath or affirmation; department to develop form, time. [MSA § 28.1701(2)]

Sec. 1b. (1) The department shall develop a form which shall be used by the department to obtain information from all prisoners regarding assets of the prisoners.

(2) Upon being developed, the form shall be submitted to each person who is a prisoner as of the date the form is developed and to every person who thereafter is sentenced to imprisonment under the jurisdiction of the department. The form may be resubmitted to a prisoner by the department for purposes of obtaining current information regarding assets of the prisoner.

(3) Every prisoner shall complete the form or provide for completion of the form and the prisoner shall swear or affirm under oath that to the best of his or her knowledge the information provided is complete and accurate.

(4) The department shall have developed the form provided for under this section not later than 30 days after the effective date of this section.

**History:**
Pub Acts 1935, No. 253, § 1b, as added by Pub Acts 1984, No. 282, imd eff December 20, 1984.

**Michigan Digest references:**
Poor Persons § 11.
Prisons and Jails §§1.05, 4, 4.50, 5.
Statutes § 76.

**LEXIS-NEXIS™ Michigan analytical references:**
Michigan Law and Practice, Convicts and Prisons § 4.
Michigan Law and Practice, Education § 136.

**Research references:**
60 Am Jur 2d, Penal and Correctional Institutions § 11.

## § 800.402. Report to attorney general by director, contents.
[MSA § 28.1702]

Sec. 2. The director shall forward to the attorney general a report on each prisoner containing a completed form under section 1b together with all other information available on the assets of the prisoner and an estimate of the total cost of care for that prisoner.

**History:**
Pub Acts 1935, No. 253, § 2, imd eff June 8, 1935; amended by Pub Acts 1984, No. 282, imd eff December 20, 1984.

**Statutory references:**
Section 1b, above referred to, is § 800.401b.

**Michigan Digest references:**
Poor Persons § 11.
Prisons and Jails §§1.05, 4, 4.50, 5.
Statutes § 76.

**LEXIS-NEXIS™ Michigan analytical references:**
Michigan Law and Practice, Convicts and Prisons § 4.
Michigan Law and Practice, Education § 136.

**Research references:**
60 Am Jur 2d, Penal and Correctional Institutions § 11.

## § 800.403. Reports, investigation; cost of care of prisoner, reimbursement of state; reimbursement of state; limitation.
[MSA § 28.1703]

Sec. 3. (1) The attorney general shall investigate or cause to be investigated all reports furnished under section 2.

(2) If the attorney general upon completing the investigation under subsection (1) has good cause to believe that a prisoner has sufficient assets to recover not less than 10% of the estimated cost of care of the prisoner or 10% of the estimated cost of care of the prisoner for 2 years, whichever is less, the attorney general shall seek to secure reimbursement for the expense of the state of Michigan for the cost of care of that prisoner.

(3) Not more than 90% of the value of the assets of the prisoner may be used for purposes of securing costs and reimbursement under this act.

**History:**
Pub Acts 1935, No. 253, § 3, imd eff June 8, 1935; amended by Pub Acts 1984, No. 282, imd eff December 20, 1984.

**Statutory references:**
Section 2, above referred to, is § 800.402.

**Michigan Digest references:**
Poor Persons § 11.
Prisons and Jails §§1.05, 4, 4.50, 5.
Statutes § 76.

**LEXIS-NEXIS™ Michigan analytical references:**
Michigan Law and Practice, Convicts and Prisons § 4.
Michigan Law and Practice, Education § 136.

**Research references:**
60 Am Jur 2d, Penal and Correctional Institutions § 11.

### CASE NOTES

On reading of language of State Correctional Facility Reimbursement Act as obligating Attorney General to seek reimbursement for state care of prisoner when his assets are such that recovery of not less than ten percent of cost of care is possible, Attorney General is not barred by Act from seeking reimbursement within his discretion merely because possible recovery would be less than ten percent. State Treasurer v Cuellar (1991) 190 Mich App 464, 476 NW2d 644, app den (1992) 440 Mich 861, 486 NW2d 687, reconsideration den (1992, Mich) 489 NW2d 473.

## § 800.403a. Complete financial information, cooperation by prisoner; failure to cooperate, effect [MSA § 28.1703(1)]

Sec. 3a. (1) A prisoner shall fully cooperate with the state by providing complete financial information for purposes under this act.

(2) The failure of a prisoner to fully cooperate as provided in subsection (1) may be considered for purposes of a parole determination under section 35 of Act No. 232 of the Public Acts of 1953, being section 791.235 of the Michigan Compiled Laws.

**History:**
Pub Acts 1935, No. 253, § 3a, as added by Pub Acts 1984, No. 282, imd eff December 20, 1984.

**Michigan Digest references:**
Poor Persons § 11.
Prisons and Jails §§1.05, 4, 4.505,
Statutes § 76.

**LEXIS-NEXIS™ Michigan analytical references:**
Michigan Law and Practice, Convicts and Prisons § 4.
Michigan Law and Practice, Education § 136.

**Research references:**
60 Am Jur 2d, Penal and Correctional Institutions § 11.

## § 800.404. Exclusive jurisdiction of circuit court; complaint by attorney general, contents; order to show cause, issuance; service of complaint and order upon prisoner; methods; time; hearing; finding of assets subject to claim; order to reimburse state; amount of reimbursement; prisoner's obligation to provide support, consideration at hearing; order to reimburse state, failure to comply; order to show cause; contempt of court; cost of proceedings, liability of prisoner's assets; proceedings by state to recover cost of care of prisoner, commencement. [MSA § 28.1704]

Sec. 4. (1) The circuit court shall have exclusive jurisdiction over all proceedings under this act. The attorney general may file a complaint in the circuit court for the county from which a prisoner was sentenced, stating that the person is or has been a prisoner in a state correctional facility, that there is good cause to believe that the prisoner has assets, and praying that the assets be used to reimburse the state for the expenses incurred or to be incurred, or both, by the state for the costs of care of the person as a prisoner.

(2) Upon the filing of the complaint under subsection (1), the court shall issue an order to show cause why the prayer of the complainant should not be granted. The complaint and order shall be served upon the prisoner personally or, if the prisoner is confined in a state correctional facility, by registered mail addressed to the prisoner in care of the chief administrator of the state correctional facility where the prisoner is housed, at least 30 days before the date of hearing on the complaint and order.

(3) At the time of the hearing on the complaint and order, if it appears that the prisoner has any assets which ought to be subjected to the claim of the state under this act, the court shall issue an order requiring any person, corporation, or other legal entity possessed or having custody of those assets to appropriate and apply the assets or a portion thereof toward reimbursing the state as provided for under this act.

(4) The amount of reimbursement under this act shall not be in excess of the per capita cost of care for maintaining prisoners in the state correctional facility in which the prisoner is housed.

(5) At the hearing on the complaint and order and before entering any order on behalf of the state against the defendant, the court shall take into consideration any legal obligation of the defendant to support a spouse, minor children, or other dependents and any moral obligation to support dependents to whom the defendant is providing or has in fact provided support.

(6) If the person, corporation, or other legal entity shall neglect or refuse to comply with and order under subsection (3), the court shall order the person, corporation, or other legal entity to appear before the court at such time as the court may direct and to show cause why the person, corporation, or other legal entity should not be considered in contempt of court.

(7) If, in the opinion of the court, the assets of the prisoner are sufficient to pay the costs of the proceedings under this act, the assets shall be liable for those costs upon order of the court.

(8) The state may recover the expenses incurred or to be incurred, or both, by the state for the cost of care of the prisoner during the entire period or periods the person is a prisoner in a state correctional facility. The state may commence proceedings under this act until the prisoner has been finally discharged on the sentence and is no longer under the jurisdiction of the department.

**History:**
Pub Acts 1935, No. 253, § 4, imd eff June 8, 1935; amended by Pub Acts 1984, No. 282, imd eff December 20, 1984.

**Michigan Digest references:**
Constitutional Law § 66.
Garnishment § 42.
Injunctions § 134.
Poor Persons § 11.

Prisons and Jails §§ 1.05, 4.50.
Statutes § 76.

**LEXIS-NEXIS™ Michigan analytical references:**
Michigan Law and Practice, Constitutional Law § 344.
Michigan Law and Practice, Convicts and Prisons § 4.
Michigan Law and Practice, Education § 136.

**Research references:**
60 Am Jur 2d, Penal and Correctional Institutions § 11.

## CASE NOTES

### 1. Retroactive operation of act.

Prison Reimbursement Act imposes a civil liability on all prisoners able to pay whether they were sentenced before or after the effective date of the act, but such liability does not extend to any period of imprisonment prior to the effective date of such act. Auditor General v Olezniczak (1942) 302 Mich 336, 4 NW2d 679.

Retrospective obligation was not imposed by Prison Reimbursement Act. Auditor General v Olezniczak (1942) 302 Mich 336, 4 NW2d 679.

Estates of prisoners sentenced prior to operation of this act are liable for support and maintenance. Op Atty Gen, December 19, 1935.

### 2. Validity, construction and application of act.

Provision of this act, that reimbursement shall not be in excess of per capita cost of maintaining prisoners, provided an amount subject to mathematical computation, whereby court without exercise of its discretion could determine whether prisoner had estate which ought to be subjected to claim of state for his keep. Auditor General v Hall (1942) 300 Mich 215, 1 NW2d 516, 139 ALR 1022.

In action by auditor general of state, to recover cost of keeping and maintaining defendant as a prisoner, trial court properly held, that provision of this act, providing that reimbursement shall not be in excess of per capita cost of maintaining prisoners, did not provide for exercise of discretion by court but instead provided rule for mathematical computation, and, therefore, did not leave to court power to exercise discretion as defendant claimed. Auditor General v Hall (1942) 300 Mich 215, 1 NW2d 516, 139 ALR 1022.

Provision of this act requiring prisoner to pay for his keep and maintenance if he has sufficient estate, and vesting court with power to take into consideration the moral and legal obligations of prisoner, applied with equal force to all prisoners having an estate, and was not unreasonable classification so as to render act unconstitutional. Auditor General v Hall (1942) 300 Mich 215, 1 NW2d 516, 139 ALR 1022.

This statute, obligating a prisoner to pay for his keep and maintenance if he has sufficient estate, is civil rather than criminal in character, as act does not impose a personal judgment or liability against prisoner, but provides for establishing a lien upon his estate by ancillary proceeding in rem. Auditor General v Hall (1942) 300 Mich 215, 1 NW2d 516, 139 ALR 1022.

Under this act, obligation for prisoner's keep and maintenance is imposed upon him, to be paid from his estate, if he has any at time of his conviction, or subsequently acquires any while imprisoned. Auditor General v Hall (1942) 300 Mich 215, 1 NW2d 516, 139 ALR 1022.

Reimbursement of the state pursuant to the State Correctional Facility Reimbursement Act from a state prison inmate's disability pension benefits is limited by the garnishment restrictions of the Consumer Credit Protection Act to no more than sixty percent of such benefits where the inmate is not supporting a spouse or a dependent child. State Treasurer v Gardner (1997) 222 Mich App 62, 564 NW2d 51.

The property exemptions from levy and sale of the Revised Judicature Act (§ 600.6023; MCL § 600.6023) do not apply to reimbursement sought by the state under the State Correctional Facility Reimbursement Act. State Treasurer v Gardner (1997) 222 Mich App 62, 564 NW2d 51.

Statute mandating that trial court "take into consideration" defendant's legal or moral support obligations before entering order on behalf of state against him precluded order of reimbursement out of defendant's federal income tax refund for costs of his incarceration in state correctional facility, in absence of evidentiary hearing refuting defendant's claimed support obligations to wife, daughter, and stepchildren. State Treasurer v Downer (1993) 199 Mich App 447, 502 NW2d 704.

The statute which provides that prisoners may be required to reimburse the state for the cost of their imprisonment is not unconstitutionally vague. State Treasurer v Wilson (1986) 150 Mich App 78, 388 NW2d 312.

A resident of a state penal institution has the statutory duty to pay for the cost of his incarceration where possessed of any estate. State, Michigan State Treasurer v Turner (1981) 110 Mich App 228, 312 NW2d 418; State Treasurer on behalf of Department of Corrections v Brown (1983) 125 Mich App 620, 337 NW2d 23.

The circuit court from which a prisoner in a state penal institution was sentenced, upon petition by the auditor general or a prosecuting attorney for the county stating that he has reason to believe that the prisoner is possessed of an estate which may be subject to payment of the expenses of the incarceration and paying for the appointment of a guardian for the prisoner, must issue a citation to show cause why the petition may not be granted, and, following a hearing, if it appears that the prisoner is possessed of such an estate, the court must appoint a guardian and require the guardian to apply the estate to the reimbursement of the state for the expenses of the prisoner's incarceration. State, Michigan State Treasurer v Turner (1981) 110 Mich App 228, 312 NW2d 418.

Department of corrections may assess transportation charge upon inmates who participate in work-pass program only if transportation is actually furnished, and same amount may be charged for transportation of all participants in work-pass program even though distance may vary in individual cases. Op Atty Gen, November 1, 1977, No. 5237.

**3. Availability of federal pension, etc., income.**

Exemption of pension-derived funds from taxation and creditors' claims does not mean that they are unavailable for support of veteran while confined in a state prison. Auditor General v Olezniczak (1942) 302 Mich 336, 4 NW2d 679.

Veterans' adjusted compensation bonus bonds were exempt from claim of state for reimbursement for expense of maintenance of defendant in state prison under Prison Reimbursement Act. Auditor General v Olezniczak (1942) 302 Mich 336, 4 NW2d 679.

Deposits in bank, having been accumulated out of veteran's pension and insurance payments, express purpose of which was to provide veteran with needed support, were not exempt from claim of state for reimbursement for expense of maintenance of defendant in state prison under Prison Reimbursement Act. Auditor General v Olezniczak (1942) 302 Mich 336, 4 NW2d 679.

United States savings and treasury bonds, though purchased with funds received by guardian of veteran from veterans' administration, were not exempt from claim of state for reimbursement for expense of maintenance of defendant in state prison under Prison Reimbursement Act. Auditor General v Olezniczak (1942) 302 Mich 336, 4 NW2d 679.

Prisoner's monthly disability pension payments are earnings as defined by the Consumer Credit Protection Act, and the protections of that act limit garnishment under the State Correctional Facility Reimbursement Act to sixty percent of prisoner's pension. State Treasurer v Gardner (1997) 222 Mich App 62, 564 NW2d 51.

The state is not precluded by federal law from seeking reimbursement for the cost of a prison inmate's incarceration from the inmate's accumulated social security disability payments where the inmate, because his total care and maintenance is provided by the department of corrections, has no need for his social security disability benefits (42 USC 407). State Treasurer on behalf of Department of Corrections v Brown (1983) 125 Mich App 620, 337 NW2d 23.

State treasurer's action against prisoner and prisoner's former employer under Michigan's State Correctional Facility Reimbursement Act (SCFRA) was preempted by provision of federal Employee Retirement Income Security Act (ERISA) that proscribed alienation and assignment of plan benefits such as by garnishments; court order directing employer to deposit retiree's pension benefits into retiree's prison account from which treasurer could withdraw monies to partially reimburse state for costs of retiree's incarceration was invalid as assignment of pension plan benefits in violation of ERISA. Roberts v Baugh (1997, ED Mich) 986 F Supp 1074.

Estates of convicts otherwise liable under this act, are not exempt from charge for support and maintenance by reason of having their origin in pension granted by federal government. Op Atty Gen, January 15, 1936.

**4. Wages of prisoners.**

The Department of Corrections may not make deductions from the wages or bonuses of a prisoner working for correctional industries to reimburse the state for the cost of maintenance of the prisoner. Op Atty Gen, November 21, 1989, No. 6606.

**5. Estate of prisoner.**

The state's cost of maintaining a prisoner may be recovered from the estate of a prisoner consisting of property owned by the prisoner other than wages or bonuses of the prisoner earned while working for correctional industries. Op Atty Gen, November 21, 1989, No. 6606.

**§ 800.404a. Cost of care of prisoner, reimbursement to state; attorney general; remedies; enforcement procedure; restraining order; exception; appointment of receiver; enforcement of judgment, prohibition.** [MSA § 28.1705]

Sec. 4a. (1) Except as provided in subsection (3), in seeking to secure reimbursement under this act, the attorney general may use any remedy, interim order, or enforcement procedure allowed by law or court rule including an ex parte restraining order to restrain the prisoner or any other person or legal entity in possession or having custody of the estate of the prisoner from disposing of certain property pending a hearing on an order to show cause why the particular property should not be applied to reimburse the state as provided for under this act.

(2) To protect and maintain assets pending resolution of an action under this act, the court, upon request, may appoint a receiver.

(3) The attorney general or a prosecuting attorney shall not enforce any judgment obtained under this act by means of execution against the homestead of the prisoner.

**History:**
Pub Acts 1935, No. 253, § 4a, imd eff June 8, 1935; amended by Pub Acts 1984, No. 282, imd eff December 20, 1984.

**Michigan Digest references:**
Poor Persons § 11.
Prisons and Jails §§1.05, 4, 4.50, 5.
Statutes § 76.

**LEXIS-NEXIS™ Michigan analytical references:**
Michigan Law and Practice, Constitutional Law § 344.
Michigan Law and Practice, Convicts and Prisons § 4.
Michigan Law and Practice, Education § 136.

**Research references:**
60 Am Jur 2d, Penal and Correctional Institutions § 11.

**Legal periodicals:**
Fryer, Note, Bearing the Burden of Strict Scrutiny In the Wake of Simon & Shuster, Inc. v. Members of the New York State Crime Victims Board: A Constitutional Analysis of Michigan's "Son of Sam" Law, 70 U Det Mercy L R 1:191 (1992).

## § 800.404b. Enforcement of provisions of act; assistance of prosecuting attorney; reimbursement for cost of care of prisoner in work camp; prohibition. [MSA § 28.1706]

Sec. 4b. (1) The attorney general of this state shall enforce the provisions of this act except that the attorney general may request the prosecuting attorney of the county in which the prisoner was sentenced or the prosecuting attorney of the county in which any asset of a prisoner is located to make an investigation or assist in legal proceedings under this act.

(2) The attorney general shall not seek reimbursement under this act for the cost of care of a prisoner in a work camp if the department is being or has been reimbursed for those costs by the prisoner pursuant to section 65c of Act No. 232 of the Public Acts of 1953, being section 791.265c of the Michigan Compiled Laws.

**History:**
Pub Acts 1935, No. 253, § 4b, imd eff June 8, 1935; amended by Pub Acts 1984, No. 282, imd eff December 20, 1984.

**Michigan Digest references:**
Poor Persons § 11.
Prisons and Jails §§1.05, 4, 4.50, 5.
Statutes § 76.

**LEXIS-NEXIS™ Michigan analytical references:**
Michigan Law and Practice, Constitutional Law § 344.
Michigan Law and Practice, Convicts and Prisons § 4.
Michigan Law and Practice, Education § 136.

**Research references:**
60 Am Jur 2d, Penal and Correctional Institutions § 11.

**Legal periodicals:**
Fryer, Note, Bearing the Burden of Strict Scrutiny In the Wake of Simon & Shuster, Inc. v. Members of the New York State Crime Victims Board: A Constitutional Analysis of Michigan's "Son of Sam" Law, 70 U Det Mercy L R 1:191 (1992).

## § 800.405. Information and assistance to attorney general and prosecuting attorney by certain officials. [MSA § 28.1707]

Sec. 5. The sentencing judge, the sheriff of the county, the chief administrator of the state correctional facility, and the department of treasury shall furnish to the attorney general or prosecuting attorney all information and assistance possible to enable the attorney general or prosecuting attorney to secure reimbursement for the state under this act.

**History:**
Pub Acts 1935, No. 253, § 5, imd eff June 8, 1935; amended by Pub Acts 1984, No. 282, imd eff December 20, 1984.

**Michigan Digest references:**
Poor Persons § 11.
Prisons and Jails §§1.05, 4, 4.50, 5.
Statutes § 76.

**LEXIS-NEXIS™ Michigan analytical references:**
Michigan Law and Practice, Constitutional Law § 344.

Michigan Law and Practice, Convicts and Prisons § 4.
Michigan Law and Practice, Education § 136.

**Research references:**
60 Am Jur 2d, Penal and Correctional Institutions § 11.

## § 800.406. Cost of investigation, payment; balance, credited to general fund; determination of amount due state; evidence. [MSA § 28.1708]

Sec. 6. (1) The costs of any investigations under this act shall be paid from the reimbursements secured under this act, and the balance of the reimbursements shall be credited to the general fund of the state to be available for general fund purposes.

(2) The department of treasury may determine the amount due the state in cases under this act and render statements thereof, and such sworn statement shall be considered prima facie evidence of the amount due.

**History:**
Pub Acts 1935, No. 253, § 6, imd eff June 8, 1935; amended by Pub Acts 1984, No. 282, imd eff December 20, 1984.

**Michigan Digest references:**
Poor Persons § 11.
Prisons and Jails §§1.05, 4, 4.50, 5.
Statutes § 76.

**LEXIS-NEXIS™ Michigan analytical references:**
Michigan Law and Practice, Constitutional Law § 344.
Michigan Law and Practice, Convicts and Prisons § 4.
Michigan Law and Practice, Education § 136.

**Research references:**
60 Am Jur 2d, Penal and Correctional Institutions § 11.

## § 800.407. [Repealed] [MSA § 28.1709]

**History:**
Pub Acts 1935, No. 253, imd eff June 8, 1935; **repealed** by Pub Acts 1984, No. 282, imd eff December 20, 1984.

**Editor's notes:**
Former § 800.407 provided for the construction of the Prison Reimbursement Act relative to moneys saved from the prisoner's earnings.

---

# REIMBURSEMENT OF COUNTY FOR PROSECUTION AND PRISON MAINTENANCE EXPENSES

Act 16, 1978, p 42, imd eff February 12, 1978.

AN ACT to provide reimbursement to counties for expenses relating to certain felonies, for expenses incurred by implementing special jurisdictional duties, and for expenses incurred in maintaining escapees from correctional institutions; and to require reports. (Amended by Pub Acts 1987, No. 272, imd eff December 29, 1987, by § 2 eff April 1, 1988.).

*The People of the State of Michigan enact:*

## § 800.451. State correctional facility, definition. [MSA § 28.1714(1)]

Sec. 1. As used in this act, "state correctional facility" means a facility or institution which houses an inmate population under the jurisdiction of the department of corrections. State correctional facility includes a correctional camp, community correction center, state prison, and a state reformatory.

**History:**
Pub Acts 1978, No. 16, § 1, imd eff February 12, 1978.

## § 800.452. Reimbursement of county by state; expenses for fees of jurors, witnesses and attorneys; new felonies; submission of monthly costs to department of corrections; payment; determination of reasonableness conclusive; state agency's responsibility for duties; dates; reimbursement for fees; calculation; limit; exceptions. [MSA § 28.1714(2)]

Sec. 2. (1) The state shall reimburse each county in which a state correctional facility is located for the reasonable and actual costs incurred by the county for juror's fees, witness fees, fees of attorneys appointed by the court for the defendant, transcript fees, and for a proportion of the fees for the office of the prosecuting attorney as determined under subsection (3), in cases of new felony offenses committed by inmates of state correctional facilities during a period of state incarceration, new felonies committed during escape and cases of escape from custody as prescribed in section 65a(3) of Act No. 232 of the Public Acts of 1953, being section 791.265 of the Michigan Compiled Laws.

(2) Each county shall submit monthly its itemized costs as described in this section to the state agency designated in subsection (3). After determination by the state agency designated in subsection (3) of the reasonableness of the amount to be paid, payment shall be made in accordance with the accounting laws of the state. The determination of reasonableness by the state agency designated in subsection (3) shall be conclusive.

(3) The state agency responsible for the duties prescribed in subsections (2) and (4) shall be as follows:

(a) Before October 1, 1988, the department of corrections.

(b) On and after October 1, 1988, the department of management and budget.

(4) The amount of reimbursement for the fees of the prosecuting attorney under subsection (1) for any case, subject to the determination of reasonableness by the state agency designated in subsection (3), shall be based upon the actual time spent in prosecuting the case, and shall be calculated at a rate equal to 70% of the hourly rate or flat fee paid to court-appointed defense attorneys in the county. However, the reimbursement for a single case shall not exceed $1,000.00 unless the case is either of the following:

(a) A felony offense for which the maximum punishment is life imprisonment. In which case the reimbursement shall not exceed $10,000.00.

(b) A case that involves 12 or more hours of actual trial time, in which case the reimbursement shall not exceed $10,000.00. As used in this subdivision, "actual trial time" means the trial hours recorded on the court record beginning when juror selection begins and ending when the jury begins deliberation in the case. If there is no jury in the case, actual trial time means the trial hours recorded on the court record.

**History:**
Pub Acts 1978, No. 16, § 2, imd eff February 12, 1978; amended by Pub Acts 1987, No. 272, imd eff December 29, 1987, by § 2 eff April 1, 1988.

**§ 800.453. Reimbursement of county by state; additional jurisdictional duties in circuit court; submission of quarterly itemized costs to state court administrative officer; payment; determination of reasonableness conclusive.** [MSA § 28.1714(3)]

Sec. 3. (1) The state shall reimburse each county for the reasonable and actual costs incurred by that county for implementing additional jurisdictional duties in the circuit court imposed upon that county by law because that county is specifically named in the law as having jurisdiction.

(2) Each county shall submit quarterly its itemized costs as described in this section to the state court administrative office. After determination by the state court administrator of the reasonableness of the amount to be paid, payment shall be made in accordance with the accounting laws of the state. The determination of reasonableness by the state court administrator shall be conclusive.

**History:**
Pub Acts 1978, No. 16, § 3, imd eff February 12, 1978.

**§ 800.454. Reimbursement of county for costs of previously incarcerated state prisoner; conditions for reimbursement; daily limitation; inapplicability of provision; submission of monthly itemized costs to department of corrections; payment; determination of reasonableness conclusive.** [MSA § 28.1714(4)]

Sec. 4. (1) When a state committed prisoner who was incarcerated in a state correctional facility has escaped, not returned pursuant to agreement, or violated the terms of his or her parole and has been apprehended pursuant to an order of the department of corrections and is held in a county jail awaiting disposition of his or her case, the department of corrections shall reimburse the county holding the prisoner for the actual and reasonable daily costs, not to exceed $35.00 per day, incurred by the county in holding the prisoner. This section shall not apply to the holding of prisoners awaiting prosecution on new felony charges.

§ 800.454                                                    Prisons

(2) Each county shall submit monthly its itemized costs as described in this section to the department of corrections. After determination of reasonableness of the amount to be paid, payment shall be made in accordance with the accounting laws of the state. The determination of reasonableness by the department of corrections shall be conclusive.

**History:**
Pub Acts 1978, No. 16, § 4, imd eff February 12, 1978; amended by Pub Acts 1987, No. 272, imd eff December 29, 1987, by § 2 eff April 1, 1988.

**Michigan Digest references:**
Counties § 40.
Prisons and Jails § 2.35.

### CASE NOTES

The italicized language of 1995 Enrolled HB 4410, section 305(3), which attempts to authorize state reimbursement of counties for housing parolees convicted of new felonies contrary to the provisions of section 4(1) of 1978 PA 16, violates Const 1963, art 4, § 25, and is therefore unconstitutional and void. The remaining provisions of 1995 PA 242, including the non-italicized portions of section 305(3), supra, are severable. Atty Gen Op, August 12, 1996, No. 6912.

## § 800.455. Cost of proceedings, transfer or treatment of mentally ill prisoner; reimbursement of county; itemized costs; determination of reasonableness; payment. [MSA § 28.1714(5)]

Sec. 5. (1) The state shall reimburse each county in which a state correctional facility is located for the reasonable and actual costs of the following expenses incurred by that county for implementing jurisdictional duties in the probate court imposed upon that county by chapter 10 of the mental health code, Act No. 258 of the Public Acts of 1974, being sections 330.2001 to 330.2050 of the Michigan Compiled Laws, with respect to proceedings for the transfer of an allegedly mentally ill prisoner who is confined in a state correctional facility in that county, to the center for forensic psychiatry program for treatment, or with respect to proceedings for the treatment of an allegedly mentally ill prisoner within a state correctional facility:

(a) The expense of legal counsel appointed to represent an indigent prisoner in the proceeding.

(b) Compensation paid to each juror who is either summoned for voir dire or impaneled on a jury, if a jury trial is demanded in the proceeding.

(c) Compensation paid to each witness subpoenaed to the proceeding by the prisoner.

(d) The expense of the preparation of a transcript of the proceeding.

(2) Each county shall submit quarterly its itemized costs as described in subsection (1) to the chief probate judge of the county. After determination by the chief probate judge of the reasonableness of the amount to be paid, payment shall be made in accordance with

the accounting laws of the state. The determination of reasonableness by the chief probate judge shall be conclusive.

**History:**
Pub Acts 1978, No. 16, § 5, as added by Pub Acts 1984, No. 409, eff March 29, 1985.

## COUNTY ESCAPED PRISONER PROSECUTION PROGRAM; MICHIGAN DEPARTMENT OF MANAGEMENT AND BUDGET; MICHIGAN DEPARTMENT OF CORRECTIONS

Executive Reorganization Order 1993-4, p 2459, eff July 27, 1993

### § 800.461. County escaped prisoner prosecution program, transfer from Department of Management and Budget. [MSA § 3.29(290)]

Whereas, Article V, Section 2, of the Constitution of the State of Michigan of 1963 empowers the Governor to make changes in the organization of the Executive Branch or in the assignment of functions among its units which he considers necessary for efficient administration; and

Whereas, the County Escaped Prisoner Prosecution Program was created within the Department of Management and Budget by Act No. 272 of the Public Acts of 1987, as amended, being Sections 800.452 et seq. of the Michigan Compiled Laws; and

Whereas, the functions, duties and responsibilities assigned to the County Escaped Prisoner Prosecution Program can be more effectively organized and carried out under the supervision and direction of the head of the Department of Corrections; and

Whereas, it is necessary in the interests of efficient administration and effectiveness of government to effect changes in the organization of the Executive Branch of government.

Now, Therefore, I, John Engler, Governor of the State of Michigan, pursuant to the powers vested in me by the Constitution of the State of Michigan of 1963 and the laws of the State of Michigan, do hereby order the following:

1. All the statutory authority, powers, duties, functions and responsibilities, including the functions of budgeting, procurement and management-related functions, of the County Escaped Prisoner Prosecution Program are hereby transferred from the Department of Management and Budget to the Department of Corrections, by a Type II transfer, as defined by Section 3 of Act No. 380 of the Public Acts of 1965, as amended, being Section 16.103 of the Michigan Compiled Laws.

2. The Director of the Office of Contract Management of the Department of Management and Budget shall provide executive direction and supervision for the implementation of the transfer.

The assigned functions shall be administered under the direction and supervision of the Department of Corrections, and all prescribed functions of rule making, reimbursements and maintaining records shall be transferred to the Department of Corrections.

3. All records, personnel, property and unexpended balances of appropriations, allocations and other funds used, held, employed, available or to be made available to the County Escaped Prisoner Prosecution Program for the activities transferred are hereby transferred to the Department of Corrections to the extent required to provide for the efficient and effective operation of the County Escaped Prisoner Prosecution Program.

4. The Director of the Department of Corrections shall make internal organizational changes as may be administratively necessary to complete the realignment of responsibilities prescribed by this Order.

5. The Director of the Office of Contract Management of the Department of Management and Budget and the Director of the Department of Corrections shall immediately initiate coordination to facilitate the transfer and develop a memorandum of record identifying any pending settlements, issues of compliance with applicable federal and state laws and regulations, or obligations to be resolved by the County Escaped Prisoner Prosecution Program.

6. All rules, orders, contracts and agreements relating to the assigned functions lawfully adopted prior to the effective date of this Order shall continue to be effective until revised, amended or repealed.

7. Any suit, action or other proceeding lawfully commenced by, against or before any entity affected by this Order shall not abate by reason of the taking effect of this Order. Any suit, action or other proceeding may be maintained by, against or before the appropriate successor of any entity affected by this Order.

In fulfillment of the requirement of Article V, Section 2, of the Constitution of the State of Michigan of 1963, the provisions of this Executive Order shall become effective 60 days after the filing of this Order.

**History:**
Executive Reorganization Order No. 1993-4 was promulgated as Executive Order No. 1993-10, eff July 27, 1993.

# CHAPTER 801
# JAILS AND WORKHOUSES

## COUNTY JAILS AND THE REGULATION THEREOF
### RS 1846, Ch 171

| | | |
|---|---|---|
| § 801.1 | | Jails, use as prisons; indicted persons; committed persons; federal prisoners. |
| § 801.2 | | Solitary imprisonment; execution of sentence. |
| § 801.3 | | Intercourse with other persons. |
| § 801.4 | | County jail; charges, payment, exception. |
| § 801.4a | | County jail; charges, payment; ordinance violations; exception. |
| § 801.5 | | County jail; contracts for supplies; private donations of clothing; reimbursement of cost of medical supplies; prisoner reimbursement to county. |
| § 801.5a | | Reimbursement of county for medical supplies and medical care to prisoners; prisoner or insurance; cooperation of prisoner; refusal of cooperation, reduction of term, prohibition. |
| § 801.6 | | County jail; separation of prisoners. |
| § 801.7 | | Visitors, counsel; private conversations prohibited. |
| § 801.8 | | Prisoners' food, expense. |
| § 801.9 | | Hard labor sentence; annual account, proceeds. |
| § 801.10 | | Prisoners; work on public highways, streets, alleys, roads, or railroad crossings; work in quarry, pit, or yard; performance of work for nonprofit charitable organizations or other labor; duty of sheriff; use of prisoner labor for private benefit or financial gain prohibited; violation of subsection (2) as civil infraction; penalty; sheriff deriving private benefit or financial gain from provision of food to prisoners as civil infraction; penalty. |
| § 801.11 | | Working conditions, transportation, meals, lodging. |
| § 801.12 | | Compensation, record, report. |
| § 801.13 | | Jail of contiguous county; designation, removal of prisoners. |
| §§801.14, 801.15 [Repealed] | | |
| §§801.16–801.21 [Repealed] | | |
| § 801.22 | | Keeper's calendar of prisoners; contents, delivery to circuit court. |
| § 801.23 | | Discharge of unindicted persons. |
| § 801.25 | | Punishment of refractory prisoners; person confined on criminal charge or conviction. |
| § 801.26 | | [Repealed] |
| § 801.27 | | Effect of law on power of jailer to preserve order. |

## COUNTY JAIL OVERCROWDING EMERGENCY POWERS ACT
### Act 325 of 1982

| | | |
|---|---|---|
| § 801.51 | | Definitions. |
| § 801.52 | | Jail population exceeding rated design capacity; certification. |
| § 801.52a | | Reporting prisoner population counts. |
| § 801.53 | | Declaration of state of emergency. |
| § 801.54 | | Notification of declaration. |
| § 801.55 | | Reduction of county jail prisoner population; initial procedures. |

# Jails and Workhouses

| § 801.56 | Failure to reduce jail population to 90% of rated design capacity within 14 days; sentence review and reduction; failure of certain actions to reduce population to prescribed levels; prisoner information to chief circuit judge; classification of prisoners; sentence duration; corrections department report; evaluation, amendments to overcrowding state of emergency procedures. |
|---|---|
| § 801.57 | Failure to reduce jail population to 90% of rated design capacity within 28 days; additional sentence reductions. |
| § 801.58 | Deferral of acceptance for incarceration; exceptions; deferring acceptance for incarceration of certain persons. |
| § 801.59 | End of state of emergency; notification. |
| § 801.60 | Listing of crimes for which incarceration not deferrable. |
| § 801.61 | Limitations on act taking effect. |
| § 801.62 | Probationary periods; effect of act. |
| § 801.63 | Limitation on successive sentence reductions; authority to grant good time. |
| § 801.64 | Effective date. |

## COUNTY JAIL OVERCROWDING ACT–DEPARTMENT OF MANAGEMENT AND BUDGET–OFFICE OF THE ATTORNEY GENERAL

### Executive Reorganization Order 1994-6

| § 801.71 | Transfer of powers and duties of former office of criminal justice under the county jail overcrowding act from department of management and budget to office of attorney general by a type II transfer. |
|---|---|

## PRISONER REIMBURSEMENT TO THE COUNTY

### Act 118 of 1984

| § 801.81 | Prisoner reimbursement to county. |
|---|---|
| § 801.82 | County jail; house of correction. |
| § 801.83 | Reimbursement for expenses; form. |
| § 801.84 | List. |
| § 801.85 | Cooperation of prisoner required; refusal to cooperate. |
| § 801.86 | Investigation by county board of commissioners. |
| § 801.87 | Civil action for reimbursement; consideration by court; money judgment; order. |
| § 801.88 | Civil action for reimbursement; circuit court; venue; ex parte restraining order; hearing on order to show cause; appointment of receiver. |
| § 801.89 | Enforcement of judgment, limitations. |
| § 801.90 | Civil action to recover and enforce money judgment; district court; venue. |
| § 801.91 | Information and assistance furnished county attorneys to secure reimbursement. |
| § 801.92 | Reimbursements credited to general county fund; determination, sworn statements. |
| § 801.93 | Conditions for passage of act. |

## Jails and Workhouses

### GENERAL PROVISIONS RELATING TO JAILS, AND THE CONFINEMENT OF PRISONERS THEREIN

**RS 1846, Ch 148**

| | |
|---|---|
| § 801.101 | United States prisoners; duty of sheriff to receive and keep. |
| § 801.102 | Liability of sheriff for safe keeping. |
| § 801.103 | Separation of prisoners; civil and criminal. |
| § 801.104 | Separation of prisoners; male and female. |
| § 801.105 | Violation; liability to injured persons; misdemeanor. |
| § 801.106 | Jails in use, continuation. |
| § 801.107 | Designation of jail in another county; officer to act. |
| § 801.108 | Copy of designation, service on sheriff. |
| § 801.109 | Responsibility of sheriff for safe keeping of prisoners. |
| § 801.110 | Effect on prisoner admitted to jail liberties. |
| § 801.111 | Effect on subsequent prisoner entitled to jail liberties. |
| § 801.112 | Right of prisoner entitled to jail liberties. |
| § 801.113 | Revocation of order. |
| § 801.114 | Removal of prisoners. |
| § 801.115 | Removal of prisoners in case of fire; prisoner not deemed escaped. |
| §§801.116, 801.117 | [Repealed] |
| § 801.119 | Conveyance of prisoners through other counties; right of officers. |
| § 801.120 | Prisoner not deemed escaped; officers or prisoners not liable to civil arrest. |

### WORK FARMS, FACTORIES AND SHOPS

**Act 78 of 1917**

| | |
|---|---|
| § 801.201 | County workhouse; power of county to acquire and own. |
| § 801.202 | Commission for management; election, terms, vacancies, eligibility, oath. |
| § 801.203 | Adoption of rules; superintendent; appointment, powers, oath, duties, bond; employes; appropriation of moneys. |
| § 801.204 | Expenses; meetings; duties; rules; record of rules or orders; conflicts of interests; employment of sentenced persons, restrictions; Open Meetings Act, compliance; Freedom of Information Act, compliance. |
| § 801.205 | Books of account, contents; quarterly statement; annual balancing. |
| § 801.206 | Reports to supervisors; removal of officials or employes. |
| § 801.207 | Superintendent; duties. |
| § 801.208 | Counties without workhouse, contract with commission; publication. |
| § 801.209 | Counties without workhouse, contract with commission; sentence by court to workhouse. |
| § 801.210 | Transfer of convicted persons to workhouse; employment; fees. |
| § 801.211 | Maintenance expense; tax levy. |
| § 801.212 | Commitment of prisoner, six months limit; employment. |
| § 801.214 | Record of infractions; effect of good behavior. |
| § 801.215 | Realty, powers of commission. |
| § 801.217 | Declaration of necessity. |

# Jails and Workhouses

## DAY PAROLE OF PRISONERS

### Act 60 of 1962

| | |
|---|---|
| § 801.251 | Privilege of leaving jail during necessary and reasonable hours; purposes; limitations; "jail" defined. |
| § 801.252 | Collection of earnings; deposit in trust account; record of account; garnishment of earnings. |
| § 801.253 | Employed prisoner, liability for board; lunch; accounting for payments; transportation. |
| § 801.254 | Disbursement of earnings; purposes. |
| § 801.255 | County department of social welfare; clerk of court; collection and disbursement of earnings. |
| § 801.256 | Support of prisoner's dependents; investigation and report. |
| § 801.257 | Reduction of term; approval; exception. |
| § 801.258 | Violation of conditions, effect. |

## WEAPONS, LIQUOR AND CONTROLLED SUBSTANCES IN JAILS

### Act 7 of 1981

| | |
|---|---|
| § 801.261 | Definitions. |
| § 801.262 | Weapons in jail prohibited. |
| § 801.263 | Alcohol, controlled substances in jail prohibited. |
| § 801.264 | Alcohol, controlled substances in jail, exceptions. |
| § 801.265 | Violation as felony; penalty; exception. |
| § 801.266 | Repeal. |
| § 801.267 | Effective date. |

## REIMBURSEMENT OF CITIES FOR MEDICAL SUPPLIES OR CARE OF PRISONERS

### Act 14 of 1982

| | |
|---|---|
| § 801.301 | Reimbursement of city for medical supplies and medical care to prisoners; prisoner or insurance; cooperation of prisoner; violation, fine, restitution. |

# COUNTY JAILS AND THE REGULATION THEREOF

## RS 1846, Ch 171

### § 801.1. Jails, use as prisons; indicted persons; committed persons; federal prisoners. [MSA § 28.1721]

Sec. 1. The common jails in the several counties of this state in charge of the respective sheriffs shall be used as prisons:

First, For the detention of persons charged with offenses and duly committed for trial;

Second, For the confinement of persons committed pursuant to a sentence upon conviction of an offense, and of all other persons duly committed for any cause authorized by law; and the provi-

# Jails and Workhouses § 801.1

sions of this section shall extend to persons detained in or committed to any such jail when duly authorized by or under the authority of any court or officer of the United States, as well as by the courts and magistrates of this state: Provided, however, That all persons detained or committed to such jails by the authority of the courts of the United States, or any officer of the United States, shall be received in said county jails only in cases where the cost of the care and maintenance of such persons shall be paid by the United States, at actual cost thereof, to be fixed and determined by the Michigan welfare commission upon application of the sheriffs of the respective counties of this state, and not otherwise.

**History:**
RS 1846, Ch. 171, § 1; amended by Pub Acts 1875, No. 125, eff August 3, 1875; 1927, No. 67, imd eff April 25, 1927.

**Prior codification:**
CL 1929, § 17668; CL 1915, § 2522; HOW § 9634; CL 1897, § 2650; CL 1871, § 8018; CL 1857, § 6129.

**Cross references:**
Counties required to provide jails to be constructed according to approved plans, § 45.16.
Warden and deputies in counties between 180,000 and 250,000 population, § 46.2.
Powers of sheriff, § 51.75.
Right of cities to use county jail, § 90.8.
Duty of state bacteriologist to make free examination and analysis, § 333.9621.
Supervision and control of jails and houses of correction by department of corrections, § 791.262.
United States prisoners, § 801.101.

**Michigan Digest references:**
Prisons and Jails § 1.

**Michigan Civ Jur references:**
Counties § 51.50.

**Research references:**
60 Am Jur 2d, Penal and Correctional Institutions, § 1.
54 Am Jur Trials 425, Asserting Claims of Unconstitutional Prison Conditions.

### CASE NOTES

**1. Location of county jail.**
Common jail of each county must be located at county seat. Op Atty Gen, 1925-1926, p 176.

**2. Liability for expense of keeping prisoners.**
In the absence of any statute the expenses of detaining persons arrested for violating city ordinances are not chargeable upon the county. People ex rel. Mixer v Board of Supervisors (1873) 26 Mich 422.

**3. Liability for injuries to prisoners.**
In the absence of statute a county as one of the political divisions of the state is not liable for injury to a respondent's health caused by the unhealthful condition of the jail in which he was confined while awaiting trial on a criminal charge. Webster v Hillsdale County (1894) 99 Mich 259, 58 NW 317.

A prisoner, in order to state a cause of action against the department of corrections for injuries received while incarcerated, must be (1) a state-sentenced prisoner, committed to the department for custody, and (2) held in a penal institution over which the department has jurisdiction and power to promulgate rules and standards. Mitchell v Michigan Dep't of Corrections (1982) 113 Mich App 739, 318 NW2d 507.

**4. Keeping and treatment of prisoners.**

Every prisoner or detainee has a right to receive medical care under circumstances in which a reasonable person would seek medical care; prison or jail authorities must make available a level of medical care reasonably designed to meet the inmate's routine and emergency health care needs; a prisoner or detainee is entitled to have both his physical needs and his psychological needs met. Brewer v Perrin (1984) 132 Mich App 520, 349 NW2d 198.

A two-step test is applied in evaluating a prisoner's or detainee's claim that jail or prison officials failed to provide him necessary medical care and treatment: it requires deliberate indifference on the part of the officials and it requires the prisoner's or detainee's medical needs to be serious; to show deliberate indifference the plaintiff must show either denied or unreasonably delayed access to a physician for diagnosis or treatment of a discomfort-causing ailment, or failure to provide prescribed treatment; a medical need is serious if it is one that has been diagnosed by a physician as mandating treatment or one that is so obvious that even a lay person would easily recognize the necessity for a doctor's attention. Brewer v Perrin (1984) 132 Mich App 520, 349 NW2d 198.

Nothing in Constitution of United States requires that jail establish grievance procedure; however, such would be desirable as it would increase communication between inmates and jail authorities and would allow opportunity for differences to be reconciled prior to resort to courts. O'Bryan v County of Saginaw (1977, ED Mich) 437 F Supp 582, supp op (1978, ED Mich) 446 F Supp 436, remanded without op (1980, CA6 Mich) 620 F2d 303, on remand (1981, ED Mich) 529 F Supp 206, affd on other grounds (1984, CA6 Mich) 741 F2d 283 and (disapproved on other grounds as stated in Ward v Washtenaw County Sheriff's Dep't (1989, CA6 Mich) 881 F2d 325).

Where only means of summoning guards by prisoners was rattling bars, which was prohibited by jail rules, or yelling, county jail was ordered to devise and implement effective method for summoning guards to be consistent with inmates' right to physical security and least restrictive means test. O'Bryan v County of Saginaw (1977, ED Mich) 437 F Supp 582, supp op (1978, ED Mich) 446 F Supp 436, remanded without op (1980, CA6 Mich) 620 F2d 303, on remand (1981, ED Mich) 529 F Supp 206, affd on other grounds (1984, CA6 Mich) 741 F2d 283 and (disapproved on other grounds as stated in Ward v Washtenaw County Sheriff's Dep't (1989, CA6 Mich) 881 F2d 325).

Where inmates in county jail have gone through withdrawal from drugs or alcohol without treatment, jail was ordered to institute drug and alcohol withdrawal treatment program in order to screen out individuals with those problems on admission to jail and to house them in separate environment designed to treat withdrawal problems. O'Bryan v County of Saginaw (1977, ED Mich) 437 F Supp 582, supp op (1978, ED Mich) 446 F Supp 436, remanded without op (1980, CA6 Mich) 620 F2d 303, on remand (1981, ED Mich) 529 F Supp 206, affd on other grounds (1984, CA6 Mich) 741 F2d 283 and (disapproved on other grounds as stated in Ward v Washtenaw County Sheriff's Dep't (1989, CA6 Mich) 881 F2d 325).

Right of prisoner to exercise is fundamental and confinement for long periods of time without opportunity for regular exercise is deprivation of due process as guaranteed by Fourteenth Amendment and cruel and unusual punishment as prohibited by Eighth Amendment. O'Bryan v County of Saginaw (1977, ED Mich) 437 F Supp 582, supp op (1978, ED Mich) 446 F Supp 436, remanded without op (1980, CA6 Mich) 620 F2d 303, on remand (1981, ED Mich) 529 F Supp 206, affd on other grounds (1984, CA6 Mich) 741 F2d 283 and (disapproved on other grounds as stated in Ward v Washtenaw County Sheriff's Dep't (1989, CA6 Mich) 881 F2d 325).

Where county jail inmates were not allowed out of their cells for exercise other than for 15-minute periods of exercise on jail roof at infrequent intervals except that inmates in single cells were allowed out of their cells onto catwalk in front of cells part of each day, such exercise program was constitutionally deficient but would be sufficient if county jail conscientiously administered program of calisthenics for minimum of one-half hour per day, together with opportunity for more extensive outdoor exercise when weather so permitted. O'Bryan v County of Saginaw (1977, ED Mich) 437 F Supp 582, supp op (1978, ED Mich) 446 F Supp 436, remanded without op (1980, CA6 Mich) 620 F2d 303, on remand (1981, ED Mich) 529 F Supp 206, affd on other grounds (1984, CA6 Mich) 741 F2d 283 and (disapproved on other grounds as stated in Ward v Washtenaw County Sheriff's Dep't (1989, CA6 Mich) 881 F2d 325).

Where only medical screening done by county jail as part of admission process was series of six questions which inquired as to any known physical problems and whether inmate was under doctor's care or receiving any prescription drugs, defendants were ordered to develop and implement physical examination which would be sufficient to protect health of individual inmates and jail population in general to be administered to each inmate as part of admission process. O'Bryan v County of Saginaw (1977, ED Mich) 437 F Supp 582, supp op (1978, ED Mich) 446 F Supp 436, remanded without op (1980, CA6 Mich) 620 F2d 303, on remand (1981, ED Mich) 529 F Supp 206, affd on other grounds (1984, CA6 Mich) 741 F2d 283 and (disapproved on other grounds as stated in Ward v Washtenaw County Sheriff's Dep't (1989, CA6 Mich) 881 F2d 325).

Pretrial detainees may not be subjected to any hardship except those absolutely required for purposes of confinement only and there is nothing in need to detain prisoner pending trial that requires that he be substantially restricted in his ability to communicate by telephone. O'Bryan v County of Saginaw (1977, ED Mich) 437 F Supp 582, supp op (1978, ED Mich) 446 F Supp 436, remanded without op (1980, CA6 Mich) 620 F2d 303, on remand (1981, ED Mich) 529 F Supp 206, affd on other grounds (1984, CA6 Mich) 741 F2d 283 and (disapproved on other grounds as stated in Ward v Washtenaw County Sheriff's Dep't (1989, CA6 Mich) 881 F2d 325).

## § 801.2. Solitary imprisonment; execution of sentence. [MSA § 28.1722]

Sec. 2. When any convict shall be sentenced to solitary imprisonment and hard labor in any jail, the keeper thereof shall execute such sentence of solitary imprisonment, by confining the convict in one of the cells, if there be any in such jail, and if there be none, then in the most retired and solitary part of such jail.

**History:**
RS 1846, Ch. 171, § 2.

**Prior codification:**
CL 1929, § 17669; CL 1915, § 2523; HOW § 9635; CL 1897, § 2651; CL 1871, § 8019; CL 1857, § 6130.

**Cross references:**
Power of court to order solitary confinement, § 769.2.
Hard labor, § 801.9.

**Michigan Digest references:**
Prisons and Jails § 2.

**ALR notes:**
Validity, construction, and application of state statute criminalizing possession of contraband by individual in penal or correctional institution, 45 ALR5th 767.

**Research references:**
21 Am Jur 2d, Criminal Law § 607.

## CASE NOTES

As to the right in relation to a prisoner confined on civil process, see Leach v Whitbeck (1908) 151 Mich 327, 115 NW 253.

### § 801.3. Intercourse with other persons. [MSA § 28.1723]

Sec. 3. No intercourse shall be allowed with any convict in solitary imprisonment, except for the conveyance of food, and other necessary purposes, unless some minister of the gospel shall be disposed to visit him, in the manner hereinafter provided.

**History:**
RS 1846, Ch. 171, § 3.

**Prior codification:**
CL 1929, § 17670; CL 1915, § 2524; HOW § 9636; CL 1897, § 2652; CL 1871, § 8020; CL 1857, § 6131.

**Michigan Digest references:**
Prisons and Jails § 2.

**ALR notes:**
Validity, construction, and application of state statute criminalizing possession of contraband by individual in penal or correctional institution, 45 ALR5th 767.

**Research references:**
21 Am Jur 2d, Criminal Law § 607.

### § 801.4. County jail; charges, payment, exception. [MSA § 28.1724]

Sec. 4. Except as provided in sections 5 and 5a, all charges and expenses of safekeeping and maintaining prisoners and persons charged with an offense, shall be paid from the county treasury, the accounts therefor being first settled and allowed by the county board of commissioners.

**History:**
RS 1846, Ch. 171, § 4; amended by Pub Acts 1982, No. 16, imd eff February 25, 1982; 1984, No. 119, imd eff June 1, 1984 (see 1984 note below).

**Prior codification:**
CL 1929, § 17671; CL 1915, § 2525; HOW § 9637; CL 1897, § 2653; CL 1871, § 8021; CL 1857, § 6132.

**Editor's notes:**
**Pub Acts 1984, No. 119, § 2,** imd eff June 1, 1984, provides:
"Section 2. This amendatory act shall not take effect unless all of the following bills of the 82nd Legislature are enacted into law:
"(a) House Bill No. 4590 [which became Act No. 118 of 1984].
"(b) House Bill No. 5120 [which became Act No. 120 of 1984]."

**Statutory references:**
Sections 5 and 5a, above referred to, are §§801.5 and 801.5a.

**Michigan Digest references:**
Counties §§32, 38.
Hospitals § 1.

## Jails and Workhouses § 801.4

**ALR notes:**
Validity, construction, and application of state statute criminalizing possession of contraband by individual in penal or correctional institution, 45 ALR5th 767.

**Michigan Civ Jur references:**
Counties § 89.

**Research references:**
60 Am Jur 2d, Penal and Correctional Institutions §§13–16.

### CASE NOTES

**1. Expenses of keeping prisoners.**

The word "charged" used in a statute concerning county jails and the charges and expenses of safekeeping and maintaining prisoners and persons charged with an offense does not refer to formal arraignment on the warrant. University Emergency Services, P.C. v Detroit (1984) 141 Mich App 512, 367 NW2d 344.

The determination of whether an officer is authorized to make an arrest ordinarily depends, in the first instance, on state law; whether the person making the arrest wears a state or local badge, or whether he is a private citizen, he acts pursuant to state authority and medical expenses attendant to the arrest are, therefore, chargeable to the county; under the general laws, the expense of enforcing the criminal statutes of the state must be borne by the counties. University Emergency Services, P.C. v Detroit (1984) 141 Mich App 512, 367 NW2d 344.

A statute regarding the charges and expenses of safekeeping and maintaining prisoners and persons charged with an offense requires that charges of maintaining prisoners shall be paid from the county treasury, the accounts therefor being first settled and allowed by the county board of commissioners; a county may be determined to have waived any protection it may have under this statute to audit and verify such charges and expenses where the circumstances indicate such a waiver. University Emergency Services, P.C. v Detroit (1984) 141 Mich App 512, 367 NW2d 344.

The statute placing responsibility for the cost of maintaining persons charged with offenses on the county applies to medical expenses incurred prior to as well as subsequent to formal arraignment; the statutory requirement of "charged with an offense" is satisfied if formal charges are subsequently brought. Zieger Osteopathic Hospital, Inc. v Wayne County (1984) 139 Mich App 630, 363 NW2d 28.

Counties, by statute, are responsible for the expenses of safekeeping and maintaining prisoners and persons charged with an offense or with a violation of a city, village or township ordinance; persons whose liberty has been restrained are prisoners within the meaning of the statute; accordingly, medical expenses resulting from the treatment of persons who have been arrested by police officers of a city in the county and who are taken by the city police officers to a hospital for treatment are expenses for which the county rather than the city is responsible. St. Mary's Hospital v Saginaw County (1984) 139 Mich App 647, 363 NW2d 32.

A county is responsible for the expenses of maintaining persons committed to the county jail; however, a county is not responsible for providing continued medical care for an inmate after he is discharged from custody regardless of whether the illness or injury preexisted or arose during the period of incarceration. Borgess Hospital v County of Berrien (1982) 114 Mich App 385, 319 NW2d 354.

Subject to certain exceptions, county is responsible for medical expenses of county jail inmates. Op Atty Gen, February 25, 1976, No. 4957.

County has no authority to seek reimbursement from inmate for cost of any medical care provided. Op Atty Gen, February 25, 1976, No. 4957.

County is responsible for providing medical care to county jail inmates only during period such persons are actually incarcerated. Op Atty Gen, February 25, 1976, No. 4957.

County is responsible for hospitalization of criminal wounded by city police officer while violating state criminal law. Op Atty Gen, June 30, 1948, No. 793.

**2. – United States prisoners.**

County cannot recover from sheriff

**§ 801.4**                                                            **Jails and Workhouses**

moneys received for boarding federal prisoners in excess of per diem allowance for boarding state prisoners. Bay County v Marvin (1929) 247 Mich 529, 226 NW 247.

**3. – violators of city ordinances.**

Offenses against city ordinances are not "criminal cases," and the city, not the county, must stand the expense of detaining persons arrested for such offenses. People ex rel. Mixer v Board of Supervisors (1873) 26 Mich 422.

**4. Medicaid.**

Inmate of county jail is not eligible for medical assistance under Medicaid. Op Atty Gen, February 25, 1976, No. 4957.

## § 801.4a. County jail; charges, payment; ordinance violations; exception. [MSA § 28.1724(1)]

Sec. 4a. Except as provided in sections 5 and 5a, all charges and expenses of safekeeping and maintaining persons in the county jail charged with violations of city, village, or township ordinances shall be paid from the county treasury if a district court of the first or second class has jurisdiction of the offense.

> **History:**
> RS 1846, Ch. 171, § 4a, as added by Pub Acts 1969, No. 274, imd eff August 11, 1969, by § 2 eff September 1, 1969; amended by Pub Acts 1982, No. 16, imd eff February 25, 1982; 1984, No. 119, imd eff June 1, 1984 (see 1984 note below).
>
> **Editor's notes:**
> **Pub Acts 1984, No. 119, § 2,** imd eff June 1, 1984, provides:
> "Section 2. This amendatory act shall not take effect unless all of the following bills of the 82nd Legislature are enacted into law:
> "(a) House Bill No. 4590 [which became Act No. 118 of 1984].
> "(b) House Bill No. 5120 [which became Act No. 120 of 1984]."
>
> **Statutory references:**
> Sections 5 and 5a, above referred to, are §§801.5 and 801.5a.
>
> **Cross references:**
> Note to § 801.4.
>
> **Michigan Civ Jur references:**
> Counties § 89.
>
> **Research references:**
> 60 Am Jur 2d, Penal and Correctional Institutions §§13–16.

## § 801.5. County jail; contracts for supplies; private donations of clothing; reimbursement of cost of medical supplies; prisoner reimbursement to county. [MSA § 28.1725]

Sec. 5. (1) The county board of commissioners may provide by contract for all necessary supplies for the use of the jail, including fuel and food, clothing, bedding, and medical attendance, for prisoners committed on criminal charges.

(2) Private donations of clothing for prisoners awaiting trial shall be accepted for them by the sheriff.

(3) The county board of commissioners may provide for reimbursement of the cost of supplies for medical attendance as provided under section 5a.

(4) The county board of commissioners or the county executive or designee of the county executive may provide that the care and

# Jails and Workhouses § 801.5a

support of a prisoner be paid by the prisoner's estate or property and may provide for reimbursement of all charges and expenses of maintaining a prisoner pursuant to the prisoner reimbursement to the county act.

**History:**
RS 1846, Ch. 171, § 5; amended by Pub Acts 1972, No. 152, imd eff May 26, 1972; 1982, No. 16, imd eff February 25, 1982; 1984, No. 119, imd eff June 1, 1984 (see 1984 note below).

**Prior codification:**
CL 1929, § 17672; CL 1915, § 2526; HOW § 9638; CL 1897, § 2654; CL 1871, § 8022; CL 1857, § 6133.

**Editor's notes:**
Pub Acts 1984, No. 119, § 2, imd eff June 1, 1984, provides:
"Section 2. This amendatory act shall not take effect unless all of the following bills of the 82nd Legislature are enacted into law:
"(a) House Bill No. 4590 [which became Act No. 118 of 1984].
"(b) House Bill No. 5120 [which became Act No. 120 of 1984]."

**Statutory references:**
Section 5a, above referred to, is 801.5a.

**Cross references:**
Contracts between county board and sheriff, where latter on salary basis, for board and laundry of prisoners, § 45.405.

**Michigan Digest references:**
Counties § 38.
Prisons and Jails § 4.
Public Contracts §§1 et seq.

**ALR notes:**
Validity, construction, and application of state statute criminalizing possession of contraband by individual in penal or correctional institution, 45 ALR5th 767.

**Research references:**
60 Am Jur 2d, Penal and Correctional Institutions §§13-16.

## § 801.5a. Reimbursement of county for medical supplies and medical care to prisoners; prisoner or insurance; cooperation of prisoner; refusal of cooperation, reduction of term, prohibition. [MSA § 28.1725(1)]

Sec. 5a. (1) The county board of commissioners may seek reimbursement for expenses incurred in providing medical care and treatment pursuant to sections 4 to 5. If a county board of commissioners seeks reimbursement pursuant to this section, reimbursement shall be sought only in the following order:
 (a) From the prisoner or person charged.
 (b) From insurance companies, health care corporations, or other sources if the prisoner or person charged is covered by an insurance policy, a certificate issued by a health care corporation, or other source for those expenses.
(2) A prisoner in a county jail shall cooperate with the county in seeking reimbursement under subsection (1) for medical expenses incurred by the county for that prisoner.

## § 801.5a             Jails and Workhouses

(3) A prisoner who wilfully refuses to cooperate as provided in subsection (2) shall not receive a reduction in his or her term under section 7 of Act No. 60 of the Public Acts of 1962, being section 801.257 of the Michigan Compiled Laws.

**History:**
RS 1846, Ch. 171, § 5a, as added by Pub Acts 1982, No. 16, imd eff February 25, 1982.

**Statutory references:**
Sections 4 to 5 are §§801.4, 801.4a and 801.5.

**Michigan Digest references:**
Prisons and Jails §§4, 4.5.

**Research references:**
60 Am Jur 2d, Penal and Correctional Institutions §§13–16.

### CASE NOTES

Every prisoner or detainee has a right to receive medical care under circumstances in which a reasonable person would seek medical care; prison or jail authorities must make available a level of medical care reasonably designed to meet the inmate's routine and emergency health care needs; a prisoner or detainee is entitled to have both his physical needs and his psychological needs met. Rushing v Wayne County (1984) 138 Mich App 121, 358 NW2d 904, vacated on other grounds, app den (1986) 424 Mich 876, app den (1988) 430 Mich 867, 449 NW2d 106, later proceeding (1989, Mich) 1989 Mich LEXIS 32 and vacated on other grounds, on reconsideration (1989) 433 Mich 917, 449 NW2d 410 and revd on other grounds, in part, vacated on other grounds (1990) 436 Mich 247, 462 NW2d 23, cert den (1991) 499 US 920, 113 L Ed 2d 245, 111 S Ct 1310.

## § 801.6. County jail; separation of prisoners. [MSA § 28.1726]

Sec. 6. It shall be the duty of the keepers of the said prisons, to keep the prisoners committed to their charge, as far as may be practicable, separate and apart from each other, and to prevent all conversation between the said prisoners.

**History:**
RS 1846, Ch. 171, § 6.

**Prior codification:**
CL 1929, § 17673; CL 1915, § 2527; HOW § 9639; CL 1897, § 2655; CL 1871, § 8023; CL 1857, § 6134.

**Cross references:**
Jail inmates infected with disease, removal and hospitalization, § 327.24.

**Michigan Digest references:**
Prisons and Jails § 2.

**LEXIS-NEXIS™ Michigan analytical references:**
Michigan Law and Practice, Convicts and Prisons § 4.

**ALR notes:**
Validity, construction, and application of state statute criminalizing possession of contraband by individual in penal or correctional institution, 45 ALR5th 767.

## § 801.7. Visitors, counsel; private conversations prohibited.
[MSA § 28.1727]

Sec. 7. Prisoners detained for trial may converse with their counsel, and with such other persons as the keeper, in his discretion, may allow; prisoners under sentence shall not be permitted to hold any conversation with any person except the keepers or inspectors of the prison, unless in the presence of a keeper or inspector.

**History:**
RS 1846, Ch. 171, § 7.

**Prior codification:**
CL 1929, § 17674; CL 1915, § 2528; HOW § 9640; CL 1897, § 2656; CL 1871, § 8024; CL 1857, § 6135.

**Cross references:**
Supervision and inspection of local jails, § 791.262.

**Michigan Digest references:**
Prisons and Jails § 2.

**LEXIS-NEXIS™ Michigan analytical references:**
Michigan Law and Practice, Convicts and Prisons § 4.

**ALR notes:**
Validity, construction, and application of state statute criminalizing possession of contraband by individual in penal or correctional institution, 45 ALR5th 767.

**Michigan Civ Jur references:**
Counties § 51.50.

**Research references:**
60 Am Jur 2d, Penal and Correctional Institutions § 50.

### CASE NOTES

**1. Visitors.**
Pre-trial detainees have no constitutional right to contact visitation from spouses, relatives, children, and friends, where barrier visitation is permitted, since no-contact visitation rule does not constitute punishment for purposes of due process analysis, but rather reasonably relates to jail security. O'Bryan v County of Saginaw (1984, CA6 Mich) 741 F2d 283.

**2. Access to courts.**
Funadamental right of access to courts requires that jail authorities assist inmates in preparation and filing of meaningful legal papers by providing prisoners with adequate law libraries or adequate assistance from persons trained in law. O'Bryan v County of Saginaw (1977, ED Mich) 437 F Supp 582, supp op (1978, ED Mich) 446 F Supp 436, remanded without op (1980, CA6 Mich) 620 F2d 303, on remand (1981, ED Mich) 529 F Supp 206, affd on other grounds (1984, CA6 Mich) 741 F2d 283 and (disapproved on other grounds as stated in Ward v Washtenaw County Sheriff's Dep't (1989, CA6 Mich) 881 F2d 325).

**3. Telephone calls.**
Where policy of county jail allowed inmate one telephone call when first admitted and one upon returning from court appearance and any additional calls could be placed by guards on behalf of inmate, such limitations were impermissible but would be sufficient if present policy was supplemented by policy allowing unlimited local and long distance collect calls for 10 minutes per week per inmate and additional 10 minutes in lieu of personal visitation. O'Bryan v County of Saginaw (1977, ED Mich) 437 F Supp 582, supp op (1978, ED Mich) 446 F Supp 436, remanded without op (1980, CA6 Mich) 620 F2d 303, on remand (1981, ED Mich) 529 F Supp 206, affd on other grounds (1984, CA6

Mich) 741 F2d 283 and (disapproved on other grounds as stated in Ward v Washtenaw County Sheriff's Dep't (1989, CA6 Mich) 881 F2d 325).

**4. Printed matter.**

Where county jail did not allow inmates to receive books or magazines which were brought in by visitors, it was held that pretrial detainees had unqualified right to receive any publication which is legally available to members of public generally, regardless of whether they receive such publications through mail or from some other source. O'Bryan v County of Saginaw (1977, ED Mich) 437 F Supp 582, supp op (1978, ED Mich) 446 F Supp 436, remanded without op (1980, CA6 Mich) 620 F2d 303, on remand (1981, ED Mich) 529 F Supp 206, affd on other grounds (1984, CA6 Mich) 741 F2d 283 and (disapproved as stated in Ward v Washtenaw County Sheriff's Dep't (1989, CA6 Mich) 881 F2d 325).

County sheriff has authority to adopt rule requiring that inmate be allowed to receive magazines and books only from publishers, since rule falls under state regulation authorizing local prison administrators to adopt rules necessary to the safety, security, or function of facility or harmony of inmates, and regulation is content neutral and necessary to serve legitimate and neutral objective of jail security. Ward v Washtenaw County Sheriff's Dept (1989, CA6 Mich) 881 F2d 325.

## § 801.8. Prisoners' food, expense. [MSA § 28.1728]

Sec. 8. Prisoners detained for trial, and those under sentence, shall be provided with a sufficient quantity of wholesome food, at the expense of the county; and prisoners detained for trial, may, at their own expense, and under the direction of the keeper, be supplied with any other proper articles of food.

**History:**
RS 1846, Ch. 171, § 8.

**Prior codification:**
CL 1929, § 17675; CL 1915, § 2529; HOW § 9641; CL 1897, § 2657; CL 1871, § 8025; CL 1857, § 6136.

**Cross references:**
Contracts between county board and sheriff, where latter on salary basis, for board and laundry of prisoners, § 45.405.

**Michigan Digest references:**
Prisons and Jails § 4.

**LEXIS-NEXIS™ Michigan analytical references:**
Michigan Law and Practice, Convicts and Prisons § 4.

## § 801.9. Hard labor sentence; annual account, proceeds. [MSA § 28.1729]

Sec. 9. It shall be the duty of the keepers of the said several prisons, whenever any person shall be sentenced to hard labor therein, and any mode of labor shall be provided, to cause such prisoner to be kept constantly employed during every day, except Sunday; and annually to account with the board of supervisors of the county for the proceeds of such labor.

**History:**
RS 1846, Ch. 171, § 9.

**Prior codification:**
CL 1929, § 17676; CL 1915, § 2530; HOW § 9642; CL 1897, § 2658; CL 1871, § 8026; CL 1857, § 6137.

**Jails and Workhouses** § 801.10

**Former acts:**
Law prior to 1846, see section 8 of Pub Acts 1840, No. 39.

**Michigan Digest references:**
Prisons and Jails § 3.

**LEXIS-NEXIS™ Michigan analytical references:**
Michigan Law and Practice, Convicts and Prisons § 5.

**Michigan Civ Jur references:**
Counties § 51.50.

**Research references:**
60 Am Jur 2d, Penal and Correctional Institutions §§34–38.

**§ 801.10. Prisoners; work on public highways, streets, alleys, roads, or railroad crossings; work in quarry, pit, or yard; performance of work for nonprofit charitable organizations or other labor; duty of sheriff; use of prisoner labor for private benefit or financial gain prohibited; violation of subsection (2) as civil infraction; penalty; sheriff deriving private benefit or financial gain from provision of food to prisoners as civil infraction; penalty.** [MSA § 28.1730]

Sec. 10. (1) The county board of commissioners of any county, by resolution passed at any regular or special session, may order that prisoners over the age of 18 years under a sentence of imprisonment in the county jail, capable of performing manual labor, shall be required to work upon the public highways, streets, alleys, public roads, or railroad crossings in the county, or in any quarry, pit, or yard in the preparation or construction of materials for public highways, streets, alleys, roads, or railroad crossings in the county, to perform work for nonprofit charitable organizations including, but not limited to, churches and synagogues, or to perform any other lawful labor for the benefit of the county. When a resolution under this section is passed, the sheriff shall cause the prisoners to be put at work in the manner provided in the resolution of the county board of commissioners. The board of county road commissioners and the village or city authorities of any village or city in the county or the authorities in charge of any county institution may make application to have the prisoners work in any township, city, village, or institution in a manner prescribed by the county board of commissioners, and the county board of commissioners shall determine in which township, city, or village the prisoners shall work.

(2) A person, including a public official or public employee, shall not sell, hire, lease, loan, contract for, or otherwise use the labor of prisoners for his or her own private benefit or financial gain. A person who violates this subsection is responsible for a state civil infraction and may be ordered to pay a civil fine of not more than $500.00.

(3) A sheriff shall not derive any private benefit or financial gain from the provision of food to prisoners in the jail, whether by retaining the difference between money budgeted for food and money expended for food, or by any other method. This subsection

§ 801.10                                          Jails and Workhouses

does not prevent a sheriff from receiving a salary for duties that include supervising the operation of the jail. A sheriff who violates this subsection is responsible for a state civil infraction and may be ordered to pay a civil fine of not more than $500.00.

**History:**
RS 1846, Ch. 171, § 10; amended by Pub Acts 1861, No. 141, eff June 15, 1861; 1909, No. 10, eff September 1, 1909; 1915, No. 132, eff August 24, 1915; 1960, No. 71, eff August 17, 1960; 1984, No. 41, imd eff March 26, 1984; 1988, No. 402, imd eff December 27, 1988.
Amended by Pub Acts 1996, No. 178, imd eff April 18, 1996.

**Prior codification:**
CL 1929, § 17677; CL 1915, § 2531; HOW § 9643; CL 1897, § 2659; CL 1871, § 8027; CL 1857, § 6138.

**Effect of amendment notes:**
**The 1996 amendment** deleted subsection (4); and made other, substantive, changes throughout the section.

**Cross references:**
Use of convicts in state prisons on public projects, § 800.101.

**Michigan Digest references:**
Prisons and Jails § 3.

**LEXIS-NEXIS™ Michigan analytical references:**
Michigan Law and Practice, Convicts and Prisons § 5.

**Michigan Civ Jur references:**
Counties § 51.50.

**Research references:**
60 Am Jur 2d, Penal and Correctional Institutions §§ 34–38.

### CASE NOTES

Board of commissioners of county may, by resolution, order prisoners under sentence in county jail to work upon public projects. Op Atty Gen, June 28, 1976, No. 5061.

County has no power to agree to indemnify sheriff and save him harmless from liability for injury to county prisoners engaged in work directed by sheriff. Op Atty Gen, July 8, 1959, No. 3377.

A county has no liability for injuries or illness incurred by county prisoners while performing lawful labor for the benefit of the county. Op Atty Gen, January 6, 1958, No. 3160.

Board of supervisors of a county may pass resolution requiring prisoners to work on the public highways, streets, alleys or roads notwithstanding the county is not operated under the county road system. Op Atty Gen, 1916, p 214.

## § 801.11. Working conditions, transportation, meals, lodging. [MSA § 28.1731]

Sec. 11. All work performed by any such prisoners shall be performed under the direction of the highway commissioner of the township or the authorities of the city, village or institution where the work is done. All such prisoners while engaged in such work shall be under the control and custody of the sheriff. All tools necessary for use by such prisoners and all materials upon which work is to be performed shall be furnished by the township, city, village or institution in which the work is done. The sheriff shall

**Jails and Workhouses** § 801.12

take such precautionary measures as may be deemed necessary to prevent the escape of prisoners employed under the provisions of this act, and in case any prisoner employed shall escape, it shall be deemed to be an escape from the jail: Provided, That no additional deputy sheriff shall be appointed to guard such prisoners while so at work without the previous authorization of the board of supervisors. The board of supervisors is hereby vested with authority to reimburse the sheriff for any expenses incurred in conveying such prisoners to and from any such road, street, alley, highway, quarry, pit, yard, or institution or in properly guarding them while beyond the confines of the county jail: Provided, That all meals and food shall be furnished by the sheriff to such prisoners in the same manner as though they were confined in the county jail, except in cases where such prisoners are employed in or for a county institution providing board for inmates, in which case all meals and food shall be furnished by said institution: Provided further, That the board of supervisors shall have authority to provide for keeping such prisoners at places other than the county jail while they are performing such work as is authorized under the provisions of this act.

**History:**
RS 1846, Ch. 171, § 11; amended by Pub Acts 1909, No. 10, eff September 1, 1909; 1915, No. 132, eff August 24, 1915.

**Prior codification:**
CL 1929, § 17678; CL 1915, § 2532; HOW § 9644; CL 1897, § 2660; CL 1871, § 8028; CL 1857, § 6139.

**Cross references:**
Contracts between county board and sheriff, where latter on salary basis, for board and laundry of prisoners, § 45.405.

**Michigan Digest references:**
Prisons and Jails §§3, 4.

**Michigan Civ Jur references:**
Counties § 51.50.

**Research references:**
60 Am Jur 2d, Penal and Correctional Institutions §§34–38.

### § 801.12. Compensation, record, report. [MSA § 28.1732]

Sec. 12. No prisoner shall be entitled to any compensation either from the county, township, city or village in which he is employed for any services performed in accordance with the requirements of this act. It shall be the duty of the sheriff to keep a record of the number of days worked by each prisoner and the township, city or village in which such work was performed, and report in full to the board of supervisors at each regular session.

**History:**
RS 1846, Ch. 171, § 12; amended by Pub Acts 1861, No. 141, eff June 15, 1861; 1909, No. 10, eff September 1, 1909.

**Prior codification:**
CL 1929, § 17679; CL 1915, § 2533; HOW § 9645; CL 1897, § 2661; CL 1871, § 8029; CL 1857, § 6140.

§ 801.12                                                     Jails and Workhouses

**Michigan Digest references:**
Prisons and Jails § 3.

**Research references:**
60 Am Jur 2d, Penal and Correctional Institutions §§34–38.

## § 801.13. Jail of contiguous county; designation, removal of prisoners. [MSA § 28.1733]

Sec. 13. The provisions contained in chapter one hundred and forty-eight [148], in regard to the designation of the jail of a contiguous county for the use of any county; to the removal of prisoners in such cases; and to the removal of prisoners when danger shall be apprehended from fire or contagious disease, shall extend to prisoners confined upon any criminal process, or for a contempt, or under sentence, in like manner as to prisoners confined in civil cases.

**History:**
RS 1846, Ch. 171, § 13.

**Prior codification:**
CL 1929, § 17680; CL 1915, § 2534; HOW § 9646; CL 1897, § 2662; CL 1871, § 8030; CL 1857, § 6141.

**Statutory references:**
Chapter 148, above referred to, is §§801.107 et seq.

**Michigan Digest references:**
Prisons and Jails § 6.

## §§801.14, 801.15. [Repealed]   [MSA §§28.1734, 28.1735]

**History:**
RS 1846, Ch. 171; **repealed** by Pub Acts 1974, No. 258, by § 1102(1) eff August 6, 1975.

**Editor's notes:**
Former §§801.14 and 801.15 dealt with insane convicts. For current provisions, see §§330.2000 et seq.

## §§801.16–801.21. [Repealed]   [MSA §§28.1736–28.1741]

**History:**
RS 1846, Ch. 171; **repealed** by Pub Acts 1959, No. 7, eff March 19, 1960.

**Editor's notes:**
Former §§801.16–801.21 related to inspection of county jails. See § 791.262 as to inspection of local jails.

## § 801.22. Keeper's calendar of prisoners; contents, delivery to circuit court. [MSA § 28.1742]

Sec. 22. It shall be the duty of the keeper of every county prison to present to every circuit court to be held in his county, at the opening of such court, a calendar stating:

First, The name of every prisoner then detained in such prison;

**Jails and Workhouses** § 801.25

Second, The time when such prisoner was committed, and by virtue of what process or precept; and,

Third, The cause of the detention of every such person.

**History:**
RS 1846, Ch. 171, § 22; amended by Pub Acts 1850, No. 275, imd eff April 2, 1850; 1875, No. 146, eff August 3, 1875.

**Prior codification:**
CL 1929, § 17689; CL 1915, § 2543; HOW § 9655; CL 1897, § 2671; CL 1871, § 8039; CL 1857, § 6150.

**Research references:**
41 Am Jur 2d, Indictments and Informations § 13.

### § 801.23. Discharge of unindicted persons. [MSA § 28.1743]

Sec. 23. It shall be the duty of such court during the term thereof to inquire into the cause of the commitment of every person confined in such prison upon any criminal charge who shall not have been indicted, or against whom no information shall have been filed, and unless satisfactory cause shall be shown to such court for detaining such person in custody or upon bail, as the case may require, to cause such person to be discharged.

**History:**
RS 1846, Ch. 171, § 23; amended by Pub Acts 1850, No. 275, imd eff April 2, 1850; 1875, No. 146, eff August 3, 1875.

**Prior codification:**
CL 1929, § 17690; CL 1915, § 2544; HOW § 9656; CL 1897, § 2672; CL 1871, § 8040; CL 1857, § 6151.

**Editor's notes:**
Sec. 24. (Repealed.).
This section provided when a prisoner might not be removed on habeas corpus. It was repealed by Pub Acts 1915, No. 314, eff January 1, 1916. For present law on this subject, see MCR 3.303(A).

**LEXIS-NEXIS™ Michigan analytical references:**
Michigan Law and Practice, Convicts and Prisons § 6.

**Research references:**
41 Am Jur 2d, Indictments and Informations § 13.

### § 801.25. Punishment of refractory prisoners; person confined on criminal charge or conviction. [MSA § 28.1744]

Sec. 25. If any person confined in any jail, upon a conviction or charge of any criminal offense, shall be refractory or disorderly, or shall wilfully or wantonly destroy or injure any article of bedding, or other furniture, or a door or window, or any other part of such prison, the sheriff of the county, after due inquiry, may cause such person to be kept in solitary confinement, not more than ten [10] days for any one [1] offense; and during such solitary confinement, he shall be fed with bread and water only, unless other food shall be necessary for the preservation of his health.

**History:**
RS 1846, Ch. 171, § 25.

**Prior codification:**
CL 1929, § 17691; CL 1915, § 2545; HOW § 9658; CL 1897, § 2674; CL 1871, § 8042; CL 1857, § 6153.

**Michigan Digest references:**
Prisons and Jails § 2.

**Michigan Civ Jur references:**
Counties § 51.50.

**Research references:**
60 Am Jur 2d, Penal and Correctional Institutions §§41 et seq.
16 Fed Proc, L Ed, Habeas Corpus § 41:110.

## § 801.26. [Repealed] [MSA § 28.1745]

**History:**
CL 1929, § 17692;CL 1915, § 2546; HOW § 9659; CL 1897, § 2675; CL 1871, § 8043; CL 1857, § 6154; RS 1846, Ch 171; **repealed** by Pub Acts 1991, No. 145, imd eff November 25, 1991.

**Editor's notes:**
Former § 801.26 dealt with punishment and liability of persons convicted before a justice of the peace for destruction of jail property.

## § 801.27. Effect of law on power of jailer to preserve order. [MSA § 28.1746]

Sec. 27. Nothing contained in the two [2] preceding sections, shall be construed to take from any sheriff or jailer, any part of the authority with which he was before invested by law, to preserve order and enforce strict discipline among all the prisoners in his custody.

**History:**
RS 1846, Ch. 171, § 27.

**Prior codification:**
CL 1929, § 17693; CL 1915, § 2547; HOW § 9660; CL 1897, § 2676; CL 1871, § 8044; CL 1857, § 6155.

**Editor's notes:**
Secs. 28–30. (Repealed.).
These sections, which were CL 1929, §§17694–17696, provided penalties for breaking or attempting to break jail. They were repealed by the Penal Code, Pub Acts 1931, No. 328, p 739, eff September 18, 1931, which contained provisions superseding them, see §§750.194 et seq.

---

# COUNTY JAIL OVERCROWDING EMERGENCY POWERS ACT

Act 325, 1982, p 1380, eff February 8, 1983.

AN ACT to authorize county sheriffs to declare a county jail overcrowding state of emergency; to prescribe the powers and duties of certain judges, county sheriffs, and other county officials; and to provide remedies for a county jail overcrowding state of emergency.

**Jails and Workhouses** § 801.51

*The People of the State of Michigan enact:*

**Popular Name:**
Jail Overcrowding Emergency Powers Act.

## § 801.51. Definitions. [MSA § 28.1748(1)]

Sec. 1. As used in this act:

(a) "Chief circuit judge" means any of the following:

(i) The circuit judge in a judicial circuit having only 1 circuit judge.

(ii) Except in the county of Wayne, the chief judge of the circuit court in a judicial circuit having 2 or more circuit judges.

(iii) In the county of Wayne, the executive chief judge of the circuit court in the third judicial circuit and the recorder's court of the city of Detroit.

(b) "Chief district judge" means the chief district judge or only district judge in a district court district.

(c) "Commission of corrections" means the state commission of corrections.

(d) "County jail" means a facility operated by a county for the physical detention and correction of persons charged with or convicted of criminal offenses and ordinance violations, persons found guilty of civil or criminal contempt, and juveniles detained by court order, or a facility which houses prisoners pursuant to an agreement authorized under Act No. 164 of the Public Acts of 1861, as amended, being sections 802.1 to 802.21 of the Michigan Compiled Laws.

(e) "Department of corrections" means the state department of corrections.

(f) "Prisoner" means a person who is currently being physically detained in a county jail.

(g) "Rated design capacity" means the actual available bed space of the general population of a county jail as determined by the department of corrections, subject to applicable rules including variances to those rules granted by the commission of corrections.

**History:**
Pub Acts 1982, No. 325, § 1, eff February 8, 1983.

**Michigan Digest references:**
Constitutional Law § 67.
Judges §§9, 14.
Prisons and Jails §§1.05, 1.25, 1.60, 6.50.

**Michigan Civ Jur references:**
Counties § 51.50.

**Research references:**
60 Am Jur 2d, Penal and Correctional Institutions § 44.5.

## § 801.51

### CASE NOTES

County jail overcrowding act does not infringe on Governor's power of executive clemency. Kent County Prosecutor v Kent County Sheriff (1987) 428 Mich 314, 409 NW2d 202.

Acts taken by a chief circuit judge pursuant to the provisions of the act are an exercise of the chief circuit judge's administrative authority and may be undertaken without first having a trial or evidentiary hearing. Muskegon County Bd. of Comm'rs v Muskegon Circuit Judge (1991) 188 Mich App 270, 469 NW2d 441.

The disqualification of a chief circuit judge from presiding in an action brought by the county sheriff and county prosecutor against the county board of commissioners seeking funds and personnel to alleviate overcrowding at the county jail in itself does not disqualify the chief circuit judge from exercising the administrative authority granted by the act. Muskegon County Bd. of Comm'rs v Muskegon Circuit Judge (1991) 188 Mich App 270, 469 NW2d 441.

A chief circuit judge of a county experiencing overcrowding of its jail may not order, in the exercise of the administrative authority granted by the county jail overcrowding act, the transfer of prisoners from the overcrowded jail to the jail in another county where there is no overcrowding. Muskegon County Bd. of Comm'rs v Muskegon Circuit Judge (1991) 188 Mich App 270, 469 NW2d 441.

## § 801.52. Jail population exceeding rated design capacity; certification. [MSA § 28.1748(2)]

Sec. 2. If the general prisoner population of a county jail exceeds 100% of the rated design capacity of the county jail or a percentage of rated design capacity less than 100% as set by a court prior to the effective date of this act for 7 consecutive days or for a lesser number of days as set by a court prior to the effective date of this act, the sheriff for that county shall certify that fact in writing, by first class mail or personal delivery, to the chief circuit judge, the chief district judge, and each municipal court judge in the county in which the county jail is located, the chairperson of the county board of commissioners, and the county executive in a county in which a county executive is elected.

**History:**
Pub Acts 1982, No. 325, § 2, eff February 8, 1983.

**Michigan Digest references:**
Prisons and Jails §§1.05, 1.25, 1.60, 6.50.

**Michigan Civ Jur references:**
Counties § 51.50.

**Research references:**
60 Am Jur 2d, Penal and Correctional Institutions § 44.5.

**Legal periodicals:**
Koenig, Advocating Consistent Sentencing of Prisoners: Deconstructing the Michigan Myth that Retroactive Application of Lesser Penalties for Crimes Violates the Governor's Power of Commutation, 16 T.M. Cooley L Rev 61 (1999).

## § 801.52a. Reporting prisoner population counts. [MSA § 28.1748(2a)]

Sec. 2a. The prisoner population counts required for any purpose under this act shall be reported as being taken between the hours of 12:01 a.m. and 4:00 a.m. on each day on which a count is conducted.

**History:**
Pub Acts 1982, No. 325, § 2a, as added by Pub Acts 1988, No. 399, imd eff December 27, 1988.

**Michigan Digest references:**
Prisons and Jails §§1.05, 1.25, 1.60, 6.50.

**Michigan Civ Jur references:**
Counties § 51.50.

**Research references:**
60 Am Jur 2d, Penal and Correctional Institutions § 44.5.

## § 801.53. Declaration of state of emergency. [MSA § 28.1748(3)]

Sec. 3. If a majority of the judges and county officials notified pursuant to section 2 do not find within 3 business days after certification that the sheriff acted in error, the sheriff shall declare a county jail overcrowding state of emergency.

**History:**
Pub Acts 1982, No. 325, § 3, eff February 8, 1983.

**Statutory references:**
Section 2, above referred to, is § 801.52.

**Michigan Digest references:**
Prisons and Jails §§1.05, 1.25, 1.60, 6.50.

**Michigan Civ Jur references:**
Counties § 51.50.

**Research references:**
60 Am Jur 2d, Penal and Correctional Institutions § 44.5.

### CASE NOTES

The [former] Prison Overcrowding Emergency Powers Act is constitutional and does not contravene the governor's exclusive power of commutation with respect to sentences imposed after January 26, 1981, and with respect to sentences imposed before that date only insofar as the governor's actions which trigger the reductions in sentence are discretionary rather than mandatory. Oakland County Prosecuting Attorney v Michigan Dep't of Corrections (1981) 411 Mich 183, 305 NW2d 515.

The governor may, upon appropriate certification by the commission of corrections, declare a prison overcrowding state of emergency in the event the population of the prison system exceeds the rated design capacity for thirty consecutive days. A formal rescission of a previous emergency declaration, which has served its purpose, is not requisite to a new declaration of emergency. Op Atty Gen, August 30, 1983, No. 6182.

## § 801.54. Notification of declaration. [MSA § 28.1748(4)]

Sec. 4. Upon the declaration of a county jail overcrowding state of emergency pursuant to section 3, the sheriff shall notify all of the following persons in writing, by first class mail or personal delivery, that a county jail overcrowding state of emergency has been declared:

## § 801.54          Jails and Workhouses

(a) The judges and county officials notified pursuant to section 2.

(b) The county prosecutor.

(c) The chief law enforcement official of each state, county, and municipal law enforcement agency located in the county.

**History:**
Pub Acts 1982, No. 325, § 4, eff February 8, 1983.

**Statutory references:**
Sections 2 and 3, above referred to, are §§801.52 and 801.53.

**Michigan Digest references:**
Prisons and Jails §§1.05, 1.25, 1.60, 6.50.

**Michigan Civ Jur references:**
Counties § 51.50.

**Research references:**
60 Am Jur 2d, Penal and Correctional Institutions § 44.5.

## § 801.55. Reduction of county jail prisoner population; initial procedures. [MSA § 28.1748(5)]

Sec. 5. The sheriff, the persons notified pursuant to section 4, and other circuit, district, municipal, and recorder's court judges may attempt to reduce the prisoner population of the county jail through any available means which are already within the scope of their individual and collective legal authority, including, but not limited to, the following:

(a) Judicial review of bail for possible bail reduction, release on recognizance, or conditional release of prisoners in the county jail.

(b) Prosecutorial pre-trial diversion.

(c) Judicial use of probation, fines, community service orders, restitution, and delayed sentencing as alternatives to commitment to jail.

(d) Use of work-release, community programs, and other alternative housing arrangements by the sheriff, if the programs and alternative housing arrangements are authorized by law.

(e) Review of agreements which allow other units of government to house their prisoners in the overcrowded county jail to determine whether the agreements may be terminated.

(f) Entering into agreements which allow the sheriff for the county in which the overcrowded county jail is located to house prisoners in facilities operated by other units of government.

(g) Refusal by the sheriff to house persons who are not required by law to be housed in the county jail.

(h) Acceleration of the transfer of prisoners sentenced to the state prison system, and prisoners otherwise under the jurisdiction of the department of corrections, to the department of corrections.

(i) Judicial acceleration of pending court proceedings for prisoners under the jurisdiction of the department of corrections who will be returned to the department of corrections regardless of the outcome of the pending proceedings.

(j) Reduction of waiting time for prisoners awaiting examination by the center for forensic psychiatry.

(k) Alternative booking, processing, and housing arrangements, including the use of appearance tickets instead of booking at the county jail and the use of weekend arraignment, for categories of cases considered appropriate by the persons notified pursuant to section 4.

(l) Acceptance by the courts of credit cards for payments of bonds, fines, and court costs.

(m) Use of community mental health and private mental health resources in the county as alternatives to housing prisoners in the county jail for those prisoners who qualify for placement in the programs and for whom placement in the programs is appropriate.

(n) Use of community and private substance abuse programs and other therapeutic programs as alternatives to housing prisoners in the county jail for those prisoners who qualify for placement in the programs and for whom placement in the programs is appropriate.

(o) Preparation of a long-range plan for addressing the county jail overcrowding problem, including recommendations to the county board of commissioners on construction of new jail facilities and funding for construction or other options designed to alleviate the overcrowding problem.

(p) Review of sentencing procedures, including the elimination of delays in preparing presentence reports for prisoners awaiting sentence, and staggering the dates on which prisoners will start serving a jail sentence to minimize fluctuating demands on jail capacity.

**History:**
Pub Acts 1982, No. 325, § 5, eff February 8, 1983.

**Statutory references:**
Section 4, above referred to, is § 801.54.

**Michigan Digest references:**
Prisons and Jails §§1.05, 1.25, 1.60, 6.50.

**Michigan Civ Jur references:**
Counties § 51.50.

**Research references:**
60 Am Jur 2d, Penal and Correctional Institutions § 44.5.

### CASE NOTES

The county jail overcrowding act unconstitutionally usurps the governor's exclusive power of commutation since implementation of the act would result in the release of jail prisoners prior to the expiration of their validly imposed determinate sentences. Kent County Prosecutor v Kent County Sheriff (1984) 133 Mich App 611, 350 NW2d 298, affd (1986) 425 Mich 718, 391 NW2d 341, reh gr (1986) 426 Mich 1201 and later proceeding (1987) 428 Mich 314, 409 NW2d 202.

**§ 801.56. Failure to reduce jail population to 90% of rated design capacity within 14 days; sentence review and reduction; failure of certain actions to reduce population to prescribed levels; prisoner information to chief circuit judge; classification of prisoners; sentence duration; corrections department report; evaluation, amendments to overcrowding state of emergency procedures.** [MSA § 28.1748(6)]

Sec. 6. (1) The further actions prescribed in subsections (2) to (4) and in sections 7 and 8 shall be required unless the actions taken pursuant to section 5 reduce the county's jail population to the higher of the following:

(a) 90% of rated design capacity or a percentage of rated design capacity less than 90% as set by a court prior to February 8, 1983.

(b) A prisoner population such that the jail has the following number of empty beds:

(i) For a jail with a rated design capacity of less than 500 beds, at least 10 empty beds.

(ii) For a jail with a rated design capacity of 500 beds or more, at least 25 empty beds.

(2) If the actions taken pursuant to section 5 do not reduce the county jail's population to the level prescribed in subsection (1) within 14 days of the declaration of the county jail overcrowding state of emergency, the sheriff shall present to the chief circuit judge for the county in which the jail is located the following information for each prisoner sentenced to and housed in the county jail on that date:

(a) The name of each prisoner.

(b) The offense for which the prisoner was convicted.

(c) The length of sentence imposed for the prisoner.

(d) The date on which the prisoner began serving his or her sentence.

(e) The date on which the prisoner will be released from the jail according to the terms of his or her sentence, including computations for good time.

(f) The name of the judge who imposed the sentence.

(3) After the chief circuit judge for the county in which the jail is located reviews the information presented by the sheriff pursuant to subsection (2), the chief circuit judge shall, for purposes of county jail population reduction, classify the prisoners into 2 groups: those prisoners who, if released, would present a high risk to the public safety, and those who, if released, would not present a high risk to the public safety. The chief circuit judge shall also determine a minimum and a maximum percentage by which the sentences can be reduced. The sheriff shall reduce the sentences of all prisoners who, if released, would not present a high risk to the public safety by an equal percentage which is within the minimum and maximum percentages determined by the chief circuit judge.

(4) The sentences of prisoners sentenced to and housed in the county jail after the fourteenth day of the county jail overcrowding state of emergency may continue to be reduced in the same manner

as prescribed in subsections (2) and (3), but shall not be reduced after the county jail overcrowding state of emergency is ended or after the sheriff orders a sentence reduction pursuant to section 7, whichever occurs first.

(5) Not later than 18 months after the effective date of the 1988 amendatory act that added this subsection and amended subsection (1), the office of facility services of the department of corrections, in cooperation with the Michigan sheriffs' association, shall report to the chairpersons of the senate and house standing committees responsible for legislation concerning corrections. The report shall evaluate the effect on the overcrowding state of emergency procedures of the amendments to subsection (1) made by the 1988 amendatory act that added this subsection for the 12 months beginning on the effective date of that 1988 amendatory act.

**History:**
Pub Acts 1982, No. 325, § 6, eff February 8, 1983; amended by Pub Acts 1988, No. 399, imd eff December 27, 1988.

**Statutory references:**
Sections 5, 7 and 8, above referred to, are §§801.55, 801.57 and 801.58.

**Michigan Digest references:**
Counties § 57.
Prisons and Jails §§1.05, 1.25,1.45, 1.60, 6, 6.50.
Superintending Control § 9.

**Michigan Civ Jur references:**
Counties § 51.50.

**Research references:**
60 Am Jur 2d, Penal and Correctional Institutions § 44.5.

### CASE NOTES

**1. Constitutionality.**
County Jail Overcrowding Act, providing for reduction of inmate sentences when jail reached certain capacity, was found to be unconstitutional, based on finding that its provisions usurped governor's exclusive power of commutation and that there was no constitutional grant of power to legislature over determinate sentences. Kent County Prosecutor v Kent County Sheriff (1986) 425 Mich 718, 391 NW2d 341, reh gr (1986) 426 Mich 1201 and later proceeding (1987) 428 Mich 314, 409 NW2d 202.

1982 PA 325, §§6 and 7, which authorize a county sheriff to reduce the fixed sentences of prisoners committed or imprisoned in the county jail, are unconstitutional because they are violative of Const 1963, art 5, § 14. Op Atty Gen, February 16, 1983, No. 6131.

**2. Classification of prisoners.**
The provision of the act requiring the chief circuit judge of a county in which an overcrowded jail is located to classify prisoners into groups whose release would present high and low risk to the public safety vests in the chief circuit judge broad discretion relative to the criteria used to make the classifications. Muskegon County Bd. of Comm'rs v Muskegon Circuit Judge (1991) 188 Mich App 270, 469 NW2d 441.

An action for superintending control brought by a county board of commissioners is not an appropriate means to test the validity of the criteria used by the chief judge of the county's circuit court in classifying prisoners for the purpose of the county jail overcrowding act. Muskegon County Bd. of Comm'rs v Muskegon Circuit Judge (1991) 188 Mich App 270, 469 NW2d 441.

## § 801.57. Failure to reduce jail population to 90% of rated design capacity within 28 days; additional sentence reductions. [MSA § 28.1748(7)]

Sec. 7. If the actions taken pursuant to sections 5 and 6 do not reduce the county jail's population to the level prescribed in section 6(1) within 28 days of the declaration of the county jail overcrowding state of emergency, the original sentences, not including good time, of all prisoners sentenced to and housed in the county jail on that date shall be equally reduced by the sheriff by the least possible percentage reduction necessary, not to exceed 30%, to reduce the county jail's prisoner population to the level prescribed in section 6(1).

**History:**
Pub Acts 1982, No. 325, § 7, eff February 8, 1983; amended by Pub Acts 1988, No. 399, imd eff December 27, 1988.

**Statutory references:**
Sections 5 and 6, above referred to, are §§801.55 and 801.56.

**Michigan Digest references:**
Judges § 9.
Prisons and Jails §§1.05, 1.25, 1.60, 6.50.
Sheriffs and Constables § 13.

**Michigan Civ Jur references:**
Counties § 51.50.

**Research references:**
60 Am Jur 2d, Penal and Correctional Institutions § 44.5.

### CASE NOTES

The chief circuit judge of a county in which there is county jail overcrowding is without authority to direct the sheriff of the county not to release any prisoners who were classified as high-risk prisoners by the judge pursuant to the act, because the act requires the sheriff to release high-risk prisoners under certain circumstances. Muskegon County Bd. of Comm'rs v Muskegon Circuit Judge (1991) 188 Mich App 270, 469 NW2d 441.

1982 PA 325, §§6 and 7, which authorize a county sheriff to reduce the fixed sentences of prisoners committed or imprisoned in the county jail, are unconstitutional because they are violative of Const 1963, art 5, § 14. Op Atty Gen, February 16, 1983, No. 6131.

## § 801.58. Deferral of acceptance for incarceration; exceptions; deferring acceptance for incarceration of certain persons. [MSA § 28.1748(8)]

Sec. 8. (1) Except as otherwise provided in this subsection and subsection (2), if the actions taken pursuant to sections 5, 6, and 7 do not reduce the county jail's population to the level prescribed in section 6(1) within 42 days of the declaration of the county jail overcrowding state of emergency, the sheriff shall defer acceptance for incarceration in the general population of the county jail persons sentenced to or otherwise committed to the county jail for incarceration until the county jail overcrowding state of emergency is ended pursuant to section 9, except that the sheriff shall not defer

**Jails and Workhouses** § 801.59

acceptance for incarceration all persons under sentence for or charged with violent or assaultive crimes, sex offenses, escape from prison or jail, controlled substance offenses, or weapons offenses.

(2) The sheriff shall not defer acceptance of a prisoner for incarceration into the general population of the county jail if both of the following occur:

(a) The sheriff or the sentencing judge presents to the chief circuit judge for the county in which the county jail is located information alleging that deferring acceptance of the prisoner for incarceration would constitute a threat to public safety.

(b) The chief circuit judge, based upon the presence of a threat to public safety, approves of accepting the prisoner for incarceration.

**History:**
Pub Acts 1982, No. 325, § 8, eff February 8, 1983; amended by Pub Acts 1988, No. 399, imd eff December 27, 1988.

**Statutory references:**
Sections 5–7 and 9, above referred to, are §§801.55, 801.56, 801.57 and 801.59.

**Michigan Digest references:**
Prisons and Jails §§1.05, 1.25, 1.60, 6.50.

**Michigan Civ Jur references:**
Counties § 51.50.

**Research references:**
60 Am Jur 2d, Penal and Correctional Institutions § 44.5.

## § 801.59. End of state of emergency; notification. [MSA § 28.1748(9)]

Sec. 9. If either of the following occur, the sheriff shall certify that fact in writing by first class mail or personal delivery, to the judges and county officials notified pursuant to section 2 and, unless a majority of the judges and county officials so notified find within 3 business days after receipt of the certification pursuant to this section that the sheriff has acted in error, the sheriff shall end the county jail overcrowding state of emergency:

(a) At any time during the county jail overcrowding state of emergency, the general prisoner population of the county jail is reduced to the level prescribed in section 6(1).

(b) The county jail's population is not reduced to the level prescribed in section 6(1) within 70 days after the declaration of the county jail overcrowding state of emergency.

**History:**
Pub Acts 1982, No. 325, § 9, eff February 8, 1983; amended by Pub Acts 1988, No. 399, imd eff December 27.

**Statutory references:**
Sections 2 and 6, above referred to, are §§801.52 and 801.56.

**Michigan Digest references:**
Prisons and Jails §§1.05, 1.25, 1.60, 6.50.

**Michigan Civ Jur references:**
Counties § 51.50.

**Research references:**
60 Am Jur 2d, Penal and Correctional Institutions § 44.5.

### CASE NOTES

The governor, upon appropriate certification of the commission of corrections, shall formally rescind the previous declaration of prison overcrowding state of emergency before declaring a new prison overcrowding state of emergency. Op Atty Gen, April 5, 1984, No. 6215.

## § 801.60. Listing of crimes for which incarceration not deferrable. [MSA § 28.1748(10)]

Sec. 10. For purposes of section 8, a listing of violent or assaultive crimes, sex offenses, escape from prison or jail offenses, controlled substance offenses, and weapons offenses shall be developed by the office of criminal justice in the department of management and budget.

**History:**
Pub Acts 1982, No. 325, § 10, eff February 8, 1983.

**Statutory references:**
Section 8, above referred to, is § 801.58.

**Michigan Digest references:**
Prisons and Jails §§1.05, 1.25, 1.60, 6.50.

**Michigan Civ Jur references:**
Counties § 51.50.

**Research references:**
60 Am Jur 2d, Penal and Correctional Institutions § 44.5.

## § 801.61. Limitations on act taking effect. [MSA § 28.1748(11)]

Sec. 11. The provisions of this act shall not be applicable if a county jail population exceeds rated design capacity as the direct result of loss of bed space due to a natural disaster or deliberate destruction of property.

**History:**
Pub Acts 1982, No. 325, § 11, eff February 8, 1983.

**Michigan Civ Jur references:**
Counties § 51.50.

**Research references:**
60 Am Jur 2d, Penal and Correctional Institutions § 44.5.

## § 801.62. Probationary periods; effect of act. [MSA § 28.1748(12)]

Sec. 12. This act shall apply to prisoners sentenced to a county jail as a condition of probation but shall not reduce or otherwise affect the total probationary period imposed by the court.

**History:**
Pub Acts 1982, No. 325, § 12, eff February 8, 1983.

**Michigan Civ Jur references:**
Counties § 51.50.

**Research references:**
60 Am Jur 2d, Penal and Correctional Institutions § 44.5.

### § 801.63. Limitation on successive sentence reductions; authority to grant good time. [MSA § 28.1748(13)]

Sec. 13. If the provisions of this act are invoked more than once with respect to an individual prisoner, sentence reductions granted to that prisoner pursuant to section 7 shall not exceed 35% of the prisoner's original sentence. This section shall not limit a sheriff's authority to grant a prisoner good time as authorized by law.

**History:**
Pub Acts 1982, No. 325, § 13, eff February 8, 1983.

**Statutory references:**
Section 7, above referred to, is § 801.57.

**Michigan Civ Jur references:**
Counties § 51.50.

**Research references:**
60 Am Jur 2d, Penal and Correctional Institutions § 44.5.

### § 801.64. Effective date. [MSA § 28.1748(14)]

Sec. 14. This act shall take effect upon the expiration of 60 days after it is enacted into law.

**History:**
Pub Acts 1982, No. 325, § 14, eff February 8, 1983.

**Michigan Civ Jur references:**
Counties § 51.50.

**Research references:**
60 Am Jur 2d, Penal and Correctional Institutions § 44.5.

## COUNTY JAIL OVERCROWDING ACT–DEPARTMENT OF MANAGEMENT AND BUDGET–OFFICE OF THE ATTORNEY GENERAL

Executive Reorganization Order 1994-6, eff June 12, 1994

### § 801.71. Transfer of powers and duties of former office of criminal justice under the county jail overcrowding act from department of management and budget to office of attorney general by a type II transfer. [MSA § 28.1748(21)]

WHEREAS, Article V, Section 2, of the Constitution of the State of Michigan of 1963 empowers the Governor to make changes in the organization of the Executive Branch or in the assignment of functions among its units which he considers necessary for efficient administration; and

WHEREAS, the County Jail Overcrowding Act (the "Act") was created by Act No. 325 of the Public Acts of 1982, being Section 801.51 et seq. of the Michigan Compiled Laws; and

WHEREAS, Section 10 of the Act, being Section 801.60 of the Michigan Compiled Laws, requires the Office of Criminal Justice in the Department of Management and Budget to develop a listing of violent or assaultive crimes, sex offenses, escape from prison or jail offenses, controlled substance offenses, and weapons offenses to be used by county sheriffs as a guideline on who may not be deferred from jail incarceration under the Act; and

WHEREAS, the statute creating the Office of Criminal Justice contained a sunset provision of March 30, 1987, and the Office no longer exists; and

WHEREAS, the responsibility outlined in this section requires legal expertise on criminal justice matters that no longer is available within the Department of Management and Budget; and

WHEREAS, the Office of the Attorney General has the legal expertise required to carry out the responsibilities contained in Section 10 of the Act.

NOW, THEREFORE, I, John Engler, Governor of the State of Michigan, pursuant to the powers vested in me by the Constitution of the State of Michigan of 1963 and the laws of the State of Michigan, do hereby order the following:

1. All the authority, powers, duties, functions and responsibilities contained in Section 10 of Act No. 325 of the Public Acts of 1982, being Section 801.60 of the Michigan Compiled Laws, are hereby transferred from the Department of Management and Budget to the Office of the Attorney General, by a Type II transfer, as defined by Section 3 of Act No. 380 of the Public Acts of 1965, as amended, being Section 16.103 of the Michigan Compiled Laws.

2. The Director of the Office of Contract Management of the Department of Management and Budget shall provide executive direction and supervision for the implementation of the transfer. The assigned functions shall be administered under the direction and supervision of the Attorney General.

3. All records, property and unexpended balances of appropriations, allocations and other funds used, held, employed, available or to be made available to the Department of Management and Budget for the activities transferred are hereby transferred to the Office of the Attorney General to the extent required to provide for efficient and effective operation.

4. The Director of the Office of Contract Management of the Department of Management and Budget and the Attorney General shall immediately initiate coordination to facilitate the transfer.

5. All rules, orders, contracts and agreements relating to the

assigned functions lawfully adopted prior to the effective date of this Order shall continue to be effective until revised, amended or repealed.

6. Any suit, action or other proceeding lawfully commenced by, against or before any entity affected by this Order shall not abate by reason of the taking effect of this Order. Any suit, action or other proceeding may be maintained by, against or before the appropriate successor of any entity affected by this Order.

In fulfillment of the requirement of Article V, Section 2, of the Constitution of the State of Michigan of 1963, the provisions of this Executive Order shall become effective 60 days after filing.

**History:**
Executive Reorganization Order No. 1994-6 was promulgated on April 12, 1994, as Executive Order No. 1994-10, eff June 12, 1994.

# PRISONER REIMBURSEMENT TO THE COUNTY

Act 118, 1984, p 271, imd eff June 1, 1984.

An act regarding county jails and prisoners housed therein; to provide certain powers and duties of county officials; and to provide for the reimbursement of certain expenses incurred by counties in regard to prisoners confined in county jails. (Amended by Pub Acts 1996, No. 544, eff 90 days after final adjournment of Legislature (see Mich. Const. note below).).

*The People of the State of Michigan enact:*

**Editor's notes:**
**Michigan Constitution of 1963, Art. IV, § 27,** provides:
"No act shall take effect until the expiration of 90 days from the end of the session at which it was passed, but the legislature may give immediate effect to acts by a two-thirds vote of the members elected to and serving in each house."

**Effect of amendment notes:**
**The 1996 amendment** substituted "confined in" for "sentenced to"; and made a grammatical change.

## § 801.81. Prisoner reimbursement to county. [MSA § 28.1770(1)]

Sec. 1. This act shall be known and may be cited as "the prisoner reimbursement to the county act."

**History:**
Pub Acts 1984, No. 118, § 1, imd eff June 1, 1984.

**Michigan Digest references:**
Counties § 56.
Prisons and Jails §§1.05, 1.55, 4.50, 5.60.

**LEXIS-NEXIS™ Michigan analytical references:**
Michigan Law and Practice, Convicts and Prisons § 2.

**Michigan Civ Jur references:**
Counties § 89.

**Research references:**
60 Am Jur 2d, Penal and Correctional Institutions § 11.

**Legal periodicals:**
Sable, Casenote, The Fruits of Crime, Victims, & New York's Son of Sam Law: Simon and Schuster, Inc. v. Members of the New York State Crime Victims Board, 1992 Detroit C L Rev 4:1185.

Fryer, Note, Bearing the Burden of Strict Scrutiny In the Wake of Simon & Shuster, Inc. v. Members of the New York State Crime Victims Board: A Constitutional Analysis of Michigan's "Son of Sam" Law, 70 U Det Mercy L R 1:191 (1992).

### CASE NOTES

A county's violation of the Prisoner Reimbursement to the County Act (PRCA) by obtaining ex parte orders from the judge assigned to the defendants' criminal cases, seizing the defendants' bond monies for reimbursement of the expenses of incarcerating the defendants in the county jail could be actionable under the federal civil rights law notwithstanding that the PRCA includes postdeprivation remedies. Mudge v Macomb County (1998) 458 Mich 87, 580 NW2d 845.

A county's claim for the defense of recoupment under the Prisoner Reimbursement to the County Act (PRCA) could be raised by counterclaim after the time for bringing an action under the statute has expired as long as the plaintiff's action claiming that the county's violation of the PRCA constituted a federal civil rights violation was timely. Mudge v Macomb County (1998) 458 Mich 87, 580 NW2d 845.

The Prisoner Reimbursement to the County Act is a county's exclusive remedy for seeking reimbursement of incarceration expenses from an inmate of that county's jail. Mudge v. Macomb County (1995) 210 Mich App 436, 534 NW2d 539.

A circuit court while having subject-matter jurisdiction to adjudicate matters brought pursuant to the Prisoner Reimbursement to the County Act, may not exercise properly that jurisdiction in the absence of the filing of a formal complaint. Mudge v. Macomb County (1995) 210 Mich App 436, 534 NW2d 539.

A circuit court while having subject-matter jurisdiction to adjudicate matters brought pursuant to the Prisoner Reimbursement to the County Act, may not exercise properly that jurisdiction in the absence of the filing of a formal complaint and summons. Mudge v. Macomb County (1995) 210 Mich App 436, 534 NW2d 539.

The Prisoner Reimbursement to the County Act is a county's exclusive remedy for seeking reimbursement of incarceration expenses from an inmate of that county's jail. Mudge v. Macomb County (1995) 210 Mich App 436, 534 NW2d 539.

### § 801.82. County jail; house of correction. [MSA § 28.1770(2)]

Sec. 2. For purposes of this act, "county jail" includes a house of correction under Act No. 278 of the Public Acts of 1911, being sections 802.202 to 802.204 of the Michigan Compiled Laws.

**History:**
Pub Acts 1984, No. 118, § 2, imd eff June 1, 1984; amended by Pub Acts 1985, No. 58, imd eff June 14, 1985 (see 1985 note below).

**Editor's notes:**
**Pub Acts 1985, No. 58,** § **2,** imd eff June 14, 1985, provides:
"Section 2. The amendatory act shall not take effect unless all of the following bills of the 83rd Legislature are enacted into law:
"(a) House Bill No. 4392 [which became Act No. 61 of 1985].
"(b) House Bill No. 4393 [which became Act No. 44 of 1985].

**Jails and Workhouses** § 801.83

"(c) House Bill No. 4395 [which became Act No. 46 of 1985].
"(d) House Bill No. 4394 [which became Act No. 45 of 1985].
"(e) House Bill No. 4396 [which became Act No. 47 of 1985].
"(f) House Bill No. 4403 [which became Act No. 54 of 1985].
"(g) House Bill No. 4398 [which became Act No. 49 of 1985].
"(h) House Bill No. 4404 [which became Act No. 55 of 1985].
"(i) House Bill No. 4401 [which became Act No. 52 of 1985].
"(j) House Bill No. 4399 [which became Act No. 50 of 1985].
"(k) House Bill No. 4417 [which became Act No. 56 of 1985].
"(l) House Bill No. 4400 [which became Act No. 51 of 1985].
"(m) House Bill No. 4423 [which became Act No. 60 of 1985].
"(n) House Bill No. 4402 [which became Act No. 53 of 1985].
"(o) House Bill No. 4397 [which became Act No. 48 of 1985].
"(p) House Bill No. 4418 [which became Act No. 57 of 1985].
"(q) House Bill No. 4422 [which became Act No. 59 of 1985]."

**Michigan Digest references:**
Prisons and Jails § 1.55.

**LEXIS-NEXIS™ Michigan analytical references:**
Michigan Law and Practice, Convicts and Prisons § 2.

**Michigan Civ Jur references:**
Counties § 89.

**Research references:**
60 Am Jur 2d, Penal and Correctional Institutions § 11.

## § 801.83. Reimbursement for expenses; form. [MSA § 28.1770(3)]

Sec. 3. (1) The county may seek reimbursement for any expenses incurred by the county in relation to a charge for which a person was sentenced to a county jail as follows:

(a) From each person who is or was a prisoner, not more than $60.00 per day for the expenses of maintaining that prisoner or the actual per diem cost of maintaining that prisoner, whichever is less, for the entire period of time the person was confined in the county jail, including any period of pretrial detention.

(b) To investigate the financial status of the person.

(c) Any other expenses incurred by the county to collect payments under this act.

(2) Reimbursement under this act may be ordered as a probation condition entered pursuant to section 3 of chapter XI of the code of criminal procedure, 1927 PA 175, MCL 771.3.

(3) Before seeking any reimbursement under this act, the county shall develop a form to be used for determining the financial status of prisoners. The form shall provide for obtaining the age and marital status of a prisoner, number and ages of children of a prisoner, number and ages of other dependents, type and value of real estate, type and value of personal property, cash and bank accounts, type and value of investments, pensions and annuities, and any other personalty of significant cash value. The county shall use the form when investigating the financial status of prisoners.

**History:**
Pub Acts 1984, No. 118, § 3, imd eff June 1, 1984; amended by Pub Acts 1994, No. 212, imd eff June 23, 1994.

## § 801.83

Amended by Pub Acts 1996, No. 544, eff 90 days from end of 1996 legislative session (see Mich. Const. note below); 1998, No. 450, imd eff December 30, 1998, by enacting § 2 eff August 1, 1999 (see 1998 note below).

**Editor's notes:**
**Michigan Constitution of 1963, Art. IV, § 27,** provides:
"No act shall take effect until the expiration of 90 days from the end of the session at which it was passed, but the legislature may give immediate effect to acts by a two-thirds vote of the members elected to and serving in each house."

**Pub Acts 1998, No. 450, enacting § 1,** imd eff December 30, 1998, by enacting § 2 eff August 1, 1999, provides:
"Enacting section 1. This amendatory act does not take effect unless House Bill No. 4364 of the 89th Legislature [Pub Acts 1998, No. 449] is enacted into law."

**Effect of amendment notes:**
**The 1994 amendment** in subsection (1), substituted "$60.00" for "$30.00"; and in subsection (2) made grammatical changes, deleting "the" in three instances.

**The 1996 amendment** in subsection (1) opening paragraph inserted ", or for which a person was imprisoned as a pretrial detainee on a charge or charges that resulted in conviction for a felony,".

**The 1998 amendment** in subsection (1), in the opening paragraph, substituted "a" for "the" preceding "charge" and deleted "or charges" following "charge" and, in paragraph (c) deleted "in order" following "county"; added subsection (2); and redesignated former subsection (2) as subsection (3).

**Michigan Digest references:**
Prisons and Jails § 1.55.

**LEXIS-NEXIS™ Michigan analytical references:**
Michigan Law and Practice, Convicts and Prisons § 2.

**Michigan Civ Jur references:**
Counties § 89.

**Research references:**
60 Am Jur 2d, Penal and Correctional Institutions § 11.

**Legal periodicals:**
Fryer, Note, Bearing the Burden of Strict Scrutiny In the Wake of Simon & Shuster, Inc. v. Members of the New York State Crime Victims Board: A Constitutional Analysis of Michigan's "Son of Sam" Law, 70 U Det Mercy L R 1:191 (1992).

### CASE NOTES

The Prisoner Reimbursement to the County Act is a county's exclusive remedy for seeking reimbursement of incarceration expenses from an inmate of that county's jail. Mudge v Macomb County (1995) 210 Mich App 436, 534 NW2d 539.

The Legislature has provided a method for a county to seek reimbursement for expenses for maintaining a prisoner; a county attorney may file a civil action to seek such reimbursement. People v Gonyo (1988) 173 Mich App 716, 434 NW2d 223.

## § 801.84. List. [MSA § 28.1770(4)]

Sec. 4. At, and in accordance with, the request of the county board of commissioners or of the county executive or a designee of the county executive, the sheriff of the county shall forward to the board, county executive, or designee of the county executive a list containing the name of each sentenced prisoner and each pretrial detainee whose prosecution resulted in conviction for a felony, the term of sentence or the period of pretrial detention, and the date of admission, together with information regarding the financial status of each prisoner, as required by the county board of commissioners, the county executive, or designee of the county executive.

**History:**
Pub Acts 1984, No. 118, § 4, imd eff June 1, 1984.
Amended by Pub Acts 1996, No. 544, eff 90 days after final adjournment of Legislature (see Mich. Const. note below).

**Editor's notes:**
**Michigan Constitution of 1963, Art. IV, § 27,** provides:
"No act shall take effect until the expiration of 90 days from the end of the session at which it was passed, but the legislature may give immediate effect to acts by a two-thirds vote of the members elected to and serving in each house."

**Effect of amendment notes:**
**The 1996 amendment** added "and each pretrial detainee whose prosecution resulted in conviction for a felony"; and also added "or the period of pretrial detention".

**Michigan Digest references:**
Prisons and Jails § 1.55.

**LEXIS-NEXIS™ Michigan analytical references:**
Michigan Law and Practice, Convicts and Prisons § 2.

**Michigan Civ Jur references:**
Counties § 89.

**Research references:**
60 Am Jur 2d, Penal and Correctional Institutions § 11.

**Legal periodicals:**
Fryer, Note, Bearing the Burden of Strict Scrutiny In the Wake of Simon & Shuster, Inc. v. Members of the New York State Crime Victims Board: A Constitutional Analysis of Michigan's "Son of Sam" Law, 70 U Det Mercy L R 1:191 (1992).

## § 801.85. Cooperation of prisoner required; refusal to cooperate. [MSA § 28.1770(5)]

Sec. 5. (1) A prisoner in a county jail shall cooperate with the county in seeking reimbursement under this act for expenses incurred by the county for that prisoner.

(2) A prisoner who willfully refuses to cooperate as provided in subsection (1) shall not receive a reduction in his or her term under section 7 of 1962 PA 60, MCL 801.257. If a prisoner is ordered to reimburse the county under this act as a probation condition entered pursuant to section 3 of chapter XI of the code of criminal procedure, 1927 PA 175, MCL 771.3, the prisoner is in addition subject to probation revocation as provided in section 4 of chapter XI of the code of criminal procedure, 1927 PA 175, MCL 771.4.

**History:**
Pub Acts 1984, No. 118, § 5, imd eff June 1, 1984.
Amended by Pub Acts 1998, No. 450, imd eff December 30, 1998, by enacting § 2 eff August 1, 1999 (see 1998 note below).

**Editor's notes:**
**Pub Acts 1998, No. 450, enacting § 1,** imd eff December 30, 1998, by enacting § 2 eff August 1, 1999, provides:
"Enacting section 1. This amendatory act does not take effect unless House Bill No. 4364 of the 89th Legislature [Pub Acts 1998, No. 449] is enacted into law."

**Effect of amendment notes:**
**The 1998 amendment** in subsection (2), substituted "willfully" for "wilfully", changed the style of statutory references, and added the second sentence.

**Michigan Digest references:**
Prisons and Jails § 1.55.

**LEXIS-NEXIS™ Michigan analytical references:**
Michigan Law and Practice, Convicts and Prisons § 2.

**Michigan Civ Jur references:**
Counties § 89.

**Research references:**
60 Am Jur 2d, Penal and Correctional Institutions § 11.

## § 801.86. Investigation by county board of commissioners. [MSA § 28.1770(6)]

Sec. 6. The county board of commissioners or the county executive may investigate or cause to be investigated all the reports under section 4 furnished by the sheriff for the purpose of securing reimbursement for the expenses incurred by the county in regard to prisoners as provided for under this act.

**History:**
Pub Acts 1984, No. 118, § 6, imd eff June 1, 1984.

**Statutory references:**
Section 4, above referred to, is § 801.84.

**Michigan Digest references:**
Prisons and Jails § 1.55.

**LEXIS-NEXIS™ Michigan analytical references:**
Michigan Law and Practice, Convicts and Prisons § 2.

**Michigan Civ Jur references:**
Counties § 89.

**Research references:**
60 Am Jur 2d, Penal and Correctional Institutions § 11.

## § 801.87. Civil action for reimbursement; consideration by court; money judgment; order. [MSA § 28.1770(7)]

Sec. 7. (1) Within 12 months after the release from a county jail of a sentenced prisoner or a pretrial detainee whose prosecution resulted in conviction for a felony, an attorney for that county may

**Jails and Workhouses** § 801.87

file a civil action to seek reimbursement from that person for maintenance and support of that person while he or she is or was confined in the jail, or for any other expense for which the county may be reimbursed under section 3, as provided in this section and sections 8 to 10.

(2) A civil action brought under this act shall be instituted in the name of the county in which the jail is located and shall state the following, as applicable:

(a) In the case of a prisoner sentenced to the jail, the date and place of sentence, the length of time set forth in the sentence, the length of time actually served, and the amount or amounts due to the county pursuant to section 3.

(b) In the case of a person imprisoned as a pretrial detainee on a charge or charges that resulted in conviction for a felony, the length of pretrial detention and the amount or amounts due to the county pursuant to section 3.

(3) Before entering any order on behalf of the county against the defendant, the court shall take into consideration any legal obligation of the defendant to support a spouse, minor children, or other dependents and any moral obligation to support dependents to whom the defendant is providing or has in fact provided support.

(4) The court may enter a money judgment against the defendant and may order that the defendant's property is liable for reimbursement for maintenance and support of the defendant as a prisoner and for other expenses reimbursable under section 3.

**History:**
Pub Acts 1984, No. 118, § 7, imd eff June 1, 1984; amended by Pub Acts 1994, No. 212, imd eff June 23, 1994.
Amended by Pub Acts 1996, No. 544, eff 90 days after final adjournment of Legislature (see Mich. Const. note below).

**Editor's notes:**
**Michigan Constitution of 1963, Art. IV, § 27,** provides:
"No act shall take effect until the expiration of 90 days from the end of the session at which it was passed, but the legislature may give immediate effect to acts by a two-thirds vote of the members elected to and serving in each house."

**Effect of amendment notes:**
**The 1994 amendment** in subsection (1), substituted "12 months" for "6 months".
**The 1996 amendment** revised subsection (1) and subsection (2), opening paragraph and paragraph (a); and added subsection (2), paragraph (b).

**Statutory references:**
Sections 3 and 8 to 10, above referred to, are §§801.83, 801.88, 801.89 and 801.90.

**Michigan Digest references:**
Prisons and Jails § 1.55.

**LEXIS-NEXIS™ Michigan analytical references:**
Michigan Law and Practice, Convicts and Prisons § 2.

**Michigan Civ Jur references:**
Counties § 89.

## § 801.87

**Research references:**
60 Am Jur 2d, Penal and Correctional Institutions § 11.

**Legal periodicals:**
Fryer, Note, Bearing the Burden of Strict Scrutiny In the Wake of Simon & Shuster, Inc. v. Members of the New York State Crime Victims Board: A Constitutional Analysis of Michigan's "Son of Sam" Law, 70 U Det Mercy L R 1:191 (1992).

### CASE NOTES

The Prisoner Reimbursement to the County Act is a county's exclusive remedy for seeking reimbursement of incarceration expenses from an inmate of that county's jail. Mudge v. Macomb County (1995) 210 Mich App 436, 534 NW2d 539.

The Legislature has provided a method for a county to seek reimbursement for expenses for maintaining a prisoner; a county attorney may file a civil action to seek such reimbursement. People v. Gonyo (1988) 173 Mich App 716, 434 NW2d 223.

## § 801.88. Civil action for reimbursement; circuit court; venue; ex parte restraining order; hearing on order to show cause; appointment of receiver. [MSA § 28.1770(8)]

Sec. 8. (1) Consistent with section 7, the county may file the civil action in the circuit court. If the defendant is still a prisoner in the county jail or is a prisoner in a state correctional facility, venue is proper in the county in which the jail or correctional facility is located.

(2) If necessary to protect the county's right to obtain reimbursement under this act against the disposition of known property, the county, in accordance with rules of the supreme court of this state, may seek issuance of an ex parte restraining order to restrain the defendant from disposing of the property pending a hearing on an order to show cause why the particular property should not be applied to reimbursement of the county for the maintenance and support of the defendant as a prisoner.

(3) To protect and maintain the property pending resolution of the matter, the court, upon request, may appoint a receiver.

**History:**
Pub Acts 1984, No. 118, § 8, imd eff June 1, 1984.
Amended by Pub Acts 1996, No. 544, eff 90 days after final adjournment of Legislature (see Mich. Const. note below).

**Editor's notes:**
**Michigan Constitution of 1963, Art. IV, § 27,** provides:
"No act shall take effect until the expiration of 90 days from the end of the session at which it was passed, but the legislature may give immediate effect to acts by a two-thirds vote of the members elected to and serving in each house."

**Effect of amendment notes:**
**The 1996 amendment** in subsection (1), inserted "or is a prisoner in a state correctional facility" and "or correctional facility".

**Statutory references:**
Section 7, above referred to, is § 801.87.

**Michigan Digest references:**
Prisons and Jails § 1.55.

**LEXIS-NEXIS™ Michigan analytical references:**
Michigan Law and Practice, Convicts and Prisons § 2.

**Michigan Civ Jur references:**
Counties § 89.

**Research references:**
60 Am Jur 2d, Penal and Correctional Institutions § 11.

## § 801.89. Enforcement of judgment, limitations. [MSA § 28.1770(9)]

Sec. 9. The county shall not enforce any judgment obtained under this act by means of execution against the homestead of the defendant.

**History:**
Pub Acts 1984, No. 118, § 9, imd eff June 1, 1984.

**Michigan Digest references:**
Prisons and Jails § 1.55.

**LEXIS-NEXIS™ Michigan analytical references:**
Michigan Law and Practice, Convicts and Prisons § 2.

**Michigan Civ Jur references:**
Counties § 89.

**Research references:**
60 Am Jur 2d, Penal and Correctional Institutions § 11.

## § 801.90. Civil action to recover and enforce money judgment; district court; venue. [MSA § 28.1770(10)]

Sec. 10. Consistent with section 7, the county may file the civil action in the district court to recover a money judgment and to enforce that judgment in the same manner as other money judgments entered by the district court. If the defendant is still a prisoner in the county jail, venue in a district of the first class is proper in the county where the county jail is located and in a district of the second or third class is proper in the district where the county jail is located. If the defendant is a prisoner in a state correctional facility, venue is proper in the county in which the state correctional facility is located.

**History:**
Pub Acts 1984, No. 118, § 10, imd eff June 1, 1984.
Amended by Pub Acts 1996, No. 544, eff 90 days after final adjournment of Legislature (see Mich. Const. note below).

**Editor's notes:**
**Michigan Constitution of 1963, Art. IV, § 27,** provides:
"No act shall take effect until the expiration of 90 days from the end of the session at which it was passed, but the legislature may give immediate effect to acts by a two-thirds vote of the members elected to and serving in each house."

**Effect of amendment notes:**
**The 1996 amendment** added the last sentence, which reads "If the

§ 801.90

defendant is a prisoner in a state correctional facility, venue is proper in the county in which the state correctional facility is located".

**Statutory references:**
Section 7, above referred to, is § 801.87.

**Michigan Digest references:**
Prisons and Jails § 1.55.

**LEXIS-NEXIS™ Michigan analytical references:**
Michigan Law and Practice, Convicts and Prisons § 2.

**Michigan Civ Jur references:**
Counties § 89.

**Research references:**
60 Am Jur 2d, Penal and Correctional Institutions § 11.

**Legal periodicals:**
Fryer, Note, Bearing the Burden of Strict Scrutiny In the Wake of Simon & Shuster, Inc. v. Members of the New York State Crime Victims Board: A Constitutional Analysis of Michigan's "Son of Sam" Law, 70 U Det Mercy L R 1:191 (1992).

## § 801.91. Information and assistance furnished county attorneys to secure reimbursement. [MSA § 28.1770(11)]

Sec. 11. The sentencing judge and the sheriff of any county in which a prisoner's property is located shall furnish to the attorney for the county all information and assistance possible to enable the attorney to secure reimbursement for the county under this act.

**History:**
Pub Acts 1984, No. 118, § 11, imd eff June 1, 1984.

**LEXIS-NEXIS™ Michigan analytical references:**
Michigan Law and Practice, Convicts and Prisons § 2.

**Michigan Civ Jur references:**
Counties § 89.

**Research references:**
60 Am Jur 2d, Penal and Correctional Institutions § 11.

**Legal periodicals:**
Fryer, Note, Bearing the Burden of Strict Scrutiny In the Wake of Simon & Shuster, Inc. v. Members of the New York State Crime Victims Board: A Constitutional Analysis of Michigan's "Son of Sam" Law, 70 U Det Mercy L R 1:191 (1992).

## § 801.92. Reimbursements credited to general county fund; determination, sworn statements. [MSA § 28.1770(12)]

Sec. 12. The reimbursements secured under this act shall be credited to the general fund of the county to be available for general fund purposes. The county treasurer may determine the amount due the county under this act and render sworn statements thereof. These sworn statements shall be considered prima facie evidence of the amount due.

**History:**
Pub Acts 1984, No. 118, § 12, imd eff June 1, 1984.

**Jails and Workhouses** § 801.101

**LEXIS-NEXIS™ Michigan analytical references:**
Michigan Law and Practice, Convicts and Prisons § 2.

**Michigan Civ Jur references:**
Counties § 89.

**Research references:**
60 Am Jur 2d, Penal and Correctional Institutions § 11.

**§ 801.93. Conditions for passage of act.** [MSA § 28.1770(13)]

Sec. 13. This act shall not take effect unless all of the following bills of the 82nd Legislature are enacted into law:
  (a) House Bill No. 4589.
  (b) House Bill No. 5120.
  (c) House Bill No. 5173.

**History:**
Pub Acts 1984, No. 118, § 13, imd eff June 1, 1984.

**Editor's notes:**
House Bill No. 4589, House Bill No. 5120 and House Bill No. 5173 of the 82nd Legislature, above referred to, became Public Act Nos. 119, 120 and 121, respectively, of 1984.

**LEXIS-NEXIS™ Michigan analytical references:**
Michigan Law and Practice, Convicts and Prisons § 2.

**Michigan Civ Jur references:**
Counties § 89.

**Research references:**
60 Am Jur 2d, Penal and Correctional Institutions § 11.

## GENERAL PROVISIONS RELATING TO JAILS, AND THE CONFINEMENT OF PRISONERS THEREIN

RS 1846, Ch 148

**§ 801.101. United States prisoners; duty of sheriff to receive and keep.** [MSA § 28.1751]

Sec. 1. The sheriffs of the several counties of this state shall receive into their respective jails and keep all prisoners who are committed to the same, by virtue of any civil process, issued by any court of record instituted under the authority of the United States, until they are discharged by the due course of the laws of the United States, in the same manner as if such prisoner had been committed by virtue of process in civil actions issued under the authority of this state, and every such sheriff may receive to his own use such sums of money as shall be payable by the United States for the use of the jails.

**History:**
RS 1846, Ch. 148, § 1; amended by Pub Acts 1855, No. 163, eff February 13, 1855; 1960, No. 64, eff August 17, 1960.

## § 801.101

**Prior codification:**
CL 1929, § 17697; CL 1915, § 14760; HOW § 8939; CL 1897, § 10532; CL 1871, § 7362; CL 1857, § 5575.

**Michigan Digest references:**
Prisons and Jails §§1 et seq.
Sheriffs and Constables § 18.

**Michigan Civ Jur references:**
Counties § 51.50.

**Research references:**
27 Am Jur 2d, Escape, Prison Breaking, and Rescue §§21–24.
60 Am Jur 2d, Penal and Correctional Institutions § 8.
22 Am Jur Pl & Pr Forms, Rev, Sheriffs, Police, and Constables, Form 7.

### CASE NOTES

**1. Sheriff as United States jailer.**
In the receiving, keeping and caring for prisoners of the United States committed to a county jail, the sheriff is not a sheriff, but a jailer of the United States. Bay County v Marvin (1929) 247 Mich 529, 226 NW 247.

**2. Payment of costs of maintenance of United States prisoners.**
The sheriff is the proper party under section 5547, USRS (18 USC 699), with whom a contract is to be made for the boarding of federal prisoners, and the money paid to him as jailer of the United States is not a public fund of the county but belongs to the sheriff. Bay County v Marvin (1929) 247 Mich 529, 226 NW 247.

Payment of cost of maintenance, medical care and treatment of federal prisoners, which has been determined by the state welfare commission, may be made a condition of the acceptance of such prisoners by county jails. Op Atty Gen, 1926–1928, p 743.

**3. Persons detained as witnesses.**
Persons detained as witnesses must be regarded as persons held upon civil process and must be so treated. Leach v Whitbeck (1908) 151 Mich 327, 115 NW 253.

## § 801.102. Liability of sheriff for safe keeping. [MSA § 28.1752]

Sec. 2. Every sheriff or keeper of a prison, to whose jail any prisoner shall be committed, by any marshal or other officer of the United States, as provided in the preceding section, shall be answerable for the safe keeping of such prisoner, in the courts of the United States, according to the laws thereof.

**History:**
RS 1846, Ch. 148, § 2.

**Prior codification:**
CL 1929, § 17698; CL 1915, § 14761; HOW § 8940; CL 1897, § 10533; CL 1871, § 7363; CL 1857, § 5576.

**Research references:**
27 Am Jur 2d, Escape, Prison Breaking, and Rescue §§21–24.
60 Am Jur 2d, Penal and Correctional Institutions § 8.
22 Am Jur Pl & Pr Forms, Rev, Sheriffs, Police, and Constables, Form 7.

## § 801.103. Separation of prisoners; civil and criminal. [MSA § 28.1753]

Sec. 3. Prisoners arrested on civil process, other than for civil contempt, shall be kept in rooms separate and distinct from those in which prisoners detained on a criminal charge or conviction are confined. Prisoners arrested for civil contempt shall not be housed with other prisoners detained on criminal charges, except those detained on a misdemeanor charge. Except as otherwise provided in this section, prisoners arrested on civil and criminal process shall not be put or kept in the same room.

**History:**
RS 1846, Ch. 148, § 3; amended by Pub Acts 1986, No. 156, imd eff July 7, 1986.

**Prior codification:**
CL 1929, § 17699; CL 1915, § 14762; HOW § 8941; CL 1897, § 10534; CL 1871, § 7364; CL 1857, § 5577.

**Michigan Digest references:**
Prisons and Jails § 2.

**Research references:**
60 Am Jur 2d, Penal and Correctional Institutions §§3–5.

### CASE NOTES

The incarceration among felons of one arrested for contempt of court in failing to pay alimony is in violation of this section, where he has simply been charged with contempt without pronouncement of judgment. Oxford v Berry (1918) 204 Mich 197, 170 NW 83.

Solitary confinement is unlawful in case of prisoners arrested on civil process. Leach v Whitbeck (1908) 151 Mich 327, 115 NW 253.

Witnesses who are committed in default of bail for their appearance to testify on behalf of the people in a criminal case must be regarded as "prisoners held upon civil process," within the meaning of this section. In re Lewellyn (1895) 104 Mich 318, 62 NW 554.

## § 801.104. Separation of prisoners; male and female. [MSA § 28.1754]

Sec. 4. Male and female prisoners, unless they are husband and wife, shall not be put, kept, or confined in the same room in any jail, lock-up, holding center, or holding cell.

**History:**
RS 1846, Ch. 148, § 4; amended by Pub Acts 1986, No. 156, imd eff July 7, 1986.

**Prior codification:**
CL 1929, § 17700; CL 1915, § 14763; HOW § 8942; CL 1897, § 10535; CL 1871, § 7365; CL 1857, § 5578.

**Michigan Digest references:**
Prisons and Jails § 2.

**Research references:**
60 Am Jur 2d, Penal and Correctional Institutions §§3–5.

## § 801.105. Violation; liability to injured persons; misdemeanor. [MSA § 28.1755]

Sec. 5. A sheriff or other officer who violates the provisions of either

**§ 801.105**

section 3 or section 4 shall be liable to the party injured for damages and, in addition, is guilty of a misdemeanor.

**History:**
RS 1846, Ch. 148, § 5; amended by Pub Acts 1986, No. 156, imd eff July 7, 1986.

**Prior codification:**
CL 1929, § 17701; CL 1915, § 14764; HOW § 8943; CL 1897, § 10536; CL 1871, § 7366; CL 1857, § 5579.

**Statutory references:**
Sections 3 and 4, above referred to, are §§801.103 and 801.104.

**Cross references:**
Punishment for misdemeanor, § 750.504.

**Michigan Digest references:**
Penalties and Forfeitures §§1 et seq.

**Research references:**
60 Am Jur 2d, Penal and Correctional Institutions §§3-5.
2A Am Jur Pleading & Practice Forms, Rev, Assault and Battery, Form 195.4.

## § 801.106. Jails in use, continuation. [MSA § 28.1756]

Sec. 6. The buildings now used as jails and prisons in the respective counties of this state, shall be and continue the jails of the said counties respectively, until other buildings shall be designated or erected for that purpose, according to law.

**History:**
RS 1846, Ch. 148, § 6.

**Prior codification:**
CL 1929, § 17702; CL 1915, § 14765; HOW § 8944; CL 1897, § 10537; CL 1871, § 7367; CL 1857, § 5580.

**Michigan Digest references:**
Civil Arrest and Bail §§81 et seq, 90.
Criminal Law and Procedure § 739.
Prisons and Jails §§4, 6.
Process § 38.

**Research references:**
60 Am Jur 2d, Penal and Correctional Institutions §§8-10.

## § 801.107. Designation of jail in another county; officer to act. [MSA § 28.1757]

Sec. 7. If in any county there shall not be a jail, or the jail erected shall become unfit or unsafe for the confinement of prisoners, or shall be destroyed by fire or otherwise, the circuit judge of the circuit court, or any circuit court commissioner for such county, and in the upper peninsula, the district judge of the district court for such county, shall by an instrument in writing, to be filed with the clerk of the county, designate the jail of some other county for the confinement of the prisoners of such county; which shall thereupon, to all intents and purposes, except as herein otherwise provided,

# Jails and Workhouses § 801.108

become the jail of the county for which it shall have been so designated.

**History:**
RS 1846, Ch. 148, § 7; amended by Pub Acts 1855, No. 25, imd eff February 7, 1855.

**Prior codification:**
CL 1929, § 17703; CL 1915, § 14766; HOW § 8945; CL 1897, § 10538; CL 1871, § 7368; CL 1857, § 5581.

**Former acts:**
The provision relating to the upper peninsula district court was added by amendatory Act 25 of 1855. This district was established by Const 1850, art XIX, § 1 and abolished by Pub Acts 1863, No. 150.

**Michigan Digest references:**
Civil Arrest and Bail §§81 et seq, 90.
Criminal Law and Procedure § 739.
Prisons and Jails §§4, 6.
Process § 38.

**Research references:**
60 Am Jur 2d, Penal and Correctional Institutions §§8–10.

### CASE NOTES

County may seek reimbursement from demanding authority for necessary medical expenses incurred in apprehending and returning fugitive from out-of-state jurisdiction. Op Atty Gen, February 25, 1976, No. 4957.

Where an insanitary or otherwise inadequate jail has been condemned the circuit judge may order the inmates removed to another jail, whereupon the county becomes liable for their support. Op Atty Gen, 1926–1928, p 295.

Where state medical inspector reports on unsanitary condition of a county jail he may not close such jail, but should report the matter to the circuit judge under this section. Op Atty Gen, 1911, p 323.

## § 801.108. Copy of designation, service on sheriff. [MSA § 28.1758]

Sec. 8. A copy of such instrument of designation, duly certified by the clerk of the county with whom it is filed, under the seal of the circuit or district court thereof, shall be served on the sheriff and keeper of the jail so designated, whose duty it shall be from thenceforth to receive into such jail, and there safely keep, all persons who may be lawfully confined therein, pursuant to the foregoing provisions.

**History:**
RS 1846, Ch. 148, § 8; amended by Pub Acts 1855, No. 25, imd eff February 7, 1855.

**Prior codification:**
CL 1929, § 17704; CL 1915, § 14767; HOW § 8946; CL 1897, § 10539; CL 1871, § 7369; CL 1857, § 5582.

**Michigan Digest references:**
Civil Arrest and Bail §§81 et seq, 90.
Criminal Law and Procedure § 739.
Prisons and Jails §§4, 6.
Process § 38.

### § 801.109. Responsibility of sheriff for safe keeping of prisoners. [MSA § 28.1759]

Sec. 9. Such sheriff shall be responsible for the safe keeping of the persons so committed to such jail, in the same manner and to the same extent, as if he were sheriff of the county for whose use such jail shall have been designated, and with respect to the persons so committed, shall be deemed the sheriff of such county.

**History:**
RS 1846, Ch. 148, § 9.

**Prior codification:**
CL 1929, § 17705; CL 1915, § 14768; HOW § 8947; CL 1897, § 10540; CL 1871, § 7370; CL 1857, § 5583.

**Michigan Digest references:**
Civil Arrest and Bail §§81 et seq, 90.
Criminal Law and Procedure § 739.
Prisons and Jails §§4, 6.
Process § 38.

**Research references:**
60 Am Jur 2d, Penal and Correctional Institutions §§8–10.

### § 801.110. Effect on prisoner admitted to jail liberties. [MSA § 28.1760]

Sec. 10. If any prisoner confined on civil process, shall have been admitted to the liberties of the jail of the county for which such designation shall have been made, previous to such designation, they shall, notwithstanding, be entitled to remain within such liberties, but may be removed to the jail so designated, and confined therein, by the sheriff of the county in which they were admitted to the liberties of the jail, in the same cases, and in the same manner as such sheriff might by law confine them in the jail of his own county.

**History:**
RS 1846, Ch. 148, § 10.

**Prior codification:**
CL 1929, § 17706; CL 1915, § 14769; HOW § 8948; CL 1897, § 10541; CL 1871, § 7371; CL 1857, § 5584.

**Michigan Digest references:**
Civil Arrest and Bail §§81 et seq, 90.
Criminal Law and Procedure § 739.
Prisons and Jails §§4, 6.
Process § 38.

**Research references:**
60 Am Jur 2d, Penal and Correctional Institutions §§8–10.

### § 801.111. Effect on subsequent prisoner entitled to jail liberties. [MSA § 28.1761]

Sec. 11. If any persons shall be in the custody of the sheriff of the

**Jails and Workhouses** § 801.113

county for which such designation shall have been made, subsequent to such designation, and shall be entitled, according to law, to the liberties of the jail thereof, they shall be admitted to the liberties of such jail, in the same manner, and in the same cases, as if no such designation had been made, but may be removed by such sheriff to the jail so designated, and confined therein, in the same cases and in the same manner, as such sheriff might by law confine them in the jail of his own county.

**History:**
RS 1846, Ch. 148, § 11.

**Prior codification:**
CL 1929, § 17707; CL 1915, § 14770; HOW § 8949; CL 1897, § 10542; CL 1871, § 7372; CL 1857, § 5585.

**Michigan Digest references:**
Civil Arrest and Bail §§81 et seq, 90.
Criminal Law and Procedure § 739.
Prisons and Jails §§4, 6.
Process § 38.

**Research references:**
60 Am Jur 2d, Penal and Correctional Institutions §§8–10.

### § 801.112. Right of prisoner entitled to jail liberties. [MSA § 28.1762]

Sec. 12. If any persons confined in the jail so designated on civil process, or removed there, as hereinbefore provided, shall by law be entitled to the liberties of the jail, the sheriff of the county in which the jail so designated shall be, shall admit them to the liberties of such jail, in the same manner and in the same cases, as if they had been originally arrested by such sheriff, on process directed to him.

**History:**
RS 1846, Ch. 148, § 12.

**Prior codification:**
CL 1929, § 17708; CL 1915, § 14771; HOW § 8950; CL 1897, § 10543; CL 1871, § 7373; CL 1857, § 5586.

**Michigan Digest references:**
Civil Arrest and Bail §§81 et seq, 90.
Criminal Law and Procedure § 739.
Prisons and Jails §§4, 6.
Process § 38.

**Research references:**
60 Am Jur 2d, Penal and Correctional Institutions §§8–10.

### § 801.113. Revocation of order. [MSA § 28.1763]

Sec. 13. Whenever a jail shall be erected for the county for whose use such designation shall have been made, or its jail shall have been rendered fit and safe for the confinement of prisoners, the circuit judge of the circuit court for such county, or in the upper peninsula, the district judge of the district court for such county, shall, by an instrument in writing, to be filed with the clerk of the

**§ 801.113**            **Jails and Workhouses**

county, declare that the necessity for such designation has ceased, and that the same is hereby revoked and annulled.

**History:**
RS 1846, Ch. 148, § 13; amended by Pub Acts 1855, No. 25, imd eff February 7, 1855.

**Prior codification:**
CL 1929, § 17709; CL 1915, § 14772; HOW § 8951; CL 1897, § 10544; CL 1871, § 7374; CL 1857, § 5587.

**Michigan Digest references:**
Civil Arrest and Bail §§81 et seq, 90.
Criminal Law and Procedure § 739.
Prisons and Jails §§4, 6.
Process § 38.

**Research references:**
60 Am Jur 2d, Penal and Correctional Institutions §§8–10.

## § 801.114. Removal of prisoners. [MSA § 28.1764]

Sec. 14. The clerk of the county shall immediately serve a copy of such revocation upon the sheriff thereof, whose duty it shall be to remove the prisoners belonging to his custody, and so confined without his county, to his proper jail, and if any prisoners shall have been admitted to the liberties of the jail, in such other county, they shall also be removed, and shall be entitled to the liberties of the jail of the county to which they shall be removed, in the same manner as if they had been originally arrested in such county.

**History:**
RS 1846, Ch. 148, § 14.

**Prior codification:**
CL 1929, § 17710; CL 1915, § 14773; HOW § 8952; CL 1897, § 10545; CL 1871, § 7375; CL 1857, § 5588.

**Michigan Digest references:**
Civil Arrest and Bail §§81 et seq, 90.
Criminal Law and Procedure § 739.
Prisons and Jails §§4, 6.
Process § 38.

**Research references:**
60 Am Jur 2d, Penal and Correctional Institutions §§8–10.

## § 801.115. Removal of prisoners in case of fire; prisoner not deemed escaped. [MSA § 28.1765]

Sec. 15. Whenever by reason of any jail being on fire, or any building contiguous, or near to a jail, being on fire, there shall be reason to apprehend that the prisoners confined in such jail may be injured or endangered by such fire, the sheriff or keeper of such jail may, at his discretion, remove such prisoners to some safe and convenient place, and there confine them, so long as may be necessary to avoid such danger; and such removal and confinement shall not be deemed an escape of such prisoners.

**History:**
RS 1846, Ch. 148, § 15.

## Jails and Workhouses § 801.120

**Prior codification:**
CL 1929, § 17711; CL 1915, § 14774; HOW § 8953; CL 1897, § 10546; CL 1871, § 7376; CL 1857, § 5589.

**Michigan Digest references:**
Civil Arrest and Bail §§81 et seq, 90.
Criminal Law and Procedure § 739.
Prisons and Jails §§4, 6.
Process § 38.

**Research references:**
60 Am Jur 2d, Penal and Correctional Institutions §§8–10.

### §§801.116, 801.117. [Repealed] [MSA §§28.1766, 28.1767]

**History:**
RS 1846, Ch. 148; **repealed** by Pub Acts 1981, No. 7, imd eff April 17, 1981.

**Editor's notes:**
Former § 801.116 dealt with prohibition of liquor in jails. Former § 801.117 dealt with prohibition of liquor in jails. For current provisions, see §§801.261 et seq.

Sec. 18. (Repealed.).
Former § 18 related to the duty of the sheriff to deliver all declarations, etc., served upon the sheriff directed to any prisoner, to such prisoner. It was repealed by Pub Acts 1915, No. 314, eff January 1, 1916. For current provision, see § 600.1908.

### § 801.119. Conveyance of prisoners through other counties; right of officers. [MSA § 28.1768]

Sec. 19. Any sheriff or other officer, who shall have arrested any prisoner, may pass over, across and through such parts of any other county or counties as shall be in the ordinary route of travel from the place where such prisoner shall have been arrested, to the place where he is to be conveyed and delivered, according to the command of the process by which such arrest shall have been made.

**History:**
RS 1846, Ch. 148, § 19.

**Prior codification:**
CL 1929, § 17714; CL 1915, § 14777; HOW § 8957; CL 1897, § 10550; CL 1871, § 7380; CL 1857, § 5593.

**Michigan Digest references:**
Civil Arrest and Bail §§81 et seq, 90.
Criminal Law and Procedure § 739.
Prisons and Jails §§4, 6.
Process § 38.

**Research references:**
60 Am Jur 2d, Penal and Correctional Institutions §§8–10.

### § 801.120. Prisoner not deemed escaped; officers or prisoners not liable to civil arrest. [MSA § 28.1769]

Sec. 20. Such conveyance shall not be deemed an escape; nor shall the prisoner so conveyed, or the officers having them in their

## § 801.120      Jails and Workhouses

custody, be liable to arrest on any civil process, while passing through such other county or counties.

**History:**
RS 1846, Ch. 148, § 20.

**Prior codification:**
CL 1929, § 17715; CL 1915, § 14778; HOW § 8958; CL 1897, § 10551; CL 1871, § 7381; CL 1857, § 5594.

**Michigan Digest references:**
Civil Arrest and Bail §§81 et seq, 90.
Criminal Law and Procedure § 739.
Prisons and Jails §§4, 6.
Process § 38.

**Research references:**
60 Am Jur 2d, Penal and Correctional Institutions §§8–10.

# WORK FARMS, FACTORIES AND SHOPS

Act 78, 1917, p 145, imd eff April 17, 1917.

AN ACT to establish and to provide for the conduct and maintenance of work farms, factories or shops in counties of this State and to authorize the confinement of convicted persons therein and to provide for the punishment of such persons for breaking or attempting to break out; and to permit counties not operating work farms, factories or shops to contract for the care of their prisoners with counties operating such farms, factories or shops.

*The People of the State of Michigan enact:*

## § 801.201. County workhouse; power of county to acquire and own. [MSA § 28.1791]

Sec. 1. The various counties of this state are hereby authorized to acquire, own and hold real estate and buildings within their respective boundaries to be used as work farms, factories or shops for the confinement, punishment and reformation of persons sentenced thereto, and to conduct and operate the same.

**History:**
Pub Acts 1917, No. 78, § 1, imd eff April 17, 1917.

**Prior codification:**
CL 1929, § 17720.

**Michigan Digest references:**
Criminal Law and Procedure §§739, 987.
Prisons and Jails §§1–6.

**L Ed annotations:**
Termination of public employment: right to hearing under due process clause of Fifth or Fourteenth Amendment–Supreme Court cases, 48 L Ed 2d 996.

**ALR notes:**
Validity, construction, and application of statutes making public proceedings open to the public, 38 ALR3d 1070.

**Michigan Civ Jur references:**
Counties § 51.50.

**Research references:**
60 Am Jur 2d, Penal and Correctional Institutions §§3–5, 8–10.

### § 801.202. Commission for management; election, terms, vacancies, eligibility, oath. [MSA § 28.1792]

Sec. 2. The management and direction of such work farms, factories or shops and of the convicted persons sentenced thereto, subject to the periodical visitations of the state authorities at their discretion, shall be under the authority of a nonpartisan commission to be elected for that purpose by the board of supervisors of such county. Said board of commissioners shall consist of three [3] members. The first three [3] members shall be elected by the board of supervisors, at any meeting at which a majority of the members-elect shall decide to operate under this act, as follows: One [1] member for one [1] year from and after January first [1st], following this election, one [1] for two [2] years, one [1] for three [3] years, after said January first [1st]; and annually thereafter at the regular January meeting one [1] member shall be elected for the full term of three [3] years. Vacancies shall be filled by said board of supervisors. The first [1st] commissioners shall assume their duties immediately on election. The commissioners shall be residents of the county which they serve, but no member of the board of supervisors shall be eligible during the term for which he was elected supervisor. The commissioners shall make and subscribe the constitutional oath of office and file the same with the county clerk before assuming their duties.

**History:**
Pub Acts 1917, No. 78, § 2, imd eff April 17, 1917.

**Prior codification:**
CL 1929, § 17721.

**Cross references:**
Form of oath, Const 1963, art XI, § 1.
Supervision and inspection of local jails and houses of correction, § 791.262.

**Michigan Digest references:**
Criminal Law and Procedure §§739, 987.
Prisons and Jails §§1–6.

**L Ed annotations:**
Termination of public employment: right to hearing under due process clause of Fifth or Fourteenth Amendment–Supreme Court cases, 48 L Ed 2d 996.

**ALR notes:**
Validity, construction, and application of statutes making public proceedings open to the public, 38 ALR3d 1070.

**Michigan Civ Jur references:**
Counties § 51.50.

**Research references:**
60 Am Jur 2d, Penal and Correctional Institutions §§3–5, 8–10.

## § 801.203. Adoption of rules; superintendent; appointment, powers, oath, duties, bond; employes; appropriation of moneys. [MSA § 28.1793]

Sec. 3. Said commissioners are hereby authorized and empowered to establish and adopt rules for the regulation and discipline and the work and labor of the persons confined in and on said work farm, factory or shop; and to appoint a superintendent thereof, whose term of office shall be during good behavior, the salary to be fixed by said commission. The superintendent shall have the usual powers of a deputy sheriff, shall take the constitutional oath of office before assuming his duties, same to be filed with the county clerk; and before entering such duties he shall execute to the people of the state of Michigan a bond in the penal sum of five thousand [5,000] dollars, to be approved by said commissioners, and filed with the county clerk, conditioned that he shall faithfully account for all money and property that may come into his hands by virtue of his office and faithfully perform all the duties incumbent upon him as such superintendent, according to law. It shall also be the duty of the commissioners to employ and fix the compensation of such subordinate officers, guards and employes as such commission, with the approval of the board of supervisors, may deem necessary, and prescribe their duties not otherwise prescribed by law, and to make all rules and regulations in relation to the management and government thereof as they may deem expedient. But no appropriation of moneys shall be made by said commission without the sanction of the said board of supervisors by a vote of a majority of all the members-elect.

**History:**
Pub Acts 1917, No. 78, § 3, imd eff April 17, 1917.

**Prior codification:**
CL 1929, § 17722.

**Cross references:**
Form of oath, Const 1963, art XI, § 1.

**Michigan Digest references:**
Criminal Law and Procedure §§739, 987.
Prisons and Jails §§1–6.

**L Ed annotations:**
Termination of public employment: right to hearing under due process clause of Fifth or Fourteenth Amendment–Supreme Court cases, 48 L Ed 2d 996.

**ALR notes:**
Validity, construction, and application of statutes making public proceedings open to the public, 38 ALR3d 1070.

**Michigan Civ Jur references:**
Counties § 51.50.

**Jails and Workhouses** § 801.204

**Research references:**
60 Am Jur 2d, Penal and Correctional Institutions §§3–5, 8–10.

**§ 801.204. Expenses; meetings; duties; rules; record of rules or orders; conflicts of interests; employment of sentenced persons, restrictions; Open Meetings Act, compliance; Freedom of Information Act, compliance.** [MSA § 28.1794]

Sec. 4. (1) The commissioners shall serve without fee or compensation, except actual expenses. They shall hold a meeting on the first Monday of May of each year at the county seat, and other meetings as they shall by rule appoint. One or more commissioners shall visit the work farm, factory, or shop not less than once each month. A meeting of the commissioners on the work farm, factory or shop shall be held once every 3 months, when they shall examine the management, hear and determine all complaints or questions within the province of the superintendent; and shall make rules for the government of the work farm, factory, or shop that are proper and necessary. All rules or orders of the commissioners shall be recorded in a book to be kept for that purpose. A member of the county board of commissioners, commissioners, or an officer or employee of the work farm, factory, or shop shall not be, directly or indirectly, interested in a contract, purchase, or sale for or on account of the work farm, factory or shop. A person sentenced to the work farm, factory, or shop shall not be employed in work in which a member of the county board of commissioners, commissioners, or an officer or employee of the work farm, factory, or shop has a direct or indirect interest.

(2) The business which the commissioners may perform shall be conducted at a public meeting held in compliance with Act No. 267 of the Public Acts of 1976, being sections 15.261 to 15.275 of the Michigan Compiled Laws. Public notice of the time, date, and place of the meeting shall be given in the manner required by Act No. 267 of the Public Acts of 1976.

(3) A writing prepared, owned, used, in the possession of, or retained by the commissioners in the performance of an official function shall be made available to the public in compliance with Act No. 442 of the Public Acts of 1976, being sections 15.231 to 15.246 of the Michigan Compiled Laws.

**History:**
Pub Acts 1917, No. 78, § 4, imd eff April 17, 1917; amended by Pub Acts 1977, No. 193, imd eff November 17, 1977.

**Prior codification:**
CL 1929, § 17723.

**Michigan Digest references:**
Criminal Law and Procedure §§739, 987.
Prisons and Jails §§1–6.

**L Ed annotations:**
Termination of public employment: right to hearing under due process clause of Fifth or Fourteenth Amendment–Supreme Court cases, 48 L Ed 2d 996.

**ALR notes:**
Validity, construction, and application of statutes making public proceedings open to the public, 38 ALR3d 1070.

**Michigan Civ Jur references:**
Counties § 51.50.

**Research references:**
60 Am Jur 2d, Penal and Correctional Institutions §§3–5, 8–10.

## § 801.205. Books of account, contents; quarterly statement; annual balancing. [MSA § 28.1795]

Sec. 5. The books of said work farm, factory or shop shall be so kept as to clearly exhibit the state of the inmates, number received and discharged, and the receipts from and the expenditures for and on account of each line of work, and for repairs or improvements and up-keep of the premises. A quarterly statement shall be made out which shall specify minutely all receipts and expenditures; proper vouchers for each expenditure shall accompany each statement, and the statement shall be filed with the county clerk. The accounts of said work farm shall be annually closed and balanced on December thirty-first [31st] of each year, giving a full account of the operations of the preceding year.

**History:**
Pub Acts 1917, No. 78, § 5, imd eff April 17, 1917.

**Prior codification:**
CL 1929, § 17724.

**Michigan Digest references:**
Criminal Law and Procedure §§739, 987.
Prisons and Jails §§1–6.

**L Ed annotations:**
Termination of public employment: right to hearing under due process clause of Fifth or Fourteenth Amendment–Supreme Court cases, 48 L Ed 2d 996.

**ALR notes:**
Validity, construction, and application of statutes making public proceedings open to the public, 38 ALR3d 1070.

**Michigan Civ Jur references:**
Counties § 51.50.

**Research references:**
60 Am Jur 2d, Penal and Correctional Institutions §§3–5, 8–10.

## § 801.206. Reports to supervisors; removal of officials or employes. [MSA § 28.1796]

Sec. 6. The board of supervisors of such county may require such further reports and exhibits of the condition of the management of such institution as to them may seem necessary and proper, and may, for misconduct or wilful neglect of duty, upon sufficient evidence thereof, after notice and hearing, remove any officer or employe, including the members of said commission.

**Jails and Workhouses** § 801.207

**History:**
Pub Acts 1917, No. 78, § 6, imd eff April 17, 1917.

**Prior codification:**
CL 1929, § 17725.

**Michigan Digest references:**
Criminal Law and Procedure §§739, 987.
Prisons and Jails §§1–6.

**L Ed annotations:**
Termination of public employment: right to hearing under due process clause of Fifth or Fourteenth Amendment–Supreme Court cases, 48 L Ed 2d 996.

**ALR notes:**
Validity, construction, and application of statutes making public proceedings open to the public, 38 ALR3d 1070.

**Michigan Civ Jur references:**
Counties § 51.50.

**Research references:**
60 Am Jur 2d, Penal and Correctional Institutions §§3–5, 8–10.

## § 801.207. Superintendent; duties. [MSA § 28.1797]

Sec. 7. The superintendent of the said work farm, factory or shop shall have entire control and management of all its concerns, subject to said commission, and the rules and regulations adopted for its government. He shall be responsible for the manner in which said work farm, factory or shop is managed and conducted. He shall reside on the premises, devote his entire time and attention to the business thereof and visit and examine into the condition and management of every part of the work, and of each person thereon confined, daily and as often as good order and necessity may require. He shall exercise a general supervision and direction in regard to the discipline, police and business of said work farm, factory or shop.

**History:**
Pub Acts 1917, No. 78, § 7, imd eff April 17, 1917.

**Prior codification:**
CL 1929, § 17726.

**Michigan Digest references:**
Criminal Law and Procedure §§739, 987.
Prisons and Jails §§1–6.

**L Ed annotations:**
Termination of public employment: right to hearing under due process clause of Fifth or Fourteenth Amendment–Supreme Court cases, 48 L Ed 2d 996.

**ALR notes:**
Validity, construction, and application of statutes making public proceedings open to the public, 38 ALR3d 1070.

**Michigan Civ Jur references:**
Counties § 51.50.

**Research references:**
60 Am Jur 2d, Penal and Correctional Institutions §§3–5, 8–10.

## § 801.208. Counties without workhouse, contract with commission; publication. [MSA § 28.1798]

Sec. 8. The board of supervisors of any county of the State, not owning or operating a work farm, factory or shop under the provisions of this act, shall have full power and authority to enter into an agreement with any commission organized under this act to receive and keep in or on their work farm, factory or shop, any person or persons who may be sentenced to confinement by any court or magistrate in any of said counties, for any term of not more than six [6] months. Whenever such agreement shall have been made it shall be the duty of the board of supervisors for any county in behalf of which such agreement shall have been made, to give public notice thereof in some newspaper published within said county.

**History:**
Pub Acts 1917, No. 78, § 8, imd eff April 17, 1917.

**Prior codification:**
CL 1929, § 17727.

**Michigan Digest references:**
Criminal Law and Procedure §§739, 987.
Prisons and Jails §§1–6.

**L Ed annotations:**
Termination of public employment: right to hearing under due process clause of Fifth or Fourteenth Amendment–Supreme Court cases, 48 L Ed 2d 996.

**ALR notes:**
Validity, construction, and application of statutes making public proceedings open to the public, 38 ALR3d 1070.

**Michigan Civ Jur references:**
Counties § 51.50.

**Research references:**
60 Am Jur 2d, Penal and Correctional Institutions §§3–5, 8–10.

## § 801.209. Counties without workhouse, contract with commission; sentence by court to workhouse. [MSA § 28.1799]

Sec. 9. In every county having such agreement, it shall be the duty of every court by whom any person, for any crime or misdemeanor not punishable by imprisonment, in the State prison, may be sentenced for any term of not more than 6 months, to sentence such person to the work farm, factory, or shop there to be received, kept, and employed in a manner prescribed by law and the rules and discipline of the work farm, factory, or shop; and by such warrant and commitment to cause such persons to be forthwith conveyed by some proper officer to work farm, factory, or shop.

**History:**
Pub Acts 1917, No. 78, § 9, imd eff April 17, 1917; amended by Pub Acts 1991, No. 156, imd eff November 25, 1991.

**Prior codification:**
CL 1929, § 17728.

**Michigan Digest references:**
Criminal Law and Procedure §§739, 987.
Prisons and Jails §§1–6.

**L Ed annotations:**
Termination of public employment: right to hearing under due process clause of Fifth or Fourteenth Amendment–Supreme Court cases, 48 L Ed 2d 996.

**ALR notes:**
Validity, construction, and application of statutes making public proceedings open to the public, 38 ALR3d 1070.

**Michigan Civ Jur references:**
Counties § 51.50.

**Research references:**
60 Am Jur 2d, Penal and Correctional Institutions §§3–5, 8–10.

## § 801.210. Transfer of convicted persons to workhouse; employment; fees. [MSA § 28.1800]

Sec. 10. It shall be the duty of the sheriff, constable or other officer in and for any county having such agreement with said commissioners, to whom any warrant or commitment for that purpose may be directed by any court or magistrate in such county, to convey such person so sentenced to the said work farm, factory or shop and there deliver such person to the superintendent or other proper officer of the said work farm, factory or shop, whose duty it shall be to receive such person so sentenced and to safely keep and employ such person for the term mentioned in the warrant or commitment, according to the rules and regulations of the said work farm, factory or shop; the officer thus conveying and so delivering the person or persons so sentenced shall be allowed such fees or compensation therefor as shall be prescribed or allowed by the board of supervisors for the county in which such persons shall have been convicted.

**History:**
Pub Acts 1917, No. 78, § 10, imd eff April 17, 1917.

**Prior codification:**
CL 1929, § 17729.

**Michigan Digest references:**
Criminal Law and Procedure §§739, 987.
Prisons and Jails §§1–6.

**L Ed annotations:**
Termination of public employment: right to hearing under due process clause of Fifth or Fourteenth Amendment–Supreme Court cases, 48 L Ed 2d 996.

**ALR notes:**
Validity, construction, and application of statutes making public proceedings open to the public, 38 ALR3d 1070.

**Michigan Civ Jur references:**
Counties § 51.50.

**Research references:**
60 Am Jur 2d, Penal and Correctional Institutions §§3–5, 8–10.

## § 801.211. Maintenance expense; tax levy. [MSA § 28.1801]

Sec. 11. The expense of maintaining the said work farm, factory or shop, over and above the receipts for labor of persons confined therein and for crops produced thereon, and for the support of those whose support shall not be chargeable to the county, shall be audited and paid from time to time by the board of auditors or the board of supervisors of the county in counties not having boards of auditors, and shall be raised, levied and collected as part of the general expense of said county.

**History:**
Pub Acts 1917, No. 78, § 11, imd eff April 17, 1917.

**Prior codification:**
CL 1929, § 17730.

**Michigan Digest references:**
Criminal Law and Procedure §§739, 987.
Prisons and Jails §§1–6.

**L Ed annotations:**
Termination of public employment: right to hearing under due process clause of Fifth or Fourteenth Amendment–Supreme Court cases, 48 L Ed 2d 996.

**ALR notes:**
Validity, construction, and application of statutes making public proceedings open to the public, 38 ALR3d 1070.

**Michigan Civ Jur references:**
Counties § 51.50.

**Research references:**
60 Am Jur 2d, Penal and Correctional Institutions §§3–5, 8–10.

## § 801.212. Commitment of prisoner, six months limit; employment. [MSA § 28.1802]

Sec. 12. It shall be lawful for any judge of the district or municipal court to commit persons convicted before them to the work farm, factory, or shop for a term not exceeding 6 months, notwithstanding the fact that the law or ordinance under which sentence is passed provides that the respondent shall be committed to another place of detention. And every person so sentenced shall be received upon the work farm, factory, or shop provided the capacity is not already overtaxed, and shall be kept and employed in the manner prescribed herein, and shall be subject to the rules and discipline of the work farm, factory, or shop.

**History:**
Pub Acts 1917, No. 78, § 12, imd eff April 17, 1917; amended by Pub Acts 1991, No. 156, imd eff November 25, 1991.

**Prior codification:**
CL 1929, § 17731.

**Editor's notes:**
Sec. 13. (Repealed.).
Former § 13, which was CL 1929, § 17732, provided penalties for escape

## Jails and Workhouses § 801.215

or attempt to escape. It was repealed by the Penal Code, Pub Acts 1931, No. 328, p 750, eff September 18, 1931 which contains an identical provision.

**Michigan Digest references:**
Criminal Law and Procedure §§739, 987.
Prisons and Jails §§1–6.

**L Ed annotations:**
Termination of public employment: right to hearing under due process clause of Fifth or Fourteenth Amendment–Supreme Court cases, 48 L Ed 2d 996.

**ALR notes:**
Validity, construction, and application of statutes making public proceedings open to the public, 38 ALR3d 1070.

**Michigan Civ Jur references:**
Counties § 51.50.

**Research references:**
60 Am Jur 2d, Penal and Correctional Institutions §§3–5, 8–10.

## § 801.214. Record of infractions; effect of good behavior. [MSA § 28.1803]

Sec. 14. The superintendent of said work farm, factory or shop shall cause to be kept a record of each and allctions of the rules and discipline of such work farm, factory or shop with the names of the person or persons offending, and the date and character of such offense; and every person therein detained whose name does not appear upon such record shall be entitled to a deduction of three [3] days per month from his sentence for each month he shall continue to obey all the rules of the said work farm, factory or shop.

**History:**
Pub Acts 1917, No. 78, § 14, imd eff April 17, 1917.

**Prior codification:**
CL 1929, § 17733.

**Michigan Digest references:**
Prisons and Jails § 2.

**Research references:**
60 Am Jur 2d, Penal and Correctional Institutions §§58, 59, 61–64.

## § 801.215. Realty, powers of commission. [MSA § 28.1804]

Sec. 15. Any real estate which has been or is being used for county work farm, factory or shop purposes shall, immediately upon the election of a commission pursuant to the terms of this act, be turned over to such commission pursuant to this act. And such commission, by and with the approval of a majority of all supervisors-elect of such county, given by vote at some regular meeting or special meeting called for that purpose, may sell such real estate and invest its proceeds in other real estate in said county to be used for like purposes; or in case it is decided to discontinue said farm, factory or shop then the proceeds shall be turned into the general fund of such county.

**History:**
Pub Acts 1917, No. 78, § 15, imd eff April 17, 1917.

**Prior codification:**
CL 1929, § 17734.

## § 801.217. Declaration of necessity. [MSA § 28.1806]

Sec. 17. This act is hereby declared to be immediately necessary for the preservation of the public peace, health and safety.

**History:**
Pub Acts 1917, No. 78, § 17, imd eff April 17, 1917.

**Prior codification:**
CL 1929, § 17736.

# DAY PAROLE OF PRISONERS

Act 60, 1962, p 49, eff March 28, 1963.

AN ACT to provide for the day parole of prisoners in county jails to permit them to be gainfully employed outside the jail or pursue other activities; to provide for the granting of reductions in terms of imprisonment and the regulation thereof; and to provide for the disposition of earnings from such employment. (Amended by Pub Acts 1982, No. 15, imd eff February 25, 1982 (see 1982 note below)).

*The People of the State of Michigan enact:*

**Editor's notes:**
**Pub Acts 1982, No. 15, § 2,** imd eff February 25, 1982, provides:
"Section 2. This amendatory act shall not take effect unless House Bill No. 4276 of the 81st Legislature [which became Act No. 16 of 1982] is enacted into law."

## § 801.251. Privilege of leaving jail during necessary and reasonable hours; purposes; limitations; "jail" defined. [MSA § 28.1747(1)]

Sec. 1. (1) Except as otherwise provided in subsection (2), a sentence or commitment of a person to a county jail for any reason may grant to the person the privilege of leaving the jail during necessary and reasonable hours for any of the following purposes:
　(a) Seeking employment.
　(b) Working at his or her employment.
　(c) Conducting his or her own self-employed business or occupation, including housekeeping and caring for the needs of his or her family.
　(d) Attendance at an educational institution.
　(e) Medical treatment, substance abuse treatment, mental health counseling, or psychological counseling.
A person may petition the court for such privilege at the time of

**Jails and Workhouses** § 801.252

sentence or commitment, and in the discretion of the court may renew his or her petition. The court may withdraw the privilege at any time by order entered with or without notice.

(2) A person shall not be granted the privileges described in subsection (1), except for the privilege of leaving the jail during necessary and reasonable hours for the purpose of medical treatment, substance abuse treatment, mental health counseling, or psychological counseling, if the person is housed in the jail while serving all or any part of a sentence of imprisonment for any of the following crimes:

(a) Section 145c, 520b, 520c, 520d, or 520g of the Michigan penal code, Act No. 328 of the Public Acts of 1931, being sections 750.145c, 750.520b, 750.520c, 750.520d, and 750.520g of the Michigan Compiled Laws.

(b) Murder in connection with sexual misconduct.

(c) An attempt to commit a crime described in subdivision (a) or (b).

(3) As used in this act, "jail" means a facility that is operated by a county for the detention of persons charged with, or convicted of, criminal offenses or ordinance violations, or persons found guilty of civil or criminal contempt, for not more than 1 year.

**History:**
Pub Acts 1962, No. 60, § 1, eff March 28, 1963; amended by Pub Acts 1987, No. 146, imd eff October 26, 1987.

**Michigan Digest references:**
Garnishment § 42.
Pardons and Paroles §§4 et seq.

**LEXIS-NEXIS™ Michigan analytical references:**
Michigan Law and Practice, Convicts and Prisons § 5.

**Michigan Civ Jur references:**
Counties §§50, 51.

**Research references:**
59 Am Jur 2d, Pardon and Parole §§82, 83.
Mich Pl & Pr (2nd Ed) § 70.318.65.
9 Fed Proc, L Ed, Criminal Procedure § 22:1166.

CASE NOTES

A defendant who is sentenced to a jail term and granted work release privileges may have those work release privileges revoked by the sentencing court without prior notice or hearing without violating either the statute under which the work release privileges were granted or the defendant's due process rights. People v Malmquist (1986) 155 Mich App 521, 400 NW2d 317, app den (1987) 428 Mich 854.

**§ 801.252. Collection of earnings; deposit in trust account; record of account; garnishment of earnings.** [MSA § 28.1747(2)]

Sec. 2. The sheriff, or friend of the court in alimony or nonsupport cases, shall collect the wages or salary of an employed prisoner, or

§ 801.252   Jails and Workhouses

require him to turn over his wages or salary in full when received. The officer shall deposit the same in a trust checking account and keep a ledger showing the status of the account of each prisoner. The wages or salary are not subject to garnishment in the hands of the employer or the officer during the prisoner's term.

**History:**
Pub Acts 1962, No. 60, § 2, eff March 28, 1963.

**Michigan Digest references:**
Garnishment § 42.
Pardons and Paroles §§4 et seq.

**Michigan Civ Jur references:**
Counties §§50, 51.

**Research references:**
59 Am Jur 2d, Pardon and Parole §§82, 83.
Mich Pl & Pr (2nd Ed) § 70.318.65.
9 Fed Proc, L Ed, Criminal Procedure § 22:1166.

## § 801.253. Employed prisoner, liability for board; lunch; accounting for payments; transportation. [MSA § 28.1747(3)]

Sec. 3. A gainfully employed prisoner is liable for the cost of his board in the jail as fixed by the sheriff. If necessarily absent from jail at a meal time, he shall at his request be furnished with an adequate nourishing lunch to carry to work. The sheriff or friend of the court shall charge his account, if he has one, for such board. If the prisoner is gainfully self-employed, he shall pay the sheriff for such board, in default of which his employment privilege is automatically forfeited. If the jail food is furnished directly by the county, the sheriff shall account for and pay the board payments to the county treasurer. The board of supervisors by ordinance may provide that the county furnish or pay for the transportation of employed prisoners to and from their place of employment.

**History:**
Pub Acts 1962, No. 60, § 3, eff March 28, 1963.

**Michigan Digest references:**
Garnishment § 42.
Pardons and Paroles §§4 et seq.

**Michigan Civ Jur references:**
Counties §§50, 51.

**Research references:**
59 Am Jur 2d, Pardon and Parole §§82, 83.
Mich Pl & Pr (2nd Ed) § 70.318.65.
9 Fed Proc, L Ed, Criminal Procedure § 22:1166.

**CASE NOTES**

County has no authority to seek reimbursement from inmate for cost of any medical care provided. Op Atty Gen, February 25, 1976, No. 4957.

## § 801.254. Disbursement of earnings; purposes. [MSA § 28.1747(4)]

Sec. 4. The sheriff or friend of the court shall disburse the wages or salary of an employed prisoner for only the following purposes in the order stated:

(a) Board of the prisoner;

(b) Necessary travel expense to and from work and other incidental expenses of the prisoner;

(c) Support of the prisoner's dependents, if any;

(d) Payment, either in full or ratably, of the prisoner's obligations, acknowledged by him in writing, or which have been reduced to judgment;

(e) The balance, if any, to the prisoner upon his discharge.

**History:**
Pub Acts 1962, No. 60, § 4, eff March 28, 1963.

**Michigan Digest references:**
Garnishment § 42.
Pardons and Paroles §§4 et seq.

**Forms:**
Mic Civ Prac Forms § 71.31.17.

**Michigan Civ Jur references:**
Counties §§50, 51.

**Research references:**
59 Am Jur 2d, Pardon and Parole §§82, 83.
Mich Pl & Pr (2nd Ed) § 70.318.65.
9 Fed Proc, L Ed, Criminal Procedure § 22:1166.

## § 801.255. County department of social welfare; clerk of court; collection and disbursement of earnings. [MSA § 28.1747(5)]

Sec. 5. The board of supervisors by resolution may direct that the functions of the officer under sections 2 or 4, or both, be performed by the county department of social welfare; or, if the board has not so directed, a court of record may order that the prisoner's earnings be collected and disbursed by the clerk of the court. The order shall remain in force until rescinded by the board or the court, whichever made it.

**History:**
Pub Acts 1962, No. 60, § 5, eff March 28, 1963.

**Statutory references:**
Sections 2 and 4, above referred to, are §§801.252 and 801.254.

**Michigan Digest references:**
Garnishment § 42.
Pardons and Paroles §§4 et seq.

**Michigan Civ Jur references:**
Counties §§50, 51.

**Research references:**
59 Am Jur 2d, Pardon and Parole §§82, 83.

Mich Pl & Pr (2nd Ed) § 70.318.65.
9 Fed Proc, L Ed, Criminal Procedure § 22:1166.

## § 801.256. Support of prisoner's dependents; investigation and report. [MSA § 28.1747(6)]

Sec. 6. The county department of social welfare shall at the request of the court investigate and report to the sheriff or friend of the court the amount necessary for support of the prisoner's dependents.

**History:**
Pub Acts 1962, No. 60, § 6, eff March 28, 1963.

**Michigan Digest references:**
Garnishment § 42.
Pardons and Paroles §§4 et seq.

**Michigan Civ Jur references:**
Counties §§50, 51.

**Research references:**
59 Am Jur 2d, Pardon and Parole §§82, 83.
Mich Pl & Pr (2nd Ed) § 70.318.65.
9 Fed Proc, L Ed, Criminal Procedure § 22:1166.

## § 801.257. Reduction of term; approval; exception. [MSA § 28.1747(7)]

Sec. 7. Except as provided in section 5 of the prisoner reimbursement to the county act and section 5a of chapter 171 of the Revised Statutes of 1846, being section 801.5a of the Michigan Compiled Laws, a prisoner may receive, if approved by the court, a reduction of ¼ of his or her term if his or her conduct, diligence, and general attitude merit such reduction.

**History:**
Pub Acts 1962, No. 60, § 7, eff March 28, 1963; amended by Pub Acts 1982, No. 15, imd eff February 25, 1982 (see 1982 note below); 1984, No. 120, imd eff June 1, 1984 (see 1984 note below).

**Editor's notes:**
**Pub Acts 1982, No. 15, § 2,** imd eff February 25, 1982, provides:
"Section 2. This amendatory act shall not take effect unless House Bill No. 4276 of the 81st Legislature [which became Act No. 16 of 1982] is enacted into law."
**Pub Acts 1984, No. 120, § 2,** imd eff June 1, 1984, provides:
"Section 2. This amendatory act shall not take effect unless the following bills of the 82nd Legislature are enacted into law:
"(a) House Bill No. 4589 [which became Act No. 119 of 1984].
"(b) House Bill No. 4590 [which became Act No. 118 of 1984]."

**Statutory references:**
Section 5 of the prisoner reimbursement to the county act, above referred to, is § 801.85; Section 5a of chapter 171 of the Revised Statutes of 1846 is § 801.5a.

**Michigan Digest references:**
Garnishment § 42.
Pardons and Paroles §§4 et seq.

**Michigan Civ Jur references:**
Counties §§50, 51.

**Jails and Workhouses** § 801.261

**Research references:**
59 Am Jur 2d, Pardon and Parole §§82, 83.
Mich Pl & Pr (2nd Ed) § 70.318.65.
9 Fed Proc, L Ed, Criminal Procedure § 22:1166.

**Legal periodicals:**
Koenig, Advocating Consistent Sentencing of Prisoners: Deconstructing the Michigan Myth that Retroactive Application of Lesser Penalties for Crimes Violates the Governor's Power of Commutation, 16 T.M. Cooley L Rev 61 (1999).

### § 801.258. Violation of conditions, effect. [MSA § 28.1747(8)]

Sec. 8. A prisoner who violates any condition specified by the court for his conduct, custody or employment shall be reported by the sheriff to the court, which may then order that the balance of his sentence or commitment be spent in actual confinement and that any earned reduction of his term be forfeited.

**History:**
Pub Acts 1962, No. 60, § 8, eff March 28, 1963.

**Michigan Digest references:**
Garnishment § 42.
Pardons and Paroles §§4 et seq.

**Michigan Civ Jur references:**
Counties §§50, 51.

**Research references:**
59 Am Jur 2d, Pardon and Parole §§82, 83.
Mich Pl & Pr (2nd Ed) § 70.318.65.
9 Fed Proc, L Ed, Criminal Procedure § 22:1166.

---

# WEAPONS, LIQUOR AND CONTROLLED SUBSTANCES IN JAILS

Act 7, 1981, p 24, eff June 1, 1981.

AN ACT to prohibit without authorization the bringing into jails and other specified areas any alcoholic liquor, controlled substances, weapons, and certain other items; the selling or furnishing to prisoners, and the improper disposal of any alcoholic liquor, controlled substances, weapons, and certain other items; the possession or control by prisoners of any alcoholic liquor, controlled substances, weapons, and certain other items; to prescribe a penalty; and to repeal certain acts and parts of acts.

*The People of the State of Michigan enact:*

### § 801.261. Definitions. [MSA § 28.1775(1)]

Sec. 1. As used in this act:
(a) "Alcoholic liquor" means any spiritous, vinous, malt, or fermented liquor, liquid, or compound whether or not medicated,

containing ½ of 1% or more of alcohol by volume and which is or readily can be made suitable as a beverage.

(b) "Controlled substance" means a drug, substance, or immediate precursor in schedules 1 to 5 of part 72 of Act No. 368 of the Public Acts of 1978, as amended, being sections 333.7201 to 333.7231 of the Michigan Compiled Laws.

(c) "Jail" means a municipal or county jail, work-camp, lock-up, holding center, half-way house, community corrections center, house of correction, or any other facility maintained by a municipality or county which houses prisoners.

(d) "Prisoner" means a person incarcerated in a jail or a person committed to a jail for incarceration who is a participant in a work release or vocational or educational study release program.

**History:**
Pub Acts 1981, No. 7, § 1, eff June 1, 1981; amended by Pub Acts 1985, No. 46, imd eff June 14, 1985 (see 1985 note below).

**Editor's notes:**
Pub Acts 1985, No. 46, § 2, imd eff June 14, 1985, provides:
"Section 2. This amendatory act shall not take effect unless all of the following bills of the 83rd Legislature are enacted into law:
"(a) House Bill No. 4392 [which became Act No. 61 of 1985].
"(b) House Bill No. 4393 [which became Act No. 44 of 1985].
"(c) House Bill No. 4394 [which became Act No. 45 of 1985].
"(d) House Bill No. 4396 [which became Act No. 47 of 1985].
"(e) House Bill No. 4403 [which became Act No. 54 of 1985].
"(f) House Bill No. 4398 [which became Act No. 49 of 1985].
"(g) House Bill No. 4404 [which became Act No. 55 of 1985].
"(h) House Bill No. 4401 [which became Act No. 52 of 1985].
"(i) House Bill No. 4399 [which became Act No. 50 of 1985].
"(j) House Bill No. 4417 [which became Act No. 56 of 1985].
"(k) House Bill No. 4400 [which became Act No. 51 of 1985].
"(l) House Bill No. 4423 [which became Act No. 60 of 1985].
"(m) House Bill No. 4402 [which became Act No. 53 of 1985].
"(n) House Bill No. 4397 [which became Act No. 48 of 1985].
"(o) House Bill No. 4418 [which became Act No. 57 of 1985].
"(p) House Bill No. 4421 [which became Act No. 58 of 1985].
"(q) House Bill No. 4422 [which became Act No. 59 of 1985]."

**Federal aspects:**
Prison Possession and Traffic in Contraband Articles. 18 USCS § 1791.

**Michigan Civ Jur references:**
Counties § 51.50.
Intoxicating Liquors § 166.

**Research references:**
60 Am Jur 2d, Penal and Correctional Institutions §§41, 42.

## § 801.262. Weapons in jail prohibited. [MSA § 28.1775(2)]

Sec. 2. (1) Unless authorized by the chief administrator of the jail, a person shall not do either of the following:

(a) Bring into a jail or a building appurtenant to a jail, or onto the grounds used for jail purposes, for the use or benefit of a prisoner, any weapon or other item that may be used to injure a prisoner or other person, or used to assist a prisoner in escaping from jail.

(b) Sell or furnish to a prisoner, or dispose of in a manner that allows a prisoner access to the weapon or other item, any weapon or other item which may be used to injure a prisoner or other person, or used to assist a prisoner in escaping from jail.

(2) Unless authorized by the chief administrator of the jail, a prisoner shall not possess or have under his or her control any weapon or other item that may be used to injure a prisoner or other person, or used to assist a prisoner in escaping from jail.

**History:**
Pub Acts 1981, No. 7, § 2, eff June 1, 1981.

**Federal aspects:**
Prison Possession and Traffic in Contraband Articles. 18 USCS § 1791.

**Michigan Civ Jur references:**
Counties § 51.50.
Intoxicating Liquors § 166.

**Research references:**
60 Am Jur 2d, Penal and Correctional Institutions §§41, 42.

## § 801.263. Alcohol, controlled substances in jail prohibited. [MSA § 28.1775(3)]

Sec. 3. (1) Except as provided in section 4, a person shall not bring into a jail, a building appurtenant to a jail, or the grounds used for jail purposes; sell or furnish to a prisoner; or dispose of in a manner that allows a prisoner access to an alcoholic liquor or controlled substance, any alcoholic liquor or controlled substance.

(2) Except as provided in section 4, a prisoner shall not possess or have under his or her control any alcoholic liquor or controlled substance.

**History:**
Pub Acts 1981, No. 7, § 3, eff June 1, 1981.

**Statutory references:**
Section 4, above referred to, is § 801.264.

**Federal aspects:**
Prison Possession and Traffic in Contraband Articles. 18 USCS § 1791.

**Michigan Civ Jur references:**
Counties § 51.50.
Intoxicating Liquors § 166.

**Research references:**
60 Am Jur 2d, Penal and Correctional Institutions §§41, 42.

## § 801.264. Alcohol, controlled substances in jail, exceptions. [MSA § 28.1775(4)]

Sec. 4. (1) An alcoholic liquor or controlled substance may be brought into a jail or a building appurtenant to a jail, or onto the grounds used for jail purposes; furnished to a prisoner or employee of the jail; and possessed by the prisoner or employee, if a licensed physician certifies in writing that the alcoholic liquor or controlled substance is necessary for the health of the prisoner or employee. The certificate shall contain and specify the quantity of the alcoholic liquor or controlled substance that is to be furnished the prisoner or employee; the name of the prisoner or employee; the time when the alcoholic liquor or controlled substance is to be furnished; and the reason needed. The licensed physician or his or her agent shall deliver the certificate to the chief administrator for his or her approval before furnishing a prisoner or employee of the jail any alcoholic liquor or controlled substance.

(2) Not more than 2 ounces of wine for the use of the clergy, and in addition, 1 ounce of wine for each person receiving communion may be brought into a jail or a building appurtenant to a jail or onto the grounds used for jail purposes by a person of the clergy of any religious denomination for clergy purposes.

**History:**
Pub Acts 1981, No. 7, § 4, eff June 1, 1981.

**Federal aspects:**
Prison Possession and Traffic in Contraband Articles. 18 USCS § 1791.

**Michigan Civ Jur references:**
Counties § 51.50.
Intoxicating Liquors § 166.

**Research references:**
60 Am Jur 2d, Penal and Correctional Institutions §§41, 42.

## § 801.265. Violation as felony; penalty; exception. [MSA § 28.1775(5)]

Sec. 5. (1) Except as provided in subsection (2), a person who violates this act is guilty of a felony punishable by imprisonment for not more than 5 years or a fine of not more than $1,000.00, or both.

(2) If a violation of section 3 involving a controlled substance constitutes the delivery, possession with intent to deliver, or possession of or other action involving a controlled substance that is punishable by imprisonment for more than 5 years under part 74 of the public health code, 1978 PA 368, MCL 333.7401 to 333.7461, the person shall not be prosecuted under this act for that violation.

**History:**
Pub Acts 1981, No. 7, § 5, eff June 1, 1981.
Amended by Pub Acts 1999, No. 28, imd eff May 21, 1999, by enacting § 1 eff August 1, 1999.

**Effect of amendment notes:**
**The 1999 amendment** in subsection (1), substituted "Except as provided in subsection (2), a" for "A", "felony punishable by" for "misdemeanor, subject to a fine of not more than $500.00, or", and "5 years or a fine of not more than $1,000.00" for "1 year"; and added subsection (2).

**Statutory references:**
Section 3, above referred to, is § 801.263.

**Federal aspects:**
Prison Possession and Traffic in Contraband Articles. 18 USCS § 1791.

## Jails and Workhouses § 801.267

**Michigan Civ Jur references:**
Counties § 51.50.
Intoxicating Liquors § 166.

**Research references:**
60 Am Jur 2d, Penal and Correctional Institutions §§41, 42.

### § 801.266. Repeal. [MSA § 28.1775(6)]

Sec. 6. Sections 16 and 17 of chapter 148 of the Revised Statutes of 1846, as amended, being sections 801.116 and 801.117 of the Compiled Laws of 1970, are repealed.

**History:**
Pub Acts 1981, No. 7, § 6, eff June 1, 1981.

**Statutory references:**
Sections 16 and 17 of chapter 148 of the Revised Statutes of 1846, above referred to, are §§801.116 and 801.117.

**Federal aspects:**
Prison Possession and Traffic in Contraband Articles. 18 USCS § 1791.

**Michigan Civ Jur references:**
Counties § 51.50.
Intoxicating Liquors § 166.

**Research references:**
60 Am Jur 2d, Penal and Correctional Institutions §§41, 42.

### § 801.267. Effective date. [MSA § 28.1775(7)]

Sec. 7. This act shall take effect on June 1, 1981.

**History:**
Pub Acts 1981, No. 7, § 7, eff June 1, 1981.

**Federal aspects:**
Prison Possession and Traffic in Contraband Articles. 18 USCS § 1791.

**Michigan Civ Jur references:**
Counties § 51.50.
Intoxicating Liquors § 166.

**Research references:**
60 Am Jur 2d, Penal and Correctional Institutions §§41, 42.

---

# REIMBURSEMENT OF CITIES FOR MEDICAL SUPPLIES OR CARE OF PRISONERS

Act 14, 1982, p 37, imd eff February 25, 1982.

AN ACT to provide for the reimbursement of expenses incurred by cities in providing medical supplies for or medical treatment or attendance of prisoners in city jails; and to provide civil fines for a violation of this act.

*The People of the State of Michigan enact:*

## § 801.301. Reimbursement of city for medical supplies and medical care to prisoners; prisoner or insurance; cooperation of prisoner; violation, fine, restitution. [MSA § 28.1712]

Sec. 1. (1) A city may seek reimbursement for expenses incurred in providing medical supplies and medical care and treatment for prisoners. If a city seeks reimbursement pursuant to this act, reimbursement shall be sought only in the following order:

(a) From the prisoner or person charged.

(b) From insurance companies, health care corporations, or other sources if the prisoner or person charged is covered by an insurance policy, a certificate issued by a health care corporation, or other source for those expenses.

(2) A prisoner in a city jail shall cooperate with the city in seeking reimbursement under subsection (1) for medical expenses incurred by the city for that prisoner.

(3) A prisoner who violates subsection (2) is subject to a civil fine of not more than $100.00 and may be required by the court to make restitution to the city in the amount of the medical expenses incurred for that prisoner by the city.

**History:**
Pub Acts 1982, No. 14, § 1, imd eff February 25, 1982.

**Michigan Digest references:**
Prisons and Jails §§4, 4.5.

**LEXIS-NEXIS™ Michigan analytical references:**
Michigan Law and Practice, Convicts and Prisons § 4.

**Research references:**
60 Am Jur 2d, Penal and Correctional Institutions § 16.

# CHAPTER 802

# HOUSES OF CORRECTION

## DETROIT HOUSE OF CORRECTION [Repealed]

### Act 164 of 1861 [Repealed]

§§802.1–802.21 [Repealed]

## ADMINISTRATION AND OPERATION OF WOMEN'S DIVISION [Repealed]

### Act 189 of 1975 [Repealed]

§§802.31–802.35 [Repealed]

### Act 131 of 1867 [Repealed]

§ 802.51 [Repealed]
§ 802.52 [Repealed]
§§802.53–802.55 [Repealed]
§§802.57, 802.58 [Repealed]

### Act 145 of 1869 [Repealed]

§§802.101–802.111 [Repealed]

### Act 10 of 1887 [Repealed]

§§802.151, 802.152 [Repealed]

### Act 64 of 1927 [Repealed]

§ 802.181 [Repealed]

## HOUSES OF CORRECTION IN CITIES [Repealed]

### Act 278 of 1911 [Repealed]

§§802.201–802.204 [Repealed]
§ 802.205 [Repealed]

## DETROIT HOUSE OF CORRECTION [Repealed]

Act 164, 1861, p 262, eff June 15, 1861.
[Repealed]

AN ACT to establish the Detroit house of correction and authorize the confinement of convicted persons and persons awaiting trial or sentence. (Amended by Pub Acts 1970, No. 183, imd eff August 3, 1970.).

## §§802.1–802.21. [Repealed] [MSA §§28.1811–28.1830]

**History:**
Pub Acts 1861, No. 164, eff June 15, 1861; **repealed** by Pub Acts 1985, No. 55, imd eff June 14, 1985 (see 1985 note below); **repealed** by Pub Acts 1985, No. 62, imd eff June 14, 1985.

**Editor's notes:**
**Pub Acts 1985, No. 55,** § **3,** imd eff June 14, 1985, provides:
"Section 3. This amendatory act shall not take effect unless all of the following bills of the 83rd Legislature are enacted into law:
"(a) House Bill No. 4392 [which became Act No. 61 of 1985].
"(b) House Bill No. 4393 [which became Act No. 44 of 1985].
"(c) House Bill No. 4395 [which became Act No. 46 of 1985].
"(d) House Bill No. 4394 [which became Act No. 45 of 1985].
"(e) House Bill No. 4396 [which became Act No. 47 of 1985].
"(f) House Bill No. 4403 [which became Act No. 54 of 1985].
"(g) House Bill No. 4398 [which became Act No. 49 of 1985].
"(h) House Bill No. 4401 [which became Act No. 52 of 1985].
"(i) House Bill No. 4399 [which became Act No. 50 of 1985].
"(j) House Bill No. 4417 [which became Act No. 56 of 1985].
"(k) House Bill No. 4400 [which became Act No. 51 of 1985].
"(l) House Bill No. 4423 [which became Act No. 60 of 1985].
"(m) House Bill No. 4402 [which became Act No. 53 of 1985].
"(n) House Bill No. 4397 [which became Act No. 48 of 1985].
"(o) House Bill No. 4418 [which became Act No. 57 of 1985].
"(p) House Bill No. 4421 [which became Act No. 58 of 1985].
"(q) House Bill No. 4422 [which became Act No. 59 of 1985]."
Sec. 18. (Repealed.).
Former § 18, which was CL 1929, § 17754, prescribed penalties for escapes or attempted escapes from the Detroit House of Correction. It was repealed by the Penal Code, Pub Acts 1931, No. 328, eff September 18, 1931, which contains a provision superseding it. See § 750.194.

# ADMINISTRATION AND OPERATION OF WOMEN'S DIVISION [Repealed]

Act 189, 1975, p 406, imd eff August 5, 1975.
[Repealed]

AN ACT to authorize the department of corrections to assume administration and operation of the women's division of the Detroit house of correction; to receive misdemeanant and felony prisoners from other government agencies for custody, care, and maintenance; to charge those agencies for the custody, care, and maintenance of those prisoners; and to supersede portions of certain acts.

## §§802.31–802.35. [Repealed] [MSA §§28.1860(1)–28.1860(5)]

**History:**
Pub Acts 1975, No. 189, imd eff August 5, 1975; **terminated** by its own definition, eff August 5, 1977.

**Houses of Correction** § 802.52

Act 131, 1867, p 175, eff June 27, 1867.
[Repealed]

AN ACT supplementary to an act entitled "An act to establish the Detroit house of correction, and authorize the confinement of convicted persons therein."

### § 802.51. [Repealed] [MSA § 28.1841]

**History:**
Pub Acts 1867, No. 131, eff June 27, 1866; **repealed** by Pub Acts 1985, No. 55, imd eff June 14, 1985 (see 1985 note below); **repealed** by Pub Acts 1985, No. 62, imd eff June 14, 1985.

**Editor's Note:**
Pub Acts 1985, No. 55, § 3, imd eff June 14, 1985, provides:
"Section 3. This amendatory act shall not take effect unless all of the following bills of the 83rd Legislature are enacted into law:
"(a) House Bill No. 4392 [which became Act No. 61 of 1985].
"(b) House Bill No. 4393 [which became Act No. 44 of 1985].
"(c) House Bill No. 4395 [which became Act No. 46 of 1985].
"(d) House Bill No. 4394 [which became Act No. 45 of 1985].
"(e) House Bill No. 4396 [which became Act No. 47 of 1985].
"(f) House Bill No. 4403 [which became Act No. 54 of 1985].
"(g) House Bill No. 4398 [which became Act No. 49 of 1985].
"(h) House Bill No. 4401 [which became Act No. 52 of 1985].
"(i) House Bill No. 4399 [which became Act No. 50 of 1985].
"(j) House Bill No. 4417 [which became Act No. 56 of 1985].
"(k) House Bill No. 4400 [which became Act No. 51 of 1985].
"(l) House Bill No. 4423 [which became Act No. 60 of 1985].
"(m) House Bill No. 4402 [which became Act No. 53 of 1985].
"(n) House Bill No. 4397 [which became Act No. 48 of 1985].
"(o) House Bill No. 4418 [which became Act No. 57 of 1985].
"(p) House Bill No. 4421 [which became Act No. 58 of 1985].
"(q) House Bill No. 4422 [which became Act No. 59 of 1985]."

### § 802.52. [Repealed] [MSA § 28.1842]

**History:**
Pub Acts 1867, No. 131, eff June 27, 1866; **repealed** by Pub Acts 1972, No. 179, imd eff June 16, 1972; **repealed** by Pub Acts 1985, No. 55, imd eff June 14, 1985 (see 1985 note below); **repealed** by Pub Acts 1985, No. 62, imd eff June 14, 1985.

**Editor's notes:**
Pub Acts 1985, No. 55, § 3, imd eff June 14, 1985, provides:
"Section 3. This amendatory act shall not take effect unless all of the following bills of the 83rd Legislature are enacted into law:
"(a) House Bill No. 4392 [which became Act No. 61 of 1985].
"(b) House Bill No. 4393 [which became Act No. 44 of 1985].
"(c) House Bill No. 4395 [which became Act No. 46 of 1985].
"(d) House Bill No. 4394 [which became Act No. 45 of 1985].
"(e) House Bill No. 4396 [which became Act No. 47 of 1985].
"(f) House Bill No. 4403 [which became Act No. 54 of 1985].
"(g) House Bill No. 4398 [which became Act No. 49 of 1985].
"(h) House Bill No. 4401 [which became Act No. 52 of 1985].
"(i) House Bill No. 4399 [which became Act No. 50 of 1985].
"(j) House Bill No. 4417 [which became Act No. 56 of 1985].
"(k) House Bill No. 4400 [which became Act No. 51 of 1985].
"(l) House Bill No. 4423 [which became Act No. 60 of 1985].
"(m) House Bill No. 4402 [which became Act No. 53 of 1985].

§ 802.52                                                              Houses of Correction

"(n) House Bill No. 4397 [which became Act No. 48 of 1985].
"(o) House Bill No. 4418 [which became Act No. 57 of 1985].
"(p) House Bill No. 4421 [which became Act No. 58 of 1985].
"(q) House Bill No. 4422 [which became Act No. 59 of 1985]."

## §§802.53–802.55. [Repealed]    [MSA §§28.1843–28.1845]

**History:**
    Pub Acts 1867, No. 131, eff June 27, 1866; **repealed** by Pub Acts 1985, No. 55, imd eff June 14, 1985 (see 1985 note below); **repealed** by Pub Acts 1985, No. 62, imd eff June 14, 1985.

**Editor's notes:**
    **Pub Acts 1985, No. 55, § 3,** imd eff June 14, 1985, provides:
    "Section 3. This amendatory act shall not take effect unless all of the following bills of the 83rd Legislature are enacted into law:
    "(a) House Bill No. 4392 [which became Act No. 61 of 1985].
    "(b) House Bill No. 4393 [which became Act No. 44 of 1985].
    "(c) House Bill No. 4395 [which became Act No. 46 of 1985].
    "(d) House Bill No. 4394 [which became Act No. 45 of 1985].
    "(e) House Bill No. 4396 [which became Act No. 47 of 1985].
    "(f) House Bill No. 4403 [which became Act No. 54 of 1985].
    "(g) House Bill No. 4398 [which became Act No. 49 of 1985].
    "(h) House Bill No. 4401 [which became Act No. 52 of 1985].
    "(i) House Bill No. 4399 [which became Act No. 50 of 1985].
    "(j) House Bill No. 4417 [which became Act No. 56 of 1985].
    "(k) House Bill No. 4400 [which became Act No. 51 of 1985].
    "(l) House Bill No. 4423 [which became Act No. 60 of 1985].
    "(m) House Bill No. 4402 [which became Act No. 53 of 1985].
    "(n) House Bill No. 4397 [which became Act No. 48 of 1985].
    "(o) House Bill No. 4418 [which became Act No. 57 of 1985].
    "(p) House Bill No. 4421 [which became Act No. 58 of 1985].
    "(q) House Bill No. 4422 [which became Act No. 59 of 1985]."

## §§802.57, 802.58. [Repealed]    [MSA §§28.1847, 28.1848]

**History:**
    Pub Acts 1867, No. 131, eff June 27, 1866; **repealed** by Pub Acts 1985, No. 55, imd eff June 14, 1985 (see 1985 note below); **repealed** by Pub Acts 1985, No. 62, imd eff June 14, 1985.

**Editor's Note:**
    **Pub Acts 1985, No. 55, § 3,** imd eff June 14, 1985, provides:
    "Section 3. This amendatory act shall not take effect unless all of the following bills of the 83rd Legislature are enacted into law:
    "(a) House Bill No. 4392 [which became Act No. 61 of 1985].
    "(b) House Bill No. 4393 [which became Act No. 44 of 1985].
    "(c) House Bill No. 4395 [which became Act No. 46 of 1985].
    "(d) House Bill No. 4394 [which became Act No. 45 of 1985].
    "(e) House Bill No. 4396 [which became Act No. 47 of 1985].
    "(f) House Bill No. 4403 [which became Act No. 54 of 1985].
    "(g) House Bill No. 4398 [which became Act No. 49 of 1985].
    "(h) House Bill No. 4401 [which became Act No. 52 of 1985].
    "(i) House Bill No. 4399 [which became Act No. 50 of 1985].
    "(j) House Bill No. 4417 [which became Act No. 56 of 1985].
    "(k) House Bill No. 4400 [which became Act No. 51 of 1985].
    "(l) House Bill No. 4423 [which became Act No. 60 of 1985].
    "(m) House Bill No. 4402 [which became Act No. 53 of 1985].
    "(n) House Bill No. 4397 [which became Act No. 48 of 1985].
    "(o) House Bill No. 4418 [which became Act No. 57 of 1985].
    "(p) House Bill No. 4421 [which became Act No. 58 of 1985].
    "(q) House Bill No. 4422 [which became Act No. 59 of 1985]."

**Houses of Correction** 802.152

Act 145, 1869, p 264, eff July 5, 1869.
[Repealed]

AN ACT to provide for the imprisonment and detention of convicted persons in the Detroit house of correction.

### §§802.101–802.111. [Repealed] [MSA §§28.1861–28.1871]

**History:**
Pub Acts 1869, No. 145, eff July 5, 1869; **repealed** by Pub Acts 1985, No. 55, imd eff June 14, 1985 (see 1985 note below); **repealed** by Pub Acts 1985, No. 62, imd eff June 14, 1985.

**Editor's notes:**
**Pub Acts 1985, No. 55,** § **3,** imd eff June 14, 1985, provides:
"Section 3. This amendatory act shall not take effect unless all of the following bills of the 83rd Legislature are enacted into law:
"(a) House Bill No. 4392 [which became Act No. 61 of 1985].
"(b) House Bill No. 4393 [which became Act No. 44 of 1985].
"(c) House Bill No. 4395 [which became Act No. 46 of 1985].
"(d) House Bill No. 4394 [which became Act No. 45 of 1985].
"(e) House Bill No. 4396 [which became Act No. 47 of 1985].
"(f) House Bill No. 4403 [which became Act No. 54 of 1985].
"(g) House Bill No. 4398 [which became Act No. 49 of 1985].
"(h) House Bill No. 4401 [which became Act No. 52 of 1985].
"(i) House Bill No. 4399 [which became Act No. 50 of 1985].
"(j) House Bill No. 4417 [which became Act No. 56 of 1985].
"(k) House Bill No. 4400 [which became Act No. 51 of 1985].
"(l) House Bill No. 4423 [which became Act No. 60 of 1985].
"(m) House Bill No. 4402 [which became Act No. 53 of 1985].
"(n) House Bill No. 4397 [which became Act No. 48 of 1985].
"(o) House Bill No. 4418 [which became Act No. 57 of 1985].
"(p) House Bill No. 4421 [which became Act No. 58 of 1985].
"(q) House Bill No. 4422 [which became Act No. 59 of 1985]."

Act 10, 1887, p 9, imd eff February 5, 1887.
[Repealed]

AN ACT to provide for the confinement of certain prisoners in the Detroit house of correction.

### §§802.151, 802.152. [Repealed] [MSA §§28.1881, 28.1882]

**History:**
Pub Acts 1887, No. 10, imd eff February 5, 1887; **repealed** by Pub Acts 1985, No. 55, imd eff June 14, 1985 (see 1985 note below); **repealed** by Pub Acts 1985, No. 62, imd eff June 14, 1985.

**Editor's notes:**
**Pub Acts 1985, No. 55,** § **3,** imd eff June 14, 1985, provides:
"Section 3. This amendatory act shall not take effect unless all of the following bills of the 83rd Legislature are enacted into law:
"(a) House Bill No. 4392 [which became Act No. 61 of 1985].
"(b) House Bill No. 4393 [which became Act No. 44 of 1985].
"(c) House Bill No. 4395 [which became Act No. 46 of 1985].
"(d) House Bill No. 4394 [which became Act No. 45 of 1985].
"(e) House Bill No. 4396 [which became Act No. 47 of 1985].
"(f) House Bill No. 4403 [which became Act No. 54 of 1985].
"(g) House Bill No. 4398 [which became Act No. 49 of 1985].
"(h) House Bill No. 4401 [which became Act No. 52 of 1985].
"(i) House Bill No. 4399 [which became Act No. 50 of 1985].

"(j) House Bill No. 4417 [which became Act No. 56 of 1985].
"(k) House Bill No. 4400 [which became Act No. 51 of 1985].
"(l) House Bill No. 4423 [which became Act No. 60 of 1985].
"(m) House Bill No. 4402 [which became Act No. 53 of 1985].
"(n) House Bill No. 4397 [which became Act No. 48 of 1985].
"(o) House Bill No. 4418 [which became Act No. 57 of 1985].
"(p) House Bill No. 4421 [which became Act No. 58 of 1985].
"(q) House Bill No. 4422 [which became Act No. 59 of 1985].″

Act 64, 1927, p 81, eff September 5, 1927.
[Repealed]

AN ACT relating to confinement of prisoners in the Detroit house of correction, and providing for compensation therefor.

## § 802.181. [Repealed] [MSA § 28.1891]

**History:**
Pub Acts 1927, No. 64, eff September 5, 1927; **repealed** by Pub Acts 1985, No. 55, imd eff June 14, 1985 (see 1985 note below); **repealed** by Pub Acts 1985, No. 62, imd eff June 14, 1985.

**Editor's notes:**
**Pub Acts 1985, No. 55, § 3,** imd eff June 14, 1985, provides:
"Section 3. This amendatory act shall not take effect unless all of the following bills of the 83rd Legislature are enacted into law:
"(a) House Bill No. 4392 [which became Act No. 61 of 1985].
"(b) House Bill No. 4393 [which became Act No. 44 of 1985].
"(c) House Bill No. 4395 [which became Act No. 46 of 1985].
"(d) House Bill No. 4394 [which became Act No. 45 of 1985].
"(e) House Bill No. 4396 [which became Act No. 47 of 1985].
"(f) House Bill No. 4403 [which became Act No. 54 of 1985].
"(g) House Bill No. 4398 [which became Act No. 49 of 1985].
"(h) House Bill No. 4401 [which became Act No. 52 of 1985].
"(i) House Bill No. 4399 [which became Act No. 50 of 1985].
"(j) House Bill No. 4417 [which became Act No. 56 of 1985].
"(k) House Bill No. 4400 [which became Act No. 51 of 1985].
"(l) House Bill No. 4423 [which became Act No. 60 of 1985].
"(m) House Bill No. 4402 [which became Act No. 53 of 1985].
"(n) House Bill No. 4397 [which became Act No. 48 of 1985].
"(o) House Bill No. 4418 [which became Act No. 57 of 1985].
"(p) House Bill No. 4421 [which became Act No. 58 of 1985].
"(q) House Bill No. 4422 [which became Act No. 59 of 1985].″

# HOUSES OF CORRECTION IN CITIES [Repealed]

Act 278, 1911, p 479, eff August 1, 1911.
[Repealed]

AN ACT to authorize the establishment of houses of correction in cities and to authorize the sentencing of persons convicted of crime thereto, and the confinement and detention of persons charged with or convicted of crime therein, and to fix and prescribe the duties and powers of all city, state and county officers with regard thereto.

**Houses of Correction** § 802.205

## §§802.201–802.204. [Repealed] [MSA §§28.1901–28.1904]

**History:**
Pub Acts 1911, No. 278, eff August 1, 1911; **repealed** by Pub Acts 1985, No. 62, imd eff June 14, 1985.

## § 802.205. [Repealed] [MSA § 28.1905]

**History:**
Pub Acts 1911, No. 278, eff August 1, 1911; **repealed** by Pub Acts 1985, No. 55, imd eff June 14, 1985 (see 1985 note below); **repealed** by Pub Acts 1985, No. 62, imd eff June 14, 1985.

**Editor's notes:**
**Pub Acts 1985, No. 55, § 3,** imd eff June 14, 1985, provides:
"Section 3. This amendatory act shall not take effect unless all of the following bills of the 83rd Legislature are enacted into law:
 "(a) House Bill No. 4392 [which became Act No. 61 of 1985].
 "(b) House Bill No. 4393 [which became Act No. 44 of 1985].
 "(c) House Bill No. 4395 [which became Act No. 46 of 1985].
 "(d) House Bill No. 4394 [which became Act No. 45 of 1985].
 "(e) House Bill No. 4396 [which became Act No. 47 of 1985].
 "(f) House Bill No. 4403 [which became Act No. 54 of 1985].
 "(g) House Bill No. 4398 [which became Act No. 49 of 1985].
 "(h) House Bill No. 4401 [which became Act No. 52 of 1985].
 "(i) House Bill No. 4399 [which became Act No. 50 of 1985].
 "(j) House Bill No. 4417 [which became Act No. 56 of 1985].
 "(k) House Bill No. 4400 [which became Act No. 51 of 1985].
 "(l) House Bill No. 4423 [which became Act No. 60 of 1985].
 "(m) House Bill No. 4402 [which became Act No. 53 of 1985].
 "(n) House Bill No. 4397 [which became Act No. 48 of 1985].
 "(o) House Bill No. 4418 [which became Act No. 57 of 1985].
 "(p) House Bill No. 4421 [which became Act No. 58 of 1985].
 "(q) House Bill No. 4422 [which became Act No. 59 of 1985]."

# CHAPTER 803

# YOUTH TRAINING AND REHABILITATION

## HOUSE OF CORRECTION FOR JUVENILE OFFENDERS [Repealed]

### Act 78 of 1855 [Repealed]

§§803.11–803.15 [Repealed]
§ 803.23 [Repealed]

## MICHIGAN INDUSTRIAL SCHOOL FOR BOYS [Repealed]

### Act 114 of 1893 [Repealed]

§§803.51–803.55 [Repealed]

## BOYS' TRAINING SCHOOL [Repealed]

### Act 185 of 1925 [Repealed]

§§803.101–803.113 [Repealed]

## ACQUISITION OF NEW, SALE OF OLD LAND AND FACILITIES FOR BOYS' VOCATIONAL SCHOOL

### Act 20 of 1946 (Ex Sess) [Repealed]

§§803.201–803.209 [Repealed]

### Act 181 of 1956

| | |
|---|---|
| § 803.211 | Boys' vocational school; acquisition of site; studies, plans; approval required. |
| § 803.212 | Appropriation. |
| § 803.213 | Assistance in carrying out purposes of act. |
| § 803.214 | Release of appropriations; reversion of unexpended balance; appropriation not deemed future commitment. |
| § 803.215 | Other provisions repealed. |

## THE JUVENILE FACILITIES ACT

### Act 73 of 1988

| | |
|---|---|
| § 803.221 | Short title. |
| § 803.222 | Definitions. |
| § 803.223 | Annual report. |
| § 803.224 | Inquiry; report. |
| § 803.225 | Commitment report; petition to conduct review hearing; combining annual report with review hearing. |
| § 803.225a | Community placement and discharge from wardship; chemical testing for DNA identification profiling; providing samples; manner; consent; hearing or court order not required; "sample" defined. |
| § 803.226 | Contracts. |
| § 803.227 | Conditional effective date. |
| § 803.228 | Effective date. |

## YOUTH REHABILITATION SERVICES ACT

### Act 150 of 1974

| | |
|---|---|
| § 803.301 | Short title. |
| § 803.302 | Definitions. |
| § 803.302a | County as county juvenile agency; powers; revocation of authorization. |
| § 803.303 | Youth agency; powers and duties. |
| § 803.304 | Youth agency; additional powers and duties. |
| § 803.305 | Cost of public ward's care. |
| § 803.306 | Absence of public ward from facility or residence; penalty. |
| § 803.306a | Escape from facility or residence; notification; orders; applicability of subsection (1); "escape" defined. |
| § 803.307 | Duration of public wardship; discharge or release; delayed sentence; sentencing as adult offender. |
| § 803.307a | Chemical testing for DNA identification; samples provided by public ward; collection; transmission to department of state police; manner; rules; consent, hearing, or court hearing not required; "sample" defined. |
| § 803.308 | Records confidential; exceptions. |
| § 803.309 | Repeal; references in repealed statutes. |

## REHABILITATION CAMP FOR MALE DELINQUENT YOUTH

### Act 229 of 1962

| | |
|---|---|
| § 803.317 | Conservation rehabilitation camp for male delinquent youth; establishment; operations; program; trainees; camp facilities. |

## REHABILITATION CAMP FOR MALE DELINQUENT YOUTH

### Act 145 of 1963

| | |
|---|---|
| § 803.321 | Establishment of camp. |
| § 803.322 | Selection of trainees; custody. |
| § 803.323 | Appropriation; cost of facilities. |

## Camp LaVictoire

### Act 145 of 1965

| | |
|---|---|
| § 803.331 | Camp LaVictoire; transfer to social welfare department. |
| § 803.332 | Preparation and execution of documents. |
| § 803.333 | Operation as conservation-rehabilitation camp. |

# HOUSE OF CORRECTION FOR JUVENILE OFFENDERS [Repealed]

### Act 78, 1855
### [Repealed]

**§§803.11–803.15.  [Repealed]**   [MSA §§28.1932–28.1936]

**History:**
Pub Acts 1855, No. 78, imd eff February 10, 1855; **repealed** by Pub Acts 1949, No. 31, eff September 23, 1949.

§ 803.23. [Repealed] [MSA § 28.1938]

**History:**
Pub Acts 1855, No. 78, imd eff February 10, 1855; **repealed** by Pub Acts 1949, No. 31, eff September 23, 1949.

## MICHIGAN INDUSTRIAL SCHOOL FOR BOYS [Repealed]

Act 114, 1893, p 155, imd eff May 26, 1893.
[Repealed]

AN ACT to provide for a board of trustees for the management and control of the Michigan industrial school for boys and to repeal all acts in conflict with this act.

§§803.51–803.55. [Repealed] [MSA §§28.1951–28.1955]

**History:**
Pub Acts 1893, No. 114, imd eff May 26, 1893; **repealed** by Pub Acts 1949, No. 30, eff September 23, 1949.

## BOYS' TRAINING SCHOOL [Repealed]

Act 185, 1925, p 263, eff August 27, 1925.
[Repealed]

AN ACT to provide a state agency for the correction, education, care and protection of boys in conflict with society; to establish a boys' training school under the control of the Michigan social welfare commission; to prescribe who may be admitted thereto, the powers and duties of the officers immediately in charge of said school, the character and extent of education, discipline and training to be enforced and provided therein; to provide for the temporary use of other state facilities in certain cases of boys committed to the state department of social welfare; to provide for the temporary use of the boys' training school by the counties and at the expense of the counties for the care of delinquent boys who are mentally or physically unable to profit from the education provided therein; and to provide penalties for violations of certain provisions of this act. (Amended by Pub Acts 1944 (Ex Sess), No. 10, imd eff February 19, 1944; 1953, No. 122, eff October 2, 1953; 1961, No. 13, imd eff May 9, 1961.).

§§803.101-803.113. [Repealed] [MSA §§28.1961-28.1973]

**History:**
Pub Acts 1925, No. 185, eff August 27, 1925; **repealed** by Pub Acts 1974, No. 150, imd eff June 12, 1974.

**Editor's notes:**
For current provisions, see Youth Rehabilitation Services Act, §§803.301 et seq.

## ACQUISITION OF NEW, SALE OF OLD LAND AND FACILITIES FOR BOYS' VOCATIONAL SCHOOL

Act 20, 1946 (Ex Sess), p 41, imd eff February 26, 1946.
[Repealed]

AN ACT to provide for the acquisition of adequate lands and facilities for the boys' vocational school, and the disposition of the present site and facilities; to prescribe the powers and duties of the state administrative board; and to prescribe the powers and duties of certain state officials, boards and commissions with respect thereto. (Amended by Pub Acts 1947, No. 177, imd eff June 11, 1947.).

§§803.201-803.209. [Repealed] [MSA §§28.1984(1)-28.1984(9)]

**History:**
Pub Acts 1946 (Ex Sess), No. 20, imd eff February 26, 1893; **repealed** by Pub Acts 1956, No. 181, imd eff April 16, 1956.

Act 181, 1956, p 336, imd eff April 16, 1956.

AN ACT to authorize the department of social welfare to acquire options on a site for and to purchase, subject to the approval of the state administrative board, a site for a boys' vocational school; to authorize planning for site utilization and the preparation of plans; to make appropriations therefor and to repeal certain acts and parts of acts.

*The People of the State of Michigan enact:*

### § 803.211. Boys' vocational school; acquisition of site; studies, plans; approval required. [MSA § 28.1984(11)]

Sec. 1. The department of social welfare is authorized and directed to obtain options and to purchase a site or sites for the location of a boys' vocational school, to make studies and investigations as to size and type of construction for said school and to prepare preliminary plans and obtain the estimated cost thereof: Provided, That any purchase of a site or sites shall be subject to approval by the state administrative board as to price and accounting procedures.

**History:**
Pub Acts 1956, No. 181, § 1, imd eff April 16, 1956.

## § 803.212. Appropriation. [MSA § 28.1984(12)]

Sec. 2. For the purposes of section 1 there is hereby appropriated the sum of $200,000.00 from the general fund of the state. The amounts hereby appropriated shall be paid out of the state treasury at such times and in such manner as is or may be provided by law.

**History:**
Pub Acts 1956, No. 181, § 2, imd eff April 16, 1956.

**Statutory references:**
Section 1, above referred to, is § 803.211.

## § 803.213. Assistance in carrying out purposes of act. [MSA § 28.1984(13)]

Sec. 3. The department of social welfare is authorized to call upon any state agency for assistance in carrying out the purposes of this act.

**History:**
Pub Acts 1956, No. 181, § 3, imd eff April 16, 1956.

## § 803.214. Release of appropriations; reversion of unexpended balance; appropriation not deemed future commitment. [MSA § 28.1984(14)]

Sec. 4. Expenditures under the provisions of this act shall be authorized when the release of the appropriations is approved by the state administrative board. No agency included within the provisions of this act shall make any commitments for any project until after the release of the appropriation. The board may approve the release of a part of any appropriation for the purpose of preparing such plans or for such studies or investigations as may be necessary.

It is hereby provided that any unexpended balance in any of the appropriations made under this act shall not revert to the fund from which appropriated at the close of the fiscal year, but shall continue until the purposes for which the same were appropriated have been completed.

Any appropriation under the provisions of this act for preliminary plans shall not be deemed a commitment on the part of the legislature for any future appropriations.

**History:**
Pub Acts 1956, No. 181, § 4, imd eff April 16, 1956.

## § 803.215. Other provisions repealed. [MSA § 28.1984(15)]

Sec. 5. Act No. 20 of the Public Acts of the first extra session of 1946, as amended, being sections 803.201 to 803.209, inclusive, is hereby repealed.

**History:**
Pub Acts 1956, No. 181, § 5, imd eff April 16, 1956.

## THE JUVENILE FACILITIES ACT

Act 73, 1988, p 200, imd eff March 28, 1988.

An act to provide for certain responsibilities and duties of the family independence agency and county juvenile agencies and certain facilities, institutions, and agencies; and to provide for the preparation of certain reports pertaining to certain juveniles. (Amended by Pub Acts 1998, No. 521, imd eff January 12, 1999 (see 1998 note below).).

*The People of the State of Michigan enact:*

**Editor's notes:**
**Pub Acts 1998, No. 521, enacting § 1,** imd eff January 12, 1999, provides:
"Enacting section 1. This amendatory act does not take effect unless all of the following bills of the 89th Legislature are enacted into law:
"(a) Senate Bill No. 1183 [Pub Acts 1998, No. 516].
"(b) Senate Bill No. 1184 [Pub Acts 1998, No. 517].
"(c) Senate Bill No. 1185 [Pub Acts 1998, No. 518].
"(d) Senate Bill No. 1186 [Pub Acts 1998, No. 519].
"(e) Senate Bill No. 1187 [Pub Acts 1998, No. 478].
"(f) Senate Bill No. 1196 [Pub Acts 1998, No. 528].
"(g) Senate Bill No. 1197 [Pub Acts 1998, No. 529]."

**Effect of amendment notes:**
**The 1998 amendment** substituted "family independence agency and county juvenile agencies" for "department of social services".

### § 803.221. Short title. [MSA § 25.399(221)]

Sec. 1. This act shall be known and may be cited as "the juvenile facilities act".

### § 803.222. Definitions. [MSA § 25.399(222)]

Sec. 2. As used in this act:
(a) "County juvenile agency" means that term as defined in section 2 of the county juvenile agency act.
(b) "Department" means the family independence agency.
(c) "Juvenile" means a person within the jurisdiction of the family division of the circuit court under section 2(a) of chapter XIIA of 1939 PA 288, MCL 712A.2, or within the jurisdiction of the circuit court under section 606 of the revised judicature act of 1961, 1961 PA 236, MCL 600.606.
(d) "Juvenile facility" means a county facility, an institution operated as an agency of the county or the family division of circuit court, or an institution or agency described in the youth rehabilitation services act, 1974 PA 150, MCL 803.301 to 803.309, to which a juvenile has been committed under section 18(1)(e) of chapter XIIA of 1939 PA 288, MCL 712A.18, or under section 27a of chapter IV or section 1 of chapter IX of the code of criminal procedure, 1927 PA 175, MCL 764.27a and 769.1.

**Youth Training and Rehabilitation** § 803.223

**History:**
Pub Acts 1988, No. 73, § 2, imd eff March 28, 1988.
Amended by Pub Acts 1996, No. 416, by § 2 eff January 1, 1998 (see 1996 note below); 1998, No. 521, imd eff January 12, 1999 (see 1998 note below).

**Editor's notes:**
**Pub Acts 1996, No. 416,** § **3,** by § 2 eff January 1, 1998, provides:
"Section 3. This amendatory act shall not take effect unless Senate Bill No. 1052 of the 88th Legislature [Pub Acts 1996, No. 388] is enacted into law."
**Pub Acts 1998, No. 521, enacting** § **1,** imd eff January 12, 1999, provides:
"Enacting section 1. This amendatory act does not take effect unless all of the following bills of the 89th Legislature are enacted into law:
"(a) Senate Bill No. 1183 [Pub Acts 1998, No. 516].
"(b) Senate Bill No. 1184 [Pub Acts 1998, No. 517].
"(c) Senate Bill No. 1185 [Pub Acts 1998, No. 518].
"(d) Senate Bill No. 1186 [Pub Acts 1998, No. 519].
"(e) Senate Bill No. 1187 [Pub Acts 1998, No. 478].
"(f) Senate Bill No. 1196 [Pub Acts 1998, No. 528].
"(g) Senate Bill No. 1197 [Pub Acts 1998, No. 529]."

**Effect of amendment notes:**
**The 1996 amendment** in paragraph (a) substituted "family independence agency" for "department of social services"; in paragraph (b) substituted "family division of the circuit court" for "juvenile division of the probate court"; and in paragraph (c), substituted "or the family division of the circuit court" for "or the juvenile division of the probate court".
**The 1998 amendment** added paragraph (a); redesignated former paragraphs (a)–(c) as (b)–(d); changed the style of statutory references throughout; in paragraph (d), as redesignated, substituted "an" for "a state" preceding "institution"; and made grammatical changes.

**Statutory references:**
Section 2 of the county juvenile agency act is § 45.622.

## § 803.223. Annual report. [MSA § 25.399(223)]

Sec. 3. If a juvenile is committed to a juvenile facility, the department or county juvenile agency, as applicable, shall prepare for the court that committed the juvenile an annual report stating the services being provided to the juvenile, where the juvenile has been placed, and the juvenile's progress in that placement.

**History:**
Pub Acts 1988, No. 73, § 3, imd eff March 28, 1988.
Amended by Pub Acts 1998, No. 521, imd eff January 12, 1999 (see 1998 note below).

**Editor's notes:**
**Pub Acts 1998, No. 521, enacting** § **1,** imd eff January 12, 1999, provides:
"Enacting section 1. This amendatory act does not take effect unless all of the following bills of the 89th Legislature are enacted into law:
"(a) Senate Bill No. 1183 [Pub Acts 1998, No. 516].
"(b) Senate Bill No. 1184 [Pub Acts 1998, No. 517].
"(c) Senate Bill No. 1185 [Pub Acts 1998, No. 518].
"(d) Senate Bill No. 1186 [Pub Acts 1998, No. 519].
"(e) Senate Bill No. 1187 [Pub Acts 1998, No. 478].
"(f) Senate Bill No. 1196 [Pub Acts 1998, No. 528].
"(g) Senate Bill No. 1197 [Pub Acts 1998, No. 529]."

**Effect of amendment notes:**
The **1998 amendment** inserted "or county juvenile agency, as applicable,"; inserted "an" preceding "annual" and substituted "report" for "reports".

## § 803.224. Inquiry; report. [MSA § 25.399(224)]

Sec. 4. (1) If a juvenile within the jurisdiction of the circuit court under section 606 of the revised judicature act of 1961, 1961 PA 236, MCL 600.606, is committed to a juvenile facility pending trial, the department or county juvenile agency, as applicable, shall inquire into the juvenile's antecedents, character, and circumstances and shall report in writing to the court before the juvenile's sentencing.

(2) A report prepared under subsection (1) shall include all of the following:

(a) An evaluation of and a prognosis for the juvenile's adjustment in the community based on factual information contained in the report.

(b) A recommendation as to whether the juvenile is more likely to be rehabilitated by the services and facilities available in adult programs and procedures than in juvenile programs and procedures.

(c) A recommendation as to what disposition is in the best interests of the public welfare and the protection of the public security.

**History:**
Pub Acts 1988, No. 73, § 4, imd eff March 28, 1988.
Amended by Pub Acts 1996, No. 416, by § 2 eff January 1, 1998 (see 1996 note below); 1998, No. 521, imd eff January 12, 1999 (see 1998 note below).

**Editor's notes:**
**Pub Acts 1996, No. 416, § 3,** by § 2 eff January 1, 1998, provides:
"Section 3. This amendatory act shall not take effect unless Senate Bill No. 1052 of the 88th Legislature [Pub Acts 1996, No. 388] is enacted into law."

**Pub Acts 1998, No. 521, enacting § 1,** imd eff January 12, 1999, provides:
"Enacting section 1. This amendatory act does not take effect unless all of the following bills of the 89th Legislature are enacted into law:
"(a) Senate Bill No. 1183 [Pub Acts 1998, No. 516].
"(b) Senate Bill No. 1184 [Pub Acts 1998, No. 517].
"(c) Senate Bill No. 1185 [Pub Acts 1998, No. 518].
"(d) Senate Bill No. 1186 [Pub Acts 1998, No. 519].
"(e) Senate Bill No. 1187 [Pub Acts 1998, No. 478].
"(f) Senate Bill No. 1196 [Pub Acts 1998, No. 528].
"(g) Senate Bill No. 1197 [Pub Acts 1998, No. 529]."

**Effect of amendment notes:**
The **1996 amendment** made grammatical changes.
The **1998 amendment** changed the style of statutory reference; deleted ", or within the jurisdiction of the recorder's court of the city of Detroit under section 10a(1)(c) of Act No. 369 of the Public Acts of 1919, being section 725.10a of the Michigan Compiled Laws" following the statutory reference; and inserted "or county juvenile agency, as applicable,".

## § 803.225. Commitment report; petition to conduct review hearing; combining annual report with review hearing. [MSA § 25.399(225)]

Sec. 5. (1) Before a juvenile hearing under section 18d of chapter XIIA of 1939 PA 288, MCL 712A.18d, or under section 1b of chapter IX of the code of criminal procedure, 1927 PA 175, MCL 769.1b, the department or county juvenile agency, as applicable, shall prepare a commitment report for the court. A commitment report shall include all of the following:

(a) The services and programs currently being utilized by, or offered to, the juvenile and the juvenile's participation in those services and programs.

(b) Where the juvenile currently resides and the juvenile's behavior in his or her current placement.

(c) The juvenile's efforts toward rehabilitation.

(d) Recommendations for the juvenile's release or continued custody.

(2) If the department or county juvenile agency, as applicable, believes that the juvenile has been rehabilitated and does not present a serious risk to public safety, the department or county juvenile agency may petition the court to conduct a review hearing at any time before the juvenile becomes 19 years of age or, if the committing court has continued jurisdiction over the juvenile, at any time before the juvenile becomes 21 years of age.

(3) The annual report required by section 3 may be combined with a review hearing under this section.

**History:**
Pub Acts 1988, No. 73, § 5, imd eff March 28, 1988.
Amended by Pub Acts 1998, No. 521, imd eff January 12, 1999 (see 1998 note below).

**Editor's notes:**
**Pub Acts 1998, No. 521, enacting § 1,** imd eff January 12, 1999, provides:
"Enacting section 1. This amendatory act does not take effect unless all of the following bills of the 89th Legislature are enacted into law:
"(a) Senate Bill No. 1183 [Pub Acts 1998, No. 516].
"(b) Senate Bill No. 1184 [Pub Acts 1998, No. 517].
"(c) Senate Bill No. 1185 [Pub Acts 1998, No. 518].
"(d) Senate Bill No. 1186 [Pub Acts 1998, No. 519].
"(e) Senate Bill No. 1187 [Pub Acts 1998, No. 478].
"(f) Senate Bill No. 1196 [Pub Acts 1998, No. 528].
"(g) Senate Bill No. 1197 [Pub Acts 1998, No. 529]."

**Effect of amendment notes:**
**The 1998 amendment** in subsection (1), changed the style of statutory references and inserted "or county juvenile agency, as applicable"; and in subsection (2), inserted "or county juvenile agency, as possible", inserted "or county juvenile agency" preceding "may", and made grammatical changes.

**Statutory references:**
Section 3 is § 803.223.

## § 803.225a. Community placement and discharge from wardship; chemical testing for DNA identification profiling; providing samples; manner; consent; hearing or court order not required; "sample" defined. [MSA § 25.399(225a)]

Sec. 5a. (1) A juvenile convicted of or found responsible for a violation of section 91, 316, or 317 of the Michigan penal code, 1931 PA 328, MCL 750.91, 750.316, and 750.317, or a violation or attempted violation of section 349, 520b, 520c, 520d, 520e, or 520g of the Michigan penal code, 1931 PA 328, MCL 750.349, 750.520b, 750.520c, 750.520d, 750.520e, and 750.520g, who is under the supervision of the department or a county juvenile agency under section 18 of chapter XIIA of 1939 PA 288, MCL 712A.18, shall not be placed in a community placement of any kind and shall not be discharged from wardship until he or she has provided samples for chemical testing for DNA identification profiling or a determination of the sample's genetic markers and has provided samples for a determination of his or her secretor status. However, if, at the time the juvenile is to be discharged from wardship, the department of state police already has a sample from the juvenile that meets the requirements of the rules promulgated under the DNA identification profiling system act, 1990 PA 250, MCL 28.171 to 28.176, the juvenile is not required to provide another sample.

(2) The samples required to be collected under this section shall be collected by the department or county juvenile agency, as applicable, and transmitted by the department or county juvenile agency to the department of state police in the manner prescribed by rules promulgated under the DNA identification profiling system act, 1990 PA 250, MCL 28.171 to 28.176.

(3) The department or county juvenile agency may collect a sample under this section regardless of whether the juvenile consents to the collection. The department or county juvenile agency is not required to give the juvenile an opportunity for a hearing or obtain a court order before collecting the sample.

(4) As used in this section, "sample" means a portion of a juvenile's blood, saliva, or tissue collected from the juvenile.

**History:**
Pub Acts 1988, No. 73, § 5a, as added by Pub Acts 1996, No. 511, imd eff January 9, 1997, by § 2 eff January 1, 1997 (see 1996 note below); amended by Pub Acts 1998, No. 521, imd eff January 12, 1999 (see 1998 note below).

**Editor's notes:**
**Pub Acts 1996, No. 511, § 3,** imd eff January 9, 1997, by § 2 eff January 1, 1997, provides:
"Section 3. This amendatory act shall not take effect unless all of the following bills of the 88th Legislature are enacted into law:
"(a) House Bill No. 5783 [Pub Acts 1996, No. 507].
"(b) House Bill No. 5912 [Pub Acts 1996, No. 508].
"(c) House Bill No. 6062 [Pub Acts 1996, No. 512]."
**Pub Acts 1998, No. 521, enacting § 1,** imd eff January 12, 1999, provides:
"Enacting section 1. This amendatory act does not take effect unless all of the following bills of the 89th Legislature are enacted into law:

**Youth Training and Rehabilitation** § 803.227

"(a) Senate Bill No. 1183 [Pub Acts 1998, No. 516].
"(b) Senate Bill No. 1184 [Pub Acts 1998, No. 517].
"(c) Senate Bill No. 1185 [Pub Acts 1998, No. 518].
"(d) Senate Bill No. 1186 [Pub Acts 1998, No. 519].
"(e) Senate Bill No. 1187 [Pub Acts 1998, No. 478].
"(f) Senate Bill No. 1196 [Pub Acts 1998, No. 528].
"(g) Senate Bill No. 1197 [Pub Acts 1998, No. 529]."

**Effect of amendment notes:**
**The 1998 amendment** changed the style of statutory references throughout; in subsection 91), substituted "department or a county juvenile agency" for "family independence agency"; in subsection (2), inserted "or county juvenile agency, as applicable" and inserted "or county juvenile agency" preceding "to"; and in subsection (3), inserted "or county juvenile agency" in two instances.

### § 803.226. Contracts. [MSA § 25.399(226)]

Sec. 6. The department and a county juvenile agency may enter into contracts necessary to carry out the duties and responsibilities of this act.

**History:**
Pub Acts 1988, No. 73, § 6, imd eff March 28, 1988.
Amended by Pub Acts 1998, No. 521, imd eff January 12, 1999 (see 1998 note below).

**Editor's notes:**
**Pub Acts 1998, No. 521, enacting § 1,** imd eff January 12, 1999, provides:
"Enacting section 1. This amendatory act does not take effect unless all of the following bills of the 89th Legislature are enacted into law:
"(a) Senate Bill No. 1183 [Pub Acts 1998, No. 516].
"(b) Senate Bill No. 1184 [Pub Acts 1998, No. 517].
"(c) Senate Bill No. 1185 [Pub Acts 1998, No. 518].
"(d) Senate Bill No. 1186 [Pub Acts 1998, No. 519].
"(e) Senate Bill No. 1187 [Pub Acts 1998, No. 478].
"(f) Senate Bill No. 1196 [Pub Acts 1998, No. 528].
"(g) Senate Bill No. 1197 [Pub Acts 1998, No. 529]."

**Effect of amendment notes:**
**The 1998 amendment** inserted "and a county juvenile agency".

### § 803.227. Conditional effective date. [MSA § 25.399(227)]

Sec. 7. This act shall not take effect unless all of the following bills of the 84th Legislature are enacted into law:
(a) House Bill No. 4731.
(b) House Bill No. 4733.
(c) House Bill No. 4741.
(d) House Bill No. 4748.
(e) House Bill No. 4750.
(f) House Bill No. 5203.
(g) Senate Bill No. 137.
(h) Senate Bill No. 604.
(i) Senate Bill No. 605.
(j) Senate Bill No. 607.
(k) Senate Bill No. 608.
(l) Senate Bill No. 609.

## § 803.228. Effective date. [MSA § 25.399(228)]

Sec. 8. This act shall take effect October 1, 1988.

**History:**
Added by Pub Acts 1988, No. 73, imd eff March 28; as amended by Pub Acts 1988, No. 176, imd eff June 21.

# YOUTH REHABILITATION SERVICES ACT

Act 150, 1974, p 327, imd eff June 12, 1974.

An act to provide for the acceptance, care, and discharge of youths committed as public wards; to prescribe the liability for the cost of services for public wards; to prescribe procedures for the return of public wards who absent themselves without permission; to provide a penalty for the violation of this act; and to repeal acts and parts of acts. (Amended by Pub Acts 1996, No. 512, imd eff January 9, 1997, by § 2 eff January 1, 1997 (see 1996 note below); 1998, No. 517, imd eff January 12, 1999 (see 1998 note below).).

*The People of the State of Michigan enact:*

**Editor's notes:**
**Pub Acts 1996, No. 512,** § **3,** imd eff January 9, 1997, by § 2 eff January 1, 1997, provides:

"Section 3. This amendatory act shall not take effect unless all of the following bills of the 88th Legislature are enacted into law:
"(a) House Bill No. 5783 [Pub Acts 1996, No. 507].
"(b) House Bill No. 5912 [Pub Acts 1996, No. 508].
"(c) House Bill No. 6061 [Pub Acts 1996, No. 511]."

**Pub Acts 1998, No. 517, enacting** § **1,** imd eff January 12, 1999, provides:

"Enacting section 1. This amendatory act does not take effect unless all of the following bills of the 89th Legislature are enacted into law:
"(a) Senate Bill No. 1183 [Pub Acts 1998, No. 516].
"(b) Senate Bill No. 1185 [Pub Acts 1998, No. 518].
"(c) Senate Bill No. 1186 [Pub Acts 1998, No. 519].
"(d) Senate Bill No. 1187 [Pub Acts 1998, No. 478].
"(e) Senate Bill No. 1196 [Pub Acts 1998, No. 528].
"(f) Senate Bill No. 1197 [Pub Acts 1998, No. 529]."

**Effect of amendment notes:**
**The 1996 amendment** inserted a comma after the word "acceptance"; deleted "and"; inserted ", and discharge"; deleted "of social services" and "certain".

**The 1998 amendment** substituted "as public" for "to the department as state"; deleted "of counties" following "liability"; and substituted "public" for "state" in two instances.

## § 803.301. Short title. [MSA § 25.399(51)]

Sec. 1. This act shall be known and may be cited as the "youth rehabilitation services act".

**Cross references:**
Social welfare department, powers and duties, see § 400.14.

**Youth Training and Rehabilitation** § 803.302

**Michigan Digest references:**
Probate Courts § 28.

§ **803.302. Definitions.** [MSA § 25.399(52)]

Sec. 2. As used in this act:

(a) "County juvenile agency" means that term as defined in section 2 of the county juvenile agency act.

(b) "Department" means the family independence agency.

(c) "Public ward" means either of the following:

(i) A youth accepted for care by a youth agency who is at least 12 years of age when committed to the youth agency by the juvenile division of the probate court or the family division of circuit court under section 18(1)(e) of chapter XIIA of 1939 PA 288, MCL 712A.18, if the court acquired jurisdiction over the youth under section 2(a) or (d) o f chapter XIIA of 1939 PA 288, MCL 712A.2, and the act for which the youth is committed occurred before his or her seventeenth birthday.

(ii) A youth accepted for care by a youth agency who is at least 14 years of age when committed to the youth agency by a court of general criminal jurisdiction under section 1 of chapter IX of the code of criminal procedure, 1927 PA 175, MCL 769.1, if the act for which the youth is committed occurred before his or her seventeenth birthday.

(d) "Youth agency" means either the department or a county juvenile agency, whichever has responsibility over a public ward.

**History:**
Pub Acts 1974, No. 150, § 2, imd eff June 12, 1974; amended by Pub Acts 1988, No. 76, imd eff March 28, 1988, by § 3 eff October 1, 1988 (see 1988 note below).
Amended by Pub Acts 1996, No. 253, imd eff June 12, 1996, by § 2 eff January 1, 1997 (see 1996 note below); 1996, No. 417, by § 2 eff January 1, 1998 (see 1996 note below); 1998, No. 517, imd eff January 12, 1999 (see 1998 note below).

**Editor's notes:**
**Pub Acts 1988, No. 76,** § **2,** imd eff March 28, 1988, by § 3 eff October 1, 1988 (amended by Pub Acts 1988, No. 179, § 1), provides:
"Section 2. This amendatory act shall not take effect unless all of the following bills of the 84th Legislature are enacted into law:
"(a) House Bill No. 4731 [which became Act No. 51 of 1988].
"(b) House Bill No. 4733 [which became Act No. 52 of 1988].
"(c) House Bill No. 4741 [which became Act No. 53 of 1988].
"(d) House Bill No. 4748 [which became Act No. 67 of 1988].
"(e) House Bill No. 4750 [which became Act No. 54 of 1988].
"(f) House Bill No. 5203 [which became Act No. 182 of 1988].
"(g) Senate Bill No. 137 [which became Act No. 64 of 1988].
"(h) Senate Bill No. 601 [which became Act No. 73 of 1988].
"(i) Senate Bill No. 604 [which became Act No. 74 of 1988].
"(j) Senate Bill No. 605 [which became Act No. 75 of 1988].
"(k) Senate Bill No. 608 [which became Act No. 77 of 1988].
"(l) Senate Bill No. 609 [which became Act No. 78 of 1988]."
**Pub Acts 1996, No. 253,** § **3,** imd eff June 12, 1996, by § 2 eff January 1, 1997, provides:
"Section 3. This amendatory act shall not take effect unless all of the following bills of the 88th Legislature are enacted into law:

"(a) Senate Bill No. 281 [Pub Acts 1996, No. 248].
"(b) Senate Bill No. 283 [Pub Acts 1996, No. 249].
"(c) Senate Bill No. 682 [Pub Acts 1996, No. 244].
"(d) Senate Bill No. 689 [Pub Acts 1996, No. 250].
"(e) Senate Bill No. 699 [Pub Acts 1996, No. 247].
"(f) Senate Bill No. 724 [Pub Acts 1996, No. 254].
"(g) Senate Bill No. 867 [Pub Acts 1996, No. 255].
"(h) Senate Bill No. 870 [Pub Acts 1996, No. 256].
"(i) House Bill No. 4037 [Pub Acts 1996, No. 257].
"(j) House Bill No. 4038 [Pub Acts 1996, No. 258].
"(k) House Bill No. 4044 [Pub Acts 1996, No. 245].
"(l) House Bill No. 4371 [Pub Acts 1996, No. 246].
"(m) House Bill No. 4445 [Pub Acts 1996, No. 259].
"(n) House Bill No. 4486 [Pub Acts 1996, No. 260].
"(o) House Bill No. 4487 [Pub Acts 1996, No. 261].
"(p) House Bill No. 4490 [Pub Acts 1996, No. 262]."

**Pub Acts 1996, No. 417,** § 3, by § 2 eff January 1, 1998, provides:
"Section 3. This amendatory act shall not take effect unless Senate Bill No. 1052 of the 88th Legislature [Pub Acts 1996, No. 388] is enacted into law."

**Pub Acts 1998, No. 517, enacting** § 1, imd eff January 12, 1999, provides:
"Enacting section 1. This amendatory act does not take effect unless all of the following bills of the 89th Legislature are enacted into law:
"(a) Senate Bill No. 1183 [Pub Acts 1998, No. 516].
"(b) Senate Bill No. 1185 [Pub Acts 1998, No. 518].
"(c) Senate Bill No. 1186 [Pub Acts 1998, No. 519].
"(d) Senate Bill No. 1187 [Pub Acts 1998, No. 478].
"(e) Senate Bill No. 1196 [Pub Acts 1998, No. 528].
"(f) Senate Bill No. 1197 [Pub Acts 1998, No. 529]."

**Effect of amendment notes:**
**The first 1996 amendment (Pub Act 253)** in paragraph (a), replaced "state department of social services" with "family independence agency."; in paragraph (b), subparagraph (ii), replaced "15" with "14"; and made grammatical changes.

**The second 1996 amendment (Pub Act 417)** in paragraph (b), subparagraph (i), substituted "the" for "a" and inserted "court or the family division of circuit"; and in paragraph (b), subparagraph (ii), substituted "person" for "youth".

**The 1998 amendment** added paragraphs (a) and (d); redesignated former paragraphs (a) and (b) as (b) and (c); substantially revised paragraph (c) as redesignated and changed the style of statutory references therein.

**Statutory references:**
Section 2 of the county juvenile agency act is § 45.622.

**Michigan Digest references:**
Probate Courts § 28.

**LEXIS-NEXIS™ Michigan analytical references:**
Michigan Law and Practice, Convicts and Prisons § 2.

### CASE NOTES

**1-10. [Reserved for use in future supplementation.]**

**11. Construction and effect.**

A private foster home is in many ways the private counterpart to state institutions under purview of department of social welfare charged with caring for dependent, neglected and delinquent children, and these state institutions are distinguished from "public schools" by §§340.251 and 400.207. Traverse City Sch. Dist. v AG (1971) 384 Mich 390, 185 NW2d 9.

Neither state social welfare commission nor state administrative board has authority to grant easement to state highway department or to city of Lansing for construction of way open to public travel over property owned by state and used in connection with boys' vocational school; special legislative authorization would be required for granting of such easement. Op Atty Gen, November 18, 1955, No. 2327.

Interpretation of former § 803.102, prior to 1953 amendment, with respect to admission of certain types of boys to boys' vocational school. Op Atty Gen, September 22, 1947, No. 585.

## § 803.302a. County as county juvenile agency; powers; revocation of authorization. [MSA § 25.399(52a)]

Sec. 2a. (1) On the date a county becomes a county juvenile agency under the county juvenile agency act, the county juvenile agency shall assume responsibility for all public wards for which the department had responsibility and for which the county had financial liability under section 5 immediately before the county became a county juvenile agency.

(2) If the county revokes authorization for the county juvenile agency under the county juvenile agency act, the department shall assume responsibility for the public wards for which the county juvenile agency had responsibility on the effective date of revocation.

**History:**
Pub Acts 1974, No. 150, § 2a, as added by Pub Acts 1998, No. 517, imd eff January 12, 1999 (see 1998 note below).

**Editor's notes:**
Pub Acts 1998, No. 517, enacting § 1, imd eff January 12, 1999, provides:
"Enacting section 1. This amendatory act does not take effect unless all of the following bills of the 89th Legislature are enacted into law:
"(a) Senate Bill No. 1183 [Pub Acts 1998, No. 516].
"(b) Senate Bill No. 1185 [Pub Acts 1998, No. 518].
"(c) Senate Bill No. 1186 [Pub Acts 1998, No. 519].
"(d) Senate Bill No. 1187 [Pub Acts 1998, No. 478].
"(e) Senate Bill No. 1196 [Pub Acts 1998, No. 528].
"(f) Senate Bill No. 1197 [Pub Acts 1998, No. 529]."

**Statutory references:**
Section 5, above referred to, is § 803.305.

**Michigan Digest references:**
Probate Courts § 28.

## § 803.303. Youth agency; powers and duties. [MSA § 25.399(53)]

Sec. 3. (1) A youth agency may receive and accept youths as public wards for purposes of care and rehabilitation. A youth agency shall accept a youth properly committed to it in accordance with law. Only 1 youth agency has responsibility for a youth at any time. The department shall not receive or accept youths as public wards for a county if that county is a county juvenile agency that assumed responsibility for public wards committed by the juvenile division of

§ 803.303          Youth Training and Rehabilitation

probate court, family division of circuit court, or court of general criminal jurisdiction for that county.

(2) Custody of a public ward under this act is as follows:

(a) If the department accepts the youth or responsibility for the youth is transferred to the department as provided in section 2a, the state, represented by the department director or his or her designate, has custody from the time of acceptance until the youth is discharged from wardship under section 7 or responsibility for the youth is transferred to a county juvenile agency under section 2a.

(b) If a county juvenile agency accepts the youth or responsibility for the youth is transferred to the county juvenile agency under section 2a, the county has custody from the time of acceptance or transfer until the youth is discharged from wardship under section 7 or responsibility for the youth is transferred to the department under section 2a. For custody purposes, the county is represented by the county department director designated by the following:

(i) For a county that has adopted a charter under 1966 PA 293, MCL 45.501 to 45.521, the county executive or chief administrative officer.

(ii) For a county that has adopted an optional unified form of county government under 1973 PA 139, MCL 45.551 to 45.573, the county executive or county manager.

(iii) For a county not described in subparagraph (i) or (ii), the county board of commissioners.

(3) If a public ward is placed in a residential facility other than his or her own home, the youth agency shall provide the youth's food, clothing, housing, educational, medical, and treatment needs. The youth agency may consent to routine nonsurgical medical care or to emergency medical treatment of the youth, but consent for nonemergency elective surgery shall be given by the youth's parent or legal guardian. If a public ward is placed in his or her own home, the youth agency shall provide counseling services and may establish reasonable conditions under which the youth will be permitted to remain in the home, but the youth's parents retain all other parental rights and duties.

**History:**
Pub Acts 1974, No. 150, § 3, imd eff June 12, 1974.
Amended by Pub Acts 1998, No. 517, imd eff January 12, 1999 (see 1998 note below).

**Editor's notes:**
**Pub Acts 1998, No. 517, enacting § 1,** imd eff January 12, 1999, provides:
"Enacting section 1. This amendatory act does not take effect unless all of the following bills of the 89th Legislature are enacted into law:
"(a) Senate Bill No. 1183 [Pub Acts 1998, No. 516].
"(b) Senate Bill No. 1185 [Pub Acts 1998, No. 518].
"(c) Senate Bill No. 1186 [Pub Acts 1998, No. 519].
"(d) Senate Bill No. 1187 [Pub Acts 1998, No. 478].
"(e) Senate Bill No. 1196 [Pub Acts 1998, No. 528].
"(f) Senate Bill No. 1197 [Pub Acts 1998, No. 529]."

## Youth Training and Rehabilitation § 803.304

**Effect of amendment notes:**
The **1998 amendment** substantially revised the former section and divided the section into subsections (1), (2) and (3).

**Statutory references:**
Sections 2a and 7, above referred to, are §§803.302a and 803.307.

**Michigan Digest references:**
Probate Courts § 28.

### § 803.304. Youth agency; additional powers and duties.
[MSA § 25.399(54)]

Sec. 4. (1) A youth agency may establish facilities and programs for the care of public wards. A youth agency shall supervise and operate facilities and programs or contract for the care of public wards, including institutions, halfway houses, youth camps, diagnostic centers, regional detention facilities and treatment centers, group homes, supervision in the community, or other child welfare services.

(2) A youth agency may utilize the facilities, services, or personnel of any approved agency of this state and its political subdivisions or of any licensed private agency for the care and rehabilitation of public wards. A youth agency may contract with the family division of circuit court for the care and rehabilitation of public wards.

(3) A youth agency may supervise a public ward placed in private home care.

(4) A public ward may be placed in any facility, residence, or program described in this section. If the youth agency determines the best interests of a public ward require the involvement of another state or county entity, other than the department of corrections, then the youth agency and that state or county entity shall determine an appropriate care and treatment plan for the public ward. A youth agency may place a public ward in a mental institution under the mental health code, 1974 PA 258, MCL 330.1001 to 330.2106, unless the public ward resides with his or her parents. If the public ward resides with his or her parents, placement in a mental institution requires consent of the custodial parent. If placement in a mental institution occurs, the public ward shall be returned to the youth agency's custody upon release from the mental institution.

(5) When necessary, a youth agency may place a public ward in a public or private institution or agency incorporated under the laws of another state or country and approved or licensed by that state's or country's approving or licensing agency, provided that the program which the youth agency seeks to place a public ward meets licensing laws, requirements, and rules required for the placement of a public ward with a public or private institution or agency in Michigan. However, if 1 or more appropriate juvenile residential care providers located or doing business in this state have bed space available, the youth agency shall use that space rather than a space available by a provider located or doing business in another state. This requirement does not apply if the provider located or doing

business in another state offers a specialized program that is not available in this state. For purposes of placements by the department only, "appropriate juvenile residential care provider" means a private nonprofit entity domiciled in this state that is licensed by the department of consumer and industry services and that entered into 1 or more contracts with the department to provide residential care services for youths on or before the effective date of the amendatory act that added this sentence.

**History:**
Pub Acts 1974, No. 150, § 4, imd eff June 12, 1974; amended by Pub Acts 1984, No. 325, imd eff December 26, 1984; 1988, No. 76, imd eff March 28, 1988, by § 3 eff October 1, 1988 (see 1988 note below).
Amended by Pub Acts 1998, No. 517, imd eff January 12, 1999 (see 1998 note below).

**Editor's notes:**
**Pub Acts 1988, No. 76, § 2,** imd eff March 28, 1988, by § 3 eff October 1, 1988, provides:
"Section 2. This amendatory act shall not take effect unless all of the following bills of the 84th Legislature are enacted into law:
"(a) House Bill No. 4731 [which became Act No. 51 of 1988].
"(b) House Bill No. 4733 [which became Act No. 52 of 1988].
"(c) House Bill No. 4741 [which became Act No. 53 of 1988].
"(d) House Bill No. 4748 [which became Act No. 67 of 1988].
"(e)House Bill No. 4750 [which became Act No. 54 of 1988].
"(f) House Bill No. 5203 [which became Act No. 182 of 1988].
"(g) Senate Bill No. 137 [which became Act No. 64 of 1988].
"(h) Senate Bill No. 601 [which became Act No. 73 of 1988].
"(i) Senate Bill No. 604 [which became Act No. 74 of 1988].
"(j) Senate Bill No. 605 [which became Act No. 75 of 1988].
"(k) Senate Bill No. 608 [which became Act No. 77 of 1988].
"(l) Senate Bill No. 609 [which became Act No. 78 of 1988]."
**Pub Acts 1988, No. 179, § 1,** provides:
"Section 1. Enacting section 3 of Act No. 76 of the Public Acts of 1988 is amended to read as follows:
"Section 3. This amendatory act shall take effect October 1, 1988."
**Pub Acts 1998, No. 517, enacting § 1,** imd eff January 12, 1999, provides:
"Enacting section 1. This amendatory act does not take effect unless all of the following bills of the 89th Legislature are enacted into law:
"(a) Senate Bill No. 1183 [Pub Acts 1998, No. 516].
"(b) Senate Bill No. 1185 [Pub Acts 1998, No. 518].
"(c) Senate Bill No. 1186 [Pub Acts 1998, No. 519].
"(d) Senate Bill No. 1187 [Pub Acts 1998, No. 478].
"(e) Senate Bill No. 1196 [Pub Acts 1998, No. 528].
"(f) Senate Bill No. 1197 [Pub Acts 1998, No. 529]."

**Effect of amendment notes:**
**The 1998 amendment** made the following substitutions throughout: "A youth agency" for "The department", "youth agency" for "department", and "public" for "state"; in subsection (2), substituted "family" for "juvenile" and "circuit" for "the probate"; in subsection (4), deleted "under this act" following "ward", substituted "or county entity" for "agency", substituted "youth" for "department, together with that", inserted "and that state or county entity", substituted "under" for "by the department pursuant to", substituted "requires" for "shall be with the", inserted "in a mental institution", inserted "youth agency's" preceding "custody", deleted "of the department" following "custody", and changed the style of statutory references; substantially revised subsection (5); and made minor grammatical changes.

**Cross references:**
Regulation of state institutions, § 21.71.
State department of social services, §§400.1 et seq.

**Michigan Digest references:**
Probate Courts § 28.

**LEXIS-NEXIS™ Michigan analytical references:**
Michigan Law and Practice, Convicts and Prisons § 2.

### CASE NOTES

**1-10. [Reserved for use in future supplementation.]**

**11. Admission and discharge.**
Under former statute, neither girls nor boys were eligible for parole from such institution for lack of statutory authority and neither girls nor boys were eligible for admission to said institution after reaching seventeenth birthday. Op Atty Gen, May 12, 1952, No. 1539.

Juvenile institute commission was not justified in ruling that new commitment was necessary before inmate of school could be returned thereto after order for admission to mental hospital had been made under former § 330.31. Op Atty Gen, March 13, 1947, No. 185.

Practice of discharging inmate of school when order for admission to hospital had been made by probate court following certificate filed by school superintendent under former § 330.31, was improper. Op Atty Gen, March 13, 1947, No. 185.

Under former statute, it was not mandatory that juvenile institute commission retain jurisdiction over boy in vocational school until he attained age of 19 years, for commission's jurisdiction ended upon boy's graduation, or his discharge from institution. Op Atty Gen, May 8, 1946, No. 0-4591.

Under former statute, boy committed to vocational school remained subject to law governing school, length of time specified in commitment by court being unimportant. Op Atty Gen, May 8, 1946, No. 0-4591.

Under former statute, maximum period of confinement for boy committed prior to February 19, 1946 ended when boy attained age of 17 or 18 years. Op Atty Gen, May 8, 1946, No. 0-4591.

Under former statute, the period of commitment was no longer fixed by court order, but, since the 1944 amendment, by the statutory provisions: until graduation (§ 803.105), until temporary release (§ 803.108), or until the age of 18 (§ 803.109). Op Atty Gen, February 6, 1945, No. 0-3097.

Under former statutes, prior to amendment, boy on parole from industrial school when act became effective and returned for any reason was entitled to allowance on graduation or honorable discharge. Op Atty Gen, 1925-1926, p 132.

**12. Medical care.**
Prior to 1953 amendment of former § 803.102, if boy admitted to school was found not to be free from any chronic or contagious disease or mental or physical defect which would be menace to those already in school, he could be returned to juvenile division of probate court which committed him, where proper medical care or other disposition might be determined upon by court, as provided in § 712A.18. Op Atty Gen, May 17, 1946, No. 0-4692.

**13. Parole.**
Under former statute, boys were not eligible for parole from such institutions for lack of statutory authority. Op Atty Gen, May 12, 1952, No. 1539.

**14. Leave of absence.**
Under former statute, juvenile court had no power to revoke temporary leave of absence granted by boys' vocational school. If boy on leave had committed new offense, court might again take him under its jurisdiction and commit him to school for new offense, or simply notify school of commission of new offense, whereupon superintendent of school might order boy returned to school to be retained until such time as law required that he be discharged. Op Atty Gen, May 17, 1946, No. 0-4692.

Former juvenile institute commission retained jurisdiction of boy while he was on temporary leave of absence. Op Atty Gen, May 8, 1946, No. 0-4591.

## § 803.305. Cost of public ward's care. [MSA § 25.399(55)]

Sec. 5. (1) Except as provided in subsection (3), the county from which the public ward is committed is liable to the state for 50% of the cost of his or her care, but this amount may be reduced by the use of funds from the annual original foster care grant of the state to the county, or otherwise, for any period in respect to which the department has made a finding that the county is unable to bear 50% of the cost of care. If the department reduces a county's liability under this section, the director shall inform the respective chairpersons of the appropriations committees of the senate and house of representatives at least 14 days before granting the reduction. The county of residence of the public ward is liable to the state, rather than the county from which the youth was committed, if the juvenile division of the probate court or the family division of circuit court of the county of residence withheld consent to a transfer of proceedings under section 2 of chapter XIIA of 1939 PA 288, MCL 712A.2, as determined by the department. The finding that the county is unable to bear 50% of the expense shall be based on a study of the financial resources and necessary expenditures of the county made by the department.

(2) The department shall determine the cost of care on a per diem basis using the initial annual allotment of appropriations for the current fiscal year exclusive of capital outlay and the projected occupancy figures upon which that allotment was based. That cost of care applies in determining required reimbursement to the state for care provided during the calendar year immediately following the beginning of the current fiscal year for which the state expenditures were allotted.

(3) A county that is a county juvenile agency is liable for the entire cost of a public ward's care while he or she is committed to the county juvenile agency.

**History:**
Pub Acts 1974, No. 150, § 5, imd eff June 12, 1974; amended by Pub Acts 1980, No. 305, imd eff December 1, 1980 (see 1980 note below); 1984, No. 325, imd eff December 26, 1984.

Amended by Pub Acts 1996, No. 417, by § 2 eff January 1, 1998 (see 1996 note below); 1998, No. 517, imd eff January 12, 1999 (see 1998 note below).

**Editor's notes:**
**Pub Acts 1980, No. 305,** § **2,** imd eff December 1, 1980, provides:
"Section 2. This amendatory act shall not take effect unless the following House Bills of the 1980 regular session of the legislature are enacted into law:
"(a) House Bill No. 5819 [which became Act No. 329 of 1980].
"(b) House Bill No. 5818 [which became Act No. 306 of 1980]."
**Pub Acts 1996, No. 417,** § **3,** by § 2 eff January 1, 1998, provides:
"Section 3. This amendatory act shall not take effect unless Senate Bill No. 1052 of the 88th Legislature [Pub Acts 1996, No. 388] is enacted into law."
**Pub Acts 1998, No. 517, enacting** § **1,** imd eff January 12, 1999, provides:
"Enacting section 1. This amendatory act does not take effect unless all of the following bills of the 89th Legislature are enacted into law:

## Youth Training and Rehabilitation § 803.306

"(a) Senate Bill No. 1183 [Pub Acts 1998, No. 516].
"(b) Senate Bill No. 1185 [Pub Acts 1998, No. 518].
"(c) Senate Bill No. 1186 [Pub Acts 1998, No. 519].
"(d) Senate Bill No. 1187 [Pub Acts 1998, No. 478].
"(e) Senate Bill No. 1196 [Pub Acts 1998, No. 528].
"(f) Senate Bill No. 1197 [Pub Acts 1998, No. 529]."

**Effect of amendment notes:**
**The 1996 amendment** made changes throughout the section.

**The 1998 amendment** in subsection (1), substituted "Except as provided in subsection (3)" for "The", substituted "public" for "state" preceding "ward" in each instance, and changed the style of statutory references; in subsection (2), inserted "department shall determine the", deleted "shall be determined by the department" following "care", substituted "That" for "The" preceding "cost", and deleted "so determined" preceding "applies"; and added subsection (3).

**Michigan Digest references:**
Probate Courts § 28.

### CASE NOTES

**1-10. [Reserved for use in future supplementation.]**

**11. Costs and expenses.**

**12. – in general.**
Under former statute, the financial responsibility of the department of social welfare ceased whenever a boy committed to boys' vocational school was released or discharged therefrom and left the premises if the department fully observed the requirements of former § 803.112, relative to suitable clothing, transportation to destination and sustenance for not to exceed 30 days. Op Atty Gen, October 14, 1950, No. 1289.

**13. – of minor called to testify.**
Under former statute, boys' vocational school was not required to pay transportation expenses of boy called from school as witness in court, nor expenses of official taking boy into court to testify. Op Atty Gen, September 4, 1946, No. 0-5021.

**14. – medical expenses.**
Medical care of boy paroled to his parents under former § 803.108 was responsibility of his parents and not state; if boy's parents were unable to pay for his care, then he became burden of county of his legal settlement unless his care would be assumed under Afflicted Children's Act by crippled children's commission. Op Atty Gen, March 19, 1946, No. 0-4499.

**15. – returning escapee to school.**
Attorney general found no provision in former statute empowering juvenile institute commission to send anyone into another state to apprehend and return escaped student, nor any provision for payment of expense of his return from another state. Op Atty Gen, May 8, 1946, No. 0-4591.

**16. Reimbursement.**
In absence of statute specifically dealing with question, state could not require reimbursement from minor's estate for expenses of incarcerating minor in state institution such as boys' training school. In re Estate of Plummer (1972) 42 Mich App 603, 202 NW2d 429.

## § 803.306. Absence of public ward from facility or residence; penalty. [MSA § 25.399(56)]

Sec. 6. (1) A public ward shall not absent himself or herself from the facility or residence in which he or she has been placed without the youth agency's prior approval. A public ward who violates this provision may be returned to the facility in which he or she was placed by a peace officer without a warrant. A person who knows the

## § 803.306            Youth Training and Rehabilitation

whereabouts of a public ward who violates this subsection shall immediately notify the youth agency and the nearest peace officer.

(2) A person who induces or assists a public ward to violate subsection (1) or who fails to give the notice required in subsection (1) is guilty of a misdemeanor punishable by imprisonment for not more than 90 days or a fine of not more than $100.00, or both.

**History:**
Pub Acts 1974, No. 150, § 6, imd eff June 12, 1974.
Amended by Pub Acts 1998, No. 517, imd eff January 12, 1999 (see 1998 note below).

**Editor's notes:**
**Pub Acts 1998, No. 517, enacting § 1,** imd eff January 12, 1999, provides:
"Enacting section 1. This amendatory act does not take effect unless all of the following bills of the 89th Legislature are enacted into law:
"(a) Senate Bill No. 1183 [Pub Acts 1998, No. 516].
"(b) Senate Bill No. 1185 [Pub Acts 1998, No. 518].
"(c) Senate Bill No. 1186 [Pub Acts 1998, No. 519].
"(d) Senate Bill No. 1187 [Pub Acts 1998, No. 478].
"(e) Senate Bill No. 1196 [Pub Acts 1998, No. 528].
"(f) Senate Bill No. 1197 [Pub Acts 1998, No. 529]."

**Effect of amendment notes:**
**The 1998 amendment** substituted "public" for "state" in each instance throughout; in subsection (1), inserted "or herself, inserted "or her" in two instances, inserted "the youth agency's", deleted "of the department" following "approval", substituted "who knows" for "having knowledge of", and substituted "subsection" for "provision"; and in subsection (2), inserted "punishable by imprisonment for not more than 90 days or a fine of not more than $100.00, or both".

**Michigan Digest references:**
Probate Courts § 28.

### CASE NOTES

**1-10. [Reserved for use in future supplementation.]**

**11. Construction and effect.**
The Youth Rehabilitation Services Act provides that a peace officer may take into custody without a warrant or order of the probate court a ward of the state who, without prior approval of the Department of Social Services, has left the facility or residence in which he or she has been placed. Op Atty Gen, June 19, 1986, No. 6374.

## § 803.306a. Escape from facility or residence; notification; orders; applicability of subsection (1); "escape" defined. [MSA § 25.399(56a)]

Sec. 6a. (1) If a public ward described in subsection (2) escapes from a facility or residence in which he or she has been placed, other than his or her own home or the home of his or her parent or guardian, the individual at that facility or residence responsible for maintaining custody of the public ward at the time of the escape shall immediately notify 1 of the following of the escape or cause 1 of the following to be immediately notified of the escape:

    (a) If the escape occurs in a city, village, or township that has a police department, that police department.

**Youth Training and Rehabilitation** § 803.306a

(b) If subdivision (a) does not apply, 1 of the following:

(i) The sheriff department of the county where the escape occurs.

(ii) The department of state police post having jurisdiction over the area where the escape occurs.

(2) Subsection (1) applies if the public ward is a public ward under an order of any of the following:

(a) The juvenile division of the probate court or the family division of circuit court under section 2(a)(1) of chapter XIIA of 1939 PA 288, MCL 712A.2.

(b) The circuit court under section 606 of the revised judicature act of 1961, 1961 PA 236, MCL 600.606.

(c) The recorder's court of the city of Detroit under section 10a(1)(c) of former 1919 PA 369.

(3) A police agency that receives notification of an escape under subsection (1) shall enter that notification into the law enforcement information network without undue delay.

(4) As used in this section, "escape" means to leave without lawful authority or to fail to return to custody when required.

**History:**
Pub Acts 1974, No. 150, § 6a, as added by Pub Acts 1996, No. 481, imd eff December 27, 1996, by § 2 eff January 1, 1997 (see 1996 note below); amended by Pub Acts 1998, No. 517, imd eff January 12, 1999 (see 1998 note below).

**Editor's notes:**
**Pub Acts 1996, No. 481, § 3,** imd eff December 27, 1996, by § 2 eff January 1, 1997, provides:

"Section 3. This amendatory act shall not take effect unless all of the following bills of the 88th Legislature are enacted into law:

"(a) Senate Bill No. 1027 [Pub Acts 1996, No. 482].

"(b) Senate Bill No. 1028 [Pub Acts 1996, No. 483]."

**Pub Acts 1998, No. 517, enacting § 1,** imd eff January 12, 1999, provides:

"Enacting section 1. This amendatory act does not take effect unless all of the following bills of the 89th Legislature are enacted into law:

"(a) Senate Bill No. 1183 [Pub Acts 1998, No. 516].

"(b) Senate Bill No. 1185 [Pub Acts 1998, No. 518].

"(c) Senate Bill No. 1186 [Pub Acts 1998, No. 519].

"(d) Senate Bill No. 1187 [Pub Acts 1998, No. 478].

"(e) Senate Bill No. 1196 [Pub Acts 1998, No. 528].

"(f) Senate Bill No. 1197 [Pub Acts 1998, No. 529]."

**Effect of amendment notes:**
**The 1998 amendment** substituted "public" for "state" throughout; in the initial paragraph of subsection (1), substituted "responsible" for "having responsibility"; in paragraph (1)(a), substituted "that" for "the" preceding "police" and deleted "of that city, village, or township" following "department" the second time it appears; in paragraph (1)(b), substituted "If" for "Except as provided in", inserted "does not apply" and substituted "where" for "in which" in each instance; in subsection (2), substituted "under" for "pursuant to" and changed the style of statutory references.

**Michigan Digest references:**
Probate Courts § 28.

**ALR notes:**
Validity, construction, and application of juvenile escape statutes, 46 ALR5th 523.

**Research references:**
47 Am Jur 2d, Juv Cts §§52, 53, 58.

## § 803.307. Duration of public wardship; discharge or release; delayed sentence; sentencing as adult offender. [MSA § 25.399(57)]

Sec. 7. (1) A youth accepted by a youth agency remains a public ward until discharged from public wardship with the approval of any of the following and, if placed in an institution, shall remain until released with the approval of any of the following:

(a) If the youth was committed to a youth agency under section 18(1)(e) of chapter XIIA of 1939 PA 288, MCL 712A.18, and the youth was adjudicated as being in the court's jurisdiction under section 2(a) of chapter XIIA of 1939 PA 288, MCL 712A.2, with the approval of the family division of circuit court.

(b) If the youth was committed to a youth agency under section 1 of chapter IX of the code of criminal procedure, 1927 PA 175, MCL 769.1, with the approval of the court of general criminal jurisdiction under section 1b of chapter IX of the code of criminal procedure, 1927 PA 175, MCL 769.1b.

(2) Except as otherwise provided in this section, a youth accepted as a public ward shall be automatically discharged from public wardship upon reaching the age of 19. Except as provided in subsection (3), a youth committed to a youth agency under section 18(1)(e) of chapter XIIA of 1939 PA 288, MCL 712A.18, for an offense that, if committed by an adult, would be a violation or attempted violation of section 72, 83, 84, 86, 88, 89, 91, 110a(2), 186a, 316, 317, 349, 520b, 520c, 520d, 520g, 529, 529a, 530, or 531 of the Michigan penal code, 1931 PA 328, MCL 750.72, 750.83, 750.84, 750.86, 750.88, 750.89, 750.91, 750.110a, 750.186a, 750.316, 750.317, 750.349, 750.520b, 750.520c, 750.520d, 750.520g, 750.529, 750.529a, 750.530, and 750.531, or section 7401(2)(a)(i) or 7403(2)(a)(i) of the public health code, 1978 PA 368, MCL 333.7401 and 333.7403, shall be automatically discharged from public wardship upon reaching the age of 21. Except as provided in subsection (4), a youth committed to a youth agency under section 1 of chapter IX of the code of criminal procedure, 1927 PA 175, MCL 769.1, shall be automatically discharged from public wardship upon reaching the age of 21.

(3) If the family division of circuit court imposes a delayed sentence on the youth under section 18(1)(n) of chapter XIIA of 1939 PA 288, MCL 712A.18, the youth shall be discharged from public wardship and committed under the court's order.

(4) If a court of general criminal jurisdiction sentences the youth to a sentence provided by law for an adult offender under section 1b of chapter IX of the code of criminal procedure, 1927 PA 175, MCL 769.1b, the youth shall be discharged from public wardship and committed under the court's order.

## Youth Training and Rehabilitation § 803.307

**History:**
Pub Acts 1974, No. 150, § 7, imd eff June 12, 1974; amended by Pub Acts 1988, No. 76, imd eff March 28, 1988, by § 3 eff October 1, 1988 (see 1988 note below).

Amended by Pub Acts 1991, No. 90, imd eff July 31, 1991; 1994, No. 198, imd eff June 21, 1994, by § 2 eff October 1, 1994 (see 1994 note below); 1996, No. 245, imd eff June 12, 1996, by § 3 eff January 1, 1997 (see 1996 note below); 1996, No. 246, imd eff June 12, 1996, by § 3 eff January 1, 1997 (see 1996 note below); 1996, No. 417, by § 2 eff January 1, 1998 (see 1996 note below); 1998, No. 517, imd eff January 12, 1999 (see 1998 note below).

**Editor's notes:**
**Pub Acts 1988, No. 76, § 2,** imd eff March 28, 1988, by § 3 eff October 1, 1988 (amended by Pub Acts 1988, No. 179, § 1), provides:

"Section 2. This amendatory act shall not take effect unless all of the following bills of the 84th Legislature are enacted into law:

"(a) House Bill No. 4731 [which became Act No. 51 of 1988].
"(b) House Bill No. 4733 [which became Act No. 52 of 1988].
"(c) House Bill No. 4741 [which became Act No. 53 of 1988].
"(d) House Bill No. 4748 [which became Act No. 67 of 1988].
"(e) House Bill No. 4750 [which became Act No. 54 of 1988].
"(f) House Bill No. 5203 [which became Act No. 182 of 1988].
"(g) Senate Bill No. 137 [which became Act No. 64 of 1988].
"(h) Senate Bill No. 601 [which became Act No. 73 of 1988].
"(i) Senate Bill No. 604 [which became Act No. 74 of 1988].
"(j) Senate Bill No. 605 [which became Act No. 75 of 1988].
"(k) Senate Bill No. 608 [which became Act No. 77 of 1988].
"(l) Senate Bill No. 609 [which became Act No. 78 of 1988]."

**Pub Acts 1994, No. 198, § 3,** imd eff June 21, 1994, by § 2 eff October 1, 1994, provides:

"Section 3. This amendatory act shall not take effect unless Senate Bill No. 773 of the 87th Legislature (which became Pub Acts 1994, No. 191) is enacted into law."

**Pub Acts 1996, No. 245, §§2, 4,** imd eff June 12, 1996, by § 3 eff January 1, 1997, provide:

"Section 2. This amendatory act applies to offenses committed on or after its effective date.

"Section 4. This amendatory act shall not take effect unless all of following bills of the 88th Legislature are enacted into law:

"(a) Senate Bill No. 281 [Pub Acts 1996, No. 248].
"(b) Senate Bill No. 283 [Pub Acts 1996, No. 249].
"(c) Senate Bill No. 682 [Pub Acts 1996, No. 244].
"(d) Senate Bill No. 689 [Pub Acts 1996, No. 250].
"(e) Senate Bill No. 699 [Pub Acts 1996, No. 247].
"(f) Senate Bill No. 700 [Pub Acts 1996, No. 253].
"(g) Senate Bill No. 724 [Pub Acts 1996, No. 254].
"(h) Senate Bill No. 867 [Pub Acts 1996, No. 255].
"(i) Senate Bill No. 870 [Pub Acts 1996, No. 256].
"(j) House Bill No. 4037 [Pub Acts 1996, No. 257].
"(k) House Bill No. 4038 [Pub Acts 1996, No. 258].
"(l) House Bill No. 4371 [Pub Acts 1996, No. 246].
"(m) House Bill No. 4445 [Pub Acts 1996, No. 259].
"(n) House Bill No. 4486 [Pub Acts 1996, No. 260].
"(o) House Bill No. 4487 [Pub Acts 1996, No. 261].
"(p) House Bill No. 4490 [Pub Acts 1996, No. 262]."

**Pub Acts 1996, No. 246, §§2, 4,** imd eff June 12, 1996, by § 3 eff January 1, 1997, provide:

"Section 2. This amendatory act applies to offenses committed on or after its effective date.

"Section 4. This amendatory act shall not take effect unless all of following bills of the 88th Legislature are enacted into law:

"(a) Senate Bill No. 281 [Pub Acts 1996, No. 248].

§ 803.307      Youth Training and Rehabilitation

"(b) Senate Bill No. 283 [Pub Acts 1996, No. 249].
"(c) Senate Bill No. 682 [Pub Acts 1996, No. 244].
"(d) Senate Bill No. 689 [Pub Acts 1996, No. 250].
"(e) Senate Bill No. 699 [Pub Acts 1996, No. 247].
"(f) Senate Bill No. 700 [Pub Acts 1996, No. 253].
"(g) Senate Bill No. 724 [Pub Acts 1996, No. 254].
"(h) Senate Bill No. 867 [Pub Acts 1996, No. 255].
"(i) Senate Bill No. 870 [Pub Acts 1996, No. 256].
"(j) House Bill No. 4037 [Pub Acts 1996, No. 257].
"(k) House Bill No. 4038 [Pub Acts 1996, No. 258].
"(l) House Bill No. 4044 [Pub Acts 1996, No. 245].
"(m) House Bill No. 4445 [Pub Acts 1996, No. 259].
"(n) House Bill No. 4486 [Pub Acts 1996, No. 260].
"(o) House Bill No. 4487 [Pub Acts 1996, No. 261].
"(p) House Bill No. 4490 [Pub Acts 1996, No. 262]."

**Pub Acts 1996, No. 417, § 3,** by § 2 eff January 1, 1998, provides:

"Section 3. This amendatory act shall not take effect unless Senate Bill No. 1052 of the 88th Legislature [Pub Acts 1996, No. 388] is enacted into law."

**Pub Acts 1998, No. 517, enacting § 1,** imd eff January 12, 1999, provides:

"Enacting section 1. This amendatory act does not take effect unless all of the following bills of the 89th Legislature are enacted into law:

"(a) Senate Bill No. 1183 [Pub Acts 1998, No. 516].
"(b) Senate Bill No. 1185 [Pub Acts 1998, No. 518].
"(c) Senate Bill No. 1186 [Pub Acts 1998, No. 519].
"(d) Senate Bill No. 1187 [Pub Acts 1998, No. 478].
"(e) Senate Bill No. 1196 [Pub Acts 1998, No. 528].
"(f) Senate Bill No. 1197 [Pub Acts 1998, No. 529]."

**Effect of amendment notes:**

The **1994 amendment** in subsection (1), deleted former paragraph (a) which read: "Until June 1, 1991 and except as otherwise provided in subdivisions (b) and (d), with the approval of the youth parole and review board under section 121 of the social welfare act, Act No. 280 of the Public Acts of 1939, being section 400.121 of the Michigan Compiled Laws."; redesignated former paragraphs (b)–(d) as (a)–(c); in subsection (2) inserted "529a," and "750.529a," and deleted "the code of criminal procedure" preceding "Act No. 175" and ", being section 769.1 of the Michigan Compiled Laws," following "of 1927"; and made grammatical changes.

The **first 1996 amendment (Pub Act 245)** amended the statutory provisions found in subsection (2).

The **second 1996 amendment (Pub Act 246)** added subsections (3) and (4).

The **third 1996 amendment (Pub Act 417)** in subsection (1), paragraphs (a) and (b) and subsection (3), substituted "family division of circuit" for "juvenile division of the probate".

The **1998 amendment** substituted "public" for "state" throughout; substituted "a youth agency" for "the department" throughout; changed the style of statutory references throughout; substituted "a youth agency remains a public" for "the department shall remain" in the initial paragraph of subsection (1); deleted former paragraph (a) of subsection (1) and redesignated former paragraphs (b) and (c) as (a) and (b); and deleted the last sentence of paragraph (1)(a) as redesignated;

**Michigan Digest references:**
  Juvenile Proceedings § 33.
  Probate Courts § 28.

**LEXIS-NEXIS™ Michigan analytical references:**
  Michigan Law and Practice, Convicts and Prisons § 6.

# Youth Training and Rehabilitation § 803.307a

**CASE NOTES**

1-10. [Reserved for use in future supplementation.]

11. **Construction, operation and effect.**
A probate court which places a juvenile offender with the Department of Social Services pursuant to the Youth Rehabilitation Services Act has no authority to specify the length of the juvenile's commitment. In re Jackson (1987) 163 Mich App 105, 414 NW2d 156, app den (1987) 429 Mich 885.

**§ 803.307a. Chemical testing for DNA identification; samples provided by public ward; collection; transmission to department of state police; manner; rules; consent, hearing, or court hearing not required; "sample" defined.** [MSA § 25.399(57a)]

Sec. 7a. (1) A public ward under a youth agency's jurisdiction for a violation of section 91, 316, or 317 of the Michigan penal code, 1931 PA 328, MCL 750.91, 750.316, and 750.317, or a violation or attempted violation of section 349, 520b, 520c, 520d, 520e, or 520g of the Michigan penal code, 1931 PA 328, MCL 750.349, 750.520b, 750.520c, 750.520d, 750.520e, and 750.520g, shall not be placed in a community placement of any kind and shall not be discharged from wardship until he or she has provided samples for chemical testing for DNA identification profiling or a determination of the sample's genetic markers and has provided samples for a determination of his or her secretor status. However, if at the time the public ward is to be discharged from public wardship the department of state police already has a sample from the public ward that meets the requirements of the rules promulgated under the DNA identification profiling system act, 1990 PA 250, MCL 28.171 to 28.176, the public ward is not required to provide another sample.

(2) The samples required to be collected under this section shall be collected by the youth agency and transmitted to the department of state police in the manner prescribed by rules promulgated under the DNA identification profiling system act, 1990 PA 250, MCL 28.171 to 28.176.

(3) The youth agency may collect a sample under this section regardless of whether the public ward consents t o the collection. The youth agency is not required to give the public ward an opportunity for a hearing or obtain a court order before collecting the sample.

(4) As used in this section, "sample" means a portion of a public ward's blood, saliva, or tissue collected from the public ward.

**History:**
Pub Acts 1974, No. 150, § 7a, as added by Pub Acts 1996, No. 512, imd eff January 9, 1997, by § 2 eff January 1, 1997 (see 1996 note below); amended by Pub Acts 1998, No. 517, imd eff January 12, 1999 (see 1998 note below).

**Editor's notes:**
**Pub Acts 1996, No. 512,** § **3,** imd eff January 9, 1997, by § 2 eff January 1, 1997, provides:
"Section 3. This amendatory act shall not take effect unless all of the following bills of the 88th Legislature are enacted into law:

§ 803.307a             **Youth Training and Rehabilitation**

"(a) House Bill No. 5783 [Pub Acts 1996, No. 507].
"(b) House Bill No. 5912 [Pub Acts 1996, No. 508].
"(c) House Bill No. 6061 [Pub Acts 1996, No. 511]."
**Pub Acts 1998, No. 517, enacting** § 1, imd eff January 12, 1999, provides:
"Enacting section 1. This amendatory act does not take effect unless all of the following bills of the 89th Legislature are enacted into law:
"(a) Senate Bill No. 1183 [Pub Acts 1998, No. 516].
"(b) Senate Bill No. 1185 [Pub Acts 1998, No. 518].
"(c) Senate Bill No. 1186 [Pub Acts 1998, No. 519].
"(d) Senate Bill No. 1187 [Pub Acts 1998, No. 478].
"(e) Senate Bill No. 1196 [Pub Acts 1998, No. 528].
"(f) Senate Bill No. 1197 [Pub Acts 1998, No. 529]."

**Effect of amendment notes:**
The **1998 amendment** substituted "public" for "state" and "youth agency" for "department" throughout; changed the style of statutory references throughout; in subsection (1), substituted "a youth agency's" for "the"; and in subsection (2), deleted "by the department" following "transmitted".

**Michigan Digest references:**
Probate Courts § 28.

## § 803.308. Records confidential; exceptions. [MSA § 25.399(58)]

Sec. 8. All records of a youth agency pertaining to a public ward are confidential and shall not be made public except as follows:

(a) If the person is less than 18 years of age, by the agency's authorization when necessary for the person's best interests.

(b) If the person is 18 years of age or older, by his or her consent.

**History:**
Pub Acts 1974, No. 150, § 8, imd eff June 12, 1974.
Amended by Pub Acts 1998, No. 517, imd eff January 12, 1999 (see 1998 note below).

**Editor's notes:**
**Pub Acts 1998, No. 517, enacting** § 1, imd eff January 12, 1999, provides:
"Enacting section 1. This amendatory act does not take effect unless all of the following bills of the 89th Legislature are enacted into law:
"(a) Senate Bill No. 1183 [Pub Acts 1998, No. 516].
"(b) Senate Bill No. 1185 [Pub Acts 1998, No. 518].
"(c) Senate Bill No. 1186 [Pub Acts 1998, No. 519].
"(d) Senate Bill No. 1187 [Pub Acts 1998, No. 478].
"(e) Senate Bill No. 1196 [Pub Acts 1998, No. 528].
"(f) Senate Bill No. 1197 [Pub Acts 1998, No. 529]."

**Effect of amendment notes:**
The **1998 amendment** in the initial paragraph, substituted "a youth agency" for "department", "public" for "state", and "except as follows" for "unless"; in paragraph (a), substituted "less than 18 years of" for "under the", deleted "of majority" following "age", inserted "agency's", deleted "of the department" following "authorization", deleted "deemed" preceding "necessary", inserted "person's" and deleted "of the youth" following "interests"; and, in paragraph (b), substituted "is 18 years of age or older" for "has attained the age of majority", and inserted "or her".

**Youth Training and Rehabilitation** § 803.317

**Michigan Digest references:**
Probate Courts § 28.

**§ 803.309. Repeal; references in repealed statutes.** [MSA § 25.399(59)]

Sec. 9. Act No. 183 of the Public Acts of 1925, being sections 804.101 to 804.113 of the Compiled Laws of 1970, and Act No. 185 of the Public Acts of 1925, being sections 803.101 to 803.113 of the Compiled Laws of 1970, are repealed. References in all laws to these acts, the girls' training school, or the boys' training school shall be deemed to refer to the department or institutions operated by the department under this act.

**Michigan Digest references:**
Probate Courts § 28.

## REHABILITATION CAMP FOR MALE DELINQUENT YOUTH

Act 229, 1962, imd eff July 12, 1962.

AN ACT to make appropriations for various state institutions, departments, commissions, boards, agencies and certain state purposes related to public welfare services for the fiscal year ending June 30, 1963, to provide for the expenditure of such appropriations, and to provide for the disposition of fees and other income received by the various state agencies.

*The People of the State of Michigan enact:*

**§ 803.317. Conservation rehabilitation camp for male delinquent youth; establishment; operations; program; trainees; camp facilities.**

Sec. 17. The state department of social welfare shall establish and operate on publicly-owned land a conservation rehabilitation camp for male delinquent youth committed to that department.

The state department of social welfare shall be responsible for the rehabilitation program which shall include academic education, vocational training and personal and vocational counseling by qualified personnel.

The state department of social welfare may select as trainees male youth who have been committed to the department and whose rehabilitation will be furthered by this conservation education-training experience. Any person selected as a trainee shall remain in the custody of the department of social welfare.

In addition to any other amounts appropriated, there is hereby appropriated from the general fund for the fiscal year ending June 30, 1963 to the state department of social welfare the sum of

§ 803.317    Youth Training and Rehabilitation

$80,000.00, or as much thereof as may be necessary, for the construction and renovation of camp facilities.

In addition to any other amounts appropriated, there is hereby appropriated from the general fund for the fiscal year ending June 30, 1963 to the state department of social welfare the sum of $100,000.00, or as much thereof as may be necessary, for the operation of camp facilities herein provided. Any expenses incurred by any state department at the request of the state department of social welfare acting under the authority of this act shall be reimbursed from funds appropriated under this act.

**History:**
Pub Acts 1962, No. 229, imd eff July 12, 1962.

## REHABILITATION CAMP FOR MALE DELINQUENT YOUTH

Act 145, 1963, p 200, imd eff May 14.

AN ACT to authorize the establishment and maintenance of youth conservation rehabilitation camps; to define the powers and duties of the department of social welfare; and to make appropriations therefor.

*The People of the State of Michigan enact:*

### § 803.321. Establishment of camp. [MSA § 25.399(1)]

Sec. 1. The department of social welfare shall establish and operate on publicly-owned land a conservation rehabilitation camp for male delinquent youth committed to that department.

**Former acts:**
Section 17 of Act No. 229 of 1962, in language similar to that used in this act, also provided for the establishment of rehabilitation camps. Act No. 229 was an appropriation act and was not published in full; however, section 17 thereof was carried as a note to § 400.14.

**Cross references:**
Powers, duties and functions of department of social welfare transferred to department of social services, see § 16.552.

### § 803.322. Selection of trainees; custody. [MSA § 25.399(2)]

Sec. 2. The department of social welfare may select as trainees male youth who have been committed to the department and whose rehabilitation will be furthered by this conservation education-training experience. Any person selected as a trainee shall remain in the custody of the department of social welfare.

### § 803.323. Appropriation; cost of facilities. [MSA § 25.399(3)]

Sec. 3. There is hereby appropriated from the general fund for the fiscal year ending June 30, 1964 to the department of social welfare the sum of $50,000.00, or as much thereof as may be necessary, for the completion of construction and renovation of camp facilities. Total cost of such facilities including equipment shall not exceed the $50,000.00 appropriated herein and the $80,000.00 appropriated in Act No. 229 of the Public Acts of 1962.

## Camp LaVictoire

Act 145, 1965, p 231, imd eff July 12.

AN ACT to transfer camp LaVictoire from the state department of corrections to the state department of social welfare; and to authorize its operation as a conservation-rehabilitation camp.

*The People of the State of Michigan enact:*

### § 803.331. Camp LaVictoire; transfer to social welfare department. [MSA § 25.399(21)]

Sec. 1. The buildings and physical assets comprising camp LaVictoire are hereby transferred from the state department of corrections to the state department of social welfare.

**Cross references:**
Powers, duties and functions of department of social welfare transferred to department of social services, see § 16.552.

### § 803.332. Preparation and execution of documents. [MSA § 25.399(22)]

Sec. 2. The attorney general shall prepare and have executed the necessary deeds and documents to carry out the provisions of this act.

### § 803.333. Operation as conservation-rehabilitation camp. [MSA § 25.399(23)]

Sec. 3. The state department of social welfare is authorized to operate camp LaVictoire as a conservation-rehabilitation camp.

# CHAPTER 804

# GIRLS' TRAINING SCHOOLS

## GIRLS' TRAINING SCHOOL [Repealed]

### Act 133 of 1879 [Repealed]

§§804.10–804.18 [Repealed]

### Act 117 of 1893 [Repealed]

§§804.51–804.54 [Repealed]

### Act 183 of 1925 [Repealed]

§§804.101–804.113 [Repealed]

## HOUSE OF GOOD SHEPHERD AT DETROIT [Repealed]

### Act 271 of 1887 [Repealed]

§ 804.151 [Repealed]

---

## GIRLS' TRAINING SCHOOL [Repealed]

Act 133, 1879, p 133, imd eff May 31, 1879.
[Repealed]

AN ACT to establish an institution under the name and style of the Michigan reform school for girls.

### §§804.10–804.18. [Repealed] [MSA §§28.2001–28.2007]

**History:**
Pub Acts 1879, No. 133, imd eff May 31, 1879; **repealed** by Pub Acts 1949, No. 29, eff September 23, 1949.

Sections 1–9. (Superseded.). This act was How §§9827–9835. Section 1 established an institution under the name of the "Michigan reform school for girls." Section 2 vested supervision of the institution in a board of control and was superseded by Pub Acts 1891, No. 140, which created a state board of prison inspectors. The act of 1891 was superseded by Pub Acts 1893, No. 117, which was in turn repealed by Pub Acts 1949, No. 28. Sections 3–5 related to the construction of the institution and the other sections to the powers and duties of the old board. Public Acts 1925, No. 183, repealed so much of this act as was inconsistent therewith. Sec. 16. (Repealed.). Former § 16 provided for a biennial report to the legislature and was repealed by Pub Acts 1881, No. 206. Sec. 17. (Obsolete.). Former § 17 provided for the assessment of the appropriations for 1879–1880. Sec. 21. (Repealed.). Former § 21, which was CL 1929, § 17839, provided penalties for assisting inmates of the home to

**804.18**                                **Girls' Training Schools**

escape, and for knowingly marrying such persons. It was repealed by the Penal Code, Pub Acts 1931, No. 328, eff September 18, 1931, which contains a section superseding it, see § 750.185. Sec. 22. (Repealed.). Former § 22 dealt with the school agent. It was repealed by Pub Acts 1919, No. 261, eff August 14, 1919.

Act 117, 1893, p 168, imd eff May 26, 1893.
[Repealed]

AN ACT to provide for the control and management of the industrial home for girls, and to repeal all acts and parts of acts in conflict with the provisions of this act.

## §§804.51–804.54. [Repealed] [MSA §§28.2011–28.2014]

**History:**
Pub Acts 1893, No. 117, §§1–4, imd eff May 26, 1893; **repealed** by Pub Acts 1949, No. 28, eff September 23, 1949.

Act 183, 1925, p 259, eff August 27, 1925.
[Repealed]

AN ACT to establish at Adrian the girls' training school, continuing said school under the control of the Michigan social welfare commission; prescribing who may be admitted thereto, the powers and duties of the officers immediately in charge of said school, the character and extent of discipline and training to be enforced and provided therein, the compensation of the officers, teachers and other assistants appointed or hired in said institution, and penalties for violations of certain provisions of this act. (Amended by Pub Acts 1949, No. 175, eff September 23, 1949.).

## §§804.101–804.113. [Repealed] [MSA §§28.2021–28.2033]

**History:**
Pub Acts 1925, No. 183, eff August 27, 1925; **repealed** by Pub Acts 1974, No. 150, imd eff June 12, 1974.

**Editor's notes:**
For current provisions see youth rehabilitation services act, §§803.301 et seq.

---

# HOUSE OF GOOD SHEPHERD AT DETROIT [Repealed]

Act 271, 1887, p 370, eff September 28, 1887.
[Repealed]

AN ACT to allow the commitment and detention of female children to the house of the good shepherd at Detroit.

## § 804.151. [Repealed] [MSA § 28.2041]

**History:**
Pub Acts 1887, No. 271, eff September 28, 1887; **repealed** by Pub Acts 1964, No. 256, eff August 28, 1964.

# CHAPTER 830

# STATE BUILDING PROGRAMS

## POSTWAR BUILDING PROGRAM FOR UNIVERSITY OF MICHIGAN AND STATE COLLEGE OF AGRICULTURE

### Act 1 of 1946 (Ex Sess)

§§830.1–830.5 [Repealed]

§ 830.2  Construction and equipment authorized at university of Michigan; public necessity declared; appropriations; postwar victory building board, membership.

§ 830.3  Construction and equipment authorized at state college of agriculture; public necessity declared; appropriations.

§ 830.4  Postwar victory building board empowered to take steps needed to make federal funds available.

§ 830.5  Repeal.

## POSTWAR EMERGENCY HOSPITAL BUILDING PROGRAM

### Act 2 of 1946 (1st Ex Sess)

§§830.31–830.33 [Repealed]

§ 830.32  Postwar victory building board authorized to take steps necessary to make federal funds available.

§ 830.33  Delete this section

## STATE INSTITUTIONS [EXECUTED]

### Act 10 of 1946 [EXECUTED]

§§830.51–830.54 [Repealed]

## POSTWAR BUILDING PROGRAM FOR WAYNE UNIVERSITY AND VARIOUS STATE COLLEGES [EXECUTED]

### Act 11 of 1946 (Ex Sess) [EXECUTED]

§§830.71–830.74 [Repealed]

## STATE BUILDING AND CONSTRUCTION [EXECUTED]

### Act 313 of 1947 [EXECUTED]

§§830.101–830.105 [Repealed]

## STATE BUILDING AND CONSTRUCTION [EXECUTED]

### Act 46 of 1948 (1st Ex Sess) [EXECUTED]

§§830.111–830.116 [Repealed]

## POSTWAR VICTORY BUILDING BOARD ABOLISHED [EXECUTED]

### Act 155 of 1949 [EXECUTED]

§ 830.121 [Repealed]

## UNIVERSITY OF MICHIGAN; MICHIGAN STATE COLLEGE [EXECUTED]

### Act 314 of 1947 [EXECUTED]

§ 830.151 [Repealed]

## UNIVERSITY OF MICHIGAN [EXECUTED]

### Act 35 of 1950 (Ex Sess) [EXECUTED]

§§830.171–830.173 [Repealed]

## PERCY JONES HOSPITAL AT BATTLE CREEK [EXECUTED]

### Act 34 of 1950 (Ex Sess) [EXECUTED]

§§830.201–830.202 [Repealed]

## BUILDING DIVISION OF DEPARTMENT OF ADMINISTRATION [EXECUTED]

### Act 37 of 1950 [EXECUTED]

§§830.251–830.253 [Repealed]

## MENTAL HEALTH INSTITUTIONS [EXECUTED]

### Act 45 of 1951 [EXECUTED]

§§830.301–830.304 [Repealed]

## STATE OFFICE BUILDING

### Act 4 of 1951 (1st Ex Sess)

§ 830.401  Agencies authorized to enter into leases, contracts, etc., required to finance and construct state office building; duty and authority of state administrative board.
§ 830.402  Previous leases, contracts, etc., ratified.
§ 830.403  Contracts and leases not required to be approved by legislature.
§ 830.404  Custody and disbursement of funds.

## STATE BUILDING AUTHORITY

### Act 183 of 1964

§ 830.411  Definitions.
§ 830.411a  Declaration of necessity and purpose.
§ 830.412  State building authority created; general powers; trustees; organization, meetings and voting; handling of funds.

**State Building Programs** 830.5

| § 830.413 | Additional powers of state building authority; Freedom of Information Act, compliance. |
|---|---|
| § 830.414 | Acquisition of property. |
| § 830.415 | Conveyance to building authority of property owned by state. |
| § 830.416 | Leases; required provisions; term. |
| § 830.417 | Lease of facilities from authority; approval; payment of true rental; leasing of furnishings or equipment. |
| § 830.418 | Revenue obligations generally. |
| § 830.418a | Reserve fund; creation; use; income or interest earned; limitations on use, withdrawal. |
| § 830.419 | Obligations; statutory first lien; enforcement. |
| § 830.419a | Contract with bondholders; moneys and deposits, security. |
| § 830.420 | State indebtedness. |
| § 830.421 | Tax exemption. |
| § 830.421a | Personal liability or accountability, limitation. |
| § 830.422 | Investment by fiduciaries. |
| § 830.423 | Public purpose; construction. |
| § 830.424 | Act as additional or alternative method; supplemental and additional to powers conferred by other laws. |
| § 830.425 | Advisory opinion on constitutionality; effect of partial invalidity. |

PLANNING OF PROPOSED STATE BUILDING PROJECTS [Repealed]

**Act 242 of 1976 [Repealed]**

§§830.501–830.505 [Repealed]

---

## POSTWAR BUILDING PROGRAM FOR UNIVERSITY OF MICHIGAN AND STATE COLLEGE OF AGRICULTURE [EXECUTED]

Act 1, 1946 (Ex Sess), p 9, imd eff February 18, 1946.
[EXECUTED]

AN ACT declaring an emergency in the administration of the affairs of the university of Michigan and Michigan state college of agriculture and applied science, approving a postwar victory building program for said institutions, and making certain appropriations therefor; and repealing certain acts and parts of acts.

*The People of the State of Michigan enact:*

**§§830.1–830.5. [Executed]**   [MSA §§15.954(1)–15.954(5)]

**History:**
Pub Acts 1946 (Ex Sess), No. 1, §§1–5, imd eff February 18, 1946; **executed**.

## POSTWAR EMERGENCY HOSPITAL BUILDING PROGRAM
## [EXECUTED]

Act 2, 1946 (1st Ex Sess), p 11, imd eff February 18, 1946.
[EXECUTED]

AN ACT declaring an emergency in the facilities of the state hospitals, approving a postwar emergency hospital building program, providing for the acquisition of certain lands, and making certain appropriations therefor; and repealing certain acts and parts of acts.

*The People of the State of Michigan enact:*

**§§830.31–830.33. [Executed]**  [MSA §§14.862(1)–14.862(3)]

**History:**
Pub Acts 1946 (1st Ex Sess), No. 2, §§1–3, imd eff February 18, 1946; **executed.**

**Editor's notes:**
The postwar victory building board established under the provisions of this act were abolished by Pub Acts 1949, No. 155, eff September 23, 1949.


## STATE INSTITUTIONS [EXECUTED]

Act 10, 1946,
[EXECUTED]

**§§830.51–830.54. [Executed]**

**History:**
Pub Acts 1946, No. 10; **executed.**

**Editor's notes:**
Former §§830.51–830.54 approved and made appropriations for a postwar emergency building and construction program at certain state institutions.


## POSTWAR BUILDING PROGRAM FOR WAYNE UNIVERSITY AND VARIOUS STATE COLLEGES
## [EXECUTED]

Act 11, 1946 (Ex Sess), p 34, imd eff February 25, 1946.
[EXECUTED]

AN ACT declaring an emergency in the administration of the affairs of the Wayne university, Michigan college of mining and technol-

**State Building Programs** 830.116

ogy, central Michigan college of education, Michigan state normal college, northern Michigan college of education and western Michigan college of education, approving a postwar victory building program for said institutions, making certain appropriations therefor, and to repeal certain acts and parts of acts.

### §§830.71–830.74.  [Executed] [MSA §§15.2121–15.2124]

**History:**
Pub Acts 1946 (Ex Sess), No. 11, imd eff February 25, 1946; **executed.**

**Editor's notes:**
Former §§830.71–830.74 approved and made appropriations for a postwar victory building program for certain educational institutions.

## STATE BUILDING AND CONSTRUCTION [EXECUTED]

Act 313, 1947
[EXECUTED]

### §§830.101–830.105.  [Executed]

**History:**
Pub Acts 1947, No. 313; **executed.**

**Editor's notes:**
Former §§830.101–830.105 approved and made appropriations for certain state building and construction purposes and for the acquisition of certain land and property at state institutions.

## STATE BUILDING AND CONSTRUCTION [EXECUTED]

Act 46, 1948 (1st Ex Sess)
[EXECUTED]

### §§830.111–830.116.  [Executed]

**History:**
Pub Acts 1948 (1st Ex Sess), No. 56; **executed.**

**Editor's notes:**
Former §§830.111–830.116 made additional appropriations for the completion of building projects under construction at certain state institutions and for the construction of other emergency projects at certain state institutions.

## POSTWAR VICTORY BUILDING BOARD ABOLISHED [EXECUTED]

Act 155, 1949
[EXECUTED]

### §830.121. [Executed]

**History:**
Pub Acts 1949, No. 155; **executed**.

**Editor's notes:**
Former § 830.121 abolished the postwar victory building board.

## UNIVERSITY OF MICHIGAN; MICHIGAN STATE COLLEGE [EXECUTED]

Act 314, 1947
[EXECUTED]

### §830.151. [Executed]

**History:**
Pub Acts 1947, No. 314; **executed**.

**Editor's notes:**
Former § 830.151 made additional appropriations for construction and equipment of buildings at the University of Michigan and Michigan State College.

## UNIVERSITY OF MICHIGAN [EXECUTED]

Act 35, 1950 (Ex Sess)
[EXECUTED]

### §§830.171–830.173. [Executed]

**History:**
Pub Acts 1950 (Ex Sess), No. 35; **executed**.

**Editor's notes:**
Former §§830.171–830.173 made appropriations for certain building construction purposes at the University of Michigan.

**State Building Programs**   **830.304**

## PERCY JONES HOSPITAL AT BATTLE CREEK [EXECUTED]

Act 34, 1950 (Ex Sess)
[EXECUTED]

### §§830.201–830.202. [Executed]

**History:**
Pub Acts 1950 (Ex Sess), No. 34; **executed**.

**Editor's notes:**
Former §§830.201–830.202 authorized and made an appropriation for the acquisition of Percy Jones General Hospital in Battle Creek.

## BUILDING DIVISION OF DEPARTMENT OF ADMINISTRATION [EXECUTED]

Act 37, 1950
[EXECUTED]

### §§830.251–830.253. [Executed]

**History:**
Pub Acts 1950 (Ex Sess), No. 37; **executed**.

**Editor's notes:**
Former §§830.251–830.253 made an appropriation to the building division of the department of administration to complete detailed engineering specifications.

## MENTAL HEALTH INSTITUTIONS [EXECUTED]

Act 45, 1951
[EXECUTED]

### §§830.301–830.304. [Executed]

**History:**
Pub Acts 1951, No. 45, §§1–4; **executed**.

**Editor's notes:**
Former §§830.301–830.304 made appropriations from the state hospital bulding fund for capital outlay purposes with respect to state mental institutions.

## STATE OFFICE BUILDING

Act 4, 1951 (1st Ex Sess), p 614, imd eff August 23, 1951.

AN ACT to authorize and ratify acts of the state administrative board, the state department of administration and the trustees of the state employees' retirement funds in connection with the financing and construction of a new state office building in the city of Lansing; and to prescribe the powers and duties of the state treasurer.

*The People of the State of Michigan enact:*

### § 830.401. Agencies authorized to enter into leases, contracts, etc., required to finance and construct state office building; duty and authority of state administrative board. [MSA § 3.447(11)]

Sec. 1. The state department of administration and the trustees of the state employees' retirement funds, jointly and severally, are hereby authorized and empowered to enter into and execute all leases, contracts and agreements, and take any and all necessary steps, required to finance and provide for the construction of a new state office building on block 108, original plat of the city of Lansing: Provided, That the state administrative board shall approve each of the foregoing acts: And provided further, That the state administrative board may direct any of the foregoing acts to be performed by the state department of administration.

**History:**
Pub Acts 1951 (1st Ex Sess), No. 4, § 1, imd eff August 23, 1951.

### § 830.402. Previous leases, contracts, etc., ratified. [MSA § 3.447(12)]

Sec. 2. Any and all leases, contracts and agreements, and steps heretofore taken by the state administrative board, the state department of administration and the trustees of the state employees' retirement funds, jointly or severally, in connection with the financing and construction of a new state office building in the city of Lansing, are hereby ratified and declared valid.

**History:**
Pub Acts 1951 (1st Ex Sess), No. 4, § 2, imd eff August 23, 1951.

### § 830.403. Contracts and leases not required to be approved by legislature. [MSA § 3.447(13)]

Sec. 3. Notwithstanding the provisions of Acts No. 315 and No. 316 of the Public Acts of 1947, no such contract or lease, whether heretofore or hereafter executed, shall require the approval of the legislature to become effective.

**History:**
Pub Acts 1951 (1st Ex Sess), No. 4, § 3, imd eff August 23, 1951.

### § 830.404. Custody and disbursement of funds. [MSA § 3.447(14)]

Sec. 4. The state treasurer is hereby authorized and empowered to take custody of such funds as may be deposited with him for the execution of the contracts, leases and agreements entered into under the terms of section 1 of this act, and to disburse said funds in accordance with the accounting laws of the state.

**History:**
Pub Acts 1951 (1st Ex Sess), No. 4, § 4, imd eff August 23, 1951.

## STATE BUILDING AUTHORITY

Act 183, 1964, p 247, imd eff May 19, 1964.

AN ACT creating the state building authority with power to acquire, construct, furnish, equip, own, improve, enlarge, operate, mortgage, and maintain facilities for the use of the state or any of its agencies; to act as a developer or co-owner of facilities as a condominium project for the use of the state or any of its agencies; to authorize the execution of leases pertaining to those facilities by the building authority with the state or any of its agencies; to authorize the payment of true rentals by the state; to provide for the issuance of revenue obligations by the building authority to be paid from the true rentals to be paid by the state and other resources and security provided for and pledged by the building authority; to authorize the creation of funds; to authorize the conveyance of lands by the state or any of its agencies for the purposes authorized in this act; to authorize the appointment of a trustee for bondholders; to permit remedies for the benefit of parties in interest; to provide for other powers and duties of the authority; and to provide for other matters in relation to the authority and its obligations. (Amended by Pub Acts 1988, No. 248, imd eff July 11, 1988; 1994, No. 252, imd eff July 5, 1994.).

*The People of the State of Michigan enact:*

### § 830.411. Definitions. [MSA § 3.447(101)]

Sec. 1. As used in this act:
　(a) "Building authority" means the state building authority created by this act.
　(b) "State" means the legislative, executive, and judicial branches of state government and includes institutions of higher education.
　(c) "Existing facilities" means all existing buildings and other facilities, the sites for the buildings or facilities, and furnishings

§ 830.411                                          **State Building Programs**

or equipment for the buildings or facilities located on real property acquired by the building authority under the terms of this act.

(d) "Facilities" means furnishings or equipment, existing facilities, and all new buildings, parking structures and lots, and other facilities, the sites for the buildings, structures, or facilities, and furnishings or equipment for the buildings, structures, or facilities in any way acquired or constructed by the building authority under this act.

(e) "True rental" means the rental required to be paid by the state to the building authority under a lease between the state and the building authority entered into under this act. The true rental shall be paid by the state to the building authority or its assignee periodically as specified in the lease with the building authority and shall be in periodic amounts that do not exceed the economic or market value to the state of the leased facilities. The economic or market value to the state of the leased facilities shall be determined by the state administrative board before the execution of a lease by the state under this act by an appraisal made by or for the state using commonly employed procedures that will fairly determine economic or market value. When using procedures commonly employed by appraisers, an appraisal may set forth a range for the true rental that reflects variations that may occur in the components upon which the appraisal is based. If a lease is only for furnishings or equipment, the state administrative board may employ an appraiser to determine the economic or market value to the state of the furnishings or equipment, or the state administrative board may approve an alternative method to determine the economic or market value to the state of the furnishings or equipment. The alternative method may include the determination of the economic or market value to the state by a person who is in the business of leasing furnishings or equipment.

(f) "Board" means the board of trustees of the building authority.

(g) "Bond" or "obligation" means a bond, note, or other debt obligation issued by the building authority under section 8.

(h) "Institution of higher education" means a college or university listed in section 4 or 5 of article VIII of the state constitution of 1963 or described in section 6 of article VIII of the state constitution of 1963 or a community or junior college established under section 7 of article VIII of the state constitution of 1963.

(i) "Equipment" means machinery, hardware, or any other type of equipment or a group of integrally related equipment, which shall meet all of the following:

  (i) The equipment or the predominant portion of the group of integrally related equipment is located in or is physically connected to a state occupied building or facility or is located on state owned property.

  (ii) The portion of the group of integrally related equipment that is not described in subparagraph (i) is integral to the functioning of the integrally related equipment described in subparagraph (i).

(iii) The projected useful life of the equipment is 5 years or more.

(j) "Party in interest" includes an owner of an obligation issued under this act; a counterparty to an agreement relating to security or management of payment, revenue, or interest rate exposure, including, but not limited to, a bank, bond insurance provider, or security firm, as its interest appears; and a trustee or fiduciary duly designated by the building authority or otherwise to act on behalf of 1 or more owners or counterparties.

**History:**
Pub Acts 1964, No. 183, § 1, imd eff May 19, 1964; amended by Pub Acts 1976, No. 240, eff March 31, 1977, by § 2 eff September 30, 1976; 1981, No. 183, imd eff December 23, 1981; 1988, No. 248, imd eff July 11, 1988; 1994, No. 252, imd eff July 5, 1994.

**Effect of amendment notes:**
The **1994 amendment** in paragraph (e), substituted "a" for "any" in two instances, substituted "When" for "An appraisal, when", and inserted "an appraisal"; in paragraph (g) deleted "or 'bonds'" following "Bond", "or 'obligations'" following "obligation", and "or 'notes'" following "notes" and made grammatical changes; in paragraph (h) substituted "Institution" for "Institutions"; and added new paragraphs (i) and (j).

**Former acts:**
This act is substantially similar to former § 291.101–291.115 , except insofar as the former act limited the purposes for which buildings and facilities might be acquired.

**Statutory references:**
Section 8, above referred to, is § 830.418 .

**Michigan Digest references:**
Municipal and Public Bonds §§1, 40, 41.
State of Michigan §§10, 12, 15, 19, 24.
Taxes § 57.

**ALR notes:**
Power of governmental unit to issue bonds as implying power to refund them, 1 ALR2d 134.
What constitutes a "public sale", 4 ALR2d 575.

**Michigan Civ Jur references:**
State of Michigan § 14.20.

**Research references:**
64 Am Jur 2d, Public Securities and Obligations §§105, 210.
71 Am Jur 2d, State and Local Taxation §§336 et seq.
76 Am Jur 2d, Trusts § 385.

### CASE NOTES

**1. Validity.**
Under State Building Authority Act providing for lease by state of property from authority, contractual obligation, enforceable, in court of claims, would be imposed upon future legislatures to appropriate amounts each year sufficient to pay period rentals to authority for true rents falling due in future years. In re Request for Advisory Opinion Enrolled Senate Bill etc. (1977) 400 Mich 311, 254 NW2d 544.

§ 830.411 State Building Programs

State building Authority Act provision for issuance of bonds by authority to be repaid from proceeds derived from true rental payments by state under leases of property from authority would be held not to involve pledge of general obligation of state for repayment of bonds within meaning of constitutional limitations on issuance or evidence of state debt or borrowing of money by state, where bonds in question purported to be revenue bonds payable only from revenue generated by payment of true rentals under terms of leases, involving no indication on part of state to bonds under Act which specifically required disclaimer of pledge of state's general obligation. In re Request for Advisory Opinion Enrolled Senate Bill etc. (1977) 400 Mich 311, 254 NW2d 544.

Fact that state's rental obligation would be paid from general tax fund would be held not to vitiate true nature of revenue bonds provided for under State Building Authority Act as would render them subject to constitutional limitations on state borrowing under otherwise valid provision of Act authorizing building authority to issue bonds to be repaid from proceeds derived from true rental payments by state under leases of property from building authority. In re Request for Advisory Opinion Enrolled Senate Bill etc. (1977) 400 Mich 311, 254 NW2d 544.

State Building Authority Act provision authorizing state to lease property from authority would be held not to involve state debt in violation of constitutional limitations on power of legislature to borrow money and issue evidence of debt. In re Request for Advisory Opinion Enrolled Senate Bill etc. (1977) 400 Mich 311, 254 NW2d 544.

**2. Bonds.**

The State Building Authority may not issue bonds that are repayable over a period extending one year beyond the economic life of the project, as determined by the State Administrative Board, to be financed by the proceeds of the bonds. Op Atty Gen, October 22, 1987, No. 6477.

## § 830.411a. Declaration of necessity and purpose. [MSA § 3.447(101a)]

Sec. 1a. The legislature finds all of the following:

(a) That there is a present need for the state, its agencies, and departments, in order to carry out necessary governmental functions and enterprises and to provide necessary services to the people of the state as mandated or permitted by constitution and law, to do both of the following:

(i) Rent, lease, or otherwise acquire additional buildings, together with necessary parking structures and lots, facilities, furnishings, equipment, and sites.

(ii) Renovate or restore properties owned or used by the state.

(b) That the state now rents and leases from private owners at a substantial cost space and furnishings or equipment in many communities in order to provide services, and as the state continues to grow it will be necessary to rent or lease substantial additional space and furnishings or equipment from private owners at substantial additional cost to provide services.

(c) That the state building authority is created by this act with the powers granted in this act to do both of the following:

(i) Provide additional space and furnishings or equipment in the best locations and in the most economical and efficient manner.

(ii) Improve existing facilities through the restoration or renovation of those facilities.

**History:**
Pub Acts 1964, No. 183, § 1a, as added by Pub Acts 1976, No. 240, eff March 31, 1977, by § 2 eff September 30, 1976; amended by Pub Acts 1988, No. 248, imd eff July 11, 1988.

## § 830.412. State building authority created; general powers; trustees; organization, meetings and voting; handling of funds. [MSA § 3.447(102)]

Sec. 2. (1) The State building authority is created, is made a body corporate, separate and distinct from the state, and may sue and be sued, pled and be impleaded, contract and be contracted with, have a corporate seal, and enjoy and carry out all powers granted it in this act. Funds of the authority shall be handled in the same manner and by the same provisions of law which apply to state funds.

(2) The building authority shall be governed by a board of trustees consisting of 5 members appointed by the governor, with the advice and consent of the senate, for terms of 4 years. In appointing the first members of the board, the governor shall designate 2 to serve for 4 years, 1 to serve for 3 years, 1 to serve for 2 years, and 1 to serve for 1 year.

(3) A vacancy in office of a member of the board, whether caused by resignation, death, expiration of office, or otherwise, shall be filled by appointment by the governor with the advice and consent of the senate. Each member of the board shall enter upon his or her duties after appointment and shall qualify by taking and filing the constitutional oath of office. A member of the board shall hold office until the appointment and qualification of a successor. A person holding an elective or appointive office with the state shall not be appointed to the board.

(4) After designation and qualification of the members of the board, the board shall organize. The business which the board of trustees may perform shall be conducted at a public meeting the the board of trustees held in compliance with Act No. 267 of the Public Acts of 1976, being sections 15.261 to 15.275 of the Michigan Compiled Laws. Public notice of the time, date, and place of the meeting shall be given in the manner required by Act No. 267 of the Public Acts of 1976. A quorum for the transaction of business shall consist of 3 of the members of the board. An action of the board requires a concurring vote by a majority of the board.

**History:**
Pub Acts 1964, No. 183, § 2, imd eff May 19, 1964; amended by Pub Acts 1976, No. 240, eff March 31, 1977, by § 2 eff September 30, 1976; 1978, No. 199, imd eff June 4, 1978.

**Michigan Digest references:**
Municipal and Public Bonds §§1, 40, 41.
State of Michigan §§10, 12, 15, 19, 24.
Taxes § 57.

**ALR notes:**
Power of governmental unit to issue bonds as implying power to refund them, 1 ALR2d 134.
What constitutes a "public sale", 4 ALR2d 575.

**Michigan Civ Jur references:**
State of Michigan § 14.20.

**Research references:**
64 Am Jur 2d, Public Securities and Obligations §§105, 210.
71 Am Jur 2d, State and Local Taxation §§336 et seq.
76 Am Jur 2d, Trusts § 385.

## § 830.413. Additional powers of state building authority; Freedom of Information Act, compliance. [MSA § 3.447(103)]

Sec. 3. The building authority may do any of the following:

(a) Adopt bylaws for the regulation of its affairs and the conduct of its business.

(b) Adopt an official seal.

(c) Maintain a principal office at a place within this state.

(d) Sue and be sued in its own name and plead and be impleaded.

(e) Acquire, construct, furnish, equip, improve, restore, renovate, enlarge, own, operate, and maintain facilities that are approved by concurrent resolution of the legislature for the use of the state or an agency of the state.

(f) Acquire in the name of the building authority, hold, and dispose of real and personal property, or an interest in real and personal property, in the exercise of its powers and the performance of its duties.

(g) Act as a developer or co-owner of a facility that is a condominium project under the condominium act, Act No. 59 of the Public Acts of 1978, as amended, being sections 559.101 to 559.275 of the Michigan Compiled Laws, in the exercise of its powers and the performance of its duties.

(h) Borrow money for a corporate purpose as prescribed in this act, issue negotiable revenue bonds payable solely from the true rental except to the extent paid from the proceeds of sale of revenue obligations and any additional security provided for and pledged by the building authority in the resolution authorizing revenue obligations under section 8, and provide for the payment of the bonds and the rights of the holders of the bonds and mortgage facilities in favor of the holders of bonds issued under this act.

(i) Make and enter into contracts, leases, and other instruments necessary or incident to the performance of its duties and the execution of its powers. A lease may include provisions for construction, improvement, restoration, renovation, operation, use, and disposition of the facilities on payment of the bonds. If the cost of a contract for construction, materials, or services, other than compensation for personal or professional services, involves an expenditure of more than $5,000.00, the building authority shall make a written contract with the lowest qualified bidder, after advertisement for not less than 2 consecutive weeks in a newspaper of general circulation in this state, and in other publications as determined by the building authority.

**State Building Programs** § 830.413

(j) Employ and fix the compensation of consulting engineers, architects, superintendents, managers, and other construction, accounting, appraisal, and financial experts, attorneys, and other employees and agents as the authority determines are necessary to perform its duties and functions under this act.

(k) Receive and accept from a federal agency grants for or in aid of the construction of facilities and receive and accept aid or contributions from any source of either money, property, labor, or other things of value, to be held, used, and applied only for the purposes for which the grants and contributions were made.

(l) Require fidelity bonds from employees handling money of the building authority. The bonds shall be in sums and subject to the terms and conditions that the board considers satisfactory.

(m) Do all acts necessary or, in the opinion of the building authority, convenient to carry out the powers expressly granted.

(n) Require that final actions of the board are entered in the journal of the board. A writing prepared, owned, used, in the possession of, or retained by the board in the performance of an official function shall be made available to the public in compliance with the freedom of information act, Act No. 442 of the Public Acts of 1976, as amended, being sections 15.231 to 15.246 of the Michigan Compiled Laws.

(o) Require that the books and records of account of the building authority are audited annually by the auditor general, or if the auditor general is unable to act, by an independent certified public accountant appointed by the auditor general.

(p) Make and enter into contracts for insurance, letters of credit, and commitments to purchase its revenue obligations, or enter into other transactions to provide separate security to assure the timely payment of any revenue obligations of the building authority. A contract of the building authority permitted by this section shall not be a general obligation of the state or building authority.

**History:**
Pub Acts 1964, No. 183, § 3, imd eff May 19, 1964; amended by Pub Acts 1976, No. 240, eff March 31, 1977, by § 2 eff September 30, 1976; 1978, No. 199, imd eff June 4, 1978; 1981, No. 183, imd eff December 23, 1981; 1988, No. 248, imd eff July 11, 1988.

**Statutory references:**
Section 8 is § 830.418.

**Michigan Digest references:**
Municipal and Public Bonds §§1, 40, 41.
State of Michigan §§10, 12, 15, 19, 24.
Taxes § 57.

**ALR notes:**
Power of governmental unit to issue bonds as implying power to refund them, 1 ALR2d 134.
What constitutes a "public sale", 4 ALR2d 575.

**Michigan Civ Jur references:**
State of Michigan § 14.20.

**Research references:**
64 Am Jur 2d, Public Securities and Obligations §§105, 210.
71 Am Jur 2d, State and Local Taxation §§336 et seq.
76 Am Jur 2d, Trusts § 385.

**Legal periodicals:**
Government contractor defense, 1984 Tr Law Guide 1.

## § 830.414. Acquisition of property. [MSA § 3.447(104)]

Sec. 4. The building authority may acquire property by purchase, construction, lease, gift, devise, or condemnation, and for the purpose of condemnation, it may proceed under the provisions of Act No. 149 of the Public Acts of 1911, as amended, being sections 213.21 to 213.41 of the Michigan Compiled Laws, or any other appropriate statute.

**History:**
Pub Acts 1964, No. 183, § 4, imd eff May 19, 1964; amended by Pub Acts 1976, No. 240, eff March 31, 1977, by § 2 eff September 30, 1976.

**Michigan Digest references:**
Municipal and Public Bonds §§1, 40, 41.
State of Michigan §§10, 12, 15, 19, 24.
Taxes § 57.

**ALR notes:**
Power of governmental unit to issue bonds as implying power to refund them, 1 ALR2d 134.
What constitutes a "public sale", 4 ALR2d 575.

**Michigan Civ Jur references:**
State of Michigan § 14.20.

**Research references:**
64 Am Jur 2d, Public Securities and Obligations §§105, 210.
71 Am Jur 2d, State and Local Taxation §§336 et seq.
76 Am Jur 2d, Trusts § 385.

## § 830.415. Conveyance to building authority of property owned by state. [MSA § 3.447(105)]

Sec. 5. (1) Property owned by the state may be conveyed to the building authority for any purpose expressed in this act, subject, however, to prior approval by the state administrative board, by the attorney general, and by concurrent resolution of the legislature concurred in by a majority of the members elected to and serving in each house. The votes and names of the members voting on the resolution shall be entered in the journal. After approval as provided in this subsection, a conveyance shall be executed for and on behalf of the state by the governor and secretary of state, or in the event of the absence or disability of either of them, by the lieutenant governor or deputy secretary of state.

(2) In addition to other authority granted by law, property owned by an institution of higher education may be conveyed to the building authority for any purpose expressed in this act, subject, however, to approval by the governing body of the institution of higher education, by the state administrative board, and by concur-

rent resolution of the legislature concurred in by a majority of the members elected to and serving in each house. The votes and names of the members voting on the resolution shall be entered in the journal. After approval as provided in this subsection, a conveyance shall be executed for and on behalf of the institution of higher education by authorized officers of the institution of higher education. In addition to other authority granted by law, an institution of higher education may enter into a lease with the building authority under section 6 for the period provided in that section.

**History:**
Pub Acts 1964, No. 183, § 5, imd eff May 19, 1964; amended by Pub Acts 1976, No. 240, eff March 31, 1977, by § 2 eff September 30, 1976; 1993, No. 35, imd eff May 11, 1993 (see 1993 note below); 1994, No. 252, imd eff July 5, 1994.

**Editor's notes:**
**Pub Acts 1993, No. 35, § 2,** imd eff May 11, 1993, provides:
"Section 2. This amendatory act shall not take effect unless Senate Bill No. 363 of the 87th Legislature [which became Act No. 19 of 1993] is enacted into law."

**Effect of amendment notes:**
**The 1994 amendment** in subsection (2), added "In addition to other authority granted by law, an institution of higher education may enter into a lease with the building authority under section 6 for the period provided in that section."

**Statutory references:**
Section 6, above referred to, is § 830.416.

**Michigan Digest references:**
Municipal and Public Bonds §§1, 40, 41.
State of Michigan §§10, 12, 15, 19, 24.
Taxes § 57.

**ALR notes:**
Power of governmental unit to issue bonds as implying power to refund them, 1 ALR2d 134.
What constitutes a "public sale", 4 ALR2d 575.

**Michigan Civ Jur references:**
State of Michigan § 14.20.

**Research references:**
64 Am Jur 2d, Public Securities and Obligations §§105, 210.
71 Am Jur 2d, State and Local Taxation §§336 et seq.
76 Am Jur 2d, Trusts § 385.

## § 830.416. Leases; required provisions; term. [MSA § 3.447(106)]

Sec. 6. The building authority may lease existing facilities or facilities defined by this act for the purposes specified in this act, to the state, or any of its agencies acting on its behalf. A lease authorized by this act shall be for a period not exceeding 40 years from the date of execution of the lease, and shall contain provisions for the payment of true rental by the state to the building authority. If bonds are issued by the building authority in accordance with the authorization provided in section 8 for the purpose of financing all or

§ 830.416

part of the cost of facilities, the true rental shall be fixed in the lease. A lease may contain other provisions relative to the construction, operation, use, and disposition of the facilities on payment of the bonds, and improvement of the facilities and remedies available to the authority upon default by the state of any of the state's obligations under the lease within the scope and purposes provided in this act as may be agreed upon.

**History:**
Pub Acts 1964, No. 183, § 6, imd eff May 19, 1964; amended by Pub Acts 1976, No. 240, eff March 31, 1977, by § 2 eff September 30, 1976; 1980, No. 240, imd eff July 24, 1980; 1981, No. 183, imd eff December 23, 1981.

**Statutory references:**
Section 8, above referred to, is § 830.418.

**Michigan Digest references:**
Municipal and Public Bonds §§1, 40, 41.
State of Michigan §§10, 12, 15, 19, 24.
Taxes § 57.

**ALR notes:**
Power of governmental unit to issue bonds as implying power to refund them, 1 ALR2d 134.
What constitutes a "public sale", 4 ALR2d 575.

**Michigan Civ Jur references:**
State of Michigan § 14.20.

**Research references:**
64 Am Jur 2d, Public Securities and Obligations §§105, 210.
71 Am Jur 2d, State and Local Taxation §§336 et seq.
76 Am Jur 2d, Trusts § 385.

## § 830.417. Lease of facilities from authority; approval; payment of true rental; leasing of furnishings or equipment.
[MSA § 3.447(107)]

Sec. 7. (1) The state may lease facilities from the building authority for public purposes within the concepts provided in this act, upon terms and conditions agreed upon and subject to the limitations and provisions provided in section 6. Before execution, a lease shall be approved by the state administrative board and, except as provided in subsection (3), by concurrent resolution of the legislature concurred in by a majority of the members elected to and serving in each house. The votes and names of the members voting shall be entered in the journal. The lease as approved by the building authority and the administrative board, and if required, the legislature or an institution of higher education, may provide for a determinable true rental as a range as permitted under section 1(e).

(2) If a lease is approved containing a true rental stated as a range, then actual rental to be paid under the lease shall be fixed at an amount certified by the appraiser and, after the certification, shall be approved by the state administrative board and the building authority. The appraiser shall not certify, and the board and authority shall not approve, a true rental amount unless the amount is fixed within or below the stated range. A lease shall not be

executed more than 3 years after its approval by the legislature. The state shall pay to the building authority or its assignee the true rental at the times, in the manner, and at the place specified in the lease. The governor and the budget director shall include in the annual budget of the state for each year an amount fully sufficient to pay the true rental required to be paid by the state to the building authority or its assignee required by any lease under this act. If the lease is for an institution of higher education, then in addition, the lease shall be authorized by the institution of higher education and signed by its authorized officers.

(3) The state, except institutions of higher education, may lease from the building authority property that is comprised only of furnishings or equipment if all of the following requirements are met:

(a) Before a lease that is only for furnishings or equipment is executed, the general form of the lease shall be approved by concurrent resolution of the legislature concurred in by a majority of the members elected to and serving in each house. The form of the lease approved by the legislature need not contain a description of the property to be leased or the rental or a rental range. However, before the state executes the lease, the description of the property to be leased and the rental shall be approved by the state administrative board as provided in subsection (2). The concurrent resolution of the legislature approving the form of lease shall also approve a maximum amount of furnishings and equipment that may be leased during the 2 years following the approval of the lease pursuant to the form of lease approved.

(b) A lease that is only for furnishings or equipment shall be executed only if the furnishings or equipment are for use by a state agency as determined under the management and budget act, Act No. 431 of the Public Acts of 1984, being sections 18.1101 to 18.1594 of the Michigan Compiled Laws.

**History:**
Pub Acts 1964, No. 183, § 7, imd eff May 19, 1964; amended by Pub Acts 1976, No. 240, eff March 31, 1977, by § 2 eff September 30, 1976; 1981, No. 183, imd eff December 23, 1981; 1988, No. 248, imd eff July 11, 1988; 1994, No. 252, imd eff July 5, 1994.

**Effect of amendment notes:**
**The 1994 amendment** reorganized former subsection (1) into subsections (1) and (2), redesignating former subsection (2) as (3); changed the time period in subsection (2) from one year to three years; changed the time period in subsection (3), paragraph (a) from 12 months to two years; and made other revisions.

**Statutory references:**
Sections 1 and 6, above referred to, are §§830.411 and 830.416.

**Michigan Digest references:**
Municipal and Public Bonds §§1, 40, 41.
State of Michigan §§10, 12, 15, 19, 24.
Taxes § 57.

**ALR notes:**
Power of governmental unit to issue bonds as implying power to refund them, 1 ALR2d 134.
What constitutes a "public sale", 4 ALR2d 575.

**Michigan Civ Jur references:**
State of Michigan § 14.20.

**Research references:**
64 Am Jur 2d, Public Securities and Obligations §§105, 210.
71 Am Jur 2d, State and Local Taxation §§336 et seq.
76 Am Jur 2d, Trusts § 385.

## § 830.418. Revenue obligations generally. [MSA § 3.447(108)]

Sec. 8. (1) By resolution or resolutions of its board, the building authority may provide for the issuance of revenue obligations, which may include revenue bonds, revenue notes, or other evidences of revenue indebtedness, and refunding revenue bonds or notes, or other refunding evidences of indebtedness, the obligations for which shall not become a general obligation of this state or a charge against this state, but all revenue obligations and the interest on the revenue obligations and the call premiums for the revenue obligations shall be payable solely from true rental, except to the extent paid from the proceeds of sale of revenue obligations and any additional security provided for and pledged, or from other funds as provided in this act, and each revenue obligation shall have such a statement printed on the face of the revenue obligation. If the resolution of the building authority provides for interest coupons to be attached to a revenue obligation, each interest coupon shall have a statement printed on the coupon that the coupon is not a general obligation of this state or the building authority but is payable solely from certain revenues as specified in the revenue obligation. Revenue obligations may be issued for the purpose of paying part or all of the costs of the facilities or for the purpose of refunding or advance refunding, in whole or in part, outstanding revenue obligations issued pursuant to this act whether the obligations to be refunded or advance refunded have matured or are redeemable or shall mature or become redeemable after being refunded. The cost of the facilities may include an allowance for legal, engineering, architectural, and consulting services; interest on revenue obligations becoming due before the collection of the first true rental available for the payment of those revenue obligations; a reserve for the payment of principal, interest, and redemption premiums on the revenue obligations of the authority; and other necessary incidental expenses including, but not limited to, placement fees; fees or charges for insurance, letters of credit, lines of credit, remarketing agreements, or commitments to purchase obligations issued pursuant to this act; fees or charges associated with an agreement to manage payment, revenue, or interest rate exposure; or any other fees or charges for any other security provided to assure timely payment of the obligations.

(2) The proceeds of a revenue obligation issue may be used to pay the cost of facilities that are subject to more than 1 lease if either subdivision (a) or (b) is true:

(a) Both of the following are true:

(i) The resolution authorizing the revenue obligations provides for the use of a specific allocable portion of the revenue

**State Building Programs** § 830.418

obligation proceeds to pay the estimated cost of each of the facilities, together with the allocable portion of the reserves, discount, interest on the obligations becoming due before the first true rental available for payment of the obligations, and obligation issuance expense with respect to each facility.

(ii) The true rental and other funds of the building authority and other security as provided in this act available for the revenue obligations including other funds as provided in this act are sufficient to pay the allocable portion of the revenue obligation issue for which the true rental and other funds and security are pledged.

(b) The obligation is part of an interim financing pool described in subsection (23).

(3) Revenue obligations that refund outstanding obligations may include the payment of interest accrued, or to accrue, to the earliest or any subsequent date of redemption, purchase, or maturity of the revenue obligations to be refunded, redemption premium, if any, and any commission, service fee, and other expense necessary to be paid in connection with revenue obligations that refund outstanding obligations. Proceeds of refunding revenue obligations may also be used to pay part of the cost of issuance of the refunding revenue obligations, interest on the refunding revenue obligations, a reserve for the payment of principal, interest, and redemption premiums on the refunding revenue obligations, and other necessary incidental expenses including, but not limited to, placement fees; fees or charges for insurance, letters of credit, lines of credit, remarketing agreements, or commitments to purchase obligations issued pursuant to this act; fees or charges associated with an agreement to manage payment, revenue, or interest rate exposure; or any other fees or charges for any other security provided to assure timely payment of the obligations. The building authority may also provide for the withdrawal of any funds from a reserve created for the payment of principal, interest, and redemption premiums on the refunded obligations and for the deposit of those funds in the reserve for the payment of principal, interest, and redemption premiums on the refunding obligations or may provide for use of that reserve money to pay principal, interest, and redemption premiums on the obligations to be refunded. Obligations issued to refund outstanding obligations may be issued in a principal amount greater than, the same as, or less than the principal amount of the obligations to be refunded, and subject to the maximum rate of interest provided in subsection (8), may bear interest rates that are higher than, the same as, or lower than the interest rates of the obligations to be refunded. If obligations are issued to refund outstanding obligations of the authority, a lease whose rental has been pledged for repayment of the obligations to be refunded shall not be terminated solely by reason of the payment or provision for payment of the obligations to be refunded, and the lease and all of the rights and obligations under the lease remain in full force and effect in accordance with its terms.

§ 830.418

(4) Except as otherwise provided in this section, the building authority shall use income or profit derived from the investment of money in a fund or account of the building authority, including the proceeds of sale of the revenue obligations, only for the purpose of paying principal, interest, and redemption premiums on the revenue obligations of the building authority, or for any purpose for which the proceeds of the revenue obligations may be used under this act, as determined by the resolution of the board authorizing the issuance of revenue obligations.

(5) Within limits considered appropriate and established by the board, the board may authorize by resolution a member of the board or the person appointed by the building authority as its chief operating officer or chief staff person, if the authorization limits or prescribes the maximum interest rates, minimum price, maximum principal amount, and the latest maturity date of the obligations, to do any of the following:

(a) Determine interest rates or methods for determining interest rates for, maturities of, principal amounts of, denominations of, dates of issuance of, interest payment dates for, redemption rights and the terms under which redemption rights may be waived, transferred, or sold, prepayment rights with respect to, the purchase price of, and the type of funds for settlement of obligations.

(b) Determine which, if any, letter of credit, line of credit, standby note or bond purchase agreement, bond insurance, or other agreement providing security or liquidity for obligations of the building authority, approved by the board, provides a cost savings and should be entered into in connection with the issuance of the obligations of the building authority.

(c) Take any other action on behalf of the board within limitations established by the board as the board considers necessary in connection with the issuance of obligations of the building authority.

(6) To the extent provided by resolution of the board, principal of, and interest and redemption premiums on, revenue obligations issued for the purpose of paying all or part of the cost of the facilities shall be secured by and payable only from any or all of the following sources:

(a) The true rental derived from the facilities constructed or acquired with the proceeds of the revenue obligations.

(b) The proceeds of revenue obligations.

(c) The reserve, if any, established for the payment of principal of, or interest or redemption premiums on, the obligations.

(d) The proceeds of insurance, a letter of credit, or a line of credit acquired as security for the revenue obligations.

(e) The proceeds of obligations issued to refund the revenue obligations.

(f) The proceeds of the foreclosure or enforcement of a mortgage, security interest, or deed of trust on the facilities financed by the revenue obligations granted by the authority as security for the revenue obligations.

(g) Other funds of the authority not previously pledged for other obligations of the authority, including funds of the authority derived from rentals and other revenues, investment income or profit, or funds or accounts relating to other facilities, and payments received pursuant to an agreement to manage payment, revenue, or interest rate exposure as provided in subsection (22).

(h) Investment earnings and profits on any or all of the sources described in subdivisions (a) to (g).

(7) To the extent provided by resolution of the board, principal of, and interest and redemption premiums on, refunding revenue obligations shall be secured by and payable only from any or all of the following sources:

(a) The true rental derived from the facilities constructed or acquired with the proceeds of the obligations being refunded.

(b) The proceeds of the refunding obligations.

(c) The reserve, if any, established for the payment of the principal of, or interest and redemption premiums on, the refunding obligations or the obligations to be refunded.

(d) The proceeds of insurance, a letter of credit, or a line of credit acquired as security for the revenue obligations.

(e) The proceeds of obligations issued to refund the refunding obligations.

(f) The proceeds of the foreclosure or enforcement of any mortgage, security interest, or deed of trust on the facilities financed from the proceeds of the obligations being refunded, granted by the authority as security for the refunding obligations.

(g) Other funds of the authority not previously pledged for other obligations of the authority, including other funds of the authority derived from rentals and other revenues, investment income or profit, or funds or accounts relating to other facilities, and payments received pursuant to an agreement to manage payment, revenue, or interest rate exposure as provided in subsection (22).

(h) Investment earnings or profits on any of the sources described in subdivisions (a) to (g).

(8) Obligations issued under this act may be either serial obligations or term obligations, or any combination of serial or term obligations. The obligations shall mature not more than 40 years from their date, and in any event not more than 1 year from the due date of the last true rental pledged for the payment of the obligations, and may bear interest at fixed or variable interest rates, or may be without stated interest, but the net interest rate or rates of interest, taking into account any discount on the sale of the obligations, shall not exceed 18% or a higher rate if permitted by the municipal finance act, 1943 PA 202, MCL 131.1 to 139.3. The obligations may be sold at a discount.

(9) Except as otherwise provided in this subsection, in the resolution or resolutions authorizing the issuance of the obligations, the board shall determine the principal amount of the obligations to be

## § 830.418 State Building Programs

issued, the registration provisions, the date of issuance, the obligation numbers, the obligation denominations, the obligation designations, the obligation maturities, the interest payment dates, the paying agent or paying agents or the method of selection of the agent or agents, the rights of prior redemption of the obligations, and the terms under which redemption rights may be waived, transferred, or sold, the rights of the holders to require prepayment of the principal of or interest on the obligations, the maximum rate of interest, the method of execution of the obligations, and such other provisions respecting the obligations, the rights of the holders of the obligations, the security for the obligations, and the procedures for disbursement of the obligation proceeds and for the investment of the proceeds of obligations and money for the payment of obligations. Rather than making the determinations required by this subsection, the board may authorize a person identified in subsection (5) to make the determinations and take the actions authorized under subsection (5).

(10) The board in the resolution or resolutions authorizing the issuance of obligations may provide for the assignment of the true rental to be paid by the state under the lease or leases to 1 of the paying agents for the obligations or to a trustee, as provided in this act, in which case the state shall pay the rental to the paying agent or trustee. For the purposes and within the limitations set forth in this act, the board may by resolution covenant to issue or cause to be issued, or use its best efforts to issue or cause to be issued, refunding revenue obligations to refund obligations issued under this act.

(11) The board in the resolution, or resolutions, authorizing the obligations may provide for the terms and conditions upon which the holders of the obligations, or a portion of the obligations or a trustee for the obligations, is entitled to the appointment of a receiver. The receiver may enter and take possession of the facility, may lease and maintain the facility, may prescribe rentals and collect, receive, and apply income and revenues thereafter arising from the facility in the same manner and to the same extent that the authority is so authorized. The resolution or resolutions may provide for the appointment of a trustee for the holders of the obligations, may give to the trustee the appropriate rights, duties, remedies, and powers, with or without the execution of a deed of trust or mortgage, necessary and appropriate to secure the obligations, and may provide that the principal of and interest on any obligations issued under this act shall be secured by a mortgage, security interest, or deed of trust covering the facility, which mortgage, security interest, or deed of trust may contain the covenants, agreements, and remedies as will properly safeguard the obligations as may be provided for in the resolution or resolutions authorizing the obligations, including the right to sell the facility upon foreclosure sale, not inconsistent with this act.

(12) All obligations and the interest coupons, if any, attached to the obligations are declared to be fully negotiable and to have all of the qualities incident to negotiable instruments under the uniform

**State Building Programs** § 830.418

commercial code, 1962 PA 174, MCL 440.1101 to 440.11102, subject only to the provisions for registration of the obligations that may appear on the obligations. The obligations and interest on the obligations are exempt from all taxation by the state or any of its political subdivisions.

(13) Unless an exception from prior approval is available pursuant to subsection (18), the issuance of the obligations is subject to approval of the department of treasury under the municipal finance act, 1943 PA 202, MCL 131.1 to 139.3. However, the municipal finance act, 1943 PA 202, MCL 131.1 to 139.3, except as otherwise provided in this act, is not applicable to the issuance of obligations. The department of treasury shall issue its order of approval when it has determined all of the following:

(a) That the revenues, properties, and other securities pledged for revenue obligations are sufficient.

(b) That, to the extent authorized by the building authority, insurance, letters of credit, irrevocable commitments to purchase revenue obligations, or other transactions to provide separate security to assure timely payment of any revenue obligations of the building authority have been provided, and in fact, those transactions do provide resources, when taken with true rental and proceeds authorized by this act, for the prompt repayment of the revenue obligations.

(c) That the purpose for which the revenue obligations are issued and the manner in which the revenue obligations are proposed to be issued comply with this act.

(14) When prior approval is required, the department of treasury may approve the issuance from time to time of obligations to refinance by refunding any obligations at the same time it approves the issuance of the obligations to be refunded. If the department of treasury approves a pool of obligations established under subsection (23), that approval is an approval of all obligations issued within that pool. The department of treasury may require the building authority to file with the department of treasury periodic reports and information as the department of treasury considers necessary. The department of treasury has the enforcement and remedial powers with respect to the building authority and its obligations as are provided by the municipal finance act, 1943 PA 202, MCL 131.1 to 139.3, or other provisions of law.

(15) The obligations may be sold at private or at public sale under the procedures and subject to the conditions prescribed by resolution of the board.

(16) The building authority may issue additional obligations of equal standing with respect to the pledge of the true rentals and additional security provided pursuant to this act with previously issued obligations of the building authority issued to acquire or construct a facility or facilities, or to refund the obligations, for the purpose of completing, or making additions, improvements, or replacements to, the facility or facilities for which the previous obligations of the authority were issued or to refund all or part of

§ 830.418  State Building Programs

obligations previously issued for such a facility, under the terms and conditions provided in the resolution authorizing the previous issue of obligations.

(17) The authority shall not have obligations outstanding at any 1 time for any of its corporate purposes in a principal amount totaling more than $2,700,000,000.00, which limitations shall not include principal appreciation as provided in subsection (20) or obligations or portions of obligations used to pay for any of the following:

(a) Amounts set aside for payment of interest becoming due before the collection of the first true rental available.

(b) Amounts set aside for a reserve for payment of principal, interest, and redemption premiums.

(c) Costs of issuance of the obligations and the discount, if any, on sale.

(d) The sums expected to be set aside for the purposes provided in this subsection for any obligations authorized by the authority but not sold. The amount set aside or expected to be set aside for the purposes provided in this subsection shall be conclusively determined by a certificate setting forth the amounts executed by the executive director of the building authority. In addition, there shall be excluded from the limitation obligations issued to refund prior obligations if those prior obligations will not be retired within 90 days after the date of issuance of the refunding obligations. If an obligation is issued to retire a prior obligation within 90 days after the date of issuance of the refunding obligation, the obligation is counted against the limitation when the refunded obligation is retired.

(18) The requirement of subsection (13) for obtaining the prior approval of the department of treasury before issuing obligations under this section is subject to sections 10 and 11 of chapter III of the municipal finance act, 1943 PA 202, MCL 133.10 and 133.11, and the department of treasury has the same authority as provided by section 11 of chapter III of the municipal finance act, 1943 PA 202, MCL 133.11, to issue an order providing or denying an exception from the prior approval required by subsection (13) for obligations authorized by this act.

(19) The authority may apply and pledge, if not already pledged, all or any unpledged part of the true rental and other revenues of a facility; income and profit from the investment of money pertaining to a facility; and money in a fund or account of the authority pertaining to a facility to pay the principal, interest, and redemption premiums on revenue obligations of the authority other than those to which the true rental and other revenues, investment income, or profit or funds or accounts pertain; to pay amounts due under an agreement to manage payment, revenue, or interest rate exposure regardless of the obligations or investments to which the agreement relates; or to pay part or all of the cost of additional facilities to be acquired by the authority for the use of the state. The authority may establish a separate fund into which the rental and other revenues,

**State Building Programs** § 830.418

investment income or profit, or money of such a fund or account shall be deposited to be used to pay principal, interest, and redemption premiums on outstanding obligations of the authority or to acquire facilities for the use of the state. The authority shall not acquire a facility unless the acquisition is approved by the state administrative board and by a concurrent resolution of the legislature approved by a majority of the members elected to and serving in each house. The authority may pledge any or all of the foregoing to the payment of revenue obligations of the authority other than those to which they pertain. If the true rental and other revenues, investment income or profit, or the money in funds or accounts to be applied as specified in this subsection pertain to a facility leased to the state and an institution of higher education pursuant to a lease executed and delivered before January 1, 1983, no application or pledge thereof may be made unless approved by the institution of higher education.

(20) If the authority issues an obligation that appreciates in principal amount, the amount of principal appreciation each year on that obligation, after the date of original issuance, shall not be considered to be principal indebtedness for the purposes of the limitation in subsection (17) or any other limitation. The appreciation of principal after the date of original issue shall be considered interest and shall be within the interest rate limitations set forth in this act.

(21) Of the $2,700,000,000.00 authorized under subsection (17), priority shall be determined by the joint capital outlay committee.

(22) In connection with an obligation issued previously or to be issued under this act or an investment made previously or to be made, the board may by resolution authorize and approve the execution and delivery of an agreement to manage payment, revenue, or interest rate exposure. The agreement may include, but is not limited to, an interest rate exchange agreement, an agreement providing for payment or receipt of money based on levels of or changes in interest rates, an agreement to exchange cash flows or series of payments, or an agreement providing for or incorporating interest rate caps, collars, floors, or locks. Subject to a prior pledge or lien created under this act, a payment to be made by the building authority under an agreement described in this subsection is payable, together with other obligations of the building authority, from those sources described in subsections (6) and (7), all with the parity or priority and upon the conditions set forth in the board's resolution. An agreement entered into under this subsection is not a general obligation of the state or the building authority, and the agreement does not count against the limitation on outstanding obligations contained in subsection (17).

(23) The building authority may authorize by resolution a pool of obligations to meet interim financing needs. A pool may be issued in 1 or more series, may relate to 1 or more projects, and is subject to all of the following:

(a) The board's resolution approving the pool shall state at least all of the following:

(i) The name or designation of the pool to distinguish it from any other pool issued under this subsection.

(ii) The latest date by which an obligation issued under the pool must mature, which shall not be later than 5 years after the date on which the pool is established. The duration of the pool shall be the time from the date on which the pool is established to the latest possible maturity date of obligations issued pursuant to the pool, or sooner as provided by resolution.

(iii) The maximum par amount of obligations that may be outstanding at any time during the duration of the pool. The resolution may state the maximum par amount of obligations that may be issued pursuant to the pool.

(iv) Other terms of the obligations as provided in subsection (8) or the limits within which the chief operating officer, chief staff person, or member of the board shall determine those terms as provided in subsection (5).

(v) The security for obligations issued pursuant to the pool.

(vi) Other provisions, not inconsistent with the terms of this act, that the board determines to be necessary or appropriate to the pool.

(b) Proceeds of obligations issued as part of a pool established under this subsection may be used for any of the purposes for which revenue obligations of the building authority may be used as described in subsection (1). However, an obligation shall not be issued with respect to a facility unless all of the following are true:

(i) The board approves the financing of the facility pursuant to the pool, which approval may be made at the same time as or after the establishment of the pool.

(ii) The board approves the proposed form of lease for the facility, which approval may be made prior to, at the same time as, or after the establishment of the pool.

(iii) The state administrative board, an institution of higher education, if applicable, and the legislature have approved the form of the lease as required by section 7, which approval may be made prior to, at the same time as, or after the establishment of the pool.

(iv) The aggregate amounts of obligations issued and outstanding with respect to a facility under a pool, together with other obligations that may have been issued and are outstanding with respect to the facility under this act do not exceed the cost of the facility, including allowable interest costs, as approved by the state administrative board, an institution of higher education, if applicable, and the legislature.

(v) On or before the issuance of obligations the proceeds of which are to finance the acquisition, construction, renovation, or rehabilitation of the facility, the building authority and the state, and, if applicable, an institution of higher education, enter into the lease or an agreement to construct or acquire the facility, which lease or agreement sets forth the terms and conditions under which the building authority will finance the construction or acquisition of the facility for lease to the state or to the state and any applicable institution of higher education.

**History:**
Pub Acts 1964, No. 183, § 8, imd eff May 19, 1964; amended by Pub Acts 1976, No. 240, eff March 31, 1977, by § 2 eff September 30, 1976; 1980, No. 240, imd eff July 24, 1980; 1981, No. 183, imd eff December 23, 1981; 1983, No. 156, imd eff July 24, 1983; 1985, No. 206, imd eff December 27, 1985; 1987, No. 119, imd eff July 20, 1987; 1993, No. 35, imd eff May 11, 1993 (see 1993 note below); 1994, No. 252, imd eff July 5, 1994.

Amended by Pub Acts 1997, No. 127, imd eff November 5, 1997.

**Editor's notes:**
**Pub Acts 1993, No. 35, § 2,** imd eff May 11, 1993, provides:
"Section 2. This amendatory act shall not take effect unless Senate Bill No. 363 of the 87th Legislature [which became Act No. 19 of 1993] is enacted into law."

**Effect of amendment notes:**
**The 1994 amendment** added subsections (22) and (23); and made numerous other revisions throughout the section.

**The 1997 amendment** replaced "the" with "this" before "state" in three instances in subsection (1); made stylistic changes to statutory references in subsections (8), (12), (13), (14), and (18); and replaced "$2,000,000,000.00" with "$2,700,000,000.00" in subsections (17) and (21).

**Statutory references:**
Section 7 is § 830.417.

**Michigan Digest references:**
Municipal and Public Bonds §§1, 40, 41.
State of Michigan §§10, 12, 15, 19, 24.
Taxes § 57.

**ALR notes:**
Power of governmental unit to issue bonds as implying power to refund them, 1 ALR2d 134.
What constitutes a "public sale", 4 ALR2d 575.

**Michigan Civ Jur references:**
State of Michigan § 14.20.

**Research references:**
64 Am Jur 2d, Public Securities and Obligations §§105, 210.
71 Am Jur 2d, State and Local Taxation §§336 et seq.
76 Am Jur 2d, Trusts § 385.

### CASE NOTES

The State Building Authority may not issue bonds that are repayable over a period extending one year beyond the economic life of the project, as determined by the State Administrative Board, to be financed by the proceeds of the bonds. Op Atty Gen, October 22, 1987, No. 6477.

## § 830.418a. Reserve fund; creation; use; income or interest earned; limitations on use, withdrawal. [MSA § 3.447(108a)]

Sec. 8a. The building authority may create and establish a special fund or funds to secure any issue of obligations, referred to as a reserve fund, and shall pay into the reserve fund any proceeds of

§ 830.418a

sale of any issue of obligations to the extent provided in the resolution of the building authority authorizing the issuance thereof and any other money derived from true rental, investment income, or any lease or facility which may be available to the authority for the purpose of the fund. All money held in any reserve fund, except as provided in this section or section 8, shall be used solely for the payment of the principal of the obligations for which the fund was established, the payment of interest on the obligations for which the fund was established, or the payment of any redemption premium required to be paid when the obligations are redeemed before maturity. Money in the reserve fund shall not be withdrawn except for the purpose of paying principal of and interest on the obligations for which the fund was established maturing and becoming due and for the payment of which other money of the authority is not available or as otherwise provided in this act. Except as provided in section 8, any income or interest earned by, or increment to, the reserve fund due to the investment or reinvestment of the reserve fund may only be withdrawn and used for any purposes for which obligations may be issued and to pay interest and to pay at maturity, purchase, or call for redemption obligations of the building authority for which the fund was established, as the building authority determines in the resolution authorizing the obligations.

**History:**
Pub Acts 1964, No. 183, § 8a, as added by Pub Acts 1980, No. 240, imd eff July 24, 1980; amended by Pub Acts 1981, No. 183, imd eff December 23, 1981; 1983, No. 156, imd eff July 24, 1983.

**Statutory references:**
Section 8, above referred to, is § 830.418.

## § 830.419. Obligations; statutory first lien; enforcement.
[MSA § 3.447(109)]

Sec. 9. A board resolution authorizing the issuance of an obligation, or an agreement relating to the security of the obligation or agreement to manage payment, revenue, or interest rate exposure with respect to the obligation, may assign, pledge, and create a statutory first lien, and 1 or more subordinate liens, on the true rental for a facility and on the other revenues, funds, and accounts described in section 8 to and in favor of parties in interest. An assignment or pledge made by the building authority is valid and binding from the date of delivery of the obligation, or as applicable, an agreement related to security or management of payment, revenue, or interest rate exposure. The lien of the assignment and pledge is effective without physical delivery or further action and is valid and binding against parties having claims of any kind against the building authority irrespective of whether the parties have notice of the lien and pledge. The resolution, and any instrument by which the assignment or pledge is made or created, need not be recorded. By suit, action, mandamus, or other proceedings, a party in interest may protect and enforce the statutory first lien and any

**State Building Programs** § 830.420

and all rights of the parties in interest under the laws of the state, or under a resolution authorizing the issuance of the obligation, or as applicable, an agreement related to security or management of payment, revenue, or interest rate exposure, and may enforce and compel the performance of all duties required by this act, the resolution, or the lease to be performed by the building authority, the state, or any officers of the state. An action, mandamus, or other proceedings may be brought by a party in interest concerning an obligation or agreement under this act directly against the state to compel the performance of the duties of the state required by this act, the resolution, or the lease.

**History:**
Pub Acts 1964, No. 183, § 9, imd eff May 19, 1964; amended by Pub Acts 1976, No. 240, eff March 31, 1977, by § 2 eff September 30, 1976; 1983, No. 156, imd eff July 24, 1983; 1994, No. 252, imd eff July 5, 1994.

**Effect of amendment notes:**
The 1994 amendment made revisions throughout this section.

**Michigan Digest references:**
Municipal and Public Bonds §§1, 40, 41.
State of Michigan §§10, 12, 15, 19, 24.
Taxes § 57.

**ALR notes:**
Power of governmental unit to issue bonds as implying power to refund them, 1 ALR2d 134.
What constitutes a "public sale", 4 ALR2d 575.

**Michigan Civ Jur references:**
State of Michigan § 14.20.

**Research references:**
64 Am Jur 2d, Public Securities and Obligations §§105, 210.
71 Am Jur 2d, State and Local Taxation §§336 et seq.
76 Am Jur 2d, Trusts § 385.

## § 830.419a. Contract with bondholders; moneys and deposits, security. [MSA § 3.447(109a)]

Sec. 9a. The building authority may contract with the holders of its bonds as to the custody, collection, securing, investment, and payment of any moneys of the building authority. Moneys of the building authority and deposits of such moneys may be secured in the manner determined by the building authority. Banks and trust companies may give security for such deposits.

**History:**
Pub Acts 1964, No. 183, § 9a, as added by Pub Acts 1976, No. 240, eff March 31, 1977, by § 2 eff September 30, 1976.

## § 830.420. State indebtedness. [MSA § 3.447(110)]

Sec. 10. This act shall not be construed or interpreted as to authorize or permit the incurring of indebtedness of the state contrary to the provisions of the state constitution.

### § 830.420

**History:**
Pub Acts 1964, No. 183, § 10, imd eff May 19, 1964; amended by Pub Acts 1976, No. 240, eff March 31, 1977, by § 2 eff September 30, 1976.

**Michigan Digest references:**
Municipal and Public Bonds §§1, 40, 41.
State of Michigan §§10, 12, 15, 19, 24.
Taxes § 57.

**ALR notes:**
Power of governmental unit to issue bonds as implying power to refund them, 1 ALR2d 134.
What constitutes a "public sale", 4 ALR2d 575.

**Michigan Civ Jur references:**
State of Michigan § 14.20.

**Research references:**
64 Am Jur 2d, Public Securities and Obligations §§105, 210.
71 Am Jur 2d, State and Local Taxation §§336 et seq.
76 Am Jur 2d, Trusts § 385.

### § 830.421. Tax exemption. [MSA § 3.447(111)]

Sec. 11. Property owned and acquired by the building authority in accordance with this act shall be exempt from taxes levied by the state or its political subdivisions and taxing districts. The building authority shall not be required to pay taxes or assessments upon its activities or upon its income or revenues.

**History:**
Pub Acts 1964, No. 183, § 11, imd eff May 19, 1964; amended by Pub Acts 1976, No. 240, eff March 31, 1977, by § 2 eff September 30, 1976.

**Michigan Digest references:**
Municipal and Public Bonds §§1, 40, 41.
State of Michigan §§10, 12, 15, 19, 24.
Taxes § 57.

**ALR notes:**
Power of governmental unit to issue bonds as implying power to refund them, 1 ALR2d 134.
What constitutes a "public sale", 4 ALR2d 575.

**Michigan Civ Jur references:**
State of Michigan § 14.20.

**Research references:**
64 Am Jur 2d, Public Securities and Obligations §§105, 210.
71 Am Jur 2d, State and Local Taxation §§336 et seq.
76 Am Jur 2d, Trusts § 385.

### § 830.421a. Personal liability or accountability, limitation. [MSA § 3.447(111a)]

Sec. 11a. The members of the authority and persons executing notes or bonds shall not be liable personally on the notes or bonds, or be subject to personal liability or accountability by reason of the issuance thereof.

**History:**
Pub Acts 1964, No. 183, § 11a, as added by Pub Acts 1976, No. 240, eff March 31, 1977, by § 2 eff September 30, 1976.

**State Building Programs** § 830.423

### § 830.422. Investment by fiduciaries. [MSA § 3.447(112)]

Sec. 12. Bonds issued by the building authority under this act are securities in which banks, bankers, savings banks, trust companies, savings and loan associations, investment companies, and other persons carrying on a banking business, insurance companies, insurance associations, and other persons carrying on an insurance business, and administrators, executors, guardians, trustees, and other fiduciaries may properly and legally invest funds belonging to them or within their control.

**History:**
Pub Acts 1964, No. 183, § 12, imd eff May 19, 1964; amended by Pub Acts 1976, No. 240, eff March 31, 1977, by § 2 eff September 30, 1976.

**Michigan Digest references:**
Municipal and Public Bonds §§1, 40, 41.
State of Michigan §§10, 12, 15, 19, 24.
Taxes § 57.

**ALR notes:**
Power of governmental unit to issue bonds as implying power to refund them, 1 ALR2d 134.
What constitutes a "public sale", 4 ALR2d 575.

**Michigan Civ Jur references:**
State of Michigan § 14.20.

**Research references:**
64 Am Jur 2d, Public Securities and Obligations §§105, 210.
71 Am Jur 2d, State and Local Taxation §§336 et seq.
76 Am Jur 2d, Trusts § 385.

### § 830.423. Public purpose; construction. [MSA § 3.447(113)]

Sec. 13. It is hereby found, determined, and declared that the creation of the building authority and the carrying out of its corporate purposes are in all respects for the benefit of the people of the state and constitute a public purpose and that the facilities to be acquired are necessary for the public welfare of the people of the state, and that the building authority will be performing an essential governmental function in the exercise of the power conferred upon it by this act. This act shall be liberally construed to effect the intents and purposes hereof.

**History:**
Pub Acts 1964, No. 183, § 13, imd eff May 19, 1964; reenacted without change by Pub Acts 1976, No. 240, eff March 31, 1977, by § 2 eff September 30, 1976.

**Michigan Digest references:**
Municipal and Public Bonds §§1, 40, 41.
State of Michigan §§10, 12, 15, 19, 24.
Taxes § 57.

**ALR notes:**
Power of governmental unit to issue bonds as implying power to refund them, 1 ALR2d 134.
What constitutes a "public sale", 4 ALR2d 575.

**§ 830.423**

**Michigan Civ Jur references:**
State of Michigan § 14.20.

**Research references:**
64 Am Jur 2d, Public Securities and Obligations §§105, 210.
71 Am Jur 2d, State and Local Taxation §§336 et seq.
76 Am Jur 2d, Trusts § 385.

## § 830.424. Act as additional or alternative method; supplemental and additional to powers conferred by other laws. [MSA § 3.447(114)]

Sec. 14. This act shall be deemed to provide an additional or alternative method for accomplishing the purposes authorized hereby. This act shall be regarded as supplemental and additional to powers conferred by other laws and shall not be regarded as in derogation of any powers presently existing.

**History:**
Pub Acts 1964, No. 183, § 14, imd eff May 19, 1964; amended by Pub Acts 1976, No. 240, eff March 31, 1977, by § 2 eff September 30, 1976.

**Michigan Digest references:**
Municipal and Public Bonds §§1, 40, 41.
State of Michigan §§10, 12, 15, 19, 24.
Taxes § 57.

**ALR notes:**
Power of governmental unit to issue bonds as implying power to refund them, 1 ALR2d 134.
What constitutes a "public sale", 4 ALR2d 575.

**Michigan Civ Jur references:**
State of Michigan § 14.20.

**Research references:**
64 Am Jur 2d, Public Securities and Obligations §§105, 210.
71 Am Jur 2d, State and Local Taxation §§336 et seq.
76 Am Jur 2d, Trusts § 385.

## § 830.425. Advisory opinion on constitutionality; effect of partial invalidity. [MSA § 3.447(115)]

Sec. 15. Pursuant to section 8 of article 3 of the state constitution of 1963, it is the intent of the legislature to request by concurrent resolution the opinion of the supreme court as to the constitutionality of this 1976 amendatory act as amended. Notwithstanding section 5 of chapter 1 of the Revised Statutes of 1846, being section 8.5 of the Michigan Compiled Laws, if the supreme court's advisory opinion finds any portion of this act, as amended, to be invalid, the entire act shall be invalid.

**History:**
Pub Acts 1964, No. 183, § 15, as added by Pub Acts 1976, No. 240, eff March 31, 1977, by § 2 eff September 30, 1976.

**Statutory references:**
Section 5 of RS 1846, Ch. 1, above referred to, is § 8.5.

**Michigan Digest references:**
Municipal and Public Bonds §§1, 40, 41.

State of Michigan §§10, 12, 15, 19, 24.
Taxes § 57.

**ALR notes:**
Power of governmental unit to issue bonds as implying power to refund them, 1 ALR2d 134.
What constitutes a "public sale", 4 ALR2d 575.

**Michigan Civ Jur references:**
State of Michigan § 14.20.

**Research references:**
64 Am Jur 2d, Public Securities and Obligations §§105, 210.
71 Am Jur 2d, State and Local Taxation §§336 et seq.
76 Am Jur 2d, Trusts § 385.

# PLANNING OF PROPOSED STATE BUILDING PROJECTS [Repealed]

Act 242, 1976, p 691, imd eff August 8, 1976.
[Repealed]

AN ACT to provide for preliminary studies and planning of proposed building projects for state purposes.

## §§830.501–830.505. [Repealed] [MSA §§3.440(1)–3.440(5)]

**History:**
Pub Acts 1976, No. 242, §§1–5, imd eff August 8, 1976; **repealed** by Pub Acts 1984, No. 431, imd eff March 29, 1985.

# Michigan Compiled Laws Service

**CUMULATIVE SUPPLEMENT TO VOLUME 71**

Issued April 2004

*Includes Legislation and annotations through the end of the 2003 Regular Session of the Legislature.*

For the latest enactments and annotations, see the MCLS Advance Legislative Service and Quarterly Update Pamphlets.

LexisNexis™

LexisNexis, the knowledge burst logo, and Michie are trademarks of Reed Elsevier Properties Inc., used under license. Matthew Bender is a registered trademark of Matthew Bender Properties Inc.

© 2004 Matthew Bender & Company, Inc., a member of the LexisNexis Group.
All rights reserved.

No copyright is claimed in the text of statutes, regulations and excerpts from opinions quoted within this work. Permission to copy material exceeding fair use, 17 U.S.C. §107, may be licensed for a fee of $1 per page per copy from the Copyright Clearance Center, 222 Rosewood Drive, Danvers, MA, 01923, telephone (978) 750-8400.

Editorial Offices
701 East Water Street, Charlottesville, VA 22902 (800) 446-3410
www.lexis.com

ISBN 0-327-16001-2

5719213

# THIS VOLUME CONTAINS

**Statutes:**

This volume of the Michigan Compiled Laws Service, as supplemented, contains the full text of the general laws of a permanent nature enacted by, and in force through, the 2003 Regular Legislative Session (2003 PA 322).

For the latest enactments, consult the MCLS Advance Legislative Service and MCLS Quarterly Updates. You can also call LexisNexis™ at 1-800-833-9844.

**Case notes and other annotation and reference materials:**

This publication contains annotations taken from decisions of the Michigan Supreme Court, Michigan Court of Appeals and the appropriate federal courts issued as of March 1, 2004.

The case notes and other annotation and reference materials construing and applying the statutes in this volume have been updated through the following:

    Mich Atty Gen Op 7143 (2003)
    1    Ave Maria L Rev 215
    2003  Det CL Rev 507
    83   Mich B J 72
    10   Mich J Gender & Law 189
    25   Mich J Int'l L 211
    9    Mich J Race & L 235
    101  Mich L Rev 1102
    10   Mich Telecomm Tech L Rev 175
    20   T.M. Cooley L Rev 361
    81   U Det Mercy L Rev 141
    37   U Mich J L Ref 599
    47   Wayne L Rev 1431

---

**SHEPARD'S® Citations Service.** For further research of authorities referenced here, use SHEPARD'S to be sure your case or statute is still good law and to find additional authorities that support your position. SHEPARD'S is available exclusively from LexisNexis™.

# CHAPTER 791

# DEPARTMENT OF CORRECTIONS

## DEPARTMENT OF CORRECTIONS

### Act 232 of 1953

#### CHAPTER IV
#### BUREAU OF PENAL INSTITUTIONS

§ 791.268a  Visits from minors; conditions; restrictions; "minor" defined.

## LOCAL CORRECTIONS OFFICERS TRAINING ACT

### Act 125 of 2003

| | |
|---|---|
| § 791.531 | Short title. |
| § 791.532 | Definitions. |
| § 791.533 | Sheriffs coordinating and training office; creation; head of office; chief executive officer; executive secretary. |
| § 791.534 | Qualifications and appointment of members; vacancy; reappointment; terms. |
| § 791.535 | Chairperson; vice-chairperson; designation; terms; reelection; meetings; conduct; compensation. |
| § 791.536 | Holding public office or employment; disqualification prohibited. |
| § 791.537 | Administrative support services. |
| § 791.538 | Standards and requirements. |
| § 791.539 | Local corrections officers advisory board; creation; qualifications and appointment of members; terms; vacancy; reappointment; compensation; development and recommendation of standards and requirements; training facilities. |
| § 791.540 | Annual report. |
| § 791.541 | Local corrections officer; certification. |
| § 791.542 | Local corrections officer; evidence of employment; certification. |
| § 791.543 | Local corrections officer; certification; conditions. |
| § 791.543a | Collective bargaining agreement; temporary transfer or assignment. |
| § 791.544 | Duties of council. |
| § 791.545 | Local corrections officers training fund; creation in state treasury; administration; source of funds; use; eligibility of counties to receive grants; reimbursement of fee; unexpended funds. |
| § 791.546 | Acceptance of funds, grants, and gifts. |

## DEPARTMENT OF CORRECTIONS
Act 232, 1953, p 407, eff October 2, 1953.

### CHAPTER I
### DEPARTMENT OF CORRECTIONS

**§ 791.201. Establishment; administration by Michigan corrections commission; membership of commission, political affiliation, oath, holding other position, term, vacancies, removal, compensation and expenses; director; executive office, place of meetings. [MSA § 28.2271]**

#### LexisNexis™ and Other Annotations

**Michigan Digest references:**
Zoning § 18.

**LexisNexis™ Michigan analytical references:**
Michigan Law and Practice, Convicts and Prisons § 2.

**§ 791.201a. Short title.**

Sec. 1a. This act shall be known and may be cited as the "corrections code of 1953".

**History:**
Pub Act 1953, No. 232, § 1a, as added by Pub Acts 2002, No. 212, imd eff April 29, 2002.

**§ 791.202. Commission, organization; meetings; quorum; administrative authority and duty; Open Meetings Act, compliance. [MSA § 28.2272]**

#### LexisNexis™ and Other Annotations

**Michigan Digest references:**
Municipal Corporations § 118.50.
Pardons and Paroles § 4.
Zoning § 18.

**LexisNexis™ Michigan analytical references:**
Michigan Law and Practice, Convicts and Prisons § 2.
Michigan Law and Practice, Criminal Law and Procedure § 877.

**§ 791.203. Director of corrections; appointment, qualifications, term, removal, compensation and expenses, chief administrative officer of commission, powers and duties. [MSA § 28.2273]**

#### LexisNexis™ and Other Annotations

**Michigan Digest references:**
Prisons and Jails § 2.40.

**LexisNexis™ Michigan analytical references:**
Michigan Law and Practice, Convicts and Prisons §§2, 6.

**Department of Corrections** § 791.205a

### CASE NOTES

Deputy director of the Department of Corrections' Bureau of Correctional Facilities has authority to overrule a warden's award of special good time credit made pursuant to MCLS § 800.33(12), which is not an exception to the general grant of power and authority provided the director and assistant directors of the Department of Corrections under MCLS §§791.203, 791.205; the statutory grant of power gives the director and assistant directors full power and authority to supervise and control the affairs of the department, and such full power and authority includes discretionary decisions regarding the length of time that prisoners must serve. Edmond v Dep't of Corr. (2002) 254 Mich App 154, 656 NW2d 842.

## § 791.204. Jurisdiction of department. [MSA § 28.2274]

### LexisNexis™ and Other Annotations

**Michigan Digest references:**
Constitutional Law §§66, 89, 326, 371.
Criminal Law and Procedure § 754.60.
Pardons and Paroles §§2, 5, 6.
Prisons and Jails §§1, 1.05, 1.25, 1.35, 1.45, 1.50, 4.
Statutes § 26.
Zoning § 18.

**LexisNexis™ Michigan analytical references:**
Michigan Law and Practice, Convicts and Prisons § 2.

## § 791.205. Assistant directors; appointment, powers and duties. [MSA § 28.2275]

### LexisNexis™ and Other Annotations

**Michigan Digest references:**
Prisons and Jails § 2.40.

**LexisNexis™ Michigan analytical references:**
Michigan Law and Practice, Convicts and Prisons § 6.

### CASE NOTES

Deputy director of the Department of Corrections' Bureau of Correctional Facilities has authority to overrule a warden's award of special good time credit made pursuant to MCLS § 800.33(12), which is not an exception to the general grant of power and authority provided the director and assistant directors of the Department of Corrections under MCLS §§791.203, 791.205; the statutory grant of power gives the director and assistant directors full power and authority to supervise and control the affairs of the department, and such full power and authority includes discretionary decisions regarding the length of time that prisoners must serve. Edmond v Dep't of Corr. (2002) 254 Mich App 154, 656 NW2d 842.

## § 791.205a. Employment or appointment by department of person convicted or charged with felony. [MSA § 28.2275a]

### LexisNexis™ and Other Annotations

**Michigan Digest references:**
Worker's Disability Compensation §§152, 153, 248.15.

§ 791.205a  MCLS Cumulative Supplement

LexisNexis™ Michigan analytical references:
Michigan Law and Practice, Workmen's Compensation § 91.

CASE NOTES

Employer could not re–employ the employee because the employee had been convicted of a felony; pursuant to MCLS § 418.361(1), the employer was not liable to pay partial disability benefits to the employee for the employee's loss of wage–earning capacity attributable to his work–related injury. Sweatt v Dep't of Corr. (2003) 468 Mich 172, 661 NW2d 201.

## § 791.206. Rules generally. [MSA § 28.2276]

### LexisNexis™ and Other Annotations

**Michigan Digest references:**
Combinations and Monopolies § 12.
Mandamus § 115.
Pardons and Paroles §§4, 5.
Prisons and Jails §§1.05, 1.35, 1.50, 4.

**LexisNexis™ Michigan analytical references:**
Michigan Law and Practice, Convicts and Prisons § 2.
Michigan Law and Practice, Criminal Law and Procedure § 877.
Michigan Law and Practice, Unfair Competition § 7.

### CASE NOTES

**1. Construction, operation and effect.**

Plaintiffs' claims under the Michigan Antitrust Reform Act dismissed because the conduct complained of, that defendant State of Michigan entered into exclusive inmate telephone agreements under which inmates were restricted to collect only calls for which the plaintiff recipients were being charged excessive rates and surcharges, fell within the governmental exception to the act, which applies when a unit of government, in this case, the Michigan Department of Corrections, is acting in a subject matter area in which it is authorized to act. Miranda v Michigan, 168 F Supp 2d 685 (ED Mich 2001).

## § 791.216. Comprehensive plan for establishment of correctional facilities, development; approval by legislature; determination of need for facility; notice of proposed establishment of facility; local advisory board, creation; duties; officers; public hearing as to potential site; time; attendance; procedures for addressing; exclusion; public notice; minutes; final site selection; finding of compliance with act; transmittal of finding and notice; option to lease or purchase property; time for exercising. [MSA § 28.2286]

### LexisNexis™ and Other Annotations

**LexisNexis™ Michigan analytical references:**
Michigan Law and Practice, Convicts and Prisons § 2.

## § 791.220e. Scott correctional facility; western Wayne correctional facility; capacity limits; increase. [MSA § 28.2290(5)]

Sec. 20e. ◆

[(1) Except as provided in subsection (2), not more than 880

**Department of Corrections** § 791.220g

prisoners shall be housed at the Scott correctional facility and not more than 925 prisoners shall be housed at the western Wayne correctional facility.

(2) If a new housing unit is constructed within the security perimeter of either facility listed in subsection (1), the capacity limits listed in subsection (1) for that facility are increased by the designated capacity of the new housing unit.]

**History:**
Amended by Pub Acts 2002, No. 670, imd eff December 26, 2002, by enacting § 1 eff March 1, 2003 (see 2002 note below).

**Editor's notes:**
Pub Acts 2002, No. 670, enacting § 2, imd eff December 26, 2002, by enacting § 1 eff March 1, 2003, provides:

"Enacting section 2. This amendatory act does not take effect unless all of the following bills of the 91st Legislature are enacted into law:
"(a) House Bill No. 5394 [Pub Acts 2002, No. 665].
"(b) House Bill No. 5395 [Pub Acts 2002, No. 666]."

**Effect of amendment notes:**
The 2002 amendment rewrote the entire section.

## § 791.220g. Youth correctional facility. [MSA § 28.2290(7)]

Sec. 20g. (1) The department may establish a youth correctional facility which shall house only prisoners committed to the jurisdiction of the department who are 19 years of age or less[. If the department establishes or contracts with a private vendor for the operation of a youth correctional facility, following intake processing in a department operated facility, the department shall house all male prisoners who are 16 years of age or less at the youth correctional facility unless the department determines that the prisoner should be housed at a different facility for reasons of security, safety, or because of the prisoner's specialized physical or mental health care needs.] ◆

[(2) Except as provided in subsection (3), a prisoner who is 16 years of age or less and housed at a youth correctional facility shall only be placed in a general population housing unit with prisoners who are 16 years of age or less.

(3) A prisoner who becomes 17 years of age while being housed at a youth correctional facility and who has a satisfactory prison record may remain in a general population housing unit for no more than 1 year with prisoners who are 16 years of age or less.

(4) Except as provided in subsection (3), a prisoner who is 16 years of age or less and housed at a youth correctional facility shall not be allowed to be in the proximity of a prisoner who is 17 years of age or more without the presence and direct supervision of custody personnel in the immediate vicinity.

(5)] ◆ The department may establish and operate the youth correctional facility or may contract on behalf of the state with a private vendor for the construction or operation, or both, of the youth correctional facility. If the department contracts with a private vendor to construct, rehabilitate, develop, renovate, or

§ 791.220g

operate any existing or anticipated facility pursuant to this section, the department shall require a written certification from the private vendor regarding all of the following:

(a) If practicable to efficiently and effectively complete the project, the private vendor shall follow a competitive bid process for the construction, rehabilitation, development, or renovation of the facility, and this process shall be open to all Michigan residents and firms. The private vendor shall not discriminate against any contractor on the basis of its affiliation or nonaffiliation with any collective bargaining organization.

(b) The private vendor shall make a good faith effort to employ, if qualified, Michigan residents at the facility.

(c) The private vendor shall make a good faith effort to employ or contract with Michigan residents and firms to construct, rehabilitate, develop, or renovate the facility.

[(6)] ◆ If the department contracts with a private vendor for the operation of the youth correctional facility, the department shall require by contract that the personnel employed by the private vendor in the operation of the facility be certified as correctional officers to the same extent as would be required if those personnel were employed in a correctional facility operated by the department. The department also shall require by contract that the private vendor meet requirements specified by the department regarding security, protection of the public, inspections by the department, programming, liability and insurance, conditions of confinement, educational services required under subsection ◆ [(11)], and any other issues the department considers necessary for the operation of the youth correctional facility. The department shall also require that the contract include provisions to protect the public's interest if the private vendor defaults on the contract. Before finalizing a contract with a private vendor for the construction or operation of the youth correctional facility, the department shall submit the proposed contract to the standing committees of the senate and the house of representatives having jurisdiction of corrections issues, the corrections subcommittees of the standing committees on appropriations of the senate and the house of representatives, and, with regard to proposed construction contracts, the joint committee on capital outlay. A contract between the department and a private vendor for the construction or operation of the youth correctional facility shall be contingent upon appropriation of the required funding. If the department contracts with a private vendor under this section, the selection of that private vendor shall be by open, competitive bid.

[(7)] ◆ The department shall not site a youth correctional facility under this section in a city, village, or township unless the local legislative body of that city, village, or township adopts a resolution approving the location.

[(8)] ◆ A private vendor operating a youth correctional facility under a contract under this section shall not do any of the following, unless directed to do so by the department policy:

## Department of Corrections § 791.220g

(a) Calculate inmate release and parole eligibility dates.
(b) Award good time or disciplinary credits, or impose disciplinary time.
(c) Approve inmates for extensions of limits of confinement.

[(9)] ◆ The youth correctional facility shall be open to visits during all business hours, and during nonbusiness hours unless an emergency prevents it, by any elected state senator or state representative.

[(10)] ◆ Once each year, the department shall report on the operation of the facility. Copies of the report shall be submitted to the chairpersons of the house and senate committees responsible for legislation on corrections or judicial issues, and to the clerk of the house of representatives and the secretary of the senate.

[(11)] ◆ Regardless of whether the department itself operates the youth correctional facility or contracts with a private vendor to operate the youth correctional facility, all of the following educational services shall be provided for juvenile prisoners housed at the facility who have not earned a high school diploma or received a general education certificate (GED):

(a) The department or private vendor shall require that a prisoner whose academic achievement level is not sufficient to allow the prisoner to participate effectively in a program leading to the attainment of a GED certificate participate in classes that will prepare him or her to participate effectively in the GED program, and shall provide those classes in the facility.

(b) The department or private vendor shall require that a prisoner who successfully completes classes described in subdivision (a), or whose academic achievement level is otherwise sufficient, participate in classes leading to the attainment of a GED certificate, and shall provide those classes.

[(12)] ◆ Neither the department nor the private vendor shall seek to have the youth correctional facility authorized as a public school academy under the revised school code, 1976 PA 451, MCL 380.1 to 380.1852.

[(13)] ◆ A private vendor that operates the youth correctional facility under a contract with the department shall provide written notice of its intention to discontinue its operation of the facility. This subsection does not authorize or limit liability for a breach or default of contract. If the reason for the discontinuance is that the private vendor intends not to renew the contract, the notice shall be delivered to the director of the department at least 1 year before the contract expiration date. If the discontinuance is for any other reason, the notice shall be delivered to the director of the department at least 6 months before the date on which the private vendor will discontinue its operation of the facility. This subsection does not authorize or limit liability for a breach or default of contract.

**History:**
Amended by Pub Acts 2000, No. 211, imd eff June 27, 2000.

**Effect of amendment notes:**
The **2000 amendment** in subsection (1), substituted the second sen-

### § 791.220g

tence for "and who were within the jurisdiction of 1 of the following courts:", and deleted former paragraphs (1)(a), (1)(b), and (1)(c); added subsections (2)–(4); and redesignated former subsections (2)–(10) as subsections (5)–(13).

#### LexisNexis™ and Other Annotations

**LexisNexis™ Michigan analytical references:**
Michigan Law and Practice, Convicts and Prisons § 2.

### § 791.220h. Order of restitution; deductions and payments. [MSA § 28.2290(8)]

#### LexisNexis™ and Other Annotations

**LexisNexis™ Michigan analytical references:**
Michigan Law and Practice, Criminal Law and Procedure § 3.

## CHAPTER II
## BUREAU OF PROBATION

### § 791.222. Probation officers for courts; appointment, supervision and removal; grounds; misdemeanor, probation recovery camps. [MSA § 28.2292]

#### LexisNexis™ and Other Annotations

**LexisNexis™ Michigan analytical references:**
Michigan Law and Practice, Courts § 86.

### § 791.223a. Probation personnel, circuit and recorders court, state employees, supervision and direction; county probation personnel, transfer to state classified civil service; election; date; new employees, status; remaining employee of county, funds to county, use; plan, civil service commission, provisions; applicability of act; county responsibilities. [MSA § 28.2293(1)]

#### LexisNexis™ and Other Annotations

**LexisNexis™ Michigan analytical references:**
Michigan Law and Practice, Courts § 86.

### § 791.225. Expenses of administering probation service covering more than one county; service grants, uniform rules. [MSA § 28.2295]

#### LexisNexis™ and Other Annotations

**Michigan Digest references:**
Constitutional Law § 48.
Counties § 39.

## Department of Corrections § 791.225a

**§ 791.225a. Supervision fees; collection; records; payment; waiver; determination; allocation of money collected for other obligations; administrative costs; enhanced services; unpaid amounts. [MSA § 28.2295(1)]**

Sec. 25a. (1) The department shall collect supervision fees ordered under section 13(2) of chapter II or section 1 or 3c of chapter XI of the code of criminal procedure, ◆ [1927 PA 175, MCL 762.13, 771.1, and 771.3c]. The department shall maintain records of supervision fees ordered by the court, including records of payment by persons subject to supervision fees and any amounts of supervision fees past due and owing.

(2) A supervision fee is payable when the order of delayed sentence or order of probation is entered, unless the court allows a person who is subject to a supervision fee to pay the fee in monthly installments.

(3) The department shall waive any applicable supervision fee for a person who is transferred to another state under the interstate compact entered into pursuant to ◆ [1935 PA 89, MCL 798.101 to 798.103, or the interstate compact entered into pursuant to 2002 PA 40, MCL 3.1011 to 3.1012], for the months during which he or she is in another state. The department shall collect a supervision fee of not more than ◆ [$135.00] per month for each month of supervision in this state for an offender transferred to this state under ◆ [an] interstate compact. In determining the amount of the fee, the department shall consider the offender's projected income and financial resources. The department shall use the following table of projected monthly income in determining the amount of the fee:

| Projected Monthly Income | Amount of Fee |
|---|---|
| $     0-249.99 | $ 0.00 |
| $250.00-499.99 | $10.00 |
| $500.00-749.99 | ◆ [$25.00] |
| ◆ [$750.00-999.99] | ◆ [$40.00] |
| [$1,000.00 or more | 5% of monthly income, but not more than $135.00] |

The department may collect a higher amount than indicated by the table, up to the maximum of ◆ [$135.00] for each month of supervision in this state, if the department determines that the offender has sufficient assets or other financial resources to warrant the higher amount. If the department collects a higher amount, the amount and the reasons for collecting that amount shall be stated in the department records.

(4) If a person who is subject to a supervision fee is also subject to any combination of fines, costs, restitution orders, assessments, or payments arising out of the same criminal proceeding, the allocation of money collected for those obligations shall be as otherwise provided in the code of criminal procedure, ◆ [1927 PA 175, MCL 760.1 to 777.69].

(5) Twenty percent of the money collected by the department under this section shall be allocated for administrative costs incurred by the department in collecting supervision fees and for

enhanced services, as described in this subsection. Enhanced services include, but are not limited to, the purchase of services for offenders such as counseling, employment training, employment placement, or education; public transportation expenses related to training, counseling, or employment; enhancement of staff performance through specialized training and equipment purchase; and purchase of items for offender employment. The department shall develop priorities for expending the money for enhanced services in consultation with circuit judges in this state. At the end of each fiscal year, the unexpended balance of the money allocated for administrative costs and enhanced services shall be available for carryforward to be used for the purposes described in this subsection in subsequent fiscal years. ◆

(6) If a person has not paid the full amount of a supervision fee upon being discharged from probation, or upon termination of the period of delayed sentence for a person subject to delayed sentence, the department shall review and compare the actual income of the person during the period of probation or delayed sentence with the income amount projected when the supervision fee was ordered. If the department determines that the person's actual income did not equal or exceed the projected income, the department shall waive any unpaid amount in excess of the total amount that the person would have been ordered to pay if the person's income had been accurately projected, unless the court order states that a higher amount was ordered due to available assets or other financial resources. Any unpaid amounts not waived by the department shall be reported to the department of treasury. The department of treasury shall attempt to collect the unpaid balances pursuant to section 30a of ◆ [1941 PA 122, MCL 205.30a]. Money collected under this subsection shall not be allocated for the purposes described in subsection (5).

**History:**
Amended by Pub Acts 2002, No. 502, imd eff July 16, 2002.

**Effect of amendment notes:**
　**The 2002 amendment** in subsections (1), (4) and (6) changed the style of the statutory citation; in subsection (3), opening paragraph substituted "1935 PA 89, MCL 798.101 to 798.103, or the interstate compact entered into pursuant to 2002 PA 40, MCL 3.1011 to 3.1012" for "Act No. 89 of the Public Acts of 1935, being sections 798.101 to 798.103 of the Michigan Compiled Laws", "$135.00" for "$30.00" and "an" for "that"; in subsection (3), table substituted "$25.00" for "$20.00", "$750.00-999.99" for "$750.00 or more", "$40.00" for "$30.00", added "$1,000.00 or more 5% of monthly income, but not more than $135.00"; in subsection (3), closing paragraph substituted "$135.00" for "$30.00"; and in subsection (5) deleted the last sentence which read: "Money received by the department pursuant to this subsection in the fiscal year ending September 30, 1994 is appropriated for the purposes described in this subsection.".

**Department of Corrections** § 791.233

**§ 791.229. Privileged or confidential communications; access to records, reports, and case histories; confidential relationship inviolate.** [MSA § 28.2299]

LexisNexis™ and Other Annotations

**Michigan Digest references:**
Constitutional Law §§280, 283.
Criminal Law and Procedure §§733.55, 733.70.
Records § 7.
Witnesses § 174.10.

## CHAPTER III

## BUREAU OF PARDONS AND PAROLES; PAROLE BOARD

**§ 791.231. Bureau of field services; establishment; supervision by deputy director, appointment, tenure, powers, duties; parole officers; secretarial; assistants; quarters.** [MSA § 28.2301]

LexisNexis™ and Other Annotations

**Michigan Digest references:**
Criminal Law and Procedure § 1001.

**LexisNexis™ Michigan analytical references:**
Michigan Law and Practice, Criminal Law and Procedure § 877.

**§ 791.231a. Parole board; establishment; members; terms, reappointment, removal, vacancies, qualifications; compensation; chairperson; designation, powers and duties; appointment and training function.** [MSA § 28.2301(1)]

LexisNexis™ and Other Annotations

**LexisNexis™ Michigan analytical references:**
Michigan Law and Practice, Criminal Law and Procedure § 877.

**§ 791.233. Grant of parole; conditions; paroles-in-custody; rules.** [MSA § 28.2303]

LexisNexis™ and Other Annotations

**Michigan Digest references:**
Criminal Law and Procedure § 754.60.
Pardons and Paroles § 4—6.

**LexisNexis™ Michigan analytical references:**
Michigan Law and Practice, Criminal Law and Procedure §§875, 877.
Michigan Law and Practice, Statutes § 34.

**Legal periodicals:**
Deming, Criminal Law: Michigan's Sentencing Guidelines, 79 Mich B J 652 (2000).

§ 791.233b

## § 791.233b. Eligibility for parole; minimum term required to be served; ineligibility for special parole. [MSA § 28.2303(3)]

### LexisNexis™ and Other Annotations

**Michigan Digest references:**
  Assault and Battery § 1.
  Constitutional Law § 67.
  Criminal Law and Procedure §§264.10, 731.20, 733.50, 737, 741, 743.50, 765.
  Criminal Sexual Conduct § 43.
  Homicide § 148.
  Pardons and Paroles §§4—6.
  Prisons and Jails § 2.40.
  Statutes § 189.

**LexisNexis™ Michigan analytical references:**
  Michigan Law and Practice, Criminal Law and Procedure §§875, 877.
  Michigan Law and Practice, Statutes § 34.

**Legal periodicals:**
  Deming, Criminal Law: Michigan's Sentencing Guidelines, 79 Mich B J 652 (2000).

### CASE NOTES

**4. Nonparolable offense**
Habeas relief was properly denied where an inmate's plea agreement was not illusory as the inmate avoided a trial on a first-degree murder charge that was punishable by life without parole and instead was given the opportunity for parole. McAdoo v Elo (2003, CA6 Mich) 346 F3d 159, 2003 FED App 339P.

Habeas relief was properly denied where, inter alia, an inmate's plea agreement was not illusory as the inmate avoided a trial on a first-degree murder charge that was punishable by life without parole and instead was given the opportunity for parole. McAdoo v Elo (2003, CA6 Mich) 346 F3d 159, 2003 FED App 339P.

## § 791.233d. Samples for chemical testing. [MSA § 28.2303(5)]

Sec. 33d. (1) A prisoner ◆ shall not be released on parole, placed in a community placement facility of any kind, including a community corrections center or a community residential home, or discharged upon completion of his or her maximum sentence until he or she has provided samples for chemical testing for DNA identification profiling or a determination of the sample's genetic markers and has provided samples for a determination of his or her secretor status. However, if at the time the prisoner is to be released, placed, or discharged the department of state police already has a sample from the prisoner that meets the requirements of ◆ the DNA identification profiling system act, ◆ [ 1990 PA 250, MCL 28.171 to 28.176 ], the prisoner is not required to provide another sample [ or pay the fee required under subsection (4) ].

(2) The samples required to be collected under this section shall be collected by the department and transmitted by the department to the department of state police in the manner prescribed ◆ under the DNA identification profiling system act, ◆ [ 1990 PA 250, MCL 28.171 to 28.176 ].

## Department of Corrections § 791.233d

(3) The department may collect a sample under this section regardless of whether the prisoner consents to the collection. The department is not required to give the prisoner an opportunity for a hearing or obtain a court order before collecting the sample.

[(4) A prisoner shall pay an assessment of $60.00. The department shall transmit the assessments or portions of assessments collected to the department of treasury for the department of state police forensic science division to defray the costs associated with the requirements of DNA profiling and DNA retention prescribed under the DNA identification profiling system act, 1990 PA 250, MCL 28.171 to 28.176.

(5) The DNA profiles of DNA samples received under this section shall only be disclosed as follows:

(a) To a criminal justice agency for law enforcement identification purposes.

(b) In a judicial proceeding as authorized or required by a court.

(c) To a defendant in a criminal case if the DNA profile is used in conjunction with a charge against the defendant.

(d) For an academic, research, statistical analysis, or protocol developmental purpose only if personal identifications are removed.]

(6) ◆ As used in this section, "sample" means a portion of a prisoner's blood, saliva, or tissue collected from the prisoner.

**History:**
Amended by Pub Acts 2001, No. 86, imd eff July 26, 2001, by enacting § 1 eff January 1, 2002 (see 2001 note below).

**Editor's notes:**
**Pub Acts 2001, No. 86, enacting § 2,** imd eff July 26, 2001, by enacting § 1 eff January 1, 2002, provides:

"Enacting section 2. This amendatory act does not take effect unless all of the following bills of the 91st Legislature are enacted into law:

"(a) Senate Bill No. 389 [Pub Acts 2001, No. 87].
"(b) Senate Bill No. 393 [Pub Acts 2001, No. 90].
"(c) Senate Bill No. 394 [Pub Acts 2001, No. 84].
"(d) House Bill No. 4610 [Pub Acts 2001, No. 88].
"(e) House Bill No. 4611 [Pub Acts 2001, No. 91].
"(f) House Bill No. 4613 [Pub Acts 2001, No. 89].
"(g) House Bill No. 4633 [Pub Acts 2001, No. 85]."

**Effect of amendment notes:**
**The 2001 amendment** substantially revised subsection (1); in subsection (2), deleted "by rules promulgated" following "prescribed", and changed the style of statutory references; added subsections (4) and (5); and redesignated former subsection (4) as subsection (6).

### LexisNexis™ and Other Annotations

**LexisNexis™ Michigan analytical references:**
Michigan Law and Practice, Criminal Law and Procedure § 877.

### § 791.233e. Parole guidelines; purpose; mandatory and discretionary factors; nondiscrimination; promulgation of rules; departure from guidelines; review of guidelines; proposed revisions. [MSA § 28.2303(6)]

#### LexisNexis™ and Other Annotations

**Michigan Digest references:**
Pardons and Paroles § 5.

**LexisNexis™ Michigan analytical references:**
Michigan Law and Practice, Criminal Law and Procedure § 877.

### § 791.234. Prisoners subject to jurisdiction of parole board; indeterminate and other sentences; termination of sentence; interview; release on parole; discretion of parole board; appeal to circuit court; cooperation with law enforcement by prisoner violating § 333.7401; conviction before effective date of amendatory act; definitions. [MSA § 28.2304]

Sec. 34. (1) Except as provided in section 34a, a prisoner sentenced to an indeterminate sentence and confined in a state correctional facility with a minimum in terms of years other than a prisoner subject to disciplinary time is subject to the jurisdiction of the parole board when the prisoner has served a period of time equal to the minimum sentence imposed by the court for the crime of which he or she was convicted, less good time and disciplinary credits, if applicable.

(2) Except as provided in section 34a, a prisoner subject to disciplinary time sentenced to an indeterminate sentence and confined in a state correctional facility with a minimum in terms of years is subject to the jurisdiction of the parole board when the prisoner has served a period of time equal to the minimum sentence imposed by the court for the crime of which he or she was convicted.

(3) If a prisoner other than a prisoner subject to disciplinary time is sentenced for consecutive terms, whether received at the same time or at any time during the life of the original sentence, the parole board has jurisdiction over the prisoner for purposes of parole when the prisoner has served the total time of the added minimum terms, less the good time and disciplinary credits allowed by statute. The maximum terms of the sentences shall be added to compute the new maximum term under this subsection, and discharge shall be issued only after the total of the maximum sentences has been served less good time and disciplinary credits, unless the prisoner is paroled and discharged upon satisfactory completion of the parole.

(4) If a prisoner subject to disciplinary time is sentenced for consecutive terms, whether received at the same time or at any time during the life of the original sentence, the parole board has jurisdiction over the prisoner for purposes of parole when the prisoner has served the total time of the added minimum terms. The maximum terms of the sentences shall be added to compute the new maximum term under this subsection, and discharge shall be issued

only after the total of the maximum sentences has been served, unless the prisoner is paroled and discharged upon satisfactory completion of the parole.

(5) If a prisoner other than a prisoner subject to disciplinary time has 1 or more consecutive terms remaining to serve in addition to the term he or she is serving, the parole board may terminate the sentence the prisoner is presently serving at any time after the minimum term of the sentence has been served.

(6) A prisoner under sentence for life, other than a prisoner sentenced for life for murder in the first degree ◆ or sentenced for life for a violation of chapter XXXIII of the Michigan penal code, 1931 PA 328, MCL 750.200 to 750.212a, who has served 10 calendar years of the sentence in the case of a prisoner sentenced for ◆ [a] crime committed before October 1, 1992, or, except as provided in subsection (10), who has served 20 calendar years of the sentence in the case of a prisoner sentenced to imprisonment for life for violating or conspiring to violate section 7401(2)(a)(i) of the public health code, 1978 PA 368, MCL 333.7401, who has another conviction for a serious crime, or, except as provided in subsection (10), who has served 17-½ calendar years of the sentence in the case of a prisoner sentenced to imprisonment for life for violating or conspiring to violate section 7401(2)(a)(i) of the public health code, 1978 PA 368, MCL 333.7401, who does not have another conviction for a serious crime, or who has served 15 calendar years of the sentence in the case of a prisoner sentenced for ◆ [a] crime committed on or after October 1, 1992, is subject to the jurisdiction of the parole board and may be released on parole by the parole board, subject to the following conditions:

(a) At the conclusion of 10 calendar years of the prisoner's sentence and thereafter as determined by the parole board until the prisoner is paroled, discharged, or deceased, and in accordance with the procedures described in subsection (7), 1 member of the parole board shall interview the prisoner. The interview schedule prescribed in this subdivision applies to all prisoners to whom this subsection is applicable, regardless of the date on which they were sentenced.

(b) In addition to the interview schedule prescribed in subdivision (a), the parole board shall review the prisoner's file at the conclusion of 15 calendar years of the prisoner's sentence and every 5 years thereafter until the prisoner is paroled, discharged, or deceased. A prisoner whose file is to be reviewed under this subdivision shall be notified of the upcoming file review at least 30 days before the file review takes place and shall be allowed to submit written statements or documentary evidence for the parole board's consideration in conducting the file review.

(c) A decision to grant or deny parole to a prisoner so sentenced shall not be made until after a public hearing held in the manner prescribed for pardons and commutations in sections 44 and 45. Notice of the public hearing shall be given to the sentencing judge, or the judge's successor in office, and parole shall not be granted

**§ 791.234**

if the sentencing judge, or the judge's successor in office, files written objections to the granting of the parole within 30 days of receipt of the notice of hearing. The written objections shall be made part of the prisoner's file.

(d) A parole granted under this subsection shall be for a period of not less than 4 years and subject to the usual rules pertaining to paroles granted by the parole board. A parole ordered under this subsection is not valid until the transcript of the record is filed with the attorney general whose certification of receipt of the transcript shall be returnable to the office of the parole board within 5 days. Except for medical records protected under section 2157 of the revised judicature act of 1961, 1961 PA 236, MCL 600.2157, the file of a prisoner granted a parole under this subsection is a public record.

(e) A parole shall not be granted under this subsection in the case of a prisoner who is otherwise prohibited by law from parole consideration. In such cases the interview procedures in section 44 shall be followed.

(7) An interview conducted under subsection (6)(a) is subject to both of the following requirements:

(a) The prisoner shall be given written notice, not less than 30 days before the interview date, stating that the interview will be conducted.

(b) The prisoner may be represented at the interview by an individual of his or her choice. The representative shall not be another prisoner. A prisoner is not entitled to appointed counsel at public expense. The prisoner or representative may present relevant evidence in favor of holding a public hearing as described in subsection (6)(b).

(8) In determining whether a prisoner convicted of violating or conspiring to violate section 7401(2)(a)(i) of the public health code, 1978 PA 368, MCL 333.7401, and sentenced to imprisonment for life before October 1, 1998 is to be released on parole, the parole board shall consider all of the following:

(a) Whether the violation was part of a continuing series of violations of section 7401 or 7403 of the public health code, 1978 PA 368, MCL 333.7401 and 333.7403, by that individual.

(b) Whether the violation was committed by the individual in concert with 5 or more other individuals.

(c) Any of the following:

(i) Whether the individual was a principal administrator, organizer, or leader of an entity that the individual knew or had reason to know was organized, in whole or in part, to commit violations of section 7401 or 7403 of the public health code, 1978 PA 368, MCL 333.7401 and 333.7403, and whether the violation for which the individual was convicted was committed to further the interests of that entity.

(ii) Whether the individual was a principal administrator, organizer, or leader of an entity that the individual knew or had reason to know committed violations of section 7401 or 7403 of

**Department of Corrections** § 791.234

the public health code, 1978 PA 368, MCL 333.7401 and 333.7403, and whether the violation for which the individual was convicted was committed to further the interests of that entity.

(iii) Whether the violation was committed in a drug-free school zone.

(iv) Whether the violation involved the delivery of a controlled substance to an individual less than 17 years of age or possession with intent to deliver a controlled substance to an individual less than 17 years of age.

(9) Except as provided in section 34a, a prisoner's release on parole is discretionary with the parole board. The action of the parole board in granting a parole is appealable by the prosecutor of the county from which the prisoner was committed or the victim of the crime for which the prisoner was convicted. The appeal shall be to the circuit court in the county from which the prisoner was committed, by leave of the court.

(10) If the sentencing judge, or his or her successor in office, determines on the record that a prisoner described in subsection (6) sentenced to imprisonment for life for violating or conspiring to violate section 7401(2)(a)(i) of the public health code, 1978 PA 368, MCL 333.7401, has cooperated with law enforcement, the prisoner is subject to the jurisdiction of the parole board and may be released on parole as provided in subsection (6), 2-½ years earlier than the time otherwise indicated in subsection (6). The prisoner is considered to have cooperated with law enforcement if the court determines on the record that the prisoner had no relevant or useful information to provide. The court shall not make a determination that the prisoner failed or refused to cooperate with law enforcement on grounds that the defendant exercised his or her constitutional right to trial by jury. If the court determines at sentencing that the defendant cooperated with law enforcement, the court shall include its determination in the judgment of sentence.

[(11) An individual convicted of violating or conspiring to violate section 7401(2)(a)(ii) or 7403(2)(a)(ii) of the public health code, 1978 PA 368, MCL 333.7401 and 333.7403, before the effective date of the amendatory act that added this subsection is eligible for parole after serving the minimum of each sentence imposed for that violation or 10 years of each sentence imposed for that violation, whichever is less.

(12) An individual convicted of violating or conspiring to violate section 7401(2)(a)(iii) or 7403(2)(a)(iii) of the public health code, 1978 PA 368, MCL 333.7401 and 333.7403, before the effective date of the amendatory act that added this subsection is eligible for parole after serving the minimum of each sentence imposed for that violation or 5 years of each sentence imposed for that violation, whichever is less.

(13) An individual convicted of violating or conspiring to violate section 7401(2)(a)(iv) or 7403(2)(a)(iv) of the public health code, 1978 PA 368, MCL 333.7401 and 333.7403, before the effective date of the

§ 791.234

amendatory act that added this subsection who is sentenced to a term of imprisonment that is consecutive to a term of imprisonment imposed for any other violation of section 7401(2)(a)(i) to (iv) or section 7403(2)(a)(i) to (iv) is eligible for parole after serving ½ of the minimum sentence imposed for each violation of section 7401(2)(a)(iv) or 7403(2)(a)(iv). This subsection does not apply if the sentence was imposed for a conviction for a new offense committed while the individual is on probation or parole.

(14) The parole board shall provide notice to the prosecuting attorney of the county in which the individual was convicted before granting parole to the individual under subsection (11), (12), or (13).

(15)] ◆ As used in this section:

(a) "Serious crime" means violating or conspiring to violate article 7 of the public health code, 1978 PA 368, MCL 333.7101 to 333.7545, that is punishable by imprisonment for more than 4 years, or an offense against a person in violation of section 83, 84, 86, 87, 88, 89, 316, 317, 321, 349, 349a, 350, 397, 520b, 520c, 520d, 520g, 529, 529a, or 530 of the Michigan penal code, 1931 PA 328, MCL 750.83, 750.84, 750.86, 750.87, 750.88, 750.89, 750.316, 750.317, 750.321, 750.349, 750.349a, 750.350, 750.397, 750.520b, 750.520c, 750.520d, 750.520g, 750.529, 750.529a, and 750.530.

(b) "State correctional facility" means a facility that houses prisoners committed to the jurisdiction of the department, and includes a youth correctional facility operated under section 20g by the department or a private vendor.

**History:**
Amended by Pub Acts 2002, No. 670, imd eff December 26, 2002, by enacting § 1 eff March 1, 2003 (see 2002 note below).

**Editor's notes:**
Pub Acts 2002, No. 670, enacting § 2, imd eff December 26, 2002, by enacting § 1 eff March 1, 2003, provides:
"Enacting section 2. This amendatory act does not take effect unless all of the following bills of the 91st Legislature are enacted into law:
"(a) House Bill No. 5394 [Pub Acts 2002, No. 665].
"(b) House Bill No. 5395 [Pub Acts 2002, No. 666]."

**Effect of amendment notes:**
The 2002 amendment in subsection (6), opening paragraph, following "first degree" deleted a comma, following "sentenced for" substituted "a" for "any other" in two instances; added subsections (11)–(14); and redesignated former subsection (11) as (15).

**Statutory references:**
Sections 20g, 34a, 44 and 45, above referred to, are §§791.220g, 791.234a, 791.244 and 791.245.

### LexisNexis™ and Other Annotations

**Michigan Digest references:**
Assault and Battery § 1.
Constitutional Law §§283, 286.50, 326, 339.
Controlled Substances §§1, 20.
Criminal Law and Procedure §§128, 733.50, 741.
Criminal Sexual Conduct § 43.
Former Jeopardy § 3.

## Department of Corrections § 791.234

Homicide § 149.
Pardons and Paroles §§2, 4, 5.
Prisons and Jails § 9.
State of Michigan § 26.

**LexisNexis™ Michigan analytical references:**
Michigan Law and Practice, Criminal Law and Procedure §§877, 878.
Michigan Law and Practice, Public Health and Welfare § 173.

### CASE NOTES

**2. Constitutionality.**

Federal district court, which dismissed petition for habeas corpus relief without prejudice due to petitioner's failure to exhaust state court remedies, nevertheless expressed its view that Michigan statutory amendment, eliminating appeals by prisoners from parole board decisions, while retaining appeals by the prosecution and by victims, implicates Equal Protection concerns. Matson v Mich Parole Bd. (2001, ED Mich) 175 F Supp 2d 925.

**3. Construction, operation and effect.**

Defendant who offered to cooperate 12 years after his conviction was deemed to have cooperated under the statute if he provided law enforcement with any specific information pertaining to the execution of law enforcement duties, even if law enforcement ultimately deems the information irrelevant to its current duties or investigations, or otherwise has no use for the information. People v Matelic (2001) 249 Mich App 1, 641 NW2d 252.

**4. Parole eligibility; life imprisonment.**

Where a trial court noted in sentencing that defendant could be considered for parole despite his life sentence for second degree murder, the parole board's subsequent consideration and refusal to pursue parole proceedings did not invalidate the life sentence because the parole board had obtained jurisdiction over defendant under MCLS § 791.234(6) and defendant had, in fact, been considered for parole. People v Moore (2003) 468 Mich 573, 664 NW2d 700.

The legislature's authorization of parole eligibility for drug lifers, who on release on parole would remain under the surveillance of prison authorities, does not encroach on the governor's commutation power. People v Matelic (2001) 249 Mich App 1, 641 NW2d 252.

Once the court determined that defendant had cooperated with federal law enforcement agencies, the statutory requirements were satisfied and the court should have certified defendant as eligible for early parole consideration. People v Tomasovich (2002) 249 Mich App 282, 642 NW2d 682.

An inmate serving a parolable life sentence is not entitled to a written explanation for the parole board's decision of "no interest" in taking further action after the prisoner's statutorily mandated interview, and the parole board's decision of "no interest" is not appealable to the circuit court; the statute requires that every inmate serving a parolable life sentence be interviewed by a member of the parole board after serving ten years, and every five years thereafter, but the prisoner is not entitled to a written explanation of the reasons why the prisoner was not advanced to the next stage of the parole process, and a prisoner does not have the right to a written explanation until after the parole board makes a final determination not to release the prisoner after a public hearing; the parole board's decision of "no interest" is not appealable, and only the ultimate decision to grant or deny parole of an inmate serving a parolable life sentence is appealable. Gilmore v Parole Bd., 247 Mich App 205, 635 NW2d 345 (2001).

The statutory requirement that the parole board develop parole guidelines governing the exercise of the board's discretion as to the release of prisoners on parole does not apply to prisoners serving parolable life sentences until the parole board is faced with the decision whether to release the prisoner on parole; under the statutory scheme for prisoners serving parolable life sentences, a release decision is not confronted until after the prisoner has been interviewed, has avoided judicial veto, and has advanced through a public hearing, at

## § 791.234

which time the board must either grant or deny parole. Jackson v Dep't of Corr., 247 Mich App 380, 636 NW2d 305 (2001).

A sentencing judge's recommendation in the judgment of a life sentence that defendant not be granted parole does not violate the so-called "lifer law" because the sentencing judge would still be required to file written objections to a grant of parole within 30 days of receipt of the notice of hearing. People v Garza, 246 Mich App 251, 631 NW2d 764 (2001).

**5. Date of minimum expiration.**

Michigan Department of Corrections had the authority to forfeit disciplinary credits earned by the inmate on a sentence that had been completed by serving the maximum term less disciplinary credits, based on prison misconduct by the inmate occurring while serving a sentence that was ordered to be served consecutive to the earlier sentence, when credits were explicitly tied to an inmate's parole eligibility date and discharge date, MCL §§791.234 and 800.33, thus credits did not determine when a sentence expired or was completed, but only when an inmate was subject to parole or discharge, and the statutory scheme set forth no mechanism for, or manner of, recognizing that a consecutive sentence was somehow completed or expired at the moment the time served and credits equal the maximum sentence, and made clear that credits were a matter of grace and were subject to forfeiture. Ryan v Dep't of Corr. (2003) 259 Mich App 26, 672 NW2d 535, app dismd (2004, Mich) 2004 Mich LEXIS 2.

## § 791.234a. Placement in special alternative incarceration unit; eligibility requirements; minimum sentence required for certain violations; participation prohibited by sentencing judge; eligibility determination by department; notice; prisoner consent to placement; minimum and maximum placement period; parole; suspension or revocation of parole; annual report to legislature. [MSA § 28.2304(1)]

### LexisNexis™ and Other Annotations

**Michigan Digest references:**
Criminal Law and Procedure § 796.50.

**LexisNexis™ Michigan analytical references:**
Michigan Law and Practice, Criminal Law and Procedure §§719, 751, 871.

## § 791.235. Release of prisoner on parole; procedure. [MSA § 28.2305]

### LexisNexis™ and Other Annotations

**Michigan Digest references:**
Pardons and Paroles §§2, 4, 5.
State of Michigan § 26.

**LexisNexis™ Michigan analytical references:**
Michigan Law and Practice, Criminal Law and Procedure § 877.

**Department of Corrections** § 791.236

**§ 791.236. Order of parole; signature of chairperson; notice; amendment; rescission; conditions; supervision; restitution; payment of parole supervision fee; condition requiring payment of assessment or minimum state cost; compliance with §§28.721 to 28.732; violation of §§333.7401 to 333.7545; condition requiring housing in community corrections center or community residential home; condition requiring payment by parolee; review to ensure payment of restitution; report of violation; registration of parolee; condition to protect named person; "violent felony" defined. [MSA § 28.2306]**

Sec. 36. (1) All paroles shall be ordered by the parole board and shall be signed by the chairperson. Written notice of the order shall be given to the sheriff or other police officer of the municipality or county in which the prisoner was convicted, and to the sheriff or other local police officer of the municipality or county to which the paroled prisoner is sent.

(2) A parole order may be amended or rescinded at the discretion of the parole board for cause. If a paroled prisoner who is required to register pursuant to the sex offenders registration act, 1994 PA 295, MCL 28.721 to 28.732, willfully violates that act, the parole board shall rescind the parole. If a prisoner convicted of violating or conspiring to violate section 7401(2)(a)(i) or (ii) or 7403(2)(a)(i) or (ii) of the public health code, 1978 PA 368, MCL 333.7401 and 333.7403, is released on parole and violates or conspires to violate article 7 of the public health code, 1978 PA 368, MCL 333.7401 to 333.7545, and that violation or conspiracy to violate is punishable by imprisonment for 4 or more years, or commits a violent felony during his or her release on parole, parole shall be ◆ [rescinded].

(3) A parole shall not be rescinded unless an interview is conducted by 1 member of the parole board. The purpose of the interview is to consider and act upon information received by the board after the original parole release decision. A rescission interview shall be conducted within 45 days after receiving the new information. At least 10 days before the interview, the parolee shall receive a copy or summary of the new evidence that is the basis for the interview. An amendment to a parole order shall be in writing and is not effective until notice of the amendment is given to the parolee.

(4) When a parole order is issued, the order shall contain the conditions of the parole and shall specifically provide proper means of supervision of the paroled prisoner in accordance with the rules of the bureau of field services.

(5) The parole order shall contain a condition to pay restitution to the victim of the prisoner's crime or the victim's estate if the prisoner was ordered to make restitution pursuant to the crime victim's rights act, 1985 PA 87, MCL 780.751 to 780.834, or the code of criminal procedure, 1927 PA 175, MCL 760.1 to ◆ [777.69].

(6) The parole order shall contain a condition requiring the parolee to pay a parole supervision fee as prescribed in section 36a.

(7) The parole order shall contain a condition requiring the

§ 791.236            MCLS Cumulative Supplement

parolee to pay any assessment the prisoner was ordered to pay pursuant to section 5 of 1989 PA 196, MCL 780.905.

[(8) The parole order shall contain a condition requiring the parolee to pay the minimum state cost prescribed by section 1j of chapter IX of the code of criminal procedure, 1927 PA 175, MCL 769.1j, if the minimum state cost has not been paid.

(9)] ◆ If the parolee is required to be registered under the sex offenders registration act, 1994 PA 295, MCL 28.721 to 28.732, the parole order shall contain a condition requiring the parolee to comply with that act.

[(10)] ◆ If a prisoner convicted of violating or conspiring to violate section 7401(2)(a)(i) or (ii) or 7403(2)(a)(i) or (ii) of the public health code, 1978 PA 368, MCL 333.7401 and 333.7403, is released on parole, the parole order shall contain a notice that if the parolee violates or conspires to violate article 7 of the public health code, 1978 PA 368, MCL 333.7401 to 333.7545, and that violation or conspiracy to violate is punishable by imprisonment for 4 or more years, or commits a violent felony during his or her release on parole, parole shall be ◆ [rescinded].

[(11)] ◆ A parole order issued for a prisoner subject to disciplinary time may contain a condition requiring the parolee to be housed in a community corrections center or a community residential home for not less than the first 30 days but not more than the first 180 days of his or her term of parole. As used in this subsection, "community corrections center" and "community residential home" mean those terms as defined in section 65a.

[(12)] ◆ The parole order shall contain a condition requiring the parolee to pay the following amounts owed by the prisoner, if applicable:

   (a) The balance of filing fees and costs ordered to be paid under section 2963 of the revised judicature act of 1961, 1961 PA 236, MCL 600.2963.

   (b) The balance of any filing fee ordered to be paid by a federal court under section 1915 of title 28 of the United States Code, 28 U.S.C. 1915 and any unpaid order of costs assessed against the prisoner.

[(13)] ◆ In each case in which payment of restitution is ordered as a condition of parole, a parole officer assigned to a case shall review the case not less than twice yearly to ensure that restitution is being paid as ordered. The final review shall be conducted not less than 60 days before the expiration of the parole period. If the parole officer determines that restitution is not being paid as ordered, the parole officer shall file a written report of the violation with the parole board on a form prescribed by the parole board. The report shall include a statement of the amount of arrearage and any reasons for the arrearage known by the parole officer. The parole board shall immediately provide a copy of the report to the court, the prosecuting attorney, and the victim.

[(14)] ◆ If a parolee is required to register pursuant to the sex offenders registration act, 1994 PA 295, MCL 28.721 to 28.732, the

**Department of Corrections** § 791.236a

parole officer shall register the parolee as provided in that act.

[(15)] ◆ If the parole order contains a condition intended to protect 1 or more named persons, the department shall enter those provisions of the parole order into the corrections management information system, accessible by the law enforcement information network. If the parole board ◆ [rescinds] a parole order described in this subsection, the department within 3 business days shall remove from the corrections management information system the provisions of that parole order.

[(16)] ◆ As used in this section, "violent felony" means an offense against a person in violation of section 82, 83, 84, 86, 87, 88, 89, 316, 317, 321, 349, 349a, 350, 397, 520b, 520c, 520d, 520e, 520g, 529, 529a, or 530 of the Michigan penal code, 1931 PA 328, MCL 750.82, 750.83, 750.84, 750.86, 750.87, 750.88, 750.89, 750.316, 750.317, 750.321, 750.349, 750.349a, 750.350, 750.397, 750.520b, 750.520c, 750.520d, 750.520e, 750.520g, 750.529, 750.529a, and 750.530.

**History:**
Amended by Pub Acts 2003, No. 75, imd eff July 22, 2003, by enacting § 1 eff October 1, 2003.

**Effect of amendment notes:**
**The 2003 amendment** in subsections (2) and (10), following "parole shall be" substituted "rescinded" for "revoked"; in subsection (5), following "MCL 760.1 to" substituted "777.69" for "776.22"; added subsection (8); redesignated former subsections (8)–(15) as (9)–(16); and in subsection (15), following "parole board" substituted "rescinds" for "revokes".

**Statutory references:**
Sections 36a and 65a, above referred to, are §§791.236a and 791.265a.

LexisNexis™ and Other Annotations

**LexisNexis™ Michigan analytical references:**
Michigan Law and Practice, Criminal Law and Procedure § 877.

**§ 791.236a. Collection of supervision fee by parole board; limitation; payment; determination of amount; allocation of money collected for other obligations; waiver of fee; determination and collection of fee for offender transferred to state under interstate compact; administrative costs; unpaid amounts. [MSA § 28.2306(1)]**

Sec. 36a. (1) The parole board shall include in each order of parole that the department of corrections shall collect a parole supervision fee of not more than ◆ [$135.00] multiplied by the number of months of parole ordered, but not more than 60 months. The fee is payable when the parole order is entered, but the fee may be paid in monthly installments if the parole board approves installment payments for that parolee. In determining the amount of the fee, the parole board shall consider the parolee's projected income and financial resources. The parole board shall use the following table of projected monthly income in determining the amount of the fee to be ordered:

## § 791.236a

| Projected Monthly Income | Amount of Fee |
|---|---|
| $0-249.99 | $ 0.00 |
| $250.00-499.99 | $10.00 |
| $500.00-749.99 | [$25.00] ◆ |
| [$750.00-999.99] ◆ | [$40.00] ◆ |
| [$1,000.00 or more | 5% of monthly income, but not more than $135.00] |

The parole board may order a higher amount than indicated by the table, up to the maximum of ◆ [$135.00] multiplied by the number of months of parole ordered but not more than 60 months, if the parole board determines that the parolee has sufficient assets or other financial resources to warrant the higher amount. If the parole board orders a higher amount, the amount and the reasons for ordering that amount shall be stated in the parole order. ◆

(2) ◆ If a person who is subject to a supervision fee ◆ is also subject to any combination of fines, costs, restitution, assessments, or payments arising out of the same criminal proceeding, the allocation of money collected for those obligations shall be as provided in section 22 of chapter XV of the code of criminal procedure, ◆ [1927 PA 175, MCL 775.22].

(3) ◆ A person shall not be subject to more than 1 parole supervision fee at the same time. If a parole supervision fee is ordered for a parolee for any month or months during which that parolee already is subject to a parole supervision fee, the department shall waive the fee having the shorter remaining duration.

(4) ◆ The department shall waive the parole supervision fee for a parolee who is transferred to another state under the interstate compact entered into pursuant to ◆ [1935 PA 89, MCL 798.101 to 798.103, or the interstate compact entered into pursuant to 2002 PA 40, MCL 3.1011 to 3.1012], for the months during which he or she is in another state. The department shall collect a parole supervision fee of not more than ◆ [$135.00] per month for each month of parole supervision in this state for an offender transferred to this state under ◆ [an] interstate compact. In determining the amount of the fee, the department shall consider the parolee's projected income and financial resources. The department shall use the following table of projected monthly income in determining the amount of the fee:

| Projected Monthly Income | Amount of Fee |
|---|---|
| $0-249.99 | $ 0.00 |
| $250.00-499.99 | $10.00 |
| $500.00-749.99 | [$25.00] ◆ |
| [$750.00-999.99] ◆ | [$40.00] ◆ |
| [$1,000.00 or more | 5% of monthly income, but not more than $135.00] |

The department may collect a higher amount than indicated by the table, up to the maximum of ◆ [$135.00] for each month of parole supervision in this state, if the department determines that the parolee has sufficient assets or other financial resources to warrant the higher amount. If the department collects a higher amount, the amount and the reasons for collecting that amount

**Department of Corrections** § 791.236a

shall be stated in the department records.

(5) ◆ Twenty percent of the money collected by the department under this section shall be allocated for administrative costs incurred by the department in collecting parole supervision fees and for enhanced services, as described in this subsection. Enhanced services include, but are not limited to, the purchase of services for parolees such as counseling, employment training, employment placement, or education; public transportation expenses related to training, counseling, or employment; enhancement of staff performance through specialized training and equipment purchase; and purchase of items for parolee employment. At the end of each fiscal year, the unexpended balance of the money allocated for administrative costs and enhanced services shall be available for carryforward to be used for the purposes described in this subsection in subsequent fiscal years. ◆

(6) ◆ If a parolee has not paid the full amount of the parole supervision fee upon being discharged from parole, the department shall review and compare the actual income of the person during the period of parole with the income amount projected when the parole supervision fee was ordered. If the department determines that the parolee's actual income did not equal or exceed the projected income, the department shall waive any unpaid amount in excess of the total amount that the parolee would have been ordered to pay if the parolee's income had been accurately projected, unless the parole order states that a higher amount was ordered due to available assets or other financial resources. Any unpaid amounts not waived by the department shall be reported to the department of treasury. The department of treasury shall attempt to collect the unpaid balances pursuant to section 30a of ◆ [1941 PA 122, MCL 205.30a]. Money collected under this subsection shall not be allocated for the purposes described in subsection ◆ (5).

**History:**
Amended by Pub Acts 2002, No. 502, imd eff July 16, 2002.

**Effect of amendment notes:**
The **2002 amendment** in subsection (1), opening and closing paragraphs substituted "$135.00" for "$30.00"; in subsection (1), table substituted "$25.00" for "$20.00", "$750.00-999.99" for "$750.00 or more", "$40.00" for "$30.00", added "$1,000.00 or more 5% of monthly income, but not more than $135.00"; deleted former subsection (2) and redesignated subsections (3) through (7) as (2) through (6); in subsection (2) deleted "imposed on or after May 1, 1994" after "fee", changed the style of statutory citation; in subsection (4), opening paragraph, substituted "1935 PA 89, MCL 798.101 to 798.103, or the interstate compact entered into pursuant to 2002 PA 40, MCL 3.1011 to 3.1012" for "Act No. 89 of the Public Acts of 1935, being sections 798.101 to 798.102 of the Michigan Compiled Laws", "$135.00" for "$30.00", "an" for "that"; in subsection (4) table, substituted "$25.00" for "$20.00", "$750.00-999.99" for "$750.00 or more", "$40.00" for "$30.00", added "$1,000.00 or more 5% of monthly income, but not more than $135.00"; in subsection (4), closing paragraph substituted "$135.00" for "$30.00"; in subsection (5) deleted the last sentence which read: "Money received by the department pursuant to this subsection in the fiscal year ending September 30, 1994 is appropriated for the purposes described in this subsection."; in subsection (6) changed the style of statutory citation and substituted "(5)" for "(6)".

## § 791.238

**§ 791.238. Custody of paroled prisoner; warrant for return; incarceration pending hearing; treatment as escaped prisoner; time during parole violation not counted as time served; forfeiture of good time; committing crime while on parole; construction of parole.** [MSA § 28.2308]

### LexisNexis™ and Other Annotations

**Michigan Digest references:**
Criminal Law and Procedure §§731.20, 743.50.
Pardons and Paroles §§4, 8.

**LexisNexis™ Michigan analytical references:**
Michigan Law and Practice, Criminal Law and Procedure §§875, 877.

**§ 791.239. Prisoner on parole, arrest without warrant on reasonable suspicion of parole violation.** [MSA § 28.2309]

### LexisNexis™ and Other Annotations

**Michigan Digest references:**
Criminal Law and Procedure § 307.
Pardons and Paroles § 6.
Search and Seizure §§2, 7.50, 37.20.

**LexisNexis™ Michigan analytical references:**
Michigan Law and Practice, Criminal Law and Procedure §§122, 123, 877.

**§ 791.239a. Parole violation; preliminary or fact-finding hearing; procedure.** [MSA § 28.2309(1)]

### LexisNexis™ and Other Annotations

**LexisNexis™ Michigan analytical references:**
Michigan Law and Practice, Criminal Law and Procedure § 877.

**§ 791.240a. Parole violation; right to hearing; hearing, notice, time, location; rights; postponement; sufficiency of evidence; reinstatement to parole, or finding of violation and revocation of parole; noncompliance with restitution order; notice; hearing; representation by counsel; rights; finding, recommendation, disposition of charges; written statement, findings of fact, reasons.** [MSA § 28.2310(1)]

### LexisNexis™ and Other Annotations

**Michigan Digest references:**
Criminal Law and Procedure §§247.210, 247.285, 248.
Mandamus § 95.
Pardons and Paroles § 9.

**LexisNexis™ Michigan analytical references:**
Michigan Law and Practice, Criminal Law and Procedure § 877.
Michigan Law and Practice, Remedies § 232.

**Department of Corrections** § 791.243

### CASE NOTES

**9. Hearing.**

A state prison inmate's challenges to the revocation of his parole and to the warden's decision not to award him special good time sentence credits and not to restore previously forfeited or not earned credits were denied, where (1) the state's holding of the parole revocation hearing within two months of the inmate's arrest was reasonable and the state's violation of the state statutory requirement that revocation hearings be held within 45 days of arrest did not constitute a federal constitutional violation for habeas corpus purposes, and (2) the forfeiture of good time sentence credits for misconduct was expressly authorized by state law. Moore v Hofbauer, 144 F Supp 2d 877 (ED Mich 2001).

**11. – Time of hearing.**

Parolee accused of a parole violation was not entitled to a discharge from prison where a fact–finding hearing on the parole violation charge was not held within 45 days, as required by MCLS § 791.240a(1); the appropriate remedy was a writ of mandamus. Jones v Dep't of Corr. (2003) 468 Mich 646, 664 NW2d 717.

### § 791.241. Decision of parole board; order. [MSA § 28.2311]

**LexisNexis™ and Other Annotations**

**LexisNexis™ Michigan analytical references:**
Michigan Law and Practice, Criminal Law and Procedure § 877.

### § 791.242. Certificate of discharge; minimum period of parole respecting certain crimes. [MSA § 28.2312]

**LexisNexis™ and Other Annotations**

**Michigan Digest references:**
Pardons and Paroles §§1, 4.

**LexisNexis™ Michigan analytical references:**
Michigan Law and Practice, Criminal Law and Procedure § 877.

### CASE NOTES

The provision of the penal institutions, pardon, probation, and parole act stating that a paroled prisoner will receive a final order of discharge if the prisoner performs all conditions and obligations of his parole for the period fixed in the order and obeys all the rules and regulations adopted by the parole board does not violate the separation of powers doctrine under the state constitution; the statute simply provides a condition precedent to the parole board's authority to enter a final order of discharge and does not interfere with the governor's exclusive power under the state constitution to grant commutations and pardons. Wayne County Prosecutor v Department of Corrections (2000) 242 Mich App 148, 617 NW2d 921.

### § 791.243. Pardons, reprieves and commutations; form and contents of application. [MSA § 28.2313]

**LexisNexis™ and Other Annotations**

**LexisNexis™ Michigan analytical references:**
Michigan Law and Practice, Criminal Law and Procedure § 878.

### § 791.244. Parole board interview of prisoner serving sentence for first degree murder or sentence of imprisonment for life without parole; board duties upon own initiation of receipt of application for reprieve, commutation, or pardon; files as public record. [MSA § 28.2314]

#### LexisNexis™ and Other Annotations

**Michigan Digest references:**
Pardons and Paroles § 5.

**LexisNexis™ Michigan analytical references:**
Michigan Law and Practice, Criminal Law and Procedure §§877, 878.

### § 791.246. Parole board, decisions and recommendations by majority vote of board or panel. [MSA § 28.2316]

#### LexisNexis™ and Other Annotations

**Michigan Digest references:**
Pardons and Paroles §§4, 5.

**LexisNexis™ Michigan analytical references:**
Michigan Law and Practice, Criminal Law and Procedure § 877.

## CHAPTER IIIA
## [HEARINGS DIVISION]

### § 791.251. Hearings division; creation; appointment and duties of hearing administrator; duties of hearings division; supervision and qualifications of hearing officer. [MSA § 28.2320(51)]

#### LexisNexis™ and Other Annotations

**Michigan Digest references:**
Administrative Law § 4.10.
Civil Rights §§25, 26, 36, 42.
Constitutional Law § 173.
Convicts § 1.
Judgments § 18.05.
Libel and Slander § 40.
Officers and Public Employees § 69.
Prisons and Jails §§1.05, 2.15, 2.55, 2.110, 2.115, 2.120, 2.140, 4.20, 6, 6.10, 6.40.

**LexisNexis™ Michigan analytical references:**
Michigan Law and Practice, Convicts and Prisons § 3.

### § 791.252. Hearing; procedures. [MSA § 28.2320(52)]

#### LexisNexis™ and Other Annotations

**Michigan Digest references:**
Prisons and Jails §§2.110, 2.125, 6, 6.10.

**Department of Corrections** § 791.255

§ 791.254. Rehearing; motion of department or request of party; circumstances; time for filing request; procedure; amendment or vacation of decision; rules. [MSA § 28.2320(54)]

### LexisNexis™ and Other Annotations

**Michigan Digest references:**
Constitutional Law § 223.
Prisons and Jails § 2.135.

§ 791.255. Judicial review, petition by prisoner. [MSA § 28.2320(55)]

### LexisNexis™ and Other Annotations

**Michigan Digest references:**
Constitutional Law § 223.
Prisons and Jails §§1.05, 2.105, 2.110, 2.135, 2.140.

**LexisNexis™ Michigan analytical references:**
Michigan Law and Practice, Convicts and Prisons § 4.

### CASE NOTES

Prisoner's application for direct review was timely where it was submitted to the circuit court, with a claim of indigency under MCLS § 600.2963(1), within the 60-day limitation period of MCLS § 791.255(2), and, then, resubmitted with the required filing fee and documents, in conformity with a circuit court order and within the 21-day requirement of MCLS § 600.2963(1). Keenan v Dep't of Corr. (2002) 250 Mich App 628, 649 NW2d 133.

An application for direct review submitted with a claim of indigency is timely if submitted within the 60-day limitation period of MCLS § 791.255(2), just as an application submitted with the filing fee within the 60-day limitation period would be timely. However, if the prisoner fails to abide by the circuit court order regarding the payment of a filing fee within the 21-day time limit, the action will not be filed by the circuit court. Keenan v Dep't of Corr. (2002) 250 Mich App 628, 649 NW2d 133.

An application for direct review is filed for purposes of MCLS § 791.255(2) when it is submitted to, and received by, the circuit court for filing with either the filing fee or a claim of indigency within the sixty-day time limitation imposed by the statute. Keenan v Dep't of Corr. (2002) 250 Mich App 628, 649 NW2d 133.

§ 791.262 MCLS Cumulative Supplement

## CHAPTER IV
## BUREAU OF PENAL INSTITUTIONS

**§ 791.262. Definitions; administration of facilities by bureau; supervision and inspection of jails and lockups; variance; limit on supervision, inspection and promulgation of rules and standards; provision of advice and services; enforcement of orders; sheriff's residence; commission member, visitation and inspection of jail or lockup; recordkeeping; violations.** [MSA § 28.2322]

*LexisNexis™ and Other Annotations*

**Michigan Digest references:**
Constitutional Law § 89.
Nuisances § 28.
Prisons and Jails §§1, 1.05, 1.20, 1.25, 1.35, 1.45, 1.50, 4.
Statutes § 160.

**§ 791.262b. Housing two inmates in county jail cell designed and constructed for single occupancy; conditions; classification system; prohibitions; doors; visual supervision; indemnification for expense or damages; limitations on housing percentage.** [MSA § 28.2322(2)]

Sec. 62b. (1) The rules and standards promulgated under section 62(3) shall not prohibit the housing of 2 inmates in a county jail cell which is designed and constructed for single occupancy and which meets ◆ [either] of the following conditions:
  (a) The ◆ cell is at least 65 square feet in area ◆ [and] provides unrestricted access to a day area which is available for use by the inmates other than those inmates being disciplined. The day area shall be available at least 14 hours per day and shall contain an average of at least 20 additional square feet of space per inmate.
  [(b) The cell is at least 55 square feet in area and both of the 2 inmates housed in the cell participate in a day parole program for not less than 32 hours per week.]
(2) For purposes of housing inmates as provided for under this section, the sheriff of the county shall develop and implement a classification system classifying the county jail population according to all of the following:
  (a) Behavior characteristics.
  (b) Similar physical characteristics.
  (c) Age.
  (d) Type of crime committed and criminal history.
  (e) Gender.
(3) The classification system under subsection (2) shall be submitted to and approved by the department. Any classification system in effect on December 31, 1987 ◆ shall continue in effect until changed as provided in this subsection.

**Department of Corrections** § 791.263a

(4) A person who has no prior criminal convictions may only be housed with another inmate who does not have a prior felony conviction.

(5) Cells in which 2 inmates are housed shall have doors which allow visual supervision, and inmates shall be under visual supervision at least every hour.

(6) An inmate who is subject to section 33b(a) to (cc) ◆ shall not be housed in a cell with another inmate as provided for under this section, unless the sentencing judge authorizes the inmate for ◆ [that] housing.

(7) If the state incurs any expense or is liable for damages on any judgment for an action brought as the result of a county housing 2 inmates in a cell as provided ◆ [in] this section, the county in which the action arose shall fully indemnify the state for the expense or damages.

(8) No more than 75% of the total inmate population may be housed 2 to a cell and pretrial inmates must be housed in separate cell blocks or housing units from sentenced inmates. In any jail facility with 5 or more floors, pretrial inmates shall be housed on separate floors from sentenced inmates.

**History:**
Amended by Pub Acts 2000, No. 211, imd eff June 27, 2000.

**Effect of amendment notes:**
The **2000 amendment** in subsection (1), substituted "either" for "both"; in paragraph (1)(a), deleted "basic" preceding "cell", redesignated former paragraph (1)(b) as a portion of paragraph (1)(a), and substituted ". The cell" for "and" following "feet in area"; added current paragraph (1)(b); in subsection (6), changed the style of statutory references, and substituted "that" for "such" preceding "housing"; and in subsection (7), substituted "in for" for "under" following "provided".

**Statutory references:**
Section 62 is 791.262.

## § 791.263. Wardens; appointment; personnel; "correctional facility" explained. [MSA § 28.2323]

### LexisNexis™ and Other Annotations

**LexisNexis™ Michigan analytical references:**
Michigan Law and Practice, Convicts and Prisons § 2.

## § 791.263a. Compensation of correctional or youth correctional facility employees injured by inmate assault or injured during riot; exception; definitions. [MSA § 28.2323(1)]

### LexisNexis™ and Other Annotations

**Michigan Digest references:**
Prisons and Jails §§5, 5.70.

## § 791.264. Classification of prisoners; classification committee; information; filing; investigation; computation of sentence; recomputation based on amended judgment. [MSA § 28.2324]

Sec. 64. (1) The assistant director in charge of the bureau of ◆ [correctional facilities] shall ◆ classify the prisoners in ◆ [correctional facilities. The assistant director] shall ◆ [appoint] a classification committee from the staff of ◆ [each correctional facility], which committee shall perform ◆ [services in a] manner as the assistant director in charge of the bureau of ◆ [correctional facilities requires.

(2) Each] classification committee ◆ [shall] obtain and file complete information with regard to each prisoner ◆ [when the] prisoner is received in ◆ [a correctional facility. The] clerk of the court and ◆ all probation officers and other officials ◆ [ shall send information] in their possession or under their control to each ◆ classification committee when ◆ [requested to do so, in the] manner as they ◆ [are] directed. When all such existing available records have been assembled, each ◆ classification committee shall determine whether any further investigation is necessary, and, if so, ◆ shall make ◆ [that] investigation. ◆ [The] information shall be filed with the parole board so as to be readily available when the parole of the prisoner is to be considered.

[(3) The length of a prisoner's sentence shall be computed by the record office of the correctional facility, for use by the classification committee, based upon the certified copy of the judgment of sentence delivered with the prisoner. Except as provided in subsection (4), if the judgment of sentence does not specify whether the sentence shall run consecutively to or concurrently with any other sentence that the prisoner is serving, the sentence shall be computed as if it is to be served concurrently.

(4) If the conviction is for a violation of section 193, 195(2), 197(2), 227b, or 349a of the Michigan penal code, 1931 PA 328, MCL 750.193, 750.195, 750.197, 750.227b, and 750.349a, the sentence shall be computed as if it is to be served consecutively, unless the judgment of sentence specifies that the sentence shall run concurrently.

(5) If a sentence that did not specify whether it was to be served concurrently or consecutively is computed under subsection (3) or (4), or if the conviction is for a violation of section 193, 195(2), 197(2), 227b, or 349a of the Michigan penal code, 1931 PA 328, MCL 750.193, 750.195, 750.197, 750.227b, and 750.349a, and the judgment of sentence specifies that the sentence shall run concurrently, the department shall notify the sentencing judge, the prosecuting attorney, and the affected prisoner of the computation not later than 7 days after the sentence is computed.

(6) If, at any time after receiving the original judgment of sentence, the department receives an amended judgment of sentence specifying that the sentence should be computed in a different manner, the sentence shall be recomputed accordingly.]

## Department of Corrections § 791.265f

**History:**
Amended by Pub Acts 2000, No. 221, imd eff June 27, 2000, by enacting § 1 eff October 1, 2000 (see 2000 note below).

**Editor's notes:**
Pub Acts 2000, No. 221, enacting § 2, imd eff June 27, 2000, by enacting § 1 eff October 1, 2000, provides:
"Enacting section 2. This amendatory act does not take effect unless House Bill No. 4238 of the 90th Legislature [Pub Acts 2000, No. 220] is enacted into law."

**Effect of amendment notes:**
The 2000 amendment divided the former full section into subsections (1) and (2), and substantially revised these subsections; and added subsections (3), (4), and (5).

### § 791.265. Transfer or retransfer of prisoners; confinement in secure correctional facility; "offender" defined; transfer of offenders to country of citizenship; notification to judge and prosecutor; objections; "secure correctional facility" defined. [MSA § 28.2325]

**LexisNexis™ and Other Annotations**

**Michigan Digest references:**
Statutes § 55.

**LexisNexis™ Michigan analytical references:**
Michigan Law and Practice, Convicts and Prisons § 4.

### § 791.265a. Extending limits of confinement; rules; escape from custody; eligibility for extensions of limits of confinement; placement in community residential home; definitions. [MSA § 28.2325(1)]

**LexisNexis™ and Other Annotations**

**Michigan Digest references:**
Convicts § 1.
Prisons and Jails §§2.35, 3, 7.

### § 791.265b. Disabled prisoner, power of director to transfer, duration of transfer; powers and duties of department; terms defined. [MSA § 28.2325(2)]

**LexisNexis™ and Other Annotations**

**Michigan Digest references:**
Prisons and Jails §§4.30, 6.10, 6.50.

### § 791.265f. Type of housing for prisoners convicted of assaultive crimes; prohibition of opening facilities or entering contracts for dwellings originally intended to house one family. [MSA § 28.2325(6)]

**LexisNexis™ and Other Annotations**

**LexisNexis™ Michigan analytical references:**
Michigan Law and Practice, Convicts and Prisons § 4.

## § 791.265g. Definitions. [MSA § 28.2325(7)]

### LexisNexis™ and Other Annotations

**Michigan Digest references:**
Criminal Law and Procedure § 307.
Prisons and Jails § 8.
Search and Seizure §§7.50, 11.

## § 791.265h. Placement of prisoner not meeting community status criteria; criteria requirements; location of community corrections center for prisoner placement; operation of center serving more than one county; conditions; limit on number of prisoners to be placed in center; prisoner curfew; random checking of prisoners allowed off premises. [MSA § 28.2325(8)]

### LexisNexis™ and Other Annotations

**LexisNexis™ Michigan analytical references:**
Michigan Law and Practice, Convicts and Prisons § 4.

## § 791.265i. Citizens' council in municipality where community corrections center located; members, appointment, residency requirements; chairperson; meetings; meeting with center supervisor; report by supervisor on prisoner numbers, activities, etc.; designee to act on supervisor's behalf; notice by council of placement believed in violation of criteria; review of record, reclassification of prisoner; annual report by council; duties of council. [MSA § 28.2325(9)]

### LexisNexis™ and Other Annotations

**LexisNexis™ Michigan analytical references:**
Michigan Law and Practice, Convicts and Prisons § 4.

## § 791.267a. Nonemergency medical, dental, or optometric services; intentional injury; copayment or payment by prisoner; on-site medical treatment; report on feasibility and cost. [MSA § 28.2327(1)]

### LexisNexis™ and Other Annotations

**LexisNexis™ Michigan analytical references:**
Michigan Law and Practice, Convicts and Prisons § 4.

## § 791.268a. Visits from minors; conditions; restrictions; "minor" defined.

Sec. 68a. (1) Except as otherwise provided in subsection (2), a prisoner may be permitted to receive visits from a minor brother, sister, stepbrother, stepsister, half brother, or half sister if that minor is on the prisoner's approved visitor list.

(2) Notwithstanding subsection (1), the department may do any of the following:

(a) Place limits on visiting hours, establish reasonable rules of conduct, and establish uniform quotas at each institution for visits to prisoners to promote order and security in the institutions and to prevent interference with institutional routine or disruption of a prisoner's programming.

(b) Establish requirements for who must accompany the minor on the visit.

(c) Deny, restrict, or terminate visits as determined necessary by the department for the order and security of the institution.

(3) As used in this section, "minor" means a person who is less than 18 years of age.

**History:**
   Pub Acts 1953, No. 232, § 68a, as added by Pub Acts 2001, No. 8, imd eff May 25, 2001.

## § 791.269a. Subjecting visitor to pat down search; condition; waiver; definitions. [MSA § 28.2329(1)]

### LexisNexis™ and Other Annotations

**LexisNexis™ Michigan analytical references:**
   Michigan Law and Practice, Convicts and Prisons § 4.

## CHAPTER V
## BUREAU OF PRISON INDUSTRIES

## § 791.270. Monitoring of telephone communications; conditions; disclosure of obtained information; evidence in criminal prosecution; definitions. [MSA § 28.2330]

### LexisNexis™ and Other Annotations

**LexisNexis™ Michigan analytical references:**
   Michigan Law and Practice, Convicts and Prisons § 4.

---

# CORRECTIONAL OFFICERS' TRAINING ACT OF 1982

Act 415, 1982, p 1616, eff March 30, 1983.

An act to improve the training and education of state ◆ correctional officers; to provide for the certification of state correctional officers and the development of standards and requirements for state ◆ correctional officers; to provide for the creation of a correctional officers' training council and a central training academy; and to prescribe the powers and duties of certain state agencies. (Amended by Pub Acts 2003, No. 121, imd eff July 29, 2003, by enacting § 2 eff October 1, 2003 (see 2003 note below).)

*The People of the State of Michigan enact:*

§ 791.270     MCLS Cumulative Supplement

**Effect of amendment notes:**
   The **2003 amendment** deleted "and local" preceding "correctional officers" in two places.

## § 791.502. Definitions. [MSA § 28.2355(2)]

Sec. 2. As used in this act:
   (a) "Central training academy" means the central training academy established pursuant to section 15.
   (b) "Correctional facility" means ◆ [a] facility or institution which houses an inmate population under the jurisdiction of the department of corrections.
   ◆
   (c) "Council" means the correctional officers' training council created under section 3.
   (d) "Department" means the state department of corrections.
   (e) "Executive secretary" means the executive secretary of the council.
   ◆
   [(f)] ◆ "State correctional officer" means any person employed by the department in a correctional facility as a correctional officer or a corrections medical aide, or that person's immediate supervisor.

**History:**
   Amended by Pub Acts 2003, No. 121, imd eff July 24, 2003, by enacting § 2 eff October 1, 2003 (see 2003 note below).

**Editor's notes:**
   **Pub Acts 2003, No. 121, enacting § 3,** imd eff July 29, 2003, by enacting § 2 eff October 1, 2003, provides:
   "Enacting section 3. This amendatory act does not take effect unless all of the following bills of the 92nd Legislature are enacted into law:
   "(a) House Bill No. 4515 [Pub Acts 2003, No. 125].
   "(b) House Bill No. 4517 [Pub Acts 2003, No. 124].".

**Effect of amendment notes:**
   The **2003 amendment** in paragraph (b) substituted "a" for "either of the following: (i) A" following "means" and deleted former subparagraph (ii) which read "A municipal or county jail, work camp, lockup, holding center, halfway house, community corrections center, or any other facility maintained by a municipality or county which houses adult prisoners."; deleted former paragraph (f) which read " 'Local correctional officer' means any person employed by a unit of local government in a correctional facility as a correctional officer, or that person's immediate supervisor."; and redesignated former paragraph (g) as paragraph (f).

**Statutory references:**
   Sections 3 and 15, above referred to, are §§791.503 and 791.515.

## § 791.503. Correctional officers' training council; creation; duties; membership. [MSA § 28.2355(3)]

Sec. 3. The correctional officer's training council is created within the department and shall establish standards regarding training and education as prescribed in this act. The council shall consist of ◆ [8] members appointed by the governor. The members shall be appointed as follows:

**Department of Corrections** § 791.504

(a) One member shall represent state corrections officers.

[(b)] ◆ One member shall represent the ◆ [department].

[(c)] ◆ One member shall represent the ◆ [department of management and budget].

[(d)] ◆ One member shall represent the state personnel director.

[(e)] ◆ Two members shall represent the public at large.

[(f)] ◆ Two members shall represent the academic community, at least 1 of whom shall represent Michigan community colleges.

**History:**
Amended by Pub Acts 2003, No. 121, imd eff July 24, 2003, by enacting § 2 eff October 1, 2003 (see 2003 note below).

**Editor's notes:**
Pub Acts 2003, No. 121, enacting § 3, imd eff July 29, 2003, by enacting § 2 eff October 1, 2003, provides:
"Enacting section 3. This amendatory act does not take effect unless all of the following bills of the 92nd Legislature are enacted into law:
"(a) House Bill No. 4515 [Pub Acts 2003, No. 125].
"(b) House Bill No. 4517 [Pub Acts 2003, No. 124].".

**Effect of amendment notes:**
The 2003 amendment in the introductory paragraph substituted "8" for "10" following "shall consist of"; deleted former paragraphs (b) and (c) which read: "(b) One member shall represent local corrections officers." and "(c) One member shall represent local agencies which maintain jails, corrections, or temporary holding facilities."; redesignated paragraphs (d)—(h) as paragraphs (b)—(f); in paragraph (b) substituted "department" for "Michigan commission of corrections"; and in paragraph (c) substituted "department of management and budget" for "office of criminal justice".

## § 791.504. Council members; terms; appointment; vacancy; reappointment. [MSA § 28.2355(4)]

Sec. 4. (1) All members of the council shall hold office for a term of 3 years[.] ◆ Successors shall be appointed in the same manner as the original appointment.

(2) A person appointed as a member to fill a vacancy created other than by expiration of a term shall be appointed in the same manner as the original appointment for the remainder of the unexpired term of the member whom the person is to succeed.

(3) Any member may be reappointed for additional terms.

**History:**
Amended by Pub Acts 2003, No. 121, imd eff July 24, 2003, by enacting § 2 eff October 1, 2003 (see 2003 note below).

**Editor's notes:**
Pub Acts 2003, No. 121, enacting § 3, imd eff July 29, 2003, by enacting § 2 eff October 1, 2003, provides:
"Enacting section 3. This amendatory act does not take effect unless all of the following bills of the 92nd Legislature are enacted into law:
"(a) House Bill No. 4515 [Pub Acts 2003, No. 125].
"(b) House Bill No. 4517 [Pub Acts 2003, No. 124].".

§ 791.504

**Effect of amendment notes:**
The 2003 amendment in subsection (1) substituted a period for ", except that of the members first appointed 3 shall have a term of 1 year, 4 shall have a term of 2 years, and 3 shall have a term of 3 years.".

**§ 791.505. Council chairperson and vice-chairperson; designation; terms of office; reelection; location and number of council meetings; special meetings; establishment of procedures and requirements; conduct of business at public meeting; public notice; compensation; expenses.** [MSA § 28.2355(5)]

Sec. 5. (1) The council shall designate from among its members a chairperson and a vice-chairperson who shall serve for 1-year terms and who may be reelected.

(2) The council shall meet at least 4 times in each year at Lansing. The council shall hold special meetings when called by the chairperson or, in the absence of the chairperson, by the vice-chairperson, or when called by the chairperson upon the written request of ◆ [4] members of the council. The council shall establish its own procedures and requirements with respect to quorum, place, and conduct of its meeting and other matters.

(3) The business which the council may perform shall be conducted at a public meeting of the council held in compliance with the open meetings act, ◆ [ 1976 PA 267, MCL 15.261 to 15.275]. Public notice of the time, date, and place of the meeting shall be given in the manner required by ◆ [the open meetings act, 1976 PA 267, MCL 15.261 to 15.275].

(4) The members of the council shall serve without compensation but shall be entitled to their actual expenses in attending meetings and in the performance of their duties under this act.

**History:**
Amended by Pub Acts 2003, No. 121, imd eff July 24, 2003, by enacting § 2 eff October 1, 2003 (see 2003 note below).

**Editor's notes:**
Pub Acts 2003, No. 121, enacting § 3, imd eff July 29, 2003, by enacting § 2 eff October 1, 2003, provides:
"Enacting section 3. This amendatory act does not take effect unless all of the following bills of the 92nd Legislature are enacted into law:
"(a) House Bill No. 4515 [Pub Acts 2003, No. 125].
"(b) House Bill No. 4517 [Pub Acts 2003, No. 124].".

**Effect of amendment notes:**
The 2003 amendment in subsection (2) substituted "4" for "5" following "written request of"; in subsection (3) substituted "1976 PA 267, MCL 15.261 to 15.275" for "Act No. 267 of the Public Acts of 1976, as amended, being sections 15.261 to 15.275 of the Michigan Compiled Laws" and "the open meetings act, 1976 PA 367, MCL 15.261 to 15.275" for "Act No. 267 of the Public Acts of 1976, as amended".

**§ 791.514.** [Repealed] [MSA § 28.2355(14)]

**History:**
Repealed by Pub Acts 2003, No. 121, enacting § 1, imd eff July 29, 2003, by enacting § 2 eff October 1, 2003 (see 2003 note below).

**Department of Corrections** § 791.515

**Editor's notes:**
Pub Acts 2003, No. 121, enacting § 3, imd eff July 29, 2003, by enacting § 2 eff October 1, 2003, provides:
"Enacting section 3. This amendatory act does not take effect unless all of the following bills of the 92nd Legislature are enacted into law:
"(a) House Bill No. 4515 [Pub Acts 2003, No. 125].
"(b) House Bill No. 4517 [Pub Acts 2003, No. 124].".
Former § 791.514 pertained to minimum standards and requirements for local correctional officers; development.

**§ 791.515. Central training academy; establishment; provision of funds; separate appropriation.** [MSA § 28.2355(15)]

Sec. 15. The department shall establish a central training academy for use as an employee training center for state ◆ correctional officers. Funds necessary for the establishment and use of the training academy shall be provided by the department and supported by separate appropriation.

**History:**
Amended by Pub Acts 2003, No. 121, imd eff July 24, 2003, by enacting § 2 eff October 1, 2003 (see 2003 note below).

**Editor's notes:**
Pub Acts 2003, No. 121, enacting § 3, imd eff July 29, 2003, by enacting § 2 eff October 1, 2003, provides:
"Enacting section 3. This amendatory act does not take effect unless all of the following bills of the 92nd Legislature are enacted into law:
"(a) House Bill No. 4515 [Pub Acts 2003, No. 125].
"(b) House Bill No. 4517 [Pub Acts 2003, No. 124].".

**Effect of amendment notes:**
The 2003 amendment deleted "and local" following "center for state".

---

# LOCAL CORRECTIONS OFFICERS TRAINING ACT

Act 125, 2003, imd eff August 1, 2003, by enacting § 1 eff October 1, 2003 (see 2003 note below).

AN ACT to improve the training and education of local corrections officers; to provide for the certification of local corrections officers and the development of standards and requirements for local corrections officers; to provide for the creation of a sheriffs coordinating and training office and a local corrections advisory board; and to prescribe the powers and duties of certain local and state officers and agencies.

*The People of the State of Michigan enact:*

**Editor's notes:**
Pub Acts 2003, No. 125, enacting § 2, imd eff August 1, 2003, by enacting § 1 eff October 1, 2003, provides:
"Enacting section 2. This act does not take effect unless all of the following bills of the 92nd Legislature are enacted into law:
"(a) House Bill No. 4516 [Pub Acts 2003, No. 121].
"(b) House Bill No. 4517 [Pub Acts 2003, No. 124].".

## § 791.531. Short title.

Sec. 1. This act shall be known and may be cited as the "local corrections officers training act".

**History:**
Pub Acts 2003, No. 125, § 1, imd eff August 1, 2003, by enacting § 1 eff October 1, 2003 (see 2003 note below).

**Editor's notes:**
Pub Acts 2003, No. 125, enacting § 2, imd eff August 1, 2003, by enacting § 1 eff October 1, 2003, provides:
"Enacting section 2. This act does not take effect unless all of the following bills of the 92nd Legislature are enacted into law:
"(a) House Bill No. 4516 [Pub Acts 2003, No. 121].
"(b) House Bill No. 4517 [Pub Acts 2003, No. 124]."

## § 791.532. Definitions.

Sec. 2. As used in this act:

(a) "Board" means the local corrections officers advisory board created in section 9.

(b) "Council" means the sheriffs coordinating and training council described in section 4.

(c) "Executive secretary" means the executive secretary of the council.

(d) "Local correctional facility" means county jail, work camp, or any other facility maintained by a county that houses adult prisoners.

(e) "Local corrections officer" means any person employed by a county sheriff in a local correctional facility as a corrections officer or that person's supervisor or administrator.

(f) "Office" means the sheriffs coordinating and training office created in section 3.

**History:**
Pub Acts 2003, No. 125, § 2, imd eff August 1, 2003, by enacting § 1 eff October 1, 2003 (see 2003 note below).

**Editor's notes:**
Pub Acts 2003, No. 125, enacting § 2, imd eff August 1, 2003, by enacting § 1 eff October 1, 2003, provides:
"Enacting section 2. This act does not take effect unless all of the following bills of the 92nd Legislature are enacted into law:
"(a) House Bill No. 4516 [Pub Acts 2003, No. 121].
"(b) House Bill No. 4517 [Pub Acts 2003, No. 124]."

**Statutory references:**
Sections 3, 4 and 9, above referred to, are §§791.533, 791.534 and 791.539.

## § 791.533. Sheriffs coordinating and training office; creation; head of office; chief executive officer; executive secretary.

Sec. 3. (1) The sheriffs coordinating and training office is created as an autonomous entity in the department of corrections. The department is not fiscally or programmatically responsible or liable for any of the responsibilities or duties of the office, council, or board contained in this act.

(2) The head of the office is the sheriffs coordinating and training council.

(3) The chief executive officer of the office is the executive secretary, who shall be appointed by the council and who shall hold office at the pleasure of the council. The executive secretary shall perform the functions and duties as may be assigned by the council. The council may employ other persons as it considers necessary to implement the intent and purpose of this act.

**History:**
Pub Acts 2003, No. 125, § 3, imd eff August 1, 2003, by enacting § 1 eff October 1, 2003 (see 2003 note below).

**Editor's notes:**
Pub Acts 2003, No. 125, enacting § 2, imd eff August 1, 2003, by enacting § 1 eff October 1, 2003, provides:

"Enacting section 2. This act does not take effect unless all of the following bills of the 92nd Legislature are enacted into law:
"(a) House Bill No. 4516 [Pub Acts 2003, No. 121].
"(b) House Bill No. 4517 [Pub Acts 2003, No. 124]."

## § 791.534. Qualifications and appointment of members; vacancy; reappointment; terms.

Sec. 4. (1) The council consists of 7 members selected as follows:
  (a) The president of the Michigan sheriffs' association.
  (b) One member appointed to the council for a 1-year term, to be elected by the Michigan sheriffs' association, who shall be a sheriff from a county having a population of over 400,000.
  (c) One member appointed to the council for a 1-year term, to be elected by the Michigan sheriffs' association, who shall be a sheriff from a county having a population of between 100,000 and 400,000.
  (d) One member appointed to the council for a 1-year term, to be elected by the Michigan sheriffs' association, who shall be a sheriff from a county having a population under 100,000.
  (e) Two members appointed to the council for terms of 1 year each, who shall be elected by the deputy sheriff's association of Michigan.
  (f) One member appointed to the council for a 1-year term, who shall be elected by the jail administrators committee of the Michigan sheriffs' association.

(2) A member shall vacate his or her appointment upon termination of his or her official position as a sheriff or a deputy sheriff. A vacancy shall be filled in the same manner as the original appointment. A member appointed to fill a vacancy created other than by expiration of a term shall be appointed for the unexpired term of the member whom he or she is to succeed in the same manner as the original appointment. Any member may be reappointed for additional terms.

(3) The terms of the members first appointed shall begin January 1, 2004.

§ 791.534

**History:**
Pub Acts 2003, No. 125, § 4, imd eff August 1, 2003, by enacting § 1 eff October 1, 2003 (see 2003 note below).

**Editor's notes:**
Pub Acts 2003, No. 125, enacting § 2, imd eff August 1, 2003, by enacting § 1 eff October 1, 2003, provides:
"Enacting section 2. This act does not take effect unless all of the following bills of the 92nd Legislature are enacted into law:
"(a) House Bill No. 4516 [Pub Acts 2003, No. 121].
"(b) House Bill No. 4517 [Pub Acts 2003, No. 124]."

## § 791.535. Chairperson; vice-chairperson; designation; terms; reelection; meetings; conduct; compensation.

Sec. 5. (1) The council shall designate from among its members a chairperson and vice-chairperson, who shall serve for 1-year terms and who may be reelected.

(2) The council shall meet at least 4 times in each year and shall hold special meetings when called by the chairperson or, in the absence of the chairperson, by the vice-chairperson or when called by the chairperson upon the written request of 3 members of the council. The council shall establish its own procedures and requirements with respect to quorum, place, and conduct of its meetings and other matters.

(3) The business that the council may perform shall be conducted at a public meeting of the council held in compliance with the open meetings act, 1976 PA 267, MCL 15.261 to 15.275, and public notice of the time, date, and place of the meeting shall be given in the manner required by that act.

(4) The members of the council shall serve without compensation but shall be entitled to their actual expenses in attending meetings and in the performance of their duties.

**History:**
Pub Acts 2003, No. 125, § 5, imd eff August 1, 2003, by enacting § 1 eff October 1, 2003 (see 2003 note below).

**Editor's notes:**
Pub Acts 2003, No. 125, enacting § 2, imd eff August 1, 2003, by enacting § 1 eff October 1, 2003, provides:
"Enacting section 2. This act does not take effect unless all of the following bills of the 92nd Legislature are enacted into law:
"(a) House Bill No. 4516 [Pub Acts 2003, No. 121].
"(b) House Bill No. 4517 [Pub Acts 2003, No. 124]."

## § 791.536. Holding public office or employment; disqualification prohibited.

Sec. 6. A member of the council shall not be disqualified from holding any public office or employment by reason of his or her appointment or membership on the council and shall not forfeit that public office or employment by reason of his or her appointment to the council, notwithstanding the provisions of any general, special, or local law, ordinance, or city charter.

**Department of Corrections** § 791.538

**History:**
Pub Acts 2003, No. 125, § 6, imd eff August 1, 2003, by enacting § 1 eff October 1, 2003 (see 2003 note below).

**Editor's notes:**
Pub Acts 2003, No. 125, enacting § 2, imd eff August 1, 2003, by enacting § 1 eff October 1, 2003, provides:
"Enacting section 2. This act does not take effect unless all of the following bills of the 92nd Legislature are enacted into law:
"(a) House Bill No. 4516 [Pub Acts 2003, No. 121].
"(b) House Bill No. 4517 [Pub Acts 2003, No. 124]."

## § 791.537. Administrative support services.

Sec. 7. Administrative support services for the council and executive secretary shall be provided by the council as provided by separate appropriation for the council.

**History:**
Pub Acts 2003, No. 125, § 7, imd eff August 1, 2003, by enacting § 1 eff October 1, 2003 (see 2003 note below).

**Editor's notes:**
Pub Acts 2003, No. 125, enacting § 2, imd eff August 1, 2003, by enacting § 1 eff October 1, 2003, provides:
"Enacting section 2. This act does not take effect unless all of the following bills of the 92nd Legislature are enacted into law:
"(a) House Bill No. 4516 [Pub Acts 2003, No. 121].
"(b) House Bill No. 4517 [Pub Acts 2003, No. 124]."

## § 791.538. Standards and requirements.

Sec. 8. Not later than October 1, 2004 and as often as necessary after that, the council shall approve minimum standards and requirements for local corrections officers with respect to the following:

(a) Recruitment, selection, and certification of new local corrections officers based upon at least, but not limited to, work experience, educational achievement, and physical and mental fitness.

(b) New employee and continuing training programs.

(c) Recertification process.

(d) Course content of the vocational certificate program, the central training academy, and continuing training programs. The course content shall include education and training on how to identify and manage prisoners with a mental illness.

(e) Decertification process.

**History:**
Pub Acts 2003, No. 125, § 8, imd eff August 1, 2003, by enacting § 1 eff October 1, 2003 (see 2003 note below).

**Editor's notes:**
Pub Acts 2003, No. 125, enacting § 2, imd eff August 1, 2003, by enacting § 1 eff October 1, 2003, provides:
"Enacting section 2. This act does not take effect unless all of the following bills of the 92nd Legislature are enacted into law:
"(a) House Bill No. 4516 [Pub Acts 2003, No. 121].
"(b) House Bill No. 4517 [Pub Acts 2003, No. 124]."

## § 791.539. Local corrections officers advisory board; creation; qualifications and appointment of members; terms; vacancy; reappointment; compensation; development and recommendation of standards and requirements; training facilities.

Sec. 9. (1) The local corrections officers advisory board is created within the council. The board shall consist of 9 members appointed by the council, as follows:

(a) Three members of the board shall be members of the deputy sheriff's association of Michigan.

(b) Three members of the board shall be members of the Michigan sheriffs' association.

(c) One member of the board shall be a member of the police officers association of Michigan.

(d) One member of the board shall be a member of the fraternal order of police.

(e) One member of the board shall be a member of the Michigan association of counties.

(2) All members of the board shall hold office for terms of 3 years each, except that of the members first appointed 3 shall serve for terms of 1 year each, 3 shall serve for terms of 2 years each, and 3 shall serve for terms of 3 years each. Successors shall be appointed in the same manner as the original appointment.

(3) A person appointed as a member to fill a vacancy created other than by expiration of a term shall be appointed in the same manner as the original appointment for the remainder of the unexpired term of the member whom the person is to succeed.

(4) Any member may be reappointed for additional terms.

(5) The members of the board shall serve without compensation but shall be entitled to their actual expenses in attending meetings and in the performance of their duties.

(6) Not later than April 1, 2004 and as often as necessary after that, the board shall develop and recommend minimum standards and requirements for local corrections officers and shall submit those standards and requirements to the council for the council's approval under section 8.

(7) The board shall recommend to the council all facilities that the board approves for providing training to local corrections officers under this act.

**History:**
Pub Acts 2003, No. 125, § 9, imd eff August 1, 2003, by enacting § 1 eff October 1, 2003 (see 2003 note below).

**Editor's notes:**
Pub Acts 2003, No. 125, enacting § 2, imd eff August 1, 2003, by enacting § 1 eff October 1, 2003, provides:

"Enacting section 2. This act does not take effect unless all of the following bills of the 92nd Legislature are enacted into law:
"(a) House Bill No. 4516 [Pub Acts 2003, No. 121].
"(b) House Bill No. 4517 [Pub Acts 2003, No. 124]."

**Statutory references:**
Section 8, above referred to, is § 791.538.

**Department of Corrections** § 791.542

### § 791.540. Annual report.

Sec. 10. The board shall make an annual report to the council that includes pertinent data regarding the standards and requirements established and an evaluation on the effectiveness of local corrections officer training programs.

**History:**
Pub Acts 2003, No. 125, § 10, imd eff August 1, 2003, by enacting § 1 eff October 1, 2003 (see 2003 note below).

**Editor's notes:**
Pub Acts 2003, No. 125, enacting § 2, imd eff August 1, 2003, by enacting § 1 eff October 1, 2003, provides:
"Enacting section 2. This act does not take effect unless all of the following bills of the 92nd Legislature are enacted into law:
"(a) House Bill No. 4516 [Pub Acts 2003, No. 121].
"(b) House Bill No. 4517 [Pub Acts 2003, No. 124]."

### § 791.541. Local corrections officer; certification.

Sec. 11. Beginning April 1, 2004, a person shall not be a local corrections officer unless he or she is certified or recertified by the council as provided in section 12 or 13. The council shall certify those persons and recertify on an annual basis those persons who satisfy the criteria set forth in section 12 or 13.

**History:**
Pub Acts 2003, No. 125, § 11, imd eff August 1, 2003, by enacting § 1 eff October 1, 2003 (see 2003 note below).

**Editor's notes:**
Pub Acts 2003, No. 125, enacting § 2, imd eff August 1, 2003, by enacting § 1 eff October 1, 2003, provides:
"Enacting section 2. This act does not take effect unless all of the following bills of the 92nd Legislature are enacted into law:
"(a) House Bill No. 4516 [Pub Acts 2003, No. 121].
"(b) House Bill No. 4517 [Pub Acts 2003, No. 124]."

**Statutory references:**
Sections 12 and 13, above referred to, are §§791.542 and 791.543.

### § 791.542. Local corrections officer; evidence of employment; certification.

Sec. 12. Effective January 1, 2005, a person who is employed as a local corrections officer before January 1, 2005, upon furnishing the council satisfactory evidence of his or her employment as a local corrections officer, shall be certified and recertified by the council as a local corrections officer if he or she applies to the council for certification not later than April 1, 2004.

**History:**
Pub Acts 2003, No. 125, § 12, imd eff August 1, 2003, by enacting § 1 eff October 1, 2003 (see 2003 note below).

**Editor's notes:**
Pub Acts 2003, No. 125, enacting § 2, imd eff August 1, 2003, by enacting § 1 eff October 1, 2003, provides:
"Enacting section 2. This act does not take effect unless all of the

following bills of the 92nd Legislature are enacted into law:
"(a) House Bill No. 4516 [Pub Acts 2003, No. 121].
"(b) House Bill No. 4517 [Pub Acts 2003, No. 124]."

### § 791.543. Local corrections officer; certification; conditions.

Sec. 13. A person who was not employed as a local corrections officer before January 1, 2005 but who becomes employed as a local corrections officer on or after January 1, 2005 shall not be certified or recertified by the council unless he or she meets all of the following conditions:

(a) He or she is a citizen of the United States and is 18 years of age or older.

(b) He or she has obtained a high school diploma or attained a passing score on the general education development test indicating a high school graduation level.

(c) Not later than 12 months after becoming employed as a local corrections officer, he or she has fulfilled other standards and requirements developed by the board and approved by the council for certification.

(d) He or she has fulfilled standards and requirements developed by the council upon the recommendation of the board for recertification.

**History:**
Pub Acts 2003, No. 125, § 13, imd eff August 1, 2003, by enacting § 1 eff October 1, 2003 (see 2003 note below).

**Editor's notes:**
Pub Acts 2003, No. 125, enacting § 2, imd eff August 1, 2003, by enacting § 1 eff October 1, 2003, provides:
"Enacting section 2. This act does not take effect unless all of the following bills of the 92nd Legislature are enacted into law:
"(a) House Bill No. 4516 [Pub Acts 2003, No. 121].
"(b) House Bill No. 4517 [Pub Acts 2003, No. 124]."

### § 791.543a. Collective bargaining agreement; temporary transfer or assignment.

Sec. 13a. Nothing in this act supersedes a right granted under a collective bargaining agreement. A person who exercises a right pursuant to a collective bargaining agreement that results in that person being required to obtain certification under this act shall be allowed not less than 2 years to obtain that certification at the expense of the employer. Nothing in this act prohibits the county sheriff from temporarily transferring or assigning an uncertified employee to a position normally requiring certification or from using an uncertified employee to function as a corrections officer during any period of emergency.

**History:**
Pub Acts 2003, No. 125, § 13a, imd eff August 1, 2003, by enacting § 1 eff October 1, 2003 (see 2003 note below).

**Editor's notes:**
Pub Acts 2003, No. 125, enacting § 2, imd eff August 1, 2003, by

**Department of Corrections** § 791.545

enacting § 1 eff October 1, 2003, provides:
"Enacting section 2. This act does not take effect unless all of the following bills of the 92nd Legislature are enacted into law:
"(a) House Bill No. 4516 [Pub Acts 2003, No. 121].
"(b) House Bill No. 4517 [Pub Acts 2003, No. 124]."

## § 791.544. Duties of council.

Sec. 14. The council may do all of the following:
(a) Enter into agreements with other public or private agencies or organizations to implement the intent of this act.
(b) Cooperate with and assist other public or private agencies or organizations to implement the intent of this act.
(c) Make recommendations to the legislature on matters pertaining to its responsibilities under this act.

**History:**
Pub Acts 2003, No. 125, § 14, imd eff August 1, 2003, by enacting § 1 eff October 1, 2003 (see 2003 note below).

**Editor's notes:**
Pub Acts 2003, No. 125, enacting § 2, imd eff August 1, 2003, by enacting § 1 eff October 1, 2003, provides:
"Enacting section 2. This act does not take effect unless all of the following bills of the 92nd Legislature are enacted into law:
"(a) House Bill No. 4516 [Pub Acts 2003, No. 121].
"(b) House Bill No. 4517 [Pub Acts 2003, No. 124]."

## § 791.545. Local corrections officers training fund; creation in state treasury; administration; source of funds; use; eligibility of counties to receive grants; reimbursement of fee; unexpended funds.

Sec. 15. (1) The local corrections officers training fund is created in the state treasury. The fund shall be administered by the council, which shall expend the fund only as provided in this section.

(2) There shall be credited to the local corrections officer training fund all revenue received from fees and civil fines collected under section 4b of 1846 RS 171, MCL 801.4b, and funds from any other source provided by law.

(3) The council shall use the fund only to defray the costs of continuing education, certification, recertification, decertification, and training of local corrections officers; the personnel and administrative costs of the office, board, and council; and other expenditures related to the requirements of this act. Only counties that forward to the fund 100% of fees collected under section 4b of 1846 RS 171, MCL 801.4b, are eligible to receive grants from the fund. A county that receives funds from the council under this section shall use those funds only for costs relating to the continuing education, certification, recertification, and training of local corrections officers in that county and shall not use those funds to supplant current spending by the county for those purposes, including state grants and training funds.

(4) The council, upon written request, shall reimburse the full

§ 791.545

amount of any fee paid by a person under section 4b of 1846 RS 171, MCL 801.4b, if the person was incarcerated pending trial and was found not guilty or the prosecution against the person was terminated for any reason. The council shall create and make available to all local correctional facilities in this state a written form explaining the provisions of this subsection. The form shall include the address to which the reimbursement request should be sent.

(5) Unexpended funds remaining in the fund at the end of the fiscal year shall remain in the fund and shall not revert to the general fund.

**History:**
Pub Acts 2003, No. 125, § 15, imd eff August 1, 2003, by enacting § 1 eff October 1, 2003 (see 2003 note below).

**Editor's notes:**
**Pub Acts 2003, No. 125, enacting § 2,** imd eff August 1, 2003, by enacting § 1 eff October 1, 2003, provides:
"Enacting section 2. This act does not take effect unless all of the following bills of the 92nd Legislature are enacted into law:
"(a) House Bill No. 4516 [Pub Acts 2003, No. 121].
"(b) House Bill No. 4517 [Pub Acts 2003, No. 124]."

## § 791.546. Acceptance of funds, grants, and gifts.

Sec. 16. The council may accept funds, grants, and gifts from any public or private source which shall be used to defray the expenses incident to implementing its responsibilities under this act.

**History:**
Pub Acts 2003, No. 125, § 16, imd eff August 1, 2003, by enacting § 1 eff October 1, 2003 (see 2003 note below).

**Editor's notes:**
**Pub Acts 2003, No. 125, enacting § 2,** imd eff August 1, 2003, by enacting § 1 eff October 1, 2003, provides:
"Enacting section 2. This act does not take effect unless all of the following bills of the 92nd Legislature are enacted into law:
"(a) House Bill No. 4516 [Pub Acts 2003, No. 121].
"(b) House Bill No. 4517 [Pub Acts 2003, No. 124]."

# CHAPTER 798

# CORRECTIONS

## SPECIAL ALTERNATIVE INCARCERATION ACT

Act 287, 1988, p 760, imd eff August 1, 1988.

**§ 798.11. Title of act.** [MSA § 28.2356(1)]

### LexisNexis™ and Other Annotations

**Michigan Digest references:**
Criminal Law and Procedure §§730.50, 731.20, 743.50, 754.70, 776.190.
Pardons and Paroles § 8.

**§ 798.14. Program of work and exercise; term of incarceration; aftercare residential pilot program; facility construction.** [MSA § 28.2356(4)]

### LexisNexis™ and Other Annotations

**LexisNexis™ Michigan analytical references:**
Michigan Law and Practice, Criminal Law and Procedure § 871.

## INTERSTATE COMPACTS

Act 89, 1935, p 143, imd eff May 27, 1935.

**§ 798.101. Probation and parole; interstate compact; permitting paroled prisoner to reside in other state; supervision by receiving state; retaking paroled person from receiving state; transporting retaken prisoner; regulations; ratification of compact; renunciation of compact; effect; notice.** [MSA § 28.1361]

### LexisNexis™ and Other Annotations

**LexisNexis™ Michigan analytical references:**
Michigan Law and Practice, Criminal Law and Procedure § 877.

# CHAPTER 800

# PRISONS

## MICHIGAN STATE INDUSTRIES ADVISORY BOARD–MICHIGAN DEPARTMENT OF CORRECTIONS–EXECUTIVE REORGANIZATION

### Executive Reorganization Order 2001-3

§ 800.351  Transfer of powers and duties of Michigan state industries advisory board to director of Michigan department of corrections by Type III transfer.

## PRISON CODE

Act 118, 1893, p 170, imd eff May 26, 1893.

**§ 800.33. Record of major misconduct charges as part of parole eligibility report; reduction from sentence; good time, disciplinary credits, special disciplinary credits; forfeiture; disciplinary credit committee; rules; good time committee; powers of warden and parole board; prisoner subject to disciplinary time; reduction of credits by court order. [MSA § 28.1403]**

### LexisNexis™ and Other Annotations

**Michigan Digest references:**
Administrative Law § 3.60.
Constitutional Law §§170, 225, 326, 328.
Criminal Law and Procedure §§123, 730, 731.20, 741, 743.50, 745, 765.
Former Jeopardy §§4, 7.
Habeas Corpus § 16.
Homicide § 148.
Pardons and Paroles § 10.
Prisons and Jails §§1.05, 2.10, 2.35, 2.40, 2.50, 2.80, 2.110, 5.
Probate Courts § 5.
Statutes § 129.

**LexisNexis™ Michigan analytical references:**
Michigan Law and Practice, Convicts and Prisons §§2, 6.
Michigan Law and Practice, Criminal Law and Procedure §§837, 839.

### CASE NOTES

**2. Construction, operation and effect.**

Deputy director of the Department of Corrections' Bureau of Correctional Facilities has authority to overrule a warden's award of special good time credit made pursuant to MCLS § 800.33(12), which is not an exception to the general grant of power and authority provided the director and assistant directors of the Department of Corrections under MCLS §§791.203, 791.205; the statutory grant of power gives the director and assistant directors full power and authority to supervise and control the affairs of the department, and such full power and authority includes discretionary decisions regarding the length of time that prisoners must serve. Edmond v Dep't of Corr. (2002) 254 Mich App 154, 656 NW2d 842.

The state and the state department of corrections were not liable for constitutional torts when it rearrested and reincarcerated prisoners after recalculating their sentence credits where (1) any claim that the prisoners' arrest lacked probable cause could not form the basis for liability because the claim was never pleaded or tried by express or implied consent of the parties, (2) the claim that the prisoners were placed in administrative segregation after being returned to prison was not properly before the court, and (3) while the failure of the prisoners to have a hearing before the sentencing court to determine whether they should be returned to prison could constitute a due process violation, the denial of that right was caused by the sentencing courts, and not the state or department of corrections. Reid v Department of Corrections (2000) 239 Mich App 621, 609 NW2d 215.

**8. Forfeiture of good time.**

**11. – Discretion of warden.**

Michigan Department of Corrections had the authority to forfeit disciplinary credits earned by the inmate on a sentence that had been completed by serving the maximum term less disciplinary credits, based on prison misconduct by the inmate occurring while serving a sentence that was ordered to be served consecutive to the earlier sentence, when credits were explicitly tied to an inmate's parole eligibility date and discharge date, MCL §§791.234 and 800.33, thus credits did not determine when a sentence expired or was completed, but only when an inmate was subject to parole or discharge, and the statutory scheme set forth no mechanism for, or manner of, recognizing that a consecutive sentence was somehow completed or expired at the moment the time served and credits equal the maximum sentence, and made clear that credits were a matter of grace and were subject to forfeiture. Ryan v Dep't of Corr. (2003) 259 Mich App 26, 672 NW2d 535, app dismd (2004, Mich) 2004 Mich LEXIS 2.

**12. Judicial intervention.**

An official with the department of corrections was protected by qualified immunity from liability in suit brought by prisoners who were rearrested and reincarcerated following a recalculation of their sentencing credits, where (1) the official acted in good faith when he relied on the advice of counsel in deciding to rearrest of the prisoners, (2) it was the sentencing court's issuance of the ex parte orders for the prisoners' arrest and not the official's request for such orders that caused the prisoners to be arrested and arguably violated the constitutional prohibition against ex post facto laws. Thomas v McGinnis (2000) 239 Mich App 636, 609 NW2d 222.

**§ 800.43. Receipt or possession of certain material; prohibition; list; notice; appeal; limits on amount.** [MSA § 28.1412]

### LexisNexis™ and Other Annotations

**LexisNexis™ Michigan analytical references:**
Michigan Law and Practice, Convicts and Prisons § 4.

**§ 800.49. Conveyance of convict to prison; fees and expenses; payment.** [MSA § 28.1418]

Sec. 49. The fees and actual expenses of sheriffs in conveying convicts to ◆ [a] prison shall be made out in a bill containing the ◆ [fees or expenses], and shall be presented to the warden when the prisoner is delivered at the prison. The warden shall certify on it that the prisoner has been received, and the bill, including the sheriff's actual expenses in returning to the county from ◆ [where] the prisoner was sent, shall be audited by the ◆ [state treasurer] and paid from the state treasury. Before drawing his [or her] warrant the ◆ [state treasurer] shall correct any errors in ◆ [the] bill as to form, items, or amount, and the sheriff shall be paid for ◆ [the] services, his [or her] actual traveling expenses and the expenses of the convict, and the sum of ◆ [$3.00] for each and every day so employed.

**History:**
Amended by Pub Acts 2002, No. 89, imd eff March 26, 2002.

**Effect of amendment notes:**
The 2002 amendment substituted "state treasurer" for "auditor general" in two instances, inserted "or her" in two instances, following "conveying convicts to" substituted "a" for "either", following "bill containing the" substituted "fees or expenses" for "items thereof", following "county from" substituted "where" for "whence", following "shall be paid for" substituted "the" for "such" and following "and the sum of" substituted "$3.00" for "three dollars".

### § 800.61. Escaped convicts; measures for apprehension; reward; sentence. [MSA § 28.1430]

Sec. 61. Whenever any convict shall escape from ◆ [a] prison, ◆ the warden ◆ [shall] take all proper measures for the apprehension of ◆ [the] convict, and for that purpose he [or she] may offer a reward not exceeding ◆ [$50.00] for the apprehension and delivery of ◆ [that] convict; but with the consent of his [or her] board ◆ [the] reward may be increased to a sum not exceeding ◆ [$500.00]. All suitable rewards and other sums of money, necessarily paid for advertising and apprehending any convict who may escape from prison, shall be audited by the ◆ [state treasurer], and paid out of the state treasury. If any prisoner shall be retaken, the time between the escape and his [or her] recommittal shall not be computed as part of the term of imprisonment, but he [or she] shall remain in the prison a sufficient length of time after the term of his [or her] sentence would have expired, if he [or she] had not escaped, to equal the period of time he [or she] may have been absent by reason of ◆ [the] escape.

**History:**
Amended by Pub Acts 2002, No. 89, imd eff March 26, 2002.

**Effect of amendment notes:**
The 2002 amendment inserted "or she" and "or her" throughout, following "shall escape from" substituted "a" for "either", following "prison," deleted "it shall be the duty of", following "the warden" substituted "shall" for "to", following "apprehension of" substituted "the" for "such", following "reward not exceeding" substituted "$50.00" for "fifty dollars", following "apprehension and delivery of" substituted "that" for "such", preceding "reward may be increased" substituted "the" for "such", following "sum not exceeding" substituted "$500.00" for "five hundred dollars", following "audited by the" substituted "state treasurer" for "auditor general" and following "absent by reason of" substituted "the "for "such".

#### LexisNexis™ and Other Annotations

**LexisNexis™ Michigan analytical references:**
Michigan Law and Practice, Rewards § 1.

§ 800.101       MCLS Cumulative Supplement

# EMPLOYMENT OF CONVICTS FOR PUBLIC PROJECTS
Act 181, 1911, p 305, eff August 1, 1911.

**§ 800.101. Convicts; employment on public projects; control; compensation; disposition of moneys.** [MSA § 28.1511]

*LexisNexis™ and Other Annotations*

**LexisNexis™ Michigan analytical references:**
Michigan Law and Practice, Convicts and Prisons § 5.

**§ 800.101a. Employment on state highways; requisition, order; control; compensation, disposition.** [MSA § 28.1512]

*LexisNexis™ and Other Annotations*

**LexisNexis™ Michigan analytical references:**
Michigan Law and Practice, Convicts and Prisons § 5.

**§ 800.102. Class of labor prohibited.** [MSA § 28.1513]

*LexisNexis™ and Other Annotations*

**LexisNexis™ Michigan analytical references:**
Michigan Law and Practice, Convicts and Prisons § 5.

---

# LIQUOR, NARCOTICS AND WEAPONS
Act 17, 1909, p 32, eff September 1, 1909.

**§ 800.281. Liquor, drugs and controlled substances; prohibited distribution.** [MSA § 28.1621]

*LexisNexis™ and Other Annotations*

**Michigan Digest references:**
Constitutional Law §§326, 371.
Controlled Substances § 20.
Criminal Law and Procedure §§99, 730.10.
Intoxicating Liquors §§78, 88.
Prisons and Jails §§1.05, 2.30, 2.85, 2.95.
Search and Seizure § 11.
Statutes § 33.

**LexisNexis™ Michigan analytical references:**
Michigan Law and Practice, Convicts and Prisons § 4.
Michigan Law and Practice, Public Health and Welfare § 173.

# Prisons § 800.322

## § 800.283. Weapons or implements for escape; furnishing prohibited; possession or control of weapons or implements. [MSA § 28.1623]

### LexisNexis™ and Other Annotations

**Michigan Digest references:**
Constitutional Law §§212, 276, 371.
Criminal Law and Procedure §§16, 97, 97.65.
Prisons and Jails §§1.05, 2.10, 2.100.
Statutes §§34, 114.

### CASE NOTES

**2. Construction and effect.**
Language of MCL § 800.283(4) fortified the court's conclusion that a conviction for violating the Michigan statute constituted a "violent felony" within the meaning of the Armed Career Criminal Act, 18 USCS § 924(e); the Michigan statute proscribed the possession of a weapon or other implement which might be used to injure another prisoner or person, and there was no legitimate, recreational, or innocent purpose for possessing an item the statute proscribed. United States v Gibson (2003, ED Mich) 293 F Supp 2d 776.

## § 800.284. Searching of visitors. [MSA § 28.1624]

### LexisNexis™ and Other Annotations

**LexisNexis™ Michigan analytical references:**
Michigan Law and Practice, Convicts and Prisons § 4.

---

# CORRECTIONAL INDUSTRIES ACT

Act 15, 1968, p 25, imd eff April 5, 1968.

## § 800.321. Short title. [MSA § 28.1540(1)]

### LexisNexis™ and Other Annotations

**Michigan Digest references:**
Labor Organizations and Disputes § 4.

**LexisNexis™ Michigan analytical references:**
Michigan Law and Practice, Convicts and Prisons § 5.

## § 800.322. "Correctional industries products" and "youth correctional facility" defined. [MSA § 28.1540(2)]

### LexisNexis™ and Other Annotations

**LexisNexis™ Michigan analytical references:**
Michigan Law and Practice, Convicts and Prisons § 5.

## § 800.326. Sale, exchange, or purchase of correctional industries products; availability of agricultural products to nonprofit charitable organizations or family independence agency; use of inmate labor. [MSA § 28.1540(6)]

#### LexisNexis™ and Other Annotations

**LexisNexis™ Michigan analytical references:**
Michigan Law and Practice, Convicts and Prisons § 5.

## § 800.327. Employment of inmates; types of employment. [MSA § 28.1540(7)]

#### LexisNexis™ and Other Annotations

**LexisNexis™ Michigan analytical references:**
Michigan Law and Practice, Convicts and Prisons § 5.

## § 800.327a. Assignment of inmates to work in private manufacturing or service enterprise. [MSA § 28.1540(7a)]

#### LexisNexis™ and Other Annotations

**LexisNexis™ Michigan analytical references:**
Michigan Law and Practice, Convicts and Prisons § 5.

## § 800.332. Schedule of payments or allowances to inmates or dependents. [MSA § 28.1540(12)]

#### LexisNexis™ and Other Annotations

**Michigan Digest references:**
Prisons and Jails § 3.40.

---

# MICHIGAN STATE INDUSTRIES ADVISORY BOARD–MICHIGAN DEPARTMENT OF CORRECTIONS–EXECUTIVE REORGANIZATION

Executive Reorganization Order 2001-3, eff December 2, 2001

## § 800.351. Transfer of powers and duties of Michigan state industries advisory board to director of Michigan department of corrections by Type III transfer.

WHEREAS, Article V, Section 1, of the Constitution of the state of Michigan of 1963 vests the executive power in the Governor; and

WHEREAS, Article V, Section 2, of the Constitution of the state of Michigan of 1963 empowers the Governor to make changes in the organization of the Executive Branch or in the assignment of functions among its units which he considers necessary for efficient administration; and

WHEREAS, the Michigan State Industries advisory Board

("Board") was created within the Michigan Department of Corrections pursuant to Executive Order 1993-15, being section 800.341 of the Michigan Compiled Laws; and

WHEREAS, the functions, duties and responsibilities assigned to the Board can more effectively be carried out by the Director of the Michigan Department of Corrections in consultation with the businesses and workers of the state; and

WHEREAS, it is necessary in the interests of efficient administration and effectiveness of government to effect changes in the organization of the Executive Branch of government.

NOW, THEREFORE, I, John Engler, Governor of the state of Michigan, pursuant to the powers vested in me by the Constitution of the state of Michigan of 1963 and the laws of the state of Michigan, do hereby order the following:

1. All the statutory authority, powers, duties, functions and responsibilities of the Michigan State Industries Advisory Board are hereby transferred to the Director of the Michigan Department of Corrections by a Type III transfer, as defined in Section 3 of Act No. 380 of the Public Acts of 1965, as amended, being Section 16.103 of the Michigan Compiled Laws.

2. The Director of the Michigan Department of Corrections shall provide executive direction and supervision for the implementation of the transfer made under this Order. The assigned functions shall be administered under the direction and supervision of the Director of the Michigan Department of Corrections.

3. The Director of the Michigan Department of Corrections shall administer the assigned functions transferred by this Order in such ways as to promote efficient administration and shall make internal organizational changes as may be administratively necessary to complete the realignment of responsibilities prescribed by this Order.

4. All records of the Michigan State Industries Advisory Board are hereby transferred to the Michigan Department of Corrections.

5. The Michigan State Industries Advisory Board is hereby abolished.

In fulfillment of the requirement of Article V, Section 2, of the Constitution of the state of Michigan of 1963, the provisions of this Executive Order shall become effective sixty (60) days from the filing of this Order.

**History:**
Executive Reorganization Order No. 2001-3 was promulgated October 2, 2001, as Executive Order No. 2001-7, eff December 2, 2001.

§ 800.401                  MCLS Cumulative Supplement

# STATE CORRECTIONAL FACILITY REIMBURSEMENT ACT

Act 253, 1935, p 434, imd eff June 8, 1935.

## § 800.401. Title of act. [MSA § 28.1701]

### LexisNexis™ and Other Annotations

**Michigan Digest references:**
Costs and Allowances §§105.15, 105.355, 105.445.
Infants § 54.
Prisons and Jails § 4.50.

**LexisNexis™ Michigan analytical references:**
Michigan Law and Practice, Convicts and Prisons § 4.
Michigan Law and Practice, Education § 131.

## § 800.401a. Definitions. [MSA § 28.1701(1)]

### LexisNexis™ and Other Annotations

**Michigan Digest references:**
Prisons and Jails § 4.50.

**LexisNexis™ Michigan analytical references:**
Michigan Law and Practice, Convicts and Prisons § 4.
Michigan Law and Practice, State § 4.

### CASE NOTES

Employee Retirement Income Security Act (ERISA) did not bar an order directing pension fund payments to an inmate to be paid directly to his prison account because ERISA did not protect payments after they had been made to the beneficiary, the pension payments were made to an account in the inmate's name, and, therefore, there was no assignment or alienation of funds barred by ERISA; hence, the payments were "assets" as contemplated by MCL § 800.401a when the warden subsequently disbursed funds under the State Correctional Facility Reimbursement Act to repay the state for the inmate's costs. People v Gottschalk (2003, Mich) 468 Mich 901, 660 NW2d 714.

## § 800.403. Reports, investigation; cost of care of prisoner, reimbursement of state; reimbursement of state; limitation. [MSA § 28.1703]

### LexisNexis™ and Other Annotations

**Michigan Digest references:**
Prisons and Jails §§1.05, 1.55, 4.50.

# Prisons § 800.404

**LexisNexis™ Michigan analytical references:**
Michigan Law and Practice, Convicts and Prisons § 4.

**§ 800.404. Exclusive jurisdiction of circuit court; complaint by attorney general, contents; order to show cause, issuance; service of complaint and order upon prisoner; methods; time; hearing; finding of assets subject to claim; order to reimburse state; amount of reimbursement; prisoner's obligation to provide support, consideration at hearing; order to reimburse state, failure to comply; order to show cause; contempt of court; cost of proceedings, liability of prisoner's assets; proceedings by state to recover cost of care of prisoner, commencement.** [MSA § 28.1704]

### LexisNexis™ and Other Annotations

**Michigan Digest references:**
Constitutional Law §§66, 326.
Injunctions § 134.
Prisons and Jails §§1.05, 4.50.

**LexisNexis™ Michigan analytical references:**
Michigan Law and Practice, Convicts and Prisons § 4.
Michigan Law and Practice, State § 4.

### CASE NOTES

**5. Estate of prisoner.**

Employee Retirement Income Security Act (ERISA) did not bar an order directing pension fund payments to an inmate to be paid directly to his prison account because ERISA did not protect payments after they had been made to the beneficiary, the pension payments were made to an account in the inmate's name, and, therefore, there was no assignment or alienation of funds barred by ERISA; hence, the payments were within the inmate's estate as contemplated by MCL § 800.404(3) when the warden subsequently disbursed funds under the State Correctional Facility Reimbursement Act to repay the state for the inmate's costs. People v Gottschalk (2003, Mich) 468 Mich 901, 660 NW2d 714.

Employee Retirement Income Security Act (ERISA) did not bar an order directing pension fund payments to an inmate to be paid directly to his prison account because ERISA did not protect payments after they had been made to the beneficiary, the pension payments were made to an account in the inmate's name, and, therefore, there was no assignment or alienation of funds barred by ERISA; hence, the payments were within the inmate's estate as contemplated by MCL § 800.404(3) when the warden subsequently disbursed funds under the State Correctional Facility Reimbursement Act to repay the state for the inmate's costs. People v Gottschalk (2003, Mich) 468 Mich 901, 660 NW2d 714.

§ 800.454    MCLS Cumulative Supplement

## REIMBURSEMENT OF COUNTY FOR PROSECUTION AND PRISON MAINTENANCE EXPENSES

Act 16, 1978, p 42, imd eff February 12, 1978.

**§ 800.454. Reimbursement of county for costs of previously incarcerated state prisoner; conditions for reimbursement; daily limitation; inapplicability of provision; submission of monthly itemized costs to department of corrections; payment; determination of reasonableness conclusive.** [MSA § 28.1714(4)]

**LexisNexis™ and Other Annotations**

**Michigan Digest references:**
  Counties § 40.
  Prisons and Jails § 2.35.

# CHAPTER 801

# JAILS AND WORKHOUSES

## COUNTY JAILS AND THE REGULATION THEREOF
### RS 1846, Ch 171

§ 801.4b  Payment of fee by inmate; collection; forwarding fees to local corrections officers training fund; disposition; failure to pay fee as civil infraction; civil fine; enforcement; refund.

## COUNTY JAILS AND THE REGULATION THEREOF
### RS 1846, Ch 171

**§ 801.4. County jail; charges, payment, exception. [MSA § 28.1724]**

### LexisNexis™ and Other Annotations

**Michigan Digest references:**
Counties § 32.
Hospitals § 1.

**LexisNexis™ Michigan analytical references:**
Michigan Law and Practice, Counties § 78.

**§ 801.4b. Payment of fee by inmate; collection; forwarding fees to local corrections officers training fund; disposition; failure to pay fee as civil infraction; civil fine; enforcement; refund.**

Sec. 4b. (1) Beginning August 1, 2003, each person who is incarcerated in the county jail shall pay a fee of $12.00 to the county sheriff when the person is admitted into the jail.

(2) The county sheriff may collect a fee owed under this section by withdrawing that amount from any inmate account maintained by the sheriff for that inmate.

(3) Except as provided in subsections (4) and (5), the sheriff, once each calendar quarter, shall forward all fees collected under this section to the local corrections officers training fund created in the local corrections officers training act.

(4) The revenue derived from fees collected under this section shall be directed in the manner provided in subsection (5) in a county for which the sheriffs coordinating and training council has certified that the county's standards and requirements for the training of local corrections officers equals or exceeds the standards and requirements approved by the sheriffs coordinating and training council under the local corrections officers training act.

(5) In a county that meets the criteria in subsection (4), both of the following apply:

### § 801.4b

(a) Once each calendar quarter, the sheriff shall forward $2.00 of each fee collected to the state treasurer for deposit in the local corrections officers training fund created in the local corrections officers training act.

(b) The remaining $10.00 of each fee shall be retained in that county, to be used only for costs relating to the continuing education, certification, recertification, and training of local corrections officers and inmate programs including substance abuse and mental health programs in that county. However, revenue from the fees shall not be used to supplant current spending by the county for continuing education, certification, recertification, and training of local corrections officers.

(6) An inmate who fails to pay a fee owed under this section before being discharged from the jail is responsible for a state civil infraction and may be ordered to pay a civil fine of $100.00. An appearance ticket may be issued to a person who fails to pay a fee owed under this section. The appearance ticket may be issued by the sheriff or a deputy sheriff. The county prosecutor for the county in which the jail is located is responsible for enforcing the state civil infraction. A civil fine collected under this section shall be paid as provided under section 8831 of the revised judicature act of 1961, 1961 PA 236, MCL 600.8831.

(7) A person who is incarcerated in a jail pending trial or arraignment is entitled to a full refund of the fee paid under this section if the prosecution against him or her is terminated for any reason or if he or she is found not guilty of the charges. Each person required to pay a fee under this section shall be given a written form explaining the circumstances under which he or she may request a refund under this subsection. The form shall be as prescribed in section 15 of the local corrections officers training act.

**History:**
RS 1846, No. 171, § 4b, as added by Pub Acts 2003, No. 124, imd eff August 1, 2003, by enacting § 2 eff October 1, 2003 (see 2003 note below).

**Editor's notes:**
"Enacting section 2. This amendatory act does not take effect unless all of the following bills of the 92nd Legislature are enacted into law:
(a) House Bill No. 4515 [Pub Act 2003, No. 525].
(b) House Bill No. 4516 [Pub Act 2003, No. 521].".

**Statutory references:**
Section 15 of the local corrections officers training act, above referred to, is § 791.545.

## § 801.6. County jail; separation of prisoners. [MSA § 28.1726]

### LexisNexis™ and Other Annotations

**LexisNexis™ Michigan analytical references:**
Michigan Law and Practice, Convicts and Prisons § 4.

# Jails and Workhouses § 801.23

**§ 801.7. Visitors, counsel; private conversations prohibited.** [MSA § 28.1727]

### LexisNexis™ and Other Annotations

**LexisNexis™ Michigan analytical references:**
Michigan Law and Practice, Convicts and Prisons § 4.

**§ 801.8. Prisoners' food, expense.** [MSA § 28.1728]

### LexisNexis™ and Other Annotations

**LexisNexis™ Michigan analytical references:**
Michigan Law and Practice, Convicts and Prisons § 4.

**§ 801.9. Hard labor sentence; annual account, proceeds.** [MSA § 28.1729]

### LexisNexis™ and Other Annotations

**LexisNexis™ Michigan analytical references:**
Michigan Law and Practice, Convicts and Prisons § 5.

**§ 801.10. Prisoners; work on public highways, streets, alleys, roads, or railroad crossings; work in quarry, pit, or yard; performance of work for nonprofit charitable organizations or other labor; duty of sheriff; use of prisoner labor for private benefit or financial gain prohibited; violation of subsection (2) as civil infraction; penalty; sheriff deriving private benefit or financial gain from provision of food to prisoners as civil infraction; penalty.** [MSA § 28.1730]

### LexisNexis™ and Other Annotations

**LexisNexis™ Michigan analytical references:**
Michigan Law and Practice, Convicts and Prisons § 5.

**§ 801.23. Discharge of unindicted persons.** [MSA § 28.1743]

### LexisNexis™ and Other Annotations

**LexisNexis™ Michigan analytical references:**
Michigan Law and Practice, Convicts and Prisons § 6.

§ 801.51                    MCLS Cumulative Supplement

## COUNTY JAIL OVERCROWDING EMERGENCY POWERS ACT

Act 325, 1982, p 1380, eff February 8, 1983.

### § 801.51. Definitions. [MSA § 28.1748(1)]

#### LexisNexis™ and Other Annotations

**Michigan Digest references:**
Constitutional Law § 67.
Judges §§9, 14.
Prisons and Jails §§1.05, 1.25, 1.60, 6.50.

### § 801.56. Failure to reduce jail population to 90% of rated design capacity within 14 days; sentence review and reduction; failure of certain actions to reduce population to prescribed levels; prisoner information to chief circuit judge; classification of prisoners; sentence duration; corrections department report; evaluation, amendments to overcrowding state of emergency procedures. [MSA § 28.1748(6)]

#### LexisNexis™ and Other Annotations

**Michigan Digest references:**
Counties § 57.
Prisons and Jails §§1.45, 1.60, 6.
Superintending Control § 9.

### § 801.57. Failure to reduce jail population to 90% of rated design capacity within 28 days; additional sentence reductions. [MSA § 28.1748(7)]

#### LexisNexis™ and Other Annotations

**Michigan Digest references:**
Judges § 9.
Sheriffs and Constables § 13.

---

## PRISONER REIMBURSEMENT TO THE COUNTY

Act 118, 1984, p 271, imd eff June 1, 1984.

### § 801.81. Prisoner reimbursement to county. [MSA § 28.1770(1)]

#### LexisNexis™ and Other Annotations

**Michigan Digest references:**
Counties § 56.
Courts § 99.
Prisons and Jails §§1.05, 1.55, 4.50, 5.60.

**LexisNexis™ Michigan analytical references:**
Michigan Law and Practice, Convicts and Prisoners § 2.
Michigan Law and Practice, Counties § 78.
Michigan Law and Practice, Real Property § 161.

## GENERAL PROVISIONS RELATING TO JAILS, AND THE CONFINEMENT OF PRISONERS THEREIN

RS 1846, Ch 148

**§ 801.119. Conveyance of prisoners through other counties; right of officers. [MSA § 28.1768]**

### LexisNexis™ and Other Annotations

**LexisNexis™ Michigan analytical references:**
Michigan Law and Practice, Sheriffs and Constables § 4.

## WORK FARMS, FACTORIES AND SHOPS

Act 78, 1917, p 145, imd eff April 17, 1917.

**§ 801.210. Transfer of convicted persons to workhouse; employment; fees. [MSA § 28.1800]**

### LexisNexis™ and Other Annotations

**LexisNexis™ Michigan analytical references:**
Michigan Law and Practice, Convicts and Prisoners § 4.

## DAY PAROLE OF PRISONERS

Act 60, 1962, p 49, eff March 28, 1963.

**§ 801.251. Privilege of leaving jail during necessary and reasonable hours; purposes; limitations; "jail" defined. [MSA § 28.1747(1)]**

### LexisNexis™ and Other Annotations

**Michigan Digest references:**
Criminal Law and Procedure § 730.10.

**LexisNexis™ Michigan analytical references:**
Michigan Law and Practice, Convicts and Prisoners § 5.

## § 801.257

**§ 801.257. Reduction of term; approval; exception.** [MSA § 28.1747(7)]

### LexisNexis™ and Other Annotations

**Michigan Digest references:**
Constitutional Law § 328.
Criminal Law and Procedure §§730, 762.

---

# REIMBURSEMENT OF CITIES FOR MEDICAL SUPPLIES OR CARE OF PRISONERS

Act 14, 1982, p 37, imd eff February 25, 1982.

**§ 801.301. Reimbursement of city for medical supplies and medical care to prisoners; prisoner or insurance; cooperation of prisoner; violation, fine, restitution.** [MSA § 28.1712]

### LexisNexis™ and Other Annotations

**LexisNexis™ Michigan analytical references:**
Michigan Law and Practice, Convicts and Prisons § 4.

# CHAPTER 803
# YOUTH TRAINING AND REHABILITATION

THE JUVENILE FACILITIES ACT
Act 73, 1988, p 200, imd eff March 28, 1988.

**§ 803.225a. Community placement and discharge from wardship; chemical testing for DNA identification profiling; exception; providing samples; manner; consent; hearing or court order not required; disclosure; assessment; "felony" and "sample" defined.** [MSA § 25.399(225a)]

Sec. 5a. (1) A juvenile ◆ who is under the supervision of the department or a county juvenile agency under section 18 of chapter XIIA of[ the probate code of 1939,] 1939 PA 288, MCL 712A.18, shall not be placed in a community placement of any kind and shall not be discharged from wardship until he or she has provided samples for chemical testing for DNA identification profiling or a determination of the sample's genetic markers and has provided samples for a determination of his or her secretor status ◆ [ if any of the following apply:

(a) The juvenile has been found responsible for a violation of section 83, 91, 316, 317, or 321 of the Michigan penal code, 1931 PA 328, MCL 750.83, 750.91, 750.316, 750.317, and 750.321, or a violation or attempted violation of section 349, 520b, 520c, 520d, 520e, or 520g of the Michigan penal code, 1931 PA 328, MCL 750.349, 750.520b, 750.520c, 750.520d, 750.520e, and 750.520g, or a violation of section 167(1)(c) or (f) or 335a of the Michigan penal code, 1931 PA 328, MCL 750.167 and 750.335a, or a local ordinance substantially corresponding to section 167(1)(c) or (f) or 335a of the Michigan penal code, 1931 PA 328, MCL 750.167 and 750.335a.

(b) The juvenile has been convicted of a felony or attempted felony, or any of the following misdemeanors, or local ordinances substantially corresponding to the following misdemeanors:

(i) A violation of section 145a of the Michigan penal code, 1931 PA 328, MCL 750.145a, enticing a child for immoral purposes.

(ii) A violation of section 167(1)(c), (f), or (i) of the Michigan penal code, 1931 PA 328, MCL 750.167, disorderly person by window peeping, engaging in indecent or obscene conduct in public, or loitering in a house of ill fame or prostitution.

(iii) A violation of section 335a of the Michigan penal code, 1931 PA 328, MCL 750.335a, indecent exposure.

(iv) A violation of section 451 of the Michigan penal code, 1931 PA 328, MCL 750.451, first and second prostitution violations.

§ 803.225a

(v) A violation of section 454 of the Michigan penal code, 1931 PA 328, MCL 750.454, leasing a house for purposes of prostitution.

(vi) A violation of section 462 of the Michigan penal code, 1931 PA 328, MCL 750.462, female under the age of 17 in a house of prostitution.

(2) Notwithstanding subsection (1), if at the time the juvenile is convicted of or found responsible for the violation the investigating law enforcement agency or the department of state police already has a sample from the juvenile that meets the requirements of the DNA identification profiling system act, 1990 PA 250, MCL 28.171 to 28.176, the juvenile is not required to provide another sample or pay the fee required under subsection (6).

(3)] ◆ The samples required to be collected under this section shall be collected by the department or county juvenile agency, as applicable, and transmitted by the department or county juvenile agency to the department of state police in the manner prescribed ◆ under the DNA identification profiling system act, 1990 PA 250, MCL 28.171 to 28.176.

[(4)] ◆ The department or county juvenile agency may collect a sample under this section regardless of whether the juvenile consents to the collection. The department or county juvenile agency is not required to give the juvenile an opportunity for a hearing or obtain a court order before collecting the sample.

[(5) The DNA profiles of DNA samples received under this section shall only be disclosed as follows:

(a) To a criminal justice agency for law enforcement identification purposes.

(b) In a judicial proceeding as authorized or required by a court.

(c) To a defendant in a criminal case if the DNA profile is used in conjunction with a charge against the defendant.

(d) For an academic, research, statistical analysis, or protocol developmental purpose only if personal identifications are removed.

(6) A juvenile found responsible for or convicted of 1 or more crimes listed in subsection (1) shall pay an assessment of $60.00. The juvenile agency shall transmit the assessments or portions of assessments collected to the department of treasury for the department of state police forensic science division to defray the costs associated with the requirements of DNA profiling and DNA retention prescribed under the DNA identification profiling system act, 1990 PA 250, MCL 28.171 to 28.176.

(7)] ◆ As used in this section[ :] ◆

[(a) "Felony" means a violation of a penal law of this state for which the offender may be punished by imprisonment for more than 1 year or an offense expressly designated by law to be a felony.

(b) "Sample"] means a portion of a juvenile's blood, saliva, or tissue collected from the juvenile.

**Youth Training and Rehabilitation** § 803.307

**History:**
Amended by Pub Acts 2001, No. 90, imd eff July 26, 2001, by enacting § 1 eff January 1, 2002 (see 2001 note below).

**Editor's notes:**
Pub Acts 2001, No. 90, enacting § 2, imd eff July 26, 2001, by enacting § 1 eff January 1, 2002, provides:

"Enacting section 2. This amendatory act does not take effect unless all of the following bills of the 91st Legislature are enacted into law:
"(a) Senate Bill No. 389 [Pub Acts 2001, No. 87].
"(b) Senate Bill No. 394 [Pub Acts 2001, No. 84].
"(c) House Bill No. 4610 [Pub Acts 2001, No. 88].
"(d) House Bill No. 4611 [Pub Acts 2001, No. 91].
"(e) House Bill No. 4612 [Pub Acts 2001, No. 86].
"(f) House Bill No. 4613 [Pub Acts 2001, No. 89].
"(g) House Bill No. 4633 [Pub Acts 2001, No. 85]."

**Effect of amendment notes:**
The 2001 amendment revised this section to such an extent that a detailed comparison would be impracticable.

## YOUTH REHABILITATION SERVICES ACT
Act 150, 1974, p 327, imd eff June 12, 1974.

**§ 803.301. Short title.** [MSA § 25.399(51)]

### LexisNexis™ and Other Annotations

**Michigan Digest references:**
Probate Courts § 28.

**LexisNexis™ Michigan analytical references:**
Michigan Law and Practice, Parent and Child § 45.

**§ 803.302. Definitions.** [MSA § 25.399(52)]

### LexisNexis™ and Other Annotations

**LexisNexis™ Michigan analytical references:**
Michigan Law and Practice, Convicts and Prisons § 2.

**§ 803.307. Duration of public wardship; discharge or release; delayed sentence; sentencing as adult offender.** [MSA § 25.399(57)]

### LexisNexis™ and Other Annotations

**Michigan Digest references:**
Juvenile Proceedings § 48.

**LexisNexis™ Michigan analytical references:**
Michigan Law and Practice, Convicts and Prisons § 6.

## § 803.307a. Chemical testing for DNA identification; samples provided by public ward; collection; transmission to department of state police; manner; consent, hearing, or court hearing not required; disclosure; assessments; "felony" and "sample" defined. [MSA § 25.399(57a)]

Sec. 7a. (1) A public ward under a youth agency's jurisdiction ◆ shall not be placed in a community placement of any kind and shall not be discharged from wardship until he or she has provided samples for chemical testing for DNA identification profiling or a determination of the sample's genetic markers and has provided samples for a determination of his or her secretor status ◆ [ if any of the following apply:

(a) The public ward has been found responsible for a violation of section 83, 91, 316, 317, or 321 of the Michigan penal code, 1931 PA 328, MCL 750.83, 750.91, 750.316, 750.317, and 750.321, or a violation or attempted violation of section 349, 520b, 520c, 520d, 520e, or 520g of the Michigan penal code, 1931 PA 328, MCL 750.349, 750.520b, 750.520c, 750.520d, 750.520e, and 750.520g, or a violation of section 167(1)(c) or (f) or 335a of the Michigan penal code, 1931 PA 328, MCL 750.167 and 750.335a, or a local ordinance substantially corresponding to section 167(1)(c) or (f) or 335a of the Michigan penal code, 1931 PA 328, MCL 750.167 and 750.335a.

(b) The public ward has been convicted of a felony or attempted felony, or any of the following misdemeanors, or local ordinances that are substantially corresponding to the following misdemeanors:

(i) A violation of section 145a of the Michigan penal code, 1931 PA 328, MCL 750.145a, enticing a child for immoral purposes.

(ii) A violation of section 167(1)(c), (f), or (i) of the Michigan penal code, 1931 PA 328, MCL 750.167, disorderly person by window peeping, engaging in indecent or obscene conduct in public, or loitering in a house of ill fame or prostitution.

(iii) A violation of section 335a of the Michigan penal code, 1931 PA 328, MCL 750.335a, indecent exposure.

(iv) A violation of section 451 of the Michigan penal code, 1931 PA 328, MCL 750.451, first and second prostitution violations.

(v) A violation of section 454 of the Michigan penal code, 1931 PA 328, MCL 750.454, leasing a house for purposes of prostitution.

(vi) A violation of section 462 of the Michigan penal code, 1931 PA 328, MCL 750.462, female under the age of 17 in a house of prostitution.

(2) Notwithstanding subsection (1), if at the time the public ward is convicted of or found responsible for the violation the investigating law enforcement agency or the department of state police already has a sample from the public ward that meets the requirements of the DNA identification profiling system act, 1990 PA 250,

## Youth Training and Rehabilitation § 803.307a

MCL 28.171 to 28.176, the public ward is not required to provide another sample or pay the fee required under subsection (6).

(3)] ◆ The samples required to be collected under this section shall be collected by the youth agency and transmitted to the department of state police in the manner prescribed ◆ under the DNA identification profiling system act, 1990 PA 250, MCL 28.171 to 28.176.

[(4)] ◆ The youth agency may collect a sample under this section regardless of whether the public ward consents to the collection. The youth agency is not required to give the public ward an opportunity for a hearing or obtain a court order before collecting the sample.

[(5) The DNA profiles of DNA samples received under this section shall only be disclosed as follows:
 (a) To a criminal justice agency for law enforcement identification purposes.
 (b) In a judicial proceeding as authorized or required by a court.
 (c) To a defendant in a criminal case if the DNA profile is used in conjunction with a charge against the defendant.
 (d) For an academic, research, statistical analysis, or protocol developmental purpose only if personal identifications are removed.

(6) A public ward found responsible for or convicted of 1 or more crimes listed in subsection (1) shall pay an assessment of $60.00. The department shall transmit the assessments or portions of assessments collected to the department of treasury for the department of state police forensic science division to defray the costs associated with the requirements of DNA profiling and DNA retention prescribed under the DNA identification profiling system act, 1990 PA 250, MCL 28.171 to 28.176.

(7)] ◆ As used in this section[:] ◆
 [(a) "Felony" means a violation of a penal law of this state for which the offender may be punished by imprisonment for more than 1 year or an offense expressly designated by law to be a felony.
 (b) "Sample"] means a portion of a public ward's blood, saliva, or tissue collected from the public ward.

**History:**
 Amended by Pub Acts 2001, No. 84, imd eff July 26, 2001, by enacting § 1 eff January 1, 2002 (see 2001 note below); 2001, No. 85, imd eff July 26, 2001, by enacting § 1 eff January 1, 2002 (see 2001 note below).

**Editor's notes:**
 Pub Acts 2001, No. 84, enacting § 2, imd eff July 26, 2001, by enacting § 1 eff January 1, 2002, provides:
 "Enacting section 2. This amendatory act does not take effect unless all of the following bills of the 91st Legislature are enacted into law:
  "(a) Senate Bill No. 389 [Pub Acts 2001, No. 87].
  "(b) Senate Bill No. 393 [Pub Acts 2001, No. 90].
  "(c) House Bill No. 4610 [Pub Acts 2001, No. 88].
  "(d) House Bill No. 4611 [Pub Acts 2001, No. 91].
  "(e) House Bill No. 4612 [Pub Acts 2001, No. 86].
  "(f) House Bill No. 4613 [Pub Acts 2001, No. 89].
  "(g) House Bill No. 4633 [Pub Acts 2001, No. 85]."

## § 803.307a

**Pub Acts 2001, No. 85, enacting § 2,** imd eff July 26, 2001, by enacting § 1 eff January 1, 2002, provides:

"Enacting section 2. This amendatory act does not take effect unless all of the following bills of the 91st Legislature are enacted into law:

"(a) Senate Bill No. 389 [Pub Acts 2001, No. 87].
"(b) Senate Bill No. 393 [Pub Acts 2001, No. 90].
"(c) Senate Bill No. 394 [Pub Acts 2001, No. 84].
"(d) House Bill No. 4610 [Pub Acts 2001, No. 88].
"(e) House Bill No. 4611 [Pub Acts 2001, No. 91].
"(f) House Bill No. 4612 [Pub Acts 2001, No. 86].
"(g) House Bill No. 4613 [Pub Acts 2001, No. 89]."

**Effect of amendment notes:**

**The first 2001 amendment (Pub Act 84)** revised this section to the extent that a detailed comparison would be impracticable.

**The second 2001 amendment (Pub Act 85)** revised this section to the extent that a detailed comparison would be impracticable.

# CHAPTER 830

# STATE BUILDING PROGRAMS

## STATE BUILDING AUTHORITY

Act 183, 1964, p 247, imd eff May 19, 1964.

**§ 830.411. Definitions.** [MSA § 3.447(101)]

### LexisNexis™ and Other Annotations

**Michigan Digest references:**
Constitutional Law §§228, 361.

**§ 830.418. Revenue obligations generally.** [MSA § 3.447(108)]

Sec. 8. (1) By resolution or resolutions of its board, the building authority may provide for the issuance of revenue obligations, which may include revenue bonds, revenue notes, or other evidences of revenue indebtedness, and refunding revenue bonds or notes, or other refunding evidences of indebtedness, the obligations for which shall not become a general obligation of this state or a charge against this state, but all revenue obligations and the interest on the revenue obligations and the call premiums for the revenue obligations shall be payable solely from true rental, except to the extent paid from the proceeds of sale of revenue obligations and any additional security provided for and pledged, or from other funds as provided in this act, and each revenue obligation shall have such a statement printed on the face of the revenue obligation. If the resolution of the building authority provides for interest coupons to be attached to a revenue obligation, each interest coupon shall have a statement printed on the coupon that the coupon is not a general obligation of this state or the building authority but is payable solely from certain revenues as specified in the revenue obligation. Revenue obligations may be issued for the purpose of paying part or all of the costs of the facilities or for the purpose of refunding or advance refunding, in whole or in part, outstanding revenue obligations issued pursuant to this act whether the obligations to be refunded or advance refunded have matured or are redeemable or shall mature or become redeemable after being refunded. The cost of the facilities may include an allowance for legal, engineering, architectural, and consulting services; interest on revenue obligations becoming due before the collection of the first true rental available for the payment of those revenue obligations; a reserve for the payment of principal, interest, and redemption premiums on the revenue obligations of the authority; and other necessary incidental expenses including, but not limited to, placement fees; fees or charges for insurance, letters of credit, lines of credit, remarketing agreements, or commit-

## § 830.418

ments to purchase obligations issued pursuant to this act; fees or charges associated with an agreement to manage payment, revenue, or interest rate exposure; or any other fees or charges for any other security provided to assure timely payment of the obligations.

(2) The proceeds of a revenue obligation issue may be used to pay the cost of facilities that are subject to more than 1 lease if either subdivision (a) or (b) is true:

(a) Both of the following are true:

(i) The resolution authorizing the revenue obligations provides for the use of a specific allocable portion of the revenue obligation proceeds to pay the estimated cost of each of the facilities, together with the allocable portion of the reserves, discount, interest on the obligations becoming due before the first true rental available for payment of the obligations, and obligation issuance expense with respect to each facility.

(ii) The true rental and other funds of the building authority and other security as provided in this act available for the revenue obligations including other funds as provided in this act are sufficient to pay the allocable portion of the revenue obligation issue for which the true rental and other funds and security are pledged.

(b) The obligation is part of an interim financing pool described in subsection ◆ [ (20) ].

(3) Revenue obligations that refund outstanding obligations may include the payment of interest accrued, or to accrue, to the earliest or any subsequent date of redemption, purchase, or maturity of the revenue obligations to be refunded, redemption premium, if any, and any commission, service fee, and other expense necessary to be paid in connection with revenue obligations that refund outstanding obligations. Proceeds of refunding revenue obligations may also be used to pay part of the cost of issuance of the refunding revenue obligations, interest on the refunding revenue obligations, a reserve for the payment of principal, interest, and redemption premiums on the refunding revenue obligations, and other necessary incidental expenses including, but not limited to, placement fees; fees or charges for insurance, letters of credit, lines of credit, remarketing agreements, or commitments to purchase obligations issued pursuant to this act; fees or charges associated with an agreement to manage payment, revenue, or interest rate exposure; or any other fees or charges for any other security provided to assure timely payment of the obligations. The building authority may also provide for the withdrawal of any funds from a reserve created for the payment of principal, interest, and redemption premiums on the refunded obligations and for the deposit of those funds in the reserve for the payment of principal, interest, and redemption premiums on the refunding obligations or may provide for use of that reserve money to pay principal, interest, and redemption premiums on the obligations to be refunded. Obligations issued to refund outstanding obligations may be issued in a principal amount greater than, the same as, or less than the principal amount of the obligations to be

refunded, and subject to the maximum rate of interest provided in subsection (8), may bear interest rates that are higher than, the same as, or lower than the interest rates of the obligations to be refunded. If obligations are issued to refund outstanding obligations of the authority, a lease whose rental has been pledged for repayment of the obligations to be refunded shall not be terminated solely by reason of the payment or provision for payment of the obligations to be refunded, and the lease and all of the rights and obligations under the lease remain in full force and effect in accordance with its terms.

(4) Except as otherwise provided in this section, the building authority shall use income or profit derived from the investment of money in a fund or account of the building authority, including the proceeds of sale of the revenue obligations, only for the purpose of paying principal, interest, and redemption premiums on the revenue obligations of the building authority, or for any purpose for which the proceeds of the revenue obligations may be used under this act, as determined by the resolution of the board authorizing the issuance of revenue obligations.

(5) Within limits considered appropriate and established by the board, the board may authorize by resolution a member of the board or the person appointed by the building authority as its chief operating officer or chief staff person, if the authorization limits or prescribes the maximum interest rates, minimum price, maximum principal amount, and the latest maturity date of the obligations, to do any of the following:

(a) Determine interest rates or methods for determining interest rates for, maturities of, principal amounts of, denominations of, dates of issuance of, interest payment dates for, redemption rights and the terms under which redemption rights may be waived, transferred, or sold, prepayment rights with respect to, the purchase price of, and the type of funds for settlement of obligations.

(b) Determine which, if any, letter of credit, line of credit, standby note or bond purchase agreement, bond insurance, or other agreement providing security or liquidity for obligations of the building authority, approved by the board, provides a cost savings and should be entered into in connection with the issuance of the obligations of the building authority.

(c) Take any other action on behalf of the board within limitations established by the board as the board considers necessary in connection with the issuance of obligations of the building authority.

(6) To the extent provided by resolution of the board, principal of, and interest and redemption premiums on, revenue obligations issued for the purpose of paying all or part of the cost of the facilities shall be secured by and payable only from any or all of the following sources:

(a) The true rental derived from the facilities constructed or acquired with the proceeds of the revenue obligations.

§ 830.418

(b) The proceeds of revenue obligations.

(c) The reserve, if any, established for the payment of principal of, or interest or redemption premiums on, the obligations.

(d) The proceeds of insurance, a letter of credit, or a line of credit acquired as security for the revenue obligations.

(e) The proceeds of obligations issued to refund the revenue obligations.

(f) The proceeds of the foreclosure or enforcement of a mortgage, security interest, or deed of trust on the facilities financed by the revenue obligations granted by the authority as security for the revenue obligations.

(g) Other funds of the authority not previously pledged for other obligations of the authority, including funds of the authority derived from rentals and other revenues, investment income or profit, or funds or accounts relating to other facilities, and payments received pursuant to an agreement to manage payment, revenue, or interest rate exposure as provided in subsection ◆ [(19)].

(h) Investment earnings and profits on any or all of the sources described in subdivisions (a) to (g).

(7) To the extent provided by resolution of the board, principal of, and interest and redemption premiums on, refunding revenue obligations shall be secured by and payable only from any or all of the following sources:

(a) The true rental derived from the facilities constructed or acquired with the proceeds of the obligations being refunded.

(b) The proceeds of the refunding obligations.

(c) The reserve, if any, established for the payment of the principal of, or interest and redemption premiums on, the refunding obligations or the obligations to be refunded.

(d) The proceeds of insurance, a letter of credit, or a line of credit acquired as security for the revenue obligations.

(e) The proceeds of obligations issued to refund the refunding obligations.

(f) The proceeds of the foreclosure or enforcement of any mortgage, security interest, or deed of trust on the facilities financed from the proceeds of the obligations being refunded, granted by the authority as security for the refunding obligations.

(g) Other funds of the authority not previously pledged for other obligations of the authority, including other funds of the authority derived from rentals and other revenues, investment income or profit, or funds or accounts relating to other facilities, and payments received pursuant to an agreement to manage payment, revenue, or interest rate exposure as provided in subsection ◆ [(19)].

(h) Investment earnings or profits on any of the sources described in subdivisions (a) to (g).

(8) Obligations issued under this act may be either serial obligations or term obligations, or any combination of serial or term obligations. The obligations shall mature not more than 40 years

**State Building Programs** § 830.418

from their date, and in any event not more than 1 year from the due date of the last true rental pledged for the payment of the obligations, and may bear interest at fixed or variable interest rates, or may be without stated interest, but the net interest rate or rates of interest, taking into account any discount on the sale of the obligations, shall not exceed ◆ a ◆ rate ◆ permitted by the ◆ [revised municipal finance act, 2001 PA 34, MCL 141.2101 to 141.2821]. The obligations may be sold at a discount.

(9) Except as otherwise provided in this subsection, in the resolution or resolutions authorizing the issuance of the obligations, the board shall determine the principal amount of the obligations to be issued, the registration provisions, the date of issuance, the obligation numbers, the obligation denominations, the obligation designations, the obligation maturities, the interest payment dates, the paying agent or paying agents or the method of selection of the agent or agents, the rights of prior redemption of the obligations, and the terms under which redemption rights may be waived, transferred, or sold, the rights of the holders to require prepayment of the principal of or interest on the obligations, the maximum rate of interest, the method of execution of the obligations, and such other provisions respecting the obligations, the rights of the holders of the obligations, the security for the obligations, and the procedures for disbursement of the obligation proceeds and for the investment of the proceeds of obligations and money for the payment of obligations. Rather than making the determinations required by this subsection, the board may authorize a person identified in subsection (5) to make the determinations and take the actions authorized under subsection (5).

(10) The board in the resolution or resolutions authorizing the issuance of obligations may provide for the assignment of the true rental to be paid by the state under the lease or leases to 1 of the paying agents for the obligations or to a trustee, as provided in this act, in which case the state shall pay the rental to the paying agent or trustee. For the purposes and within the limitations set forth in this act, the board may by resolution covenant to issue or cause to be issued, or use its best efforts to issue or cause to be issued, refunding revenue obligations to refund obligations issued under this act.

(11) The board in the resolution, or resolutions, authorizing the obligations may provide for the terms and conditions upon which the holders of the obligations, or a portion of the obligations or a trustee for the obligations, is entitled to the appointment of a receiver. The receiver may enter and take possession of the facility, may lease and maintain the facility, may prescribe rentals and collect, receive, and apply income and revenues thereafter arising from the facility in the same manner and to the same extent that the authority is so authorized. The resolution or resolutions may provide for the appointment of a trustee for the holders of the obligations, may give to the trustee the appropriate rights, duties, remedies, and powers, with or without the execution of a deed of trust or mortgage, necessary and appropriate to secure the obligations, and may

## § 830.418

provide that the principal of and interest on any obligations issued under this act shall be secured by a mortgage, security interest, or deed of trust covering the facility, which mortgage, security interest, or deed of trust may contain the covenants, agreements, and remedies as will properly safeguard the obligations as may be provided for in the resolution or resolutions authorizing the obligations, including the right to sell the facility upon foreclosure sale, not inconsistent with this act.

(12) All obligations and the interest coupons, if any, attached to the obligations are declared to be fully negotiable and to have all of the qualities incident to negotiable instruments under the uniform commercial code, 1962 PA 174, MCL 440.1101 to 440.11102, subject only to the provisions for registration of the obligations that may appear on the obligations. The obligations and interest on the obligations are exempt from all taxation by ◆ [this] state or any of its political subdivisions.

◆

(13) ◆ The obligations may be sold at private or at public sale under the procedures and subject to the conditions prescribed by resolution of the board.

(14) ◆ The building authority may issue additional obligations of equal standing with respect to the pledge of the true rentals and additional security provided pursuant to this act with previously issued obligations of the building authority issued to acquire or construct a facility or facilities, or to refund the obligations, for the purpose of completing, or making additions, improvements, or replacements to, the facility or facilities for which the previous obligations of the authority were issued or to refund all or part of obligations previously issued for such a facility, under the terms and conditions provided in the resolution authorizing the previous issue of obligations.

(15) ◆ The authority shall not have obligations outstanding at any 1 time for any of its corporate purposes in a principal amount totaling more than $2,700,000,000.00, which limitations shall not include principal appreciation as provided in subsection ◆ [(17)] or obligations or portions of obligations used to pay for any of the following:

(a) Amounts set aside for payment of interest becoming due before the collection of the first true rental available.

(b) Amounts set aside for a reserve for payment of principal, interest, and redemption premiums.

(c) Costs of issuance of the obligations and the discount, if any, on sale.

(d) The sums expected to be set aside for the purposes provided in this subsection for any obligations authorized by the authority but not sold. The amount set aside or expected to be set aside for the purposes provided in this subsection shall be conclusively determined by a certificate setting forth the amounts executed by the executive director of the building authority. In addition, there shall be excluded from the limitation obligations issued to refund

**State Building Programs** § 830.418

prior obligations if those prior obligations will not be retired within 90 days after the date of issuance of the refunding obligations. If an obligation is issued to retire a prior obligation within 90 days after the date of issuance of the refunding obligation, the obligation is counted against the limitation when the refunded obligation is retired.

(16) ◆ The authority may apply and pledge, if not already pledged, all or any unpledged part of the true rental and other revenues of a facility; income and profit from the investment of money pertaining to a facility; and money in a fund or account of the authority pertaining to a facility to pay the principal, interest, and redemption premiums on revenue obligations of the authority other than those to which the true rental and other revenues, investment income, or profit or funds or accounts pertain; to pay amounts due under an agreement to manage payment, revenue, or interest rate exposure regardless of the obligations or investments to which the agreement relates; or to pay part or all of the cost of additional facilities to be acquired by the authority for the use of the state. The authority may establish a separate fund into which the rental and other revenues, investment income or profit, or money of such a fund or account shall be deposited to be used to pay principal, interest, and redemption premiums on outstanding obligations of the authority or to acquire facilities for the use of ◆ [this] state. The authority shall not acquire a facility unless the acquisition is approved by the state administrative board and by a concurrent resolution of the legislature approved by a majority of the members elected to and serving in each house. The authority may pledge any or all of the foregoing to the payment of revenue obligations of the authority other than those to which they pertain. If the true rental and other revenues, investment income or profit, or the money in funds or accounts to be applied as specified in this subsection pertain to a facility leased to the state and an institution of higher education pursuant to a lease executed and delivered before January 1, 1983, no application or pledge thereof may be made unless approved by the institution of higher education.

(17) ◆ If the authority issues an obligation that appreciates in principal amount, the amount of principal appreciation each year on that obligation, after the date of original issuance, shall not be considered to be principal indebtedness for the purposes of the limitation in subsection ◆ [(15)] or any other limitation. The appreciation of principal after the date of original issue shall be considered interest and shall be within the interest rate limitations set forth in this act.

(18) ◆ Of the $2,700,000,000.00 authorized under subsection ◆ [ (15)], priority shall be determined by the joint capital outlay committee.

(19) ◆ In connection with an obligation issued previously or to be issued under this act or an investment made previously or to be made, the board may by resolution authorize and approve the

§ 830.418

execution and delivery of an agreement to manage payment, revenue, or interest rate exposure. The agreement may include, but is not limited to, an interest rate exchange agreement, an agreement providing for payment or receipt of money based on levels of or changes in interest rates, an agreement to exchange cash flows or series of payments, or an agreement providing for or incorporating interest rate caps, collars, floors, or locks. Subject to a prior pledge or lien created under this act, a payment to be made by the building authority under an agreement described in this subsection is payable, together with other obligations of the building authority, from those sources described in subsections (6) and (7), all with the parity or priority and upon the conditions set forth in the board's resolution. An agreement entered into under this subsection is not a general obligation of ◆ [this] state or the building authority, and the agreement does not count against the limitation on outstanding obligations contained in subsection ◆ [(15)].

(20) ◆ The building authority may authorize by resolution a pool of obligations to meet interim financing needs. A pool may be issued in 1 or more series, may relate to 1 or more projects, and is subject to all of the following:

(a) The board's resolution approving the pool shall state at least all of the following:

(i) The name or designation of the pool to distinguish it from any other pool issued under this subsection.

(ii) The latest date by which an obligation issued under the pool must mature, which shall not be later than 5 years after the date on which the pool is established. The duration of the pool shall be the time from the date on which the pool is established to the latest possible maturity date of obligations issued pursuant to the pool, or sooner as provided by resolution.

(iii) The maximum par amount of obligations that may be outstanding at any time during the duration of the pool. The resolution may state the maximum par amount of obligations that may be issued pursuant to the pool.

(iv) Other terms of the obligations as provided in subsection (8) or the limits within which the chief operating officer, chief staff person, or member of the board shall determine those terms as provided in subsection (5).

(v) The security for obligations issued pursuant to the pool.

(vi) Other provisions, not inconsistent with the terms of this act, that the board determines to be necessary or appropriate to the pool.

(b) Proceeds of obligations issued as part of a pool established under this subsection may be used for any of the purposes for which revenue obligations of the building authority may be used as described in subsection (1). However, an obligation shall not be issued with respect to a facility unless all of the following are true:

(i) The board approves the financing of the facility pursuant to the pool, which approval may be made at the same time as or after the establishment of the pool.

**State Building Programs**  § 830.418

(ii) The board approves the proposed form of lease for the facility, which approval may be made prior to, at the same time as, or after the establishment of the pool.

(iii) The state administrative board, an institution of higher education, if applicable, and the legislature have approved the form of the lease as required by section 7, which approval may be made prior to, at the same time as, or after the establishment of the pool.

(iv) The aggregate amounts of obligations issued and outstanding with respect to a facility under a pool, together with other obligations that may have been issued and are outstanding with respect to the facility under this act do not exceed the cost of the facility, including allowable interest costs, as approved by the state administrative board, an institution of higher education, if applicable, and the legislature.

(v) On or before the issuance of obligations the proceeds of which are to finance the acquisition, construction, renovation, or rehabilitation of the facility, the building authority and the state, and, if applicable, an institution of higher education, enter into the lease or an agreement to construct or acquire the facility, which lease or agreement sets forth the terms and conditions under which the building authority will finance the construction or acquisition of the facility for lease to the state or to the state and any applicable institution of higher education.

[(21) Bonds and notes issued under this act are not subject to the revised municipal finance act, 2001 PA 34, MCL 141.2101 to 141.2821.

(22) The issuance of bonds and notes under this act is subject to the agency financing reporting act.]

**History:**
Amended by Pub Acts 2002, No. 382, imd eff May 24, 2002.

**Effect of amendment notes:**
The 2002 amendment in subsection (2), paragraph (b), following "in subsection" substituted "(20)" for "(23)"; in subsections (6) and (7), paragraph (g), following "in subsection" substituted "(19)" for "(22)"; in subsection (8), following "shall not exceed" deleted "18% or" and "higher", preceding "permitted by" deleted "if", changed the style of statutory reference; in subsection (12), following "taxation by" substituted "this" for "the"; deleted former subsections (13), (14) and (18); redesignated former subsections (15)–(17) as (13)–(15) and (19)–(23) as (16)–(20); in subsection (15), opening paragraph, following "in subsection" substituted "(17)" for "(20)"; in subsection (16), following "for the use of" substituted "this" for "the"; in subsections (17) and (18), following "subsection" substituted "(15)" for "(17)"; in subsection (19), following "obligation of" substituted "this" for "the", following "in subsection" substituted "(15)" for "(17)"; and added subsections (21) and (22).

**Statutory references:**
Section 7, above referred to, is § 830.417.